THE DOG LOVER'S COMPANION TO
WASHINGTON D.C. & BALTIMORE

Ann & Don Oldenburg

AVALON
TRAVEL

THE DOG LOVER'S COMPANION TO WASHINGTON D.C. & BALTIMORE
The Inside Scoop on Where to Take Your Dog
Second Edition

Ann and Don Oldenburg

Published by
Avalon Travel Publishing
1400 65th Street, Suite 250
Emeryville, CA 94608, USA

Printing History
1st edition—October 1998
2nd edition—January 2003
5 4 3 2 1

ISBN: 1-56691-472-8
ISSN: 1540-3300

Editors: Kevin McLain, Angelique S. Clarke
Copy Editor: Jeannie Trizzino
Graphics: Susan Mira Snyder
Production: Jacob Goolkasian, Alvaro Villanueva, Carey Wilson
Map Editor: Olivia Solís
Cartography: Donald Patterson
Index: Rachel Kuhn

Cover and Interior Illustrations: Phil Frank

Distributed by Publishers Group West

Printed in the United States by Worzalla

KEEPING CURRENT

Note to All Dog Lovers:

While our information is as current as possible, changes to fees, regulations, parks, roads, and trails sometimes are made after we go to press. Businesses can close, change their ownership, or change their rules. Earthquakes, fires, rainstorms, and other natural phenomena can radically change the condition of parks, hiking trails, and wilderness areas. Before you and your dog begin your travels, please be certain to call the phone numbers for each listing for updated information.

Attention Dogs of Washington D.C. & Baltimore:

Our readers mean everything to us. We explore Washington D.C., Baltimore, and the surrounding areas so that you and your people can spend true quality time together. Your input to this book is very important. In the last few years, we've heard from many wonderful dogs and their humans about new dog-friendly places, or old dog-friendly places we didn't know about. If we've missed your favorite park, beach, outdoor restaurant, hotel, or dog-friendly activity, please let us know. We'll check out the tip and if it turns out to be a good one, include it in the next edition, giving a thank-you to the dog and/or person who sent in the suggestion. Please write us—we always welcome comments and suggestions.

The Dog Lover's Companion to Washington D.C. & Baltimore
AVALON TRAVEL PUBLISHING
1400 65TH STREET, SUITE 250
EMERYVILLE, CA 94608, USA
email: atpfeedback@avalonpub.com

ACKNOWLEDGMENTS

Writing the second edition of this book was a lot like taking Chappy for a walk around the block twice: the scenery was familiar but the more we looked around, the more things had changed. One big change has been our three sons—J.B., James, and Cole—whose boyish insights, great humor and love have blessed our lives. The boys are four years older now and they were even better sports when we needed their patience and valuable assistance on the "dog book"—even if it meant going straight to a park after one of their baseball games. And, of course, they are Chappy's very best friends in the world.

We would also like to thank our mothers, Sally Trebbe and Alice Oldenburg, for their dogged encouragement, opinions, and loving kindness. And thanks to our editors, colleagues, and friends as well. Without them, writing this edition would have seemed too much like teaching an old dog new tricks.

CONTENTS

Germantown

Glen Echo

Kensington

Laytonsville

Olney

Poolesville

Potomac

Rockville

Silver Spring

Spencerville

Takoma Park

Viers Mill

Wheaton

White Oak

Adelphi

Beltsville

Bladensburg

Bowie

Brandywine

Camp Springs

Clinton

College Park

Colmar Manor

District Heights

Fort Washington

Greenbelt

Laurel

Oxon Hill

Powder Mill

Riverdale

Upper Marlboro

Brighton

Clarksville

Columbia

Elkridge

Ellicott City

Friendship

Glenwood

Highland

Jessup

Savage

Scaggsville

Woodbine

Avalon

Bengies-Chase

Catonsville

Cockeysville

Cromwell

Dundalk

Edgemere–Sparrows Point

Essex

Fullerton

Kingsville

Lake Roland

Loch Raven

Owings Mills

Parkville

Reisterstown

Timonium

Towson

Armistead

Belair-Edison

Butchers Hill

Cherry Hill

WASHINGTON D.C.– BALTIMORE AREA MAP

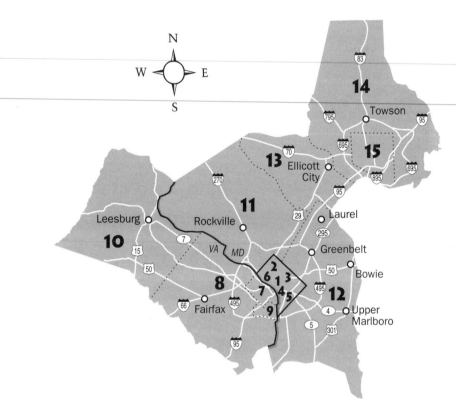

MAPS

DISTRICT OF COLUMBIA

VIRGINIA

MARYLAND

INTRODUCTION

INTRODUCTION

Outside of a dog, a book is probably man's best friend; and inside of a dog, it's too dark to read.

—Groucho Marx

We really did try to find a new and clever dog quote to lead off the new second edition of this guidebook. We considered humorist Dave Barry's funny and apt line that "dogs feel very strongly that they should always go with you in the car, in case the need should arise for them to bark violently at nothing right in your ear." And O. A. Battista's observation: "A dog is one of the remaining reasons why some people can be persuaded to go for a walk." Like those and others, Daniel Pinkwater's comment that "the old saw about old dogs and new tricks only applies to certain people" also seemed relevant to the concept of this book.

But, in the end, we were like the old dog that couldn't learn a new trick. We stuck with the Groucho Marx quote above that began our first edition, because, well, we did put the dog inside the book instead. It's easier to read than the other way, more humane to your furry best friend, too.

This book is designed to make you and your pooch even better best friends. There's nothing a dog likes better than a joy ride—his wet nose stuck out the window, wind blowing in his furry face, saliva flying, with not a care in the world. Come to think of it, there's nothing *we* like better (except nix the flying saliva part). So we tried to capture some of that wind-in-the-face spirit in the joy rides, wilderness excursions, long walks in the parks, eatery hopping, city-hydrant sniffing, sleepovers, and other dog-friendly things to do that we've detailed and reviewed in these pages. And if your pup is lucky, all of these pages are destined to become dog-eared around your house.

By now, everyone has noticed that taking dogs out in public is making a huge comeback in the United States. Long ago, the most dignified members of society took their manicured and groomed canines everywhere with them, no questions asked. That changed as the *Homo sapiens* population exponentially multiplied and our canine companions were relegated to the proverbial doghouse.

But folks today are weary of leaving their Buddys and Bowsers behind and whimpering at the window. There was a time when our very own pooch, Chappy, would hear the keys jingle, our sons' footsteps to the front door, and he'd race to our feet to beg the way only dogs know how to beg. His eyes big and pleading, his tail wagging the rest of his body like crazy, and then, alas, his best hopes were quickly dashed, leaving him in that pathetic hangdog posture as we closed the door behind us. He'd quickly scamper to the wing chair upstairs and press his wet nose against the bay window, watching us back down the driveway without you-know-who along. When we returned, he'd still be at the window, waiting. Oh, the guilt and shame every dog owner has known at one time or another!

But, travel experts are bowled over by the surge in the demand of canine-sensitive clients who want to take their furry friends with them—wherever they go. More accommodations have opened their doors to dogs, from bare-bones budget motels to the classiest digs in town. Parks, restaurants, fairs, and festivals, too, are reconciling with the new canine consciousness—right here in the nation's capital and Baltimore.

We know this firsthand because Chappy has been going everywhere with us—including just about everywhere we've visited in researching this guide for the good of his out-and-about brethren. Since assisting us on the first edition of this book, he has continued to be our doggy barometer on the road, our Charles Kuralt of the canine countryside. Funny thing is, he was born for the job.

You see, Chappy is a Tibetan terrier. That's the smart, medium-size, shaggy-haired breed traditionally raised and pampered by the Dalai Lamas of Tibet to be nothing more than a loyal and loving member of the family. So our tail-wagger doesn't know squat about chasing sheep, can't herd cattle, finds flushing pheasants from tall grass to be perplexing behavior, won't fetch, gets nervous around water, and runs from fights—and this time around, on the second edition, he's a few years older and a bit more gimpy. He'll raise holy hell if he thinks his family's threatened, but otherwise our pooch is a lover, not a fighter. He's more likely to chant "Om" than roam far from home. He's bred to be a connoisseur of canicular culture, a pursuer of poochy possibilities, an aficionado of arf! And no matter how old he gets, he'll never think of himself—anymore than any of us would—as a lonely left-behind.

Oh yeah. Another thing he is: Tibetan terriers are considered to be luck dogs in their homeland. They bring good fortune (along with some chewed furniture and rug stains as pups) to those who take care of them—namely us. Chappy figures that when all else fails, when he's hidden one too many of the boys' toys, or barked at nothing to wake us in the wee hours, he's still the luck dog. It's his ace in the hole. In Tibet it's bad luck just to contemplate sending your Tibetan terrier off to doggy Siberia. In fact, these snow-loving dogs are so revered in Tibet that sometimes they're referred to as holy, though in our case, it's more like, "Holy cow! What did Chappy do this time?"

Why did we get this pedigreed fluff ball with a Buddhist background—besides the luck factor, that is? As novelist Robert Benchley put it, "A dog teaches a boy fidelity, perseverance, and to turn around three times before lying down." When our first of three sons was three years old, we wanted J. B. (now a strapping 15-year-old) to learn those values—especially the latter one—from owning and caring for a dog of his own. Because Tibetans are one of a few breeds that don't shed and rarely affect people who suffer from allergies to animals, we also figured his "highness" wouldn't congest Grandma Oldenburg's upper respiratory system when she came for a visit. We totally fell in love with the clumsy little puppy we met at the breeder's home that week soon after Christmas. So did our two younger sons, James and Coley—once they arrived. We've been lucky in love with him ever since.

Meanwhile, Chappy has proven to be as lucky as a saintly dashboard statuette in our travels in search of dog-friendly fun and facilities. Start taking your poochster out on the town and you'll quickly find out, as we did, that dogs can be fine traveling companions. Unlike some people we know (Boys, that's enough now! Boys, don't make me stop this car!), Chappy is so thrilled to be included on our joy rides that he never complains, never asks if we're there yet, never squabbles in the backseat, never has to stop along the highway to pee (Oops! Wrong on that one!), never gets bored, never stomps on imaginary brakes or asks why we didn't go the other way, never recommends "stopping and asking someone," and never turns his nose up at food we give him.

By now, Chappy's so used to coming along that when he hears the keys jingle, he goes directly to the drawer where we keep his leash. He fully understands the words "walk" and "park," and at times seems to enunciate "park." Or is that just "bark?" Either way, he's learned how to curl up on the back seat and travel like the champion he coulda been—even when we pull into a park and find a disheartening rejection of a sign that reads No Dogs Allowed. Why, that shouldn't happen to a dog, much less to Chappy.

Generally, dogs love wherever you take them—though some places are better suited for them than others, and they know it. Over the last several years of four-legged legwork on this book, we learned that there are pockets of intense dog-lovers around the Washington-Baltimore area. We also learned that many rangers in beautiful parks and many friendly restaurateurs and hoteliers will jump through hoops to make your doggy feel at home away from home. Most important, we learned that if you really want to include your pup on your journeys through everyday life, going just about anywhere, you can. And you can feel good about doing it.

Indeed, Chappy's dogged responses to the people and places we visited have helped us rate these experiences—from a dog's perspective. He doesn't exactly paw the ground like Mr. Ed, and he isn't real picky either. A tree, a patch of grass, some new smells, hey, even some old smells, and he's a happy Chappy. But he did remind us many times to look at the way things are through his eyes. What more can a dog ask? We learned that just because a park is pretty to humans doesn't mean it's going to be a treat for dogs. Just because Old Town, Alexandria, is one of the great dog-loving communities and a charming place to walk your pup, doesn't mean Chappy loves it all the time—sometimes there's a little too much noisy traffic in those colonial, cobblestoned environs for him.

So if you find Chappy's opinions butting into these chapters, that's because he's the proxy for all dogs in these pages. He's the everydog. The interview with the dog on the street. He's the John Doe of dogs. Others lent a hand, too. The kind folks at SPCAs and Humane Associations throughout the area offered suggestions. Friends who knew dogs or who knew the territory added their two cents. Folks we crossed paths and tangled leashes with helped point us in new directions. But the bottom line is that Chappy was the canine critic. He's the average dog's dog. As Andy Rooney once barked, "The average dog is a nicer person than the average person."

Before we get into the meat of the matter (a phrase Chappy insisted on), let's do some basic training. Forget "Fetch." Never mind "Stay." These notes, pointers, and tips are on how to use *The Dog Lover's Companion to Washington D.C. & Baltimore* and what you need to keep in mind when you and the pooch are hardnosing the highway, strolling through a hotel lobby, or hiking the hinterlands.

THE PAWS RATING SCALE

Having said all of that, this book (with Chappy's blessing) really is intended to be a guide for places you *and* your dog can enjoy together. So you'll find that in rating the parks, recreation areas, and beaches, we gave the highest scores to the ones we enjoyed as much as Chappy did. Because we have three boys (ages 15, 9, and 6), we probably looked at parks with an eye for family fun and function as well. We also know that for many people, Little Snookums is their child—maybe even their only child. No problem: As you already know, Chappy, too, is one of our family (though he's the only one of us who occasionally drinks from the toilet).

Chappy's not a big, loping adventurous member of the family, and he's not a particularly hardy dog either. His genetic makeup is better suited to the care of higher-consciousness beings somewhere in the Himalayas, maybe with a little meditating on nirvana mixed in. Doing the research, the poor pup even tore a ligament in his rear leg (though he's mostly recovered now). But we tried to take into account all kinds of dogs when rating places.

If it was quiet, the walk gentle, and the smells plentiful, Chappy was happiest, but we also looked for other factors—water, cleanliness, off-leash allowances (legal and not-so-legal), shade, breeze, facilities, terrain, quality of trails, wildlife, friendliness, other dogs, and more. The originators of the Dog Lover's Companion series came up with the highly regarded, time-honored "Paws Rating Scale" for the first book of this kind, and we used it as our guideline, too. Here's how the icons work:

Fire Hydrant (🐾): A park designated with this symbol only rates good enough to be a pit stop and nothing more. This is the lowest rating possible and means the place is "worth a squat." You know, when Fido gets that pained look in the car, and you're in this neighborhood already? Other than for lifting a leg there, these parks have no redeeming doggy value to warrant a visit.

One paw (🐾): Better than a fire hydrant rating, but not by much, one-paw places usually are either small community parks mostly devoted to kids and playgrounds and ball games, but offering a patch of grass for a pooch. Or they are parks that might have earned a higher rating if only they weren't so trashy, hard to find, or simply lacking in characteristics to set them apart from the same old, same old. Once in a while a national treasure of a parkland earns only one paw when it prohibits pups from its properties except for that gravelly fire road and one campground area—but often we don't bother to include those parks since dogs are considered second-class citizens there.

Two paws (🐾 🐾): This is a decent place to stop, with some of the characteristics that make tails wag. You probably wouldn't make plans to visit a two-paw park unless you live within walking distance—in which case you're probably fortunate. You certainly wouldn't go far out of your way to drive here or figure on spending much time on these grounds. If you were heading in that direction already and wanted to plan for some leg-stretching time out of the car, this would be it.

Three paws (🐾 🐾 🐾): Bigger, better in every way—there are more trees, and the grass is greener (figuratively and literally speaking). Maybe this park offers a sweet panoramic view or a particularly pleasant path cutting through woods worthy of exploring. It probably doesn't have water a dog can take a dip in, but it may offer some other treat that sets it apart—perhaps an off-leash zone or a regular doggy social on Saturday mornings or a variety of terrain to keep the chew-master fascinated. Lots of exceptional parks that miss on one or two counts earn this rating. By the way, we also rate in increments; a park that can't quite scale the highest peaks of our standards but comes darn close just might earn slightly better marks (such as 🐾 🐾 🐾 ½).

Four paws (🐾 🐾 🐾 🐾): This is top of the line, folks, the best of the best. This is the highest rating we give a place, and it means you'll come close to finding doggy nirvana here. When we've found a park that offers room for dogs to romp in a stream, run in acre after acre of open fields, hike through enchanted forests, and take in nature in all its glory, we rate it four paws. These over-achieving locations tend to be beautiful spots for humans as well—whether rugged and mountainous or well manicured and country-clubbish. They offer unusually wonderful outings for you and your dog, hours worth of fun and excitement—sometimes days. Repeat appeal? Yes, these are the parks you'll plan to return to with the pooch, and she'll be happy you do. Four-paw places are so wonderful that they are the destinations and not the detours.

A few more things: If you see a symbol of a dog running (🐕), that means the place is one of the increasingly common—though still controversial—areas that sanction dogs to run leash free. Like some regions of the country where authorities have recognized the value of official off-leash properties, our region is starting to give dogs that wink and a nod. Arlington County in Virginia has pioneered this kind of benevolence toward Bowsers and their companions. Fairfax County has sniffed the trail as well, opening several off-leash parks for dogs since we wrote the first edition. Some locations in Maryland have either considered and tabled the proposal (Baltimore City, for instance) or are trying it as an experiment (Bowie). Stay tuned there.

Chappy's opinion? The fact that every dedicated dog park we've seen is so overused suggests the popularity of the idea. But, in reality, it also means that these great ideas quickly become fenced-in dirt ground where grass won't grow and dog poop, when picked up as required, ends up as a mountain of filthy stench piled in a big disposal can at one end of the area. And Chappy's not so fond of the over-aggressive dogs that inevitably show up at these sites with their dimwit humans. Yes, the rules give plenty of permission to the good citizens to show bad dogs and their humanoid companions to the gate (and don't let it hit you in the behind on the way out!), but that doesn't stop the incidents. Frankly, while Chappy supports the concept of leash-free zones, he'd just as soon stay on a long leash and visit an incredibly beautiful national or regional park.

Now and then in this book, you'll see a people symbol (🚶). This indicates that the park offers something exceptional for the humans. Hey, the chauffeur should get tossed a bone once in a while!

We are proud and happy to say we personally visited every park in this book. We even visited many that didn't make these pages for various reasons you don't want to know. In areas where you'll find an exceptional park or two, we didn't include some of the perfectly fine but otherwise ordinary community parks. On the other hand, in a few locales where dog-friendly havens are few and far between, we included some small and undistinguished parks because that's about all there are if you happen to be driving through.

The directions we've given for each location are from our own many wrong turns and from our now badly refolded, marked-up maps. Usually we try to direct you from the nearest big highway or from a likely starting point. The maps in this book, as you'll see, may not be as detailed as you might need. So, unless you're familiar with the turf, we recommend you consult your own map before heading out. We used a lot of American Automobile Association maps (free to members), and we also found that ADC map books of each county are hard to beat for detail. They're available at almost every drug store and book store.

HE? SHE? IT?

Our dog, Chappy, is a he, so you might find in reading this book that we've referred to dogs in the masculine sense more often than in the feminine. That's not meant to slight dogs deserving a "she." It's *not* a political statement. Let's just say that it's our fault and no one else's. We've tried not to exclude any dog by breed or gender. We've tried alternating references to him and her; we never use "it," since dogs are beings and "its" are not. But we do tend to think "Chappy" when describing these places, so forgive us if you count more he's than she's in these pages. Forgive us, and then get over it. You should be in a four-paw park enjoying your canine companion instead of counting pronouns anyway.

BONE APPÉTIT!

Unlike Parisians who think nothing of bringing their poodles with them to ze cafés de Paris, restaurants that pull out the chair and snap the napkin across a pooch's lap are few and far between in the Washington and Baltimore areas. Some might say, *"vive la différence!"* It's a cultural thing that dogs don't understand.

The laws in Maryland, Virginia, and the District are essentially the same in this regard. Health codes prohibit dogs from going inside restaurants unless they're guide dogs. But we've found there's some margin for error, or for interpretation of the law, shall we say, when dining premises are outside. While some restaurant managers won't budge on this, others distinguish between

outdoor patios that are fenced in, railed in, walled, or otherwise partially enclosed, and those that simply provide tables and chairs outside.

We tried to find restaurants that had outdoor tables, restaurants that on nice days—generally late spring, summer, and into fall—allow you to keep your dog at your feet or, second best, leashed near you though not actually on the premises. We also included restaurants and eateries that offer carryout food when the fare is especially worthy or when the locations feature nearby benches for dining with the dog or that are near a good park and convenient for picking up a picnic lunch. No, we didn't include every Chinese carryout restaurant—there are simply too many of them. And for philosophical and practical reasons we didn't include the usual suspects from the world of fast food; we didn't want to even go there. Besides, you know these places are everywhere without our pointing them out and contributing to the blight of high calories, high-fat food, obesity in America, and uh, never mind; don't get us started.

You'll find that leniency on serving patrons with pups outdoors varies from location to location, from town to town, even on which hostess or manager seats you on a particular night. We've eaten outdoors at restaurants that happily invited Chappy to sit at our ankles while we dined, even brought him a bowl of water and a treat. The same restaurants might reject the doggy idea another time when it's too busy. Some of the restaurants we've listed as dog friendly in this book may even snub you and the pooch when you arrive. Keep in mind that restaurant policies change, people aren't always consistent, managers come and go, and, as your mother taught you, the good graces of strangers can't always be counted on.

When traveling with a dog, sometimes you can bend the rules or make up new ones with friendly restaurant proprietors. On the approach, however, the nicer you and your dog are—the more polite, the more respectful of others—the better chance you'll have of getting seated. Often just showing that you have good intentions and a sweet pup can get you a table.

But if you're turned down, don't take offense. Don't scream and shout. Don't walk out in a huff. These aren't moral judgments the restaurant managers are making. Don't take it personally. Fussing about rules that are beyond the control of a hard-working waiter or hostess isn't going to change a twit for others following in your paw prints. It certainly isn't going to change overnight a culture that usually without question separates dogs and food service. But if you act like a bonehead, it might convince folks that the rules are right to begin with.

Some other restaurant rules of etiquette: If you do get seated with your dog, say, at an outdoor table, keep her at floor level. A dog's face, tongue out and dripping, ready to pounce where food is served, won't make you welcome guests. How other patrons respond to your pooch nearby may well determine whether this magic moment happens again—ever. Dogs in restaurants should be barely seen and never heard. One serious no-no is letting your dining dog beg—from you or from other nearby diners. Nobody wants to dig in to a lovely, aged filet mignon with béarnaise sauce only to meet eye to eye with a craving gourmet mutt at the next table. Staying unobtrusive at a restaurant also includes being clean. If not for your own pleasure, certainly for that of other patrons, don't bring a dirty dog to a restaurant.

ROOM SERVICE

Hotels change policies, too. And this second edition is a testament to that fact. No sooner does one hotel that a few years ago greeted Rover with doggy chocolates and chilled bowls of water do a turnabout in policy, than another suddenly lays down the welcome mat to any mutt that needs a place to stay. Go figure. This second time around, we found a wide variety of responses to our inquiries about dogs staying at hotels. Some of them charge high dog fees and many require deposits that are returned if the room is unharmed. Some require that you stay in a room designated for smokers. (We'd rather smell a wet dog!) Others request that you not leave your dog alone in the room—which makes good sense because a dog left alone in unfamiliar surroundings is a license for trouble, no matter how good the pay-per-view show is.

Some hotels ask that you always be present with your dog or take your dog out when housekeeping arrives to make the beds, clean toilets, and otherwise neaten up. Many put weight restrictions on accepting dogs—though we never once walked into a hotel lobby and faced a weigh-in at the check-in counter. A few required that you clear the dog by getting the manager's approval over the telephone before arriving.

A lot of red tape, you say? Most hotels simply don't allow dogs at all—not in rooms, not in their lobbies, not by the pool, nowhere on their property.

The point is that if dog lovers want to encourage hotels and the hotel industry to loosen policies on dog guests, we can't fuel the debate by providing bad examples and nightmare incidents. In the first edition, a concierge at one fancy hotel in Washington told us how its dog-friendly policy suddenly got more restrictive one night after a mastiff client left in the room alone at dinnertime acted like a crazed rock 'n' roller and tore the place apart. By the second edition, the hotel had changed hands, and dogs are no longer invited to the party. But many hoteliers know that most dog guests are wonderful, well-behaved, and trouble-free. They don't poop where they shouldn't, they don't chew the antique furniture, they don't leave their signature in the lobby, they don't keep the neighbors up all night, they don't slam doors, and they don't steal the towels.

Good etiquette goes a long way when there's room in the inn for the pupster. Some tips worth following:

Check-In: When checking in, keep the pup on a short leash. The first sign of potential trouble to a desk clerk is your dog wandering the lobby signing the fern urn, while you're signing the guest book.

Time to Get Real: If your pooch isn't house-trained at home, don't even think about taking her to a hotel. Even experienced dogs can have accidents in new and unusual places, especially confined ones like a hotel room. Some will want to mark off new territory. So be prepared. Buy that local newspaper down in the lobby before going up to the room (they're not just for wrapping fish). Try to avoid inevitable problems by taking the pooch outside for walks regularly. We've noted whether hotels have plentiful grassy areas outside around the parking lot or down the street. Use them.

Security Blankets: Chappy doesn't shed, but most dogs do and some dogs so profusely you wonder why they aren't bald. You know if yours does. It's helpful to you and the hotel personnel if you bring along an old blanket, preferably one the dog is emotionally attached to, and spread it out in the corner where you want the pup to sleep. Not only does this help to keep fur from flying and you from pulling your hair out, but it provides your dog with a comfort zone in the room.

Home Alone: As we've already mentioned but think important enough to mention again, don't leave your dog alone in the room. Hotels don't want to have to deal with your sweet pooch who turns into a yapping, whining, rampaging monster when left behind. One hotel manager told us his policy was plain and simple: He calls the city's animal control department and has the dog removed if patrons break this rule and the lonely dog causes trouble. A few hotels provide dog-sitting service as an alternative to patrons who might otherwise be tempted to "let Spike sleep while we're gone." But the bottom line is, if you bring Spike along when traveling, you need to take full responsibility for him.

Through the Back Door? No dice on sneaking dogs into hotels whose policies ban them. That isn't acceptable behavior. We found far more hotels than we ever guessed that accept dogs. Because more people are traveling with their pups, more hotels are accommodating them—and lots of them are doing so happily. Besides, smuggling in the dog makes you and him tense the entire stay. Sounds like fun, huh?

At Your Service: Don't forget the wonders of room service at mealtime when you're traveling with a dog. The same hotel restaurant that wouldn't think of seating Rover will gladly bring the same meal to the privacy of your room. You might want to pack your pup's food and water dishes just to help keep him from making a mess.

Do Not Disturb the Staff: Next to opening the door and finding naked people or a dead body, the last thing housekeeping folks at hotels want to find when they come to clean a room—besides a 50-cent tip—is a growling dog. If you have to leave your dog alone momentarily, perhaps to go downstairs for a newspaper, hang the Do Not Disturb sign outside your door. And don't forget to leave a decent tip for maids who accepted your pooch without complaint. Though we dog lovers would like to think otherwise, it is beyond the call of duty for these folks. Housekeepers do extra work when a dog stays overnight. Just like every good pooch, good hoteliers deserve a pat on the head, too.

The room rates we quote in the book are for two adults and a dog in most cases. We generally asked hotels for their double rate—which usually means two double beds. But in the hotel biz, there's always a range of prices—including weekend deals, seasonal variations, special event–related rates, and so on. At one hotel, all we had to do was hesitate when quoted a price and the desk clerk immediately dropped the rate by $35 a night. Use our quotes as a guide and call ahead for exact dates and rates.

We also tried to steer you and your dog to decent places to stay. Some are modest hotels offering few amenities beyond cleanliness, comfort, and convenience. Others, like the Four Seasons Hotel in Georgetown, are first-class adventures for you and your furry traveling companion. We urge that no matter where you're going, always double-check in advance about the current policy regarding dogs.

SAFETY AND HEALTH PROVISIONS

You've picked a four-paw park or the distant wilderness of one of our day trips, and you're ready to head off. Before you do, like a good Boy Scout, make

sure you're prepared for your trip. You need to think of your dog's needs ahead of time. Even though most ventures will go without a hitch or glitch, for your dog's sake you need to be ready for trouble. Here are some pointers:

Water: Water is the first consideration—and oddly, it's the necessity most often forgotten. Water, water everywhere and not a drop to drink? It happens. Out on some trail miles from anywhere, or in the middle of a waterless park on a sunny summer day, being without your own supply of water can be devastating. Don't assume there's always a source of water. Dogs can dehydrate quickly when they're out and about—especially in the heat.

Always carry water with you. Whether it's a thermos, a bottle of designer spring water, or one of those spiffy devices that will purify water instantly, just make sure you have some. Offer it to your thirsty pooch often, no matter what the weather, no matter whether he's asking for it. Manufacturers make nifty collapsible water dishes for dogs that serious hikers like, but your pup can easily drink from an upside-down Frisbee (a good trick), from a cup, or from your cupped hands. Just make sure she drinks plenty.

Doggy Bags: Some folks swear by taking along a "doggy bag" where ever they go with the pup. Nothing fancy is required. A grocery bag (preferably empty) left in the trunk will do fine. But it takes the effort out of remembering things you'll always need when traveling with the dog.

Include a can opener, for instance, since few other tools easily open cans of dog food—especially when you're 25 miles from the nearest 7-Eleven store. You might want to keep a small sealed bag of your pup's favorite dry food, too.

Throw in a couple of cheap plastic bowls—those old yellowed Tupperware ones shoved to the back of the cabinet will work fine, and so will old plastic margarine tubs. That old leash you replaced? Include it. Leashes break, and if you're in the middle of a national park without a spare when that happens, you've got problems.

If your roving Rover is on any kind of medication (Glycoflex for that limpy knee, hydroxyzine for the itchy spot, heartworm pills in case of extended trips, whatever), take a few extras. That's just in case you get waylaid by the beauty of your destination and, being the spontaneous, fun-loving folks you are, you decide to stay another day or week.

A rawhide bone has saved many a night on the road, believe us. A pooper-scooper or stash of plastic bags is a must. A couple of old towels, maybe a blanket. Your pup needs to have current rabies and ID tags on his collar in case of getting separated, but in a crisis away from home, acting fast can make a big difference in finding her. One great idea we came across is to photocopy an 8-by 11-inch "Missing" or "Lost Dog" poster with your dog's photo and specifics on it—including how to reach you there and at home, plus a phone number for a neighbor back at home. On a long trip you may even want to bring along a copy of your dog's rabies certificate. Also, snap one of those barrel-type IDs on your dog's collar, too, showing the name, address, and phone number of where you'll be vacationing. That way if she should get lost, at least the finder won't be calling your empty house. That's about it.

First Aid Kits: A first aid kit is a good idea when taking your dog to the ends of the Earth—even if it only seems that far. As landscape artist John Muir once said, "Whenever we go in the wilderness, we find more than we seek."

Most of us know the usual first aid items for humans, but there are some additionals to assemble when preparing for emergencies involving your dog. For instance, get some Vetrap—a bandage that sticks to fur better without pulling out the hair. Kwik-Stop or styptic powder are coagulants that help to stop blood flow if your pooch gets cut.

If you're roaming in the backwoods, bring along tick tweezers; we adore our handy pair of hemostats because they're so useful in so many ways. But you might even consider a product called Tick Release that forces those dirty, evil critters to back out of there. Other items: strong antibiotic ointment, rectal thermometer, white petroleum jelly, sterile non-adherent bandage pads, antihistamine medication such as Benadryl (in case of allergic reaction), hydrogen peroxide (for cleansing wounds), a self-adhering Ace athletic bandage, Pepto-Bismol tablets (dogs eat stuff they shouldn't), Maalox coated or buffered aspirin, a small pair of scissors, ear and eye ointment such as Terramycin, a disposable razor, Q-tips, and a bandanna. And if you don't know how to perform CPR on a dog, it is a life-saving possibility you can ask your veterinarian about.

Pest Control: Fleas and ticks are not only a drag for you, but they can be a serious health threat to your beloved buddy. Many of the insects carry Lyme disease or heartworm organisms. Consult your vet about flea preventives. Ticks are a particularly big problem in our area. We pull a few of the disgusting creatures off Chap ever summer. To remove, use a device such as tweezers or hemostats or simply grasp as much of the body as you can (the head is generally embedded in the skin). Turn and twist, giving a pulling motion. Then check to make sure you have removed all of the tick. Dab the area with an antiseptic and watch it for a few days for infection.

If you want to try an all-natural insect repellent that's popular among some hikers, mix two cups of vinegar with one cup of Avon Skin So Soft lotion, one cup of water, a tablespoon of eucalyptus oil (buy it at the drug store), and a tablespoon of citronella oil, and pour the mixture into a spray bottle. Other dog lovers say just adding the Avon Skin So Soft in with your pup's conditioner after shampooing also helps keep insects at bay.

Cruising in the Car: Some dogs, like some humans, don't handle long car rides well. Car sickness happens, and it ain't a pretty picture. Some vets recommend giving dogs a half a Dramamine tablet beforehand if this is a recurring problem. That not only helps with the sickness but makes the pooch drowsy. A natural remedy is to feed the dog ginger snaps a half hour before heading out—and that's something Chappy has no problem trying, whether it works or not. Ginger is an age-old Chinese antidote to motion sickness. We know of one dog lover who bought a booster seat for his dog and insists that enabling her pup to see out the front windshield eliminated the problem. We know that has helped us a lot when we're driving.

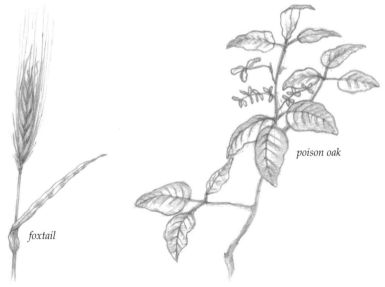

foxtail

poison oak

Pad Problems? Chappy's paw pads were calloused, the vet told us when we took him in for a checkup not too long ago. We don't suspect the wood-chip or dirt paths we'd hiked were the culprit, but paved streets and paths and road salt leftover from wintry conditions had taken a toll. Check your pooch's pads regularly whether you're hiking the park trails often or regularly walking around the block in your neighborhood. If your dog seems to be developing a pad problem, consider soaking his paws in extremely strong cold tea. The tannic acid toughens the pads, we're told. Better not to drink the tea afterward, however. For rough trail hiking, consider buying your dog a set of doggy boots. We know Chappy wouldn't be thrilled with this idea, but it might be helpful to you and yours. Many outdoor camping stores and dog catalogues carry them.

Dogs in Heat? No, this isn't the X-rated part of the book. We're talking temperature. Chappy isn't one for hot days, that's for sure. But you've got to keep a close eye on any dog that's out in the summer heat.

Not that we relish taking Chappy's rectal temperature, but that is one certain method of determining if your dog is suffering from heatstroke. The numbers would be four to seven degrees above a dog's normal temperature range of 100–102.5° F. To know what normal is for your dog, you might want to take your dog's temperature on a day when he has just awakened and is feeling fine.

If you suspect that your dog is overheating and you don't have a rectal thermometer, an alternative method is to feel his groin area for a definitive rise in body heat. If you already know what his normal temperature feels like down there, the comparison will help you detect when the degrees are elevated.

In the early stages of heat exhaustion, a dog pants relentlessly. Panting is a pooch's method of maintaining body temperature. Her oral mucous membranes will also become dry and brick red, so always check the gums for this color change. Also, a dog that's overheating tends to look for ways to help herself. She'll simply lie down and not go further, or seek out shade or bushes to lie in. Puppies and older dogs are more susceptible to heat than other dogs. Later she'll become weak and uncoordinated. Shock eventually sets in, followed by coma and death—if you don't intervene in time.

If you suspect overheating, *do not* immerse the dog in very cold water or ice; use cool water and fan the dog instead. Focus the cooling-off process on the tummy and groin areas. The goal of emergency treatment is to gradually reduce the dog's rectal temperature. Secondary complications are quite common. Obviously, if you suspect your dog is suffering from heatstroke, get her to the vet in a hurry.

If your dog is showing signs of lethargy, check her for dehydration. If you can pull the skin behind her neck away from the body, release it, and notice it doesn't return to natural position, she's dehydrated. Get the dog into the shade immediately, wet her belly and genitals, and get her to drink cool water. Joggers who take their pooches along for a warm-weather run face this problem, so check with your vet before trying to turn your lovable mutt into a marathoner. Even when just hiking the trails, dogs need to rest more frequently than you do.

The Greenhouse Effect: Oh, yeah—need we remind you? Never, *ever*, leave a dog (or child) in a closed car with the windows up in the heat. The burning summer sun can literally turn your car into an oven. Kids and dogs die every year from this kind of thoughtlessness, so don't underestimate how hot that car gets—even for a few minutes.

HAPPY CAMPERS

Taking the dog out to the great outdoors for a weekend in the pup tent? Several points worth keeping in mind when camping with your best friend:

The Leash Debate: Dream as they might of their rugged Rovers racing in the freedom and solitude of America's natural beauty, experienced campers recommend that you hike the wilderness with your dog on a leash—at all times. While the debate between dog hikers rages over on- and off-leash policies (with both sides making convincing arguments), being able to restrain your dog should you bump into a distraction (say, a bear or bobcat) might save your dog's life. Unless he minds your voice commands to a tee without a leash, your backpacking pup just might race off after a deer, squirrel, rabbit, or other creature.

On the other hand, a friend of ours broke two fingers because she had a leash wrapped around her hand when her beefy Lab took off suddenly after a squirrel. You've got to know your dog to know the best method of restraint in the woods. Of course, leash laws on public parklands usually make this a moot point anyway. We advise campers and hikers to follow those rules because dog owners who don't and whose dogs scare wildlife or get into fights with other dogs give park authorities reason to close off more parkland to dogs.

No matter how well-behaved you think your dog is, it is both impolite and dangerous to other campers not to have your dog restrained. As one person on a dog-hike Internet message board noted, "While he is your puddin, sweetums, or darlin, to the rest of the world he is an unfamiliar, 40-pound carnivore."

Don't Let Your Dog Grow Up To Be a Nuisance: Don't let your dog become a nuisance to other campers or animals. This means control her barking and scoop up after her when she poops. If you are inconsiderate, you leave a disgusting camping area for the next tent-pitcher. Also, if you're going to camp out, your dog needs to be well-behaved around other people—both adults and children—as well as other dogs. She will need to understand when playtime is over and not to bark at every hoot of an owl or rustle of a tree. If she has never been to dog school, it's never too late to start. The cost is minimal, and it will make you a better, more responsive dog owner as well as a better camper with a dog.

In Dogs We Trust: Don't venture out if you have doubts about your pooch's ability to camp out. Be ready to pack it up and leave if it doesn't go well. Try to be aware of what situations may make him act strangely or provoke an aggressive or defensive reaction. Don't take him out if you are worried in the slightest that he could injure someone.

Everything's under Control: Allow plenty of time before the sun sets to find your camping spot. If you have to camp near other campers, don't hesitate to let them know that you have a dog. Tell them that while you will keep your dog restrained at all times, they will need to heed his space, and if they have a dog, to keep theirs restrained.

Sleeping Arrangements? Use a lightweight sleeping bag folded in half with a small piece of fleece on top of him for cold nights. Most doggy campers agree it's best to bring the pup inside the tent rather than leash him outside. There are too many nocturnal critters out there to make him fit to be tied.

Keeping Current: Before you head off to a campground, make sure your dog's vaccinations are up-to-date. Out there is where dogs often encounter unvaccinated animals, not to mention skunks. Dog licenses should also be current. It doesn't hurt to check with your vet about the areas where you will be camping; some pose additional health risks for dogs and may warrant additional precautions, such as a stronger heartworm medication.

A Friend in Need: It's also a good idea to notify a friend where and when you're going camping and check in with the park rangers at the park headquarters where you'll be camping. Most campgrounds require it anyway, though some backwoods camping doesn't. But someone needs to know where you're going in case of an emergency.

The check-in is also essential to clarify what you can and can't do with your dog. Unfortunately, uncontrolled dogs and irresponsible pet owners have contributed to the sometimes hostile reactions by fellow campers and the closing of many campsites to dogs. Always ask at the camp station if dogs are allowed in the campsite and respect whatever rules the campground has regarding dogs.

TO LEASH OR NOT TO LEASH

Using a leash on your dog isn't only a decision to be made when in the backwooods of a national park or camping out on some distant mountaintop. Just walking around the block in your neighborhood raises the same issues for dedicated dog owners. It seems like darn near every time you walk your dog on a leash, an off-leash dog is going to run up and give you a scare.

Most of the time, the other dog and even his owner don't mean any harm—and won't cause any. The two pooches will just sniff each other where the sun

---

don't shine, approve or disapprove, and move on. They might even like each other and want to play. Sometimes tensions will rise and you'll notice the telltale signs of a dog fight about to happen.

Dog fights have little or nothing to do with gender and almost everything to do with the dominance of one dog over another. If two dogs are dominant and meet nose to nose (which is a very confrontational stance in dogdom), there's going to be fight. Allowing dogs to be leash-free not only raises the likelihood, it ups the ante and gives the off-leash dog an advantage.

Debates are unending on the topic in dog circles. Few issues draw a line between dog lovers more heatedly. There are those dog lovers who feel dogs should be allowed to run free—so they break the rules. There are also those dog lovers who feel that letting dogs loose will not only ruin the fun for everyone but is intimidating to their own pets, not to mention themselves. When a big and aggressive dog comes bounding up without seeming to be under any control, it can be frightening. We've heard sad dogfight stories that end with the on-leash and law-abiding dog getting the worst of it. We've heard of dog lovers who resorted to carrying pepper spray and golf clubs to ward off aggressive off-leash dogs—and in a couple of cases, their owners. Dog lovers, can't we just get along?

In this book, we use a leash-free symbol ( ) to signify places where dogs are allowed to run free. Yet most parks still and always will require that a dog be on her leash. That's not to say that there aren't some rangers who have told us that they look the other way if the dog is friendly and well-behaved. And you're going to find plenty of parks where you and your not-a-mean-bone-in-her-body pooch are the only ones around, and that leash snaps off so easily. But of course friendly and well-behaved dogs aren't usually the problem.

That's also not to say that there aren't parks, such as the amazing canine hangout at Battery Kemble Park in Washington, where most of the dogs, dozens of them at times, run wild with almost no hassles. Basically, our recommendation is that you should expect leash laws just about everywhere nowadays. Abide by them. Remember that the one result of dogs running free and causing trouble in public places is more No Dogs Allowed signs in public places—something no dog lover wants.

IT'S A DOG! IT'S A PLANE!

Planning to travel on an airplane with your dog? Our first rule is to reconsider. Air travel is an iffy proposition for pups and the changing official policies and even unofficial attitudes of the major air carriers towards flying animals makes it all the more iffier. Add the fact that dogs die in the cargo holds of airplanes every year—especially in summer months when the plane is delayed at the airport and it gets too hot for man or beast in there—and there's a lot to think over. Some airlines go so far as to embargo all pet travel in their baggage compartments. But don't count on the airline reservation folks to give you advice in your dog's best interest. "Shoulda woulda" doesn't work if your dog is overheating at 20,000 feet.

Other aspects of air travel for dogs, though not as alarming, are at least unpleasant. If you don't keep your pooch inside a regulation-size dog carrier at home for hours at a time, why do it when you need to fly? Some breeds of dogs don't do well in warmer conditions, either. Hey, you could be flying to New York and your pup could be heading to San Diego after that transfer in Chicago—and don't tell us your luggage never did that. It also costs a bundle to fly your dog.

Okay, those possibilities haven't deterred you? You're certain your dog won't be traumatized by being caged for hours in a strange and lonely compartment at altitudes he can't possibly contemplate? The first rule of flight is to call in advance and check on airline policies about dog travelers. Some airlines have good reputations for dealing with flying dogs. Talk it through with the customer service representative when making reservations. Find out what is required in terms of carrier size and regulations, length of flight and layovers, and so on.

For any flight you need to send water along. A small bowl three-quarters filled with frozen water and attached to the inside of the carrier will melt fast enough to quench your dog's thirst but slow enough not to spill. You need to feed the pup several hours before he boards the plane and make sure to give a last-stop for peeing, too. Longer flights are harder: If there are layovers, you can attach a sealed bag of kibble to the top side of the carrier with instructions for airline baggage personnel to feed him—and cross your fingers that they do.

Other dog-flight basics include labeling the carrier with "Live Animal" signs on each side, marking arrows pointing out its up side, and enclosing a sheet with your name, address, phone, the dog's name, and destination.

THE SCOOP ON DOG POOP

This is no news flash. At this point everyone knows that you should scoop your dog's poop. We got into a pretty good habit of tying a plastic baggy around Chappy's leash (at our end) before we set out so that we wouldn't have to worry about remembering to carry something for the job. There are numerous contraptions and devices available these days, too, for scooping up what dogs' behinds leave behind. Some parks that know its clientele is populated with pups often provide poop bags near their entrance points. This ain't fun for most of us, but it does help keep places clean and inviting for other dogs and people.

ABOUT THIS BOOK

Not for the first edition, certainly not the second, did we eat at every restaurant and stay in every hotel. That would take a lifetime to do, especially with Chappy sniffing every tree and hydrant, and marking every other clump of grass.

For those establishments that we didn't experience firsthand, we relied on our reporting skills instead of rating them. We leave that up to you. Keep in mind that businesses change hands or fold, managers change policies, and new laws are enacted. For every hotel and motel entry, we called or visited the place—with or without Chappy. But you should always call ahead first to confirm that the policies remain dog-friendly.

BEYOND THE BORDERS

You and your dog might actually want to venture beyond the boundaries of this book . . . maybe head for the Wild West or other parts of this country. Avalon Travel Publishing covers many other states and areas of the country. All of the authors are experts in their areas and have adventurous dogs who help them explore and rate the attractions. For more information on obtaining any of the other Dog Lover's Companions, visit this website: www. dogloverscompanion.com.

A DOG IN NEED

We would be remiss if we didn't encourage you to head to the local pound to see if you could give an unwanted dog a new home and a new lease on life. Especially if you don't currently have a dog and this book inspired you, consider the companionship you could bring into your life. Page through this book and look at the adventures that await you and your new best pal. To paraphrase John Lennon, the love you get is equal to the love you give—and that's no truer than with dogs.

The pet supply chain PetsMart sponsors regular, easy-to-do dog and cat adoptions at some of its stores in the Washington and Baltimore areas. Local humane societies and shelters are more than happy to assist you in taking home one of their needy and unwanted dogs—some of whom won't see another sunset unless some kind dog lover like you rescues them.

For more information, contact the local branches of the SPCA, humane society, or animal league in your county or city. Or contact the National Humane Education Society, a nonprofit group that encourages kindness to animals and the adoption of unwanted animals, at 521-A East Market Street, Leesburg, VA 20175; 703/777-8319; website: www.nhes.org.

DISTRICT
OF COLUMBIA

The canine presence has long been a part of the scenery in the nation's capital, where politicians know that every baby kissed and every dog patted is a potential vote. In fact, the savviest politicians, Washington's long line of first families, have set the tone of canine accompaniment through history. Benefiting personally and politically from the friendship of their dogs, the leaders of the Free World have valued their right-hand pooches, from Airedales and floppy-eared beagles to ordinary mutts, as best friends that help soften public images. They may be power brokers, but a lot of them are dog lovers, too. And that ought to be worth some benefit of the doubt when the independent counsel asks for grand jury testimony, right?

Even the area's most illustrious residents have deferred to the nonpartisan loyalty of four-legged confidants. George Washington knew nothing of today's PAC mentality, but he cherished his pack of foxhounds, given to him by his dear French friend the Marquis de Lafayette. Thomas Jefferson's Briards too often dined on sheep, while James Monroe judiciously governed the burgeoning nation in much the same way his favorite two dogs steered their woolly herds. John Tyler had wolfhounds and James Buchanan a Newfoundland. Abe Lincoln? Is it any surprise that the Great Emancipator's furry companion was a common mutt named "Jip"? James Garfield had a dog named Veto, which may tell you something of his relationship with Congress. Warren Harding's Airedale Laddie Boy regularly attended cabinet meetings with his master and even had his own chair; Laddie's birthday parties included dogs from the neighborhood. Teddy Roosevelt's favorite dog was a terrier named Skip who won over the Rough Rider's heart the day he confronted a wild bear as his master hunted in the Grand Canyon. Franklin Delano Roosevelt had a Scottie named Fala, who accompanied him always and stood at attention during the playing of the national anthem. Once, the Republican opposition wrongly claimed that FDR dispatched a naval destroyer to fetch Fala from the Aleutian Islands. When the president counterattacked that the GOP was attacking his little dog, the public turned nasty toward the Republican dog kickers.

Occasionally First Dogs land on newspaper front pages and make history. More than a decade before Richard Nixon was dogged by the Watergate scandal, he served as President Eisenhower's vice president and even then was under attack. His sweet cocker spaniel Checkers probably spared his political neck with what history has recorded as the "Checkers Speech." Nikita Khrushchev added to Jack Kennedy's pack of Hyannisport dogs when the Soviet premier gave the president's daughter Caroline the pups of his pooch Pushinka. Who could forget Lyndon Johnson's beagles, Him and Her? They became media darlings when pics of LBJ lifting them by their floppy ears hit the front pages and humane society supporters howled in protest. Gerald Ford's golden retriever Liberty stayed close to the president in the Oval Office.

Proving publishing is a dog-eat-dog business, George Herbert Walker Bush's springer spaniel Millie wrote a book (with First Lady Barbara Bush) that made the *New York Times* bestseller list and outsold the president's own autobiography. Presidential candidate Bob Dole and his miniature schnauzer Leader tried to return the White House to the dogs after four years of Bill Clinton's cat house—but Dole fell short by too many kibbles in the electoral college. Of course, once Clinton's address changed to 1600 Pennsylvania Avenue, the Great Schmoozer realized a dog could take the heat off and adopted Buddy. Sadly, just about a year after the Clintons left the White House, Buddy was hit by a car and killed outside his New York home. George W. Bush brought Spot, his 11-year-old English springer spaniel, to the White House— and the Republicans would argue it's the only Spot on the president's record. Spot, by the way, is the offspring of former President George Bush's dog, Millie, and was actually born in the White House in 1989. She's the only second-generation pet in presidential history. And since arriving at 1600 Pennsylvania Avenue, the Bushes have added a second pooch—a Scottish terrier named Barney.

Yup, dogs make news in this town where reporters pounce on any juicy story that can put a public figure in the doghouse, like when the *Washington Post* slipped in a scandalous item about a certain Democratic campaign strategist and his pet's illicit activities. Seems James Carville, the outspoken Democratic insider who masterminded Bill Clinton's first presidential campaign, knows a bark that's worse than a sound bite. He was walking his pet when nature (instead of the Oval Office) called. When the poop was written up in the paper, a miffed Carville complained about "leaks" in Washington: "If your dog defecates on the Capitol grounds, they put it in the paper!" Hey, a scoop is a scoop.

But the key issue to the canine citizenry hereabouts isn't politics so much as the postcard perfection of the nation's capital that largely keeps pooches in the picture. More than 1,000 acres of national capital property is parkland in this city of might. It's not all trees and green fields, mind you. Included in that gerrymandering of greenery among the concrete and marble are historic sites such as the White House, where dogs aren't formally invited. But more than 150 historic parks, squares, circles, and triangles, plus 170 manicured flower beds and 35 ornamental pools—the likes of which are found nowhere this side of that other dog-loving burg known as Paris—bejewel the low-rise city.

Those similarities aren't coincidental, by the way. The open space and parks found throughout the 67 square miles of the District of Columbia were part of the 1791 plan for the federal city designed by Frenchman Pierre L'Enfant, the *enfant terrible* architect of his day, who can be credited and blamed for the upsides and downsides of this city's layout. Dog lovers will find the colossal monuments and commemorative gardens he blueprinted to be mostly dog-accommodating as long as respect is properly paid. Lifting a leg against a statue of a Founding Father (not that that would *ever* happen) would be wrong. Very wrong. And even though the elected officials here frequently step in it, etiquette and the law require that you pick up what your doggy leaves behind.

In a city that rules, you have to expect some rules. Dog leash laws are in effect in the District: Your dog is required to be "firmly secured by a substantial leash" no longer than four feet in all parks and public areas. Scoop laws? Dog owners must "immediately remove dog excrement from any curb, gutter, alley or street." Violations risk fines of up to $300.

Parking rules are in effect as well. If driving into the District for a day of dog-walking the historic sites, there's a strategy to parking you should know. Traffic in Washington can be maddening. That's understating its effect during rush hours. So, if possible, avoid those times. Otherwise, first place to try to search for parking is the National Mall itself, along both Jefferson Drive and Madison Drive, the two main thoroughfares running the length of the Mall. You can't park along the Mall in the early morning hours, but late morning and afternoon parking is possible and people grabbing the spots tend to be tourists or locals visiting the museums who come and go. If you're lucky enough to find a space there, it's free for up to three hours.

We tend to be lucky with Chappy along. But there's another parking possibility if you're bringing along any other breed: South of the Lincoln Memorial, along Ohio Drive and West Basin Drive in West Potomac Park, you'll find some free parking without time restrictions. The alternative is to find a nearby parking garage and pay for the privilege.

Another logistical challenge for visitors is navigating. The District is divided into four directional quadrants: Northwest, Northeast, Southwest, and Southeast. Look at it this way: The division begins at the Capitol itself, with North Capitol and South Capitol Streets being the east-west boundaries and East Capitol Street and its imaginary extension through the middle of the National Mall all the way to the Lincoln Memorial being the north-south boundary.

Dogs have no problem with this, but humans tend to get confused when finding themselves at Third Street SE when their appointment's at Third Street NW. To shorten the leash on this confusion, we've ignored these divisions for all entries under the heading of the National Mall—except in their addresses. The Mall technically encompasses all four designations, you see. Oh, never mind. Other locations throughout the District are categorized by their correct quadrants. Also, because this is a national city where so much is owned and operated by the federal government, national parks are listed by their neighborhood locations.

One word of caution: Since September 11, 2001, when terrorists attacked the World Trade Center in New York City and the Pentagon here, some public spaces around the Capitol Building and the White House have been fenced or blocked with barriers to deter future terrorists. It's an inconvenience that's necessary, so consider any deterrence to terrorism you may come across when strolling with your pooch as a national prerogative and not an imposition.

Meanwhile, much of the District offers unique dog-lover opportunities that you won't find anywhere else. There's nothing quite like nuzzling up to your pooch on a warm summer evening under the stars at the National Mall, listening to the National Symphony Orchestra perform a Mozart or Beethoven ditty with the dramatically lit Capitol as the backdrop. And that special moment may come for you, as it did for us, when we embraced our pup Chappy—only to realize that Chappy's excitement wasn't the orchestra at all. Rather, he'd mistaken the magnificent Capitol dome for the most incredible hydrant he'd ever contemplated. And that's no editorial, folks, just a dog's imagination at work.

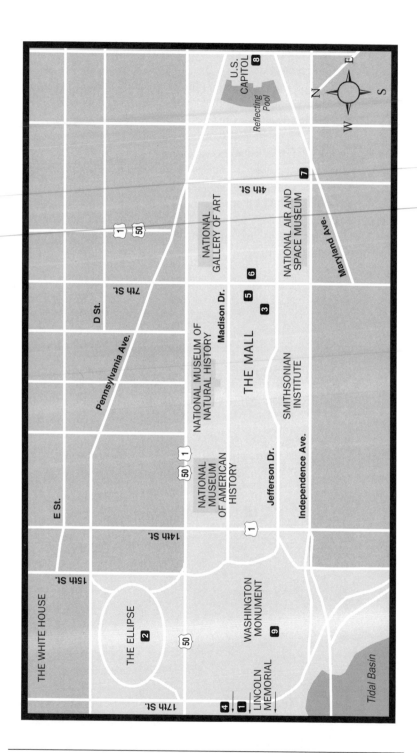

THE NATIONAL MALL

At the heart of the city, this is a memorable place where a piece of history awaits you and the pooch 'round every corner and beside every fire hydrant. A grassy 146-acre expanse with its hundreds of varieties of trees and majestic statues and fountains, it's a perfect dog-walking setting. Most of the monuments are images embedded in our national consciousness and attract hundreds of thousands of tourists annually. The celebrations, protests, demonstrations, and festivals that have been held in this national open space are among the events that mark the pages of history books. Framed by rows of old elm trees and home to the Smithsonian Institution, the National Mall has something for both you and your dog to enjoy—and to marvel at the wonder of a free society.

National Parks

1 Constitution Gardens 🐾 🐾 🐾 🐾 🐕

More than 50 acres of tree-shaded lawns and a six-acre lake—who would believe such a puppy paradise could exist smack dab in the middle of a large metropolitan area, much less the capital of the country? Dedicated in 1976 as a living legacy garden in tribute to the founding of the nation, the park's centerpiece is a memorial to the 56 signers of the Declaration of Independence that rests on the one-acre, man-made island in the middle of a six-acre lake.

Take the footbridge over to the island and check out the replicas of the signatures on the Declaration, etched there in granite. During the heat of August, Chappy turns Hemingwayesque and likes to thinks of this as his *Island in the Stream*. Pups do occasionally dive in on hot days even if they aren't supposed to.

Strolling through these gardens with your pooch (leashed, as required by law) is not only an experience in stunning scenic beauty but also a lesson in what good government can accomplish. The long stretches of pathways are partly shaded. Near the western end of this park stand the polished black granite walls of the Vietnam Veterans Memorial, inscribed with the names of those who died or are still missing from the Vietnam War. This heartfelt reminder of the horrors and futility of war is surrounded by so much green space that reverent dogs go largely unnoticed though not unappreciated. And the latest war—the one against terrorism—has changed the face of this park only slightly, with some barriers on its perimeter.

The park is located along Constitution Avenue NW, between the Washington Monument grounds and the Lincoln Memorial at Henry Bacon Drive. Parking is best along Constitution Avenue, if you're lucky and it's not rush hour (you will be towed). The gardens are open 24 hours a day but are densely dark after sunset. It is well patrolled by kind park rangers, and crime isn't a big problem on the National Mall. But as in any big city, use good judgment. 202/426-6841.

2 The Ellipse 🐾 🐾 🐾 🐾

This grand landscaped oval just south of the White House is part of what's formally known as President's Park (the other part being gregarious Lafayette Square on the other side of the White House), but nobody calls it that. The park was designed to be a pretty view for the First Family but doubles as a splendid downtown destination for dog lovers with pooches in tow (meaning leashed). Besides, strolling through these manicured lawns with the leader of the free world undoubtedly watching you from his window directly across the street is kind of cool. And there are the expected monuments; Chappy's favorite is the Boy Scouts of America statue alongside 15th Street NW where a fountain flows in season. Take that as a reminder to be a good scout hereabouts: New barriers and Secret Service checkpoints were erected in the aftermath of the September 11, 2001 terrorist attacks. Vehicles are definitely restricted here; dogs and their human companions on foot, less so. The Ellipse is located between 15th and 17th Streets NW and Constitution Avenue and E Street NW, with the best parking opportunities on side streets opposite 17th Street NW. It's open 24 hours a day, and the White House looks absolutely magnificent at night. 202/426-6841.

3 Hirshhorn Museum and Sculpture Garden 🐾 🐾 🐾 🐾

While the inside of this repository of contemporary art is off-limits even to the most art cravin' of canines, the Hirshhorn Sculpture Garden just outside is a cultural playground where leashed and well-behaved dogs are allowed to absorb some of the finer things in life—large sculptures by such notables as Rodin and Miró, in stone, bronze, and other materials.

But keep your pooch back from the artwork, puhleeze! For that matter, don't touch it yourself. Though these pieces appear to be tough as nails, even the salty sweat from human fingertips takes a terrible toll over time. So you can imagine what damage certain doggish fluids might do—no need for specifics, is there? The sculpture garden is free and located between Seventh and Ninth Streets NW on the National Mall side of the Hirshhorn. It's open daily, 10 A.M.–5:30 P.M. 202/357-3235.

4 Lincoln Memorial 🐾 🐾 🐾 🐾

This stately monument and surrounding grounds to the west side of the National Mall are an emotionally moving stopoff if you're trying to catch the spirit of official Washington with your four-footed pal. A must-see destination if you're visiting the city, this is probably a long-overlooked one if you've lived here very long.

The colossal statue of the Great Emancipator, Abraham Lincoln, seated and gazing across the Reflecting Pool toward the Capitol and the Washington Monument, is a sight to behold, especially at night when lit against the black sky. Our hyper-patriotic Chappy dared not misstep or yank the leash too taut before the imposing Mr. Lincoln.

Either side of the interior is etched with the words of the Gettysburg Address and Lincoln's Second Inaugural Address, though Chappy wouldn't sit through an entire reading of both. The greenscape surrounding the memorial and framing the stunning reflecting pool is a dog lover's dream come true, with lots of trees and spectacular views that make a walk in the capital city most positively memorable—as it was meant to be. For camera-toting dog lovers few locations offer as perfect a pic as your pooch sitting alone midway on these grand steps. ("Stay, boy, stay!") The memorial and grounds are located at 23rd Street NW, where Daniel French and Henry Bacon Drives converge. It's open 24 hours daily—and friendly park rangers are around those hours. 202/485-9875.

5 National Gallery of Art Sculpture Garden 🐾 🐾 🐾

Among the newest dog-inviting attractions on the National Mall, this outdoor garden of exquisite sculpture blended into a parkland setting opened in 2000. With fascinating pieces of durable art on display, from Scott Burton's warm red granite "seats" sculpture to Alexander Calder's painted sheet-metal sculpture "Cheval Rouge," this is an ideal cultural diversion for the pooch. On

Friday evenings, there's even a jazz band that performs at the sculpture garden's majestic fountain. Enter at any of its six entrances with your dog on leash (a short one), of course. Open Monday–Saturday from 10 A.M.–5 P.M. and Sunday from 11 A.M.–6 P.M. (plus extended hours in the summer), it is located at Seventh Street and Constitution Avenue NW. 202/737-4215.

6 National Mall 🐾 🐾 🐾 🐾 🐾

This stretch of green flat parkland that cuts a broad and magnificent swath between the United States Capitol and the Lincoln Memorial originally was planned to be an elegant, formal garden. In our rowdy, fun-loving democratic republic, this elongated plot of land, which comes as close to being sacred ground as anywhere, is a casual and informal outdoor sanctuary to those who cherish freedom.

In the summer, you and the pooch will find plenty of company here: Women in tank tops jogging (Chappy's favorite sight, uh, because many of them bring their own dogs on leashes), jogging marines with flat tops, codgers on the park benches jogging their memories, tourists just being tourists—can provide an abundance of free entertainment. Immigrant vendors peddle egg rolls, hot dogs, pizza, and patriotic T-shirts on the perimeter. Don't be surprised to find dogs running free sometimes, despite national park laws requiring leashes.

This is prime people-watching and dog-walking territory. Stick to the time-worn paths on the inner area of the Mall when accompanying your dog, especially in warm weather when crowds descend on the various museums of

DIVERSIONS

Around and Around: Bowsers aren't allowed on the fanciful merry-go-round that's a landmark near the Smithsonian Castle on the National Mall, because dizzy dogs aren't a pretty sight. But on a lovely summer day, watching tykes take the turns goin' round and round, well, even Chappy agrees life doesn't get any better than this. The colorful old-time carousel is easy to spot along Jefferson Drive on the National Mall. 202/357-2700.

Not Rinky Dink: It's small, yes, but how quaint and charming in mid-winter, when the Mall's frozen tundra is less inviting, to take the polar puppy to watch the ice skaters on the rink near the front steps of the National Sculpture Garden and the National Museum of Natural History. Rent skates if you're inspired, though the dog will have to stay outside the fence. Otherwise, buy a cup of hot chocolate or steaming java from the rink's refreshment stand and watch the spills and thrills. Between Seventh and Ninth Streets NW on Madison Drive. 202/789-7000.

the Smithsonian Institution that line the outer edges of this spectacular park. You can walk its dirt paths, run its grassy middle, sit in the shade on its many park benches beneath stately elms, throw Frisbees, play ball, or bring a blanket and work on your tan.

One time when we brought Chappy for a midwinter stroll, a serious touch football game was underway in front of the National Gallery of Art—though no Kennedys were involved. In spring, this area is the springboard for witnessing the miracle of the cherry blossoms that alter reality for a week or two around the nearby Tidal Basin and the Washington Monument—not to disregard the more than 2,000 stately American elms that grace these grounds. In summer, this is Washington at its best and brightest!

The National Mall is bordered to the north by Constitution Avenue and to the south by Independence Avenue, with Madison and Jefferson Drives the main routes running parallel through it. It's open around the clock, though it's probably advisable not to stroll here or anywhere in the grand federal canyon, for that matter, in the wee hours. There's plenty of free parking along Madison and Jefferson Drives (after 10 A.M.) and metered parking along the cross streets; only problem is that there are plenty of parkers as well. 202/426-6841.

7 United States Botanic Gardens 🐾 ½ 🐕

Inside this hothouse conservatory, which was reopened in 2002 after an extensive rehab, is a tropical rain forest hyped up on hormones—and a little oasis of tranquility. Cacti, orchids, and other subtropical species rule here, but dogs can't go inside. The outside, however, makes for a mellow breather when hiking the government turf down by the Capitol end of the Mall with your canine lobbyist along.

Out back and just across busy Independence Avenue from the Botanic Gardens is a charming piece of paradise where you and your leashed dog can dawdle amid the exterior gardens. A multitude of seasonal blooms engulf the bench and sidewalk areas around its magnificent Bartholdi Fountain, designed by the sculptor of the Statue of Liberty. This is one of the primo little parks in the city, good not so much for hiking as for meditative ambience.

The Botanic Gardens are located at Maryland Avenue and First Street SW, at the base of the Capitol building, and are open from 9 A.M. to 5 A.M. daily. The gardens' Bartholdi Park is located at Independence and Washington Avenues SW, behind the Botanic Gardens. It's open all hours, but use discretion after dark. 202/225-8333.

8 United States Capitol 🐾 🐾 🐾 ½ 🐕

Pierre L'Enfant must have loved dogs and humans. He designed this lovely 200-acre mound, which, in his words, was "a pedestal waiting for a monument." Not that the public usually puts politicians up on a pedestal any more, but the monument turned out to be the bold and beautiful United States

Capitol building. Inside is off-limits to doggy constituents, no matter what their voting record or how much they want to serve their country. But most of the surrounding grounds of the Capitol are fair play and plenty of fun play in the shadow of the national symbol of democracy in action. The exception: Those areas blocked off for safety precautions since the September 11 terrorist attacks. Concrete barricades, chain-link fencing and strategically placed cement planters definitely diminish the beauty of the Capitol grounds and its accessibility to meanderers like us. Some of the barriers have been here since the Reagan administration, when terrorists bombed the Marine Corps barracks in Beirut. Eventually, steel bollards will be erected, which will provide more aesthetically pleasing security for the Capitol.

While your senators and representatives are inside plotting their re-elections, planning their testimony before the ethics committee, and carrying on the business of the nation (or just carrying on, as the case may be), you and the pooch can be sniffing out corruption, evidence, and other scents outside.

Quorum call for canines used to take place at the expansive West Front of the Capitol, an on-leash area dominated by grassy terraces and gardens that were designed by Frederick Law Olmsted, who also planned New York's Central Park. But some of these once carefree grounds are now blocked even to pedestrian traffic—meaning you and the peaceful-minded pooch. The Capitol police force is a clear and present presence, especially closer to the Capitol building itself. Even portions of the Capitol's steps are shut down to footsters until further notice.

Stroll to the bottom of this capital hill to see the Peace Monument on the northwest side and the Garfield Monument on the southwest side. Both make worthy stop-and-sniff spots on the way down all those white marble steps to the majestic Capitol Reflecting Pool, a grand concrete pond where Chappy got an awesome though rippled view of himself and the Capitol at once—a prime photo op for dog lovers that could just make the front of your notecards.

The grassy tree-lined charms of the northwest and southeast back sides of the Capitol, opposite the Library of Congress and the Supreme Court, have major tree-lined, grassy charms as well, but have also been secured. These old trees and shady walking spaces are truly magnificent sights, though you'll have to maneuver around some of the concrete barricades erected to block terrorists from steering explosive vehicles up into the seat of legislative power. You can't miss this monumental residence of representative democracy on the east end of the National Mall between Constitution and Independence Avenues and (believe it or not) First Streets NW, NE, SW, and SE. The Capitol grounds are open 24 hours a day, though daylight visiting is recommended. 202/225-2800.

9 The Washington Monument 🐾 🐾 ½ 🐾

One of the greatest obelisks in the world, the monument dedicated to the first president stands 555 feet tall—which is the standard of height no building in the downtown Washington area can eclipse. In February 2002, the stunning tribute reopened after closing its doors to visitors for a couple of years of remodeling. Now there are plans underway to build an underground entrance to help foil potential terrorist attacks. But the panoramic sightseeing from the monument's top windows are for people only—dogs need not apply. So don't bother standing with your leashed pup in that line at the visitors' kiosk for a ticket.

The dog-friendly outside is a grassy hill surrounded by 50 United States flags that overlook the city as the four winds blow—and it does get blustery up here. During tourist season, the area provides a fascinating scene for those who opt to sit aside and observe. In warmer weather, inevitably there is one group or another staging an educational or protest presence on the properties—and it's usually interesting. Park if you can on the north side off Constitution Avenue. The Washington Monument is located at the west end of the National Mall at 15th Street NW, and is open daily, 8 A.M.–midnight. 202/426-6841.

Restaurants

Bullfeathers: This favored Hill saloon and eatery attracts congressional staffers, its name presumably a euphemism for another favorite pastime on the Hill. The patio is enclosed so a doggy dining companion isn't a welcome sight, but Chappy enjoyed the afternoon we carried out its legendary juicy burgers to one of the several small triangle parks in the neighborhood where we found a little grass, a park bench, some shade, and a lunchtime view of life a few blocks east of the Capitol. 410 First Street SE; 202/543-5005.

Le Bon Cafe: Overlooked by tourists, this is a lunch magnet for Hill staffers who come for great salads, sandwiches, and hearty soups. Vegetarians have a place on this menu, too. You and the power pooch are welcome to sit at one of the outside tables in warm weather. No dinner though—it closes at 5 P.M. 210 Second Street SE; 202/547-7200.

Pete's Carry-Out: This charming little eatery across from the Library of Congress has tables and chairs outdoors during the warm-weather months, and welcomes your dog to sit alongside you there or by the nearby tree. The Philly chicken cheese steak is a big seller among the faux-diet crowd; otherwise, it's burgers and fries. But every day of the week has its own Chinese specialty here. We've picked up a cheap breakfast with Chappy along for the ride. 212 Second Street SE; 202/544-7335.

Taverna Greek Islands: You won't be able to bring that olive-munching pup into this quaint and casual Greek restaurant where the roasted chicken is just lemony enough, and the moussaka is a heavier treat. But when the management puts the tables out on the sidewalk in summer, ask nicely and they'll usually let your dog sit beside you. 305 Pennsylvania Avenue SE; 202/547-8360.

Tune-In: There ain't nothing like this place anywhere else on Capitol Hill—or in the District for that matter. Too bad the old jukebox that once sat at the back of the bar spinning country tunes exclusively has been replaced with a CD jukebox and a bigger selection. But the servers are still 100 percent country, and the food is good old American cooking. There should be a neon sign out front that reads Good Food. Carry out the burgers, of course, but also the barbecue, fish sandwich, meatloaf, hot turkey sandwich with mashed potatoes, sausage, and egg sandwiches—you get the picture. 331 Pennsylvania Avenue SE; 202/543-2725.

Washington Monument Snack Shop: Forget this elaborate hotdog stand during the thick of tourist season (unless you're a tourist, of course), because in season it's packed tighter than a kielbasa. Housed in something of a concrete bunker with a souvenir shop in the front, it's a great spot for cooling off your dogs *and* the dog after rambling around the National Mall. And it's good for grabbing a quick frankfurter or burger, fries, ice cream—the sort of touristy chow that is also available at food service locations in each of the Smithsonian museums nearby and at mid-Mall near the carousel and the Smithsonian Institution building on Jefferson Drive. The snack shop is located at the foot of the hill that leads up to the Washington Monument, near where Madison Drive intersects 15th Street NW.

Places to Stay

Hotel Washington: Try taking your pup up to the Sky Terrace Lounge on this venerable hotel's roof just to catch one of the best panoramic skyline views of the nation's capital—short of the top perch of the Washington Monument, that is. But don't go up there at lunchtime or dinner or the busy after-work drinking hours, because the fewer the customers the better your chances of a friendly bartender or waiter saying, "Sure, go ahead," as they did for Chappy. Location—overlooking the White House—is everything at this aging 344-room hotel, circa 1918, which has been restored nicely in recent years. And dogs are welcome with no extra charges, no deposits and no questions asked. "No nothing, a dog is no problem," the front-desk receptionist reassured us. Rates start at $125. 15th Street and Pennsylvania Avenue NW, Washington, DC 20004; 202/638-5900.

Annual Events

Make a Wish, Abe: If you're in the neighborhood with your pup on February 12, usually around 11 A.M., stop by the Lincoln Memorial and take in the lineup of dignitaries trying to align their little careers with the Great Emancipator in honor of **President's Day.** The President usually shows up to place a wreath, and military bands cut loose, respectfully, of course. It's a great scene for man and best friend alike. 202/485-9875.

Getting Wiser: If your dog enjoys watching public servants cower before their idols, show up at the Washington Monument on February 22, **George Washington's birthday,** around 11 A.M. to watch congressmen and other dignitaries lay wreaths, speechify, and generally make an official and well-deserved fuss over the father of our nation. 202/619-7222.

Washington Saint Patrick's Day Parade: I'm okay, you're O'Canine? Time to celebrate that state of consciousness known as Eire on March 17. The party starts marching around 1 P.M. and goes 10 blocks with musicians, marching bands, jig dancers, fiddlers, and bagpipers (and did anyone say Guinness?). There are definitely some Irish setters in the crowd, though only an affinity for the national heritage of the day is required of pooches present. Besides, Chappy's learned to bark with a brogue on cue, which is pretty Eire-onic. With or without Gael winds blowing, this is a not-to-be-missed parade that can hardly walk a straight line follows Constitution Avenue from Seventh to 17th Streets NW. It's a rowdy good time had by all, and as always, it happens on March 17. Parking is a bit o' trouble, so get there early. 202/637-2474.

Smithsonian Kite Festival: Any annual, dog-friendly event that is going strong as a nor'easter wind after three decades deserves your and your high-flying Fido's attention. Though the main kiting takes off from the Washington Monument grounds on the Lincoln Memorial side, the festival often ranges farther. It is usually held the last Sunday of March or the first Sunday of April. Lots of people and plenty of dogs (most of them on leashes though inevitably a few are chasing Frisbees and kite tails) show up from just after sunrise and stay to about 5 P.M. Chappy loved roaming about witnessing the inexplicable desire of humanity to take wing and fly. Registration to compete usually takes place from 10 A.M. to noon and is free, as is just watching with fascination. Best on breezy days, the competition rewards design, performance, and other categories that defy the gravity of the moment. 202/357-3030.

National Cherry Blossom Festival: Locals have a love-hate relationship with this annual two-week series of festivities that attracts more than the usual hordes of tourists to witness the nearly indescribable beauty and flowering pastels of hundreds of Yoshino and Akebono cherry trees. A gift from Japan in 1912, they surround the Washington Monument grounds and frame the nearby Tidal Basin with a sight so stunning that, when they blossom in late March or early April, even lifelong Washingtonians catch their breaths momentarily while trying to discern reality. The formal festivities include not only the expected dignitary pomp and ceremonies, but also celebratory dancing, music, even a marathon.

On top of the to-do list for dog lovers is the annual **Cherry Blossom Festival Parade,** which marches up Constitution Avenue from Seventh to 17th Streets NW, between 9:30 A.M. and noon, but get there early if you want to claim a piece of concrete curb. Almost guaranteed, Mother Nature will beat you there with cold rain and snow; it's just tradition. Featuring giant balloons, floats, bands, an international Cherry Blossom princess, and a spankin' new Cherry Blossom Queen, it's probably the largest annual spectator event in Washington—which means your pooch needs to handle crowded humanity well to attend. Traffic and parking near the blossoming trees on parade day or otherwise is a nightmare, so you'd better be willing to hike a good distance from a by-the-hour lot or parking meters several blocks away. Parking lots near the intersection of 17th and I Streets on the other side of Lafayette Park might do. 202/547-1500.

If the crowds of tourists that descend discourage you and the poochster, the annual **Cherry Blossom Festival Rugby Invitational** is held the same weekend—it's psychologically separate and isn't quite so populated. Rugby is an acquired taste, of course—mostly for dark ale (just kidding). But this is a bruising good time, and Chappy loves watching teams from the United States, Canada, and Japan beat the snot out of each other in high school, college, and men's division competition. If you figure too much of this good thing isn't so bad, just take yourself and your dog down to the USA Super League men's match, which pits the Washington Rugby Football Club against the Old Blue Rugby Football Club of New York City on that mid-April Saturday at high noon. The bones break at the National Mall fields, near the Lincoln Memorial from 9 A.M. on. 703/204-4641.

Easter Egg Roll: The only dogs you'll see nosing in on this annual and time-honored egg roll on the Monday after Easter are First Dogs. Mrs. Calvin Coolidge strolled the lawns with her presidential pups wearing Easter bonnets and Mrs. Warren G. Harding greeted children with her Airedale Laddie Boy. But it's as good an excuse as any to take the pooch to the wrought-iron fence surrounding the White House. Watch the kiddies, ages 3–6, in their Easter clothes get down and dirty while rolling the eggs on the White House's South Lawn. The **National Egg Roll** usually lasts from 10 A.M. to 2 P.M. 202/456-2200.

Earth Day: Get out those old earth shoes and leash up the dog for this annual celebration of the planet. Usually held in late April, the festival unfolds on the National Mall with activist groups, greenies, and sundry earthlings (presumably) handing out literature on how to save earthly resources. 202/619-7222.

Cleaning up Your Act: Perk up those ears come late April or so for **National Park Week** when you and your fastidious four-legger can help out the folks who bring you the great outdoors—the National Park Service. Chappy doesn't know stewardship from doggy stew, but he does know an idyllic hiking trail from a littered, pock-holed, ill-kept trail. Every year since 1993, the Park Service has designated certain of its 374 parks nationwide for volunteer clean-up activities during this week. In the metropolitan area, volunteers have rolled up their sleeves and pitched in on the Potomac watershed and the Chesapeake & Ohio Canal, among others. The camaraderie is good, the tasks bring Zen-like satisfaction, and your pup just may gain self worth for doing a good deed. For parks sponsoring volunteer activities this year, call 202/208-5477 or check the Park Service online at website: www.nps.gov. And make sure to ask if it's okay to bring the pup along, because each park has its own rules.

Spike's the Name: The annual **Volleyball-on-the-Mall** competition benefiting Hostelling International and American Youth Hostels takes place on the dog-accommodating grounds near the Lincoln Memorial, 9 A.M.–7 P.M. in mid-May. It's a recreational tournament that typically draws more than 1,000 volleyball enthusiasts, players of all levels—and plenty of room along the sidelines for pups who appreciate a nice set. Round-robin play lasts all day, and going to watch makes an excellent outing if the weather's good. 202/783-0717.

As the Canines Go Rolling Along: Barking out these orders is part of a cherished summertime tradition in the nation's capital. Take the doggy to the **free outdoor concerts** performed by military bands on Tuesday, Thursday, Saturday, and Sunday evening, June–August, at the Sylvan Theater on the grounds of the Washington Monument and at the other end of the National Mall on the West Terrace of the Capitol. Check listings for times and billings. Air Force, 202/767-5658; Army, 703/696-3718; Marines, 202/433-4011; and Navy, 202/433-2525.

Dogged Culture: Nabbing front row seats might be pushing it, but strolling behind the crowd and pulling up a patch of grass with your leashed canine to catch the National Symphony Orchestra performing its traditional **free Sunday-before-Memorial Day concert** is a great way to kick off the long holiday weekend. Guest stars are the norm; the show is free and usually starts at 8 P.M. on the Capitol's West Lawn. Check local listings for the schedule. 202/416-8100.

Smithsonian Festival of American Folk Life: This is an annual bash that's perfect for dog lovers because it spreads across most of the Mall with ethnic foods cooking outdoors, craft displays under tents, musical performances on make-shift stages, and steamy humanity crowding together in the summer heat. Each year the focus is on a different foreign culture and state of the nation and, as a festive afternoon in the nation's capital, it doesn't get any better than this. Nobody worries about dogs on leash because it's just that kind of atmosphere and it's all free (except for the food). The festival takes place annually the last week of June and the first week of July. Located prominently on the National Mall between 10th and 14th Streets NW, it is open each of those days, 11 A.M.–5:30 P.M., with specially scheduled concerts and dances until 7 P.M. 202/357-2700.

Fourth of July Celebration: So what if the Beach Boys don't play a concert at the base of the Washington Monument any more? Get over it. Chappy thinks surfing is a cable television thing anyway. This annual blowout party on the National Mall and Monument grounds is a must-do. But be forewarned: If your pooch doesn't handle shoulder-to-shoulder humanity or loud fireworks well, do not bring him here—at least not for the whole day. To do so would be inhumane. Depending on the weather, the sights and sounds and people of this big time celebration can be stifling to those at knee height—human or canine.

The annual **Independence Day Parade** starts at noon along the tried-and-true parade route on Constitution Avenue, between Seventh and 17th Streets NW. For more refined culture, take the freewheeling pooch to the West Lawn of the Capitol for the National Symphony Orchestra's annual performance with guest stars and distinguished soloists—then get out while the getting is good. But make sure you show up early on the Mall to claim the best blanket territory. Big-name entertainment is always part of the deal throughout the day, so check the newspaper listings. And past nightfall, the fireworks take charge. It's a wonderful day, but if it's a hot Washington July, make sure to bring enough water and an umbrella for the pup and sunscreen for yourself. Festivities spread outward from the Washington Monument grounds and the west side of the Capitol. 202/619-7222.

Big Wheels: You don't want your politico pooch to miss the one time each year on Capitol Hill when the term "soapbox" means something other than politicians' palaver. Since 1941, youngsters have built their own gravity-propelled racing vehicles that reach speeds of about 22 mph to compete in the annual **Soap Box Derby.** It's now held in mid-July on the 800-foot downhill drop adjacent to the Capitol building on Constitution Avenue between New Jersey and Louisiana Avenues NW. 330/733-8723.

Hut-Two-Three: Get those doggies in step at the **Twilight Tattoo Military Pageant,** traditionally held Wednesday evening, mid-July–August, at the Ellipse, south of the White House. The Third United States Infantry and the United States Army Band and Chorus put on a parade and performance that portrays the history of the United States Army. 202/789-7000.

Flying Saucers on the Mall: Even though Chappy prefers afternoons stretched out on the sofa, he gets up for the annual **Alpo Canine Frisbee Championships** that culminate on the Mall for the world finals every mid-September. This is an event to behold for dog lovers and dogs alike. Not only are discs flying everywhere, but so are some talented dogs who seem to defy gravity. The competition takes place on the Lincoln Memorial side of the Washington Monument grounds. For dogs like Chappy with no knack for stealing Frisbees out of thin air, there's also plenty of leashed canine company and lots of fun among the spectators. (It may help to remind your pup that the original Frisbees were nothing more than flying pie pans.) For canines who coulda been contenders, training manuals and schedules of competitions are available by calling 800/786-9240.

A Wicket Game: A jolly time is to be had by both humankind and caninekind on the final Sunday of September, when the National Park Service and the English-Speaking Union sponsor their **annual croquet tournament.** This proper event is a magnet for mad dogs and Englishmen—and all the more fun for it. The gamesters stake out their courts on the Ellipse, along 17th Street NW. 202/234-4602.

Purebreds Prohibited: The annual **Mutts on the Mall** celebration gives mixed-breed dogs their day in the spotlight. There are plenty of fun contests, among them a look-alike competition for dogs and their owners, as well as awards for the most beautiful mutt, the best retriever, the doggy with the waggiest tail, and the best trickster. Usually held at the end of September, the mutt mania is sponsored by the Washington Humane Society and lasts all afternoon on the National Mall beside the Air and Space Museum. The modest registration fee for contestants is tax deductible and helps homeless and abused animals in the metropolitan area. 202/723-5730.

Pageant of Peace: This annual Christmas event kicks off with a midday ceremony on the Ellipse at the end of November when a crane hoists the First Lady to the top of the national Christmas tree to position the tree-top ornament. That signals the official start of all preparations for the Pageant of Peace—a tradition that even withstood the threat following the terrorist attacks in 2001.

Since dogs aren't allowed on the public White House Candlelight Tours (December 26–28), take the pup instead to see the President give his season-of-goodwill speech and light the national Christmas tree. By the first week of December, each territory and state of the Union erects in alphabetical order its own decorated native evergreens around the promenade decking that encircles the big tree. Leashed dogs are welcomed in the best holiday spirit, though cleaning up after them is a must to keep things cheery.

While we appreciated it, the intense warmth and blowing smoke from the white-hot Yule Log open-pit fire at the Pageant's side closest to Constitution Avenue worried Chappy. This festive display is a great excuse to go downtown after dark with the dog. Look for the schedule of concerts, caroling, and dance performances held on the stage at the 15th Street side of the Ellipse, where it all takes place. 202/789-7000.

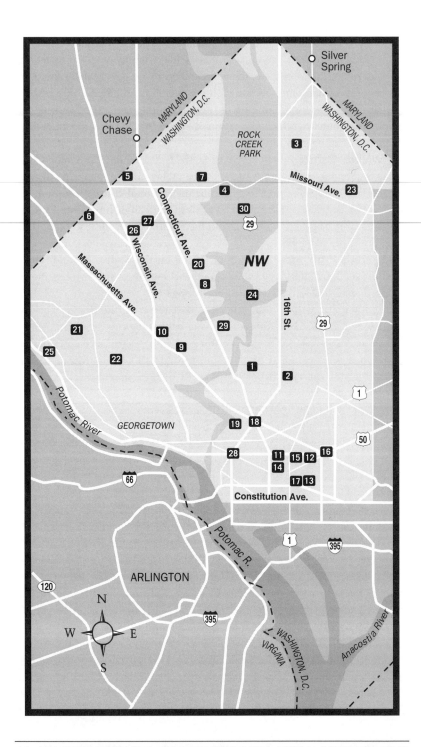

2 NORTHWEST D.C.

The District's largest quadrant is home to its most affluent residents—a fact not wasted on Chappy, who appreciates its tree-shaded sidewalks and clean and generally crime-free urban parks. Though the city's business district is located here as well, these distinct residential neighborhoods, from the stately diplomat mansions of Embassy Row and the funky old row houses of Dupont Circle to the suburban gentry of Chevy Chase, provide inviting opportunities for dog lovers in search of urban canine bliss. But take note: Some walk-about access, especially downtown around federal buildings, has been restricted by barriers, fencing, and police presence since the terrorist attacks of September 11, 2001. Keep in mind there's good reason for the inconvenience of detouring around those locations. And, as in any big city, use your noggin before walking down streets that look like trouble—even with a good dog by your side—and you'll find lots of peaceful and idyllic places to visit.

ADAMS MORGAN

Chappy adores this most ethnically diverse of all Washington neighborhoods. Its once run-down streets are now partially gentrified into an exuberant melting pot of celebrated sidewalk cafés and restaurants where English is a second language, and where you can find international cuisine from nearly every continent of the globe. Dog lovers will find shops and boutiques that range from architectural antiques to Spanish bridal stores to kente clothiers. Relatively crime free, this is a thriving business zone that differs tellingly from troubled neighborhoods nearby across 14th Street. And if you're driving in, parking can be a hassle. So stick to the sounds of the samba and the scent of salsa of these streets and don't venture far off with the pooch.

Parks, Beaches, and Recreation Areas

1 Kalorama Park 🐾 🐾 ½

The name means "beautiful view," and being that all things are relative, it is certainly that on the outskirts of the busy Adams Morgan commercial area. A comfortable park, it is close enough for the exotic scents, flavors, and sounds of this ethnically rich neighborhood to waft through the air. The playground area and sports courts draw people here, but dog lovers dominate along the broad walk and grassy hillside opposite the nearby restaurants and stores. Most dogs are on leash, as posted, in this small stretch of greenery that the "Fund for Kalorama Park" folks have worked hard to renovate and re-landscape. Benches and some shade trees add to its daylight appeal, though after dark, despite the addition of lights, you might want to head over to one of the sidewalk café tables instead and watch the passing humanity with your pup. The park is located at the intersection of Kalorama and Columbia Roads NW. It's open all hours. 202/673-7660.

2 Meridian Hill Park 🐾 🐾 ½

Chappy seemed edgy all the while we walked through this once-stately park with stone walls, concrete cast urns, and neoclassical statuary enclosing its above-street-level beauty. This national historic landmark, now also known as Malcolm X Park, originally represented an optimistic future for the surrounding neighborhood. On the hilly end of the old park, magnificent statues of Dante, Joan of Arc, and James Buchanan overlook one of the nation's longest cascading fountains. While these 12 acres are still beautiful to behold, they have fought the same good fight against urban decay and crime as the neighborhood. After dark, the park can bear a closer resemblance to a drug market than the airy urban space it was meant to be. So be advised: Watch your step and your watch. This is a daytime sojourn only.

But it really is a pretty place. A neighborhood volunteer group, "Friends of Meridian Hill," has worked hard to restore the park's appeal and prestige. Slowly it is happening. You'll even find children playing in the park at times. Nearby residents bring their dogs on leash, though some run free. Occasionally park police enforce the leash laws on these grassy slopes, but it seems like a small gesture given more serious crimes hereabouts.

EARMARK YOUR CALENDAR—SEPTEMBER

Adams Morgan Community Festival: Ready for reggae and salsa and every other kind of ethnic beat that makes your pooch walk with rhythm? This annual neighborhood celebration usually held the first or second weekend of September combines music, crafts, and food from Africa, Central and South America, and Asia. In recent years, it has expanded to span the entire weekend with activities ranging from art exhibitions and jazz bands, to an Adams-Morgan house tour, even a professional skateboarding competition, plus a fun and crowded all-out street festival with food and music the focus. It gets shoulder to shoulder at times, so pups who are skittish around mass humanity ought to stay home and listen to Latino music tapes and just say they went. In recent years, it hasn't been as copacetic as it once was—but what is in recent years? Parking isn't likely here even on off-weekends, so don't even think about it. Figure on parking blocks away and walking into one great party—which it is. The festivities are held along 18th Street between Columbia Road and Florida Avenue NW. 202/321-0938.

In 1996, an ill-conceived attempt by some dog-loving citizens led by an overly ambitious congressional staffer to create an off-leash area at the park ended up in the proverbial doghouse. The plan would have co-opted federal funds already earmarked to upgrade lighting at the park and other practical problems. It was one Washington boon*dog*gle that didn't make it through Congress after dirt-digging columnist Jack Anderson and his watchdog associate Jan Moller sniffed it out.

The park is off Florida Avenue NW, at 16th and W Streets NW. It's open all hours, but outsiders who are unfamiliar with the park and its neighborhood enter here at their own risk—especially after sunset. 202/426-6841.

Restaurants

Arbor: If you and your canine companion are strolling these international sidewalks and nothing could quite hit the spot better than an all-American cheeseburger, this is the place. When dog lovers dine at this newly revamped, plain-cookin' kitchen in decent weather, they just leash their bubbas outside of the fence that encloses the outdoors dining area and sit at a nearby table. "No problem," says the proprietor. In inclement weather, just call in the order and carry it out for doggy dining wherever it's dry. 2400 18th Street NW; 202/667-1200.

La Fourchette: *Bon jour, monsieur . . . et mon cher chien.* Sit at one of the sidewalk tables come springtime at this little piece of Paris right here in Adams Morgan and order the wonderful and right bouillabaisse. French tradition reigns in its cream sauces and seafood crepes as well. If your taste buds have ever visited the Continent, you will be hard pressed to pass by the mussels Provençal, though Chappy recommends the entrecôte Bercy. All the entrees are modestly priced and authentic. And, as in Paris, the waiter won't give your pup's presence a second thought. *Mais oui!* 2429 18th Street NW; 202/332-3077.

BRIGHTWOOD

Parks, Beaches, and Recreation Areas

🕇 Fort Stevens Park 🐾

Chappy could not have cared less that in the summer of 1864 General Jubal Early and his 20,000 rebel troops tried to invade the Union capital at this precise point near the northernmost part of the District. Nor did it matter to him that President Lincoln boosted morale of Union troops here by making a cameo appearance during the fighting. All Chappy saw were the remains of trenches and parapets—grass-covered earthwork structures where Union riflemen once held back the aborted attack. And those cannons in the back looked to him like a great place to raise a leg rather than a toast to the Yankee victory. But then Chappy's not much of a history buff. Picnicking is allowed on these grounds, though no restroom facilities facilitate that idea. As elsewhere, dogs are supposed to take this history lesson at this interesting green bump in the road on a leash.

The park is located at Piney Branch Road and Quackenbos Street NW, which borders on neighborhoods that make night walks here unwise. It's open day and night. 202/426-6841.

🕇 Rock Creek Park 🐾 🐾 🐾

Across the street from Saint John's College High School is a spacious, idyllic field of dreams—if you're a dog, that is. Okay, this is a small piece of exposed acreage of what is otherwise the well wooded and mammoth Rock Creek Park (for more information see the additional entry for Rock Creek Park in the Woodley Park section in this chapter). But this little corner has become a local dog lover's mecca, attracting the on-leash and off-leash sets especially on weekends.

Though the National Park Service requires that dogs stay on leashes, plenty don't here and authorities tend to look elsewhere since this spot isn't problematic. There's lots of shade along the edges for hot sunny days, but dogs come this way to kick out the jams and they do—running about as if there were no tomorrow, chasing Frisbees, being fancy-free. Across Military Road is an uphill ridge trail that Chappy likes to hike. Still part of Rock Creek Park, this trail winds up the side of the hill and arches into more densely forested park property.

The park is located at the intersection of Military and Glover Roads. It's open around the clock, though dog lover discretion is advised. 202/282-1063.

CHEVY CHASE

Chappy isn't the only one who confuses this country club community with the lampoonish actor of vacation-spoof notoriety (how many times has he watched Christie Brinkley dive into that pool naked?). Long before that namesake took his first pratfall, this neighborhood was growing into a getaway gateway at the District's northwesternmost boundary where Chevy Chase straddles the District line and Connecticut Avenue. At the turn of the century, the dogs who lived in these parts were chasing cattle across the dusty dirt roadways and barking at sheep in fields. Today, dogs in Chevy Chase have it much better. They live in one of the premier communities located close-in to downtown Washington.

Parks, Beaches, and Recreation Areas

5 Chevy Chase Playground 🐾

A large and entirely fenced ball field and extravagant playground complex, this streetside park provides plenty of open grassy space for running—though dogs are required to be leashed. Because it is primarily a people place that's maintained through the good graces of the neighborhood residents, it's especially important to clean up when the pooch poops. And watch out for foul balls. The best parking and entrance to the park are near the corner of 41st and Livingston Streets NW, a block off Western Avenue. It is open daylight hours. 202/673-7660.

6 Fort Bayard 🐾 🐾

Chappy loves cold weather and finds unexplainable joy in burying his face in snowdrifts, so he scampered into this quiet urban park with gusto the morning after a winter storm dropped three inches of snow on its hilly grounds. Neighborhood kids were sledding in full force and Chappy quickly got into the icy spirit. Known in the nearby community as "Lady Bug Park" for reasons one can only guess, this is one of the District's 61 Civil War defensive fortress sites, though the fortress has been replaced by a baseball field and a playground that keep kids busy in warm weather. Dogs are supposed to be leashed, and the park is small enough that it makes good sense. Picnicking under the beautiful old tall maples and oaks is a lazy, shady pastime on hot summer days.

The park is located along Western Avenue NW between River Road NW and 47th Street NW. Parking is most convenient along 47th Street. It is open dawn–dusk. 202/426-6841.

⑦ Newlands Park ☙ ½

One of the several ravine parklands in the city, this unattended two-block site with a few clear-cut trails provides runabout Rovers an utterly natural environment for romping—though, despite the nativeness of it all, the District's leash laws are in effect. On one especially hot summer day, Chappy found the considerable creek that flows across the park's back side good for splashing and exploring.

The park is located along Military Road between 28th and 30th Streets NW. It's open dawn–dusk. 202/673-7660.

Restaurants

Bread & Chocolate: Carry out anything on the menu of this European-style restaurant to a nearby bench or park. If chicken Milanese is the special of the day, Chappy recommends it. Soups and vegetarian dishes also make the cut. 5542 Connecticut Avenue NW; 202/966-7413.

The Cheesecake Factory: This often-crowded and always casual eatery's menu is longer on big salad concoctions than on its namesake cheesecakes. And that's a healthy enough reason to pick up a picnic-bagged lunch and head for the hills. Lots of chicken and greenery fill these salad bowls before all sorts of ingredients give them a name. The Santa Fe salad, with its black beans and cilantro vinaigrette goes well on hot summer days. 5345 Wisconsin Avenue NW at the Chevy Chase Pavilion; 202/364-0500.

Parthenon Greek Restaurant: Traditional Greek fare, from herbed lamb to lemony Athenian chicken, not to mention tasty fish dishes, is served at tables out front in warm weather; the proprietor has no problem with a pooch hanging out at your feet there. We made sure to sit on the table farthest from the front door, discretion being the better part of valor. Nice folks here, nice food. 5510 Connecticut Avenue NW; 202/966-7600.

Starbucks: Maybe it's their caffeine intake, but we have yet to find a Starbucks that doesn't get happily hyped about dogs. And inevitably there's

EARMARK YOUR CALENDAR—MAY

Holy Flowers! The first weekend in May? Mark it as the National Cathedral's two-day **Flower Mart and Craft Show** that colorfully spills out onto the sidewalks of the cathedral grounds with family activities, stunning flowers and plants, inspirational and other crafts, and enough food to feed the multitudes. Keep your furry flower sniffer on a leash, but buy some posies to support the cathedral gardens and grounds—a small penance to pay to help those nice enough to let you stroll here with your creature great or small all the other days of the year. Admission is free. It's located at Massachusetts and Wisconsin Avenues NW. 202/537-6200.

a comfy park bench or table right outside the door where java junkies and their calmer canines can sit and try to relax much as possible. It's certainly true at this perky place, which opens at 6 A.M.—when you need a café au lait more than ever. It's located at the intersection of Livingston Street and Connecticut Avenue, about six blocks south of Chevy Chase Circle; 202/244-9705.

Western Market: This old-fashioned neighborhood corner market stocks plenty of cold cuts, rolls, chips, and other edibles perfect for putting together a picnic at Fort Bayard Park or the Chevy Chase Playground just down the street. The only reason it lists a Maryland telephone number is that it's on that side of the dividing line, Western Avenue; 4840 Western Avenue. 301/229-7222.

CLEVELAND PARK

One local pundit described this affluent and brainy neighborhood along Connecticut Avenue north of the National Zoo as having more linear feet of built-in bookshelves per capita than any other place on earth. Not that that matters to most canines, unless shelf space is needed for this dog book. But these tree-lined streets with their neatly kept, pricey, and large-framed cottages reflecting late 19th century architecture attract the intellectual elite of the city—professionals, government officials, lawyers, academics, and journalists, among others. And they bring along their assorted setters, Labs, and other happy higher-brow breeds—so the sidewalk socializing for visiting pups is good here.

Like the other outlying areas of the old city, the neighborhood once was considered a chichi summer retreat from the sticky and swampy downtown. It's named for Grover Cleveland, the president who in 1886 ran the country from his "summer White House" hereabouts. Chappy's happy just to run its countrylike park trails. And even after-dusk strolls in this neighborhood are generally safe.

Parks, Beaches, and Recreation Areas
8 Melvin C. Hazen Trail 🐾 🐾

A great walk through the woods and nothing more, this drop-off from a busy intersection onto a path through tall woods whisks you and your pup out of urban consciousness and into an enchanted forest. Maintained by the feds, it's a road less traveled in these parts that leads in 0.4 miles to Connecticut Avenue and in 1.1 miles to Rock Creek Park. With his leash attached as required, Chappy was delighted by the isolation of it all. The distant sound of traffic clogging main arteries becomes a white noise backdrop to the song of birds far above and the rustling of winter leaves.

The trailhead is located near the intersection of Tilden Street and Reno Road NW, about 0.9 miles from the National Zoo up Connecticut Avenue and onto Tilden. It's open all hours, but because this is close to being urban wilderness and way off-street, after-dark visits aren't advised. 202/426-6841.

9 Normanstone Park 🐾 🐾

The back side of Normanstone Park, stretching along Fulton Street in the Massachusetts Heights subdivision, is all unadulterated woods and wilderness, though not great walking territory due to overgrowth. We drove around the park to its more humane side and parked as close as we could to Massachusetts Avenue. Not far up the sidewalk is a stone walkway that leads into the park and to the compelling Kahlil Gibran Memorial at the park's southern end. It's a calming circular memorial with nuggets of truth attributed to this Lebanese poet and philosopher carved in the granite benches that surround the fountain at its center. Chappy looked at the love-and-peace poet's place of honor and seemed to feel kinship, but we left before he started barking out Tibetan limericks. "There once was a terrier from Nantucket, who . . . ."

The park and memorial are located on Massachusetts Avenue between 30th and 34th Streets NW, opposite the British Embassy. They're open 24 hours a day. 202/282-1063.

10 Washington National Cathedral Grounds 🐾 🐾 ½

While tourists and worshippers tour the inspirational inside of this remarkable medieval-like cathedral, built nearly a century ago in the finest Old World tradition, both those in awe of flying buttresses and gargoyles and those with dogs are welcome to walk the sacred grounds outside on Mount Saint Alban Hill—elevated above the rest of the city.

There you and the pup will find a tree grown from a cutting of the Glastonbury Thorn in England, which legend says arose from the staff of Joseph of Arimathea. The stone-walled Bishop's Garden to the south side of the cathedral is one of the city's loveliest places to contemplate the meaning of life—or the riddle of dog spelled backwards. Even dogs like Chappy who aren't particularly introspective are allowed to stroll through its well-tended rose and herb gardens, past its calming pools, and among the boxwoods and magnolias.

Near the Bishop's Garden to the east is the miniature forest and woodland path envisioned by the cathedral's architect in 1907 to be the idyllic wildflower woodlands from which worshippers would emerge to attend services. At the southernmost corner of the cathedral grounds, where Wisconsin Avenue intersects Garfield Street, adjacent to Saint Alban's School, is the prettiest little sitting park you'll find, like out of one of those meditation exercises where you image an oasis amid the hustle and bustle. Its benches ideal for watching the passing scene, listening in on the chatter of uniformed school children, and enjoying the carillon recitals on Saturdays.

The cathedral grounds are located at Massachusetts and Wisconsin Avenues NW. Cathedral tours of the interior are available Monday–Saturday, 10 A.M.–3:15 P.M., the prime time for strolling outside—though Sundays are perfect with a pious pooch as well. 202/537-6200.

DIVERSIONS

Diplomatic Immunity: Take your diplomatic pooch for a long walking tour of the famous and elegant Embassy Row—the address of about 50 of the 150 or so foreign embassies in town. Flags fly outside the embassies, and official emblems decorate the doors and wrought-iron gates of the diplomatic missions here. Chappy found the Brazil and Pakistan embassies intriguing, and many of them are notable examples of architecture. And on any given day, there's the possibility of a rousing good demonstration—which Chappy prefers to watch from the opposite side of the street. Embassy Row extends for blocks along Massachusetts Avenue NW between Scott and Observatory Circles.

Buy a Bone: A battle of the pet shops has been raging up and down Connecticut Avenue for years. On this stretch in dog-conscious Cleveland Park, you can stop by Petco and buy a bag of rawhide bones cheaper than just about anywhere else—certainly in these parts. 3505 Connecticut Avenue NW; 202/686-0901.

Restaurants

Byblo's Deli: This ethnic-accented deli serves subs, sandwiches, falafel, other Middle Eastern cuisine. The dog-accommodating tables out front in warm weather are just the ticket when short on time and big on appetite. 3414 Connecticut Avenue NW; 202/364-6549.

Cactus Cantina: The fence enclosing the sidewalk café area of this casual and inexpensive Tex-Mex eatery in highbrow Cleveland Park means no dogs can actually sit at the tables. That would be a health department violation, says the manager. But many of her regular customers leash their dogs outside the fence and sit at the adjacent tables to enjoy pork tamales, beef fajitas, and any of the entrees from the mesquite grill—as we did with Chappy, who was perfectly content with the snippets we tossed his way. But then that's the kind of *amigo* he is. 3300 Wisconsin Avenue NW; 202/686-7222.

Cafe Deluxe: Stop by this comfy Cleveland Park institution near the National Cathedral to carry out an order of tasty grilled vegetables, old-fashioned pizza, or just a better-than-average burger. It's fast, simple, and you can park you pooch at one of the parking meters in front and not even deposit the quarter. 3228 Wisconsin Avenue NW; 202/686-2233.

Vace Italian Delicatessen and Homemade Pasta: A landmark in this neighborhood for years, its former unkempt incarnation moved across Connecticut Avenue into more spacious digs, where it can be eclectic rather than disorderly. The homemade sausage alone is reason enough to stop by, and

Chappy seconds that emotion. But the crispy thin-crust pizza is a big favorite and so is the focaccia—all great eating you and the poochini can carry out and eat on your way elsewhere. 3315 Connecticut Avenue NW; 202/363-1999.

Yes! Natural Foods: The longtime mecca of organic natural eating in the nation's capital, stop here for a quick gulp of energizing kefir (a yogurtlike drink), or pick up dried fruits and veggies, nuts, and seeds to fix your own trail mix. Fresh vegetables, vitamins and other supplements—there's so much that's good for you here that you feel healthier just walking down the aisles. And for the pup, Chappy recommends the all-natural dog treats and food. 3425 Connecticut Avenue NW; 202/363-1559.

DOWNTOWN

There's not as much wide-open parkland in these city blocks as out in the 'burbs. But by the fire hydrants-per-square-mile standard, this is dog-friendly territory. Extending northwest from the Capitol and north of Pennsylvania Avenue, this concrete canyon of government and office buildings, stores, shops, restaurants, historic sites, and even a few homes. It is bordered by North Capitol Street to the east and 16th Street behind the White House to the west. Defying neighborhood status because people mostly work and shop here, the downtown area does have pockets of residential areas and peaceful sitting parks that soften its hard-edged city streets.

While the sidewalks still roll up by the late dinner hour, the continuing downtown revitalization that started in the 1980s has spruced up Pennsylvania Avenue and the arts corridor along Seventh Street. Those evening hours are being extended, attracting more folks this way after work. The MCI Center, finished in 1997, is the hub of the retail and entertainment revitalization and the home of the NBA Wizards and NHL Capitals. And the construction of the new, gigantic Washington Convention Center is underway and scheduled for completion in 2003. It will be the largest building in the District. Should you and your dog venture to these paved environs, there is some exceptional greenery and parkland, and some up-and-coming territory—though hardly the rambling acres found farther out.

Parks, Beaches, and Recreation Areas

11 Farragut Square 🐾 🐾

With mortars aimed high, the statue of Admiral David Glasgow Farragut reigns over this small park with a triangular theme to its sidewalks and landscaping. But cute as this park is, its central location at the busy intersection of Connecticut Avenue and K Street works against its appeal to dog lovers—certainly during rush hour. Traffic jams nearby makes it noisy with automobile horns, racing engines, and frustrated motorists, something that made Chappy a mite nervous and ready to put the paw to the pedal and go. The park gets more than its share of heating-grate preachers, ne'er-do-wells, and bike messengers taking a breather. But, darn it, it ain't a bad little spot in the sun on a nice day.

Located between I and K Streets NW at Connecticut Avenue, it's open 24 hours a day, though recommended only during daylight hours. 202/426-6841.

12 Franklin Square 🐾 🐾

Of the three pearls in the string of urban green space along the K Street corridor (along with McPherson and Farragut Squares), this is the largest and airiest. At the north side is a statue of Commodore John Barry. In the middle is an open piazza with a fountain where folks with or without dogs lounge like lizards in the sun—especially at lunchtime. The well-shaded square is also well kept and, in season, blooms with a beautifully planned lineup of flowers. And although these blocks of 14th Street have been rescued from its underbelly past as the city's main strip joint and peep show zone, some riffraff still finds its way here, though it shouldn't interfere with your and the pup's pleasant day in the downtown park.

Located between K and I Streets and 14th and 13th Streets NW, the park is open all hours, though daylight hours are when you want to be there. 202/426-6841.

13 Freedom Plaza 🐾

One of the open public spaces created by the revitalization of Pennsylvania Avenue, this rectangular plaza just north of the Federal Triangle complex is mostly flatstone with a tiny bit of grass. Afternoon concerts and other events are regularly scheduled to attract the human element to its hewn mineral surfaces, and dogs can join in the crowd of onlookers and in-line skaters. Otherwise, this feels like it's between a rock and a hard place to Chappy.

Located at Pennsylvania Avenue and 13th Street NW, the Plaza is open 24 hours a day. 202/426-6841.

14 Lafayette Park 🐾 🐾 ½

This high-rent parcel of parkland across the street from the White House leaves no doubt that you're walking your dog in the nation's premier power neighborhood. One afternoon when we strolled its circular brick walkways and sprawling lawns with Chappy, the unseasonably warm winter day made it a perfect place for absorbing sunshine. Its most central feature, a huge statue of hound-loving Andy Jackson riding high in the saddle, is cast from cannons the old general captured during the War of 1812. There's the usual row of protesters and dissenters who normally commandeer this stretch in front of the White House with signboards warning against the evils of nuclear weapons and the end of the world. With the ever-present precautions against insane terrorist acts, the entire stretch of Pennsylvania Avenue between the park and the White House grounds is closed to traffic, making this all the more a dog-friendly stretch to stroll.

Chappy proved a little too curious for comfort to some of the harmless protesters who populate a few of the many benches. But he didn't protest the fact that this undoubtedly is one of the most historic urban parks per square foot in America. This polite and pretty park of oval fountains features charming statues such as the one that stands at the northeast corner dedicated to General Thaddeus Kosciuszko, the Polish Revolutionary War hero. This is a presidential park that dates back to the origins of the city. It's land that Thomas Jefferson declared a public place; FDR's confidant Bernard Baruch held court on its park benches, and Harry Truman took his famous early morning walks here.

Choicest locations for dog sitting and picnicking with the pooch start at the five modest tables near the southwest corner behind the weatherworn Comte de Rochambeau statue directly in sight of the White House. Similar tables on the northwest corner across from historic Decatur House are usually grabbed early by fanatic chess players. The other primo locale is the central Jackson statue where people-watching is de rigueur. Despite its proximity to the home of the president, after dark isn't as inviting as daylight hours.

Located directly across Pennsylvania Avenue from the White House, the park is open 24 hours a day. 202/426-6841.

15 McPherson Square 🐾 🐾

In the center of this urban block of crisscrossing sidewalks and triangular grassy spots stands a stately statue of Major General James B. McPherson, poised for Civil War buffs and head-bobbin' pigeons. Plenty of shade and park benches dot this great little nook for relaxing or picnicking to break up a downtown hiking or shopping venture with the pooch. On weekdays, the benches are populated by about equal numbers of professionals from offices of the nearby K Street "canyon" and homeless folks mostly napping in the sun, though a few panhandle. Nice thing about this park is the amenities around it—plenty of take-out joints that cater to the weekday lunchtime crowds.

Located between K and I Streets at 15th Street NW, it's open all hours, though discretion is advised. 202/426-6841.

16 Mount Vernon Place 🐾

Chinatown can be an enjoyable excursion, especially to see the ornate Friendship Archway (Seventh and H Streets NW) or to dine in one of its many Asian restaurants. This tiny park is nearby, though more handy than alluring. The centerpiece of the park is an old library building now owned by the University of the District of Columbia. The fringes around it are grassy and offer shade trees and lots of benches. Don't stop here after dark, however, since the neighborhood has known better days in terms of crime—but expects to know better days again with the new Washington Convention Center under construction nearby.

The park is located at the intersection of K Street, Massachusetts, and New York Avenues NW; it's open all hours. 202/673-7660.

🔳17 Pershing Park 🐾

Approaching this block-long city park from the 14th Street side, Chappy got all excited and started tugging on the leash. From there, it looks like a grassy park with shade trees and benches, a pleasant little shift of consciousness from urban concrete and the busy intersections that surround it.

But once in the park, what you find is more concrete—it's just a lot less busy. Only the edges of this relaxing hideaway across Pennsylvania Avenue from the handsome Willard Inter-Continental Hotel are landscaped naturally. Most of this park dedicated to celebrated Army General John Pershing is attractively tiered and paved to create an amphitheater effect, with a pool at its center that's fed by a tantalizing waterfall. To Chappy's delight, the pool is turned into a small skating rink in the winter. A nearby kiosk serves sandwiches and munchies for dining on the benches and steps. Located between 14th and 15th Streets NW on Pennsylvania Avenue, the park is open all hours. 202/426-6841.

Restaurants

Benkay: Lunchtime at this below-street-level sushi palace is an all-you-can-eat buffet with fresh and generous cuts of sushi and sashimi, as well as many noodle and tempura dishes. Load up from the buffet table and carry out your lunch to a sunny spot where you and the doggy-san can dine as one. At dinner, it's a menu-driven sushi restaurant, so call your order ahead for carryout. You do have to look for it, because this friendly garden of tasty delights really is below street level. 727 15th Street NW; 202/737-1515.

Bertolini's: Before contemplating the 100-foot-diameter granite world map next door at the United States Navy Memorial with Chappy, we stepped into this downtown link in a chain of Italian restaurants and carried out some scrumptious *pizzetta*—the restaurant's rosemary-and-Parmesan flatbread version of classic Italian bruschetta. Other Italian tasties fill out the menu. For more elaborate dining, such as the pasta with lobster, shrimp, and scallops, sit down at the outdoor seating and tables in front where an obedient dog is welcome to sit alongside. 801 Pennsylvania Avenue NW; 202/638-2140.

Bombay Club: Tired of fried chicken or hot dogs when strolling downtown with the urbanite pup? Though this fine Indian restaurant seems far too clubbish with that British sense of dignity and tallyho old chap flavor to allow hounds inside, its friendly proprietors are willing to pack food up for you, so carry away one of the tasty tandoori dishes. 815 Connecticut Avenue NW; 202/659-3727.

Bottom Line: During the warmer months, starting in April, tables emerge at sidewalk level of this underground restaurant and classic bar. You can sit with your dog at one of the outside tables and order some of the better beers and burgers in the neighborhood, plus full-meal gourmet salads. 1714 I Street NW, a half block west of Farragut Square. 202/298-8488.

Cosi: When they rehabbed this beautiful old downtown office building, they built in the corner, ground-level, this great sandwich bar that is also springing up in various locations around town. Lucky us, says Chappy. There may be cheaper lunches around, but you won't find fresher salads and more intriguing bread. The $7 Caesar chicken salad, homemade Cosi bread included, is enough for Chappy and us! And outside, there are more than a dozen new double-length park benches in the sun. K and 15th Streets NW; 202/639-8999.

Cafe Mozart: If the taste of genuine German vittles like sauerbraten and kraut and the sounds of Wagner or a foot-stomping polka band appeal to you and der Hund, stop by this friendly enclave for lunch or dinner. The German deli at the front of the restaurant makes picking up sandwiches and a big helping of hot German potato salad easy. For more elaborate meals, you can call in a carryout order for anything on the dinner menu, though Chappy considers this a wurst-case scenario. 1331 H Street NW; 202/347-5732.

Capital Deli: At the corner of L and 15th Streets NW, carry your lunch out to a nearby park bench or in good weather pull up a chair and dine with your dog at its sidewalk cafe area (no waiters here, however). Breakfast is served; for lunch, salad bar, deli sandwiches and wraps, mostly, for a quick and easy meal. 1100 15th Street NW; 202/466-5119.

Georgia Brown's: The place looks mighty fancy, what with valet parking out front, and it is. But you can carryout dishes of the low-country southern cooking here such as shrimp-and-crayfish cakes and pecan-crusted catfish. The benches of McPherson Square are directly across the street for doggy dining. 950 15th Street NW; 202/393 4499.

Havana Breeze: This busy and authentic Cuban eatery is made for carry-out with the *perro* pup. Jerked chicken from a leg-and-thigh to the whole bird is the specialty, but the platters are pleasers as well, especially the marinated pork fried pieces. 1401 K Street NW; 202/789-1470.

High Noon: At the corner of K Street and Vermont Avenue, this is a genuine breakfast and luncheon hangout. Morning hours feature coffee, bagels, and eggs "a billion ways." For lunch, it's big thick sandwiches in crusty bread, huge salads, and pastas. Outside there's sidewalk tables year around where you can sit your pup. No tables left? Carry it out across the street to McPherson Square. 927 15th Street NW; 202/682-2211.

Julia's Empanadas: Here's a quick and different carry-out-only place to grab a variety of handmade and lovingly baked empanadas to take to McPherson Square. They make 'em in several nationalities, from the spicy

Jamaican meat pies to the Chilean-style beef empanadas. 1000 Vermont Avenue NW; 202/789-1878.

La Prima Caffe: Across 14th Street from Franklin Park, this little gourmet salad and sandwich shop makes it easy to cart a lunch to a nearby park bench and relax with your little *cagnolino* with Italian-accented fare. 950 14th Street NW; 202/898-1140.

Lawsons Gourmet Provisions: Plenty of choices in this zealous version of the steam-table buffet carryouts that are everywhere downtown catering to the luncheon inclinations of the fully employed. Many of the entrées at these midday hot spots are Asian in origin, though this one serves equal portions of other kinds of cuisine. It's at the corner of 14th and I Streets NW, 1350 I Street NW; 202/789-1440.

Les Halles: The outdoor tables are set up whenever the weather allows, so a warm day even in February can put you and *vôtre chien* dining at the most authentic French bistro in Washington. Across from the Federal Triangle near Freedom Plaza, this is Chappy's favorite fancy restaurant for dinner, because that's when the owner is there and he's the one with the soft spot *au coeur* for dogs. The crudités and paté excel, and don't pass up *l'ingole* (steak) and fries, which are so *very* French. *Et mais oui,* you can also order a lovely Bordeaux from the excellent wine list. 1201 Pennsylvania Avenue NW; 202/347-6848.

Loeb's Deli: At the intersection of I Street and Vermont Avenue NW, the southeastern corner of McPherson Square, this is an authentic New York eatery right down to the attitude of the fine folks who slap pastrami and corned beef between rye as if they've been doing it forever—and they have. In warmer weather, the sidewalk dining section is huge. There's plenty of room for a baloney-snacking Bowser to sit obediently next to your feet and people-watch without anyone usually complaining. Or carry out your order to a shaded bench across the street, if the lawyers from K Street threaten to sue the pooch. They serve beer here, too. 832 15th Street NW; 202/371-1150.

Naan & Beyond: If you're looking for a new deli, this hole in the wall specializes in Indian cuisine wrapped in one of India's most popular, tandoor-baked flatbreads called naan. Chappy says the chicken tikka sandwich is a small bite of nirvana. 1710 L Street NW; 202/466-6404.

N.Y. Gourmet: If you're in the neighborhood, like we often are a block away at the *Washington Post,* this overly efficient but friendly Chinese luncheon buffet is a great place to stop in and take out lunch on weekdays. On one side is the cold buffet with salads, pepper-sauced tofu, various pasta and chicken dishes, and on the other, the hot side with various Chinese dishes, usually including orange chicken and fried rice worth investing, according to Chappy's Asian palate. He likes those meat-filled Chinese dumplings, too. Several white plastic tables outside work fine for dining with the dog. 1020 15th Street NW; 202/296-8113.

Old Ebbitt Grill: Don't go in the front door of this very popular publike restaurant located in an office-retail high-rise mall. It'll be packed with people waiting for tables—and dogs can't come in the classy entrance anyway. But on weekdays, a luncheon carryout counter opens at the back of the restaurant. The counter line is less crowded and serves a limited menu of the same great tasting foods as the sit-down digs, and you can carry your meal out to one of the benches outside the mall area. The thick and juicy hamburgers are hard to pass up—and just ask for a grilled chicken Caesar salad if you want it, even if it's not on the menu. 675 15th Street NW; 202/347-4801.

Wall Street Deli: Salad bar, homemade hoagie rolls, and deli stuffings make this quick-stop luncheon spot a convenient eatery right next door to Farragut Square. And tables out front make it dog friendly indeed. 919 18th Street NW; 202/466-4959.

Places to Stay

Hay-Adams: For a quintessential Washington experience, stay at this comfy and classy 143-room hotel that stands on the grounds where John Hay and Henry Adams built mansions during the early years of the Republic. But don't schlep into this English country setting wearing blue jeans and a T-shirt, or, worse yet, tourist clothes, because dignitaries stay here when in town, and coats and ties are the norm. Well-behaved small dogs, 10 pounds and under, and approved in advance, are welcome at no extra charge; large ones and barking ones are not. The best views of the White House across Lafayette Square are from rooms on the hotel's south side on floors five and up—which are also the most popular rooms and suites. Rates range from $265 up. 800 16th Street NW, Washington, DC 20006; 202/638-6600.

Holiday Inn–Downtown: This smaller 208-room version of the standard Holiday Inn is a block from Franklin Square. Dogs that are 25 pounds or less are welcome at a one-time, nonrefundable fee of $25. Rates range from $90 to $179. 1155 14th Street NW, Washington, DC 20005; 202/737-1200.

The Jefferson: It doesn't get much better than this: "There's no restriction on the size of the dog or the number of dogs," the concierge said matter-of-factly. Just four blocks from the White House and practically next door to the National Geographic Society, these classy digs have just as classy a welcome policy for pets. While the décor and amenities would've made Mr. Jefferson a happy man, they accommodate dogs as well as anyone here. Of course, your pooch can't dine at the lovely restaurant downstairs, but room service delivers the cuisine nonetheless. Rates start at $229. 1200 16th Street NW, Washington, DC 20036; 202/833-6200.

Lincoln Suites Downtown: This redesigned boutique hotel bills itself as "hip, edgy and gorgeous." And it is. Plus, it doesn't hesitate for a second to register dogs 30 pounds and under—though Chappy thinks they also have to

EARMARK YOUR CALENDAR

Chinese New Year Festival: You and *le petit chien* can witness the annual parade through the streets of Chinatown from the doggy vantage point of a sidewalk spot near the red-and-gold Chinatown Friendship Archway—one of the largest single-span archways in the world. The annual parade includes marching bands, traditional dragon dancers, other entertainers, and lots of onlookers. Festivities usually start at 1 P.M. at Fifth and H Streets NW, and the parade follows H Street to the Friendship Arch. Careful though: Chappy had had enough of the commotion and noise soon after arriving. The festival takes place on the Sunday closest to the Chinese New Year, which falls in late January to early-to-mid-February; the archway is located at Seventh and H Streets NW. 202/638-1041 or 202/393-2280.

All That Independence Jazz: Held on the Fourth of July, the annual **Freedom Plaza Jazz Festival** is a streetfest where you and the pooch can find refuge from the crowded humanity of the Mall and take in some cool jazz in the spirit of democracy and with elbow room for all. The music plays 2–10 P.M. and is free for the listening. Head for the sound of the sax at Freedom Plaza, Pennsylvania Avenue between 13th and 14th Streets NW. 202/783-0360.

Waiters in a Hurry?: The annual **Bastille Day Race and Celebration,** held here every July 14th since 1974, features the quickest of the city's waiters and waitresses balancing glasses of champagne on a tray while racing from the wonderfully dog-friendly Les Halles restaurant to the United States Capitol and back. There's a customer race, if getting sweaty suits you better than sipping a nice Bordeaux and watching. Surprise entertainment invariably shows up throughout the congenial day. And here's the tip: This is loads of fun and you can bring the dog. Stake out your territory at Les Halles, where the races begin and end. 1201 Pennsylvania Avenue NW. 202/347-6848.

Bite-Sized Gourmet: Sampling the specialties of some of Washington's most popular restaurants at the **Taste of DC** can burn off an afternoon, even if it won't burn off many calories. But this is the only way your pup will ever taste some of this fare, since many of the restaurants in this annual munchathon aren't dog accommodating. The pay-per-taste buffet usually takes place in mid-October along the sidewalks of Pennsylvania Avenue NW between Ninth and 14th Streets NW. 202/724-4093.

be as "hip, edgy and gorgeous" as he is. The charge is $15 a night, which is fair enough for all the marble, chrome, and carpeting in each of its 99 suites. It's a great location if you're coming to town for theater hopping. Rates start at $99. 1823 L Street NW, Washington, DC 20036; 202/223-4320.

The Madison: At any time police escorts just might roar up to a sudden stop in front of this charming hotel, their sirens blaring and lights flashing, stopping traffic and pedestrians alike, just to deliver a visiting foreign dignitary to his or her quarters. Check which foreign flag is flying next to the United States flag on the front of the building, and you'll know who's in town. Proximity to the White House and classy accommodations in this 353-room hotel attract many foreign officials and domestic business execs to this corner locale. Some of them bring their dogs, and you can too as long as the pup is 30 pounds or under and well trained. Funny how sometimes the fancier the hotel the more casual the attitude towards dogs—which is true here. Rates vary but range from $255 and up, plus a $30 per night canine charge. 15th and M Streets NW, Washington, DC 20005; 202/862-1600.

St. Regis Hotel: "We happily accept dogs," the front desk informed us. "All the way up to 20 pounds." And, indeed, this 193-room Starwood hotel conveniently located just two blocks from Lafayette Square and three from the White House is dog friendly. Chappy preferred the cozy lobby, though scents of the luncheon buffet to the left and around the corner in the hotel restaurant diverted his attention—but dogs aren't seated there. Rates range from $145 to $190, plus a daily $25 fee for the pooch. 923 16th Street NW, Washington, DC 20006; 202/638-2626.

Willard Inter-Continental Hotel: One of the great old historic hotels in the city, just two blocks from the White House, its beaux arts exterior and elegant lobby overwhelmed Chappy at first. Completely renovated in the early 1980s after the old hotel had been allowed to fall into disrepair, this gem is again historically correct and true to its period, a nice touch considering that nearly every Chief Executive from Franklin Pierce to Ike Eisenhower were patrons of the Willard. Dog lovers pay no extras to bring their pooches along, though you must sign a waiver that commits you to pay for any damages. But as Chappy discovered quickly, the staff exhibits no reluctance to accept dogs with open arms, or at least a kind pat on the noggin. And all of the hotel's 340 guest rooms and suites, decorated in dark mahogany and Queen Anne–style furnishings, accommodate dogs in a first-rate manner. Rates vary by season and availability, but start at $235. 1401 Pennsylvania Avenue NW, Washington, DC 20004. 202/628-9100 or 800/327-0200.

DUPONT CIRCLE

North of Washington's main business district and south of Adams Morgan, this neighborhood of row houses, neatly kept brownstones, galleries, and restaurants is, in spirit, Washington's Greenwich Village. Widely known as the heart of the District's gay and lesbian community, it's also home to bohemians, nihilist punks, poets, paupers, beggars, princes, thieves, and, well, you get the idea. That's life. Progressives and regressives, even a few aggressives, live creatively side-by-side in a radical environment within an establishment town that seems to appeal to our Kerouac-minded dog. It's a culturally rich and inviting area that makes walking the dog a few blocks from a used-book store to an avant-garde art gallery a pure and simple pleasure.

Parks, Beaches, and Recreation Areas

18 Dupont Circle 🐾

Despite the heavy traffic that ebbs and flows around this major city circle at the heart of Embassy Row and the hub of activity in this neighborhood, there's a certain centering that goes on amid the old men playing chess on stone tables and gay residents out for the sunshine in the park. Sure, there are the homeless and the drunks as well, but this is a big parklike circle so there's plenty of room.

The circle is located at the intersection of Massachusetts, Connecticut, and New Hampshire Avenues and P Street NW. 202/673-7660.

19 P Street Beach 🐾

Okay, it's not really a beach. It's a so-called beach. But during the dog days of summer, this isolated grassy knoll overlooking Rock Creek Parkway from Dupont Circle side has long been popular for sunbathing and the only difference between it and a real beach is no sand and no ocean. This insider spot is known as a favorite hangout of gay sun worshippers, though straight folks also enjoy it and plenty of dogs rollick about. No matter your sexual identity, the sun shines brightly on the hillsides of breathtaking daffodils across the parkway in early spring. It's open all hours, but the sunny hours are the best and safest (its after-sunset patrons didn't come for the sunshine). The park is located just off P Street NW heading west toward Georgetown on the left before crossing the P Street Bridge. 202/673-7660.

Restaurants

Bacchus: You and your furry friend can order carryout Lebanese cuisine, from *baba ghanoush* to tabbouleh to hummus; in other words, great appetizer foods for lunch or dinner when you and the pup get that Middle East yearning. 1827 Jefferson Place NW; 202/785-0734.

Burro: Totally take-out Tex-Mex is what rules at this quick-fixin's cantina. This border-style fast food won't leave you asking, *"¿Cuánto es?"* It's *bueno* tacos and burritos on the cheap, in other words. 1621 Connecticut Avenue NW; 202/483-6861.

California Pizza Kitchen: Carry out one of the many imaginative combinations of toppings that this West Coast pizza chain has cooked up. The most traditionally good is the four-cheese pizza with tomatoes, though Chappy prefers artful pizza making such as the roasted chicken-and-garlic pie. 1260 Connecticut Avenue NW; 202/331-4020.

Gabriel: Weekdays, pick up a great bargain of the tasty tapas, and on weekends you won't find a better roast suckling pig buffet—perhaps anywhere. You and the dog will have to carry out the generous portions, but this lovely Latin food is well worth it. 2121 P Street NW, in the Radisson Barcelo Hotel; 202/956-6690.

Otello: Nothing fancy about this old-fashioned Italian place or the food it serves—down-to-earth pastas with rich and hearty red sauces. So if the piazza poochini gets a cravin' for good old-fashioned spaghetti and meatballs, this is the place to carry out the meal. 1329 Connecticut Avenue NW; 202/429-0209.

Pesce: Two words—fresh fish. It's pricey and the menu changes daily because the fish prepared here is brought in daily, but this bistro-style fishery is unmatched in its artistry of creating fish served on imaginative ragoût combinations. If you have a fax machine, call the day you and the pup want to carry out lunch or dinner and they will fax you that day's entrées. 2016 P Street NW; 202/466-3474.

Skewers: As its name implies, most of the entrées at this Middle Eastern bargain restaurant are kabobs—beef, chicken, and lamb. All are tastefully prepared for carryout should you and the dog be in the neighborhood and in need of nutrition. Or maybe you just have a pita-and-hummus hankering. 1633 P Street NW; 202/387-7400.

Teaism: Think Zen mirage just off Connecticut Avenue. This townhouse restaurant that primarily serves tea is one of Chappy's favorites. Not that he drinks tea, nor can you eat on the premises with your koan-master pooch. But for greater sustenance, you can order carryout from its self-serve menu kabobs, salads, sandwiches, and stir-fries—all carefully prepared with an artistic Japanese touch and ready for a picnic. For the real Japanese thing, take out the Bento Box, with its cold salmon, veggies, and noodles arranged with the care of a Zen garden. This is fun and delicious. 2009 R Street NW; 202/667-3827.

Places to Stay

Washington Hilton and Towers: Small dogs, 25 pounds or under, are welcome at this huge hotel complex (1,123 rooms) that's a longtime Washington establishment and the scene of many fancy society balls and professional conferences. The hotel is located six blocks northwest of Dupont Circle up the hill on Connecticut Avenue in Kalorama. The dog rate is $30 a

DIVERSIONS

Good for What Ales You: Not that the pooch can go inside, mind you, because the grand old turreted Romanesque revival Heurich Mansion, located four blocks south of Dupont Circle, now accommodates the Columbia Historical Society and its kindly librarian attitude. But you and the pooch might want to pick up a six-pack of Old Heurich beer on the way. Appreciating the sight of this one-time home of 19th-century beer magnate Christian Heurich both in body and spirits seems the way to pay proper respects. 1307 New Hampshire Avenue NW; 202/785-2068.

Dog-Eared Pages: Book a casual stop by **Second Story Books,** the veritable used-book institution located a block west of Dupont Circle. Window browsing for titles is recommended for dog walkers since the shelves and stacks of books inside get cramped and Chappy gets claustrophobic around too much bookbinding. On clear days these hip bibliophiles put out crates of deep-discount books on the sidewalk for perusing the literary scene. 2000 P Street NW; 202/659-8884.

---

day; rates for rooms start at $225. 1919 Connecticut Avenue NW, Washington, DC 20009; 202/483-3000.

Westin Fairfax Hotel: Inside, the former Ritz-Carlton's canopied entrance remains a fancy and elegant, circa 1927, hotel with fireplaces, dark walnut paneling and oriental carpeting—sort of an English hunt-club setting. "Small dogs" are permitted for a one-time fee of $75. Ask for a room on one of the upper floors, where you can look out the windows to the back and see Georgetown and the Washington Monument. Rates start at $145. 2100 Massachusetts Avenue NW, Washington, DC 20008; 202/293-2100.

FOGGY BOTTOM

One of the city's oldest 19th century neighborhoods, this riverside community is home to the Kennedy Center, the State Department and George Washington University. Despite nary a park nearby, other than those crammed in green spaces between high-traffic intersections, it's decent for dog walking because of the anything-goes campus attitude and lovely vintage brick-townhouse architecture that dominates its residential streets.

Places to Stay

Watergate Hotel: Political burglary and scandal? That's what comes to mind, all right. But this 231-room hotel adjacent to the Kennedy Center is so much more than one of Washington's most exclusive addresses. Yes, some of

---

the capital's power players do reside here—among them, Bob and Elizabeth Dole, and their pup, Leader. In 1972, when the infamous break-in occurred at the Democratic National Committee headquarters in the hotel, Dole was a resident here—and also chairman of the Republican National Committee. Some coincidence, huh? He was cleared of any role in the skullduggery that led to Richard Nixon's resignation as president. And the Doles live here still.

More than a quarter of a century later, Monica Lewinsky moved in soon after making scandal headlines of her own. Some coincidence again, huh? She was next-door neighbors with Bob Dole! But for nonpartisan poochsters, this 35-year-old luxury hotel, owned by Swissôtel, goes well beyond innuendo and scandal to make a grand statement: "If small, dogs are allowed." And there's no extra charge, no deposits, no rules—except hotel dog etiquette is expected. Standard room rates start at $270. 2650 Virginia Avenue NW, Washington, DC 20037; 202/965-2300.

FOREST HILLS

There are only a few good reasons for dog lovers to wander these hidden streets of stately homes located between Connecticut Avenue and the western tree line of Rock Creek Park. Residents with wealth and clout pay a high price for privacy in these parts, so walking a leashed dog helps to distinguish you from suspicious characters who have no visible reason to be here.

Parks, Beaches, and Recreation Areas

20 Soapstone Valley Park 🐾 🐾 🐾

The harrowing descent into this ravine park (it could just as easily be called a cliffside park) didn't faze Chappy's Himalayan genetics. The sight of this sprawling drop-off that is well below roadside level, and its very old trees and irregular creeks and streams, got his Tibetan blood flowing.

Largely overlooked by local traipsers and tourists who tend to opt for the nearby Rock Creek Park instead (see the Brightwood and Woodley Park sections in this chapter), this hidden treasure sees few visitors—other than those fortunate few who live near it. This is the kind of wild and woody parkland you would hardly imagine exists smack in the middle of northwest Washington. The Connecticut Avenue high-rises that tower over its western slope make it seem even more remarkable. The fact is that this 0.75-mile stretch was once part of Rock Creek Park to the east before it got disconnected by what is now the 25-acre Hillwood estate that belonged to cereal heiress Marjorie Merriweather Post. Hillwood is a mansion and museum noted for its world-class collection of 18th- and 19th-century imperial Russian art, and perfectly pristine gardens—all open to the public, but not to pooches.

For easiest and safest access down into the ravine, park your car at the far west (to the right) end of the dead-end Audubon Terrace—the road that

DIVERSIONS

Literary License: Not only does it have entire shelves of dog-related books, but the classy **Politics & Prose** is one bookstore that mixes browsers with Bowsers. Except for the coffeeshop area downstairs, dogs are welcome to come in with their owners, and many of them do. The practice started when the proprietor used to bring in a dog that hung out all day long. Other dogs visited and the rest is history. Chappy likes the art book area directly at the back from the front entrance. Catch an evening when an author is speaking or signing books for a special treat. 5015 Connecticut Avenue NW; 202/364-1919.

Making a Pet Stop: A few blocks up from Rock Creek Park's entrance near Yuma Street and Connecticut Avenue, the **Pet Pantry** has marked off its territory. If you can't find the brands of premium dog food you want elsewhere, check with these perfectionists and they'll probably have it. Even more endearing is that they deliver within the neighborhood. 4455 Connecticut Avenue NW; 202/363-6644.

borders the park's northern length. Step gingerly down the side of the gorge. To the east (left), the park turns even more mountainous, with rocky formations that look daunting—but just follow one of the paths down into the park. This hidden park is located about 1.3 miles north of the National Zoo, off Connecticut Avenue. Turn right onto Albemarle Street, then right again onto 29th Street, which ends at Audubon Terrace and the park. It's open day and night, but with all the tricky footwork, daytime and dry-weather visits are highly recommended. 202/282-1063.

Restaurants

Cafe di Mamma: The crust really is golden brown on the pies at this self-service pizzeria that sells by the slice. Easy in, easy out. 4483 Connecticut Avenue NW; 202/686-1992.

Marvelous Market: With its fresh-from-the-oven, crusty, and chewy sourdough and Old World–style breads, this aptly named bakery almost single-handedly changed the way Washingtonians think about the most basic of dining pleasures when it opened more than a decade ago. And how perfect that there's a nice bench just outside the front door where you and the pup can relax with a warm loaf of kalamata olive bread or a traditional baguette. Specials such as the soft and tasty walnut wheat bread or any of the croissants, reputed to be the best in town, are hard to resist. And don't ignore the kitchen items such as the eggplant-based Mediterranean spread. A line sometimes forms for the 7:30 A.M. opening, and the bakery keeps rolling in the dough until 8 P.M., seven days a week. 5035 Connecticut Avenue NW; 202/686-4040.

FOXHALL

No need to bring along the swank detector because the exclusivity of this neighborhood, where the Rockefeller mansion once was the centerpiece of a massive estate, is obvious. The winding and hilly Foxhall Road remains the address of some of the District's priciest digs (and dogs), the kind of multimillion-dollar homes *Architectural Digest* calls to plead for photo shoots— and is put on hold. None of this intimidates Chappy, who likes to play the poor-dog-from-Tibet role unless his pedigree serves his agenda better. And, in these parts, pedigree does matter—for canines and humans alike.

Parks, Beaches, and Recreation Areas
21 Battery Kemble Park 🐾 🐾 🐾 🐾

Hidden between the neighborhoods of Foxhall and nearby Palisades, this bucolic 57-acre park is hilly and woodsy—and unlike any other dog-friendly park you'll find in the area. We drove into its central parking lot one sunny afternoon and counted more than two dozen dogs running off leash—on the hillside, in the parking lot, across the field nearby, down the pedestrian paths, everywhere. Reports by frequenting dog lovers confirm that a dozen or more dogs off leash is the norm—especially on weekends and weekday evenings.

Unofficially known as "the Dog Park of DC" (there are no official dog parks in the District), this place has been the subject of controversy for several years since neighborhood dog owners commandeered the national park property as an off-leash dog zone. District and national park rules require pups in parks to remain on leashes. Occasionally a park ranger shows up here and upholds the law, sending some dog owners home with hefty fines (as much as $200) for their blatant disregard. But most days, this is an unauthorized free-for-all playground for dogs—which has its pluses and minuses.

One plus is that the vast majority of regulars are well-behaved dogs owned by people who have voice control of their pups and take care of the park— even reseed its grasses that get trampled and ragged from so much canine cavorting. Rarely do dog fights break out, and most of the dogs seem to enjoy romping together, chasing balls, and racing about.

But on rare days we have seen problems such as the time two Dobermans were terrorizing several other dogs, stopping just short of fighting—including one of them bounding menacingly toward our leashed Zen-and-peace puppy Chappy from 100 feet away, before we barked some harsh commands at the intruder ourselves. When we firmly recommended to its owner that she get control of her dog, she sat on the trunk of her car working on her tan and shrugged, as if to say, "Dogs will be dogs." Only goes to show even knuckleheads are allowed to have dogs—which we knew already, right?

The other downside of the park is that there's plenty of evidence lying around that some dog owners don't clean up after their poopin' pooches. In effect, this negligence turned the hillside that otherwise would be prime for grassy somersaulting into something of a slippery slope—and a none-too-pretty picture. Too bad the learning curve is equally steep for the few inconsiderate dog owners who've made these green acres into a microcosm of the debate over on-leash and off-leash dogs in public parks.

The old park itself, meanwhile, is a marvelous meadow in the middle of the city, with two major trails for hiking—one heading southeast that follows a rippling and stony creek, and the other a broader trail to the east side that's primarily woodsy. The valley field next to the parking lot is perfect for picnicking, with a couple of grills and a picnic table, though don't count on the water fountain working and any lavish show of food is bound to attract a salivating audience. There's also history amid the blooming flower gardens in the spring and striking leaf colors of fall: A modest cannon battery that defended the nation's capital from an attack across the river during the Civil War is still maintained by the National Park Service.

The park is located north of Georgetown off Foxhall and Loughboro Roads on Chain Bridge Road; look for the park sign and entrance on the left. It's open dawn–dusk. 202/426-6841.

Restaurants

Sutton Place Gourmet: One-stop grocery shopping for the gourmet and his tasteful pooch, this is the first of what has grown into a metropolitan area chain of shops carrying fresh meats and seafood, pastries and breads, and many prepared dishes ready to take into any of the nearby parks for a scrumptious picnic. On a hot summer day, you can kick off the shoes and sit on the heated brick steps right outside with your pup and dine. 3201 New Mexico Avenue NW in Sutton Place. 202/363-5800.

GLOVER PARK

Try as he might, Chappy just can't bark out the pronunciation of this moderate income but highly sought-after neighborhood of yuppie couples with kids and dogs, older longtime residents with dogs, and empty nesters with dogs. Yeah, a few cats too—but you'd expect some diversity in this friendly community. Located north by northwest of Georgetown, this is an earthier environment of duplexes and townhouses interspersed with green spaces and tall trees. By the way, it's not pronounced "GLOW-ver" but rather "GLOVE-er" and sometimes "GLAH-ver."

Parks, Beaches, and Recreation Areas

22 Glover-Archbold Park 🐾 🐾 🐾 ½

More than 100 acres of unmanicured parkland, where paths wind about and cross Foundry Branch Creek, this piece of nature is sanctuary to some of the city's surprising array of wildlife—and provides the same getaway for you and your dog.

We were stunned by the beauty of this grand-scale parkland that stretches all the way from the upscale Spring Hill neighborhood south through Glover Park and Georgetown down to the Chesapeake & Ohio Canal and the river. Many of the trees that tower over the easily followed trails are as old as the city itself. A stream cuts across one side of its wooded valley, and in the middle is a grove of tall white birch that shimmers amid the earth colors surrounding it in midwinter and greens in summer. On its eastern side especially, trail entrances are steep downhill hikes, though the footing isn't bad unless it recently rained or snowed.

Dogs are supposed to be on a leash, though the immensity of the park beckons many a pooch companion to disregard the law. That's especially true of a fringe area at 39th and W Streets that regulars consider an unofficial off-leash dog zone, meaning you can run but you can also get caught. Keep in mind, though, that park rangers who swing by occasionally aren't the only risk; aggressive raccoons have posed some problems hereabouts, and an unleashed dog is more likely to cross their paths.

One of the better entrances to the park is located near 42nd and Davis Streets NW, at the bottom of the Spring Hill neighborhood where high-rise apartments edge the park and there's usually plenty of parking on nearby streets. A second convenient entrance is across Reservoir Road near the Georgetown University Hospital complex, though you may need to search the side streets for parking. You can also access the park from the Chesapeake & Ohio Canal directly north of Georgetown. The park runs northward from the Chesapeake & Ohio Canal nearly three miles, past Georgetown University and through prime District real estate and beyond Massachusetts Avenue to the woods behind WRC-TV and the radio station.

Open dawn until dusk daily, the park's primary border to the east is 42nd Street NW, and to the west, 44th Street NW. 202/282-1063.

Restaurants

Rockland's: This is the original that we first visited years ago after someone told us these are the best barbecued ribs in town. So go for the crusty smoked ribs and maybe take out a some orders of jalapeño cornbread to go with it. And the Caesar salad here is the real thing. 2418 Wisconsin Avenue NW; 202/333-2558.

MANOR PARK

Parks, Beaches, and Recreation Areas

23 Fort Slocum 🐾

Overgrown and wooded, this hillside acreage bordering on the District's northeast quadrant provides some open running space. Nothing much remains

---

of the Civil War fortification that once stood on these unattended grounds where cannons fired on Confederate troops advancing on Fort Stevens yonder several miles.

Located in a predominantly African-American working-class community, this underused field's only real attraction to anyone living outside the immediate neighborhood is its rich history. From here, you can look across the valley to the northwest and easily imagine what this city might have looked like some 140 years ago during the Civil War. The view hasn't changed that much from this vantage point. The park is open dawn–dark. It's located between Madison Place NW and Oglethorpe Street NW along Kansas Avenue. 202/282-1063.

MOUNT PLEASANT

Not nearly the dining and nightlife attraction of its neighbors south of Irving Street in Adams Morgan, not nearly as troubled as the Petworth neighborhood to the east across 14th Street, this older townish community is diverse and largely residential—and offers a dog-friendly environment.

Parks, Beaches, and Recreation Areas
24 Piney Branch Park 🐾 🐾
Truly a tree's branch off Rock Creek Park, neighborhood dogs rule the roost here among the clearings of heavy-use basketball courts and picnic tables that get a lot of cookout use in warm weather. It's a neighborhood thing here. The park is located at the fork in Rock Creek Parkway about a quarter mile past the National Zoo, on Piney Branch Parkway. It's open until dark. 202/282-1063.

PALISADES

Comfortably middle class with 1920s bungalows and small brick houses on the river side of MacArthur Boulevard, this close-to-downtown neighborhood just northwest of Georgetown turns distinctly poshy across MacArthur with expensive brick colonials. On the hillside directly above the Chesapeake & Ohio Canal, this is nice dog territory because it has the feel of a small town.

Parks, Beaches, and Recreation Areas
25 Palisades Park and Recreation Center 🐾 🐾
One of the lesser known tennis court parks in the District, this is one of those destinations that you pretty much need to know about to find. Not only is it buffered from the busy traffic of MacArthur Boulevard by a couple of blocks of the funky residential Palisades neighborhood, but you've even got to turn up a short street into its parking lot to find it. Even then, folks from curbside might never know that over the slight hill and under the trees are hidden and

July Fourth Parade: For a little old-fashioned, small-town patriotism this Independence Day, take the pooch over to Palisades' main street (MacArthur) on the Fourth and plop down on the sidewalk for a parade that could happen anywhere across the United States and anytime in the past 50 years—though most improbably on the streets of the nation's capital. Lots of red fire trucks, Scottish bagpipers, doofy clowns, homemade floats, and local hoke. Keep your eyes peeled for the Battery Kemble Park Barkers marching unit, up to three dozen parading pooches from the free-for-all park that extends toward Palisades from the Foxhall neighborhood. By the way, if you feel that beat and can't stay in your seat, the parade welcomes anyone to join in on the marching—including your all-American pup. The hour-long parade's staging area is at the intersection of Whitehaven Parkway and MacArthur Boulevard. The parade usually starts shortly after 10 A.M. If you like to watch, anywhere from there up along MacArthur Boulevard to Edmunds Place will do. Like the good old days, the whole affair winds down at the Palisades Park and Recreation Center for a community picnic. 202/282-2186.

often uncrowded tennis courts. Between the courts and the recreation center at the parking lot are an abundant ball field and plenty of God's green grass for pooch running. Though the leash law rules even in oft-overlooked parks such as this little gem, it's not unusual to find a rowdy dog or two running free, chasing a Frisbee, and bothering nobody since nobody is usually around.

The park is located off MacArthur Boulevard about two miles northwest of Georgetown, at Dana Street and Sherrier Place NW. It's open until dark, and the lighted tennis courts extend that a few hours. 202/282-2186.

Restaurants

Listrani's Italian Gourmet: Too bad dogs can't be seated at great little restaurants such as this Italian café, where the airiness of the place speaks for the tasty light fare served. But the good news is that there's plenty to take out from the deli-style counter at the front of the restaurant—from saucy pizzas to calamari salads to antipasti. And tying your dog to the benches in front, where customers wait for tables on busy nights, isn't a problem. 5100 MacArthur Boulevard NW; 202/363-0619.

TENLEYTOWN

Like Friendship Heights to its north and American University Park to the northwest, this quiet neighborhood is something of a throwback to small-town America where youngsters ride their bikes down tree-lined residential streets and old folks rock on porches contemplating the weeds in their lawns. A sap for Jimmy Stewart movies, Chappy likes that neo-1950s feel of the place.

Parks, Beaches, and Recreation Areas

26 Fort Reno Park 🐾 ½

Just north of the retail center and surrounding neighborhood of Tenleytown, Chappy found this large and hilly park to suit his purposes perfectly well, even if it's mostly unkempt. But the ball field, tennis courts, and soccer field get plenty of use, and students from adjacent Deal Junior High School shortcut across its wide lawns. But, otherwise, few trees and no facilities don't add up to much more than utilitarian intersection. And the skyscraping broadcast towers next door aren't a pretty sight. The park is located just off Wisconsin Avenue, five blocks past Tenley Circle (Nebraska Avenue intersection) on Belt Road. It's open dawn–dark. 202/673-7660.

27 Muhlenberg Park 🐾

A tiny block's worth of green grass and a fringe of trees in front of Murch Elementary School and not even a bench to sit on, this drive-by park might work for dogs into the frugality concept, but even nearby Fort Reno Park has a leg up on it. Located at the intersection of Nebraska Avenue and Davenport Street NW, the park is open dawn–dark. 202/673-7660.

WEST END

Wedged between upscale Georgetown, the university life of Foggy Bottom, and business- and government-dense downtown, this condo and apartment haven offers lots more office space than Chappy cares for and its personality is shaped by the prominent destinations it bridges. These blocks do offer a few dog-kind restaurants and hotels, if not much else for dog lovers.

Parks, Beaches, and Recreation Areas

28 Washington Circle 🐾

Fact is that the circles in the nation's capital just don't add up to the squares in terms of dog-ability. Part of the reason is that squares take on something of a parklike atmosphere and there's a feeling of closure, whereas circles tend to be the hubs of noisy circling traffic made for that purpose rather than a human or pooch oasis. But Chappy knows you can't fit a square peg into a round hole. For him, this circle is sort of a favorite pot to pee in and that's about all— a lovely one to be sure, and its proximity to Georgetown makes it a convenient stop for few other activities. One precaution: Cross the streets carefully because drivers tend to be looking into their left side mirrors to merge into the circular traffic pattern and not in front of them.

The circle is located at the convergence of Pennsylvania Avenue NW, K

Street NW, New Hampshire Avenue NW, and 23rd Street NW. It's open all hours. 202/673-7660.

Restaurants

Asia Nora: The Thai shellfish stew is spicy and unusual, like many of the excellent entrées on the changing menu at this Asian fusion restaurant near West End, where Thai, Japanese, Indian, and Indonesian tastes join forces. Carry out something nouveau Asian, but for dinner only; no lunch is served. 2213 M Street NW; 202/797-4860.

Legal Sea Foods: The Boston origins of this big seafood restaurant are evident in its vast menu and emphasis on daily fresh fare. Any of its many varieties of sturdier grilled fish is enough lure for us, but nostalgia for Martha's Vineyard summers often brings us back for the traditional New England lobster roll. All of it is take-out, of course, when the salty dog is along. 2020 K Street NW; 202/496-1111.

Places to Stay

Monarch Hotel: These classy and expensive accommodations boast a glassed lobby dedicated to the concept of "bringing the outside in" and about a third of the rooms that overlook the sunny courtyard gardens. But its pet policy isn't quite so insistent on bringing dogs and cats in from the outside. "We have a very strict pet policy," said a front-desk clerk sternly, as if to say "and we mean it!" Pets must be 25 pounds or under—and I wouldn't dismiss the possibility that they have a scale behind the registration desk. Check in with a dog and you must leave a $500 refundable deposit plus a nonrefundable $150 cleaning fee. And you must sign a waiver stating that you will supervise your dog at all times and keep the pup under control or in a cage when cleaning personnel come to your room.

For quick relief, don't steer your pooch to the courtyard, please! A school yard with a grove of trees and baseball field is about a half block away. Also, Rock Creek Park and Washington Circle are within easy walking distance. Room rates start at $270. 2401 M Street NW, Washington, DC 20037; 202/429-2400.

New Hampshire Suites Hotel: This splendid Best Western hotel welcomes traveling pooches without hesitation—an increasingly unusual virtue in town. Guests with dogs are kept to first floor rooms, which is a convenience to the hotel and to dog lovers (no Fido freakin' on the elevators). And, there's no extra charge. But the hotel appreciates a heads-up in advance, and asks that you bring your dog crate and never leave the pup in the room alone. Chappy likes the free continental breakfast, but what's new?

Georgetown is a brisk walk away and George Washington University's campus is nearly next door, so there's lots of interesting walking close by. Room rates range from about $95 and up. 1121 New Hampshire Avenue NW, Washington, DC 20037; 202/457-0565 or 800/762-3777.

Park Hyatt Washington:: Just three blocks from Georgetown, this 224-room modern luxury hotel offers plenty of extras, from original "name" artworks hung throughout to goose-down duvets. More importantly, it takes in canine clients with no deposit, no extra charge, and no restrictions. They're just plain nice and friendly to the furry faction here. Rates start at $275. 1201 24th Street NW, Washington, DC 20037; 202/789-1234.

WOODLEY PARK

The name's almost synonymous with the zoo. And that's not altogether fair to this first-class neighborhood north of Rock Creek Park that's home to diverse culinary opportunities, modestly elegant Victorian homes, some not-so-modest ones bordering on the park, some older high-rise apartment buildings, and two of the city's largest hotels. Young professionals find this to be a prestigious address, so there's plenty to do—plus a cluster of restaurants and eateries around Connecticut Avenue, the major artery through this community.

Parks, Beaches, and Recreation Areas

29 National Zoological Park 🐾 ◀●

Don't bring your domesticated Bowser along to the zoo if undertaking the standard visit is what you have in mind because dogs aren't allowed there—and for good reason. There are just too many caged and frustrated beasts—some 4,500 of them and 480 species, including the famous giant pandas and those weird dinosaurlike Komodo dragons that would just as soon dine on a schnauzer as befriend one. Besides, the last thing the inmates at this lovely zoo want to see is your chipper pup strutting around on the outside looking in—which is probably why the zookeepers post "no pets" at the entrances. But you can park in any of the zoo's peripheral parking lots and walk your leashed dog around the outer edges of the zoo grounds, over to nearby Rock Creek Park, or stroll up to Connecticut Avenue outside the north gate, where you can snap a photo of your pooch standing in front of the zoo's main entrance—a nice memento.

The zoo's main entrance is located along the 3000 block of Connecticut Avenue near Hawthorne Avenue; for its preferable back entrance and parking lots, look for the signs along Rock Creek Parkway near Harvard Street. The zoo grounds are open daily except Christmas Day, 6 A.M.–8 P.M. 202/673-4800 or 202/673-4717.

30 Rock Creek Park 🐾 🐾 🐾 🐾 ◀●

Let Chappy guide your leisurely wanderings in the District of Columbia, and inevitably he'll tug your leash into this sprawling national park—one of his favorite federal spaces. A testament to justice, freedom and your tax dollars at work, no other park smack-dab in the middle of a major city can match the wild beauty of these gorgeous and completely dog-friendly 1,750 acres.

Set aside by Congress in 1890 as the nation's first urban national park, it is twice the size of New York City's Central Park. This park is known for foxes and deer and more than 100 species of birds—and a natural beauty that's hard to fathom this close in. Every year, some two million visitors stroll, jog, in-line skate, ride horseback (in designated parts), bike, and old-fashioned meander these tree-shaded paths. Picnicking is a traditional summertime affair: The park provides 30 formal picnicking sites equipped with rain shelters and grills—many of them near the rollicking Rock Creek itself and requiring permits. Otherwise, a multitude of picnic sites and scattered tables for pick-up picnics require no permits.

Chappy and our gang of explorers have even indulged in late springtime snoozes on its sunny lawns following a basket luncheon—an indication of how comfortable and reasonably safe most of these park grounds are (though, as always in the city, use your better judgment). Dog lovers will find the nature to be nearly undisturbed throughout its forested four-mile length that follows the gurgling and occasionally swift Rock Creek (deep enough for doggy dipping in places) from the Potomac River through northwest Washington and into Montgomery County, Maryland. The park is dog delightful, though National Park rules require your comely companion to be on a leash. Inevitably you'll see some that aren't. But plenty of amiable and helpful park rangers take care of these sacred grounds, so ignoring leash laws risks a fine—or a stern lecture if you're lucky.

Chappy gets so focused at sniffing out tracks of wildlife and other dogs that he barely notices the thousands of daffodils blooming on the park's hillside slopes that look like wind-blown yellow seas in the spring. But you will notice. By fall, the yellow is replaced by a mixed palette of the reds, golds, yellows, and oranges from the many hardwood trees that make this park a seasonal wonderland. Even winter's spartan landscapes inspire poetic imagery with their bare simplicity. Summertime is simply plush and rich and perfect for hiking trails or walking the creek's edge.

Park newbies driving into this vast wilderness might be confused that there's no apparent main entrance. As soon as you drive past the National Zoo on Rock Creek Parkway heading north from downtown, you're already in the park—and you will know it. What you won't know as you watch the architecture of charming bridges and natural beauty of the creek from your car's window, is where to park in the park.

The first opportunity comes just north of the National Zoo. Turn left at the first intersection, Porter Street, and cross the little bridge over Rock Creek, where you bear right onto Porter. You can find free parking in the residential area and walk down to this under-used and overlooked section of the park that's visited mostly by walking-distance neighbors and serious joggers. Populated with white oaks and red maples among its many old, tall trees, this paved path features astonishing rock formations where archaeologists regularly conduct digs into our prehistoric ancestry.

North of the Porter Street exit is another prime locale. Bear left at the unclearly marked fork opposite the right-hand turn marked Piney Branch Exit. At the first stoplight, turn left onto Tilden Street and continue until you cross the aptly named Tilden Street Bridge. Immediately on the right is the always-full parking lot at the Gallery Barn and Old Pierce Mill. Continue past that lot and look for a larger lot on your left about 50 feet ahead. You'll be surrounded by a dazzling open field, jogging and hiking trails that wind north and south, a clean bathroom facility, even a pay phone that works. This is a worthy stop for man and beast—and probably the best introductory excursion into Rock Creek Park. Stop by the Rock Creek Gallery, where art shows are housed in the rustic carriage house (circa 1811–1820) that was part of the old Pierce Plantation way back when. Depending on how busy this relaxed art gallery is (and who's behind the front desk), you might be able to bring your well-behaved leashed pup inside for a peek at the current exhibition in progress. Just ask politely first.

Across the small parking lot is the 19th century Pierce Mill, a fully restored and operational grain mill that's the last survivor of 20 gristmills that operated on Rock Creek from 1664 to 1925. Dogs aren't welcome inside, where a park ranger keeps his nose to the grindstone (figuratively) during daytime hours, talking to tourists about the old mill (it closes at dark). But directly behind the mill, Rock Creek shows off with white-water cascades and a waterfall that Chappy could've played near all day.

Plenty of canine company is thereabouts, too, because this is a primo picnicking and lollygagging territory—and a hub of imaginative park activity. From Pierce Mill, it's a 1.4-mile hike south to the National Zoo and exactly twice as far south to the Chesapeake & Ohio Canal. About six miles due north is the park's nature center and planetarium, its main visitor center (by car, follow the nature center signs to the Glover Road location). The center houses displays showing how to identify wildlife and plants, as well as other exhibits, but is off-limits to dogs. Still, you can pick up useful trail information at the main desk and use the bathroom facilities. And the center's vast parking lot provides an easy starting point for the strenuous and hilly 4.5-mile Western Ridge Trail—a well-marked hike Chappy found to be abundant with sniffable nature.

The park's headquarters are located at 3545 Williamsburg Lane NW; 202/282-1063. The nature center is located at 5200 Glover Road NW; except for federal holidays, it is open Wednesday–Sunday, 9 A.M.–5 P.M., and daily during summer; 202/426-6829. Pierce Mill is open Wednesday–Sunday, 9 A.M.–5 P.M., except for federal holidays; 202/426-6908. Rock Creek Park itself is open daily throughout the year and is free. Most formal picnic groves (with grills, tables, etc.) in the park must be reserved by calling 202/673-7646, but plenty of picnicking areas are first-come, first-served. No camping is allowed in the park. Wading and swimming in Rock Creek are prohibited.

Restaurants

Austin Grill: Head to this cantina with a classic menu from deep in the heart of Texas for carryout chorizo and loaded quesadillas, or just stick to the good barbecue dishes. 2404 Wisconsin Avenue NW; 202/337-8080.

Lebanese Taverna: Carry out "Lebanese pizza" and a side of cold tabbouleh from this institution of higher culinary arts—and tell them Chappy sent you. Uh, on second thought, better not to mention Chappy here. 2641 Connecticut Avenue NW; 202/265-8681

Mrs. Simpson's: Right in front of this dignified and charming restaurant is a small outdoor patio with tables overlooking Connecticut Avenue. Dog lovers with their well-mannered dogs seated amiably by their feet dine serenely there on contemporary cuisine—lovely salads, crab cakes, grilled veggies. It also offers one of the most pleasant Sunday champagne brunches you'll find. Outside tables are available as weather permits at this exquisite little restaurant named for Wallis Simpson, who stole the heart of the Duke of Windsor. And this delightful place will steal your heart and your dog's on a sunny spring afternoon. 2915 Connecticut Avenue NW; 202/332-8700.

New Heights: Leash your dog to the rail opposite your table at the outdoor sidewalk terrace at this casual, contemporary Asian-Southwestern fusion restaurant and nobody minds one bit. Actually the only reason the kind folks here would prefer your pooch not sit inside on the patio is so he doesn't trip a waiter (by accident, of course). Order any of the excellent fish entrees—some with imaginative sauces. 2317 Calvert Street NW; 202/234-4110.

Places to Stay

Marriott Wardman Park Hotel: One of the bigger hotels in the city with more than 1,500 rooms, it impressed Chappy with the size of the lawns and walking space around the hotel—even some wooded fringes. Just down Connecticut Avenue from the National Zoo and a block north of easy access to Rock Creek Park, the location is prime turf for pooches, who can stay with their masters free of charge but with a 25-pound-and-under restrictions on size. Rates start at around $200. 2660 Woodley Road NW, Washington, DC 20008; 202/328-2000.

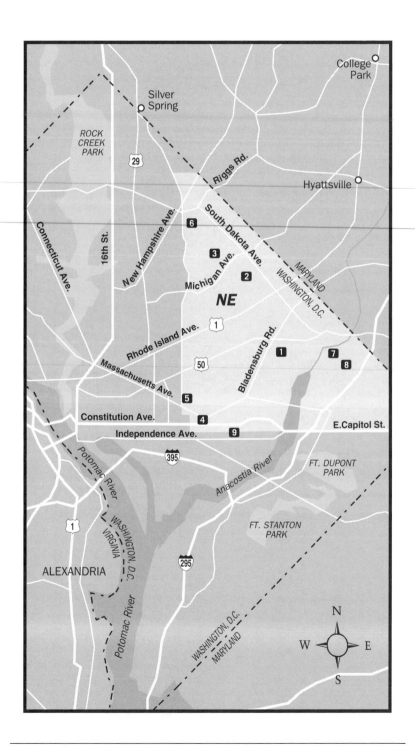

3 NORTHEAST D.C.

Bordered by North Capitol Street to the west, East Capitol Street to the south, the District line and, well, you get the idea. In fact, even folks who live in the metropolitan area have a hard time describing where Northeast begins and ends. All you and your dog have to know is that within these boundaries are some pleasantly serene middle-class townhouse neighborhoods on the rebound. And there are some addresses where you don't want to venture— even with an aggressively protective canine by your side. Generally this isn't wide-eyed tourist territory, and not where you'll be making hotel reservations if visiting. But there are some worthy destinations for dog lovers.

The most sought-after address in northeast is Capitol Hill, which also spreads into the other three District quadrants. As you might imagine, Capitol Hill teems with young congressional staffers, lobbyists, members of Congress, and other ne'er-do-wells. Huge brownstones and smaller townhomes are the mainstays, but a few apartment, condo units and townhouses being rehabbed can be found. As a rule those areas closest to the Capitol command the highest prices and are considered the safest—even though street crime and robberies are common occurrences. But the tree-shaded streets in the neighborhood "behind" the Capitol comprise a quaint and historic area.

National Parks

❶ United States National Arboretum 🐾 🐾 🐾 🐾 🐾

Even the folks at this wonderful vista of natural beauty couldn't identify the neighborhood it's in, so we went back on our promise to list national parks by their locations. Sorry, but while this is near Trinidad, Gateway, and even Fort Lincoln–New Town, this magnificent acreage isn't located in any of them. It stands on its own, and rightfully so, as far as we're concerned.

Though some of its more fragile plant collections are off-limits for rambunctious canines, this 444-acre paradise of dedicated gardens and rolling hills that suddenly drop to hidden lakes and meditative ponds beckons dogs and dog lovers alike with its sedate beauty and wide-open spaces. "Wow" is the word here—and "bow wow." For dog lovers and their pups, this is a must-see oasis along grungy New York Avenue NE.

We steered Chappy away from the magnificent bonsai, herb garden, and azalea patches because we didn't want a bull-in-the-china-shop incident. There are fragile flora areas here where dogs aren't invited; watch for those signs. Instead, we wandered in awe through the National Capitol Columns site. Its 22 white sandstone columns were removed from the United States Capitol's east portico in 1958 during an expansion project. Now, the columns rise up so suddenly from a reflecting pool surrounded by a vast meadow that you'll feel as if you've stumbled into an ancient Hellenic garden.

Traipse through the brushy woods by the Kingman Lake Overlook and let the pup play alongside the Anacostia River; or better yet (and probably cleaner), visit the large ponds that are teeming with large Japanese koi—they'll occupy the dog mentality—and yours—for a relaxing spell. Head up Hickey Hill Road to the Asian Collection, where the view of the lake from the pathway to the pagoda is Zen-sational! But these grounds are extensive, so make sure to pick up a free map to avoid driving in circles. Maps are available at the bulletin board near the visitor's entrance off New York Avenue and at the administration offices and gift shop. Follow the well-marked signs.

Picnicking is pretty much contained in a large quadrant on the back side of the arboretum near Maryland Avenue, where there is plenty of parking and some facilities. Many local residents in the know visit here during each of the four seasons to witness the spectacular changing horticulture. Spring and early summer will make a blooming idiot of any nature lover with a dazzling wealth of ferns, dogwoods, azaleas, and daffodils. Dogs need to be leashed, even if some of the roomy fields invite running free, and you'll see dogs and their companions who couldn't resist nature's invitation. Admission is free.

The arboretum is open daily, 8 A.M.–5 P.M., year-round (closed Christmas). Its two entrances are at 3501 New York Avenue NE and 24th and R Streets NE, off of Bladensburg Road. 202/245-2726.

Herb Festival: Call it urban herbology if you're poetically inclined. This annual festival put on by the Friends of the National Arboretum and the Herb Society of America introduces the identities and uses of more herbs than Chappy could sniff. Even for less sensitive humans this is herb heaven. More than a hundred varieties of herbs are on sale. There are also herbal cooking and crafting demonstrations, herbal books, herbal refreshments—the whole herbal lifestyle.

Of the dozens of formal programs at the arboretum, this one might be best for canine accompaniment—because there's plenty to take in besides the special guided tours of the fragile herb garden where dogs aren't allowed. The festival is held in early May in tents adjacent to the administration building. The National Arboretum is located at 3501 New York Avenue NE. Admission is free. 202/245-2726.

BROOKLAND

One of the neighborhoods where many African Americans moved to during the Depression, Brookland hosts the 154-acre, tree-lined campus of Catholic University of America, Trinity College next door, and the exquisite National Shrine of the Immaculate Conception—all centers of intellect and faith that Chappy likes for their broad grassy campuses. This is another neighborhood on the rebound where you'll find friendly dog lovers out and about. It is home to an interesting mix of college students, professors, and elderly middle-class residents who live for the most part in neatly kept row houses and Cape Cods that bring a welcome respite from the clamor of the inner city nearby.

Parks, Beaches, and Recreation Areas
2 Fort Bunker Hill Park 🐾

Rising above the residential neighborhood that now surrounds it, this link in the chain of city forts built during the Civil War to protect the nation's capital from a rebel offensive is high enough to overlook Catholic University. It even overlooks the United States Soldier's and Airman's Home where Abraham Lincoln's summerhouse once stood. If you and the pooch climb the path up the hill, past the abandoned water fountain and historic plaque to take in the view, you'll find some of the old fort's parapets still visible at the top, but not much else anymore. History is the only reason to head this way unless you happen to be here anyway. But it's an interesting point of view.

Open dawn–dusk and is located at 14th and Otis Streets NE. 202/426-6841.

3 Turkey Thicket Park 🐾

A small community park that borders on Brookland Elementary School, this is neighborhood greenery that promises little more than a place to stretch those dog legs. There are a couple dozen of these smaller recreation areas in this quadrant, but they're almost entirely dedicated to basketball courts, playgrounds and outside sports—not leisurely dog walks. But in a pinch, they come in handy. It's open dawn–dusk and is located at 10th Street and Michigan Avenue NE; 202/690-5185.

Restaurants

Colonel Brooks' Tavern: No dogs inside, no email or fax orders. But good restaurants are hard to find down this direction, so phone in your order from this reliable tavern's take-out menu—including a sumptuous baked salmon Caesar salad, a killer steak-and-cheese on French bread (hold the green peppers), and fried catfish, the likes of which you haven't seen since leaving Louisiana. The half rack of barbecued pork ribs served with white baked beans and coleslaw is a piece of work, too. And if you're in the neighborhood on Tuesday night, swing by for some Dixieland jazz. The tavern is open into the wee hours to accommodate exam-cramming students. 901 Monroe Street NE; 202/529-4002.

Island Jim's Crab Shack and Tiki Bar: This surprising oasis even caught our beach dog off guard. This island paradise is the neighbor of Colonel Brooks' place and the Brookland Metro station. Appropriate picnic-table décor is right for the crab-by-the-dozen menu and rum drinks. This is as close as you'll ever come to wastin' away in Margaritaville—in northeast D.C. 901 Monroe Street NE; 202/635-8454.

EARMARK YOUR CALENDAR–SUMMER

For Dogs Named Spike: More than 100 local volleyball teams compete every summer in the all-day **National Kidney Foundation Volleyball Marathon** on Catholic University's Augustinian Fields at Taylor Street and Michigan Avenue NE. And while the pooch can be a spectator only, you can register at the event (it costs $25–50 in pledges raised) and play on a short-handed team. Food, beer and sports beverages, and lots of fun follow the bouncing ball. Admission is free. The Catholic University fields are located off Michigan Avenue along Brookland Drive NE. 202/244-7900.

Celebrating Roots: Every July the **African-American Family Day Summerfest** brings music, dancing, and food to Turkey Thicket Park's modest grounds. Well-behaved dogs on leashes are welcome, but it's a neighborhood thing with lots of kids, so if your pup isn't up for that, don't go. 10th Street and Michigan Avenue NE; 202/232-3511.

CAPITOL HILL NE

The Capitol's surrounding community actually does have a life of its own beyond politics and government. Its northeast sector is an old neighborhood of townhouses inhabited by powerful residents that branches off from the Supreme Court building and the Senate office buildings. But further northeast the neighborhood borders on areas that are more impoverished than empowered. Some of these streets are historic and clean; some of them are just mean. So a word of caution: Residents here know crime is a problem, especially after twilight. Folks walking dogs aren't immune. So stick to daylight when you take in the quaint townhouse-lined streets here that originated with the beginnings of this city.

Parks, Beaches, and Recreation Areas

4 Stanton Park 🐾 ½

Northeast of the green lawns surrounding the Capitol and Union Station, this modest plot of grass and shrubs, about two blocks by one, serves its neighborhood dogs' recreational needs admirably as the stately statue of General Nathanael Greene looks on. Our visit was unremarkable except for Chappy feeling like a dog out of his territory.

The park is located at the convergence of Maryland Avenue and Massachusetts Avenue NE, between Fourth and Sixth Streets NE, and it is open all hours, although all hours aren't recommended. 202/426-6841.

5 Union Station Plaza 🐾 🐾 ½

For three long blocks south of where taxis line up at the busy plaza outside the train station, stretching to the Senate side of the Capitol building, this huge green space straddles the northwest-northeast District line and includes several miniparks whose names never appear on maps or in guidebooks. It's all anchored by the Taft Memorial Carillon (barely on the northwest side) and a pretty circular pool with multilevel fountains and falls called Lower Senate Park closer to Union Station.

Technically, the plaza is all taxis, rail commuters, and shoppers scurrying about the front of the train station and multilevel shopping mall. But the delightful parklands just beyond the impressive semicircle of flags that wave high in front of Union Station are an excellent doggy playground.

You and the pooch can chime in with the gong show that rings from the carillon-like clockwork, or just sit back and relax with all the congressional staffers who lunch and congregate at the little Congressional Park along Constitution Avenue. The restored beaux arts train station itself was modeled after the Baths of Caracalla in Rome and is an impressive depot.

Bordered by Delaware Avenue to the east, Louisiana Avenue to the west, Constitution Avenue to the south, and Union Station to the north, the plaza and parkland are open all hours, but use common sense after dark. 202/426-6841.

Restaurants

Capitol City Brewing Company: Dag nammit, you can't carry out any of this fine brew pub's stouts or ales, but you can call ahead and pick up one of its fat and juicy burgers (Chappy recommends the bleu cheese on top) or hofbrau bratwurst sandwiches, all at reasonable prices. All right already, Chappy says to include the brewmaster's sausage platter, which serves up three local sausage favorites—andouille, duck, and Thai chicken sausages grilled on an open fire, with sauerkraut, apple chutney, and horseradish mashed potatoes, for about $15. 2 Massachusetts Avenue NE; 202/842-BEER (202/842-2337).

FORT TOTTEN

Parks, Beaches, and Recreation Areas

6 Fort Totten Park 🐾

You and your dog won't need to use your imaginations to envision the fort itself, because its earthworks are still relatively intact about 50 yards up through this vast piece of hillside woods from the entrance near Crittenden Avenue NE. And there is a grassy lawn area for picnicking where the barracks stood 140 years ago, near the rifle trench that is still visible. But the park goes largely neglected and occasionally is the scene of criminal activity. Except for a city youth summer camp that uses the parkland, the long-ago firing of the 20 guns and mortars that once pointed from between the parapets is still the most activity the park has seen.

The park entrance is located at Fort Totten Drive and Crittenden Avenue NE and is open dawn–dusk, daily. 202/426-6841.

KENILWORTH

Parks, Beaches, and Recreation Areas

7 Kenilworth Aquatic Gardens 🐾 🐾 🐾 👞

Here's a change of scenery that will lift any dog's spirits—and just when Chappy showed signs of not seeing the forest for the trees after visiting so many parks. We dropped in on this 12-acre waterworld garden across the Anacostia River from the National Arboretum. Despite the on-leash requirement, Chappy was rejuvenated by the sights and unfamiliar smells of exquisite water lilies and other blooming tropical plants. And there in multitudes, so close to Chappy's Tibetan heart, were lotuses! *Om mani padme om!*

To catch this wet plant show at its best, head this way no sooner than mid-May, when they bring back the water flora from their winter hothouses. The plants remain until the threat of frost in late fall—but the gardens are open year-round.

In the winter months, emphasis changes from plant life to bird life, some 40 species including gawky blue herons, magnificent eagles, and grand ospreys hanging out like regulars at a neighborhood bar. Dog lovers and their dogs are welcome on the guided walks through the watery plant life that are scheduled regularly or by appointment from Memorial Day to Labor Day.

There is no admission charge to enter the gardens, which are open daily, 7 A.M.–4 P.M. The gardens are located off Kenilworth Avenue (I-295) near the Maryland line at Anacostia Avenue and Douglas Street NE; 202/426-6905.

8 Kenilworth Park 🐾 🐾 ½

Adjoining the Kenilworth Aquatic Gardens a half mile to the south, this 25-acre expanse of grassy open fields formerly was a city landfill. It goes to show you can teach an old dog new tricks, however, because the landfill is now filled with several soccer and rugby fields and lots of running room for man and beast alike. Leash laws dictate your dog be on one, but this park often seems nearly deserted, so you will find people letting their dogs run loose and carefree. Community plans to further develop the site into a riverside showcase remain stalled by tight finances, but the stroll alongside the river is nice and quiet as it is.

The park, which is open dawn–dusk, is located off Kenilworth Avenue (I-295) on the westernmost end of Burroughs Avenue NE. 202/426-6905.

LINCOLN PARK

Parks, Beaches, and Recreation Areas

🄈 Lincoln Park 🐾 🐾

It looks and, symbolically, it *is* huge: This large rectangular plot of urban property overlapping from the District's northeast quadrant into the southeast was paid for with money donated by freed slaves—many of whom were veterans of the Union army. It is officially called "Freedom Square," but unofficially you can think of this as Doggy Square.

On the west end is a statue of Abraham Lincoln with the Emancipation Proclamation in one hand and the other extended to an enslaved black man breaking free of his shackles. On the east side of the park, which is located between the neighborhoods of Capitol Hill and Lincoln Park, stands a statue of the renowned educator and founder of the National Council of Negro Women, Mary McLeod Bethune. You'll find plenty of neighborhood dog-loving residents and their dogs hanging out at this three-block-long oasis with lots of benches and grassy spaces. Many of the dogs run off leash despite laws to the contrary.

The neighborhood has benefited from ongoing gentrification but remains one of those enigmatic Capitol Hill locales that can be a little edgy after dark. Yuppie residents fill this greenery on weekends with their pampered pooches and infants in strollers. The park is their meeting ground where neighbors meet neighbors. Early morning and after-work hours are prime pooch time on weekdays and all daylight hours on weekends. People without dogs who move into the stately townhouses facing the park soon get dogs—because that's the common currency here.

The park is located about 10 blocks directly east of the United States Capitol Building, at 11th Street and Massachusetts Avenue NE; 202/690-5185.

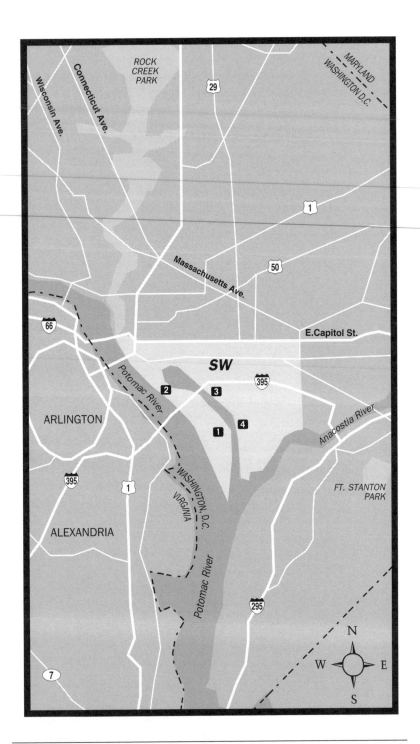

SOUTHWEST D.C.

The quadrant of the nation's capital best suited for water dogs, Southwest D.C. is bordered by the city's two historic rivers—the Potomac and the Anacostia. From the cherry tree–rimmed Tidal Basin to the Washington Channel to the bridges that span the Potomac from its waterfront, this area's charms include the most familiar of national monuments surrounded by dog-friendly parklands. It's the home of the Arena Stage and the in-town boating mecca along the waterfront. Again, because neighborhoods are few and far between the federal presence here, we have separated the national parks into their own section.

National Parks

1 East Potomac Park 🐾 🐾 🐾 🐾 🐾

You'll know you're at Hains Point, the southernmost point of this dazzling 328-acre peninsula park, when your dog freaks momentarily at the sight of *The Awakening,* a Gulliver-sized hand, face, and foot of a bearded mythic hero emerging from the ground. Once more, Chappy revealed his cultural shortcomings. He mostly disregarded the popular sculpture by J. Seward

---

Johnson and instead sniffed out nearby territory for less-than-artistic reasons. But we must admit that we've been to some art gallery openings where such behavior would've fit right in.

That said, take your pooch to see this unique sculpture while you can, because as this book goes to press there's bureaucratic rumblings about moving it elsewhere—probably to put up a parking lot.

A popular destination for locals and tourists alike, this 1.5-mile-long finger of land points south into the Potomac River from the Jefferson Memorial and the maze of traffic overpasses extending off the 14th Street Bridge. With or without the *The Awakening*, the park's real centerpiece isn't all that likely to wake up the canine visitor—one of the flattest 18-hole golf courses you will find. It is circled here by an excellent walking loop planted with Japanese cherry trees where you need to watch out for stray drives and penalty strokes whizzing past. This course is a hacker's delight.

It's safer walking along the water side of tree-lined Ohio Drive where you and the pooch can lean on the railing and watch the river go by for hours if you like. Across the river from the northeastern side are the handsome rows of Georgian houses and pillared buildings of the Army War College; the southwestern view is the landing and take-off strips of Ronald Reagan National Airport. High tide occasionally submerges part of this perimeter sidewalk, so watch your step. But there's plenty of open walking and roust-about space here.

Next to the sculpture (or were it once was) is a large field where Chappy wanted nothing more than to run and run. It's easy to drop off the children at the adjacent huge fenced playground with bathroom facilities, where you can keep an eye on them while running the pup. An abundance of picnic tables and benches provide a relaxing riverside space for humans. Indeed, during one of our visits, three dogs were running sans leash, even though regulations require a leash. Few enough people were there that it didn't bother anyone.

By the way, if *The Awakening* is still planted here, take advantage of one of the many ideal photo ops the city has to offer a dog lover and companion. If you can get your pup to sit in the mouth or gripping hand of the sculptured figure (we couldn't), the photo you take should prove to be a rare sight indeed. The park is open 8 A.M.–midnight and is located along Ohio Drive on the South side of 14th Street and I-395 from the Jefferson Memorial; look for signs to Hains Point and East Potomac Park. 202/426-6841.

2 West Potomac Park 🐾 🐾 🐾 🐾 ◀▬

A must-see for all dog lovers, this waterside park's newest attraction is the Franklin Delano Roosevelt Memorial, which since it opened in 1997 has become one of the most popular monuments in the nation's capital. But this parkland actually stretches from two of the nation's most popular memorials—

DIVERSIONS

Is That Cricket? From spring through fall, the wide-open fields of West Potomac Park get a workout with **soccer, rugby, and cricket matches,** many of them embassy teams, competing for crowds of onlookers. Weekends also see full-blown **polo matches,** with magnificent horses and riders tearing up the turf in sight of the Tidal Basin and Lincoln Memorial. There are no admission charges for you or restrictions on well-behaved pups (other than that they stay off the fields of competition). Check newspaper listings for times, which vary. The games are played at West Potomac Park between Independence Avenue SW and Ohio Drive SW; 202/426-6841.

the Lincoln and the Jefferson Memorials, which theoretically are included in East Potomac Park. Go figure.

But even the well-manicured grounds on this elongated stretch of beautiful parkland provide an unparalleled place for romp and circumstance. Picking up where East Potomac Park leaves off at the backside of Mr. Jefferson's marble columns, the park provides some surprisingly roomy grass zones where dogs can feel the Capital of the Free World under their paws. A lovely dog walk awaits you east of the memorial, along 14th Street and around the Tidal Basin.

Around the Jefferson Memorial are surprisingly roomy grass zones where dogs can feel the Capital of the Free World under their paws. A lovely dog walk awaits you to the east side of the memorial, along 14th Street and around the Tidal Basin. In early spring, this is prime Japanese cherry blossom territory with more than 3,000 blooming trees guaranteed to astound you with a beauty that surpasses description. In any other season, it's just about as pretty a walk as can be found amid a city this size. From the memorial itself, you can see the paddleboat house just over the little bridge. On a good summer day, the operator will let you take the pooch out for a memorable boat ride.

On the portico of the domed white marble Jefferson Memorial on the West Potomac Park side, dogs encounter no obstacles, no signs banning them, no judgmental glances from the tourist crowd clicking automatic lenses nonstop at all hours. This is a spectacular setting, patriotic to the hilt, a doggy photo op most certainly. Even the anarchist-to-the-bone Chappy tried saluting—or so we thought until we saw it was his rear leg he was raising. A gentle tug on the leash reminded our pup not to abuse the freedoms he enjoys. Just something to keep in mind if you take your dog all the way up the memorial's many steps for a close-up of the magnificent statue of our third president. You might want to warn him ahead of time that the rolled-up thing in Jefferson's left hand is a document and not a newspaper. Then, again, you might not want to.

Then onward across the little Inlet Bridge and along Ohio Drive to the FDR Memorial, which was unveiled in May 1997. With its back to the Tidal Basin, it is a huge 7.5 acres of public space made of more than 6,000 tons of granite. You'll find room to roam among the 12-foot granite walls bearing FDR quotations, several sculptures and friezes, waterfalls and pools, and set-off nooks and crannies. Much of its popularity is due to the hands-on (and paws-on) element here; this is a touchable memorial that fascinates visitors. Besides the centerpiece statues of FDR himself, the statue of the president's dog, Fala, will please dogs and dog lovers.

Still surrounding the park are several softball fields and a lovely soccer-rugby-polo field. Chappy raced around on his leash pretending to be a star athlete as we ran beside him, pretending not to be out of breath. Be advised not to race your dog during games, however.

From downtown Washington, follow 14th Street southwest (toward Virginia) and watch for signs to the Jefferson Memorial before crossing the George Mason Bridge (14th Street Bridge) into Virginia. From Virginia, take the George Washington Memorial Parkway to the 14th Street Bridge (Arland D. Williams Jr. Bridge). Veer to the right on I-395 into the District, and watch for the immediate exit to East Potomac Park and Ohio Drive, which will take you to West Potomac Park. West Potomac Park is open year-round, 24 hours a day, as is the FDR Memorial—but use good judgment. The Jefferson Memorial is open all hours; National Park Service rangers and interpreters are on site to answer questions and give talks from 8 A.M. to midnight every day except December 25. 202/426-6841.

Restaurants

Jefferson Memorial Concession Stand: Yeah, right, a tourist fast-food stand? Well, you cannot find a better hot dog in Washington than at this little official food kiosk opposite the T-shirt and souvenir hawkers at the entrance of the parking lot. It's a $3 foot-long dog, and the bun itself is an extravagance. 202/426-6841.

Places to Stay

Loew's L'Enfant Plaza Hotel: Funny that a place where the dominant characteristic is serious concrete, a place surrounded by office buildings and a towering freeway, goes out of its way to be pet permissible. But that's the Loew's hotel-chain policy, thank you. Not only does this hotel that mostly caters to business clients welcome dogs, it just may have some doggy treats behind the desk at check-in. Room rates start at $205. Nearby, under the Dwight Eisenhower Freeway and to the south just one block, is the grassy knoll of Banneker Park where a pup can stretch his legs and sniff the aromas from across Maine Avenue at the Washington Fish and Seafood Market Place. 480 L'Enfant Plaza SW, Washington, DC 20024; 202/484-1000.

WATERFRONT

A waterside haven for federal employees and boat-happy refugees from the pressures of the city proper, the Southwest Waterfront is within a short walk of Capitol Hill and L'Enfant Plaza. Located just north of the Anacostia River, the neighborhood is also home to theaters, restaurants, high-rise condos, and pricey townhouses. Pooches will find the river's edge as pleasant an excursion as their human companions will. And watch for major changes in this area: In March 2002, the D.C. government announced plans to redesign and revitalize this entire under-used waterfront and turn it into a gentrified mix of apartment buildings, parks, and shopping plazas.

Parks, Beaches, and Recreation Areas

3 Benjamin Banneker Park 🐾

The circular little park atop a grassy hillside surrounded by extraordinarily wide boxwoods isn't much of an attraction for dogs, unless feeding the pigeons from a park bench excites them. In the shadow of the metallic Eisenhower Freeway, the park is dedicated to the African-American mathematician and inventor whom George Washington hired to work with Pierre L'Enfant in designing the nation's capital. This is one of those cases

---

EARMARK YOUR CALENDAR

Share the Dream: On January 12, celebrate **Martin Luther King's birthday** at the wreath-laying ceremony, usually at the Lincoln Memorial, where Dr. King gave his famous and inspiring "I Have a Dream" speech. Even now, the speech sends tingles down the spine when we hear the recording played at this ceremony. Dogs and dog lovers can share in the upbeat tempo as local choirs, guest speakers, and a military color guard make this a memorable occasion. Call first; location varies from year to year. 202/619-7222.

Not Worse Than Its Bite: The **Bark Ball,** an annual and formal black-tie celebration of our favorite four-footed fur balls, is the Washington Humane Society's premiere fund-raising event. The food isn't for the dogs, the bar is open, and the dancing goes late into the night. The proceeds benefit homeless dogs in the District. It's an evening to howl about. Held in mid-June usually at the dog-friendly Loews L'Enfant Plaza Hotel but location changes so check before ordering tickets, which run about $100 per person. 202/723-5730.

DIVERSIONS

You Could Get Hooked: Nowhere in the city is quite like the **Washington Fish and Seafood Market Place,** the traditional market-place for Chesapeake Bay fishermen to sell their catches upriver to District residents. Excitement isn't all that's in the air at this market—on hot days, the scent of seafood dominates from the sides of the permanently docked barges. But most of the time the colorful characters promising to cut marked prices on the bushels of live blue crabs and ice-packed fish, oysters, shrimp, and other seagoing creatures provide great real-life theater. Hanging out at what locals referred to as "the fish wharf" can be a real education, too. How to choose fresh squid? How to fillet a flounder? Watch and learn.

Problem for Chappy was that, besides the intriguing sights and smells, the wharf is also busy and bustling—especially on weekends. He quickly suffered sensory overload. So be prepared to carry away a pound of smoked shrimp or some cooked crab cakes and find a bench in one of the little marina parks a few blocks downriver. The only noise you'll hear is the slap of water against the boats, the seagulls, and the clank of rigging. The Fish and Seafood Market Place is located at the northwest dead end of Water Street, near Memorial Bridge and across Maine Avenue from Benjamin Banneker Park. There is no telephone.

---

where the history is more interesting than the park, which is only a decent dash from Main Street and the waterfront fish markets should your pooch need breathing room or to do his duty. Located at the end of L'Enfant Plaza SW, along Maine Avenue and Ninth Street SW. 202/673-7660.

4 Gangplank Marina and Capital Yacht Club 🐾 🐾 🐾

While "waterfront" loosely describes the neighborhood bordering on this watery stretch of the District, the true city waterfront spans the length of Water Street and is home to dozens of yachts and sailboats and an array of restaurants—and little else. Any dog worth his salt will enjoy the breezy walk on either the upper or lower boardwalk between the marina and the riverside patios of the restaurants.

For Chappy, this was a welcome and sedate escape from the electrifying atmosphere at the seafood wharf nearby. The slapping of waves against the seawall, the clang of sailing rigs against the masts, and the cries of seagulls all make this a relaxed time-wasting stroll on the dock.

Three junctures that give access from the dock to Water Street connect the waterfront to small, municipal parks, such as the one at Ninth and Water Streets SW. They anchor the marina to the city with their bricked walkways, well-kept benches, and actual ship anchors that serve as centerpieces and lend visual relief to the waterfront. For dog lovers, these clean little parks are great waterside rest stops where you can enjoy carryout food from one of the nearby restaurants in the company of your seagoing pooch. The marina and mini-parks are located along the river between Sixth Street SW and the Fish and Seafood Market. The waterfront is open all hours. 202/488-8110.

Restaurants

Phillips Flagship: The wrought-iron tables and chairs on the patio out back overlooking the marina are mighty tempting to sit down with the dog and order a quick seafood salad. This is one of the last vestiges of past eating establishment in this area in transition; even its longtime competition, Hogate's, closed its doors. But this place is cavernous, seating 1,400 guests, many of whom arrive in tourist buses. But on a slow day, the kind folks here just might allow you and your pup to sit quietly at a deck table and gaze out on the calming river. Phillips isn't a risk-taking place, as its menu (including flounder stuffed with crab) attests. So ask politely first; a good server will steer you toward broiled instead of fried. And need I mention that Chappy recommends the crab cakes? You can always carry out the food to one of the nearby anchor parks that break up the stretch of commercial buildings along the waterfront. 900 Water Street SW; 202/488-8515.

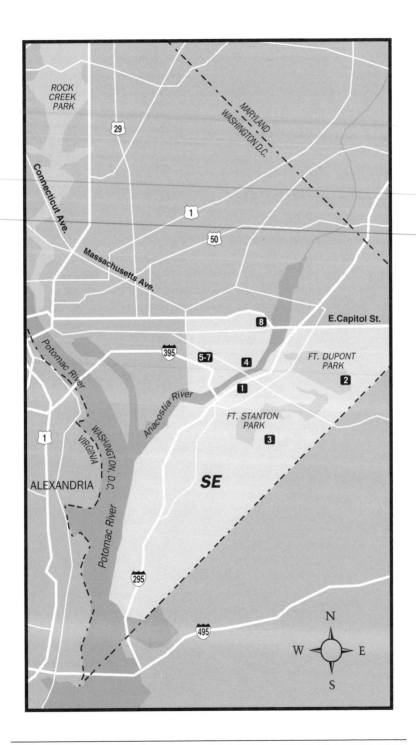

ROCK CREEK PARK

29

MARYLAND
WASHINGTON D.C.

Connecticut Ave.

1

50

Massachusetts Ave.

E.Capitol St.

8

395

5-7

4

1

FT. DUPONT PARK

2

Potomac River

Anacostia River

FT. STANTON PARK

3

WASHINGTON D.C.
VIRGINIA

1

SE

ALEXANDRIA

Potomac River

295

495

N
W ⊕ E
S

5 SOUTHEAST D.C.

Extending southeast from the United States Capitol, much of the large District quadrant lies beyond the natural boundary of the Anacostia River on the Maryland side. Many working-class residents are trying to reclaim their old neighborhoods from the scourge of poverty and violence. But many of these streets deserve the reputation as crime-ridden areas troubled by inner-city problems, including gang- and drug-related crimes and random shootings—which are also well documented in the local press and in courtrooms. Don't look for hotels here—it's not tourist turf. We recommend the same cautions that law-abiding residents practice to those who would venture with their dogs into any of the several beautiful, historic, and dog-friendly parks hereabouts.

ANACOSTIA

Economically distressed and struggling with the problems of violent crime, welfare, and unemployment that all inner cities face, this historic and once-proud neighborhood located south of the Anacostia River is troubled and overrun by run-down public housing, bail bond shops, and carryout joints.

Parks, Beaches, and Recreation Areas

1 Anacostia Park 🐾 🐾

The statuesque blue heron standing on its stilted legs in the shallows of the Anacostia River was unlike anything Chappy had ever seen. But the long-legged feathered friend wasn't unusual at this park that stretches along both banks for more than two miles. Big birds are regulars here and the boys were amazed by the ones we saw as Chappy gave us the "I gotta go bad" look.

Chap just wanted to race around on the empty soccer field where we pulled over to park amid these 1,200 acres of ball fields, picnicking spots, playgrounds, and wide-open spaces that are perfect for dog exercising—stretching all the way along the east bank to Kenilworth Park and Aquatic Gardens to the northeast.

Besides herons, you can come upon egrets, ducks, and geese because part of this park is a bird sanctuary. Occasionally a genuine U.S. Navy destroyer is in port across the river at the Navy Yard. That's appropriate since Captain John Smith of Jamestown fame four centuries ago sailed up the Potomac to a site on these grounds and introduced himself to the Nocotohtank tribe that lived here.

The Nocotohtanks are long gone. Too bad the litter isn't. You'd think this parkland would be better protected these days from thoughtless trash-tossing and garbage backwash that mars the river's edge and parts of the park. The trash and junk are good enough reason not to go closer to the water, which isn't all that clean and healthy anyway. Let's just say this isn't a good dog-dipping spot. Other than city league teams that compete on these sports fields, the park is largely used by its neighbors from the inner city and working-class communities it borders. And it's fair to say that everyone who comes here isn't taking a stroll in the park, so be cautious.

The park is open 7:30 A.M.–dark daily. The eastern bank of the park is located off Pennsylvania Avenue SE, across the John Philip Sousa Bridge from downtown and near the intersection of Minnesota Avenue SE and Nicholson Street SE. 202/426-6905.

2 Fort Dupont Park 🐾 🐾

Old Fort Dupont that was built on these hilly and forested 376 acres during the Civil War in preparation for bullets flying. Today, not much of that old fort stands, but bullets do fly here, according to crime reports. A different kind of conflict rages in the nearby inner-city neighborhoods now, where drug gangs and street crime hold many good citizens hostage in their own homes for fear of going outside their front doors. Brazen young men hang out on street corners and cruise in cars looking for trouble. Unfortunately, some of that trouble spills onto the grounds of this lovely oasis.

It's a shame, too, because this historic park is a sight to be seen. Trees believed to be more than 200 years old provide plenty of shade, and four slightly overgrown trails wind through the expanse of wooded land. One of the city's exemplary locations for seeing beautiful fall foliage, these rugged hillsides are fiery orange, yellow, and scarlet when the leaves change. You can even wander amid wild orchids growing on parts of its 340 acres. The path from the parking area at the activity center leads to what remains of the earthworks atop the ridge where Union troops once stood their ground to defend the United States Capitol across the Anacostia River.

The park is open dawn–dusk and is located at Randle Circle and Minnesota Avenue SE. From downtown Washington, take Pennsylvania Avenue across the John Philip Sousa Bridge, turn left on Minnesota Avenue SE, and go about 0.6 miles where you will see the park entrance sign to the right of the traffic circle. Another entrance is located farther south on Pennsylvania Avenue SE. 202/426-7723.

3 Fort Stanton Park 🐾

This large and woodsy park is distinct mostly because it hosts the Anacostia Museum, a Smithsonian exhibition and research center focusing on African-American heritage. The lake and playgrounds are a plus, and once there you can feel relatively secure. But with the nearby inner-city housing projects comes the crime that makes this a potentially inhospitable neighborhood. So unless you are familiar with the territory, think twice before exploring in this direction. And if it *is* familiar ground, take care anyway. The park is located north of Suitland Parkway at 1901 Fort Place SE; 202/426-7745.

CAPITOL HILL SE

The old townhouse residences and storefronts that fill in between federal buildings on this side of the Capitol and either side of Pennsylvania Avenue down toward the river make this great strolling space for dog lovers. Keep up your guard, however, and be smart. The problem hereabouts on these quaint sidewalks is that crimes such as armed robbery and muggings aren't uncommon. But the closer to the Capitol, the better the sidewalks and scenes.

Parks, Beaches, and Recreation Areas

🔟 Congressional Cemetery 🐾 ½

On a pretty rise above the north bank of the Anacostia River, this aged cemetery is a veritable "history park" that'll make you and your pooch think you've gone to dog heaven. Well, sort of. Established in 1807, it is America's first national cemetery and the final resting place of about 60,000 people. But for energetic pooches and socially inclined dog lovers, this is hardly a resting place.

"It is THE locale for dogs on Capitol Hill. It is a major dog venue," says *Washington Post* humor writer Gene Weingarten, who takes his yellow Lab "Harry S Truman" to the old graveyard usually twice a weekend to run off-leash around the grassy lawns and paved pathways among tombstones and statues. Typically, there are dozens of other dogs there, too, most of them off-leash.

But first a little history: Since the 1970s, this tombstone territory had been on death's doorstep, so to speak. The sacred grounds where the bones of some of America's most notable forefathers are buried—Apache Chief Taza, Civil War photographer Mathew B. Brady, composer John Philip Sousa, and FBI Director J. Edgar Hoover among them—was threatened by neglect, vandalism, and rampant looters.

Things started looking up in 1997 when the National Trust for Historic Preservation invigorated community and volunteer efforts to save Congressional Cemetery by adding it to its list of "America's Most Endangered Historic Places." Today, the privately owned 32-acre cemetery is a fenced, tranquil, and largely safe environment that's blessed with plenty of old trees, poop bags, trash cans, lighting, and parking—not to mention an abundance of fascinating history engraved in stone as you stroll casually about.

To plot your visits here, you must join Congressional Cemetery's Dog-Walkers group, a canine-centered organization whose members patrol the grounds daily, hold annual fundraising garage sales and spring clean-ups, among other activities. But, for the annual fee ($125 plus $25 per dog), mostly members just enjoy the cemetery, make long-lasting friends, and socialize as their pups roughhouse and run free.

Of course, there are some rules. Members are limited to two dogs per permit and the entire group is limited to 250 members so the cemetery doesn't get overrun on beautiful spring days. Dog must be self-managed; bad dogs and their humans are removed from the grounds and their membership revoked with no refund. Professional dog walkers aren't allowed in the group or the cemetery.

Open dawn to dusk, the cemetery is located at 1801 E Street SE. From the Capitol building, take Pennsylvania Avenue SE just over a mile to a left on G Street SE to the intersection of 18th Street SE. 202/543-0539.

DIVERSIONS

Market Day at Eastern Market: At this longtime Capitol Hill institution, it's fashionable to hobnob with prominent residents and not-so-prominent ones over crates of veggies, fruits, farm eggs, chickens, fish, homemade breads, and even some crafts and things. The historic **Eastern Market** is one of the last remaining vestiges of Washington's 19th- and early 20th-century public markets, and the only historic fresh food market still operating in the city. It holds court Tuesday–Saturday in the stunning red brick warehouse where you will find fresh everything, from fish to apples. Since 1963, the market has celebrated **Market Day** in mid-May with fabulous foods, crafts, games, and music.

Dogs are welcome around the outside where they can sniff the freshness and explore the meaning of marketability. Favorable space surrounds the market building itself, and there are plenty of goods there to satiate human and doggy curiosity. If your pooch needs to raise a leg or squat, go directly across Independence Avenue SE from the market to the triangle of greenery and park benches that are made to order. The market is located along Seventh Street SE one block below Pennsylvania Avenue. 202/534-7293.

After a morning at Eastern Market, your pooch just might need a snack or show of appreciation, so stop by **Doolittle's Pet Shop,** directly across Seventh Street, where accessories for the well-accessorized pup are sold with loving kindness and neighborly care. 224 Seventh Street SE; 202/544-8710.

5 Folger Park 🐾 ½

For a quick fix of green, green grass amid the miles of concrete and marble of the Capital City, this popular two-block haven is really more of a perk than a park. Location is everything, so should you be visiting the Library of Congress, this spot for Spot is only a couple of blocks south. Your dog will find it is a neighborhood favorite among dog lovers and their companions, who despite laws requiring leashes often let their pups run about off leash. The largest part of the park is all nice trees and benches with running space in the middle; the smaller section looks better suited for touch football.

Open dawn to dusk, and stick to daylight hours here. The park is located between Second and Third Streets SE, and D and E Streets SE. 202/690-5185.

6 Garfield Park 🐾

Twice the size of nearby Folger Park, this big chunk of near-the-freeway park has half the appeal and is little more than a fine how-do-you-do if your pup is sitting cross-legged in the front seat and needing immediate relief. Though only a few blocks away, the neighborhood isn't as inviting either. You'll see dogs running free, as we did, but the law in the District requires leashes in public places, and these dogs aren't all that sociable. The park is located along New Jersey and Virginia Avenues SE across from the Capitol Power Plant site. 202/690-5185.

7 Marion Park Playground 🐾

Renovated by the National Park Service and Capitol Hill neighborhood citizens, this is a clean and pleasant sitting park—a small space with wooden playground equipment and brick walkways surrounded by a wrought-iron fence in case His Honor the Pooch needs some lean green while walking 'round the Hill. Be sure to keep your dog on the leash. Daylight hours are recommended since it's a bit off the beaten track and a stone's throw from the Southeast Freeway where late-night venturing isn't good thinking.

Open all hours, the park is located at South Carolina Avenue and Fourth Street SE. 202/690-5185.

8 Robert Francis Kennedy (RFK) Stadium 🐾 ½

Once the legendary home of the Washington Senators before greedy ownership stole them away, and to the Washington Redskins before the heralded home team moved to new facilities in suburban Landover, Maryland, in 1997, this grand old stadium that was built for baseball. And it still may be used for baseball if Major League Baseball owners figure out these green fields are ripe for a team. It still hosts professional soccer games, concerts, and evangelist gatherings. But the sheen is gone. The DC Armory next door is the seasonal home to circuses, antique extravaganzas, and other shows.

But forget the indoors stuff: Outside sporty dogs will find a wide expanse of grass and the permanent scent of pigskin memories cherished by die-hard fans on the grand rectangular expanse of grass stretching from the stadium's front door all the way to 19th Street SE. Its grounds are open all hours (daylight recommended); the stadium is located at East Capitol and 22nd Streets SE. 202/547-9077.

Restaurants

Bread & Chocolate: Near the Eastern Market, this classy yet modestly priced sit-down or carryout eatery has won over many a regular with great sandwiches and even more complex dishes. Outdoor tables along Seventh Street can accommodate a low-key pup when it's not very crowded; otherwise, carry your order out to a nearby bench. Pennsylvania Avenue SE and Seventh Street SE; 202/547-2875.

Market Lunch: How many eateries serve two versions of crab cakes? Lump and spicy shredded. Chappy, an inveterate Eastern Shore pooch who knows a blue crab from the second-rate pretenders, thinks if you haven't carried out a plate here, you haven't lived the D.C. life. And he may be right.

EARMARK YOUR CALENDAR

Roses Are Red, Violets I Chew: So Chappy's attempts at verse aren't all that cultivated. All the more reason come April (National Poetry Month) to take the poetry-challenged pooch over to the steps of the Library of Congress, where dogma meets drama, and you and the pup can lunch from a bag and feel perfectly in context to read a good book of rhyme. The Library of Congress's Madison Building is located at 101 Independence Avenue SE; 202/707-5394.

Shake What? As Norman Mailer once wrote to us (for real!) about Washington: "So much power, so little poetry." Well, Norman, get thee to an outside roost near the front lawn of the Folger Shakespeare Library with your poocheo for a capital dose of dogged inspiration each April. There, you can bespeak some sonnets or even some doggerel as the annual **Shakespeare Festival** overflows from inside this library, where half the known copies of the Bard's First Folio are stored, to the outside grassy areas. Look for medievalist jugglers and other festive characters. As the Bard himself put it in *Hamlet*, act 5, line 305: "Let Hercules himself do what he may, the cat will mew and dog will have his day." Well said, William. The Folger Shakespeare Library is located at 201 East Capitol Street SE; 202/544-4600.

Feets Don't Fail Me: The Capitol Hill Classic started in 1979 and has grown into a festive annual occasion on the Hill in the first week of May, with some 2,000 runners competing in 10K and 3K foot races, plus a one-mile **Fun Run** for kids. All the races are routed through the historic neighborhoods on the Hill, from Stanton Park to Lincoln Park, along East Capitol Street to the Capitol, and back to Stanton Park. There are dogs aplenty watching from the sidewalks and front porches—but please keep your frisky critter off the actual course so he and runners don't get hurt. 202/398-5649.

The barbecue is North Carolina correct—heavy on the vinegar and smoke taste. The breakfast—scrambled eggs, pancakes, grits—can be walked over to a nearby bench to share with the flea-marketing mutt. If you wander down to the market, make sure to scribble this eccentric eatery into your schedule. 225 Seventh Street SE; 202/547-8444.

Prego Italian Gourmet Deli: Also at the Market Court across Seventh Street from Eastern Market, the tables out front make this sub and salad joint inviting for dog lovers. The swift and tasty lunches make it inviting for anyone. Chappy says give the cheese-and-coffee-bean soup a try. 210 Seventh Street SE; 202/547-8686.

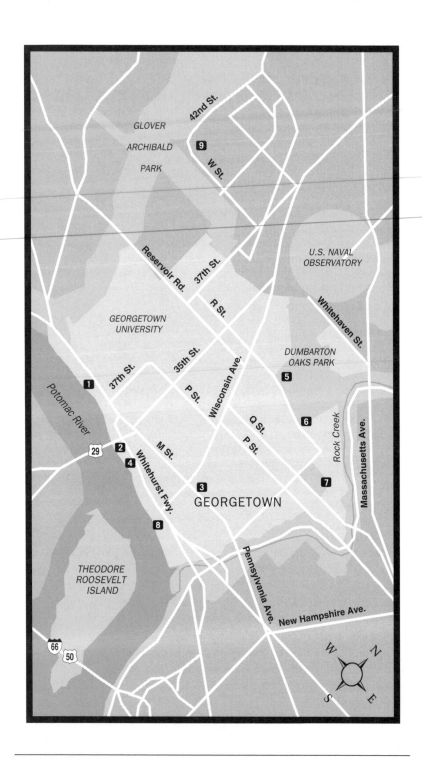

6 GEORGETOWN

Before the founding fathers carved the nation's capital from Maryland and Virginia along the Potomac, this colonial town was an Indian trading village in the 17th century and a bustling tobacco port after that. Historic Georgetown today remains a vibrant contrast to the federal city that grew up around it—and practically a separate entity in the minds of its residents.

Its dog-friendly cobblestone sidewalks are lined with federal period townhouses and some of the city's toniest addresses—some cramped but historic homes valued upwards of a million dollars, and homes where Abraham Lincoln's son, Robert Todd Lincoln, lived until his death in 1926, and where young Senator John F. Kennedy resided with his new bride, Jackie. This prestigious neighborhood's quaint shops, art galleries, boutiques, and fine restaurants concentrated along the corridor of Wisconsin Avenue and M Street attract tourists and locals alike year-round—and make these perfect strolling streets for dog lovers.

Some cautions are in order, however. Georgetown can get horribly congested, and parking is a challenge on Friday and Saturday evenings, when the nightlife kicks in full-tilt and nightlifers swarm the main sidewalks

---

leaving no safe space for pups on a leash. After dark and off the main drag, street crime has increased some in recent years—though it's hardly of the magnitude of some other District neighborhoods. Best times to walk the dog and appreciate this jewel in the belly of Washington are Sunday mornings and afternoons.

National Parks

1 Chesapeake & Ohio Canal National Historical Park
🐾 🐾 🐾 🐾 🐾

Below Georgetown proper is one of the nation's premier historic paths that's well known as one of the great dog walks of Washington—maybe in the nation. Follow in the footsteps of pioneers who 150 years ago towed canal boats and barges brimming with supplies and trade goods from the colonial port of Georgetown 184.5 miles to Cumberland, in western Maryland, then the edge of savage wilderness.

As it extends northwestward, the canal parallels the Potomac River along the back side of the Georgetown Reservoir, passing by Battery Kemble Park (in Foxhall) and through the Palisades neighborhood, up to Glen Echo, and into Maryland. The red clay path borders the canal, which can look as placid as a country stream with greenish-brown waters reflecting the trees that tower above it on both sides. For hiking with the pooch, the canal path provides a continuously level trail through the lush scenery of the Potomac River Valley. Old structures such as locks, lockhouses, and aqueducts, all remnants of the canal era, mark the canal. Some of them provided breather spots for Chappy as we hiked the edge of the canal, observing wildlife that ranges from birds to beaver.

The one downside we've found is that the towpath gets busy, with peak season May–October. Fast-traveling bicyclists love these paths and that's good reason to keep a good grip on the required leash. Most of the visitors stick to the first 14 miles of towpath from Georgetown to Great Falls. So if secluded strolling suits you and the pooch better, get started farther north at one of Maryland's canal lock sites, where you can park and walk.

You can camp along the Chesapeake & Ohio Canal Trail, although no camping sites are located within the District. You have to head into Maryland for that, too. Sites are available on a first-come, first-served basis, starting from Swain's Lock—16 miles northwest of Georgetown in the Maryland countryside. Any of the hiker-biker campgrounds found every five miles thereafter are public encampments. Each campground includes a chemical toilet, pump water (when it's not frozen), picnic tables, and a cooking grill. No reservations are necessary.

Entrance to the park in Georgetown is easiest from the Capitol Crescent Trail off the dead end of K Street NW and at Fletcher's Boat House, about two miles above Key Bridge on the towpath. A mile beyond that, you can park at a parking lot along Canal Road just beyond Chain Bridge and take the footbridge across the canal to access the towpath. Or, if you want to begin at the heart of Georgetown, start at the Chesapeake & Ohio Canal National Historical Park's Visitor Center, 1057 Thomas Jefferson Street NW. The park is open daylight hours. 202/653-5190.

2 Francis Scott Key Memorial Park 😺

This park is adjacent to Key's house where the patriot lived much of his life, including during the time he penned "The Star-Spangled Banner." Like the heroic composer, the house itself is long gone. In 1993, the lot was renovated into a memorial park featuring a limestone-columned plaza whose centerpiece is a bronze bust of Key. A 60-foot lighted flagpole bears the 15-star, 15-stripe American flag of yesteryear 24 hours a day as a modest reminder of the star-spangled mind that once resided there. The little park serves dog lovers as a contemplative waystation when walking across the Key Bridge to or from Rosslyn. The memorial park is located next to Key Bridge and M Street at 3414 Prospect Street NW. 202/653-5190.

3 Old Stone House 😺 😺

Just a lush little paradise of seasonal blooms and fragments of shade dancing on the lawn on sunny days from its pretty fruit trees, this dog-friendly hideaway is hidden behind what is thought to be the oldest pre-Revolutionary building in G-town, circa 1765. Dogs aren't allowed inside the house. But make sure to keep the pooch on the leash and scoop your dog's doodie because the small but beautiful wall-enclosed garden demands nothing less. Hideaway or not, there's no hiding here. The garden is open Wednesday–Sunday, noon–5 P.M.; it is closed holidays. It is located at 3051 M Street NW. 202/426-6851.

Parks, Beaches, and Recreation Areas

4 Capital Crescent Trail 😺 😺 😺 ½ 🐾

Missing some of the aesthetic qualities of the nearby Chesapeake & Ohio Canal towpath, this 11-mile stretch of paved biking and hiking trail (four miles of it in the District) follows what was once the railroad tracks from Georgetown to Silver Spring. It's prime dog hiking territory—so long as you stay out of the path of the speeding bicycles and sweaty joggers. That's easy to do since the trail inherited the wide space that old steam engines required, most of it more than 10 feet wide.

Hidden from view of oblivious passersby in Georgetown, the trail entrance is about a quarter of a mile past the classic white-and-green trimmed Washington Canoe Club boathouse just beyond the roughshod warehouse area beneath the Whitehurst Freeway. This is where the waterfront stretch of K Street ends under the massive stone structure of Key Bridge.

But the beauty of the tree-lined trail with glimpses now and then of the river to the west and the canal to the east surpasses its dingy beginnings. About a mile down the trail, where the fencing ends, you can climb the slight incline through the trees to the canal itself—probably the towpath's most accessible doorway in Georgetown proper. Dogs need to be on leashes here, and with cyclists racing by, it's for their own good. The trail is dedicated to the late Supreme Court Justice William O. Douglas, who used to walk these pounded dirt paths with his dog regularly and once even saved the canal from a congressional plan to fill it in and pave over it to create a "scenic road." The trail starts less than a mile beyond the end of K Street NW and is open all hours, though sticking to daylight is advisable. 202/234-4874.

5 Dumbarton Oaks Park 🐾 🐾 🐾

Behind the 19th-century Dumbarton Oaks mansion and the terraced gardens that surround it is this largely ignored 27-acre park with tranquil stretches of lawn, overgrown woods, meadows, and grottoes that back up to Rock Creek Park. Inaccessible except by foot down the carriage path to the east of the mansion, few people venture back here. Even fewer know what they're missing. Dog lovers who do often unleash their pups to let them get their yayas out—despite laws against going off leash.

"What's the harm?" said one Georgetown resident who loves to take her cavalier King Charles spaniels to the park. "Nobody's ever there." Local citizens have long intended to spruce up this best unknown park in Georgetown, but because it's far enough off the main drag and naturally unkempt, they haven't undertaken the task. This remains a hideaway worth visiting with the pup.

The park entrance is at the end of so-called Lover's Lane off R Street between 31st Street and Avon Place NW on the east side of Dumbarton Oaks. Look for a chain blocking automobile access, then go to where the path becomes soil and walk along the curving stone wall and brook, crossing a small bridge into the hidden parkland. It's open daily, 8 A.M.–dusk. 202/282-1063.

6 Montrose Park 🐾 🐾 🐾

Once the colonial site of the Richard Parrott Ropewalk, where rope rigging was made for the sailing vessels that ventured into Georgetown's harbor, this tastefully landscaped territory sandwiched between the Dumbarton Oaks proper and Oak Hill Cemetery is now one of the more fashionable doggy parks in the city.

Indeed, it is a pooch-pioneering parkland. You'll know that when you first set paw into its entrance and notice the clean-it-up container bearing glad tidings and a variety of recycled plastic baggies. A welcome sight for those conscientious among us who forgot their own scoopers, these are supplied by the good neighbors who reclaimed this land from overgrowth and neglect a few years ago.

Gardens and fountains are well kept and partitioned off by boxwoods, low brick walls, and many old trees. One weekday midafternoon when Chappy explored the grounds, three other dogs strolled near the tennis courts on the Dumbarton side of the park leash-free—despite city laws requiring dogs to be on leashes. No problem though: Residents nearby who bring their pups here have a good sense of what's tolerated and what's appropriate, and authorities don't often bother these unleashed Goergetowner pooches whose human companions bend leash laws.

Once, when a visitor was walking his Great Pyrenees puppy here off leash, it suddenly disappeared from his side. Other fellow dog-walkers immediately steered their strolls toward finding the dog—which, it turned out, had cut through the park into adjacent Rock Creek Park. Another time, a local yellow Lab went bounding toward a small contingent of serious-looking joggers. Its owner recognized the leader of the pack as then Secretary of State Warren Christopher, who maintained kind-to-animals protocol despite a grown pooch trying to plant a sloppy kiss on him.

Bring a picnic lunch to take advantage of the benches and picnic tables that are positioned in delightful gardens. Farther along the path are attractive playgrounds and a gazebo where you can relax with the dog on hot summer days. At the very back of popular and often busy Montrose Park is a small trail leading into the peaceful and hardly used Dumbarton Oaks Park (see listing above).

The park entrance is located at R Street and Avon Place NW; it's open daily dawn–dusk. 202/282-1063.

7 Rose Park 🐾 ½

The right dimensions for an inside-Georgetown neighborhood park, this little plot of grass and trees stretches down 26th Street and the corner of O Street. Early weekend mornings are busy with dogs and dog lovers sharing quality time; some pooches romp about freely despite the standard keep-'em-on-the-leash restrictions while their human counterparts read the newspaper in the sunshine. Chappy was awestruck as we threw a boomerang here and discovered the park isn't quite Aussie-appropriate in size, but the man it barely missed on its return flight never knew the difference.

The park is located at the corner of 26th and P Streets NW, just on the Georgetown-proper side of the P Street Bridge that spans Rock Creek Park. The park is open round the clock, though the wee hours aren't the most inviting—even on this edge of Georgetown where the lights are bright. 202/673-7660.

8 Washington Harbour Park 🐾 🐾 ◀●

Chappy wasn't overly impressed with this small patch-of-green park with pea gravel paths and benches. What he *adored* was that it extends along

DIVERSIONS

A Good Paddling: Dog-loving insiders in Washington know that the Runyonesque boathouse that Jack Baxter built more than 50 years ago is where you can take your pooch out for a splendid adventure. The old man's gone now and so are the days when his dog, Shadow, still slips into the river for a quick dip off the floating dock. But your water-loving pup can still do the dog-paddle here. The boating season is March–September. **Jack's Boathouse** is located at 3500 K Street NW, alongside the Potomac River, a couple of blocks below M Street. 202/337-9642.

Bow-Wow Boating Party: Take your pooch on the **Chesapeake & Ohio Canal boat rides** if he can handle 90 minutes on the water. From April to Halloween, head down to the canal at Lock 3 to ride the large mule-drawn canal boat on a trip down history lane. The park rangers wear period outfits and accommodate leashed doggy passengers whenever they can—"as long as they don't urinate on the boat or bother anyone who might be allergic to them." It's $8 for adults, $6 for seniors, $5 for kids, and dogs ride free. The launch takes place at 30th and Thomas Jefferson Streets NW, just a block below M Street. 202/653-5190.

Pharm Dogs: If you're out and about in the tree-lined walking turf along P Street east of Wisconsin Avenue and a couple of long blocks south of Montrose Park, stop in at **Morgan's Pharmacy,** a dog-friendly drugstore that's been on this corner forever. The nice folks who run it will welcome you and the leashed pooch. 3001 P Street NW; 202/337-4100.

No Fleas Please: For more than 12 years, the **Georgetown Flea Market** has peddled its collectibles every Sunday at the parking lot located at Wisconsin Avenue, 35th Street, and Whitehaven Parkway. Some 80 dealers show up regularly and a lot more browsers—many in search of nothing more than a good time. Chappy likes the various smells of old things, and we have occasionally found some finds. Open Sunday, 9 A.M.–5 P.M., the flea market is located two miles up Wisconsin Avenue from M Street between S and T Streets, near the International Safeway. 202/223-0289.

Georgetown's waterfront and provides a spectacular view of the river and Rosslyn's high-rises on the other side.

But this otherwise quiet park itself seems to take a beating—as much from the weather as from raucous college students who after a night of hard partying sometimes blow off steam with acts of random obnoxiousness. Unfortunately, the rear view of quaint-bricked Georgetown is also marred by the ugly underbelly of the Whitehurst Freeway directly over K Street.

Next door to the park is Washington Harbour proper, a contemporary and tastefully designed high-rise office and retail park set back from the river to allow plenty of mindless walking room. The boardwalk in front borders directly on the river and around the piazza where an extravagant pool and fountains are highlighted with tall columns and wild grasses. Again, the view is all and everything here: Directly south on the Potomac is the stacked pie-pan design of the Watergate Hotel, and just beyond it the majesty of the Kennedy Center.

The harbor and park are located along K Street NW between Thomas Jefferson Drive and 33rd Street NW below Georgetown. Parking can be difficult here; the best bet to find a metered space along K Street beyond 31st Street and up 31st Street. 202/944-4140.

9 Whitehaven Park 🐾 🐾 🐾

A dogleg extension of Glover-Archbold Park (see the Glover Park section of the Northwest DC chapter), this neighborhood treasure is a steep ravine into natural splendor. We parked on its upper ridge along W Street NW at 40th Place NW, where the two-hour parking is free, and slipped our way carefully down the long slope into the undeveloped woods where the few paths that exist are footworn rather than planned. It's not nearly as gigantic as Glover-Archbold Park but is no less a pretty piece of the ecosystem for an energetic exploration with the nature-loving pup.

The park is located along W Street between 37th and 42nd Streets NW. It's open 24 hours a day, though dense darkness makes it inhospitable at night. 202/282-1063

Restaurants

Aditi: Curry out? We love this venerable Indian hotspot in Georgetown, and it will prepare carryout orders for lunch and dinner on days when you've brought along the dog. The complex hot and saucy lamb or shrimp masala is ridiculously scrumptious, as are the smoky delights that come from the clay tandoori oven. For those dog days of summer when brows are glistening and appetites on the wane, pick up a selection of the delectable Indian breads—the puffy puri or stuffed *kulcha*—and maybe an order of raita, the yogurty cucumber dish that cools the palate, all to go so you and the pups can enjoy an Indian feast together. 3299 M Street NW; 202/625-6825.

Au Pied de Cochon: Out real late with the pooch and other restaurants are shuttered? Still got an appetite working, huh? This very casual, nearly degenerate, but fun institution has served late-night dinners for ages and prepares simple French food, a good cheeseburger, or an omelet with hash browns to go, so you and the pup don't go to bed hungry. Chappy still likes *au pied* because he knows it was the late-night joint where we spent our first date. 1335 Wisconsin Avenue NW; 202/333-5440.

Bistro Français: Call in a carryout order for French onion soup and ask about the specials of the day, then pick it up at the bar inside this delightful and very Parisian bistro that has long been a mainstay in Georgetown. If you're off the red meat, go with the traditional coq au vin or the rotisserie chicken with tarragon jus. If you're taking it all to a park to sit under a tree with your *petit chien,* make sure they wrap up some of their wonderful French bread. Your own bottle of bordeaux depends on what park you're going to; some ban alcoholic beverages, and we wouldn't want to break the law. 3128 M Street NW; 202/338-3830.

Booeymonger: Our favorite time to visit this longtime Georgetown eatery is on a Sunday morning. We leave with the Sunday newspaper under one arm and a take-out order of a three-egg omelet with toast and jelly and bagels under the other and walk off with the pooch to a people-watching bench nearby. Otherwise, stop by for hefty sandwiches. 3265 Prospect Street; 202/333-4810.

Champions: Is your pooch hankering for an all-American beef burger and a side of nachos with cheese? Saunter up to the bar and pick up great bar fare while your four-legged sportster hangs out front—and check out the sports memorabilia while you wait. 1206 Wisconsin Avenue; 202/965-4005.

Clyde's of Georgetown: One of Georgetown's great old saloons, it happens to serve some excellent food as well. No dogs allowed, but its top-notch burgers taste just as good under a tree as they do inside its dark clubby dining room—and they'll wrap 'em to go. Or if you're off red meat, the crab cakes are worthy. 3236 M Street NW; 202/333-9180.

Dean & DeLuca Cafe: Perfect for gourmet sandwiches and upscale salads for on-the-go canine companions who can wait outside this self-service café à la New York while you pick up lunch. There are lots of tables outside where dogs of good taste are regulars. Baguettes, cheese, and plenty of ingredients for picnicking are standard fare. 3276 M Street NW; 202/342-2500.

Enriqueta's: For genuine Mexican food, this is the place, and you and the pooch can carry it out to your own hacienda. You can get tacos anywhere so don't get them here. Rather, try something with the dark and rich mole sauce on it. 2811 M Street NW; 202/338-7772.

Filomena Ristorante: Fresh pasta made on the premises sets this longtime Georgetown pasta house apart from the other Italians. And you can carry it out just two blocks to the Washington Harbour Park and watch the Potomac flow. 1063 Wisconsin Avenue NW; 202/338-8800.

La Chaumière: Cassoulet? Escargot? Rabbit stew? You get old-fashioned country French fare at this old-fashioned country French bistro, complete with hearth and wooden walls. Too bad the dog can't sit beside you inside as they do in France, but this fine and longtime restaurant of Georgetown will package up its tempting fare and send you and your canine culinary culprit off with the goods. 2813 M Street NW; 202/338-1784.

Marvellous Market & Espresso Bar: A recent addition to G'Town's charm, this bakery will lure you by the scent of its gourmet breads and deep rich coffees. Not only is it strategically located for dog walking at the corner of Wisconsin Avenue and P Street NW, but there are six outdoor tables where a well-behaved pooch can relax while you scan the newspaper and refuel on caffeine. 202/333-2591.

Miss Saigon: We like the fisherman's soup in a hot pot at what some consider to be one of the metro area's best Vietnamese restaurants. Chappy isn't into that tangy off-sour fish flavor, but he's one wild and crazy dog for the grilled marinated meats this relaxed Vietnamese restaurant will gladly serve carryout for you and your dog. 3057 M Street NW; 202/333-5545.

Old Glory All-American Barbecue: Abundant here are red, white, and blue, and barbecue, though not necessarily in that order. Even though the setting is saloon-style, dogs not are allowed inside. But you can order at the bar and soon carry out a variety of barbecued dishes, from the tender pulled-pork sandwiches to the smoky barbecued chicken. Just don't forget to choose your style of barbecue sauce, representing several regional recipes—from the thick and tomatoey to the vinegary. 3139 M Street NW; 202/337-3406.

Riverside Grill: Probably the best choice if you're walking the pup along Washington Harbour's nice boardwalk and want to sit down for a bite, this friendly restaurant right by the water allows you to sit at one of its many outdoor tables so long as your dog sits on the opposite side of the ropes—to meet health codes. "We've got people with their dogs eating out there all the time," one waiter told us. The cuisine is continental American, steak, seafood, pasta, but that doesn't mean there's nothing fancy: Chappy recommends the chicken piccata with artichoke hearts and canapés. 3050 K Street NW; 202/342-3535.

Sushi Ko: Consider it a great privilege that an honorable restaurant such as this pioneer of sushi culinary arts in the nation's capitol will package its plump and carefully created cuts of fresh sushi and sashimi for take-out orders. The yellowfin tuna and freshwater eel are so good that it's one of only a few places to take initiates for their first stabs at sushi dining. And for the uninitiated, tempura and other Japanese dishes are available. 2309 Wisconsin Avenue NW; 202/333-4187.

Tony and Joe's: If you and the pooch are moseying around Washington Harbour, step in this seafood mecca and order some crabs to go. Then go over to the edge of the Potomac on the boardwalk and eat 'em. 3000 K Street NW; 202/944-4545.

Zed's Ethiopian: Nothing much to look at from the outside, but inside finger-snapping, lip-smacking Ethiopian food is made, and you and the pup can carry it away to sit among the columns at the Francis Scott Key Memorial just down the street. 3318 M Street NW; 202/333-4710.

EARMARK YOUR CALENDAR

Terra Firma Footing: Want to show your appreciation for all those beautiful parks you and the pup visit throughout the year? Since 1990, every year around mid-April through early May, usually during Earth Day Week, dog lovers and park lovers have converged on designated parklands in the nationwide

March for Parks. The nation's largest walking event for parks and open spaces, the march varies from one park to another, depending largely on need. Besides marching, participants repair historic buildings, plant trees, build new trails, and repair old ones—even raise funds for buying land for new community parks. About a half dozen parks each year have participated in the Maryland, D.C., and Virginia area—including Rock Creek Park, the Chesapeake and Ohio Canal National Historic Park and Sully Park. As long as the park where you choose to participate allows dogs, you can bring yours along. Call the kind National Park Service folks to find out which parks are hosting events and how to volunteer. 202/619-7222 or automated Dial-a-Park at 202/619-7275.

Perk Up the Ears: Summertime Concerts on the Canal are not only free, they're outside—so you can bring along the tone-perfect pup and hear mostly local musicians, such as the Air Force's Airmen of Note. But try to keep the pooch from howlin——unless, of course, it's a free-form jazz night when that would be quite appropriate. The shows usually take place every other Sunday at 4 P.M. at the Foundry Mall along the Chesapeake & Ohio Canal, south of M Street between 30th and Thomas Jefferson Streets NW. Schedules vary, so call first. 202/653-5190.

Places to Stay

Chesapeake & Ohio Canal National Historical Park: See the listing above for camping information in the park outside the Georgetown area.

Four Seasons Hotel: For years, this classy and posh establishment has been the lap of luxury for lap dogs and four-legged travelers of every stripe and type. And in its incomparable style, it continues to cater to canines (and their human sidekicks don't do badly here either). "We want to accommodate travels and we know pets are a big part of people's lives," said the hotel's dog-friendly publicity director Tricia Messerschmitt.

Reflecting a shortening of the leash on pet policies in the hotel industry in general, the Four Seasons has added some restrictions, however. Only dogs 15 pounds or less are now allowed and owners are asked to "be responsible" for their pets.

Still, this hotel pampers pooches with perks like no other. When you check in, the hotel provides your dog with bottled water and special doggy bowls, plus a gourmet doggy treat, such as a dog bone or chew toy. In the room, pups can relax on their own fluffy lambskin-lined doggy bed. And the staff is ready to assist you with your dog. Should you want to hit the highlights of old Georgetown for some jazz at Blues Alley or fine dining at the nearby restaurants, the hotel will find a dog sitter. "If you need a sitter, someone to walk them, a vet," said Messerschmitt, "we can arrange that for you."

Just hearing about actor Jack Lemmon bringing his standard poodle here and the circus animal trainers Siegfried and Roy checking in their two white Bengal tigers made Chappy swoon with anticipation. The hotel, said Messerschmitt, has welcomed animal guests ranging from huge boa constrictors and monkeys to jaguars. Standard rates vary but range from $335 upward. 2800 Pennsylvania Avenue NW, Washington, DC 20007; 202/342-0444.

VIRGINIA

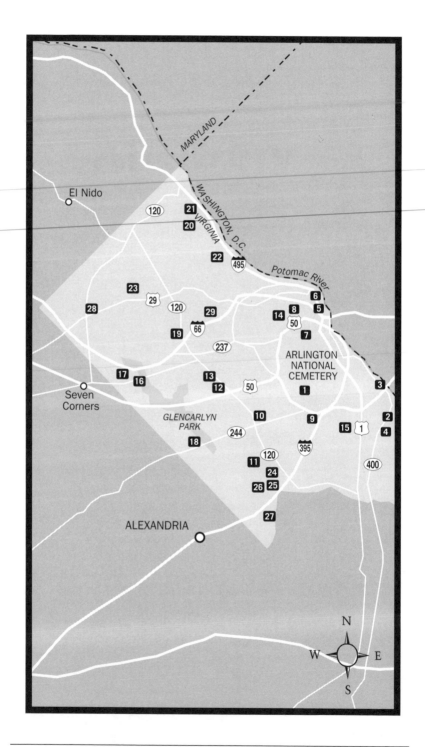

7 ARLINGTON COUNTY

Arlington may be the smallest county in the United States at 25.7 square miles, but it's got a big range of suburban parks and untamed woodlands that are perfect for romping with your dog on weekends or on sunny days when the federal government decides to shut down.

This little county was part of the territory originally claimed for the capital city of Washington back in 1791. That lasted until 1847, when Virginians caused enough ruckus that Congress voted to return what is now Arlington County (the name later derived from the home of Civil War General Robert E. Lee) and what is now the City of Alexandria back to Virginia.

Tucked almost surgically into the side of the its larger neighbor, Fairfax County, and across the Potomac River from Washington, this intimate bedroom suburb is home to pricey neighborhoods of power brokers and professionals as well as modest ethnic neighborhoods—with an abundance of nature centers and parks with wooded pathways and streams in between. It is one of Chappy's favorite destinations because it's dog friendlier than most. Plus—we have to be honest—it's close to home.

With 1,145 acres of parks and open space, Arlington is one of the most dog-friendly of the metropolitan jurisdictions, with seven (at last count) dog exercise areas, or as we've been told they are now called, Canine Community Areas, where our best friends can legally run leash free on public greenery. Spare the leash or soil the soil (poop-scooping is expected) at any of Arlington's beautiful parks—whether national, state, regional, or local—and you risk getting fined. And its state parks specify six-foot leashes.

By the way, while Arlington may be pooch sensitive, it's not always laid out to accommodate human navigational skills. By a law dating back to its split from the District of Columbia, the county cannot be divided into towns or jurisdictions, per se. Most people divide the territory into North Arlington and South Arlington. We've opted for dividing its doggy pleasures by its neighborhoods.

National Parks

❶ Arlington National Cemetery 🐾 🐾 🐾 ◄🖐

Although the grounds are kept as pristine as the spit shine on a soldier's boots, and rules like "No Jogging" exist out of respect for the many military dead buried here, you can visit the nation's most famous cemetery with your dog—if she's on a leash. Now that may not sound inviting if you're unfamiliar with its stately beauty and rolling green hills. Yes, you can pay respects here at the eternal flame marking the graves of John F. Kennedy, Jacqueline Kennedy Onassis, two of their children, and Robert F. Kennedy. Astronauts, sports figures, even actor Lee Marvin, are also buried alongside Supreme Court justices, other dignitaries, and row after row of men and women who served and defended our country. The ceremonial and somber Changing of the Guards, who stand watch 24 hours a day over the Tomb of the Unknowns, is something to see even with the well-behaved pup silent by your side—and it occurs like clockwork, every hour on the hour. But the doggish joy of this sentimental landscape isn't the memorials or the old epitaphs on simple whitewashed tombstones that date back to the country's beginnings. It's the tree-lined walks and silent dignity that you'll appreciate most with your patriotic pooch.

The cemetery is open 8 A.M.–5 P.M., October 1–April 1. In the warmer months, it stays open until 7 P.M. There's no admission fee; but the parking lot charges $1.25 for the first three hours—which is money well spent ($2 per hour thereafter). Arlington Memorial Bridge leads directly into the park from the District; from the George Washington Memorial Parkway, watch for the well-marked exits to the cemetery's entrance. 703/607-8052.

❷ Gravelly Point at National Airport 🐾 🐾 ◄🖐

Just north of the airport is a dinky parking lot wedged between the Potomac River and the north rim of the runways opposite the disgusting-sounding though quite appropriate Roaches Run. This little point sees a lot of action—including some of the canine kind. There's a ramp for launching boats so anglers and water-skiers are always coming and going. The adjacent soccer fields pack in a multicultural crowd on Sunday afternoons. And young couples after dark sometimes come here to smooch under the stars.

But the biggest attraction is the overhead view. Watching giant jet airliners come in for landing is inexplicably fascinating. One big drawback is noise (naturally). Jets are loud when you're outside of them instead of lounging in an aisle seat reading an airliner magazine. Besides the roar of jet engines, there's a bizarre post-industrial audio factor as well: Small cannons located along the air strips regularly blast blanks to flush birds from the runways between airline landings and takeoffs.

Because of the stirring view of the Potomac River (or of young couples smooching), many a picnic happens here at all times of day and night. But you had best keep your own picnic and dog away from the disturbing Roaches Run riverbank nearby, which at low tide just might expose its river rat population. For that and a lot of other reasons, including the law, keep your dog on a leash.

The park is open all hours, with after-dark jet landings (until 10 P.M.) a dramatic sight on a warm summer night. It's located next to the George Washington Memorial Parkway 0.25 miles north of National Airport. 703\ 228-4747.

3 Lady Bird and Lyndon Baines Johnson Memorial Grove
🐾 🐾 🐾 🐾

Technically within the borders of the District of Columbia (which few realize extend to the walls of the Pentagon), this 121-acre man-made island is accessible only from Virginia and was originally dedicated to the first lady whose beautification program attempted a makeover on the face of the nation.

The grove of hundreds of waterside pines and other trees commemorating Lyndon Johnson makes it pleasant as a dog-strolling park—as you'll discover, especially when it blossoms annually with more than a million daffodils and hundreds of azaleas, rhododendrons, and dogwoods. Much tamer than Theodore Roosevelt Island a few miles north, this park gives you and the dog more open space—and from the grove's wooden bridge, that stunning sight of the Pentagon is literally a stone's throw away (though best not to try it). Despite its proximity to the Pentagon, this is a peaceful park. Chappy found that the population of wild ducks and other water life here blissfully ignores even the most pugnacious of pups. But don't ignore the rules on this federal property—leashes are the standing orders.

Entrance signs for the grove are just south of the Memorial Bridge on the George Washington Memorial Parkway. 703/228-4747.

4 Mount Vernon Trail 🐾 🐾 🐾 🐾 🐾

Chappy gets ga-ga over this 17-mile-long stretch of paved pathway that winds gently along the Potomac River with picture-postcard views of the capital city, its classic bridges and monuments, and the historic river itself. Called the Mount Vernon Trail, the path starts at George Washington's classy Mount Vernon estate to the south and follows the George Washington Memorial Parkway through Arlington County and north to Great Falls.

Traffic gets heavy on the trail. But it sees mostly congenial use almost year-round by dogs, walkers, in-line skaters, and bikers who find its landscaped oasis, native woodlands, and swampy marshes a dandy sensory expedition. One of the East Coast's premier urban naturalist hikes, the trail is populated by mountain laurels, wild azaleas, redbuds, dogwoods, and crab apples—plus millions of tulips and daffodils in the spring.

Traveling on the trail's Arlington stretch takes you and your dog by two of Washington's most architecturally awesome bridges: the beaux arts archways of the Memorial Bridge, which sends traffic around the circle at the Lincoln Memorial; and the rustic Francis Scott Key Bridge, which connects high-rise Rosslyn to old and quaint Georgetown. The walkways on both bridges offer canines and humankind a bird's-eye view of one of the nation's most comely rivers. But Chappy prefers to avoid the bridges during rush hours. Early morning on weekends is prime time, since few cars are dirtying the air, and you can occasionally spot an eagle or a flock of geese passing by.

At the southernmost end of the trail in Arlington, directly across the river from the Washington Monument and the Jefferson Memorial, is a tiny park at the river's edge, anchored by the remarkable Navy and Marine Memorial. Beside the larger-than-life art nouveau aluminum sculpture of seven seagulls hovering over a beautiful breaking wave is a perfect little rest stop or pit stop, depending on your needs (portable toilets onsite). And if you and your sidekick aren't up for hiking the entire trail but want to pay a visit, this is a tasty sample with an outstanding view.

To get to the trail from the District, take any of the bridges into Virginia and follow signs to the George Washington Memorial Parkway; parking is available at several locations along the parkway. 703/228-4747.

5 Potomac Heritage Trail 🐾 🐾 🐾 🐾

For the Rough Rider mutts among us, Theodore Roosevelt Island serves as an easy gateway to this unheralded and largely untrodden 10 miles of winding and challenging trail that even some longtime residents don't know exists. With the Potomac riverbank to one side and the steep palisades rising above to the other, it cuts a magnificent hiking path on national park turf northward all the way to the American Legion Bridge (where the Beltway crosses the river to the north).

Most of the trail is relatively flat and shaded by lowland poplars, oaks, and even some pretty beech trees, making it an easy trek for pups in search of an alternative to the usual neighborhood park. But it does get rocky in places—to where you're practically climbing short inclines and creeping down the other sides. Some of its small streams require some careful stone-stepping or wading to cross, which Chappy preferred anyway. Never mind trying this after downpours, however, since it becomes a muddy slick even water dogs won't appreciate. And when the Potomac is high, this is no place to wander.

The trail is accessible from several points along the George Washington Memorial Parkway besides Theodore Roosevelt Island. The trail connects at Chain Bridge (North Glebe Road), at Turkey Run Park a couple of miles farther up, and at its northernmost end at Live Oak Drive (take the Georgetown Pike, Route 193, south, left on Balls Hill Road, and left over the Beltway (I-495) on Live Oak Drive). It's open daily dawn–dusk. 703/228-4747.

⬛ Theodore Roosevelt Island 🐾 🐾 🐾 ◀🐾

Rough and ready like the president it's named after, you won't want to miss Theodore Roosevelt Island, only a half mile from Key Bridge. This 88-acre nature sanctuary sits about 50 yards offshore in the Potomac and is dedicated to a dog-loving president whose appreciation of things natural and support of conservation puts him near the top of the Canines' Favorite Presidents list, according to a recent unscientific Chappy poll. Two and a half miles of rough-and-tumble paths cut through the island's untamed woods and swamplands (home to red and gray foxes, owls, muskrat, and other critters) and make this perfect for idle exploration. It does sport fewer facilities than some of the landscaped parks nearby, but taking a discreet leak behind an old oak tree worked just fine for Chappy and our boys.

Amid this close-in respite from the big city is a respectable commemorative plaza where a statue of the fiery 26th president overlooks four large granite tablets engraved with selections of his writings. Most dogs go for the statue to inscribe it with their own version of "Kilroy was here." Keep in mind the island is a national park site, so buckle the leash as the law requires.

The park is accessible only from the northbound lanes of the George Washington Memorial Parkway, so from the District take the Memorial Bridge or the 14th Street Bridge, or, most appropriately, the Theodore Roosevelt Bridge and take the parkway heading north. Key Bridge coming from Georgetown will put you too far above the island entrance, and getting back to it challenges even longtime residents. If you're already in Rosslyn, you're better off walking. 703/285-2598.

⬛ United States Marine Corps War Memorial 🐾 🐾 🐾 ◀🐾

Tended perfectly by U.S. Marines, the gently hilly area surrounding the Iwo Jima Memorial strikes a proud chord for Americans and attracts many a fair-weather patriot with dogs on leashes—and some on rainy days, too. The famous statue of marines hoisting a giant American flag is all the more majestic because of its backdrop: Eastward across the Potomac, the U.S. Capitol, Washington Monument, and Lincoln Memorial are all in panoramic view.

The grass always seems greener here; there are water fountains, paths, and the nearby Netherlands Carillon rings sweetly throughout the day above beds of flowers kept manicured to military perfection. Take your puppy and his leash, though you'll see some dogs running sans leash despite the rules. He'll romp on the lawns with other new canine pals while you sit on a bench, and you'll both remember why it's great to be an American. About the only time each year this isn't a fine howl-do-you-do for dogging around is in October or early November when the Marine Corps Marathon fills its grassy hillsides with marathoners and spectators. So avoid it then, unless you and the at-ease pooch want to watch the runners struggle up that last killer hill of the 26 miles.

Open 24 hours a day, the park is located off Route 110 South (turn right on Marshall Drive from Rosslyn). 703/285-2598.

Restaurants

Columbia Island Marina Snack Bar: Sit back, kick off your shoes and give those hike-weary paws a rest at the picnic tables with a picture-perfect view of sailboats tacking by and the bigger-than-life Pentagon just across the water. The barbecue is decent, and Chappy devoured a hamburger, bun and all, without any complaints. Otherwise, you can buy beer by the pitcher and the usual marina fast fare that's sure to put wind into your sails. Dogs will appreciate the sunny lawn and plenty of freshwater. Adjacent to the Lady Bird and Lyndon Baines Johnson Memorial Grove, the marina and snack bar's address is George Washington Memorial Parkway South; 202/347-0173.

Potowmack Landing: To the south on the Mount Vernon Trail heading into Alexandria, Daingerfield Island and its scenic sailboat marina provide an inviting detour for food, refreshment, and, as Chappy discovered, high-style lollygagging. In season you will find plenty of activities to ponder in the sunshine: Sailboarding right off the marina's northern point is popular, and on any given weekend regattas dominate the distant view at the river's bend. On the back side of this classy restaurant with a view is prime bass-fishing water between the boat slips. But the main restaurant is all china and crystal (though modestly priced), which means it's out of bounds for dogs' palates. The café 'round the river side is all paper plates and Styrofoam—and a great hideaway for burgers and chili dogs and brews while watching the tide come in with your seafaring pup. Self-service from the short-order counter and outside tables make it easy eating—just tie the pooch's leash to the outdoor table you want and order at the inside counter. 1 Marina Drive, just off the George Washington Memorial Parkway; 703/548-0001.

Tivoli: The Mount Vernon Trail momentarily loses its way near the Key Bridge in Rosslyn, which is excuse enough to divert your path a few blocks off the beaten path to this gourmet deli hangout on the ground floor of the Metro Mall. Carry out its continental and nouveau Italian delights from the deli and share them with four-footed friends at any of the several nearby miniparks with shaded benches. A wide variety of wines and extravagant desserts make lip-smacking great snacking—but station your dog at the newspaper box or parking meter just outside the door, because mall management does not take kindly to nonhuman creatures inside. 1700 North Moore Street; 703/524-8900.

Places to Stay

Best Western–Key Bridge: You couldn't find a better location in which to stay if you're visiting Washington. You will be within walking distance of Theodore Roosevelt Island, an excellent spot for exploring. And you'll be able to easily walk across Key Bridge into DC. Even if you're not up for that much walking there is a bit of greenery here and there near the hotel. The hotel charges an additional $25 per day for your dog and you will be put in a smoking room. A double room will cost about $99. 1850 North Fort Myer Drive, Arlington, VA, 22209; 703/522-0400 or 800/465-4329.

Quality Inn Iwo Jima: This hotel is just a quick walk away from beautiful Iwo Jima war memorial, where you and your dog can soak up some history as well as having a beautiful grassy area in which to play—on a leash of course. The dog, not you! There is only a $10 per night fee for the pet. Rooms are between $79 and $120 a night. 1501 Arlington Boulevard, Arlington, VA 22209; 703/524-5000 or 800/424-1801.

EARMARK YOUR CALENDAR

Gambling Dogs: Know those kitschy paintings of dogs playing poker? Well, the Animal Welfare League of Arlington has instituted that spirit in its annual casino night and auction, where dog lovers can gamble play money at blackjack, roulette, and dollar-wheel tables, win prizes, and snack on fancy hors d'oeuvres. The fun helps a group that's one of your dog's best friends in the county. The League holds **Casino Night** in mid-October and charges about $40 per person. Don't gamble on bringing the pooch along—this fundraiser is for human dog lovers only.

This active group also sponsors an annual **holiday photo-op,** allowing you to pose your pooch with your family and Old Saint Nick, and by Christmas you can display the photo on the mantel.

But one of the best events is the spring **Walk-for-the-Animals** fundraiser, which started in 1997, with participants and their pups either walking three miles or strolling one mile to attract pledges of donations. Top earners win great prizes like weekend getaways.

Rain or shine, the event is always a blast as dogs and humans cavort through Bluemont Park along the Washington & Old Dominion Trail on a cool May weekend. A suddenly invigorated Chappy could've hiked the long route had he not been held back by—well—by us.

Look out for the bikers and in-line skaters. We've seen more than one nasty leash-versus-skater entanglement, and it's not pretty. But this is a fun walk nonetheless, and it supports a good cause. So take a hike! For all the fun events, or to volunteer, call the Animal Welfare League of Arlington at 703/931-9241.

ARLINGTON FOREST

Parks, Beaches, and Recreation Areas

8 Lubber Run Park and Recreational Center 🐾 🐾 🐾 🐾 👞

Stop and pick up a picnic before you head here because you'll want to spend hours. One woman with her toddler on the swings told us confidentially that this sunny, charming, clean playground and accompanying wooded parkland of trees and trails are "the best kept secret in Arlington" for dogs and kids. So much for secrets.

Swings and climbing areas for even the littlest toddlers—all placed on a safe wood-chip surface—are a playful starting place next to the large parking lot. The gazebo and open grassy areas are great for running around or pulling up a green piece of ground and sunning a bit like Chappy did.

But then go to the back of the lot and follow the steep path down to the stream. That's Lubber Run, where you and your dog will find a peaceful, tree-lined path that is also a bike trail and part of the 45-mile-long Washington & Old Dominion

EARMARK YOUR CALENNAR–JUNE

Season Tickets Available: Dogs on leashes can attend the many musical acts, dance troupes, and lively theater entertainment for families held every weekend night beginning in June at Lubber Run's amphitheater. It's first-come, first-seated, so call for curtain times. And get there early enough so you and the pup can scout out dog-appropriate seats near the back. But then, every seat is a good seat at this little stage in the woods. Lubber Run Park is located off South George Mason Drive on Vermont Road and Third Street. Park closer to the theater at the Second Street entrance into the park. 703/228-6960.

Arlington County Fair: Lots of fun and commotion in the dog days of August, this annual blowout features hundreds of exhibits, carnival rides, games, food, and vendors—all reflecting the international population of the county. Dogs must keep to the outside areas, but that's where most of the fair is anyway. But be forewarned: If your dog is skittish around crowds and loud noises, give this one a second thought. Thousands of people show up for this celebration; county leash laws are in effect and make a lot of sense.

If you go, be sure to stop by the ArlingtonDogs table. Judy Green, the founder and past president of ArlingtonDogs, was a great help to us in this update of the book and she points out that the group always has a table with neat stuff like dog-bite prevention coloring books, free pet food and doggy bandannas. In fact, if you're interested in Arlington and dogs, check out the website: www.arlingtondogs.org.

The fair is free. There's shuttle bus service from three nearby sites, but don't count on getting Fido on the bus. Thomas Jefferson Community Center, 3501 Second Street South. 703/228-6400.

Trail. The stream winds back and forth underneath the idyllic pathway that leads you and the nature-loving pooch over bridges and down almost into the stream in spots. Plenty of large smooth rocks in the broad stream will prove irresistible to youngsters and some dogs who want to "paws" to refresh. You can reserve a large picnic pavilion through the park offices for parties; smaller picnic coves are everywhere for spontaneous weekend barbecues. Keep walking the path toward its end at Route 50 and you'll come to a modern but spartan amphitheater, which stages music and plays during the warm-weather months.

Clean and heated bathrooms are next to the benches nearby. If your dog can talk like Chappy does, he'll look you in the eyes and say, "Ya know, it don't get any better than this." Take Route 50 west to the North Columbus Street exit. The park's entrance is on the right at Second Street North. 703/228-6525.

ARLINGTON HEIGHTS

Parks, Beaches, and Recreation Areas

9 Towers Park 😊 ½ 🐾

Chappy tried the no-leash freedom made possible by the county's kindness at this little park and recreation area but quickly ran out of things to do. Watching a couple on the tennis courts was good for a minute maybe, then over to the basketball court where nobody was playing. Sniffing out his predecessors was fun until someone showed up with a couple of spaniels that attracted Chappy's attention. Dogs can run free of the leash in the designated area so long as they behave themselves and you pick up after them. Located at 801 South Scott Street, just off Columbia Pike and about three blocks west of Fort Myer, the park is open daily dawn–1/2 hour past dusk. 703/228-6525.

BALLSTON

Restaurants

Gaffney's Oyster and Ale House: Outdoor tables are scattered around in front of this popular restaurant/bar. Find a lenient server and surely you'll be fine with your pooch by your side on the sidewalk. 4301 North Fairfax Drive; 703/465-8800.

Pic-a-Dilly: This casual gourmet eatery used to be next to Crisp and Juicy on Lee Highway, but now has taken over this spot, formerly the Uptown Bakery. It's a dog-friendly rest stop where folks can sit in inviting Adirondack chairs out front or at the tables to the side sipping coffee and reading the paper. 3471 North Washington Boulevard; 703/527-6262.

Rio Grande: Give us enchiladas, lots of enchiladas. Good Mexican food can be found here, where outside tables get rowdy with margarita drinkers. 4301 North Fairfax Drive; 703/528-3131.

BARCROFT

Parks, Beaches, and Recreation Areas

10 Alcova Park 😊 ½

Dogs and neighbors from the 'hood take to this park of tall trees and a rambling paved pathway especially during the summer months because its many tall trees create a densely shaded oasis from searing temperatures—which is just what the doctor (er, make that *vet*) ordered. A rippling creek called Doctors Branch, believe it or not, runs directly through its well-used grounds. Modest apartment housing nearby makes this a popular "front yard," and plenty of soccer enthusiasts take up its open areas. Picnic tables await anyone wishing to sit a spell. Open daily dawn–dusk, the park is located at South George Mason Drive and Eighth Street, a long block north of Columbia Pike. 703/228-4747.

11 Barcroft Park and Playfield 🐾 🐾 🐕

Funny thing is, few dogs show up at this sports complex, despite the peaceful and underused nature trails that weave back to little Allie Freed Park and beyond that the baseball-focused Jennie Dean Park.

No real explanation for Barcroft's dogless status other than there's such an overwhelming jock presence here that the competitive-at-heart appear to dominate these grassy grounds. And there's no shortage of that breed here, especially with two of the county's premier lighted baseball fields and boundless soccer fields, not to mention lighted tennis courts, outdoor handball courts, and a basketball pit where intense pickup games go on from dawn to dusk. Picnic tables and grills and clean restrooms are pluses for the dog lover who ventures this way; overcrowded parking is the biggest minus. No one cares if you bring your dog; most don't—but only because they have games to play.

Restaurants

Chicken and Seafood Basket: Just smelling this place drives Chappy, and us, crazy. The Peruvian charcoal rotisserie chicken is juicy and plump. Or try *marucha,* which is a slice of flank steak grilled with fresh garlic. Chappy slobbers just thinking about it. Don't forget to try some yuca (also known as cassava, a root vegetable served here like a big thick French fry) on the side. 4154-A South Four Mile Run Drive; 703/998-3077.

BON AIR

Parks, Beaches, and Recreation Areas

12 Bluemont Park 🐾 🐾 🐾 🐾 🦴

You know you're barking up the right tree here because there isn't a better all-around park and recreation area in the county. You also won't find more dog lovers talking breeds and training methods, their pride and joy running at their sides. Facilities abound at the recreation center next to the front parking lot—bathrooms, a water fountain, soft drink machine, pay telephone, and picnic tables. The 10 lighted tennis courts attract plenty of public and league matches. For dog lovers out to catch a few minutes of local racquetry, the center also provides adequate shelter from a storm and is a good watering stop, as Chappy discovered on a summer day when the temps hit the 90s.

Three baseball fields behind the tennis courts usually host kid-league games that are entertaining scenes. The wide-open lawns that surround the fields are perfect for plopping down with the pup and contemplating how a seven-year-old learns to hit a baseball. Crab apple and cherry trees fill in the better dog-walking space nearby beneath full-grown, old red and sugar maples and an occasional birch, alongside the creek where shade abounds on hot days. Except for dense undergrowth along the creek itself, the park is a landscaped marvel. A paved bike path that's also perfect for in-line skating stretches along the wide and rushing waters of Four Mile Run—a section of the 45-mile Washington & Old Dominion Trail that extends across northern Virginia.

Across the creek from the ball fields is the immaculate soccer field and more space to romp and play. Many local dog owners let their water-loving canines take a dip during off hours in Four Mile Run, which can be deep in spots and gushing. Note that this is against the law. Usually no one cares about a well-behaved dog bounding into the creek, but be careful—this isn't an official off-leash area, so you can be ticketed.

There is plentiful parking at the main entrance in the lot off Wilson Boulevard and along North Manchester Street in the brick-rambler residential area. Still, on warm-weather weekends at this very popular multiple-activity destination, parking gets jam-packed, leaving you to marvel at the modern-day dilemma of heated competition for a parking space just to get into the wide-open spaces for a couple of hours. Oh well, they take paradise and put up a parking lot! The park is open daily dawn–midnight; its main entrance is located at Wilson Boulevard and North Manchester Street, and the rear entrance is at Carlin Springs Road just north of Arlington Boulevard. 703/228-4747.

13 Bon Air Park 🐾 🐾 🐾 ½

Smaller and quieter than its bustling neighbor, Bluemont Park, this is a retreat defined by the 120 varieties of roses and 3,500 other plants that grow in its thoroughly planned and lovingly tended flower beds. You will see them from the road. The two tennis courts are the most visible sight, and they get most of the use. But once you and the pooch turn into its parking lot, you'll know that *vive la différence* more than makes up for this little locale's diminutive dimensions.

The unexpected beauty of the gardens during blooming season isn't the only attraction. Four Mile Run and the Washington & Old Dominion Trail's biking and jogging path cut a playful swath through this park's more limited lawns where children play at a playground with slides and climbing equipment. Relaxation is made in the shade while your leashed dog sniffs around in the natural woods of tall pin oaks and maples that stretch lazily along Arlington Mill Road to create the park's western boundary. And there are restrooms, too.

The park is located across Wilson Boulevard from Bluemont Park at Lexington Street. 703/228-4747.

CLARENDON

To some people, Clarendon is just a Metro stop in Arlington. But comfortable residential neighborhoods border on this strip of ethnic restaurants, high-rise office buildings, and churches along Wilson and Clarendon Boulevards. There's no room for gigantic parks hereabouts, but it is dog friendly otherwise and a real community as well.

Parks, Beaches, and Recreation Areas

14 No Name Park 🐾 🐾 ½

This park has no posted name on signs or maps. It hasn't officially been recognized as a Canine Community Area by the county—at least not as of press time, despite vigorous efforts of locals. But try telling the dogs that. It's a square half block or so of grassy, fenced-in flatland, and its only purpose is to be a runabout for frisky dogs. Every evening in good weather, and especially on Fridays, welcome to the pooch social hour. You'll find any number of dogs of various breeds—six or more, usually—racing around the park leashless and carefree. Their owners congregate to chat on the Herndon Street side of the greenery, where they occasionally launch tennis balls and Frisbees for their excited dogs to chase. All seems copacetic, though some dogs playfully wrestle for a ball and chase each other like crazy at times.

You need to scoop the poop here, however, or this confined territory would quickly become an impossibility—not to mention disgusting and stinky. Besides, the big draw is that your dog can run leashless in a friendly neighborhood setting and gain some canine social skills as well. You can't very well do that if you're stepping in it.

Despite no lights (or any other facilities), on warm summer nights the dogs and owners are still there in the dark. The park is open dawn–dusk and located between Hartford and Herndon Streets, with one entrance on Key Boulevard and the other on Hartford Street. 703/228-4747.

Restaurants

Aegean Taverna: Chappy insisted on the great Greek-style lamb chops from this traditional Mediterranean eatery, whose carryout entrees include all you'd hope for to satisfy that Grecian yearn—from moussaka to stuffed grape leaves to grilled fish. With the dog along, the tables and belly dancing inside are off-limits, so carry it out and let your own belly dance at the sight of great Greek cuisine at a nearby park bench. 2950 Clarendon Boulevard; 703/841-9494.

Brooklyn Bagel Deli: Get an "Everything" bagel with veggie cream cheese and sit out on the small metal tables in front where your dog will be begging for bites. 2055 Wilson Boulevard; 703/243-4442.

Havana Cafe: Forget the charming patio tables because owners Arnold and Gloria Rodriguez won't allow dogs to sit there—as much as they wish they could. But Chappy would just as soon sit on a bench in the cute little park directly across the street near the Metro station and sample the homemade-style Cuban dishes. "We asked our mothers, 'How did Grandma cook such and such?' and that's how we make it," said Arnold. "It's 99 percent Havana; the 1 percent is the ingredients we can't get from Cuba." Try the roast pork and shrimp—and (need we add?) the black beans and rice. 3100 Clarendon Boulevard; 703/524-3611.

Red, Hot and Blue: Just up Wilson Boulevard from Rosslyn, take out some tasty Memphis-inspired pit barbecue dishes from this shop that makes take-out meals an inspiration. Chappy's favorite is the pulled pig—easy on the sauce. 1600 Wilson Boulevard; 703/276-7427.

Places to Stay

Quality Suites Courthouse Plaza: This area of Arlington is a little bit of a concrete canyon here, but it's still dog-friendly and this hotel does welcome dogs. You just may have to walk a bit to find any patch of grass. There is a $35 fee for the first night, $10 each night after that. Call for rates. 1200 North Courthouse Road, Arlington, VA 22201. 703/524-4000 or 800/228-5151.

CRYSTAL CITY

With its cluster of hotels and restaurants close to National Airport, the main drag along Jefferson Davis Drive isn't especially inviting for man or beast, being all concrete high-rises, commuter traffic, and the Pentagon at its northernmost end. But the neighborhoods to the west side are of more human proportions.

Parks, Beaches, and Recreation Areas

15 Virginia Highlands Playground 🐾 🐾

Every inch of this immense playing area is in use on a sunny Sunday afternoon—with no shortage of dog lovers and their favorite companions taking in the sights and sounds of folks getting their yayas out outside. Soccer games make it impossible to park in the parking lot, where you compete for rare spaces with the large and mostly good-natured Hispanic contingency heading for the playing fields and the sidelines where spectators picnic and cheer on their teams. Street parking isn't impossible to find, so keep looking.

A paved bike path cuts through the middle of the area separating the main soccer fields from a playground for kids under six (a rare find), basketball courts, baseball fields, and another playground for older kids. On the far end of the bike path, near the two fenced and pristine baseball fields and the picnic and grill grounds, are several packed-dirt bocce courts reflecting the international appeal here. If you're looking for a social outing with your dog, you've found it. On the downside, there are no water or restroom facilities or

EARMARK YOUR CALENDAR–APRIL

Doggone MS: If you're looking for an organized group walk linked to a do-good purpose, you won't find much better than the annual MS Walk that starts off from the Pentagon and casually (at easy dog pace) hikes across the Potomac and north up the C & O Canal towpath to Glen Echo Park in Maryland. The four-plus-hour walkathon benefits research battling multiple sclerosis. Friendly leashed dogs are welcome to accompany their humans, though the National MS Society that sponsors the walk doesn't advertise it. The Saturday event happens in mid-April and usually attracts 3,500 walkers who sign up sponsors to raise funds. There is no registration fee. Dogs must be on leashes and behave appropriately. Make sure to consider your dog's endurance level before biting off more of a walk than he can chew. 202/296-5363.

concessions, although in an emergency the neighborhood fire department is next door to the Aurora Hills Recreation and Visitors Center at the 18th Street end. Located off the Jefferson Davis Highway (Route 1) in Alexandria at 18th and Hayes Streets, next to the Pentagon City Mall, the park is open daily dawn–dusk. 703/228-6525.

Restaurants

California Pizza Kitchen: No dogs are allowed inside this innovative gourmet pizza place from the other coast. But you can carry out some of the finest pizza around with your pizza-sniffing pooch and inhale it at one of the nearby outdoor benches. The roasted garlic chicken pizza, by the way, is nearly transcendental, though the way it affects Chappy is more intestinal. Hey, it was the dog! At Pentagon Center shopping mall, 1201 South Hayes Street; 703/412-4900.

The Fashion Centre at Pentagon City: This colossus of an indoor shopping mall with its own Metro station has a lower-level food court. Except for the seeing-eye kind, dogs aren't allowed, but most of the eateries are upscale fast-food and you can easily carry it out of the mall to a nearby bench. It's located at South Hayes Street and Army Navy Drive; 703/415-2400.

Starbucks: The outdoor tables right in front of this dog-friendly java house at Pentagon Center make coffee and canines go together easily—even though the last thing Chappy needs is a cup of caffeine. Still, it's often the first thing we need, and sitting in the sun with your favorite pooch, just watching the traffic pour into the mall isn't half bad. Or is it just half good? Pentagon Center, 1201 South Hayes Street; 703/413-0566.

DOMINION HILLS

Parks, Beaches, and Recreation Areas

16 Upton Hill Regional Park 🐾 🐾 ½

The first thing you see from the long entrance into this regional park is the miniature golf course straight ahead and the baseball batting cages to the left, both cheap thrills if your dog's a good sport and doesn't mind tagging along while you bogey par-3s and take your best cuts at the fast ball. Dogs can't go in the huge swimming pool or the concession/restroom area next to the mini-golf, but beyond all the fun and games is the often-overlooked series of nature trails twisting through tall oaks and overgrown woods. The main trail leads downhill about a quarter mile to a gazebo, horseshoe, and shuffleboard zone. The attractive artificial pond provides a centerpiece for grilling and picnicking, and is a tall drink for hot dogs suffering droopy tongues. The park entrance is located at Wilson Boulevard and Patrick Henry Drive, not far from the Bluemont and Bon Air Parks (see the Bon Air section in this chapter). It's open during the seasonal months (mid-April–mid-November) dawn–dusk. 703/534-3437.

Restaurants

Hunan BBQ Express: Less than a mile west of Upton Regional Park, on Wilson Boulevard at Livingston Road, is the Dominion Hills Shopping Center, where you can get a $10 haircut at Tom's Barber Shop while the pooch watches through the window. Afterwards, indulge the more intriguing traditional Chinese food you can carry back to the park. 6017 Wilson Boulevard; 703/532-8000.

Pizza Boli: If it's standard pizza you crave, carry it out from this pie shop in any of three sizes and crusts, also in the Dominion Hills Shopping Center. Just follow your nose to the place that smells great. 6033 Wilson Boulevard; 703/534-9880.

EAST FALLS CHURCH

Parks, Beaches, and Recreation Areas

17 Benjamin Banneker Park 🐾 🐾 🐕

You'll think you're in the backyards of the nearby homes in this small area separated by a wooden fence from the soccer field next door and the bike path that leads past the creek into the woods. But this little plot of land is one of the official off-leash turfs afforded your pup by the considerate county leaders. At its entrance is a sign reminding all users to scoop behind their dogs, and usually there are plastic bags in a receptacle for poop patrolling. Every dog wants his day to run free, and this is a pretty accommodating and contained area for it. For prime social times, so-called "canine conventions" occur like clockwork on weekdays, 5–7 P.M., and on weekends, 9–10 A.M. The park is located at 16th and Sycamore Streets, near the East Falls Church Metro, and is open dawn–dusk. The community canine area is open from dawn to a half hour past dusk. 703/228-6525.

GLENCARLYN

Parks, Beaches, and Recreation Areas

18 Glencarlyn Park 🐾 🐾 🐾 🐾 🐕

Dogs don't exactly blend into the woodwork among the salamanders, turtles, and snakes exhibited inside the nature center. But Chappy was allowed into the nature center to get a drink, and no one seemed to mind. Even though he sometimes slinks around, he would never be mistaken for a snake. We stayed only long enough to take care of business, use the clean restrooms, and briefly ogle the displays. This is not a big place, so even a few visitors at once crowd it.

Outside, down the hill from the nature center, the Washington & Old Dominion Trail passes through a forest of tall oaks and maples where birders have documented more than 150 species of feathered friends. The paved path makes for a pleasant walk, strolling with baby, skateboarding, or just about anything—but, as always, keep an eye out for two-wheelers speeding 'round the bends at this junction. The park's half-mile woodland trail that crisscrosses the bike path will keep man and dog out of harm's way. A stream moves serenely through it, and the woods are delightful for dog or man, woman or child.

Folks in the know will enter the park from Fourth and Harrison Streets, where a paved path allows for driving right down to a wonderful leash-free dog park. Chappy hoofed it because, well, we didn't know any better. There's a parking lot at the top and we thought the paved path was just for bikes, until we saw smarter hounds being chauffeured down the steep hill. No matter. It was a nice hike and reminded Chappy of his mountain roots in Tibet. No? Well, okay, at least it was good for the old Chap, who has put on a few pounds since the first edition of this book.

The payoff is an official off-leash dog exercise area right next to the stream. Cross the wooden footbridge and you'll see the signs, along with the trashcans and plastic trash bags. It's dog heaven. Pooches can play up on the hillside, through the trees, down into the stream, and everywhere in between. It truly is one of the best overall areas—offering shade, trees, terrain, and water—for dogs in the area.

The park is located near Route 50, off the South Carlin Springs Road exit. Finding the entrance to the nature center in sprawling Glencarlyn Park is the challenge: Several signs pointing to the park from Glencarlyn Road steer you through a maze of dead ends and right turns amid a pleasantly funky neighborhood of saltbox homes. We turned onto Fourth Street from Carlin Springs Road and followed it until it dead-ended at a gravel parking lot. Then we took the paved path down into the park. It's not clearly marked. You'll have to explore a bit. If you want to enter by the nature center, go in on Sixth Street between Vencor Hospital and the back side of the Glencarlyn Elementary School grounds. The nature center is right past the children's garden and the big blue dinosaur sculpture and is open Tuesday–Saturday, 10 A.M.–5 P.M., and Sunday, 1 P.M.–5 P.M. The park is open dawn–dusk daily. 703/228-6535.

LARCHMONT

Parks, Beaches, and Recreation Areas

19 Lacey Woods Park 🐾 🐾 ½

Rustic wooden fencing gives this homey little neighborhood hangout a warm and friendly look. So do the hoops courts that serve as a haven for aging round-ballers who keep pickup games intense till after sunset. Beyond the would-be dream teamers is a friendly retreat where dogs and people congregate mostly after work and on weekends, where nannies and moms with toddlers take a break during spare weekday times. Trimmed with large azaleas, holly, and dogwood trees, the open fields along Frederick Street are large enough for Frisbee play and four-footed races, and the densely wooded trails nearby are fit for quick expeditions. This is one of many small but lovely community parks you'll find throughout Arlington that is dog friendly and fun. Benches, bathrooms, and lots of children help ease you in. The park is located at the corner of Washington Boulevard and George Mason Drive and is open dawn–dusk daily. 703/228-6525.

Restaurants

The Lost Dog Cafe: If you have no better reason to take your dog to nearby Lacey Woods Park, this magnificent pizza palace and microbrew bar, less than a mile west on North Washington Boulevard, is the only reason you need.

It's raining cats and dogs? Skip the park and come here instead. Just thirsty? Good enough reason, too. In fact, you don't need a better reason than that you can bring the dog. Lost Dog regulars frequently park their well-behaved tail-waggers at their feet under the table, snatching scraps of some of the most creative and wonderful gourmet pizza concoctions made anywhere. "We love 'em as long as they don't doodie anywhere," as one employee put it sensitively.

Pam McAlwee and Russ Underwood, the laid-back owners of this excellent watering hole and eatery know their dog-loving clientele well. Gracing the walls throughout its several dining rooms are huge oil paintings of dog characters jazzier than the poker dog paintings of yore. There are dog mementos everywhere, even paw prints in the concrete threshold. Dog lovers will love the menu, too. They serve just about any microbrew bearing the word "dog" in its name: Besides their own Lost Dog ale, the menu includes Dog Honey Raspberry ale, Red Dog beer, Flying Dog from Aspen, and Sea Dog from Bangor. The pizzas come in three sizes with countless toppings and combinations for $6–18. Other foods are modestly priced though immodestly scrumptious: the sea dog salad piles backfin crab, scallops, and shrimp with cilantro mayo, lettuce, and tomato on a buttery croissant. You'll woof it down, believe us. 5876 North Washington Boulevard near the Swanson Middle School; 703/237-1552.

Thai Noy: Noodles and beef to go always sounds good to Chappy. So we pretend to pamper him even though our boys gobble this mildly seasoned Thai specialty, too. 5880 North Washington Boulevard; 703/534-7474.

LYON VILLAGE
Restaurants

The Italian Store: In search of a fresh, delicious sub? Chappy always is, and the assortment here is great. They also have a fairly large gourmet food area. Then sit outside at the tables, which are right next to the Starbucks tables. It's a casual scene, especially on a warm summer day. Look for the old Vespa parked out front. In the Lyon Village Shopping Center, at Lee Highway and Spout Run; 703/528-6266.

Starbucks: Rain or shine, winter or summer, there are always a couple of plastic tables out in front of this popular place, which is right in the middle of the Lyon Village Shopping Center. Likewise, there are always people hanging out drinking their venti mocha Frappuccinos and dunking their biscotti. Dogs are a part of the regular scene. The center is at the corner of Lee Highway and Spout Run Road; 703/527-6506.

NORTH ARLINGTON

Actually several neighborhoods in a classy section of the county, the area is characterized by the exclusive Washington Golf and Country Club and beautiful parkland bordering the Potomac River.

Parks, Beaches, and Recreation Areas
20 Fort Ethan Allen Park 🐾 🐾 ½ 🐕

Picture a sunny late October day. There are leaves on the ground. A breeze is blowing. Chappy couldn't believe he was all alone at this fairly good-size dog exercise area tucked back in a residential neighborhood, but very easy to find. It is fenced in, clearly marked, and a fine place to romp. There are a couple of picnic tables scattered around for watching the pooches at play. A row of nice big trees right in the middle of the grounds is an added attraction at this serene and peaceful community canine area. The center, located off Military Road near Chain Bridge at Stafford Street and Old Glebe Road, is open from dawn to a half hour past dusk daily. 703/228-4747.

21 Gulf Branch Park 🐾 🐾 🐾 ½

What separates this nature center from the others is that its 53 acres enclose a stream valley where in springtime dogs and humans alike can witness the thrill of herring and shad feverishly swimming over each other upstream from the Potomac's salt water to the freshwater streams in their annual spawning runs.

Once the campground of Native Americans, the park is a visual feast of wildflowers and other botanical niceties, where squirrels chatter and jays squawk to rattle the forest's stillness. Though everything seems comfortably small from the limited parking lot by the nature center, hiking dogs and humans will enjoy the 0.75-mile Stream Valley Trail. It leads along this picturesque gushing creek down to the river. Don't be tempted to let your dog run free when you see how few other folks with dogs are around; posted rules require that you keep the leash on and clean up after your pet.

All picnicking and other creature comforts (including clean bathrooms) are over in the Glebe Road Park section, off 37th Street, and at the nature center, where Native American artifacts and live reptiles are displayed. Chappy developed a love-hate relationship with the fascinating glass-encased honeybee hive that buzzes before your very eyes. And take a close look at the copperhead snake in its aquarium because this is the only poisonous species of snake native to the area that you and your trail-hiking partner might encounter.

The park is located near the George Washington Memorial Parkway. From the Spout Run exit north of the Key Bridge, veer right onto Lorcum Lane at the top of the hill, then right onto Military Road, and watch for the park entrance on the left at the bottom of the hill. The nature center is open Tuesday–Saturday, 10 A.M.–5 P.M., Sunday 1–5 P.M. The park, which is located at 3608 North Military Road, is open dawn–dusk daily. 703/228-3403.

22 Potomac Overlook Regional Park 🐾 🐾 🐾 🐾 🐾

For a panoramic river view amid an ancient forest that will wow you and the pup, this is the place. Its planners have overlooked nothing in shaping an outdoors experience that's footloose and fancy-free—and for that matter just plain free. You have to drive through a residential neighborhood to find these unlikely 100 acres of winding nature trails, because the park's hidden away at the end of what looks like any other street in suburbia. Blessed little parking exists between the actual Overlook Park and the smaller Marcey Road Park at its entrance, so the trails are never overpopulated. But you and your eager hiker hound just might be left out on any given visit if you don't grab the last piece of pavement.

If you do luck into a parking spot, check out the large trail map at the tiny information center nearby and pick one of the color-coded trails for your excursion. Then go get lost in the quiet woods for hours. You and your dog will love it.

Follow the main path straight ahead and you'll come to a small area that overlooks the George Washington Memorial Parkway. Suddenly you'll emerge into an opening and hear the sound of zooming traffic. Just beyond is the Potomac River, and across it the elegant spires of Georgetown University. To the right and five miles downstream is the Washington Monument—visible even in spring when the leaves are on the trees, even better in winter when there are no leaves to part for a better look.

Leaving no stone unturned, kids will like to roll over the branches and rocks to find worms and other crawly things, giving your dog plenty to sniff. Joggers and other explorers who tackle the hilly tangle of paths are infrequent enough here, though rules still call for leashes on dogs. A spring that was a water source for the Necostin Indians who once inhabited these exquisite slopes can still serve a good drink for the pooch.

The park is located near the Spout Run exit off the George Washington Memorial Parkway: Turn right on Lorcum Lane, right again on Nellie Custis (which becomes Military Road), and another right onto Marcey Road to the park entrance. It's open dawn–dusk daily. 703/528-5406.

Restaurants

Cafe Parisien Express: In the Lee Heights Shopping Center, a few doors down from Crisp & Juicy, this tiny carryout with three outdoor tables in the front is perfect for dining with the dog if sit-down is your desire. Croissant sandwiches, omelets, and other quick dishes make for fast getaways, at cheap prices as well. 4520 Lee Highway; 703/525-3332.

Crisp & Juicy: Featuring succulent rotisserie chicken Argentinean-style with herbs and spices rubbed under the skin before slowly roasting on a spit over charcoal flames, this eatery does big business in both carryout and counter meals. Located at the corner of the small Lee Heights Shopping Center, it is worth finding even if you haven't worked up an appetite all afternoon at Potomac Overlook about a mile away. Whole chickens with a choice of three sauces (herb, spicy, and hot) run about $9 (they'll cut it up for you). For picnicking in the park, the generous and tasty sandwiches of chicken breast, or the Argentinean steak carnitas, or the Latin American chorizo with hot sauce, cooked onions, and green peppers are hard to beat. Fried yuca instead of French fries and a couple of orders of beans and rice will leave you and your dog ready to cozy up under a tree for a siesta. 4540 Lee Highway; 703/243-4222.

Thai-Thai Restaurant: These folks couldn't be kinder, and their Thai fare is wonderfully piquant and hot or not, as you like. Because it's crammed into a strip mall along a busy section of Lee Highway, there's no place to wine and dine your pooch. But they will package up a carryout order and even deliver it up to three miles. Chappy's partial to the chicken and beef satay on a bamboo skewer (with peanut sauce, of course) and so are our boys, because the

DIVERSIONS

Side by Side: Not only does Chappy appreciate the free treats usually available at **Dominion Pet & Supply Company,** but he is intrigued by the bunnies and the birds. This friendly pet shop supplies all the best dog food and supplies and even has a frequent-buyer plan for the big bags of quality kibble. 2501 North Harrison Street; 703/241-0100.

Just a couple of doors down from Dominion is a relatively new dog store called **Dogma.** The shop is filled with fun and irresistible dog goodies, but what really lures the dogs in are Mary Hogan's homemade treats. Garlicky bits or mailman-shaped biscuits, they're all so good that the boys have asked us if they can try them. Stationery, books, furniture, t-shirts, and things you didn't know you needed in dog shapes can be found here. Mary says business has been okay, and we hope it continues to increase.

Pay particular attention to the walls, where the beautiful black and white photographs by Matt Mendelsohn hang. He is an outstanding photographer who took a picture of us for our first dog book and was never given credit due to a publisher's oversight. He is excellent—his family and pet photos are a delight. If you're thinking of having a photo taken, Matt will capture you and/or your dog in a truly unique and loving way. He can be reached at 703/241-2020. The store is closed on Monday. Dogma is found at 2445 North Harrison Street. 703/237-5070.

---

spices are subtle enough for pup and child palates. Another benign dish that dogs can handle is the beef or pork *pad se-ew*. To fire up the old taste buds after dishing out some to the pup, add any of the three varieties (and temperatures) of hot spices packed with the entrees—but do so carefully. 5123 Lee Highway; 703/533-1919.

ROCK SPRING

Parks, Beaches, and Recreation Areas

23 Rock Spring Park 🐾 ½

A lovely little elongated park wedged between attractive properties in one of the last Arlington neighborhoods before crossing into Fairfax County and nearby McLean, this is a quiet, tree-shaded stop. For residents of this charming pocket of homes, its sweep of grassy knolls and benches that extends behind their backyards and across a bridged creek is their own secret garden. It's posted—dogs must be on leashes. And the dogs we encountered indeed were. The park, which is located near the intersection of North George Mason Drive off Williamsburg Boulevard and Little Falls Road, at 5800 Little Falls Road, is open from sunrise to a half hour after sunset. 703/228-6525.

SHIRLINGTON

A neighborhood that might seem like little more than an exit off the concrete ribbon of commuter-ridden I-395, this dog-friendly territory that's home to many a young professional is home to Shirlington Village—formerly a seedy warehouse area that has been renovated big time into several blocks of shops, restaurants, and movie theaters. The wide brick sidewalks and benches are inviting for the many dog lovers who find their way here, and there's lots of outdoor eating.

Parks, Beaches, and Recreation Areas

24 Fort Barnard Community Park 🐾 🐕

Brand new and proud of it, this fenced-in dog exercise area offers a nice piece of corner property for a dog to race around in. The day we visited it was cool and clear. Lola and Rocket, two big rowdy dogs, immediately ran up to Chappy, who was really in no mood for boisterous socializing. At 10 years old, he prefers to amble along in peace and stop when he pleases, not being bothered by anyone or anything. Well, Rocket and Lola were there to play. What is a dog park for, they asked!? They sniffed and cavorted and were really rough with Chap, who eventually had to sit down and snarl at them, baring his teeth like we've never seen. The mailbox in the middle of the park, used to house doggy pick-up bags, didn't appeal to him, nor did the two bowls of water in the middle of the park. He was just plain mad. He did manage to check out the one big tree in the park, but then it was time to get out of there. He left Rocket and Lola nipping and rolling all over each other as we strolled down the sidewalk outside the fence. By then, he seemed a bit proud of himself. The park is on the corner of South Pollard Street and South Walter Reed Drive. It is open from sunrise to a half hour after sunset. 703/228-6525.

25 Jennie Dean Park 🐾

The boys of summer get more out of this fine baseball complex than do dogs, but sometimes there's just nothing like a good old-fashioned baseball game, the kind kids play to right the wrongs in our day-to-day lives. Same goes for Chappy, who lasts a good three innings anytime—especially when our boys are playing. The park is located at Arlington Mill Drive and Shirlington Road, on the north side of Shirlington Village. It is open dawn–dusk. 703/228-6525.

26 Shirlington Park 🐾 🐾 🐾 🐕

A relaxing, wonderful little stretch of land running right along Four Mile Run, this park has not only a main dog exercise area, but a separate fenced-off enclosed area for small dogs. Benches make it easy to sit and wait while Fido runs around partying it up and even taking a dip—as the bigger dogs do—in the water. Trees lining the path provide some shade on hot days. Because it feels more like a natural park rather than a squared-off piece of gravel or dirt like some of the dog parks this one is particularly pleasant. The park is at 2601 South Arlington Mill Drive. It's behind a storage facility along South Four Mile Run between Shirlington Road and South Walter Reed Drive. From Four Mile Run turn onto Nelson and park behind the storage facility. We actually wound up parking across Arlington Mill and taking a bridge across. The park is open from sunrise to a half hour after sunset. 703/228-4747.

27 Utah Park 🐾 🐾 ½ 🐕

We knew we were in the right place when we saw the fenced-in gravelly area with about a dozen tennis balls lying around. Then we saw the dogs. Three of the main socializers, Gandolf, Claus, and Bilbo, came over to greet us right away. There were at least a dozen dogs running around having a grand old time. Water jugs were lined up on a picnic table. A friendly neighborhood scene was the order of the day here. From 34th Street, turn onto Utah until it connects with 32nd. Drive around the ball fields to the cul de sac next to the fenced-in dog area at 3191 Utah Street. 703/228-4747.

Restaurants

Best Buns: If you just want a loaf of olive, garlic, and herb bread, or even a little mozzarella and tomato salad with a cup of coffee, this is a good carryout place. It's attached to the Carlyle Grand Cafe, which has a pricier menu and a place to sit outside. But dogs lunching with you at Best Buns have to be tied up to a bench by the street, not near the tables. 4101 South 28th Street; 703/578-1500.

Bistro Bistro: Flowers in the window boxes in the outside eating area give this casual but delicious eatery a comfy atmosphere. See those benches, trees, and bike rack right next to the patio dining area? If you tie your pup there, the waiters will seat you at a table next to him. White chili, penne with smoked chicken, and oyster stew are house specialties, but the grilled chicken sandwich and the Get Shorty pizza won't disappoint. Chappy was happy to get meatloaf crumbs tossed his way. The bartender says dogs drop by all the time on sunny days. In Shirlington Village at 4021 South 28th Street; 703/379-0300.

Carlyle Grand Cafe: Taking advantage of the wide bricked sidewalk, these kind folks who serve an excellent Virginia trout and saucy baby-back ribs have no problem with pooches sitting at their owners' feet at the outdoor tables. 4000 South 28th Street; 703/931-0777.

WHISPERING WIND

Parks, Beaches, and Recreation Areas

28 Tuckahoe Park and Playfield 🐾 🐾 ½

Unusual and uncrowded—that's Tuckahoe. Two lighted tennis courts surprisingly are often available in a woodsy area that is great for dogs to roam around at—but on a leash, of course. There are two baseball fields that Chappy knows well since it's one of the fields where our boys learned to pitch and field. Between them there is so much open grass that while everyone else is watching the ball game, some amazing mutts are often making acrobatic Frisbee catches. A big kids' attraction is the two-story tube slide and other climbing things in a clearing amid the pines and dogwoods. Grills and picnic tables abound.

The park is located at Lee Highway and Sycamore Street, next to Bishop O'Connell High School and Tuckahoe Elementary School. It is open daily dawn–dusk. 703/228-6525.

WOODLAND

Parks, Beaches, And Recreation Areas

29 Oak Grove Park 🐾 ½

Another small neighborhood moment of serenity (except when the soccer kids are at it), what's unusual about this locale is that the entire park is elevated from street level by a stone wall and is sort of on a cloud of its own. A well-kept soccer field consumes most of the actual land up there, but there's plenty of roaming space out of bounds for leashed dogs more interested in sniffing the tall old bent trees that shade the edges. The park is open from sunrise to a half hour after sunset, and is located at the intersection of 15th Street and North Quincy Street. 703/228-6525.

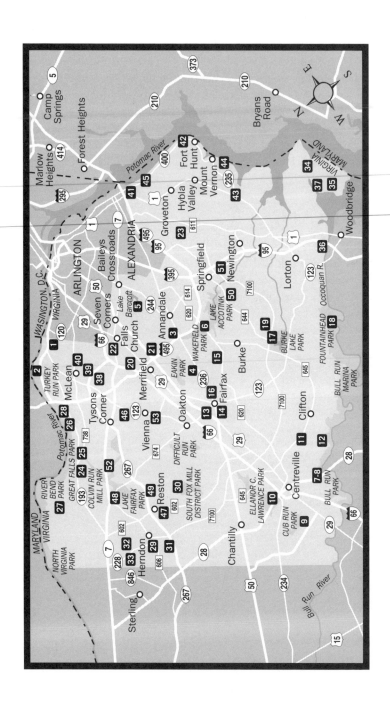

8 FAIRFAX COUNTY

One of the nation's most affluent counties, Fairfax has seen phenomenal growth in the past 30 years—transforming from farmland and undeveloped wilderness to a crowded, upscale bedroom community of the nation's capital. During the dotcom boom, in particular, the county lured lots of high-technology businesses in and as a result, now more than half the adult population lives and works right in the county instead of bothering to commute to the District of Columbia.

Covering 399 square miles, Fairfax County offers some 30,000 acres of parks. Yet the county is lagging far behind its smaller sisters—Arlington and Alexandria—in its number of off-leash dog parks. The good news: in 1999, the county adopted Standards for Fairfax County Off-Leash Dog Areas, allowing the formation of sponsoring groups for dog parks. In 2000, Fairfax County opened its first dog park in Oakton at Blake Lane Park, sponsored by Oakton Dogs. Since then, three other dog parks have been given the go-ahead: Baron Cameron, Mason District, and South Run. Two others, Chandon Park in Herndon and Lake Fairfax Park in Reston have been proposed. These leash-free spots may not be glamorous, but they are fully sanctioned, fenced-in dog parks where your pooch can put in some free-range time. As Martha Stewart would say, "that's a good thing."

They are not without rules, however, and one of the most important, for the safety and well being of us all, is that you can control your dog. Aggressive dogs really aren't welcomed at off-leash areas. And, you *must* scoop the poop—wherever you are, whether dog park or just taking a little walk around the block. Should authorities catch you not cleaning up after your dog on public land anywhere in the county, the fine is $250, the highest among all the neighboring jurisdictions and the District of Columbia. Generally, if you are walking your dog in the county, she must be on a leash. If you're in an off-leash dog area, there are a total of 19 rules, most of them geared to having control of your dog.

Fairfax County also boasts of more than three-dozen parks and recreation areas, in addition to the off-leash places, and among those, there is a wide variety—from neighborhood pit stops, to small woodsy oases, to bigger suburban parks. Most of the truly magnificent parklands with vast space, water, and the best and most facilities fall under the jurisdiction of the Northern Virginia Regional Park Authority, and the state and the national park services. Those tend to be the best and the brightest for any venturesome dog-lover's agenda, even if it does mean being on a leash.

National Parks

◼ Fort Marcy 🐾 🐾 ½

Built in 1861 to protect against the approach of troops from the South, Fort Marcy is long gone. But the cannon is still there. If you walk up the path into the woods, you'll think, hey, where's the fort? Where's anything that resembles history here?

And one piece of history *isn't* marked on this site: This is near where former White House deputy counsel Vince Foster, the Hillary Clinton friend, was found dead. Conspiracy buffs still comb the place for clues. But mostly what you find is sun filtering down on grass through the tall trees.

If you never ventured into the next clearing, it would still be a pleasant little area. But walk your pooch over that next hill and check out the small meadow with four mounds of earth, and in the clearing beyond that, you'll find the cannon—facing the Potomac as if ready to fire at the advancing enemy. Because it's not one of the bigger and better-known spots, it's easy to let your dog run around the hilly paths. Keep in mind this is national park land, and the fed's regulations require dogs to remain leashed.

To find this small gem of a park from Rosslyn, take the George Washington Memorial Parkway north about four miles past Key Bridge and look for the brown park sign on the right. The park is open dawn–dusk. 202/208-4747.

❷ Turkey Run 🐾 🐾 🐾

One reason this park rates so highly is that it gives you the chance to hike right down to the Potomac, which by historic or aesthetic standards is one fine river. If you park in lot C-1, you'll find access to three trails. One is the Potomac Heritage Trail. At 10 miles the wooded path that goes up north to the American Legion Bridge and down south to Teddy Roosevelt Island is long for most dogs—but who says you've got to hike the whole thing? Another is the Turkey Run Loop, a short 0.75-mile hike that Chappy likes better than the third, the 3.3-mile Dead Run Loop.

This is get-your-boots-on hiking, and it's on-leash hiking for dogs. The trails are steep and zigzag down to the river in a series of switchbacks. There are rough-hewn rails to hold onto in spots, and crude steps of rocks or pilings in other places. It's an adventure, and it's beautiful. The tree roots, butterflies, and chipmunks that cross your path take you far away from the noisy city that's just minutes away. It's peaceful and pretty, although rough—and its nearest neighbor is the Central Intelligence Agency.

From Rosslyn, take the George Washington Parkway north 7.5 miles and follow the signs to the park off to the right. The park is open dawn–dark. 202/208-4747.

ANNANDALE

Parks, Beaches, and Recreation Areas

❸ Annandale Community Park and Hidden Oaks Nature Center 🐾 🐾

Sigh. Another typical multi-use neighborhood park, this 52-acre locale does sport a quarter-mile, self-guided nature trail that surrounds the Hidden Oaks Nature Center located on these grounds. Put on the leash and bird-watch if you want, or photograph the wild orchids. You might come upon the railroad embankment built before the Civil War. A playground for kids offers a lot of shade on hot days for panting pups. And there's a craft gallery with regular shows.

From the Capital Beltway, take Exit 6 east onto Little River Turnpike (Route 236); turn left at the first light onto Hummer Road and go to the park entrance on left. The park is open during daylight hours. 703/941-1065.

❹ Eakin Community Park 🐾 🐾

If the entrance were a little easier to find, this park might rate higher. As it is, we discovered there are two Eakin Community Parks—and neither excels. One of them, alongside Barkley Drive, is more planned and less adventuresome with its tennis courts, ball field, and playground—and a much larger area to walk with the dog. The other, bordered by Prosperity Avenue, is much smaller and slightly unkempt.

The day we visited the little park, it had just rained and the place was a swamp filled with kamikaze mosquitoes and overgrown grass. We walked away with a lot of mud on us and on Chappy. But a positive point is the broad creek that runs along the park's back side, where an ambitious dog might dive in safely for a swim at a couple of spots. Dogs are supposed to be on a leash, as always, but we saw two that weren't. A jogging and bike trail runs through and connects both sides of this park.

From the Capital Beltway, take Exit 8 onto Route 50 west; turn left on Prosperity Avenue and go 0.7 mile to the parking lot of the smaller Eakin Park site on the left; continue past Prosperity Avenue two blocks and turn left on Barkley Drive for the larger Eakin site on the left. The park is open dawn–dusk. There is no phone.

5 Mason District Park 🐾 🐾 🐾 ◄● 🐕

With 121 acres of crisscrossing trails, this is a beautiful park for dogs and humans. There are ball fields, playgrounds, and lots of trees and grassy areas in between. Sloping hills lead through the woods for nice long (leashed) walks. An amphitheater can be found in the middle of it all. The tennis courts see a lot of action on warm days.

This has also been one of the most controversial parks around, as the Mason District Dog Opportunity Group actively pushed for an off-leash dog area and raised the close to $10,000 needed for fencing to make it happen. But some neighbors objected, claiming that its location, adjacent to Annandale's Columbia Elementary School, made it a danger to kids. On top of that, neighbors have complained about the loss of open space, as well as increased noise and odor from the dogs being so close to their homes. The result: score one for the dogs. There is a one-acre fenced-in dog park that can accommodate a maximum of 63 dogs. From the Capital Beltway, take Exit 6, go left on John Marr Drive and left on Columbia Pike. 703/941-1730.

6 Wakefield Park and Recreation Center 🐾

The big recreation center is a draw, as are the ball fields, so this ranks as another neighborhood park that is geared toward humans more so than dogs, who must be on a leash nonetheless. From the Capital Beltway, take Exit 5 to Braddock Road heading west; the park entrance is 0.2 miles on the right. The park is open dawn–dusk, although the rec center stays open later. 703/321-7081.

Restaurants

Main Street USA: You won't get even a flinch from these friendly folks if you park your dog by your feet at the outdoor patio tables and enjoy this basic American fare, from steak to prime rib. 7131 Little River Turnpike; 703/750-0777.

Sunset Grille: Carry out hearty burgers, spicy wings, and other such things from this unpretentious throwback of a roadhouse bar and grill in downtown

Annandale. And on warm evenings when they leave the front door and windows open, sit outside on your car bumper (other patrons will be out there, too) with your pooch alongside and catch some of the great live music played on its dinky stage every night except Monday. The Thursday night tradition is Bill Kirchen (formerly lead guitarist and vocals for Commander Cody) and not to be missed. He and his high-flying band, Too Much Fun, will bring a little bit of country, a little bit of rock, and a smidgen of rock-a-billy joy to you and your dog's ears. 7250 Columbia Pike; 703/658-0928.

BAILEYS CROSSROADS

Restaurants

Duangrat's: This Thai food is rated highly by all Washington culinary experts. While the crunchy papaya salad with dried shrimp can be blistering hot, other dishes on the menu come out milder—even fit for a dog's sensitive palate. Trout in banana leaves grilled with basil and cilantro is a favorite. Take a seat at either of the outside tables where the kind owners have no problem with an obedient dog lying low. 5878 Leesburg Pike; 703/820-5775.

Peking Gourmet Inn: Even George Bush (senior) couldn't bring his dog inside this old-style Chinese restaurant where, when president, he would show up with a couple of guests and Secret Service agents to order the fabulous Peking duck. His son, the one in the Oval Office, has stopped by, too. But you can order the duck to go with 15 minutes' notice. 6029 Leesburg Pike; 703/671-8088.

CENTREVILLE

Parks, Beaches, and Recreation Areas

7 Bull Run–Occoquan Trail 🐾 🐾 🐾 🐾 🐾

This 17.5-mile straight-line trail passes through 4,000 acres of some of Fairfax County's most scenic and historic parklands, but don't make the mistake of figuring it'll be a walk in the park—for you or your dog. It's more like a walk on the wild side. Extending from Bull Run Regional Park southeast into Fountainhead Regional Park, the trail passes through rough-and-tumble ravines and over steep hillsides that follow along Bull Run Creek to the gorgeous Occoquan Reservoir.

Hikers with canine sidekicks are allowed to traipse these woodlands and through its streams, as are horseback riders—but no bicycles or motor vehicles are allowed. No hunting here either, so there's no need to worry about stray gunfire; camping is restricted to Bull Run Park.

What you will find are white-tailed deer, beavers, otters, cottontail rabbits, chipmunks, and skunks, all of whom roam about here as if it were their home—which, of course, this protected sanctuary is, so behave accordingly. If your dog is like Chappy and gets weird or wired at the sight of a critter scampering (a woodchuck the size of a small dog had him bouncing like the ball on a paddleboard), keep a short lead. Dogs have to be on a leash on the trail. And, even if they didn't, some domesticated pooch whose idea of a wild-and-crazy time is fetching a tennis ball in the front yard just might get lost in these dense hemlock groves and pine stands where musket balls once flew during two major Civil War battles.

If you intend to go a spell, take ample water and some chewables. The trail passes through Bull Run Marina, which has canoes, a snack bar, restrooms, a phone, and other facilities, but that's about an 11-mile hike down the run. Take care, too, because poison ivy is alive and well here, and so are a few poisonous copperhead snakes. The trail closes at dark—and you probably don't want to be out there after dark anyway. Yikes! It's not a loop, either, so plan on a ride at the end of the hike.

To set out on the trail from Bull Run Regional Park, from I-66 west, take Exit 52 (Route 29) at Centreville; drive two miles south and turn left on Bull Run Post Office Road, which leads to the entrance. To reach the Route 28 Access Point: From I-66, take Route 28 south past the Compton Road intersection. Turn right into the small parking lot on the bluff above Bull Run to park your car. To reach the Fountainhead Regional Park Access Point: Take I-66 west to Route 123 south; about 10 miles past the City of Fairfax, turn right on Hampton Road, and go three miles to the park entrance. Call the Northern Virginia Regional Park Authority before setting out because some parts of the trail may be under renovation. And you can get a "Hiking with the Dog?" guide from the Park Authority. 703/352-5900.

8 Bull Run Regional Park 🐾 🐾 🐾 🐾 🐾

Bring your dog's jammies, because this is the best overnighter under the stars down this end of the county. Plenty of wide-open fields clearly prove irresistible for doggy fetch games and Frisbee, despite county leash laws. A few dogs always seem to be bounding about on the loose anyway. Nobody pays much attention to them, but join in at your own risk; the extensive camping here means many kindly park rangers are about.

For staying close to the campfire, hike the wide paved roadway that twists and turns through the gorgeous green vistas, often brightened by fields of Virginia bluebells and other wildflowers. Smooth enough for bicycling and carefree in-line skating, the road is bordered by well-shaded picnic grilling areas and rustic wooden shelters where panting partners can chill out before continuing. Running the distance of the road down the north side is broad and brisk Cub Run Creek; its waters turn chocolate after summer storms and will seem yucky even to gung-ho water dogs, but its rocky edge is a cool place to play.

Forgetting his etiquette lessons, Chappy tugged us over to the disc golf course where Frisbees ricocheting off trees and limbs is par, and dogs don't get in anyone's way. The miniature golf, volleyball, and huge swimming pool complex (take a look at the "tropical island" in the middle of the pool) get crowded on warm-weather weekends so that dogs are better off elsewhere in the park—such as exploring the incredible wilderness that awaits down the Bull Run–Occoquan Trail, where fewer people and lots of wildlife hang out. The hike over to the park's public shooting center, safely located more than a mile outside the park, is too far and not particularly attractive, bordering Route 66. But as long as your dog doesn't get nervous at the pop of gunfire, watching the skeet shooters from the parking lot is a blast—for a few minutes.

You can camp with your dog at one of the 150 roomy and comfortable campsites (100 with electricity) that are located away from the crowd and at the back of the park. The park's laundry facilities, showers, dump station, a camp store, and family-type recreation (including an outdoor swimming pool, miniature and disc golf, and a children's playground) make this a primo camping area for families and dogs, though you need to keep your dog with you wherever you go. The per-night fee with electricity is $16.75; without electricity, $13.25. There is an additional fee of $1 per person for more than four persons per site.

Park entry is free to residents of nearby Virginia counties; nonresident day-use fees are $5.50 per vehicle and $10 for 10 or more people. Call to reserve picnic shelters. From I-66 west, take Exit 52 (Route 29) at Centreville; drive two miles south and turn left on Bull Run Post Office Road. Follow signs to the park entrance. The park is open 10 A.M. until dark. 703/631-0550.

9 Cub Run Stream Valley Park 🐾 🐾

This hidden parkland offers nothing more than hiking and biking paths that meander through a long stretch of mostly untouched woods where the sometimes-vigorous Cub Run Stream passes by. It's an ideal place for a dog to take a dip. Theoretically, leashes are a must, but frankly, no one's around here much to uphold the law or complain—but use your better judgment. There's no main entrance, either, but access to the trails can be found here and there between the long rows of modern suburban homes that border the length of the park. You do, however, get the feeling some residents think of this as their own backyard, and who can blame them?

From I-66, exit to Route 29 south; go 1.5 miles and turn right on Pleasant Valley Road at the Virginia Run Community Center. Turn right again on White Chapel Road and look for one of the paved access paths leading into the park. The park is open dawn–dusk. There is no telephone.

Places to Stay

Bull Run Regional Park Campground: See Bull Run Regional Park in this chapter.

EARMARK YOUR CALENDAR–DECEMBER

Miracle of Lights: Northern Virginia's only **drive-through holiday lights show** is enough to electrify anyone, even pooches, not quite yet in the spirit of the Christmas holidays. More than 200,000 sparkling reminders of seasonal cheer are arranged along two miles of the Bull Run Regional Park's main drive as shapes of animals, Santa and his sleigh, and other festive displays that'll make the pup blink with awe or lie down wondering what all the hoopla is about. Then, get out of the jalopy and take in the old-fashioned outdoor holiday fair for a taste of hot chocolate and peruse country crafts and souvenirs, the band of strolling entertainers, and even a jolly old Saint Nicholas and photographer nearby. (Chappy refused Saint Nick's knee. Well, actually it was Santa who refused . . .) The annual light show runs from mid-November through early January, and a portion of the $12 per car ticket goes to deserving charities. 703/709-5437.

CHANTILLY

"Chantilly lace and a pretty face . . . ." Sorry, but the Big Bopper's corrupted any possibility of thinking of this growing burg near Washington Dulles International Airport as anything but a line in an old rock 'n' roll song. It's a little bit of country, a little bit of city, and not a bad place to find yourself with a dog.

Parks, Beaches, and Recreation Areas

10 Ellanor C. Lawrence Park 🐾 🐾 🐾 🐾 🐾

Barely hidden in the tall, aged trees behind the two-acre lily pond is Big Rocky Run, a deep creek where dogs regularly take a cool plunge. No water dog, our bath-paranoid Chappy watched from his leash (laws are in effect) by our sides as if he couldn't care less as a full-grown Saint Bernard and a black Lab frolicked shoulder deep near the edge of the best swimming hole, right by the wooden footbridge. Children stepped gingerly along stones before jumping into water nearly over their heads.

Meanwhile, Walney Pond—created originally to water livestock and provide ice in winter—is more than a picturesque centerpiece for your picnic lunch. There are tables alongside and one choice deck table on the water to the pond's south side. Colorful dragonflies skitter about the surface as folks fish from the shoreline and from the boardwalk that cuts across the placid water to the creek and to the 0.3-mile Creek Trail extending into the woods.

Leisurely is the operative word here, even on the nine well-kept trails that loop their way through these 640 historic acres. Back in colonial days this was Walney Farm, where slaves labored in the fields, dogs chased livestock and snoozed by the hearth, and gentrified Virginia landowners toasted the new republic. And there are remnants and restorations that allow you to envision life as it was in those bygone days—while your dog sniffs around. From the visitor center, which is the renovated 200-year-old farmhouse, hike the 0.4-mile historic trail (a trail map is available inside the center) to the small stone springhouse where perishables were kept cool by the spring that runs through it. The wood-chipped path from there leads to the 150-year-old red maple that somehow escaped the axes of Confederate soldiers who camped nearby and cut down most of the old trees for housing and fuel.

Farther up the path, which takes about 20 minutes to stroll, are the hardwood and evergreen woods and gullied stream where crops once grew. Other paths lead to the ruins of the old icehouse, smokehouse, and the very-much-alive beehives. The historical sites are particularly impressive in the winter when foliage doesn't distract, though the heat of the summer is inviting here for dogs because of the refreshing waters. And springtime poses fields of stunning wild posies—mayapple, bloodroot, and spring beauties. Year-round it's a pleasant hike into history.

Take I-66 west to Exit 53; turn left at the light onto Route 28, go one-quarter mile, and turn right on Walney Road. Parking at Walney Pond is one-half mile down the road on the left, and visitor center parking is 1.1 miles on the left. Grounds are open dawn–dusk daily. Visitor center hours are 9 A.M.–5 P.M. weekdays; noon–5 P.M. weekends; closed Tuesday, major holidays, and weekdays in January and February. 703/631-0013.

Restaurants

Anita's: There's one outside table somewhat separate from the others, and the waiters don't mind if you and your dog sit over there and order up enchiladas. Management just doesn't want any trouble from other customers complaining. 13921 Lee Jackson Highway; 703/378-1717.

Tasteful Meetings: Choose from 30 to 40 different sandwiches, a salad, dessert, and fruit, boxed and ready to go, for about $8.50. The grilled chicken is a favorite. But take note: It's only open weekdays, 10 A.M.–3 P.M. 14220-D Sullyfield Drive; 703/378-8080.

CLIFTON

A small and historic town on the southwest side of the county, it is surrounded by the kind of rural horse-country land that developers salivate over. The town itself is quaint and worth visiting with your dog for a lunchtime excursion or just a stroll through small-town America.

Parks, Beaches, and Recreation Areas

11 Braddock Park 🐾

Dogs can find room to roam here, but the raison d'être of this suburban park is baseball. Groups from all over the area play here day and night. There are six manicured fields with lights, and a batting cage area. In between the fields are gravel trails and some expanses of grass, so bring your dog only if the pooch is into spectator sports. Take I-66 west to Exit 53 and head south on Route 28. Go 1.3 miles and turn left on New Braddock Road. The park is 1.5 miles on the right. 703/324-8700.

12 Hemlock Overlook Regional Park 🐾

Other than serving as a midway access to the 17.5-mile Bull Run–Occoquan Trail, this isn't the best place for dogs. Or, rather, it just isn't intended for them. It's an outdoor learning center operated jointly by the Northern Virginia Regional Park Authority and George Mason University. You can park here and hike the trail—leash laws are in effect—without making any arrangements. And you'll be able to see the dense groves of 200-year-old hemlock trees the park is named for. The terrain is wild but beautiful, and it gives the feel of walking through history—this is part of the site of Bull Run, one of the most important Civil War battles.

But basically this park area is used for outdoor and team development programs for all sorts of groups, from teachers to churches to businesses—by reservation only. There are six dormitories, a dining hall, five meeting rooms, and the outdoor challenge courses.

From I-66, take the Route 123 south, turn right on Clifton Road, and drive 3.7 miles (it will seem like a lot farther); turn left on Yates Ford Road and follow it to the park entrance. The park is open dawn–dusk daily. 703/993-3754.

Restaurants

Heart in Hand: In quaint historic Clifton, this eatery across from the landmark Clifton Store will gladly seat you with the pooch at your feet at its outdoor

---

EARMARK YOUR CALENDAR–SEPTEMBER

Jumping through Hoops: The Dulles Gateway Obedience Training Club's **Show and Go Fun Match** puts dogs through the rigors and fun of a training course and rates their performances. Usually held Labor Day weekend at the Northern Virginia Community College, the course tests obedience and agility skills and costs a nominal fee for the first run-through and even less for additional run-throughs. Spectators are welcome (no charge). And that's only one of the fun things the club does. Call them at 703/273-7619; website: www.geocities.com/dgotc.

---

tables during warm seasons. But, beware—when it's too hot or sprinkling, they close the patio. The menu is a step above the usual burgers, with poached salmon, chicken dishes, quiche, and baked brie. 7145 Main Street; 703/830-4111.

FAIRFAX

Fairfax, a six-square-mile area, sits in the middle of Fairfax County and is the county seat, where many of the government offices are located. However, it isn't all politics and business here. The city itself is home to 14 parks and recreation areas—many of them small patches of green earth without facilities—where leashed dogs are welcome. But in the nearby countryside are some of the county's finest natural resources for canine carousing.

Parks, Beaches, and Recreation Areas

13 Daniels Run Park 🐾 🐾

Tall trees shade the paths, and it's very quiet. Suddenly, you feel as if you're in the Adirondacks. The streets disappear behind you, and the forest swallows you up. Okay, it's not a forest; it's a 48-acre park with the creek running through it, but you feel very much alone as the sun filters through the high-up branches. If you and your dog—who should be on a leash—want solitude, this is the place. Locals, like the cute little mutt we met named Buster, use it as a neighborhood shortcut.

From I-66, exit onto Route 123 south into Fairfax City, turn left on Main Street (Route 236), and go 1.4 miles; then turn left on Estel Road until you reach the park entrance. 703/385-7858.

14 Providence Park 🐾

Woodsy and flat, this park offers 17 acres, a playground with tepees, a picnic pavilion, and a basketball court. The only distinguishing mark is an interesting large tree between the picnic area and the basketball court. It has two limbs that spread out like a Y and lots of giant knots on it. You might like to look at it, and your dog, who must be on a leash, might like to mark it for future reference.

Take I-66 to Route 123 south into Fairfax City and go 0.6 mile past the Main Street intersection; turn right on Canfield Street to the park entrance. 703/385-7858.

15 Royal Lake Park 🐾 🐾 🐾

It seems there is no park here when you drive into the lot. But pick the two-mile path off to the right, and it will take you down to a 36-acre lake. You can walk right to the water and sit on the grass by it, or walk the 1.5-mile trail around it. Leash laws are in effect, though regulars often drop the leash and let their dogs run about. One acquaintance, a two-year-old Chesapeake Bay retriever named Kady, who loves chasing down Frisbees and dog-paddling in deep water, got a $45 ticket a while back for not obeying leash laws—so it does happen here.

This is not a park with expansive grounds, snack bars, or miniature trains, but a peaceful place to just happily cavort with your canine. Little kids dominated the day we dropped by. Tennis courts are tucked away in the woods, as is a beaten-up basketball court, but the lake is the real draw.

From the Capital Beltway, take Exit 5 to Braddock Road west; turn left on Twinbrook Road, right on Commonwealth Boulevard, then left on Gainsborough Drive to the park entrance on the left. 703/385-7858.

🔟 Van Dyck Park 🐾 🐾 ½ 🐾

Covering 20 acres, this park is an oasis in the middle of trafficky, busy, suburban Fairfax. Well-tended beds of pretty pansies arranged nicely on paved paths between tennis courts, a basketball court, playground, and picnic facilities make this seem like such a civil place. None of that rough hiking stuff happens hereabouts.

There's also a natural grassy amphitheater—maybe sinkhole is a better word—right in the middle of the park. It's perfect for playing Frisbee. Your dog must be on a leash, as always in Fairfax, and on the summer weekday we dropped by, the only action was a group of kids on the playing fields. The lawns were wide open and inviting.

Take I-66 to Route 123 south; turn left on Kenmore Drive. Take a dogleg right (no pun intended) onto University Drive and then a quick left on Layton Hall Drive, then a left on Old Lee Highway to the park entrance on the left. The park is open dawn–dusk daily. 703/385-7858.

Restaurants

Main Street Bagel and Deli: This shaded outdoor café with plenty of tables and piped-in jazz is a top-notch, dog-loving deli, and the friendly folks who run it will even bring a bowl of water if your pal starts panting. 10268 Main Street; 703/591-2966.

T. T. Reynolds: Steaks, burgers, subs, and all that he-man food that Chappy seems lured by is served at outdoor tables in back where the staff is very accommodating to well-behaved dogs. 10414 Main Street; 703/591-9292.

Places to Stay

Comfort Inn–University Center: On the outskirts of downtown Fairfax, closer to Route 66 and the pleasurable shopping of Fair Oaks Mall, these cozy quarters welcome dogs as long as they're "not big, big, big," as the desk clerk put it. A one-time fee of $25 is tacked on for the dog. Rates are about $89, including free breakfast. 11180 Main Street, Fairfax, VA 22030; 703/591-5900.

Holiday Inn–Fair Oaks: Part of the Fair Oaks Shopping Mall, this inn charges no dog fees and has no policy restricting size, though, as one manager said, "Hopefully, the dog isn't so big that it'll scare the housekeepers." Rates are about $69. If you're paying cash, you'd better have enough to cover the $150 deposit. 11787 Lee Jackson Highway, Fairfax, VA 22033; 703/352-2525.

Wellesley Inn: A couple of miles down the street from George Mason University, the Wellesley welcomes dogs under 20 pounds. There is no fee tacked on to the $69 room rate. 10327 Lee Highway, Fairfax, VA 22030; 703/359-2888.

FAIRFAX STATION

Parks, Beaches, and Recreation Areas

17 Burke Lake Park 🐾 🐾 🐾 🐾 🐾

Burke Lake Road seems to go on forever until finally, on the left, as you're nearing the intersection of Ox Road, if you look quickly you get your first glimpse of the 218-acre Burke Lake. Soon the endless subdivisions disappear and you're looking out at a placid, wide, tree-edged, peaceful oasis.

This 883-acre park has everything—open spaces, shady forest areas, trails, the lake, picnic areas, fishing, boating, golf. A little dachshund who was leash-free (like at every Fairfax County park, dogs are supposed to be on a leash) didn't know where to go first, he was so excited about the place. Chappy could relate to that. You could spend days here—and can if you opt for camping. But even if you just want to spend a hot summer afternoon in the park, it's a really pleasant place for you and your pooch.

Veer right into the park and you'll head down to the boat launch area for a breathtaking view of the expansive water. Picnic areas can be reserved, so invite friends with dogs and make a day of it. There's a volleyball area near one picnic site, a wide-open field near another picnic site, and a playground near still another. Go out on a boat and you'll see that Vesper Island, in the center of the lake, is maintained as a state waterfowl refuge. Canada geese, ducks, and herons visit the area and are best spotted in October and November, although we saw a heron standing six feet from us one July afternoon.

If you head left once you're in the park, you'll wind around by the golf course and driving range, where geese risk getting bonked on the head as they waddle about. Also on this side of the park is a complex for kids with an ice cream parlor, a miniature train, and a carousel. There's a five-mile walking trail, another trail called the Beaver Cove Nature Trail, and an 18-station fitness trail, so take your pick and head out.

There are 150 sites available for tents, tent trailers, truck campers, and travel trailers with a maximum length of 25 feet; the maximum camping time is seven consecutive days. There are no hookups, but fresh water, hot showers, restrooms, and a dump station are provided. Groceries, ice, laundry facilities, and snack items are available at the camp store (closed during winter months, as is the campground, which usually closes at the end of September for the colder months). The fee is $14 per night for up to four people.

There's no entry fee for Fairfax County residents; there's a $6 day-use fee for noncounty folks. The park is open 6 A.M.–dark. From the Capital Beltway, take Exit 5 to Braddock Road heading west; turn left on Burke Lake Road and then left on Ox Road to the park entrance on the left. 7315 Ox Road; 703/323-6600.

18 Fountainhead Regional Park 🐾 🐾 🐾 🐾 🐾

Row, row, row your dog—out into gorgeous Lake Occoquan. This park, which is at the end of some windy country roads, will truly make you feel like you're Davy Crockett. In fact, the day we visited, Chappy started growling before he got out of the car—at a pit bull sauntering by with a big log in his mouth.

Very woodsy, very remote, and very big, it is a park for a pooch who likes to explore trails. It's also one of the few that offers a way to get out on the water with your dog. Rowboats can be rented for the afternoon (and also at Bull Run Marina 6.45 miles up the trail).

Located at the widest point of the 22-mile Lake Occoquan, the park invites you to spend a pleasant afternoon of boating or lazily enjoying the ferns, dogwood, hemlock, hickory, oak, and pine trees that cover the hillside. While drowning worms from a fishing line, you might see a bald eagle, beaver, white-tailed deer, or wild turkey. Fountainhead is also where you can access the Bull Run–Occoquan Trail for serious hiking mileage. Leash laws are in effect.

The park is open mid-March through mid-November, sunrise–sunset, although in winter months it is okay to park outside the gate and walk in with your dog. From I-66, exit on Route 123 south and go past the City of Fairfax approximately 10 miles. Turn right on Hampton Road and drive three miles to the park entrance on the left. 703/250-9124.

19 Rolling Valley Park 🐾

Sitting right behind Pohick Regional Library, this is a small, suburban park. With a tiny parking lot, ball field, and playground, the offerings are standard. Add to that the fact that it's on a busy street and near a strip shopping mall. While it may be okay for a quick stop (remember to put on a leash), this little park is otherwise skippable.

From the Capital Beltway, take Exit 5 to Braddock Road west; turn left on Burke Lake Road, then left on Lee Chapel Road, left on Old Keene Mill Road, and right on Sydenstricker Road to the park entrance on the right. 703/866-0566.

Restaurants

Hopsfrog Tavern: Even American-breed dogs can't sit inside this American-cuisine restaurant for its choice burgers, steaks, ribs, or seafood, but the entire menu is available for carryout. 5745 Burke Centre Parkway; 703/239-9324.

FALLS CHURCH

Parks, Beaches, and Recreation Areas

20 Jefferson District Park 🐾

This is more golf course than park, but if you're in the neighborhood, it isn't a bad little pit stop for stretching those dog legs right and left and for free entertainment. A lot's going on here, mostly because of the basketball courts, popular for fierce pickup games. Several tennis courts next to the recently renovated miniature golf course get heavy use, though not always by someone you'd bother watching. Grassy areas surround all the courts and border the 18-hole real golf course at the back of the park where Chappy is content to watch each foursome hack away from the tees. From the Capital Beltway, take Exit 8 to Route 50 west; turn right on Gallows Road and right again on Lee Highway to the park entrance on the left at Hyson Lane. The park is open dawn–dusk. 703/573-0443.

21 Roundtree Park 🐾 🐾

Just pulling into the parking lot of this park aroused skepticism. An embankment prevents a full view of what lies below. You have to get out of the car and explore a little to find this is a better-than-average suburban park. A group was dancing happily to a boom box in the picnic pavilion area when we stopped by, putting Chappy into one of his Tibetan moods.

Following the trail and a nice low stone wall down from that entrance area will put you in a hilly open area with a playground. Stick to the path and you'll go over a creek that's almost impossible to see because of the overgrowth. From there you'll find a baseball field and a soccer field. There isn't much room to do anything more, though. But go to the right of the baseball field, or back to the playground, and pick up paths from those spots. They will lead you to a hidden dog heaven well known in the neighborhood. Although dogs are supposed to be on leashes, few ever are.

From the Capital Beltway, take Exit 8 (Route 50) east about 3.5 miles; turn right on Annandale Road and follow it about 2.5 miles to the park entrance on the left. The park is open dawn–dusk. 703/324-8700.

22 Washington & Old Dominion Railroad Regional Park 🐾 🐾 🦴

Actually a 45-mile trail blazed through some of the thickest countryside and most suburbanized neighborhoods, this high-use paved pathway runs from Shirlington in Arlington County westward through Fairfax County and all the way to Purcellville in Loudoun County. Occasionally, it expands into inviting little parklands along the way—but many of its miles are narrow and suitable mostly for biking.

Smoothly paved for jogging, in-line skating, and biking, it picks up in Fairfax County at a sunny little restful pit-stop park at the intersection of Little Falls Road and Four Mile Run Drive. Two and a half miles west, the trail sideswipes a pleasant stop at Idylwood Park, wedged between Route 66 and I-495 just off Virginia Lane. Another three to four miles along the trail and you get to North Side Park in Vienna and Eudora Park just outside the town limits, where the 33-mile bridle path for horseback riding starts to run alongside as well. Clarks Crossing Park and Difficult Run Stream Valley Park, a mile to two miles up the trail, are heavily wooded lands (some hiking trails but little else) surrounding neighborhoods.

One of the trail's sweetest respites comes less than a mile from the Reston Town Center, where it runs by two lovely lakes with a bridge and walking path cutting through several acres of greenery near the intersection of Sunset Hills Road and Old Reston Avenue. A 54-page Washington & Old Dominion Trail Guide is for sale at Northern Virginia Regional Park Authority headquarters. Call 703/352-5900.

DIVERSIONS

Disc Dogs: Local dog lovers who spell fun F-r-i-s-b-e-e belong to the **National Capital Air Canines,** a club started in 1995 to bring together area dog-disc enthusiasts and educate folks about the sport of canine disc play. The club sponsors dog-disc training clinics, play days, competitions, and socials such as Discstock and Dogtoberfest. One favorite annual event is the Howl-O-Ween costume party. These folks do all sorts of fun stuff. You can see great photos and take a look at all the events lined up on their calendar—including a Dewey Beach trip this summer—at its website: www.discdog.com.

The motto among these dog-loving Frisbee throwers? "Where the fur comes to fly!" 703/532-0709.

Restaurants

Argia's: Tables in the back of the restaurant right near the parking lot make this a spot for a nice pasta dish with a glass of chianti, your dog discreetly away from the eating but still near you. 124 North Washington Street; 703/534-1033.

Fairfax Deli: Subs, subs, and more subs. Get a hot ham and cheese, and take it down the street to Jefferson Park, sit on a bench, and watch the golfers go at it. It's a very pleasant way to do lunch. 7173 Lee Highway; 703/532-5981.

Grevey's Restaurant and Sports Bar: You can let your dog sit just outside the large eating area outdoors—open in summer—at this casual sportsy hangout that offers salads, buffalo wings, burgers, and prime rib. Some servers here get antsy about the presence of dogs, while others love it. 8130 Arlington Boulevard; 703/560-8530.

FRANCONIA

Parks, Beaches, and Recreation Areas

23 Lee District Park 🐾 🐾

Another of the county's big and popular family-style parks, this is where you'll hear a lot more umpires barking out balls and strikes than dogs barking. Tennis courts, a mini train ride, swings and slides, horseshoes, basketball—even a farmer's market that puts out veggies on Friday afternoons are all here. For you and your dog? The broad nature trails winding downward from the large picnic and playground areas through well-used woods provide a refreshing walk; and since it has no other apparent use, the life-sized red-and-yellow train caboose attracts full-bladdered pups like a giant-sized fire hydrant.

From Old Town Alexandria, take Route 1 south 1.6 miles to South Kings Highway on the right; go about 1.5 miles, turn right on a road called The Parkway, left on Dorset Drive, then left on Telegraph Road. The park entrance is on the left opposite Rose Hill Drive. The park is open Monday–Thursday, 6 A.M.–9:30 P.M.; Saturday, 9 A.M.–6 P.M.; and Sunday, noon–8 P.M. 6601 Telegraph Road; 703/922-9841.

GREAT FALLS

Parks, Beaches, and Recreation Areas

24 Colvin Run Mill Park 🐾 ½ 🐕

This may be a four-star historic site, but we just can't give it high marks for dogs. Maybe it was the docent who scrunched up her nose and said, "Well, okay, you can bring him in. But you've got to clean up behind him!"

It is a pretty little place, built between 1802 and 1811. Listed with the National Register of Historic Places, it stands on what was once a major transportation artery from the fields of the Shenandoah Valley to the busy port of Alexandria. The miller's house, dairy barn, and general store are quintessentially quaint and well worth the visit. Just don't expect them to roll out the dog-treat-lined red carpet. "We had one get off its leash, and it got a duck," the woman said of a doggy incident that obviously has lingered here.

From the Capital Beltway (I-495) take Route 7 north 5.8 miles to Colvin Run Road on the right. You'll see the grand stone-built mill as it sits just off Route 7; the parking lot's another 100 yards or so on the left. Hours vary during the seasons so call first. 10017 Colvin Run Road; 703/759-2771.

25 Great Falls Grange Park 🐾 🐾 🐕

Keep traveling up Georgetown Pike toward the village of Great Falls and you'll find this family-type park. If your dog, who must be on a leash, is into reading novels, this is a really great park—there's a very small glass-walled library on the grounds. There's one baseball field, one small playground, one small picnic area, a historic old schoolhouse, and the Grange building, once the farmhouse for the surrounding land.

From the Capital Beltway, take the Georgetown Pike west (Route 193) for six miles, past Great Falls National Park and the Riverbend turnoff, to the entrance on the right. 9818 Georgetown Pike; 703/750-1598.

26 Great Falls National Park 🐾 🐾 🐾 🐾 🐕

Bikers and hikers mostly use these acres of trails, but dogs—who must be on a leash—can find a lot of relatively flat, woodsy walking on 14 miles of trails. The park is right on the Potomac, although well above the city—too far to see it, in fact. But the big draw is the magnificent waterfall. The 77-foot cascade shows off the Potomac in a rugged, rough-and-tumble way, unlike the more placid and commonly seen parts of the river downstream closer to the city. In places the river rages a quarter-mile wide and 50 feet deep. The currents are dangerous, and warnings are posted everywhere about staying well back off the slippery rocks near the water's edge. Pawpaw trees in the park are a big draw for foxes and possums. Considered one of the great birding places in Washington, it is especially fertile turf for viewing pileated woodpeckers.

From the Capital Beltway (I-495) take the Georgetown Pike (Route 193) north to Old Dominion Drive; turn right into the park entrance. There is a year-round entrance fee of $4 if you're not a county resident. The park is open 7 a.m. until dark daily, except Christmas Day; the visitor center is open 9 a.m.–6 p.m. and is located at the intersection of Old Dominion Drive and Old Georgetown Pike; 703/285-2966.

27 Riverbend Park 🐾 🐾 🐾

Lots of duck and goose poop everywhere made us think twice about just why we were worrying about scooping! Except for Chappy's fascination with the clumps, casual strolling required paying attention to sidestepping that issue. How much could it matter with that magnificent view of the Potomac River that flows so calmly right up to your toes?

This beautiful riverside area just up the river from Great Falls covers more than 400 acres of forest, meadows, ponds, and streams along the Potomac. Carolina wren, northern orioles, purple martins, and, of course, those ducks and geese, go about their business perfectly oblivious to you and your pooch meandering along the old root-ribbed paths that lead into rather remote terrain. Densely shaded by the usual varieties of arbors overhead, this is a woods of oak, beech, sycamore, even pawpaw and sassafras. You'll hear the owls and, if you're lucky, glimpse a hawk in flight. Ann thought the riverside trail was a bit too overpopulated by nature one midsummer visit just before the park closed at dusk. "A little too buggy for my taste," she observed, swatting just behind her knee.

On the deck behind the visitor center (which closes at 5 P.M.) are boards of information about the wildlife and way of life in the parkland. Clean facilities—restrooms, water fountain, picnic tables—are a plus, as is the oversized bowl of water marked "Pet Use," which sort of set the animal-friendly tone of the park. Still, it's Fairfax, so the leash rule rules.

But at the boat launch site near the visitor center, all eyes return frequently to the river. Across the breadth of the historic Potomac, the plush and overgrown other side seems barely different than it must have been two centuries ago when a young George Washington explored these grounds. County residents pay no entrance fee; $4 per vehicle otherwise.

From the Capital Beltway (I-495) take Exit 13 to the Georgetown Pike (Route 193) west and go about 4.5 miles to Riverbend Road; turn right and go 2.3 miles, then another right on Jeffrey Road to the visitor center. The nature center is a half mile farther. Watch for deer on the way at twilight. The grounds are open 7 A.M.–8 P.M. 703/759-9018.

28 Scotts Run Nature Preserve 🐾 🐾 🐾 ½

Easy to drive right by, this little wild thing alongside what's probably the chichi-est pike in the country (the Kennedys and all manner of rich Washingtonians—from politicians to media moguls—live around here) is all nature. Actually, the 385 acres seem to be preserved at the expense of the usual civilized comforts. Nothing much seems to be happening here, certainly no facilities. The "no" signs ban bicycles, horse riding, motorcycles, leashless dogs, and alcohol from the entrance on.

But the natural-born nature is plenty if that's the neck of the woods you're looking for. Soon as we got out of the car, Chappy spotted two other dogs down the creek going ankle deep (one of them unleashed). The other dog owner made his way to his car and left as if we had invaded his private dog patch.

Genetics make our Chappy more suited to the Himalayas, so he stuck to stone stepping instead of diving in. But, never mind him, 'cause this is a wet site for pups who are inclined to splishing and splashing. Up the attractive long-decked stairway are the rough-wooded upland trails that cut through an abundance of pawpaws, dogwoods, mountain laurels, hardwoods, and more than 100 species of wildflowers in season. The trails go on and on, largely unmarked, unmanicured, but not unmanageable, until they reach the beautiful palisade along the Potomac. An interesting stopping spot for bird-watchers hoping to catch both songbirds of the forest and waterfowl from the river awaits there. It's a great place for trying to tell the woods from the trees.

From the Capital Beltway (I-495) take Exit 13 to the Georgetown Pike (Route 193) west for about six miles and look for the parking lot on the right, opposite Swinks Mill Road and before the two-lane bridge. 7400 Georgetown Pike (Route 193); 703/324-8700.

Restaurants

Old Brogue: This splendid Irish pub doesn't allow humankind's best friend at its outdoor tables because the Great Fall's Village Centre green, where it's

---

EARMARK YOUR CALENDAR–OCTOBER

Bless Me, Father: All creatures great and small and in need of some spiritual guidance should head to the Saint Francis Episcopal Church in October for the **annual blessing of the animals.** It honors Francis of Assisi, the church patron saint and the patron saint of animals. Expect to bump into rats, bunnies, cats, ponies, horses, lambs, turtles, and birds as well. 9220 Georgetown Pike (Route 193); 703/759-2082.

---

located, is off-limits to dogs. But you can carry out anything on its menu—
from burgers to crab cakes to vermicelli. 760-C Walker Road; 703/759-3309.

HERNDON
Parks, Beaches, and Recreation Areas
29 Chandon Park 🐾 ½
Herndon Dogs Inc. has been working hard to make a dog park happen at this
park, which is already home to two tennis courts, a tot play area, and a softball
field. Following in the footsteps of sister group RestonDogs Inc., Herndon
Dogs has gotten it through the approval process and, at publication time of
this book, was raising money for a fence. There's plenty of open grassy space
here for it, although this park is bordered by buildings and homes and set just
next to a modest neighborhood. From Herndon Parkway, turn into Palmer
Drive. You'll dead-end at the park. 703/435-6868.

30 Fox Mill District Park 🐾
Four-footed friends can't go on the athletic fields here, and that's what most
of this park surrounding a school is. The encompassing woods are dense and
pretty, with but a single trail starting off at the parking area across from the
football field that provides a decent walk. Posted in front of A. Scott Crossfield
Elementary School is a sign: Health Notice—No Pets Allowed on School
Property.

From I-66, exit to Route 50 west and take the first of the West Ox Road exits;
turn right on Vale Drive and go 1.3 miles to Fox Mill Road; turn left and go
two miles to the park entrance on the right. The park area is open dawn–dusk
daily. 2791 Fox Mill Road; 703/324-8700.

31 Frying Pan Park 🔥
It's not a park; it's not a farm. So what is it? Both, sort of. There are animals here
and programs for people with the animals. While that may be informative and
fun for kids, it's not a great place for dogs. Take I-66 west to Exit 57; go two
miles and turn right on Fairfax County Parkway. After about four miles, turn
left on West Ox Road (Route 608). The park entrance is about a mile on the
right. 2709 West Ox Road; 703/437-9101.

32 Runnymede Park 🐾 🐾 🐾 ½
Herndon says its sister city is Runnymede, England, and thus the name of this
park. You might feel a bit like you're in Sherwood Forest. Pull off into the
funny little driveway, and it's easy to think there isn't much here. There are
some picnic tables, a few grills, and a wall of trees. Well, there are actually 58
acres of woodsy hiking to be had here. It's billed as a community nature park
and judging from the signs for about two dozen different bird photos posted
to alert you what to watch for in the woods, it really is nature first here. All

sorts of animals call the park home: deer, foxes, beavers, squirrels, opossums, groundhogs, skunks, bats, chipmunks, turtles, rabbits, mice, voles, and others. Park rangers warn of poison ivy.

There are easy-to-follow trails that lead you back into the quiet forest. You should probably pick up a map at the front station area, not only so that you can find your way in and out, but so that you can find the pawpaw patch and the vernal ponds, breeding habitats for salamanders and toads. There are other points of interest as well. The map brochure will also explain the 43 different species of trees in the park, and you'll also learn that Sugarland Run, a stream running through the park is part of the Potomac Basin drainage system. Because of the preserve here, it's especially important to leash your dog and clean up properly after him. The park is located on Herndon Parkway, between Elden Street and Dranesville Road. 703/435-6868.

33 Stanton Park 🐾 🐾 🐾

It's amazing to find this much woodland undeveloped, but Stanton Park is right on the edge of quite a parcel of untouched trees and overgrowth. Chappy spent a good half hour just going from tree to tree toward the front of the park. There are several dozen and that was fine with him. Keep walking back into the park, however, and you'll find a little playground, along with picnic tables and grills, and trails back into the woods. No doubt many an off-leash Lab or other kind of hunting dog with a need to run has enjoyed this rustic setting, but laws say that dogs should be leashed. From Herndon Parkway turn onto Monroe Street and turn right onto Third. All the woods on your right make up the park. 703/435-6868.

Restaurants

Moseley's Burgers: This inexpensive hamburger house is a hybrid between a sit-down fern bar restaurant and a fast-food shop. Like its owner, Mark Moseley, the ever-popular former Washington Redskins placekicker, it's casual here with a sporty decor. Cheeseburgers, chicken sandwiches, chili, crispy fries, and milk shakes dominate the menu—plus there's beer here. Chappy's impressed with the Moseley Burger—two patties of 100-percent Black Angus beef ground fresh daily, with two slices of cheese, bacon, lettuce, tomato, onion, and special Moseley sauce. And, though our pup's too young to remember Moseley's legendary last-second, game-winning field goal in a blizzard that won a NFC Championship game, Chap likes that Moseley is often on hand to chat with customers and sign autographs. Dogs aren't allowed inside, but out front there are about a dozen nice tables where folks eat with their pooches regularly. "We've got customers out there with the dogs all the time. Had one just this afternoon," said the amiable Moseley on unseasonably warm January evening. 496 Elden Street; 703/203-8803.

Places to Stay

Hawthorn Suites: Upscale one- and two-bedroom suites with a complimentary breakfast is what you're paying for here. The midweek room rate is around $119, but you will be charged a $150 pet fee. Not deposit. *Fee.* 467 Herndon Parkway, Herndon, VA 20171; 703/437-5000.

Holiday Inn Express–Herndon: Part of the big chain and everything you would expect of it, this hotel accepts dogs with a $25 deposit, but has no restriction on size, bad habits, or anything else. However, you will be put in a smoking room. The woods just at the back of the facilities are where they recommend you "curb your dog" when necessary. Rates run about $119. 485 Elden Street, Herndon, VA 20170; 703/478-9777.

LORTON

Parks, Beaches, and Recreation Areas

34 Gunston Hall 🐾 🐾

The home of George Mason, one of the nation's forefathers who wrote the Virginia Declaration of Rights and collaborated on the United States Constitution, this spectacularly preserved Georgian mansion was built in 1758. Today it is open as a historical site and hosts numerous festivals each year.

The long, green lawns in front of the mansion are dog friendly enough, but once past the ticket and information office and on to the formal boxwood gardens and outlook view of the river, dogs become suspect visitors, even on a leash. If your dog doesn't mind waiting outside, the home does offer a beautiful glimpse of gentrified life as it existed 200 years ago—and some of the finest colonial woodwork to be seen in America. Entry fee for adults is $5, for students grades 1–12, $1.50. The park is open daily.

Located on Mason Neck, take Route 1 south past Fort Belvoir; turn left on Gunston Hall Road and the entrance is on the left just around the bend from Pohick Bay Regional Park. 10709 Gunston Road, on Mason Neck; 703/550-9220.

35 Mason Neck State Park 🐾 🐾 🐾

Jutting out into the Potomac River 20 miles south of Washington is this untamed peninsula, the nation's first national wildlife refuge established specifically to protect the bald eagle. Originally used only for hunting and fishing by the Dogue Indians before colonists butted in and started logging, the park today remains thousands of acres of unspoiled and protected habitat for bald eagles, hawks, deer, foxes, bobcats, and more than 200 species of songbirds.

Several clearly marked trails—all of them a mile or less—are ready for excellent wandering through tall hardwood forests with your dog on a leash no longer than six feet—the state's strict regulation. From the parking area and visitor center, the Kane's Creek Trail loop on the north side of the park heads over to the picturesque Kane's Creek, where your dog might splash around, but this isn't much of a swimming park. You can pick up the Beach Trail at the creek for a low-tide walk but a damp high-tide one along Belmont Bay, where swimming is prohibited altogether because of boat traffic. A dizzying cliff denies easy access to the Beach Trail from the main parking area.

Water and restrooms at the visitor center and a few picnic nooks are the extent of facilities at this locale. The park is open daily, 8 A.M.–dusk. The entry fee for everyone is $2 on weekends, $1 on weekdays.

From Route 1 south, turn left just past Fort Belvoir on Gunston Hall Road; go past Pohick Bay Regional Park and about a mile beyond the entrance to Gunston Hall. The entrance to Mason Neck State Park will be on the right. 7301 High Point Road; 703/550-0362.

36 Occoquan Regional Park 🐾 🐾 🐾 🐾 🐾

If dogs had country clubs, this would be one of the classiest. Trees line the long entrance driveway that leads down to the 400-acre park area on the lovely Occoquan River, and right off, it feels like you're in Beverly Hills. Pristine, well-kept, wide-open lawns give it that country-club feeling, although a historic brick kiln right in the middle of the property reminds you of the history of the place and the women suffragists who were imprisoned here in the early 1900s. It's interesting, considering that Lorton Correctional Facility, one of the District of Columbia's troublesome prisons, is just up the street.

Check out the beautiful pavilions and gazebos for picnicking high above the river, and watch the boats heading to the Potomac. Or step closer to the boat ramp area on a walkway where you stroll right beside the river and look over at the historic town of Occoquan. (The word *occoquan* derives from a Dogue Indian word meaning "at the end of the water.")

Up the road a bit in the park, there is an area of baseball fields, a snack bar, more picnic areas, and horseshoe pits—all dog territory. Chappy chatted with a boxer and a standard poodle, while an Irish setter sat in the sun lazily watching his peers, as well as the guys hitting home runs on the field. All the dogs were on leashes. That's the rule. The park has a pleasant feeling to it just the same. The snack bar area was nice and clean, water plentiful, and it never felt crowded—although there were plenty of people around.

Take I-95 to Route 123 north; travel 1.5 miles to the park entrance on the right. The park is open March–November, 6 A.M.–dark. 703/690-2121.

37 Pohick Bay Regional Park 🐾 🐾 🐾 🐾 🐾

What separates this magnificent bayside park from all the rest is plain old attitude—dogs are welcome here, *very* welcome, and it shows. Fairfax County leash laws extend to these beautiful 1,000 acres, but the dog-friendly rangers in charge are flexible. "People bring their dogs here all the time," two of them told us while petting Chappy's buzzed summer cut. "They're supposed to be on leashes, but if it's not crowded, we're not strict on that. If they're not a nuisance, off-leash is not a problem."

People aren't allowed to swim in the clear waters of Pohick Bay, which forms where the Potomac and Occoquan Rivers converge. But dogs certainly can and do. Prime doggy beach is the shaded point at the far end of the boat launch parking lot where water-happy canines jump in and play in the shallows. The doggy stroke is happening everywhere here. Alongside the boat launch and nearby docks is another favorite spot. Don't be surprised to see dogs heading off for the deeper water in boats with their humans. If you didn't bring your own boat, you can rent a sailboat, johnboat (rowboat), or paddleboat to take your furry first mate out for a day on the bay.

About five miles of great hiking trails angle throughout the heavily wooded parkland and campgrounds that border on the bay.

Other lollygagging adventures abound: No matter their handicap, dogs aren't allowed on the 18-hole golf course, but miniature golf and disc golf aren't quite so snobby. Plenty of picnic tables and grills await dog-day afternoons near the mesmerizing ebb and flow of the glistening bay, and many folks cast out a fishing line in hopes of reeling in an errant bass for lunch. If the fish aren't biting, the snack bar makes a decent microwave hamburger and corndog, and its picnic tables are on the deck overlooking the bay. Huck Finn couldn't have found a better place to waste a sunny afternoon.

Of the 150 campsites, 100 have electrical outlets and all are well kept and scenic—tucked snugly into the thick woods that surround the bayside. There is a dump station, camp store, restrooms, washers, dryers, showers, and a giant swimming pool. All sites are first class and are available on a first-come, first-served basis. Reservations are accepted. Cost per night with electricity is $16.75. There is an additional fee of $1 per person per night for more than four at a site. The park is open all year, dawn–dusk.

Limited parking means gorgeous weekends pose a problem, so go early or go during the week. But go for sure. Nonresidents pay a day-use entry fee of $4 per car. From I-95, take Exit 163, Lorton Road east. Turn right on Armistead Road, and right on Route 1 south (Richmond Highway). Turn left on Gunston Road and go four miles, past the golf course on the left, to the main entrance also on the left. From Old Town Alexandria, the park is 13 miles south: Take Route 1 past Fort Belvoir and turn left on Gunston Road; go four miles, past the golf course on the left and to the main entrance also on the left, at 6501 Pohick Bay Drive. The park is open dawn–dusk daily. 703/339-6104.

Restaurants

Historic Occoquan, an 18th century town near the Lorton area, is your best bet for strolling into eateries that are dog friendly—not to mention the pleasant possibilities of antiquing in the fine old shops and gift stores in this dog-

EARMARK YOUR CALENDAR–MARCH

Gunston Hall Kite Festival: Flying high, this festival attracts round 3,000 folks with food vendors, a puppet show, and other activities—most with strings attached. Kind dogs on leashes are welcome; Gunston staffers recommend that excitable pooches wear muzzles because there are many small children running about. The festival takes place in mid-March at Gunston Hall, 10709 Gunston Road; 703/550-9220.

friendly marina town. As we walked along the main street, a young woman handed us a menu to a nearby restaurant and invited us—Chappy, too—to come sit in the patio and have something to eat. Either she was very dog friendly or business was that slow. It was probably some combination of the two, because otherwise cats rule in this town. Chappy came across four different felines wandering the streets. He also met one Labrador who seemed to be an owner of an interior design store and another dog who appeared to be heading out for a day of boating. Chappy was happy and so were we. Several places in Occoquan have allowed us to eat at their outdoor tables.

The Garden Kitchen: This is the place where we were invited in, so we went up and sat at a table. The restaurant is located in a 150-year-old house, and the garden is off the main drag so it's quiet. Pay particular attention to the home-baked goods. There's a long menu of fruit pies, cream pies, and cheesecakes. 404 Mill Street; 703/494-2848.

Bistro Belgique Gourmande: It was hard to believe we hadn't come across this place sooner, given Don's love of Belgian beers. It's been in historic Occoquan for 10 years and fills up quickly Thursday–Sunday. It's closed Monday–Wednesday. 302 Poplar Alley, B-2. 703/494-1180.

Toby's Cafe of Occoquan: A great offering of coffees and espresso, along with gourmet sandwiches and a perfect location right next to the music store Stringfellows makes this an excellent spot for taking a break from the window shopping. 201 Union Street; 703/494-1317.

Places to Stay

Pohick Bay Regional Park Campground: See Pohick Bay Regional Park, above.

MCLEAN

Parks, Beaches, and Recreation Areas

38 Lewinsville Park 🐾 🐾

Big ball fields are the draw here for the community, though the trails are well kept and feature fitness-course props in case you're a serial exerciser. Youth football, soccer, lacrosse, and baseball dominate this turf. There's open space aplenty, some tennis courts, too. McLean Day happens here every spring, and it's inviting for dogs because there's so much wide-open grassy space surrounding the fields—though leash laws are in effect. Modest in price and in size, the popular farmer's market that sets up shop in the parking lots Friday mornings during warm months has fresh goods from cantaloupes and peaches to fresh-cut flowers and garden plants.

From the Capital Beltway (I-495), take Route 123, Dolley Madison Boulevard, toward McLean, go one mile, and turn right on Great Falls Road. Turn left at Chain Bridge Road and the park entrance is on the right. The park is open dawn–dark. 703/324-8700.

39 Marie Butler Leven Preserve 🐾 ½

Not much more than a huge field surrounded with tall woods and a small parking lot, this almost seems like a preserve not just for wildlife in the neighborhood but also for basic green space amid the ongoing tract-mansion overdevelopment of once-woodsy McLean. For dog lovers who live or happen by this area, it's a little secret where many an off-leash dog romps illegally—but don't tell on them! It's a pleasant stop, a nice field to lie on your back in the grass as you did when you were a kid and watch the summer clouds roll along the blue skies. The park is located at the intersection of Kirby Road and Loch Raven Drive. It closes at dark. 703/324-8700.

40 McLean Central Park 🐾 🐾

Right in the middle of McLean, down a bit from the CIA and the neighborhood where the Kennedys have lived for years, this tasteful small community park is just a couple of blocks from the Gourmet Giant grocery store where you just might bump grocery carts with General Colin Powell, Caspar Weinberger, or even Pat Buchanan. It's a grassy, open park, with a little bridge over a little creek. The only bad thing about this park is that it sits right at a major intersection, so you will hear the cars zoom by. But if you are in McLean and in need of a park, this one will do just fine. Dogs must be on leashes.

From I-495 (the Capital Beltway), take Route 123 to McLean and go two miles to the Old Dominion Drive; the park is on the left of the intersection at 1468 Dolly Madison Boulevard. The park closes at dark. 703/324-8700.

Restaurants

Cafe Oggi: New-style Italian fascinates Chappy. What with *fettuccine al salmone e piselli* (homemade pasta with Scottish salmon and peas) and the *osso buco di capretto* (lamb shanks in a saffron and vegetable sauce), who can blame him? So if you want spaghetti with tomato sauce, go find Chef Boyardee. Here you get sea scallops served over spinach with garlic and olive oil or a minestrone that'll perk you up when you're under the weather. Call in ahead or wait to take the order out, because your dog won't know what to do with the folded cloth napkins inside. 6671 Old Dominion Road; 703/442-7360.

Cafe Taj: Highly rated Indian cuisine and a friendly atmosphere make this a great stop in summer when the outdoor patio tables are set up. They are far enough apart that if it's not too busy, you and your dog shouldn't bother a soul—though the scent of the smoky tandoori chicken might have him licking his chops a little loudly. Hush, Chappy! Carryout is also available if you want to take your dog and dinner the half mile down Old Dominion Road to McLean Central Park and relax on a park bench. 1379 Beverly Road; 703/827-0444.

Corkie's: A neighborhood hangout, Corkie's has been in business for years. White plastic outdoor tables and chairs make for a nice eating spot, whether on warm summer evening or a comfortable Sunday brunch. Just park the pooch nearby at your feet. 6226 Old Dominion Drive; 703/533-5880.

Forbidden City: The most popular Chinese restaurant in McLean, it does a hopping carryout business that you and your dog can buy into easily enough. For simple gastronomy, its lemon chicken is prepared lightly. Showing his unadventuresome side, Chappy likes the crispy orange beef. We return regularly for the double-cooked pork—and because the owner is one of the nicest guys around. 6641 Old Dominion Drive, in McLean Square; 703/821-9000.

Italian Deli: The friendly folks who run this place also happen to make great subs. Enjoy a hero in the sun at the scattered white plastic tables out front, or get it to go. 6813 Elm Street; 703/506-1136.

Someplace Special–Gourmet Giant: Picnics for two or more include 15 different menus, ranging from $8.95 to $18.95 per person. It's best to order 24 hours in advance, however. Chappy gets miffed a bit because he's not allowed inside—but, hey, it's a grocery store! An *amazing* grocery store. At the intersection of Chain Bridge Road and Laughlin Avenue; 703/448-0800.

Starbucks: Right in the middle of McLean, this Starbucks sees nonstop action. But, as with all Starbucks shops, the tables out front are very dog-friendly. 1438 Chain Bridge Road; 703/821-1033.

At another location, this neighborhood-hangout Starbucks sits in the middle of the Chesterbrook Shopping Center and is an excellent pit stop for commuters and dogs, alike. There are only a few small tables out front, but an empty one is a welcome relief when you're out and about. 6214 Old Dominion Drive; 703/241-9480.

Three Pigs of McLean: Excellent vinegary shredded pork barbecue sandwiches, ribs, and chicken to go. 1394 Chain Bridge Road; 703/356-1700.

Panera Bread: One of several Panera restaurants in Northern Virginia, this is a new favorite, offering a nice respite from the shopping craziness of Route 7. The food is fresh and delicious, whether you opt for one of the fresh soups, maybe served in a sourdough bread bowl, or one of the salads, like our

EARMARK YOUR CALENDAR–MAY

McLean Day Festival: McLean Day is always fun and lively, but especially so on sunny days in mid-May. This festival, which has been going on annually for more than 80 years, is worth marking on the calendar. It's held on the big fields at Lewinsville Park in McLean, where you can sit and eat the bratwurst and knockwurst they grill, listen to oompah bands, and even see how your dog measures up at the dog show that happens three times during the afternoon. Booths with artwork and crafts are everywhere, as are political booths with local politicians, cheesy commercial booths, and local retailers giving away free trinkets with their logos on them. Carnival-type rides keep kids busy. The day kicks off at 9 A.M. with the annual Old Firehouse 8K run. The McLean Community Center can give you more information at 703/790-0123.

When you call the McLean Community Center, ask about the **Kids Krazy Dog Show** usually held in April. Dog owners in grades one through six show off their dogs in seven classes of competition. It's a hoot.

---

favorite—The Fandango with orange slices, walnuts, gorgonzola cheese and fat-free raspberry dressing. Chappy, of course, hopes for tidbits of turkey, bacon, or roast beef from one of the "signature sandwiches." You can sit inside by the fire; Chappy always takes a table outside. At the Pike 7 Plaza, 8365 Leesburg Pike; 703/556-3700.

Places to Stay

Best Western–Tyson's Westpark Hotel: Dogs are A-okay here, which is nice. One smelly stipulation: You have to stay in a room designated for smokers. Rates are around $165. 8401 Westpark Drive, McLean, VA 22102; 703/734-2800.

Comfort Inn–Tysons Corner: Dogs are allowed here, but there is a one-time $25 charge, on top of a room rate that's in the neighborhood of $89. 1587 Spring Hill Road, Vienna, VA 22182; 703/448-8020.

Residence Inn by Marriott: Sure, you can stay here with your dog. Just be ready to pay the astronomical $150 cleaning fee *and* a $5 pet fee. All the 96 rooms are suites, and the room rate is about $199. 8616 Westwood Center Drive, Vienna, VA 22182; 703/893-0120.

MOUNT VERNON

Parks, Beaches, and Recreation Areas

41 Belle Haven Park and Wildlife Preserve 🐾 🐾 🐾 🐾

A cozy little blanket-sitting zone, this park is one of the larger of several unassuming but high-volume riverside areas along the Mount Vernon Bike Trail, which extends 17 miles along the Virginia shoreline of the Potomac River, from the historic home of the Father of the Nation northward to the Key Bridge in Rosslyn. Bikers zoom by, some faster than the posted 15 mph speed limit, so you've got to take care crossing the path itself. This is a stop-and-start point for in-line skaters and joggers as well, with bathroom and parking facilities. But for all that commotion, it's lazy daze here: Whiffle ball, Frisbee, and fishing are about as energetic as it gets. Rugged rocks along the shoreline make it difficult for dogs to take dips, and they're supposed to be leashed anyway. So lots of dogs just hang out with loved ones for the breezes off the water.

From Mount Vernon, go north on the George Washington Memorial Parkway about six miles and watch for signs on the right just past the intersection of Belle View Boulevard. The park is open dawn–dusk. 703/768-0018.

42 Fort Hunt Park 🐾 🐾 ½

With tormentingly popular picnic grounds and recreation area six miles south of Old Town Alexandria where humans with nothing better to do while away hot summer days, Fort Hunt Park can get pretty packed. Traffic can be exasperating occasionally on weekends—especially when the old park is hosting one of its free summer Saturday concerts. In cold winter months, the grassy uplands surrounding the remnants of the Civil War fortifications are largely barren. Located at Sheridan Point along the Potomac River, the most usable bulk of this unexpectedly large and impressive park has baseball fields and picnic sites with grills and acre after acre of wide-open fields. The park ranger presence is of the mounted sort, with stables not far from the entrance. As close to the gorgeous Potomac as this spot is, the entirety of the park unfortunately is well inside the Mount Vernon Memorial Parkway and not near the river.

From Mount Vernon, drive north 2.5 miles on the George Washington Memorial Parkway, and look for the sign to the park. The park is open dawn–dusk. For more information, call the George Washington Memorial Parkway office at 703/285-1925.

43 George Washington's Grist Mill 🐾 🐾

Lest we forget, the first president of the United States was a gentleman farmer, and here's where George ground his wheat and corn into flour—even during the years of his presidency. Dogs aren't allowed inside the historic excavation and recreation of the five-floor mill, but the lovely shaded areas on the mill's side of the Dogue Run make for a nice roadside respite, but the water's a bit silty for wading. The six-foot-or-shorter leash law is in effect in this state park.

From the Beltway (I-495), take Rout 1 South (Richmond Highway) to Old Mount Vernon Road (Route 235). Turn left and then go left again onto the Mount Vernon Memorial Highway. The entrance is on the left. The park is open 10 A.M.–6 P.M., Saturday, Sunday, and holidays. 5514 Mount Vernon Memorial Highway; 703/780-3383 or 703/550-0960.

44 Mount Vernon Estate and Gardens 🐾 🐾 🐾 🐾

By George! Who would've thought those preservationist-minded ladies in the Mount Vernon Ladies' Association of the Union who went to all the trouble over the years to restore and run this historic property of George Washington would allow dogs on the property? Well, they do. You can't take your dog inside any of the buildings that are so totally founded in the founding of this nation they'll make your spine tingle. And you've got to keep the pooch on his leash at all times. There are plenty of wide-open spaces here—more than 30 acres of beautiful gardens and wooded grounds and a good many historic outdoor curiosities.

"No estate in United America is more pleasantly situated than this," Washington wrote once in a letter, and you'll undoubtedly agree, as Chappy did. Look in some of the field buildings as you work your way down the path toward the river. The carriage house has an open front and is quite a sight; so is the smokehouse with the mouth-watering scent of salty Virginia country ham inside. The re-creation of Washington's 16-sided barn was just recently completed. The newest addition on these sacred American grounds is the Forest Trail that leads a quarter mile through the woods past the general's cobble quarry, a Native American site that predates the estate, and a bridge over a steep ravine.

Farther down the peaceful older path with its canopy of old trees overhead, you will find the tomb of George and Martha, where every morning at 10 A.M. you and the dog can reverently witness the tombside ceremony. The path ends at the edge of the Potomac—an inspiring site that moved Washington in his day and will move you now.

Take George Washington Memorial Parkway eight miles south of Alexandria to the entrance. The park is open daily and all holidays; September–March, 9 A.M.–5 P.M.; April–August, 8 A.M.–5 P.M.; November–February, 9 A.M.–4 P.M. Adults, $9; senior citizens, $8.50; children 6–11 (and must be accompanied by an adult), $4.50. Mount Vernon Ladies' Association; 703/780-2000; website: www.mountvernon.org.

45 River Farm Garden Park 🐾 1/2 🐾

Located between Old Town Alexandria and Mount Vernon, River Farm was one of the original five farms on George Washington's Mount Vernon estate. But it's the gardens that are a big draw, as this is also home to the American Horticultural Society. They don't welcome dogs with open arms here, but there is a walking-tour map that leads around the beautiful grounds, and as long as your dog is on a leash and not trampling through the flowers, there's no problem in visiting. The park is open Monday–Friday, 8:30 A.M.–5 P.M.; it's open on weekends only when there's a special event. 7931 East Boulevard Drive, Alexandria. The park is halfway between Old Town and Mount Vernon on the George Washington Memorial Highway. 703/768-5700.

OAKTON

Parks, Beaches, and Recreation Areas

46 Blake Lane Park 🐾 🐾 🐕

This was Fairfax County's first official dog park. It's just a large dirt-covered, fenced-in square, but the dogs were having a good old time on the cool January day we stopped by. Chappy made his way around the edges of the park, checking out the 14 other dogs who were there. Yoshi, a German shepherd, was friendly, and two little Wheaten terriers were scampering around after tennis balls. One drawback: not much shade. The limit is 25 dogs, which happens easily in summer. To get to the park take Route 66 west, exit at Route 123 and head north, turn right on Jermantown Road. Stay on Jermantown as it becomes Blake Lane. Turn right at the second right onto Bushman Drive. The park is on the left. Park on the street and walk across the expansive grassy open park until you see the fenced-in dog park. It's open from dawn until a half hour past dusk. 703/759-2824.

Restaurants

Famous Dave's BBQ: Arguments arose over whether the Georgia chopped pork sandwich was the best or the Texas beef brisket sandwich was better. And that's not even factoring in Dave's award-winning spareribs. There is a McDonald's and a Starbucks in the shopping center where Dave's sits, not far from Blake Lane Park. But we can't imagine why you'd go to either of those when mouth-watering barbeque can be easily carried out from this Oakton favorite. Dare you to try the Devil's Spit sauce! (Although the Rich and Sassy regular stuff is dark, rich, and delicious.) 2910 Chain Bridge Road. 703/281-3800.

RESTON

One of the nation's premier "new towns," this completely planned community five miles east of Dulles Airport was started in 1962 and now encompasses within its more than 11 square miles several clustered single-home and townhouse neighborhoods surrounded by wide-open green areas, four lakes, meadows and serene spaces, golf courses, recreation areas, and 60 miles of walking and biking tails. At the center of it, as one might expect of a planned place, is the Reston Town Center—a dog-friendly hub of activity. It's neither mall nor strip center, but a walking piazza of shops and restaurants that lends itself perfectly to window-shopping with the dog and relaxing over a lunch or dinner outdoors at any of several inviting restaurant patio sections. More than 40 stores line the red-brick streets and sidewalks that converge on the large and delightfully complex Mercury Fountain.

Parks, Beaches, and Recreation Areas

47 Baron Cameron Park 🐾 🐾 🐕

For years this was park was really focused on baseball and soccer. Now the rolling hills are home to a leash-free dog park. Since the first edition of this book, RestonDogs Inc. (website: www.restondogs.org) has been hard at work to make this happen. The fenced-in area offers two nice places for dogs to romp off-leash, one for small dogs and the other for the big boys. The rims of the fields are grassy and fine for dog walking—on a leash, of course—while catching a couple of innings. Once in a while, someone's flying a model airplane over on the model airfield, which is good for a few minutes of amusement.

From I-495, take Exit 10 to the Dulles Toll Road; go about nine miles and exit onto the Reston Parkway north and take a right turn. Drive 1.2 miles and turn right on Baron Cameron Avenue. The park is a mile on the left. The entrance is at the intersection of Baron Cameron Avenue and Wiehle Avenue. 703/437-9580.

48 Lake Fairfax Park 🐾 🐾 🐾 🦴

RestonDogs is also working to open a second fenced-in dog exercise area here at this giant park complex. The 20-acre lake, 446 acres of rolling hills, paddleboats, fishing, picnicking, cross-country skiing, miniature train, and carousel all make this a user-friendly place to blow away an afternoon—and on busy summer weekends, often a little too friendly. It tends to get so packed with people here that dogs start taking a back seat to big groups of picnickers, constant traffic, and loud boom boxes.

Once you've found your parking spot, head up toward the bathroom and ticket office complex. That's where the best view of the lovely lake is. To get away from the action, you can cross over the lake and onto the campground side of the park where walking by the water's edge can be much more peaceful. No swimming in the lake, but on the other side your dog can come real close, maybe even get his feet wet. Or rent a paddleboat and take your dog for a ride away from it all.

There are 136 campsites here, all of them available by reservation, 70 of them with electrical hookups—all of them well to the back of the park, away from the crowds and ruckus that descends here on hot weekends. Some campsites are equipped for recreational vehicles; most are set up for tents and cost $12.54 a night for up to four people. Seven people are allowed per site; additional people cost $2.09 per person per night. Dogs are free but must be kept on a leash. Each site has a picnic table and grill and is close to restrooms, showers, and water spigots. You can camp here from mid-March to the end of November.

Take Route 7 west; turn left on Baron Cameron Avenue and look quickly for Lake Fairfax Drive on the left. The park is open 7 A.M.–dusk, every day. 1400 Lake Fairfax Drive. 703/471-5415.

49 Washington & Old Dominion Regional Park 🐾

Walking distance to the south of Reston Town Center are some grassy knolls that border along part of this end of the Washington & Old Dominion Railroad Regional Trail, a stretch of forest and bicycle/walking pathway that extends across Northern Virginia. The greenery along the trail gets pretty narrow here, however, and the bikes rule, so be careful if you venture this way with your dog on his leash. The entrance to the Washington & Old Dominion Regional Park is about a quarter of a mile south of the town center along the Reston Parkway. 703/352-5900.

Restaurants

Bread & Chocolate: Stop in this tiny walk-through and pick up a chicken sandwich on French bread, a latte, or maybe a croissant and head out to the fountain to sit and enjoy the day. 11928 Market Street; 703/476-4060.

Lee's Homemade Ice Cream and Deli: Behind the majestic fountain is this old-fashioned ice cream shop where milk shakes aren't a forgotten art and sandwiches are made to order. Three little outside tables or the stone benches along the courtyard make for a nice pit stop on hotter days. 11917 Freedom Drive; 703/471-8902.

Panera Bread: The Panera chain is definitely one of our new favorite restaurants. Order a bowl of clam chowder and a half a Sierra turkey sandwich or maybe a Fandango salad and then sit out at the tables and watch the skaters at the ice rink. Soup even comes served in a sourdough bread bowl, if you like to have your dish and eat it, too. In Reston Town Center; 703/437-6022.

Places to Stay

Lake Fairfax Campground: See Lake Fairfax Park, above.

Residence Inn–Herndon: The rooms are all suites—meaning they come with a full kitchen along with a living room. But here they stick you for $100 for "cleaning" and an additional $6 pet fee per night, beyond the approximately $149 per room. *Grrrr!* 315 Elden Street, Herndon, VA 22070; 703/435-0044.

DIVERSIONS

Social Scene: If you're looking for fun things to do with your dog, **RestonDogs** is the group you want to join. Activities put on by the group include monthly group dog walks, Bark Hour (a social hour for dogs and their humans), the Toys for Pups drive (collecting toys for Fairfax County Shelter Animals), and participation in events such as the Pet Fiesta and Taste of the Town at Reston Town Center. There's a nominal fee to join the group ($15 for an individual, $20 for a household), and you'll get the group newsletter, along with an invitation to the annual picnic. Check it out at www.RestonDogs.org or leave a message at 703/400-4460.

Summerfield Suites by Windham: Yes, dogs are welcome and there's even a big field in front of the hotel. But ouch! A $150 nonrefundable pet fee is attached to the stay, which runs somewhere around $149 for a suite. 13700 Coppermine Road, Herndon, VA 20171; 703/713-6800.

SPRINGFIELD

Parks, Beaches, and Recreation Areas

50 Lake Accotink Park 🐾 🐾 ½ 🐶

Crowded and busy was the overwhelming feeling at this park. There *is* water—the lake is a nice getaway, and paddleboating and fishing go on all the time at this popular spot. The small beach area also has a mini-golf course, snack bar, and playground, as well as volleyball courts crammed in next to it, so it just doesn't feel like some of the other county parks that are much more expansive. It's still head and shoulders above neighborhood parks. There's a dam over which the water flows, so the sound and look are unusual.

We didn't see a single dog the day we went, but lots of traffic showed up on foot and in cars. No reason *not* to go with a dog, however. Trails lead into the woods for nice hikes in the three-mile range.

From the Capital Beltway, take Exit 5 to Braddock Road east; go a half mile and turn right at Heming Avenue to the park's rear entrance. Or, take I-95 south to Old Keene Mill Road west; turn right on Backlick Road and left on Highland Avenue to the main entrance. The park is open daily, 6:30 A.M.–7:30 P.M. 703/569-0285.

51 South Run Park 🐾 🐾 ½ 🐕

This is one of the newest of Fairfax's official off-leash dog parks and it is usually packed with pooches. Lorton Dogs Inc. raised the funds needed to set up the one-acre play yard, tucked into the vast 192 acres of parkland here, is very popular.

The day we visited, a sunny February Sunday morning, we encountered 12 dogs before we had even gotten to the dog park. And it's a short walk from the parking lot to the dog exercise area! The lot itself is under some large electrical wires, not that it matters, but you'll know you're close when you see those.

The action in the dog park was playful and rowdy. We saw a dachshund heading in as we were heading out and were a little worried about him. Big dogs rule, and it's understandable, since big dogs need the area in which to run. Chappy, being the, er, wimp, okay, gentle, dog that he is, decided he was much happier ambling down Spartan Trail, which veers off to the left from the dog park. It was quiet. It was peaceful. It was a dirt-and-sand pathway and easy on the paws. We saw another dog owner leave the dog park and go off-leash down in this area as well saying it was just a "little too much" in the dog park for his shy and well-behaved dog.

The park can be found by taking Beltway (I-495) Exit 54, Braddock Road West. Turn left on Burke Lake Road and another left at Lee Chapel Road. When you reach Route 7100, the Fairfax County Interconnector Parkway, go left again. South Run Recreation Area will be on the right at 7550 Reservation Drive. 703/866-0566.

Places to Stay

Comfort Inn–Springfield-South: This dog-accommodating chain hotel accepts dogs under 20 pounds only. Rates vary but expect to pay about $95 a night, including breakfast. 6560 Loisdale Court, Springfield, VA 22150; 703/922-9000.

Hampton Inn–Springfield: This cozy, modest hotel takes dogs, but they can't be left alone and should be kept in carriers in the room, the front desk says. It's across the street from the Springfield Mall, which is good for shopping, but there aren't any nearby parks to walk to. Rates run about $69 per night. 6550 Loisdale Court, Springfield, VA 22150; 703/924-9444.

Motel 6: Any size dog is allowed here with no extra fee. Yippee! A double room is about $55. This is one of the few hotels that hasn't risen in price since the first edition of the book. 6868 Springfield Boulevard, Springfield, VA 22150; 703/644-5311.

EARMARK YOUR CALENDAR

Sink and Swim: Some events at Lake Accotink are more fun for kids and families, but you can bring your dog along. For example, the annual **Cardboard Boat Regatta** at Lake Accotink Park is nothing like anything you've ever been to. Even Chappy recognized how odd the scene gets as people try to float boats they've made from cardboard—with them inside! All competitors attempt to finish the course laid out on the lake, which is entertainment enough even for a cosmopolitan pooch like Chappy. There are also the usual craft displays and booths, food kiosks, carnival rides, and funky stage entertainment when soggy cardboard gets tiresome. The competition usually occurs the last weekend of May or the first weekend of June, both Saturday and Sunday. Admission is free but there's a nominal parking fee.

There are other events at Lake Accotink *just* for your dog, such as the **Boneyard Hunt** for dogs, held at Halloween. Dogs must be leashed and friendly, but you are welcome to take a short walk to the "boneyard" where treats are hidden for your dog to discover. Admission was $4 the last time it was held. For more information, call 703/569-0285 or 703/321-7082.

VIENNA

Parks, Beaches, and Recreation Areas

52 Meadowlark Gardens Regional Park 🐾 🐾

It's a shame dogs are only allowed to walk the perimeter trails of this magnificent, elegant park. Like a rich French country estate, the grounds are stately and perfectly manicured. Blooming sprays of color-coordinated flowers hang from concrete baskets on top of pillars in front of the information center, which is filled with light and even has a fireplace.

Three sparkling lakes surrounded by weeping cherry trees as well as daylilies, irises, hostas, lilacs, crab apples, and an herb garden are the center-pieces of this 95-acre park. The hostas and daylilies are the largest in the area. It's a perfect place for weddings (which it is often used for), but there's no marriage of dogs and park here. Too bad.

From I-495, take Exit 10B to Route 7 and head west. Go about three miles and turn left on Beulah Road; drive one mile to the park entrance on the right. The park is open year-round. 9750 Meadowlark Gardens Court; 703/255-3631.

53 Nottoway Park and Hunter House 🐾 🐾

This is a perfectly nice 84-acre park with a historic home that is often rented out for weddings and other events. There are shady areas for picnics. Signs say no dogs are allowed on athletic fields, but that's okay because there are

plenty of other roaming-around spaces, including nicely paved trails. Leash laws are in effect, of course.

From the Capital Beltway, take I-66 (Exit 9) heading west, take a right on Nutley Street (Route 243) heading north towards Vienna, and then turn left on Courthouse Road. The park entrance will be on the left. 9601 Courthouse Road; 703/938-7532.

Restaurants

Aaranthi: Call first on your way to a park and pick up the nicely prepared traditional Indian dishes here or go for the selection of kabobs. 409 Maple Avenue East in Danor Plaza; 703/938-0100.

Bread and Kabob: Marinated, juicy chunks of lamb are a delight here, served with the biggest pita bread we've ever seen. A favorite with locals, this little eatery is a perfect pit stop. 126 Maple Avenue West; 703/255-9696.

Cenan's Bakery: Some people think this is the best bakery in northern Virginia. See for yourself when you try one of their loaves of fresh breads, muffins, cakes, scones or bagels, or even their nice gourmet sandwiches. You can even pick up coffee and/or a nice bottle of wine. Nice little metal tables out front on the sidewalk of the shopping center make it easy to sup with your pup. 122 Branch Road SE, just off Maple Avenue; 703/242-0070.

Italian Gourmet: Pack up a picnic from this place and browse for pasta while you're at it. Then go next door to the Pie Gourmet or even walk down to the Dog World Pet Salon or the Vienna Animal Hospital. They're all tucked into the same shopping center here in the heart of Vienna. 505 Maple Avenue West; 703/938-4141.

Pie Gourmet: Cream, custard, and 35 different kinds of fruit pies can be found in this delectable bakery. Chappy's favorite is always Key lime, although he prefers a graham cracker crust. 507 Maple Avenue West; 703/281-7437.

Tequila Grande: Maybe it's a sunny Saturday morning, and you're on your way to the park. Or maybe you've just been to the park. Stop here for breakfast, lunch, or dinner. The sunrise quesadilla puts scrambled eggs into a tortilla with cheese, potatoes, onions, tomatoes, green peppers, and cilantro. Yum. The lunch and dinner platters are pretty much the usual Mexican concoctions. There's an array of enchiladas, burritos and fajitas from which to choose. When we last stopped in, the service was great and everyone was friendly. Of course, we're talking about getting it to go if you're there with your dog, because they don't have any way to accommodate pets. Chappy's always more than happy to eat his chicken taco at home. 444 Maple Avenue West; 703/255-5933.

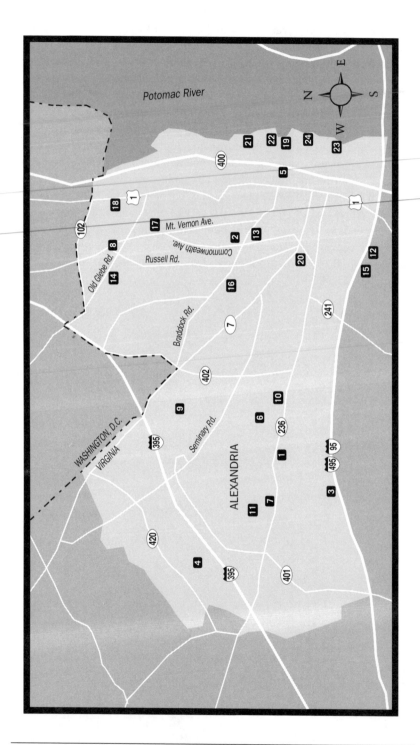

9 ALEXANDRIA

Under Virginia state law, Alexandria is its own incorporated city, and it is filled with dog parks. From the canyons of high-rise apartments around Duke and Van Dorn and Seminary, to the shaded neighborhoods whether ritzy or modest to the quaint and upscale pooch paradise of Old Town, Alexandria offers more dog areas per square foot than any other place in the area. In addition to the five fenced dog parks, there are un-fenced designated off-leash dog exercise areas. Old Town is the quaint and cobblestoned historic city that has always been particularly dog friendly, but now all of Alexandria can boast of a place for a dog to play.

ALEXANDRIA

Parks, Beaches, and Recreation Areas

1 Ben Brenman Park 🐾🐾🐾 1/2

Wow. This is a vast, beautiful place for man or beast, and there are almost always some of both here. A pond is at the center of the park and paths encircle the water. Lining the path are tall Victorian-looking streetlights. Those, with the gazebo out in the middle of the water, and the flocks of birds

DIVERSIONS

The **Animal Welfare League of Alexandria** is a dynamic, active group with special events happening almost every month. There's a Saint Patrick's Day dog show at Market Square. There's the Doggy Bone Hunt and Easter Parade in April when more than 50 dogs snatch up more than 1,000 gold foil–wrapped bones in five minutes. Dogs who've been adopted from the shelter regroup for a reunion in May. These pet photo opportunities help to raise money year-round.

Perhaps most popular are the annual Canine Games. Got a budding Mary Lou Retton dog? The Arnold Schwarzenegger of pooches? At the end of the summer, the league puts on these howlingly fun Olympics. Events include a steeplechase, obstacle course, and two water retrieval venues, along with the more traditional Frisbee, dog bowling, obedience, dog tricks, ball catch, and more. Music, refreshments, and pet-related vendors are on hand, along with a vet to answer questions and a photographer if you want to take home a souvenir photo. All dogs must be on a nonretractable leash at all times. Chappy has yet to enter this (like there's any event he could do!), but it's really popular and fun—as both spectator sport and competitive games.

Also in summer, the League puts on the **Absolutely Awesome Animal Awareness Camp of Alexandria.** No, it's not a place to send your pooch for a couple of weeks of extra-special fun, but it *is* a place to send your kids, if you have any of the human variety, to help them understand and appreciate animals. Several sessions are offered each summer. There is also a pet therapy program in which the League looks for volunteers to take their caring canines to visit elderly people in nursing homes. The league provides all necessary training, and the dog has to pass a formal evaluation and good citizenship test before getting its first patient.

The League also sponsors other events throughout the year, like the **Pet Fête,** a jazz reception, dinner, and silent auction right at the Holiday Inn of Old Town. The group is very active and would love to include you, whether you want to attend or volunteer in some way. To reach the League, call 703/838-4774; special events number, 703/838-4387; website: www.alexandriaanimals.org.

---

swooping over the water, make this a very picturesque place. But wait, there's more. Follow the paved path around the water or around the baseball field to a bridge in the back of the land. Cross over the water and you'll see volleyball areas and a fenced-in dog park. On the quiet and unusually warm wintry day we visited, we only found one dog there. She was hoping for a friend. Train tracks are right next to the park and although we weren't there to witness it, we were told that they do pass by and they can be very loud. Between the beauty of the park in general and the fenced-in leash-free area, this is easily one of the best parks around. From Duke Street near Van Dorn Street, follow the signs that lead straight into the park. 703/838-4343.

2 Braddock Road and Commonwealth Park ½ 😮 🐕

Be careful! This triangular patch of brown grass on the corner of this busy intersection worries us. It is an official off-leash exercise area, but you must have excellent confidence in your dog because it's trafficky here and there isn't much of a park. We counted five trees and a sewer drainage ditch that could swallow a Yorkie. At the southeast corner of Braddock Road and Commonwealth. 703/838-4343.

3 Cameron Run Regional Park 🧍 🐾

This isn't a spacious and grassy park for dogs; it's a water park for humans that happens to permit pets, too. And it's fairly costly. For the $10-per-adult and $9-per-child admission fee, the main attraction is the giant wave pool—where humans can pretend they're at the beach riding or dodging waves. Two smaller swimming pools with slides and the high water slides lure lines of kids of all ages. Your dog will be too hot tied up outside the pool area waiting for you while you swim, so don't even consider doing that.

If you want to visit this park system cash cow, leave your dog at home, we're sorry to say. Exceptions would be if your dog's a baseball fan (or at least your fan) and is willing to watch you take cuts in the batting cages, or if your dog

EARMARK YOUR CALENDAR

Scottish Walk: Put on your kilt. Get out the tam o'shanter. One of the biggest events of the winter is the Scottish Walk, held each year on the first weekend in December. It's a sight to behold as one Scottish clan after the other marches down Saint Asaph Street. Though it can be chilly, you'll see plenty of kilts in the parade, plus several Scottish breeds of dogs marching right along. The Scottish terriers often wear little plaid coats. You'll probably never see more Scottish deerhounds in one place at the same time. We always keep an ear open for musket fire shot off by Scottish soldiers who stop, reload, and fire periodically along the parade route. Chappy doesn't like noisy surprises and neither do the boys. Find your spot along the parade route by 10 A.M. 703/838-4200.

You can also take the high road or the low road and let your pup enjoy the **Virginia Scottish Games** that display the dances, athletic competitions, and culture of Scotland. Dogs really can learn to love the bagpipes. The two-day event usually takes place the last weekend in July at the grounds of Episcopal High School, 3901 West Braddock Road; call the Alexandria city hotline at 703/838-4200.

will caddie while you play a round of miniature golf. The batting cages and miniature golf area have separate entrances from the water complex and offer some minimal shade. The picnic zone beyond them is not remarkable and, because of the summertime crowds, takes a beating. It's small, crowded, and offers nothing more than some picnic tables for under-the-skies dining with everyone else and their cousin. The emphasis here is people, people, people—dogs are just along for the ride.

From the Beltway (I-495) take Van Dorn Street (Exit 3) north, and turn right on Eisenhower Avenue. Drive about a mile to the park on the left. The park is open 10 A.M.–8 P.M. most of the summer. The pool is closed on Labor Day. For more information, call 703/960-0767 (pool); 703/960-5714 (batting cages); 703/960-8719 (miniature golf); 703/352-5900 (picnic shelter rentals).

4 Chambliss Street Park 🐾 🐾 ½

As far as we could tell, the name of this park is actually Glen Hills Park, but the city of Alexandria lists it on the dog exercise area runs sheet at "Along Chambliss Street south of tennis courts." The park is quite pretty. Set into a big sinkhole, there is a wide-open grassy area and playground, edged in woodsy walking space. Chappy could have spent quite a bit of time here, exploring the edges while the kids played on the equipment. That would have been on a leash, however. (Chappy, not the kids.)

There is, however, also an off-leash dog exercise area that is marked with paw print posts. Best to stick to that area so that parents won't get upset with unleashed dogs running around. You know how that is. Take Beauregard Street to the point at which Chambliss veers off to the right. Follow it to the end where you'll see the sign for Glen Hills Park. 703/838-4343.

5 Chetworth Park 🐾 🐾 🐕

Tucked back into a neighborhood of modest but charming stone row houses, Chetworth Park is a little diamond in the rough. The wooden fence that surrounds the park is covered with ivy in places, giving the area the feel of someone's backyard. The little gardens inside the park add to the notion that this is a place tended with loving care. A playground sits in the back but juts out into the middle of the dog park. It's surrounded by a chain link fence. At this park, the kids are corralled; the dogs run free. The streets to Chetworth are narrow. From Route 1 going into Old Town, turn right on Bashford Lane, take a quick right on Michigan Avenue and then follow the street less than a mile to a left on Chetworth Place. It's a dead end; the park is on the left. 703/838-4343.

6 Chinquapin Park 🐾 🐾 🐕

For a modest-sized park, this popular spot handles a big checklist of outdoor activities—basketball courts, football and soccer fields, playground equipment, and tennis and volleyball courts. It's not shy of dog-friendly

Saint Patrick's Day Parade: Leave your troubles behind you when your headin' o'er to this street bash that's usually held the week before the actual day. You and your wee dog thought you'd already seen all of Ol' Town's Irishmen at the other festivals, but you hadn't now, had you? The parade features floats, Irish jig dancers, drunken blokes, and the lot, all marching down King Street soon after noon. You'll see Irish dogs here, too, and plenty of 'em—Irish setters, terriers, water spaniels, and wolfhounds. The bark of some dogs will even sound Irish to you! When the parade ends, it's to the local pubs and restaurants for a pint o' Guinness. 703/549-4535 or 703/838-4200.

Ethnic Festivals: The Irish aren't the only ones who have left their mark on Alexandria. Scheduled throughout the warm-weather months, with varying dates from year to year, these open-air celebrations of ethnic diversity in the area are a feast of foods, aromas, language, and music. They are also usually very dog friendly, as witnessed by the turnout of mutts and pups of every breed. A listing of festivals and where they're held follows. For exact dates and to check locations, call the City of Alexandria's Special Programs Division at 703/838-4844 or the Events Hotline at 703/883-4686.

Armenian Festival in May at the Market Square
Hispanic American Festival in June in Oronoco Bay Park
Irish Festival in August in the Market Square
African-American Heritage and Cultural Festival in August at the Market Square
American Indian Festival in August in Market Square
Italian Festival in September at the Market Square
Scottish Heritage Fair in September at Fort Ward Park
Cypriot Festival in October at the Market Square.

pastimes, either. Chappy took to the well-blazed hiking trails that disappear into the wooded areas and nature preserve like a duck to water. In addition to that, there is an officially sanctioned off-leash, unfenced dog exercise area just east of the loop. The park is located on at 3210 King Street next to T. C. Williams High School. It's open until dark. 703/931-1127.

7 Duke Street/Charles E. Beatley Jr. Library Park 🐾 🐾 🐕

Chappy says that some dogs are just so hard up to run leash-free and to socialize that they don't mind the fact that this dog park sits smack in the round part of an overpass road ramp, right next to the six lanes of Duke Street. That's why two dogs were zooming around chasing balls very happily when we finally found the park. We kept driving by it, looking for trees, or something. The trick here is to park at the library and then walk down to the park. Everyone does it. The park itself affords a good-sized piece of land on which to roam, so the walk is just a warm up for the fun ahead. On Duke Street, just east of the Charles E. Beatley Jr. Library. 703/838-4343.

8 Edison Street/Wildlife Sanctuary of Alexandria 🐾 🐕

There is a specially marked, official off-leash dog exercise area here, but in all honesty, this is just not a great part of town. From Mount Vernon Avenue and Glebe, go north to the first right on Reed Avenue. Turn left onto Edison and go to the dead end to the park. 703/838-4343.

9 Fort Ward Museum and Park 🐾 🐾 🐾 🦴 🐕

Just over that mound of grass is, well, more grass. And it's always greener, isn't it? But that's the fun of this 40-acre park where the fifth largest Civil War fort protecting Washington has been reconstructed. At the northwest bastion of the fort, two large mounds called earthworks are still there. It's easy to roam around and contemplate history here, which no doubt is what Chappy had in mind as he sniffed the shrubs and trees.

On summer weekends, this is a favorite spot for Revolutionary and Civil War battle reenactments, with history buffs demonstrating camp life, and British and colonial uniformed troops engaging in skirmishes. That can get a bit noisy with muskets firing blanks, even for a private first-class pooch, so think twice before marching yours this-a-way on those days.

Rather, spacious picnic areas make this a favorite destination for summer parties—dogs *et al.*—and since the place is no secret, expect a crowd on nice days.

It turns out Chappy isn't all that intrigued with American history, so he waited patiently and happily outside leashed to the front steps while the rest of us quickly visited the small museum on the grounds with exhibits of plenty of fascinating Civil War artifacts.

Just to the right of the museum building, at the front of the park, is an official off-leash dog exercise area. So walk, leashed, through history and romp, unleashed, before you go home.

The museum and park are located at 4301 West Braddock Road. Take the Seminary Road East exit off I-395 (then left on North Howard Street and right on West Braddock). They are open Tuesday–Saturday, 9 A.M.–5 P.M., and Sunday, noon–P.M. 703/838-4848.

10 Fort Williams Parkway 🐾 🐕

This is more of a ravine by the side of the road with some grass on it than a dog exercise area, but maybe we just didn't go through the woods the right way. Or maybe in a suburb you take what you can get. This was the only plot of woodsy area on Fort Williams Parkway, and it was marked as an off-leash dog area, although it just didn't seem like there was much room to roam. It's

EARMARK YOUR CALENDAR

Ghoulish Pooches: Every year a group called Doorways to Old Virginia puts on a fun and spooky event. They say dogs are most welcome to come along on this hour-long tour of the haunts of the town, if they are friendly. As they put it, "Creep through the dark night following a lantern light. Step over faded tombstones where lie old colonial bones." Led by an 18th century–attired guide, the tour is six blocks long and comes to rest in a graveyard. Tours leave from the Ramsay House Visitors Center at 221 King Street. Note: At any time of year, you can get a guided walking tour. Just ask at the Ramsay House Visitor Center, 703/548-0100.

Jingle Dogs: One of the special activities held each year in the marketplace is the annual **Christmas tree–lighting ceremony.** Kids are on parents' shoulders, dogs are on leashes, and everyone sips hot chocolate, sings carols, and watches as the lights flicker on in several decorated trees in the square. Most dogs come wearing jingle bells at the collar. Call the Alexandria Convention and Visitors Bureau at 703/838-4200.

---

more of a pit stop when a dog's gotta go. Off Duke Street, turn onto Fort Williams Parkway and travel about a mile to Dearborn Place. The park is on the corner. 703/838-4343.

11 Holmes Run Park 🐾 🐾

If you've taken the pup shopping at Landmark Shopping Center (where we hope you didn't leave her in the car on a blistering summer afternoon), she'll be pouting for some greenery in no time. Just up Van Dorn Street a short distance from the mall is this low-key stretch of woods that buffers Holmes Run.

What you'll see are some paved paths and a worn grass path by the water. They make for a nice walk, just a few blocks off the busy Duke Street area. Paths wind around the Charles Beatley Library and you can walk to the fenced-in dog park east of the building. The park is located on Holmes Run Parkway off Van Dorn Street. It's open during daylight hours. 703/883-4343.

12 Huntley Meadows Park 🐾 🐾 🐾 ½ 🐾

The only downside of this rare freshwater wetlands park is that its most compelling feature, the Heron Trail boardwalk, is now off-limits to dogs. The wooden half-mile track of sure footing that snakes through wildflower-rich meadows and wildlife-populated swamps enters a nature wonderland of herons gliding in for landings and lizards scampering underfoot. The wildlife population, so improbably hidden amid the modestly middle-class suburbs of Hybla Valley, is easily threatened by curious canines, so the three miles of land trails edging the marshlands will have to do when doggy comes along. And this flat woody bottomland does just fine, especially for long hikes and creature sightings. Spotting a pileated woodpecker pounding his noggin into a tall willow oak and coming onto a pasture of ferns growing like weeds kept our attention while Chappy sniffed the musty smells and added a few of his own. After walking most of the raised pea-gravel land trails of this one-time plantation (once owned by colonial Virginia statesman George Mason), we left Chappy tied to a shaded bench near the boardwalk entrance and walked far enough into the swamps so the boys could glimpse the frogs jumping around. No one seemed to mind—including Chappy, who was nearly lulled into a nap by the tranquility of these beautiful 1,424 acres.

Nature hiking is pretty much the extent of it here, meaning just dogging it on a leash is the pleasant pastime any time of year on these trails—with spring and summer gorgeous and lush and fall and winter full of unexpected sparse beauty. Don't worry about bikes speeding by; they're restricted to a single designated bike trail. Because there are few picnic areas and playing fields, the usual crowds go elsewhere.

From the Capital Beltway (I-495), take Exit 1 (Route 1) south for 3.5 miles; turn right at Lockheed Boulevard, and go 0.5 mile to the visitor center entrance on the left at Harrison Lane. The park is open dawn–dark. 703/768-2525.

13 Hooff's Run 🐾 ½ 🐕

Watch out for the speed bumps on Commonwealth right by this park. We thought it was just red brick, but it's raised red brick. Almost took out the underside of the van. Anyway, the park is cute. Cute? Well, it's a small rectangular plot of unfenced land right next to the Redeemed Church of Our Lord Jesus Christ. The name of the church is bigger than the building that houses it. A collie was enjoying the off-leash area the day we visited. It's obviously a neighborhood hangout. It's right by the street and it's not fenced, so take care. The park is on Commonwealth between Oak and Chapman. 703/838-4343.

14 Monticello Park 🐾 🐾 🐕

The off-leash area of the park is a little walk into the woods. You can see it from Beverly Road, where you can park and follow the path in. A big tree has fallen in the middle of the park, which is really a wooded area—no grass. Dogs who like to run around and explore woods will have a blast here. If you and your dog are more lounge-in-the-grass types, try somewhere else. From Glebe Road turn onto Russell Street and then make a right on Beverly. Go up the hill to the park on the left. 703/838-4343.

15 Stone Mansion and Stoneybrooke Park 🐾

In a pinch, this tiny pit stop works if you're in the neighborhood, but it's nothing worth going out of your way to see. The stately nature of the historic mansion seems disturbed by the tennis courts built so close. And the modern houses standing on either side of the property leave you scratching your head and wondering if nothing's sacred. Venture down the sloping green from the small parking lot to the picnic area 'round back and walk the pup on the trail heading off into the woods—but keep the leash on, lest the "neighbors" get nervous about a dog on the property.

From I-495, take Exit 2 (Telegraph Road) south; turn left on the Parkway, cross the intersection of South King's Highway, and you'll be on Stoneybrooke Drive. The park entrance is on the left. The park is open dawn–dusk. 703/750-1598.

16 Timberbranch Parkway Median 🐾 🐾 🐾 🐕

It may seem very odd to see such a highly rated park that isn't even a park, but we really fell in love with this strip of land. Maybe it was the purple crocus that covered the ground in big patches on a warm late-February day promising spring. Maybe it was the quiet, the sunny day, and the feeling that homes were well cared for. It's a fairly lengthy stretch of woodsy median that runs down the middle of the road and is also a designated off-leash exercise spot. The edges of the area are grassy and lead down to a wooded gravelly path next to a creek that runs through the middle of the land. The woods are not so dense that sunlight doesn't filter through, and yet it almost feels overgrown. Turn off Braddock Road onto Timberbranch Parkway and drive down a bit and park anywhere along the median that allows it. 703/838-4343.

Restaurants

Dancing Peppers Cantina: A nice big desk out in front of this little eatery makes for a perfect meal with your pooch. "Oh sure," said a server when asked if it was okay to have dogs. She added that it's nice to put down a bowl of water for any dog who dines there, because it's not shaded. So, go for the fajitas or the *enchiladas de Veracruz* and have a Dos Equis for us. 4111 Duke Street; 703/823-1167.

Generous George's Positive Pizza and Pasta Place: This is for true pizza lovers. There's the Cheesy Burger pizza, the Dueling Pestos pizza, the Mediterranean pizza, and just about any kind of pizza you could imagine. Or you can "build your own" as they say, and take it home. Chappy, being the cheese hound that he is, likes plain best—with extra cheese, please. 3006 Duke Street; 703/370-4303.

Thai Hut: If you or your dog get a hankering for a peanutty satay or a noodley *pad see euw,* carry it out seven days a week from this southside Alexandria Thai eatery that can make any dish as hot as you can stand it or as gentle as you like it. 408 South Van Dorn Street; 703/823-5357.

Places to Stay

Comfort Inn–Mount Vernon: No great shakes but the rooms are practical and comfy at this modest roadside chain hotel, and dogs are allowed for $20 extra per night. And the swamps and wooded trails of beautiful Huntley Meadows Park are about a mile west off Lockheed Boulevard. Rates are about $73 a night. 7212 Richmond Highway, Alexandria, VA 22306; 703/765-9000.

Days Inn–Alexandria: This is another stop in a dog-friendly hotel chain; small pets are allowed for $15 extra per night on top of a $65 room rate. Another convenience: big grassy fields stretch along the south side of the Richmond Highway nearby. 6100 Richmond Highway, Alexandria, VA 22303; 703/329-0500.

Econo Lodge–Mount Vernon: Barebones comfort at a modest price is the hallmark of this lodge that allows dogs, but dog owners must pay a one-time fee of $25, no matter how long the stay. Rooms are $55. 8849 Richmond Highway, Alexandria, VA 22309; 703/780-0300.

Red Roof Inn–Alexandria: Chappy mistakes the name of this modest chain hotel for his most annoying middle-of-the-night activity—as in, *roof, roof!* Dogs are allowed with no size limit and no doggy fee. Rate is around $71. 5975 Richmond Highway, Alexandria, VA 22303; 703/960-5200.

DEL RAY

Parks, Beaches, and Recreation Areas

17 Raymond Avenue Park 🐾 🐕

Located between Route 1 and Mount Vernon Avenue, turn onto Raymond and look for the park. On one side of the street is the Washington & Old Dominion Trail and a playground, on the other side is an official off-leash, unfenced dog exercise area.

It's a long, narrow, sloped gully, bordered on both sides by backyard fences. And it's fun for racing around. 703/838-4343.

18 Simpson Stadium Park 🐾 ½ 🐕

The word stadium here makes it sound like it's Orioles Park at Camden Yards. It's not. But it is a nice big baseball field that fills up with people all summer long. Carved out in the corner of the park, however, is a nice fenced-in, officially sanctioned patch of park in which off-leash dogs can run their own bases. Just shows there's something for everyone here. The park is right next to Route 1 on Monroe Avenue. 703/838-4775.

Restaurants

Mancini's: The lunch sandwiches and salads are delicious and for dinner this little restaurant serves up some delectable entrees. Try the white bean and shrimp salad or savor some grilled fresh salmon. There are several green plastic tables out front, perfect for dining on a warm summer night. Otherwise, get anything to go and enjoy a truly gourmet meal from a very casual setting. 1508 Mount Vernon Avenue; 703/838-3663.

St. Elmo's Coffee House: Chappy looks absurd with his black beret and sunglasses but that Beat feel is what you get at this java hut that, besides the brews, pastries, sandwiches, and soups, serves up mostly acoustic and jazzy live entertainment. The dog-friendly folks who run this joint, located in the Del Ray neighborhood just north of Old Town Alexandria, keep a large glass jar of doggy biscuits handy and will bring a bowl of water for cool-daddy dogs with a thirst. The few tables outside are where you and the pup are welcome. 2300 Mount Vernon Avenue; 703/739-9268.

OLD TOWN

Old Town—the historic seaport with cobblestone streets and brick sidewalks, quaint shops, and dozens of eateries—is rich with colonial history. A group of English and Scottish merchants started it all with a tobacco warehouse on the water in the 1740s. The settlement prospered. In 1749, lots that surveyor John West and his young assistant, George Washington, laid out went on sale. The city took on a cosmopolitan air with each new and elegant town home built. It became the hometown of Robert E. Lee, George Mason, and George Washington.

During the Civil War, Union troops occupied the town and spared it the destruction suffered by so many other Southern towns. After the war, because of the railroads that ran through and the lively shipping business, the town grew and thrived as a center of commerce. It looks today much as it did then. Somewhere along the way, it became a favorite neighborhood for dogs.

"This is dog heaven," declared one man at the market early on a Saturday morning. Indeed, Old Town may be the most dog-friendly community in the metropolitan area. Merchants give out dog treats. Dog owners host dog slumber parties. The local dog obedience school and animal welfare league are both big organizations in town. It's the kind of neighborhood where, if you walk your dog around the block, you make friends. Fast.

Stories abound of the dog owner who went to a restaurant and asked to take home a couple of bites of meat in a doggy bag. The waiter handed her a sack with three big pieces of brochette, some lamb, and some soft-shell crabs—better than she got for herself!

One of the first businesses to provide doggy snacks was the stately Burke and Herbert Bank at King and Fairfax Streets, the oldest bank in Virginia. The tellers still have treats for dogs. At the Enchanted Florist, on the corner of

Prince and Fairfax Streets, there's a bone box outside, as well as free plastic scooping bags in case you left yours at home.

A downside to Old Town is the traffic. Chappy has been here many times and still walks around with his tail down because of the metal monsters that crowd the streets. On sunny weekends, traffic can get very heavy, and people walk en masse on foot with strollers and other obstacles that come between Chappy and his precious tree sniffing. There are trees lining the

DIVERSIONS

Pup and Circumstance: More than 1,000 canines a year graduate from the **Old Town School for Dogs.** It offers doggy lessons for life, to prepare dogs for dog-friendly Old Town, where the presence of particularly well-behaved and well-trained dogs is almost expected.

The school actually sends a bus to pick up its doggy students at their homes in the morning and take them back at night. The school is located on the corner of Oronoco and Saint Asaph Streets. 529 Oronoco Street; 703/836-7643.

Fetch: Your dog will quiver. Your dog will shake. Your dog will not believe that someone actually opened a store named **Fetch** devoted to homemade treats and gifts just for dogs. The boutique offers all sorts of great dog gifts, from pretty ceramic platters to animal-fat–free treats. 101 South Saint Asaph Street; 703/518-5188.

To Market, to Market: Get up early one Saturday morning - and we do mean early - and head to **Market Square** and pick out some fresh produce from one of the oldest continuously operating markets in the country. Even if you don't want any of the turnips, tomatoes, peaches, or sunflowers peddled here, walk your dog on down for some major socializing. The best advice we can give is to get there early, because each parking meter will have a dog leashed up to it while shopping takes place in the square. No dogs are allowed on the actual plaza. The market is open 5–9 A.M. every Saturday. 301 King Street; 703/838-4770.

Holistic Hounds: Located at the edge of Old Town is **PetSage,** a pioneering holistic pet supply store that is recognized by pet owners and veterinarians regionally as a reliable source of natural products, holistic medicine, and alternative therapies for pets—plus plenty of friendly advice.

PetSage also hosts a regular schedule of by-reservation clinics and presentations, ranging from lectures by holistic veterinarians to introductory lessons in canine massage. 2391 South Dove Street, Alexandria, VA 22314; 703/299-5044 or 800/738-4584; website: www.petsage.com.

main road to the water—King Street—and Chappy generally likes to stop at every one. Of course, the law here dictates that dogs be on a leash and you must scoop the poop.

Parks, Beaches, and Recreation Areas

19 Founders Park 🐾🐾🐾 ½

Dogs congregate at this small riverside park near the southern point of little Oronoco Bay where, besides volleyball courts, the only thing is the waterfront. Take an early morning bench with your sleepy-eyed dog and catch the sunrise over the river. The grass always looks nice, the people are always friendly, and the water always gives you the feel of being somewhere other than in a city. Find the posts with little green paws and you'll know you're in the area that's been officially sanctioned as an off-leash exercise spot. Enjoy!

This is one of the saltwater pearls in the strand of tiny dog-friendly parks stretching along the Old Town waterfront. It's located at 400 North Union Street, where Oronoco Street meets the Potomac River, and is open 24 hours a day. 703/838-4343.

20 George Washington Masonic National Memorial 🐾🐾

Take the elevator up 330 feet to the observation deck on the ninth floor of this landmark everyone calls the Masonic Temple and enjoy the panoramic view of Old Town and beyond. In the George Washington Museum you can see the first president's will and testament, his family Bible, a trunk he used during the Revolutionary War, the key to the Bastille, and a clock that was stopped at the time of his death. Other floors exhibit the charitable works of Masons worldwide. But that's all for you. For your dog, who doesn't care what kind of trunk George owned unless it contains a T-bone, there's always the giant grassy hill in front of this memorial where many dogs go for exercise, even though the Masons aren't all that thrilled about it. We keep hearing that dogs are not allowed here anymore, but it's just that they ask you keep your dog on a leash, so taking advantage of all that grass to run leash-free is frowned upon. The memorial is open daily except Thanksgiving, Christmas, and New Year's, 9 A.M.–5 P.M., and is located at King Street and Callahan Drive. 703/683-2007.

21 Montgomery Park 🐾 ½

Occupying a block of land just north of the Ramada Hotel, this park is mostly grass, with a fenced-in playground where no dogs are allowed and a fenced-in dog-ground where no kids are allowed. Just kidding. In between the two, it's wide open for playing. Maybe cats go there? A couple of trees provide shade on one corner, and two picnic tables have shelters over them. The tennis courts see a lot of action here from the residents of surrounding town houses

EARMARK YOUR CALENDAR

Washington's Birthday Parade: Old Town hosts the largest parade in the country celebrating the birthday of George Washington in February. Leashed dogs are welcome to watch the festivities that march from Wilkes and Saint Asaph Streets through Old Town to Gibbon and South Fairfax Streets, starting just after noon. 703/838-4200.

Alexandria Red Cross Waterfront Festival: Oronoco Park, located on the edge of the Potomac River, makes a great spot for festivals, and Old Town loves festivals. This is one of the biggest and most fun of all the many annual festivals this town celebrates. Going on for more than 15 years, it is usually held the second weekend in June to celebrate both Alexandria's historic importance as a seaport and the vitality of the place today. It is the town's single largest event, attracting more than 100,000 people. Music plays throughout the day from a stage, and fireworks brighten the sky after dark. You and your dog can roam around the arts-and-crafts booths that line the park walkways, though chances are the pooch won't get to go on any of the kiddie rides or tours of visiting tall ships.

   The Red Cross also offers several health-check booths with health information—for humans only. The festival breaks out at Oronoco Bay Park (North Waterfront between Pendleton and Madison Streets), Founders Park, and City Marina. For specific dates and times, call the Alexandria Convention and Visitors Bureau at 703/838-4200.

and apartment complexes. Chappy, on a leash as is the rule, was happy to check this park out, but he'd rather head for one of the parks along the water. And so would we. The park is bordered by Montgomery Street, First Avenue, Royal Street, and Fairfax Street. 703/838-4343.

22 Oronoco Bay Park 🐾 🐾 🐾

A paved concrete path running along the edge attracts many walkers and many walkers of dogs. If you've had a busy day walking around Old Town, benches facing the Potomac here make a great rest stop and great boat watching. Trees line the path so that's where you and your leashed dog can find the best shade. The park is on North Fairfax Street between Pendelton and Madison; it's open 24 hours. 703/838-4343.

23 Pommander Park 🐾 🐾 ½ 🐕

Another nice little patch of prime real estate, the park is marked with the dog posts and green paw prints. There are parks on three corners of the block here, but stick with the designated leash-free area—that's why it's there. The water is peaceful, and it's pleasant to watch the kayakers go by. Chappy didn't even seem to mind the steady pounding of the work being done on the new Woodrow Wilson Bridge. The park is at the corner of Union and Gibbon Streets. 703/838-4343.

24 Waterfront Walk 🐾 🐾 ½

In this teeny-tiny park, there's a not-so-teeny-tiny cannon. There is also a grassy area rimmed by flowers and the Potomac River lapping right by the edge. Chappy stuck his head up into the wind and checked it all out, but his tail stayed down. The river is a little overpowering right here. One false step by the concrete sidewalk path and you're in the drink. Instead, Chappy likes to sniff the edges of the park and then sit on a blanket with a sandwich from a nearby deli and have a delightful picnic watching the boats on the Potomac. The park is located between Prince and King Streets on the waterfront; it's open 24 hours. 703/838-4343.

Restaurants

Firehook Bakery and Coffeehouse: Lots of dough for not much dough, doggies love this spot because it's easy to pick up some great fresh-baked bread and dash down to the waterfront. For lunch, try the focaccia. 106 North Lee Street; 703/519-8020.

Hard Times Cafe: Look, it's a chili place. The chili's great. But sometimes, especially in the company of your un-chili-trained canine, you can't do the chili. So try the chicken or tuna steak sandwiches, or the burgers. Carry 'em out, because dogs can't go inside and it's too noisy for sensitive canine ears anyway. 1404 King Street; 703/837-0050.

Irish Walk Restaurant: Near city hall, this Gaelic hangout has an outdoor patio where dog lovers and their dogs often sit back following the many parades that attract dogs to Old Town. 415 King Street; 703/548-0118.

King Street Blues: American culinary artistry at its, well, most definitively roadhouse American best, this funky place makes the cheese fries cheesy, and the roadhouse burgers thick and juicy. The Wet Wimpy burger comes with shredded pork barbecue, cheddar and jack cheese, and a fried onion tangle on top. Carry out a jambalaya po'boy and a Cobb salad, and walk the pup down to the nearby waterfront. Anything from the menu (except the Old Dominion beer and other alcoholic beverages) is good to go. 112 North Saint Asaph Street; 703/836-8800.

La Madeleine French Bakery: Country French–style café-bakeries like these are transforming the face of weekend mornings in Old Town. People park their dogs at the meters outside and dash in for croissants and fresh bread. At lunch, with the rotisserie chicken and a loaf of fancy olive bread tucked under our arms, Chappy will follow us anywhere. *Vive la France!* 500 King Street; 703/739-2854.

Misha's: Get a latte and have a lot of fun hanging around as so many folks do here. Doesn't matter if it's morning, noon or night, they're serving up the java. 102 South Patrick Street; 703/548-4089.

South Austin Grill: Pick up the tacos, enchiladas, and burritos you ordered ahead of time from the bar at this friendly and noisy down-home Tex-Mex hangout. Folks here are loads of fun and will probably beg you to bring the dog in, as they did with Chappy, but it's not allowed by law. 801 King Street; 703/684-8969.

Places to Stay

Alexandria Travelodge: Although this little two-story motel is seven blocks north of the main intersection, it's still not too bad a walk to town. There's a $25 deposit required, and you'll be put on a ground floor, but other than that, they're happy to have you and poochie. A room on a Friday night will be in the neighborhood of $64. 700 North Washington Street, Alexandria, VA 22314; 703/836-5100.

Holiday Inn—Old Town: This inn is perfectly located if you want to visit Old Town and not have to drive anywhere. Many dogs stay here during the Scottish Walk in December so book early if you're coming then, but double-check when you make a reservation. There is no extra fee and there is no deposit; they just ask that you keep your dog with you at all times and that the dog be well trained. Rates are $149 for a double on a weekend. 480 King Street, Alexandria, VA 22314; 703/549-6080.

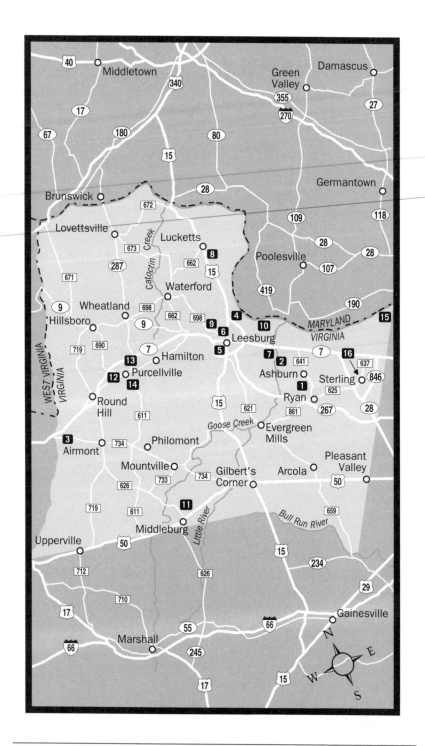

10 LOUDOUN COUNTY

Once past the congested traffic along Route 7 heading north into Loudoun County, you find *more* congested traffic! This well-heeled country cousin of the metropolitan area had acres and acres of undeveloped, scenic, open spaces when we wrote the first edition of this book. The county has seen a lot of development since then. Leesburg used to feel like it was way out there. Not anymore.

The fortunes of this lovely rural county 30 miles northwest of Washington are linked to the corporate renaissance of the Dulles International Airport corridor and hordes of urbanite commuters heading to exurbia in search of a simpler life. The county's population has doubled in the past 10 years. Planned communities such as Ashburn and Sterling, once thought of as distant enough to be hayseed hamlets, aren't considered suburbia now. Old historic towns such as graceful Leesburg and blue-blooded Middleburg that date back to the late 18th century remain residential and commercial hubs.

Alongside the crops of faux mansions that are now sprouting up in field after field, there are still some rolling green hillsides and spectacular stone-fenced estates, rich in the tradition and wealth of Virginia hunt country—

picturesque terrain where you can still hear the cry of hounds as they follow a fox's line into the dark woods. Steeped in agrarian rural tradition, you can even find some farmlands where scrappy dogs still work herds of sheep and others where dogs live chained in the back like livestock.

The dog-as-best-friend attitude is growing as the county resets its time machine. Named for the fourth Earl of Loudoun, a Scottish nobleman and governor of Virginia in 1757, it is a promising place for a dog's life. The idea of off-leash dog areas hasn't yet become a part of the collective consciousness here. Working hunting dogs are expected to be off lease, but not dogs like good old Chappy. While you will see pooches running spiritedly across its wide-open private acreage, leash laws rule in the parklands. And some places have cracked down. For example, we sure were surprised to pull up to Ashburn Park and see a big No Dogs Allowed sign. Last time we visited, we had a great time. Oh well. Ed Weil, chairperson of the Responsible Dog Ownership Group of Ashburn Farm said that a few bad apples ruined it for everyone. He and his organization are working to open a private off-leash dog park in Ashburn.

ASHBURN

Parks, Beaches, and Recreation Areas

1 Greg Crittenden Park 🐾 🐾 ½ 🦴

This peaceful, pretty complex stretches across both sides of the street here. On one side, the ball fields take up most of the land, but there is still plenty of grass and trees surrounding them in which to walk your (leashed) dog. On the left, a pond is home to geese. A small, tall windmill twirls in the sky. A fountain sprays water. An especially nice walk is the paved path around the water. The park is located at the corner of Ashburn Farm Parkway and Windmill Drive. 703/777-0343.

2 Trailside Park 🐾 🐾 ½

The in-line hockey court is no doubt a very big draw, but you could bring along a dog to sniff around the other 20 acres of land, largely dominated by ball fields. A creek—or some kind of water—runs through the park. It's nothing big or deep but perfect for cooling off hot paws on a summer day. The park at the end of Clairbourne Parkway in Ashburn Farm. 703/777-0343.

BLUEMONT

One of the county's sleepy villages, Bluemont snoozes like an old dog in the summer shade. Settled in the foothills of the Blue Ridge Mountains, it's just a couple of miles south of the West Virginia state line. Time seems to be day-dreaming at this last stop of the defunct Washington & Old Dominion Rail-

DIVERSIONS

A Day at the Races: When the steeplechase events start up in spring and again in fall, here's all you and the pooch have to remember: No dogs allowed at the Gold Cup, but pups can come to the point-to-points.

Steeplechasing in America is nearly exclusive to Virginia and Maryland. It harkens back to a time when thoroughbreds, hounds, and houndstooth jackets defined the life of landed gentry. The **Gold Cup** is all equestrian glitterati and sanctioned by the steeplechase powers that be. The **point-to-point** are less formal. They are not officially sanctioned, nor are they nearly as sanctimonious as the Gold Cup. But they are no less fascinating and still show the pomp and pretense of the sport. The country settings for these races are spectacular, the seemingly free-form horse racing is exciting to watch, and the socializing is the medium *and* the message.

Plenty of dogs will be there, for sure—undoubtedly Jack Russells or fox terriers, plus a few show-off breeds. Keep your pup on a short leash, even if some folks don't.

If you have tweed to wear, that's appropriate—though khaki or jeans do fine, too. At some point-to-points, fancy tailgating is nearly as competitive as the races. If you purchase tickets ahead of time for a reserved or rail parking space, you and the pooch will be able to stay close to your car and enjoy the luncheon spread you brought along (don't forget the candlesticks, fine silverware, and flower centerpieces). Race organizers permit alcohol (BYOB); indeed, a fruity, gin-based drink, the Pimm's Cup, is traditional among the horsy set.

Spring point-to-points run March–May; fall point-to-points run September–November. Two Middleburg point-to-points that run when springtime is getting warmer are the Middleburg Hunt Point-to-Point, held in late April, and the Bull Run Hunt Point-to-Point, usually held the first weekend in May. Both run at Glenwood Park and Racetrack, 540/338-5231, a couple of miles north of town on Route 626. Reserved parking costs about $80 and up per car; general admission (park and walk) costs about $15 per person at the gate. 703/594-3829 or 703/777-2890.

---

road. The place so convincingly retains the looks and lifestyle of yesteryear that you can almost hear the whistle blowing.

Parks, Beaches, and Recreation Areas

3 Bluemont Community Center 🚰

Not much cooking for dogs on these seven acres dedicated to people pleasures such as basketball and volleyball, a playground, a library, even an auditorium and game room. But if you come all the way to this little village to take in the annual old-fashioned country fair or the nearby Blue Ridge, this

Country Time Fun: The only train arrival scheduled hereabouts anymore comes each September to the annual **Bluemont Country Fair** when one of the locals sets up his huge model train display in the old schoolhouse. Chappy pulled us behind the schoolhouse to find the town's caboose—a nostalgic remnant from the glory days when the real railroad stopped here. Nearby, at the mountain man camp, there are demonstrations of such frontier and Native American skills as sign language, blacksmithing, beekeeping, and tomahawk throwing. These down-to-earth weekend-long festivities also feature a parade down Main Street, a 10K country road race, a pickle-making and pie-baking contest, sheepdog demonstrations, wine tastings, hay rides, pony rides for the young'uns, plenty of country barbecue and other foods, bluegrass and gospel music, and crafts. Some 5,000 folks show up each day, and leashed dogs are welcome. The fair is located throughout Bluemont, which is 17 miles west of Leesburg and about an hour's drive from Washington. Call the Loudoun County Tourism Council for more information at 800/752-6118.

plot of parkland might provide your leashed pup a welcome passing respite. The air is good. On fair days you can find the center right behind all the arts and crafts tables. You can't miss it. It's located right in the middle of town on Snickersville Turnpike and open daily dawn–dusk. 540/554-8643.

LEESBURG

Dogs like this small town that dates back to before the American Revolution. It's casually walkable—as many historic towns always have been. Just 35 miles northwest of Washington, the settlement originally called Georgetown (for George II of England) grew at the crossroads of two vital colonial roads—now Routes 7 and 15. Renamed in the mid-1700s for the notable Thomas Lightfoot Lee family whose surname is almost synonymous with Virginia, this southerly town's history is entwined with the nation's. During the War of 1812, the town even became a surrogate capital; patriots hid the Declaration of Independence and the Constitution here for safekeeping after the bloody British routed Washington. Even the famed bloodhounds of Morven Park haven't sniffed out the precise location where patriots once stashed those cultural treasures. Nor will your pooch. But with its dog-welcome attitude, its exceptional parks, musty antique shops, and nouveau historic restaurants—not to mention major dog-related events—Leesburg today has much more to offer dog lovers besides its fascinating past.

Parks, Beaches, and Recreation Areas

4 Ball's Bluff Regional Park 🐾 🐾

Driving through the subdivision of homes and town houses to get to this battlefield park hardly evokes images of Johnny Rebs pushing the advancing Yankee troops back across the Potomac River. But this engagement forced President Lincoln to rethink the Union's war strategy. The "Bluff," by the way, refers to the bluffs above the Potomac and not a battle strategy.

Behind the neatly paved streets bearing battle-related names is the single-lane road leading into the park preserving the site of the county's largest Civil War skirmish. Credit the county with keeping most of the park's 168 acres underdeveloped. The broad, 0.75-mile interpretive trail that starts from the parking lot passes the battlefield's national cemetery a quarter-mile downhill before plotting the main sites of the engagement and looping back. The few other hiking paths are *au naturel,* including those along the Potomac, and get muddy after wet weather as Chappy's paws proved. Picnic tables make this a pleasant place to bring a boxed lunch from a nearby restaurant on the Route 15 bypass just minutes away. Be forewarned, however; the park has no restrooms other than what the thicket and gorgeous forest provide. Open year-round, dawn–dusk, the park is located at the end of Ball's Bluff Road, off Battlefield Parkway and the Route 15 Leesburg Bypass. 703/737-7800.

5 Georgetown Park 🐾

Not a romp-'em-sock-'em park like you'll find on the outskirts of town, this dinky strip of greenery is the 35-mile mark of the paved Washington & Old Dominion Railroad Regional Park and Trail that cuts directly through downtown Leesburg. Besides a couple of benches and some trees, nothing much is here but bicycle riders and joggers on the old railroad trail, although it is a nice patch of grass on which to walk after you've tired of the narrow paved streets of the historic section of town. Located between Monroe and South Streets at King Street, the park and the entire 45 miles of Washington & Old Dominion Trail are open dawn–dusk. 703/729-0596.

6 Ida Lee Park Recreation Center 🐾

Folks who live around Leesburg count this 138-acre in-town recreation facility and grounds among its many blessings. This well-maintained place features a heated indoor Olympic-size swimming pool, gymnasium, library, weight room, extensive playground outside, and a lot more of little consequence to the dogs among us. Chappy found plenty of leg room on its meticulously landscaped grounds that include a hiking trail and grassy fields sprawling along the perimeter, which borders to the north on Morven Park's grounds. The recreation center is open weekdays, 6 A.M.–9 P.M.; Saturday, 9 A.M.–6 P.M.; and Sunday, noon–6 P.M., though the grounds are good for strolling just about any time. It is located on Ida Lee Drive. 703/777-1368.

DIVERSIONS

Over the River: Treat your pup to a passage on the only ferry still operating on the Potomac River. **White's Ferry** is about 3.5 miles north of downtown Leesburg. It connects cross-river on the Maryland side to a small settlement (old-time general store, snacks, gasoline, and the ferry offices) in the Chesapeake & Ohio Canal National Park. (See the Dickerson section of the Montgomery County chapter.) For about 10 awesome minutes and about 150 yards distance, you and the pooch travel midstream on this flatbed cable-drawn ferry. Foot passengers pay 50 cents to cross; automobiles go for $3 one-way and $5 round-trip. The ferry makes runs from 5 A.M. to 11 P.M., but avoid rush hour, because many exurban commuters heading into and out of Washington use it as their crossing point. Keep the pup on a leash, 'cause there's no turning back should he decide to take a swim. In rough weather, you might want to keep your dog in the car. From Leesburg, take Route 15 north for about 2.5 miles, turn right on White Ferry Road, and drive 1.5 miles to the ferry. 301/349-5200.

Howling at the Moon: The irony is that this dog-dedicated museum in a wing of the mansion at Morven Park doesn't allow your furry friend to join in this learning experience. If you live for the hunt, however, this is a must-see for you, even if your hound must wait outside. The **Museum of Hounds and Hunting** is open April–October, Tuesday–Sunday, noon–5 P.M. 703/777-2414.

Canine Christmas: Dogs get an invitation to get into the holiday spirit at the Dog School of Leesburg's **Santa Paws Workshop,** where your pooch can play games, win prizes, lap up refreshments, and have her profile photographed. The school, which trains and grooms dogs and carries a complete line of dog foods and products, features many pup-appropriate holiday gifts this time of year as well. 101 South Street SE; 703/779-1333.

7 Keep Loudoun Beautiful Park 🐾

This pleasant and tiny 3.4-acre park is more of a statement than a destination, as the name suggests. Chappy likes boat ramp parks like this one (good for canoes and small boats only), because he can dip his paws in the water without fear of falling in the deep end. There are picnic tables alongside lovely Goose Creek, so bring along the picnic basket and fishing gear. Route 7 passes by directly to the north side but the opposite acres include the old Goose Creek truss bridge and the Goose Creek Golf Course. Open dawn–dusk, the park is located on Golf Club Road 0.25 mile northwest of Goose Creek off Route 7 (Leesburg Pike). 703/777-0343.

8 Lucketts Community Park 🐾 🐾 ◀●

With 10 acres of land, this park has some room to roam. Somewhat out in the middle of nowhere, the trail network is your best bet with your best friend. Otherwise, you'll be in the midst of a soccer match or softball game. 42361 Lucketts Road at the intersection of Routes 15 and 662; 703/777-0343.

9 Morven Park 🐾 🐾 🐾 ◀●

Chappy's miffed that the guided tour inside the elegant and historic 28-room Greek revival mansion (where one-time Virginia governor and hound connoisseur Westmoreland Davis resided) doesn't allow his doggish kind. No matter, because the surrounding 1,200 acres of remarkably plush and old property welcomes dogs wholeheartedly in the spirit of the long line of hound lovers who resided here.

The boxwood gardens are extensive and a-maze-ing, so don't let a leg be raised against them, please. A carriage museum on the grounds houses more than 70 vintage horse-drawn carriages, some of which you and the pup can glimpse from the outside. No backstage passes for the pup at the Museum of Hounds and Hunting either, for fear of soiling the carpets.

Instead, we and several other dogged visitors hiked the 1.5-mile trail that starts behind the mansion and snakes through the accessible wooded area nearby. Most folks with pooches stay to the immediate 20 acres surrounding the mansion because that area is great stomping grounds for dogs and proves to be more than plenty on a sunny afternoon. Besides, territory gets wild and overgrown the farther you roam.

Bring along a picnic lunch—a lot of visitors do. Shade and drinking water are available if tongues start dragging in hot weather. This is high-society soil, so keep the pup on a leash, and be quick to pick up after him. The grounds and mansion are open April–October, noon–4:30 P.M.; Saturday, 10 A.M.–4:30 P.M.; and Sunday, 1–5 P.M.; closed Monday and national holidays. Admission is free. The park entrance is located on the north side of Leesburg off Morven Park Road on Old Waterford Road. 703/777-2414.

10 Red Rock Wilderness Overlook Regional Park 🐾 🐾

For a traipse through native Virginia woodlands, this hidden green retreat is hard to beat. Halfway around either of its two densely shaded hiking trails is a scenic cliff-top overlook of the Potomac River that sets this location apart from ordinary parks.

The first clue that we had arrived was Chappy pressing his black wet nose against the car window and barking, "Park! Park!" The rest of you will know you're there when you notice the preserved ruins of an old abandoned estate, circa 1885, surrounding the parking lot. Like a ghost farm standing testament to agrarian days gone by, the roofless walls of the granary, pumphouse, and old stone house remain. The grounds and ruins are a nice oasis with picnic tables and benches. The only other visitor was a woman who apparently had found the peaceful setting she sought to be alone with a good book.

Nose to the damp dirt path, Chappy interrupted her and then led us by his leash down the half-mile trail. (The half-mile path is to the right at the park entrance and the one-mile path is to the left.) Gigantic black crows in the tall maples and oaks cawed loudly at us. Twisted vines and Virginia crawler so entangle swaths of pines and other native trees that they look surreal. The pathway walks longer than its half mile because it's rooted and rough, though mostly level even as it approaches the cliffs. Glimpses of high-tension power lines and school buildings in the woods to the south interrupt this high adventure somewhat.

Past the barren overlook, which you cannot drive to, is the big payoff, despite a tall chain-link fence that protects visitors from a truly treacherous cliffside. What's stunning about this panoramic view is that the rough and tumble Maryland shore across the river looks so untouched by humanity that it must resemble what it looked like in colonial days. Hard to believe that this pristine riverside scene, where white birches stand out vividly against the background of the browns and greens of untamed woods, is so close to the overdeveloped, dog-eat-dog world of Washington. *Bang!* The pop of a hunter's gun on nearby private land shook us from the spell this vista cast.

With Chappy and the boys prowling through the underbrush and getting stuck in a briar patch, we returned to reality. Open dawn–dusk year-round, the park is located off the Route 15 Bypass heading east from Leesburg on Edwards Ferry Road. 703/737-7800.

Restaurants

China King's Restaurant: Chinese and carryout go hand in hand, and this old-style Asian eatery diagonally across from the courthouse will box its excellent entrées for carrying out to the countryside or just over to a bench in little Georgetown Park nearby. Chappy's partial to the Mongolian pork sans the MSG, but that's just him. 5 South King Street; 703/777-9831.

Georgetown Cafe: You can't take dogs onto the eating deck, but the owners of this stylish café say they'll whip up anything on the menu for dog lovers who call ahead or stop by to carry out a meal to a nearby park. The Reuben sandwiches and bacon cheeseburgers sell like hotcakes here. An oddity well worth the mess (Chappy didn't seem to mind the food falling) is the Gap Express, which is essentially a sloppy joe with melted cheese. You have to promise you'll power-walk those hiking trails to unclog the arteries after that one. 18 South King Street; 703/777-5000.

Laurel Brigade Inn: Fried chicken and fresh seafood are served in an authentic period setting dating back to 1759. The proprietor allows pooches to

EARMARK YOUR CALENDAR

The calendar of events in this neck of the woods is so jam-packed you'd best call the Leesburg Tourist Center for details, depending on when you're visiting. Here are some highlights:

In April, four blocks of Leesburg's historic district transform into a botanical garden for the **Leesburg Flower and Garden Festival.** More than 70 vendors set up booths with garden and landscaping displays. Musical entertainment and shows for kids, including a magician, petting zoo, puppet show, and a presentation of reptiles set the stage. It all happens around King and Market Streets. Dogs are welcome although one year, recalls an organizer, a pooch got excited and knocked over all her tickets for the door prize. That's what happens sometimes when 15,000 people are at an event.

In mid-August for more than two decades now, the entire historic downtown area turns into a **colonial street fair** for a weekend, celebrating the 1700s county court days. Hundreds of costumed colonial characters and shop owners are out and about engaging in conversation and acting up in true-to-colonial form. Reenactment regiments march and fire their muskets. This event draws large crowds because it's so doggone fun to roam through the colonial-looking Leesburg and see it come alive with colonial folks. The revenues from the celebration help to maintain and restore the county's historic buildings and cultural heritage. Alas, Chappy was too nervous around the jam-packed streets and too scared of the crack of muskets to make this a return engagement for him. And, even though August is the dog days, the temperatures were just too cookin' for our Himalayan hound.

Christmas in Leesburg is always festive and fun. The first December weekend features the town's **tree-lighting ceremony and parade** in the chilly fresh evening air. After that, old-fashioned carriage rides, pictures with Santa, and evening concerts on the courthouse steps happen about every weekend till Christmas, and so are. Call the Leesburg parks administration office for more information, 703/777-1262.

If you and the pup aren't registered to take part in this spring event, it's probably better leave your pal at home. If yours is like Chappy, he would only find all this obedience depressing anyway. But dog lovers might find the Kennel Club of Northern Virginia's annual **All-Breed Dog Show and Obedience Trial** fascinating—more than 4,000 dogs and 152 breeds participate for prizes. It's held at Morven Park's International Equestrian Center, located at Route 15 and Tutt Lane in Leesburg. Admission is charged. 703/406-2474.

sit alongside diners in the outdoor dining area. 20 West Market Street; 703/777-1010.

West Loudon Street Cafe: Tables out front are inviting and the menu is to drool for. How about a smoked salmon on toasted whole wheat? Or maybe you want to try the King Street, which is sliced turkey breast, pastrami, and Swiss cheese served on toasted rye with mustard, lettuce, and tomato. The salad platters looked really good, too. There's even house pâté, wine, and imported beer. Human and dog heaven. Located a half block off King Street, the café is right across the street from one of the public parking lots, too, so it's easy to stop in. 7A West Loudon Street; 703/777-8693.

Places to Stay

Days Inn–Leesburg: The open field nearby at this modest chain hotel on the eastside outskirts of town in the Prosperity Shopping Center makes it all the more hospitable to doggy guests. Dogs stay for an extra $6 per night, with no limitations on size. Expect to pay around $70 for a room. 721 East Market Street, Leesburg, VA 20175; 703/777-6622.

Holiday Inn–Carradoc Hall: Two miles east of Leesburg on Route 7, this is not your ordinary Holiday Inn. Carradoc Hall, you see, is an authentic colonial mansion, circa 1773, restored and expanded to include the 122-room hotel. Some of the guest quarters are in the old mansion, but most are in the newer section. Period and reproduction antiques grace the entire hotel. Outside are eight acres of country estate—old trees for pups to sniff 'n' lift, a natural spring, and plenty of green grass. All of it's hard to beat at low $59 a night. 1500 East Market Street, Leesburg, VA 20176; 703/771-9200.

MIDDLEBURG

This is definitely high-class horse country, but dogs are the next best thing around. Revolutionary War colonel and statesman Leven Powell established this vintage Virginia town at Chinn's Crossroads in 1787, and the village hasn't lost its colonial charms.

Named Middleburg because it is midway between Alexandria and Winchester on the Ashby Gap trading route (now called Route 50), the town, whose population hovers at 500–600, sits on the Loudoun side of the line dividing Loudoun and Fauquier Counties. A popular tourist attraction, its southern hospitality, and antique atmosphere of period 18th- and 19th-century buildings housing quaint shops, inns, and old-style restaurants echo the pages of history like few towns anywhere.

The original tavern, circa 1789, is the period stone building now incorporated into the Red Fox Tavern. The United Methodist Church, at the corner of Pendelton and Washington Streets, still opens its doors (though not to dogs) as

DIVERSIONS

Trailing the Gray Ghost: Drive back in time by following the tracks along Route 50 where Colonel John Singleton Mosby and his Confederate raiders traveled. This 20-mile **driving tour** starts east of Middleburg at Mount Zion Church, which served as a Civil War hospital, barracks, battleground, and burial ground, and ends at Paris, Virginia, on the slopes of the Blue Ridge Mountains. Along the route that first served as a hunting path for Native Americans are a dozen or so Mosby skirmish sites each with a tale of daring and courage. To get the descriptive guide of the driving tour, call the Mosby Heritage Area group, 540/687-4616, or pick one up at the Pink Box Visitor Center at 12 North Madison Street; 540/687-8888.

Canine canvases: When touring the narrow side streets of this quaint village, stop by the **Red Fox Fine Arts Gallery** specializing in sporting and animal paintings, including dog and hunt-country art. 7 North Liberty Street 540/687-5780.

Fresh Vittles: On Saturday from 9 A.M. to 1 P.M., local farmers congregate in the parking lot behind the Middleburg Bank for the weekly fair-weather **Middleburg Farmer's Market.** This is a pleasant pause from scurrying around hunt-country back roads or shopping Main Street, even for Chappy. He likes wet-nosing the other friendly pooches who arrive on- and off-leash. Look for the market on West Federal Street behind the Post Office; 703/777-1985.

Barking as a Second Language: If you and Rover have a communication gap, call Donnamarie of **Pax en Terra Farm,** a professional animal communicator. She can tell you what your dog (or horse, cat, bird, reptile, all species, even insects!) has been trying to tell you—if only you would listen. Animal telepathy? "I believe we all have it," says Donnamarie. "We all had it as children, but we understood that to continue would make us strange or weird." Undeterred, Donnamarie continued anyway. Now she communicates with sick pets, disturbed pets, new pets, even dead pets. Her hourly charge is $50. 540/338-5678.

a sanctuary as it did in the days following the Battle of Bull Run. Wounded soldiers from North and South retreated here from Manassas for treatment in its nave. The town was the headquarters and hiding place for Confederate Colonel John Mosby, the Gray Ghost. The town's Sharon Cemetery was the nation's first to erect a monument to the unknown war dead.

Middleburg's crooked streets and worn brick sidewalks are precious paw paths for casually touring these sites. Don't be surprised if you and your pooch make plenty of new friends while strolling aimlessly and taking in the ambiance of the capital of horse and hunt country.

Parks, Beaches, and Recreation Areas

11 Mickie Gordon Memorial Park 🐾

Chappy has known his share of grassy acreage bordering on ball fields 'cause our boys play baseball. So it didn't matter to him that this roomy park (formerly Mercer Park) a mile east of town dedicates its acres mostly to the national pastime. Hey, Chappy likes to play ball! Beyond the outfield fences is plenty of grassy space for other doggy pastimes after an afternoon of exploring in town. Plus, the lively exercise trail and small pond where local residents fish provide a quick hike and a dirty dip to energetic pups. Try to avoid game times if you're looking to romp around, however, 'cause that's when this property is packed with fans and Little Leaguers. The park is open dawn–dusk and is located at Route 50, left on Winery Lane or Carter's Farm Lane. 703/777-0343.

Restaurants

Dank's Deli: Wrought-iron outdoor tables right on the main street mean you can tie up the dog and have him near while you eat hot or cold deli sandwiches. 2 North Liberty Street; 540/687-3456.

Doc's BBQ: Chappy's nose was quivering as we pulled into a parking space right in front of the Aldie Country Store, just next to the big open-air grill still smoking from cooking some ribs. Our noses were quivering, too, so we ran in and bought some beef barbecue sandwiches, which we all gobbled pronto. Follow your nose five miles east of Middleburg on Route 50. 39285 John Mosby Highway; 703/327-6347.

Magpie's Cafe: Park your pooch at one of the plastic tables out front and be prepared to be overwhelmed by the menu of what appears to be a small café. At lunch, try the crab cake sandwiches, soups, and salads. The dinner menu kicks in at 5 P.M. or so, when entrées take over. Based on the bites he got, Chappy recommends the grilled lamb chops. 112 West Washington Street; 540/687-6443.

Scruffy's Ice Cream Parlor: If you're strolling through town with your pooch, this parlor is a must stop. This is where it all began for doggy good deeds in Middleburg, when a program called Scruffy's Strays became the Middleburg Humane Foundation. Located next door to the humane society's Second Chance Thrift Shop, Scruffy's is always open for its four-legged friends. It serves a steaming cup of joe and rich snacks such as pumpkin pie, hot-fudge brownies à la mode, and big scoops of ice cream in cinnamon waffle cones. The place sports walls decorated with dog photos that are fun to look over while waiting. It's located on West Washington Street between South Madison and South Pendleton Streets. 6 West Washington Street; 540/687-3766.

Christmas in Middleburg: If you and your pup could take only one trip to this historic town, count yourself unlucky. Then count on these festivities held annually on the first Saturday in December to inspire the kind of old-fashioned holiday spirit that's hard to find elsewhere. You'll know as soon as you arrive and see the other Christmassy canines that dogs are welcome guests for this daylong celebration in the capital of hunt country. From the **arts and crafts festival** that kicks off around mid-morning to the caroling church choirs that stop traffic along Washington Street, it's a seasonal must. Throughout town, music is in the air—an Irish guitarist at one street corner, a band of bagpipers at another. Shop owners put out mulled wines, hot chocolate, and cookies for customers making the rounds. It all culminates with the huge Christmas parade and the arrival of Santa. Keep your pup on a leash, even if some locals who know their way around town don't, because the festival attracts plenty of visitors. 540/687-8888.

Upper Crust Bakery: Keep this hot spot in mind if you want to take a lunch along to a park or steeplechase, because the kind folks who run it are happy to box it for you. They make the full measure of breads, from plain white to multigrain. Lots of cakes and pies sweeten this spot, including refrigerator pies like coconut and lemon. Have them pack a few sandwiches and toss in some of those fresh scones. 4 North Pendelton Street; 540/687-5666.

Places to Stay

Red Fox Inn and Tavern: Who would've guessed that this venerable colonial tavern and inn—billed as the "oldest original inn in America"—welcomes pooches in some of its overnight quarters. Dogs can't sleep over in the rooms at the top of the grand staircase from the dining room, where Colonel John Mosby and his Confederate raiders planned maneuvers during the Civil War. The inn occupies three separate lodges behind the original building and accepts dogs in those rooms without hesitation. Guests pay a $200 deposit for their pup, which they get back when leaving so long as the dog was well-behaved, caused no damage, and didn't bother other guests. Rooms are $150–185, Sunday–Thursday, $170–325 on weekends. 2 East Washington Street, Middleburg, VA. 20118; 540/687-6301 or 800/223-1728.

PURCELLVILLE

Don't let the stately Victorian homes lining Main Street fool you. This western Loudoun County town is blue-collar and proud of it. Dating back to the mid-1700s, Purcell's Store, as it was known then, was a commercial bump in the road between Winchester and Washington. The town prospered in the 1870s when the railroad put it on the map. Today, its antique shops attract weekend day-trippers—many with dogs accompanying. The Washington & Old Dominion Trail dead-ends its 45-mile path across northern Virginia here, bringing bikers to a halt for rest and refreshment before turning around. True to its heritage, the hot spot in town remains its old-fashioned hardware store, Nichols Hardware on 21st Street, which takes customers back a century or so.

Parks, Beaches, and Recreation Areas

12 Franklin Park 🐾

Known for its 203 acres, this park is billed as a fine family destination featuring a Starplex sports complex, a pool with four slides (plus a floating turtle and pig), a volleyball court, a few soccer fields, and two football/rugby/lacrosse fields. As a doggy destination, leash up the pooch and walk the perimeter trail at sunset, and enjoy a beautiful view of the Blue Ridge Mountains. Located between Purcellville and Round Hill off Business Route 7 on Franklin Park Drive, the park is open dawn–dusk. 703/777-0343.

13 Purcellville Pocket Park 🐾

If you and the dog are looking for a quiet bench to eat lunch, this dinky grazing park behind the Purcellville Town Hall fits the bill. Afterward, if you have any questions about the town, just ask the nice folks inside. Open daily dawn–dusk, the park is located at 130 East Main Street. 703/777-0343.

14 Washington & Old Dominion Railroad Regional Park 🐾

We know this one shows up in other locales across northern Virginia. That's because the old railroad right-of-way where locomotives traveled from 1859 to 1968 stretches its 45 miles of asphalt trail through towns and wilderness, from the Potomac to the Blue Ridge—until it gets here. Purcellville is the end of the line. This particular depot isn't exactly an impressive park or recreation stop off—yet. The town's preservation association plans to renovate and remodel the original Washington & Old Dominion Railroad station into a museum, meeting room, and public restrooms—plus a small park and fountain. The depot is located at North 21st and West O Streets; 703/729-0596.

Restaurants

Mario's Pizza and Restaurant: If it's just plain saucy pizza that you crave, carry out the tasty variety this traditional pizzeria pops out of the big ovens. 119 North 21st Street near the Washington & Old Dominion Railroad depot; 540/338-3555.

Sweet T's Ice Cream Shoppe and Deli: A local hangout in hot weather, this is the coolest place in town when the pooch needs to cool down. 860 East Main Street; 540/338-6039.

EARMARK YOUR CALENDAR

Our Town Revisited: Mid-May marks the annual **Purcellville Heritage Days** when locals put on an old-fashioned, small-town parade that marches down Main Street. The big day also features arts and crafts, barbecue, and other country-style munchings, and a full Saturday of music and festivities celebrating the town's history. Except for the fire engine sirens, this happening doesn't scare off the dogs, and a good time is had by all good men and beasts. It starts and ends at the Town Municipal Center on Main Street. 540/338-5380.

Gathering of the Vibes: The unusual thing about the Saturday morning **Purcellville Farmer's Market** is that most of the folks there are farmers—whether buying or selling. Held in the Town Hall parking lot every good-weather weekend from spring to fall, this agri-gathering is a great detour with the well-behaved pup. Pick up some bargains of fresh vegetables and fruits—many of them grown in the countryside hereabouts. Country-made pies and canned goods worth bringing home give this event an old-fashioned roadside sale feeling. 130 East Main Street; 540/338-7421.

STERLING

Parks, Beaches, and Recreation Areas

15 Algonkian Regional Park 🐾 🐾 ½

The operative word at this scenic 800-acre riverside park is "recreation." The 18-hole golf course is such a beaut because it was built for the private pleasures of industry execs before it went public. It serves nicely as a landmark for dog-appropriate activities that are restricted to its periphery, such as the quick-splash roadside water traps on greens two and five or the sun zone in the park next to the ninth tee (where you and the dog can soak up vitamin D while observing the hackers getting teed off). The par-72 course is no place for puttin' pooches like Chappy—except to get a drink or snack from the pro shop area. The sight of the many geese that reside near the first fairway and on several of the back nine that feature water got our pup-in-the-rough running afowl.

The park's popular swimming pool and miniature golf course a mile past the entrance on the west side aren't for dogs, either. The wooded nature trail that encircles this area from the parking lot to behind the row of 12 riverfront vacation cottages, however, is a casual mile-long walk where the only distraction from wildflowers and songbirds is the screams of kids cannonballing the deep end. Those lovely cottages, by the way, are a great deal for man but not beast—no dogs allowed.

DIVERSIONS

Putting Down Roots: As a tribute to your loyal pup—or to commemorate any other special event or person—you can participate in the **Plant a Memory** program at Claude Moore Park. Order a red maple, pin oak, sweet gum, sweetbay magnolia, or Carolina silverbell at the visitor center; park personnel will plant the tree where you can visit it and watch it grow. The park office sends a card to the honoree acknowledging the gift. Even if your pooch can't read the inscription, this is a sentimental way of personalizing the park. Trees range in price according to size, $60–120 each.

You can also support the park just by walking around. Check out the **March for Parks**, a coordinated nationwide annual show of support for parks in this country where people and their dogs can let their feet do the talking. It's usually held in mid-April. For these events and lots of other ones, call Claude Moore Park, 21544 Cascades Parkway; 703/444-1275.

Adopt a Pet: Mark the third Saturday of every month from noon–3 P.M. on your calendar. That's when you can combine your shopping trip for pooch supplies and a visit with some of the sweetheart pups the **Humane Society of Fairfax County** puts up for adoption at the PetsMart in the Potomac Run Shopping Center. 46220 Potomac Run Center; 703/444-6500.

Make sure to steer your leashed Rover to the main picnic and cookout areas to the east along Potomac View Road. As you might've guessed, this pastoral pocket overlooks the Potomac River where these old waters flow slowly and time stands nearly still. This is an ideal spot for the Zenlike inactivity of river watching, in which you stare into the glittering surface until the river runs through your inner self. From this vantage point, you can also gaze upon the Chesapeake & Ohio National Historical Park and Trail (see the Montgomery County chapter) on the opposite riverbank and cute Tenfoot Island just offshore.

Open year-round (hours vary by season), the park is located about 11 miles northwest from the Capital Beltway (I-495) on Route 7 then three miles north on Cascades Parkway. 703/450-4655.

16 Claude Moore Park 🐾 🐾 🐾

Chappy took to this 357-acre park like a duck to water—and there were even some of those fine-feathered friends enjoying the natural beauty of two ponds. This is the kind of sunny and untroubled place where you can cast a fishing line into the still water, steady the pole between your toes, then lie back in the tall grass for the duration—with your lazy dog alongside.

About the only noise you might hear, other than birds calling and dragon-

---

flies winging, is the march of American history along Vestal's Gap Road. As natural and unpretentious as these grounds may seem now, history once trod here. This parkland protects the sole remaining section of the colonial highway that stretched from Alexandria through Leesburg and all the way to Winchester in the early 1700s. George Washington called it "the Great Road" and used the old animal and Indian trail often for business journeys and military maneuvers from 1753 to 1799. Today, strolling the preserved and nearly pristine 0.75-mile fragment of the ancient road through the woods gives you goose bumps just knowing whose footsteps fell there—Washington, Daniel Boone, and General Braddock, among others.

Under the old oak trees nearby there are picnic tables and hiking space through the woods, where you can appraise several old buildings, including an old shanty schoolhouse. Signs at the park warn that pets must be leashed and under control at all times. Open daily dawn–dusk (though closed national holidays), the park is located on Potomac View Road (Route 637), just over a mile southwest off Route 7. The official address is 21544 Cascades Parkway. 703/444-1275.

Restaurants

Buffalo Wings Factory: Heading out to one of those great sunny afternoon parks? Stop by here and carry out a picnic lunch of barbecued chicken wings—or if you don't want to go finger-messy, order subs and sandwiches from this shopping plaza eatery. 45529 West Church Street; 703/406-0505.

MARYLAND

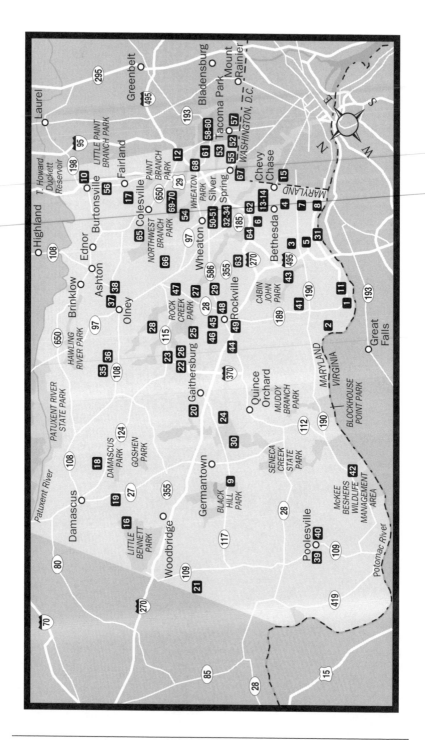

11 MONTGOMERY COUNTY

Few people probably realize that 15 years after colonists established it in 1776, Montgomery County gave up a chunk of its land—36 square miles to be exact—to the United States government to help create the imperfect diamond that would become our nation's capital.

Fewer people probably care. Dogs sure don't. But the county likes to boast about it, so we'll pass that on, just as the county likes to say it offers people a fine blend of urban sophistication and country leisure. That's pretty much true, although the country part is slowly giving way to development, as is everywhere in the DC Metro area.

In the areas close in to the District, Montgomery County is home to a bunch of federal agencies, including the National Institutes of Health, the Food and Drug Administration, the National Institute of Standards and Technology, and the National Oceanic and Atmospheric Administration. Past the federal veneer, you find some of the metropolitan area's fanciest suburbs and classiest country-club communities—and some pretty decent dog digs.

Head farther out and you can't miss the dozens of tech and heavy industrial corporations the county has reeled in to its "I-270 Technology Corridor." This is also where you find mansions with horses down the street from small old clapboard homes with chickens scratching in the backyards.

To shoppers and commuters, bumper-to-bumper traffic is the problem with no foreseeable solution. Look up "road rage" or "traffic jam" in Webster's and you might find an aerial photograph of rush hour on I-270. Weekends, when shoppers jam Rockville Pike's miles of strip shopping centers, can make for the kind of gridlock that makes Chappy lie down in the back seat and put his paws over his eyes.

But a tantalizing 27,000 acres of parkland fill in between the parking lots and asphalt and shopping plazas, making the county that consistently has been rated over the years one of the nation's wealthiest also one of the nation's richest in parklands.

Unfortunately, Maryland is lagging behind Virginia in its treatment of canine citizens, at least when it comes to sharing its pastoral state-owned property. With very few exceptions, Maryland state parks do not allow dogs to set paw on their gorgeous green acres, in this county or elsewhere across the Free State. That means the big and inviting expanses of green seen on maps, such as Seneca Creek State Park and Patuxent State Park, are off-limits to pooch patrons. In the few cases where Maryland park officials yielded to puppy power and declared an off-the-beaten-path sliver open to dogs, the concessions are hardly worth mentioning, much less worth visiting.

The good news is that Chappy found that the county's regional parks— Black Hill, Cabin John, Rock Creek, and Wheaton among them—offer plenty of grassy space, grand old trees and woods, and splash-happy water for playful pups. Perhaps best of all, the Chesapeake & Ohio Canal National Historical Park and Trail has enough dog-friendly hiking miles alongside the Potomac River to make L. L. Bean devotees and their dogs deliriously happy. The law, keep in mind, requires that dogs on public property and in parks be leashed— and cleaning up after your dogs goes without saying.

In addition to that, there has been progress on the dog park front. Canine lovers have proposed six areas to Montgomery's Department of Park and Planning. Each would include a fence or an existing barrier, such as a slope or body of water, to confine the animals. Each would be at least one acre and contain double gates, benches, and bag dispensers for dog waste. As in many places, the county does not have money in its budget for dog parks, but seems willing to help them become a reality if private funds are raised. There are six areas being considered: Aberdeen Park in North Potomac, Bonifant Landfill in Aspen Hill, Centerway Park in Gaithersburg, Evans Parkway Park in Silver Spring, Parklawn Campsite in Wheaton, and Waters Landing Park in Germantown. To check on whether any of these are open for business, try calling Terry Brooks at Parkside Headquarters at 301/495-2477.

National Parks

1 Carderock Recreation Area 🐾 🐾 ½

You won't bump into many people or dogs at this lovely and little-known park that attracts mostly in-the-know rock climbers and hikers—and pooches. But besides the rocks and hiking trails, this wilderness along the Chesapeake & Ohio Canal Trail has a picnic area with grills and a large picnic pavilion that can be rented for parties. They're good for taking a load off after tackling the local section of the Billy Goat Trail, which requires decisive footing along a rocky ridge above the Potomac, just a few rapids downstream from Great Falls. Slightly less wild is the park's recreational area, which offers fields enough for Frisbee dogs or Whiffle ball competition. Restrooms are nearby.

Take Exit 41 (Carderock) from the outer loop of the Beltway (I-495) or the Clara Barton Parkway exit (past the American Legion Bridge) on the inner loop; head west to the Carderock–Naval Surface Warfare Center exit and the park at MacArthur Boulevard. The park is open daily dawn–dusk. 301/299-3613.

2 Chesapeake & Ohio Canal National Historical Park 🐾 🐾 🐾 🐾 🐾

Never had we seen as many dogs, all on leashes, strolling around a park as we did on the sunny day we stopped at this absolute knockout of a national park. We've learned that it's always like that. Chappy was more interested in sniffing the posts that mark the walkway heading down to the canal area than anything else. The ducks swimming in the dramatic rushing water intrigued him, too.

With an average of seven drownings a year in this area of the Potomac, going into the water is forbidden. A deceptively strong current and undertow sweep people away before they know what's happened. One of the friendly park rangers told us sadly that many dogs are lost each year that way, too, when people take them off their leashes for a dip and the current carries the dog downriver. Paths right alongside the river lure the inner swimmer. But don't do it. The same ranger suggested that hot dogs can go into the canal, about 100 yards inside the park from the river. The canal varies in depth, and is often barely deep enough to wade in.

This also is an exceptional entrée to the Chesapeake & Ohio Canal hiker-biker trail that extends here from Georgetown in Washington and past here to Cumberland. Several worthy hiking trails fan off into the wilderness parts of the park. You can pick up a free trail guide from the visitor center, and the rangers will tell you which trails have been rained out or flooded. Just be sure you've got on hiking boots and a towel for your muddy canine companion.

Foot-long hot dogs top the menu at the convenient refreshment center near the parking lot, but Chappy complained a foot wasn't long enough. Alternatives included a soft pretzel, bagel with cream cheese, or an ice cream bar.

To reach the park, which is sometimes said to be in Great Falls instead of Potomac (although the mailing address is Potomac), drive north on MacArthur Boulevard until it dead-ends at the park entrance. The park closes at sunset. For more information, call the Great Falls Tavern Visitor Center at 301/299-3613.

BETHESDA

As recently as the 1940s, Bethesda was largely farmland and unpaved roads. Today, it's a crowded minimetropolis stretching a couple of blocks wide along each side of Wisconsin Avenue as it heads north from the District line into Maryland. Besides some 200 restaurants, endless shops and office high-rises, it is home to the National Institutes of Health, the massive federal government research and treatment facility that has never-ending greenery surrounding its stately medical facilities where dogs can roam and feel especially healthy. This is also home to the infamous Burning Tree, the country club that lost its tax-exempt status several years ago when it claimed in court it had no black members because black people don't play golf. Dan Quayle is an honorary member. Dogs don't have a prayer on these greens, though they do pretty well elsewhere in the moneyed and yuppified environs of Bethesda, where diminutive neighborhood parks abound.

Parks, Beaches, and Recreation Areas

🕃 Burning Tree Park 🐾

Tucked behind Burning Tree Elementary School, this is mostly a sports center for the school. But you can certainly use it for a leashed dog walk, too. Large grassy areas provide some romping space, but keep heads-up for misdirected soccer balls.

The park is open dawn–dusk. From the Beltway (I-495), take River Road north (which actually heads west) and turn right on Beech Tree. Watch for the Burning Tree entrance at the school parking lot and back to the right. 301/495-2525.

🕃 Capital Crescent Trail 🐾 🐾

Hey, buddy, watch where you're going! You'll hear that now and then strolling down this 11-mile, paved, hiker-biker trail that connects the heart of Bethesda to the heart of Georgetown. Once the right-of-way of the former Georgetown Branch Railway, the trail now cuts through urban and suburban areas and 19 various parklands—including a glorious stretch through the Chesapeake & Ohio Canal Historic Park on the north side of Georgetown. A newer section of the trail connects downtown Bethesda to downtown Silver Spring via downtown Chevy Chase.

The drawback for dog lovers? Besides the crowds it attracts, this stretch of pleasurable pavement has been overrun with folks on wheels. In-line skaters and bicyclists often exceed the posted speed limit and sometimes don't know proper passing etiquette when coming up on pedestrians and dogs. Leashes are not only required but also essential for the safety of your pup. Rangers working the trail actually started using a radar gun a while back to try to educate the whiz-by wheelers on just how fast they were going, but speed's still a problem.

So if you head this way, hike along the edge of the pavement where your pooch can easily take to the grassy skirts on the side or sniff his way through the ferns and undergrowth in the more natural stretches. Most dogs shouldn't go the full 11 miles anyway, unless they're in serious hiking shape. From Bethesda you'll probably want to start out toward Georgetown (the other way crosses more busy streets) for a mile or so and then turn back. Remember, asphalt hiking can be hard on tender dog paw pads, especially during hot summer days or in midwinter when road salts get tracked everywhere.

Pick up the trail at the Ourisman Honda parking lot near where Bethesda Avenue intersects Woodmont Avenue, less than a half mile south of the Bethesda Metro Station and a couple of blocks west of Wisconsin Avenue. It's open all hours but pounding this pavement in the dark isn't recommended. 301/495-2525.

5 Carderock Park 🐾

Yet another neighborhood park that serves as the grassy, woodsy backyard to five or six cul-de-sacs in this upscale neighborhood, this is one more testament to the community planners who schedule little green zones as nature hubs for their overdevelopment. Leashed dogs get some strolling space in the deal. The park is open daily, dawn–dusk and is located a couple of blocks off MacArthur Boulevard on 81st Street. 301/495-2525.

6 Maplewood–Alta Vista Park 🐾 🐾

A white standard poodle was playing catch with his owner when we dropped by one day. Lots of kids rode bikes and played on the playground while a group of adults chatted in the parking lot nearby. Obviously a neighborhood favorite, this park has just enough hilly areas, trees, and grassy open spaces to be fun for everyone—including the poochster on a leash.

Open dawn–dusk, the park is located south of Beltway (I-495) exit 35. Take Wisconsin Avenue less than a mile and turn right on Alta Vista Road. The park will be on the right. 301/495-2525.

7 Norwood Park 🐾 🐾 🦴

Don't crash drive into this place. The frantic pace of Wisconsin Avenue will have you speeding into this neighborhood park, but it's a one-lane entrance and we almost took out a Taurus wagon on our last visit, so be careful. Once you're safely parked, however, take a leisurely, stress-free stroll down the slope of grass next to the ball field area where you'll always find leash-free dogs—although a big sign clearly reads they must be on a leash at all times. Obviously, the trees lining the wide-open soccer field area were just too tempting. From the Beltway (I-495) take Wisconsin Avenue south and turn right on Norwood. Norwood dead-ends into the park, which is open dawn–dusk. 301/495-2525.

8 Westmoreland Hills Park 🐾 🐾

Down a steep hill, curve around to the right, pull into the parking lot, and voilà! Here's another small treasure of a neighborhood park, offering paved paths, tennis courts, and a friendly feel for a leashed dog who is bound to find some new friends who know the territory from their regular visits.

The park is open dawn–dusk. From Massachusetts Avenue heading north, go left on Elliott Road just after you've gone around Westmoreland Circle. Elliott dead-ends into the park. 301/495-2525.

Restaurants

Aangan: The Indian cuisine runs the gamut at this quiet place located just a few blocks from the town center off Georgetown Road. The friendly folks here will bag your entrées so you can carry them out to dine with your dog. Try the chicken and lamb curries, though Chappy prefers taste testing the less spicy tandoori dishes. 4920 Saint Elmo Avenue; 301/657-1262.

Athenian Plaka: Tables on the sidewalk are fine for dogs, and don't be surprised if you see other four-legged gourmets show up with their dinner companions. The traditional Greek menu, which has several tasty lamb entrées, is available for carryout, too, in case you'd rather picnic in a park. 7833 Woodmont Avenue; 301/986-1337.

Austin Grill: One block from the central intersection in Bethesda proper, this restaurant gets loud with a young and energetic crowd, so Chappy doesn't care about going in. (Good thing—he's not allowed.) You can call ahead and carry out excellent Tex-Mex salads, burritos, and fajitas. 7278 Woodmont Avenue; 301/656-1366.

Bacchus: For low-key Lebanese cuisine that you and the pooch can pick up on your way to the great outdoors or to just enjoy together at home, call in a take-out order. The hot and spicy *soujok* and any of the kabobs, even the fish, are tasty treats. Note: Bacchus is not open for lunch on weekends. 7945 Norfolk Avenue; 301/657-1722.

Bob's Famous Ice Cream: Bob's may offer only 16 flavors—as opposed to those 30-something places—but it's still a neighborhood favorite on summer nights where the action is on the sidewalk out front. 4706 Bethesda Avenue; 301/657-2963.

Cafe Bethesda: A mainstay of Bethesda, this pretty-as-a-picture restaurant will gladly send you and your dog packing with its tasty grilled chicken in a bag—or any of the items on its American-minded menu. 5027 Wilson Lane; 301/657-3383.

Cottonwood Cafe: Stop by this genteel Tex-Mex restaurant to pick up lunch for you and *el perro,* and don't be surprised to find nearly nouveau southwestern dishes that will lure you away from the enchilada and taco habit. Especially recommended are its creative chicken and turkey sandwiches. 4844 Cordell Avenue; 301/656-4844.

La Madeleine French Bakery: *Mon dieu!* Chewy inside, crisp outside, just the way a baguette ought to be! Who said real dogs don't eat quiche? This country French–style bakery and café makes serving yourself and carrying out the tasty food easy. Near the Bethesda Metro stop, at 7607 Old Georgetown Road; 301/215-9142.

Louisiana Express Company: Look for the sketched crawdaddy on the sign to find authentic Louisiana cooking, including full breakfast served every day and brunch on Sunday. Jambalaya is especially popular, and you can get it in four varieties: chicken, andouille sausage, seafood, or "the works," which is all three combined. Chappy prefers the works, but it's a little on the spicy side for him. A small order is $6.50 and a large order $10.75. The complete menu is available for carryout. 4921 Bethesda Avenue; 301/652-6945.

Trattoria Sorrento: Hearty home-style southern Italian cooking means zesty red-sauce dishes and the accompaniment of the usual trattoria entrées are available for carryout when you and your *paisano* puppy get a hankering for a pasta picnic. 4930 Cordell Avenue; 301/718-0344.

Places to Stay

Residence Inn–Bethesda: Ouch! Bring your dog, but be prepared to fork over a $100 fee, plus a $5 per night extra charge to stay in this classy 13-story hotel. That's on top of a double room rate in the neighborhood of $139 per night. 7335 Wisconsin Avenue, Bethesda, MD 20814; 301/718-0200.

BOYDS

Parks, Beaches, and Recreation Areas

9 Black Hill Regional Park 🐾 🐾 🐾 ½ 🐾

Few views are as memorable as that of Little Seneca Lake from the visitor center deck on a sunny afternoon with a leashed puppy at your side. The water in this 505-acre, artificial lake is clean, clear, and sparkles in late afternoon just as though you were at the beach. And it had better be clean, since it was created to provide both recreation and drinking water to the area. Fishing in the lake—with a license—yields largemouth bass, smallmouth bass, and catfish. Canoes and rowboats can be rented. Large picnic areas are available in the 1,854-acre park, and big groups often reserve them. Some picnic areas even have their own playgrounds, and they fill up fast at this popular park.

The park rangers here like to say that Black Hill should have been named Groundhog Regional Park because the furry rodents called "pigs in the grass" are so easily found on lakeside hills. As far as we can tell, they steer clear of dogs—even though the latter are restrained on leashes. Beavers steer clear too when they come out at dusk. There is a paved hiker-biker trail and over 10 miles of unpaved trails, often used by horse riders but otherwise perfect for paws instead of hooves (though watch where you step, 'cause horse people don't clean up after their animals like dog people do).

One cautionary note: Shade is sparse here, and you won't easily find a drinking fountain. With the lake, it's a water-water-everywhere dilemma—so BYOB for your dog and for you.

Picnic areas can be reserved May 1–October 15, through the Park Permits Office, 301/495-2525.

The park is open March 1–October 31, 6 A.M.–sunset; November 1–February 28, 7 A.M.–sunset; closed Thanksgiving, Christmas, and New Year's Day. To get to the park, take I-270 north to Exit 18, (Clarksburg Road). Go west and turn left on West Old Baltimore Road. At Lake Ridge Drive turn right into the park. 301/972-3476 or 301/972-9396.

BURTONSVILLE

Parks, Beaches, and Recreation Areas

🔟 Burtonsville Park 🐾 ½

It's a pretty safe bet that people won't be getting in the way of you and your dog here. It's just a wide-open field full of dandelions shimmering in the sun. Oh, there's a slide sitting in the middle of the grass to the left, with a teeter-totter and bench nearby. Farther down a gently sloping hill is an old basketball court and one rough ball field. Tall trees line the edge of the park near the road, but otherwise it's just wide-open acreage—no picnic pavilions or water fountains, just a nice spot to get out and stretch your legs.

The park is located just off to the left of Oursler Road, which is off Route 198, Spencerville Road. The best way to get there is to take Route 29 north, turn left on Spencerville Road and drive about 10 miles; watch carefully on the right for the sign announcing Oursler Road or you'll miss it. Turn right on Oursler Road, then left into the park. Open dawn–dusk. 301/495-2525.

CABIN JOHN

Parks, Beaches, and Recreation Areas

🔢 Cabin John Park 🐾 ½

Don't confuse this dinky five-acre park with the 540-acre Cabin John *Regional* Park on the north side of Bethesda. More of a neighborhood athletic park with basketball courts, picnic area, playground, and baseball fields, its greenery is the southernmost end of the elongated but mostly undeveloped Cabin John Creek Park and the northernmost end of the Chesapeake & Ohio Canal Historic Park. It all seems less confusing and perfectly fine for a dog on a leash when you're sitting here in the sun. Open dawn–dusk, the park is located on the righthand side of MacArthur Boulevard where it passes over the Clara Barton Parkway. 301/495-2525.

Restaurants

The Market on the Boulevard: Care for liverwurst on rye? Why yes, thank you, is Chappy's sure response. And for you? How about a chunk of salmon for dinner and a nice bottle of chardonnay to go with it. You can get wonderful gourmet carryout here. Chappy liked the Congressional sandwich—Black Forest ham with melted brie, honey mustard, lettuce, and tomato on a French roll. 7945 MacArthur Boulevard; 301/229-2526.

CALVERTON

Parks, Beaches, and Recreation Areas

12 Calverton-Fairland Park 🐾 🐾

A ramblin' kind of park that's hilly and cute, the lawns look like all baseball and football fields when you first enter it—and that's not far off the mark. Opposite the front parking lot is a picnic pavilion with tables and bathrooms, and a second grilling and picnicking pavilion is near the back of the park, behind the tennis courts. A paved trail runs through it, and between sports fields there's considerable dog-walking turf that looks primo for dog Frisbee (though leash laws are in effect) or flying a kite. And if the games have begun and you're feeling cramped, stroll due east just past that little tuft of shade trees (among the few left standing here) into smaller Galway Park, which is connected to Galway Elementary School.

The park is located at Beethoven Boulevard and Fairland Road, about a mile southeast off Route 29 (Columbia Pike), and is open dawn–dusk daily. 301/495-2525.

CHEVY CHASE

Parks, Beaches, and Recreation Areas

13 North Chevy Chase Park 🐾 🐾

No, it's not quite as small as it looks when you drive into the parking lot, which holds about eight cars. In fact, there are 31 acres of land in this park, which is good sized by neighborhood park standards. Once you get out, you'll see there's a reason more than one dog is leash-free, despite the rule that dogs must be on a leash. This neighborhood park is well known to locals and well used by tennis lovers, hoop-shooters, baseball hitters, and playground players. It is open dawn–dusk. Take the Beltway (I-495) and head south on Connecticut Avenue. Take a right onto Jones Bridge Road; the park is the first right. 301/495-2525.

14 Rock Creek Hills Park 🐾 ½

Sitting up on a hill, the ball field area was inviting, but Chappy needs trees to sniff, so he tugged us to the opposite side of the parking lot near the playground and more woodsy area where trees rim the park. He was also interested in playing Rocky and gettin' strong now, as he raced down the steps to a ravine area below and then back up again. Of course, we were more out of breath than he was. The park is open dawn–dusk. Heading north on Connecticut Avenue north, cross under the Beltway (I-495) and turn right on Saul Road. At Haverhill Drive, bear left and turn into the park on the left. 301/495-2525.

15 Rock Creek Park 🐾 🐾

Within the Montgomery County section of Rock Creek Park—not to be confused with Rock Creek *Regional* Park (see the Rockville section in this chapter)—one of the more popular spots is Meadowbrook Community Park off Beach Drive. It was here that we crossed paths with the biggest Great Dane—yes, we know that's redundant—we have ever seen. And he was not on a leash.

Dogs are supposed to be on a leash at all times, but who would argue with this creature? He was so big and black and had such pointy ears that when our oldest son first saw him, he shouted, "Mom, look! It's a pony at the park!" The dog was walking around a deserted baseball field and sniffing at some shrubbery. He commanded respect but was quite friendly. Then we saw him squish into the back of a Toyota and take off.

A couple of other leashless dogs were here as well, but not the little black bichon frisé at the playground—an obvious rule follower. The park has big open fields used for ball playing, a playground called Candy Cane City, and the bike-hike trail that leads up into Rockville or down into the District.

Take Beach Drive north past the District line and look for Meadowbrook on the right. Pull into the parking lot and walk across the bridge to the park area. It's open daily dawn–dusk. 301/495-2525.

Restaurants

Clyde's of Chevy Chase: It's hard not to order a famous Clyde's burger even at this newer location of the longtime Georgetown saloon. But Chappy tugs for the largest of the steaks served here as a perfect carryout dinner. 70 Wisconsin Circle; 301/951-9600.

La Ferme: It's too bad the vine-covered terrace is off-limits to dogs, but you can carry out dependable French cuisine for divine dining elsewhere with your four-legged Frenchy along. Much of the menu here is classic French, and the châteaubriand on a checkered tablecloth, spread on a green hillside under a tree somewhere, well, *c'est magnifique!* 7101 Brookville Road; 301/986-5255.

Starbucks: If only Starbucks had more food on the menu, Chappy would be happier about stopping here. As it is, the tables out front—even though they're right on the busy street—are great for taking a caffeine break. 8542-B Connecticut Avenue; 301/986-5187.

Places to Stay

Holiday Inn–Chevy Chase: Settle in for a night with your dog and order up room service at this 12-story hotel, but be prepared to pay a $50 "cleaning" fee.

(Don't they "clean" the room already?) Room rates are about $109 for a double. 5520 Wisconsin Avenue, Chevy Chase, MD 20815; 301/656-1500.

CLARKSBURG

Parks, Beaches, and Recreation Areas

16 Little Bennett Regional Park 🐾 🐾 🐾

Just down the road from Black Hill Regional Park, Little Bennett features camping and a much woodsier setting than Black Hill. In fact, Little Bennett is the single largest wooded area in the county with nearly 4,000 acres of forests crisscrossed by streams, although it doesn't have a large lake as most other large parks do. The meadows and scrublands interspersed throughout the park draw a mix of wildlife. If you're lucky, you can spot owls, woodcocks, and wild turkeys year-round, although Chappy never saw any when we visited. This is a great place for you if you're seeking a remote respite from the humdrum. It was a little on the desolate side for our tastes, but for hard-core campers and hikers, it would probably be heaven.

If you stop at the front gate, the friendly folks in charge will give you a map of the trails and tell you where to park. In addition, you can visit some of the historic sites in the park. In the 18th century, this was the scene of farms, gristmills, and a whiskey distillery that operated until 1907. The Kingsley Schoolhouse, built in 1893, served the community until it closed in 1935 when the Depression forced families out of the area. It is one of the few buildings that remain in a relatively unaltered state, although it is not open to the public or even learned dogs like Chappy.

Five different loops in the park offer campsites, all permitting leashed pets and insisting they never be left unattended. Some sites are for tents only. Others allow recreational vehicles. At the nature center, there is a laundry room. Reservations are not required but are recommended during the summer season, when the park is truly more a campground than a park. Rates for all tent sites are $14 per night, per site. Sites with electricity are $18. Rates are slightly less for county residents.

To get to the park, take I-270 to the Clarksburg Road exit east, and then take a left on Frederick Road. The entrance is on the right at Camping Ridge Road. The park is open daily dawn–dusk. 301/972-9222.

COLESVILLE

Parks, Beaches, and Recreation Areas

17 Cloverly Park 🐾

Ah, shade. Picnic pavilions are the first things you see here. Ball fields and a playground are beyond the pavilions in this pit stop park, which is right next to Cloverly Elementary School.

From the Beltway, take Exit 29, New Hampshire Avenue. Travel north for about 25 miles to Briggs Chaney Road. Turn right. The park is almost immediately on the left, adjacent to Cloverly Elementary School. 301/495-2525.

DAMASCUS

Parks, Beaches, and Recreation Areas

18 Damascus Recreational Park 🐾 🐾 ½ 🐾

Police were here the day we stopped by. At first, we wondered why the road was blocked. But those were just the squad cars taking up the first few spots in the parking lot next to the softball field where a rousing game between off-duty cops was underway. This is a multiuse park with ball fields, tennis courts, a playground, and even a funky red pointy sculpture reaching up into the sky right at the front gate. Art? Fire Hydrant? Tree? Chappy treats them all the same and likes to leave his signature. There are paved trails around the park that offer a pleasant if not-at-all-daunting hike. Water fountains and bathrooms offer added attractions—in that order.

From I-270, take Exit 15 (Darnestown-Germantown Road) east and turn left on Frederick Road. Turn right at Ridge Road, then right on Kings Valley Road, and look for the park entrance on the left. The park is open dawn–dusk daily. 301/495-2525.

19 Ovid Hazen Wells Recreational Park 🐾 🐾 ½ 🐾

Perched on the peak of a small mountain, this park looks over a scene like a folk art painting. There are rolling hills, crops of different colors, a church, and a winding road. Occasionally a car whizzes by. Judging from the pile of dog poop we almost stepped in, this is a popular spot for pooches and one not patrolled by anyone who enforces the leash and pooper-scooper rules. Green grass in wide-open spaces, a playground, three big picnic pavilions, and the view make this a very sweet spot, however. No water here, though, so be sure to bring some. And expect porta-potties.

From I-270, take Exit 15 (Darnestown-Germantown Road). Go east to Frederick Road and turn left. Turn right at Ridge Road (Route 27). At Skylark Road, turn left. The park, at the top of the hill on the right, is open daily, dawn–dusk. 301/495-2525.

DARNESTOWN

Parks, Beaches, and Recreation Areas

20 Darnestown Park 🐾 🐾 ½

Run until you can't anymore. There's that much land—rolling hills and wide-open grass spread out behind the tennis courts and play area in this tailored roadside park plopped amid the cows and horses in neighboring backyards. We're talkin' rural splendor in the grass here, folks, but don't expect much more than splendor.

Open daily, dawn–dusk, the park is located in the town of Darnestown, off Darnestown Road (Exit 6 west off I-270). 301/495-2525.

DICKERSON

Parks, Beaches, and Recreation Areas

21 Dickerson Conservation Park 🐾 🐾 🐾

Far Away Farm is on the road to Dickerson Conservation Park, and when you see that sign you smile because you know the people living there at one time had to say to themselves, "Are we there yet?" Passing that farm, you are far away from just about everywhere. But keep going because you're not there yet. "There" is the Dickerson Conservation Area and you'll know you're close when you see the Pepco power plant smokestack soaring into the sky and spewing out white stuff.

DIVERSIONS

White Out: White's Ferry is a throwback to another era. Pull into this town at the westernmost part of Montgomery County and check out the high-water lines marked on the little store. Rent a picnic table for $1.50, the big sign says. And, yes, that flat boat is the ferry. Here the Potomac River, in all its majesty, rules. Riding across it on the *General Jubal A. Early*, a 15-car ferry, makes you feel like a pioneer crossing long ago. The distance is short. The ride takes only a few minutes; you could almost throw a rock across—that's how far it is. And if you need to get across to Virginia, this is a lot more fun than any of the bridges downtown—certainly for dogs whom you'll want to keep on leashes going across. (Also see the Leesburg section of the Loudoun County chapter.)

The store sells snacks and bait, but it is generally open only April–October. Fishing is good here because of the Pepco plant upstream, which warms the water, they say.

The ferry runs 5 A.M. to 11 P.M., seven days a week. Foot passengers pay 50 cents to cross; automobiles go for $3 one-way and $5 round-trip. The ferry makes runs from 5 A.M. to 11 P.M., but avoid rush hour, because many exurban commuters heading into and out of Washington use it as their crossing point. To get to the ferry, take I-270 north, exit at Route 28 west (Norbeck Road), and take Route 107 west until it becomes White's Ferry Road. The ferry is at the end of the road. 24801 White's Ferry Road, Dickerson, MD 20842; 301/349-5200.

When we drove into this park, it was a little worrisome. About a half dozen pickup trucks were parked near the entrance. It was quiet. It was overcast. And it was winter, so it wasn't a green, woodsy, inviting area. It looked pretty desolate. The next thing we saw was a guy in an orange jacket carrying a gun. Yes, public hunting is allowed in parts of the area. But we pressed on because a ranger had told us it was a good place to pick up the Chesapeake & Ohio Canal Trail and see the Potomac. He was right.

We followed the entrance road to the paved parking lot and took the main path straight to the river. Chappy dug into the mud—it had rained recently—and lifted his nose into the wind by the Potomac, where it was quite breezy. He was *so* happy. Flooding around the trees made the scene swamp-like, and we didn't see a soul on the path in either direction. But the freshly strewn woodchip path and the fire someone had built recently by the water led us to believe humans had been here at some point not too long ago. And it's a natural hiking spot with some well-worn trails and lots of untouched land. The signs do say the rule is for dogs to be leashed and to take all provisions, including water. It's rugged.

Take I-270 to Darnestown Road (Route 28) west and turn left on Martinsburg Road, which is close to the Pepco plant. Look for the entrance on the right. The park is open dawn–dusk daily. 301/972-9396.

GAITHERSBURG

Parks, Beaches, and Recreation Areas

22 Blueberry Hill Park 🐾

We didn't find many thrills on this Blueberry Hill. Instead, two teenagers on bikes made faces at us and a guy in a long coat walking a pretty white leash-free Lab stared at us. What can we say? It just wasn't friendly, even though the park encompasses a fairly inviting and useful 20 open acres of grassy areas in a small suburban town house subdivision park. It was so wide open, in fact, a No Golfing sign was posted.

The park is open daily, dawn–dusk. From I-70, take the Shady Grove Road exit north. At Crabbs Branch Way, take a right and then turn left at the next big road, Redland Road. Turn left at the second street, which is Needwood Road, and follow it until you see the park on the right. 301/495-2525.

23 Centerway Park 🐾

Don't come here looking for shade. Come looking to walk around some grass with a little bit of paved path between the soccer fields and the playground equipment. Still, it was good enough for four dogs, all on leashes as is required, on one particularly sunny afternoon when we visited. But they must have been neighborhood pooches, because it's doubtful anyone would drive to get here.

The park is open dawn–dusk. Take I-270 north to Montgomery Village Avenue, turn right on Centerway Road, and left into the park. 301/495-2525.

24 Green Park 🐾 🐾 🦮

The only (at press time) fenced-in, official, off-leash dog park (a.k.a. Dog Exercise Area) in the county is located at Green Park. Here pooches have more than an acre in which to frolic. There are two fenced areas—one is 17,000 square feet and dedicated to small dogs; the other is 43,000 square feet so that the big guys can romp freely. There are lots of rules to follow, foremost being that city residents must have a current pet license. If you don't have one, go to City Hall at 31 South Summit Avenue, or call 301/258-6343. Nonresidents have to submit a Dog Exercise Area membership for each dog, which includes a completed application, current rabies certificate, and photograph of the dog, and $25. Note: The city assumes no liability; owners must be responsible for their dogs at all times. The park is open from dawn to dusk. From I-270, take Exit 9 to I-370 (Sam Eig Highway), turn right on Diamondback Drive, then left on Bickerstaff Way to the park. For more information, call 301/258-6343.

25 Johnson's Park 🐾

Shortly after the Civil War, this park (which is also called Emory Grove) was a meeting place for religious revivals. It later became a favorite baseball site for Negro League games. Now, it seems to be a favorite site for teens who cut through the woods on the edge of the almost 10-acre park to get to the pool next door. For dogs, it probably isn't as inspiring as it was for the ball players of yore or today's teens.

To get to the park, take I-270 north to Diamond Avenue and turn left as it Diamond turns into Washington Grove Lane. The park is on the left just past Midcounty Highway. It's open dawn–dusk. 301/495-2525.

26 Lake Whetstone 🐾 🐾 ½

What this little subdivision lake area lacks in acreage it makes up for in scenery. A pretty lake sits down off the busy road and is great for dawdling about and skipping a few rocks, and non-residents can easily stop and have a nice afternoon walk. There's a dock, a picnic area, and some ducks quacking around. Paved paths lead into the housing development and provide a way for a stroll with a leashed dog.

From I-270, take Montgomery Village Avenue east and go right on Islandside Drive down into the park on the left. The park is open dawn–dusk daily. 301/495-2525.

27 Redland Park 🐾 ½

Maybe it was the landscaped area of rocks and trees at the start of the paved exercise course that made us and Chappy, on a leash, feel that this was a cared-for park. A hilly loop gives it some character. It also has a playground, tennis courts, and a basketball court that attracts more sweaty humans than tongue-wagging pups.

Take I-270 to Montgomery Village Avenue, turn right on Midcounty Highway, then left at the dead end onto Shady Grove Road. Turn right onto Muncaster Mill Road, right again on Redland Road, and watch for the park entrance on the right. It's open dawn–dusk daily. 301/495-2525.

28 Stewartown Park 🐾

At least there is an island of trees shading a half dozen picnic tables where you and the leashed pooch can sit if you're tired of walking around the soccer field or tennis courts.

The park is open dawn–dusk daily. From Montgomery Village Avenue, turn right on Centerway Road and left on Goshen Road until you can turn left into the park. 301/495-2525.

29 Zoe Wadsworth Park and Woodward Park 🐾

Two parks bump up into each other in the middle of this funky little Gaithersburg neighborhood called Washington Grove. Small brown signs with arrows point to them along the narrow residential streets. Dogs should be leashed, but because this is such a 'hood affair, don't be surprised if the resident dogs are running free.

From I-270 take the Diamond Avenue exit and bear left as it turns into Washington Grove Lane. Turn a sharp right onto Center Street, which dead-ends into the park. The parks are open daily, dawn–dusk. 301/495-2525.

Restaurants

Hunan Palace Restaurant: Get your favorite kung pao chicken to go. 9011 Gaither Road; 301/947-1283.

Moby Dick: Mmm. Mmm. Love those kabobs. They'll happily wrap them up to go for you and the pooch. 105 Market Street; 301/987-7770.

Rio Grande Cafe: In the mood for enchiladas and rice? Tacos? We're always happy to have some margaritas with salt on the rocks, thank you, but with

---

EARMARK YOUR CALENDAR–DECEMBER

Bright Lights, Little Doggy: One of the only ways you can get into the gorgeous Seneca Creek State Park with a dog is to put the pup in the car and take a drive through during the **Winter Lights** show that's a big to-do every Christmas season. It's a 3.5-mile drive through a fun light show. Okay, Chappy pretty much slept through the whole thing, but we liked it and we humored us. The show runs during the entire month of December, 6 P.M.–10 P.M. on weekdays and until 11 P.M. on Saturday and Sunday. 11950 Clopper Road (Route 117); 301/258-6350.

Chappy along, it's easier to get the food here and take it home to eat and drink there. 231 Rio Boulevard; 240/632-2150.

Places to Stay

Comfort Inn–Shady Grove: "Sure! Dogs are allowed." We always like to hear that happy response. And although there is no room service at this seven-story link in the national hotel chain, several area restaurants deliver. A free continental breakfast is included with the room rate, $69 on weekends. 16216 Frederick Road, Gaithersburg, MD 20877; 301/330-0023.

Hilton–Gaithersburg: Your dog is welcome at this hotel, which is walking distance to Lake Forest Shopping Center. Lots of nice grassy areas surround the hotel, and room service is available, but expect to pay a non-refundable $100 deposit. The rate for a double on a weekend is $79. 620 Perry Parkway, Gaithersburg, MD 20877; 301/977-8900.

Holiday Inn–Gaithersburg: One bonus here is room service. There's a lake across the street, convenient for walks with the dog, but you have to cross a busy intersection of six-lane roads to get to it. A double on a weekend is $69, or $75 with breakfast. 2 Montgomery Village Avenue, Gaithersburg, MD 20879; 301/948-8900.

Residence Inn–Gaithersburg: These hotels are always a nice rest stop for you and the pooch. A one-bedroom is $79 on a weekend night, but you will be charged a non-refundable $100 pet fee. There is no room service, but each room does have a full kitchen so that you can fix your own meals. 9721 Washington Boulevard, Gaithersburg, MD 20877

GERMANTOWN

Parks, Beaches, and Recreation Areas

🔟 South Germantown Recreational Park 🐾

This is a huge park. It covers 557 acres, all flat and wide open, and it runs on both sides of the road. You know you've gone out of the park when you run into the next-door neighbor's pony or bale of hay.

But it's called a recreational park for a reason—recreation's what it does best. There are various sports fields, playground, tennis courts, and picnic areas. You and your leashed pooch could wander to the far ends of this park exploring grassy, open fields and probably not see anyone else. This isn't a fancy paved park, nor is it a rough, by-the-water, hiking park. It's more of a wide-open, come-have-fun place. So if you go, take water and mind the heat, because there isn't much shade.

Take I-270 to Clopper Road (Route 117) and head west. Turn left on Schaeffer Road and look for the park on either side. The park is open dawn–dusk daily. 301/495-2525.

GLEN ECHO

Parks, Beaches, and Recreation Areas

31 Glen Echo Park 🐾 ½ 🦴

Glen Echo is actually an old amusement park that used to offer Washingtonians who took the trolley out from town a large outdoor pool, bumper cars, a roller coaster, and other rides. It's now an art center with studios, workshops, puppet shows, and fairs like the Washington Folk Festival that's held every May or June.

The real treat on the grounds at Glen Echo, however, is the 1921 Dentzel carousel, open in the summer months only. Big multicolored animals and the old Wurlitzer organ make it a draw for little kids and big kids. The Spanish ballroom is the site of lots of dancing events on warm summer evenings. And the Puppet Theater and Adventure Theater put on many wonderful kids' shows. But all that is for people, as is the Clara Barton house—a tribute to the founder of the Red Cross.

A small park with picnic benches and a playground near the back of the complex does draw some dogs on leashes, and the grassy areas near the parking lot are nicely kept, but otherwise it's probably not worth it for your dog to come along. The park is open dawn–dusk daily. From the District, take MacArthur Boulevard out, heading north, until you see the park on the left at Goldsboro Road. 7300 MacArthur Boulevard; 301/492-6282.

KENSINGTON

Parks, Beaches, and Recreation Areas

32 Clum Kennedy Gardens 🐾 🐾

With a trellis and benches and shrubs and flowers, this sweet little park rates better than a pit stop mostly because of the fun antique hunting on nearby Howard Avenue. The stream that flows through the narrow grassy area and all the landscaping jacks it up a notch in our estimation, too, and offers a lot for dogs to sniff and you to appreciate.

From Connecticut Avenue heading north from the Beltway (I-495), turn right on Saul Road, left on Kensington Parkway, and look for the park on the right when Kensington dead-ends into Montgomery Avenue. The park is open daily, dawn–dusk. 301/495-2525.

33 Ken-Gar Palisades 😺

A 15-acre park, this place seems bigger than many of the neighborhood parks—because it is. The drawback is wide areas of chest-high weeds that are no fun and that can harbor ticks and other icky things in certain seasons. There is still plenty of good sniffing for a dog on a leash, however, including walking up the hill at the back of the park to the teeter-totter area. The park is open dawn–dusk. From Connecticut Avenue heading north from the Beltway (I-495), turn left on Wexford Drive and left on Beach Drive. Look for the park on the left. 301/495-2525.

34 Kensington Cabin Park 😺 ½

Like a sunken living room in a house, this little five-acre park area sits by the side of the road, but a couple of steps down. Look for the little log cabin com-

---

DIVERSIONS

The Land of Oz: The minute you see the **Washington Temple,** which is the home of the Church of Jesus Christ of Latter-day Saints, you will feel like Dorothy on the road to Oz. This magnificent house of worship rises up out of the suburbs just outside the Beltway and soars into the sky. Five pointed spires surround a sixth, taller one topped by a golden angel trumpeting up to the heavens. It makes you believe that all dogs really do go to heaven. Chappy, being a Tibetan terrier, was inspired, but clung to his more Buddhist tendencies, and we cleaned up after him, as you should if your pooch should leave an offering on the peaceful nature path that surrounds the temple. Of course, dogs are not allowed inside for a look at what the Latter-day Saints claim are some of the most technologically advanced religious exhibits, but, truly, the outside is what's most breathtaking. It's also good to make a note to take the trip during Christmastime when a light show is displayed on the grounds. The temple is open every day of the year, 10 A.M.–9 P.M. 9900 Stoneybrook Drive; 301/587-0144.

Flea the Fleas: If it's early spring, it's not too early to think about those pesky fleas that active dogs roaming public parks are prone to acquire. So stop by **PetsMart** just behind White Flint Mall and check out the latest anti-flea technology and get advice from the veterinary staff. 5154 Nicholson Lane, near Rockville Pike; 301/770-1343.

---

munity center, the wooden playground, and the tennis court, and then pull over and park on the street. Trees up on the hill to the back of the park interested Chappy, but it was unclear whether his interest was physiological or intellectual.

From Connecticut Avenue north at the Beltway, turn right on Beach Drive and left on Kensington Parkway. Open dawn–dusk, the park will be on the left. 301/495-2525.

Restaurants

Tea Room: Nestled among the Kensington antique shops, the Tea Room has its tables out even in the dead of winter. Stop into this casual little eatery for some hot sandwiches, or even a complete dinner with drink, which is a daily special here. On a wintry day, it's a perfect pit stop for some hot chocolate, or even tea. 3750 Howard Avenue; 301/933-1226.

LAYTONSVILLE

Parks, Beaches, and Recreation Areas

35 Laytonsville Park 🐾

Nicely designed, this 11-acre park is a pretty pit stop. Some trees were fine with Chappy for sniffing and marking. It was pleasant enough to sit for a minute on the benches and watch kids play on the playground. But if anything more than that happened, we can't recall.

Take Georgia Avenue (Route 97) north and turn left on Olney-Laytonsville Road (Route 108). Follow that to Laytonsville until it dead-ends and turn right on Laytonsville Road. Then turn left on Brink Road and look for the park on the left. The park is open dawn–dusk daily. 301/495-2525.

36 Sundown Road Park 🐾 🐾

With almost double the amount of acreage, this 20-acre park is similar to Laytonsville Park, with more grass, and it's just on the other side of town. Again, it's one of those places where there's much ado about nothing for pups. It's a nice place to stop but you wouldn't want to drive there.

Take Georgia Avenue (Route 97) north and turn left on Olney-Laytonsville Road (Route 108). Follow that to Laytonsville until it dead-ends and turn right on Laytonsville Road. Turn right on Sundown Road and look for the park on the right. The park is open dawn–dusk daily. 301/495-2525.

OLNEY

Olney is a quaint little town that was founded in the early 1800s as a community of artisans, traders, and merchants, and the friendly and creative feeling still survives. Nothing here is a dog attraction worth driving for, but if you come for the antique shops that line the main drag, be assured some pleasant parkland is close by.

Parks, Beaches, and Recreation Areas

37 Greenwood Park 🐾 🐾

From its Georgia Avenue entrance, this park looks dinky, and Chappy was ready to raise his nose and his leg to it and skedaddle. But once out of the car, you get the idea that it's a little-known oasis on the outskirts of little Olney.

Not that there's any reason to drive here unless you're in town antiquing anyway, but the paved paths that head off toward the distant school soccer fields offer a pleasant walk. Few enough folks hang out here that, even in the summer when the nearby pool is open, kind dogs are said to run leash-free— though the law requires leashes. An unpaved path leads off into thicker woods, but never mind exploring the trickle of a creek because it's entirely overrun with thistles and briars.

The park is located 11 miles north of the Beltway (I-495) on Georgia Avenue (Route 97); its entrance is on the left immediately past the intersection of Queen Elizabeth Road. It's open dawn–dusk daily. 301/495-2525.

38 Olney Manor Recreational Park 🐾 ½

The man-made lake is off to one side of this park, and it does add scenery even though you and your dog cannot jump in. But Chappy doesn't care about scenery unless it smells like a Big Mac, so the lake's looks are really just for you and for relaxing on a sunny day. Lots of grass surrounds it, and it's away from the ball fields and tennis courts. Paths by the picnic tables make for woodsy walking with a dog on a leash.

From the Beltway, take Georgia Avenue (Route 97) north, for miles and miles, and the park will be on the right at Emory Lane. It's open dawn–dusk daily. 301/495-2525.

Restaurants

Chesapeake Bagel Bakery: Fresh, hot bagels are ready all day long here. 3490 Laytonsville Road in the Olney Shopping Center; 301/570-4048.

POOLESVILLE

Parks, Beaches, and Recreation Areas

39 E. E. Halmos Park 🐾

Small and right on the road, this park made us laugh. As we pulled into the gravel drive parking area (big enough for about one car), there was a dumpster and two signs. The one on top had a picture of a dog squatting and a pile of poop behind him. Then it had a red circle around it with a line through it. We had never seen another sign quite so graphic. Most just say, "Please clean up after your dog." Coincidentally, the sign below the dog-poop sign read, "No dumping."

Take White's Ferry Road (Route 107) west until it turns into Fisher Avenue in Poolesville. Turn left on Tom Fox Avenue, right on Hughes Road, and left on Boomer Avenue until you see the park on the left. The park is open dawn–dusk daily. 301/495-2525.

40 Stevens Park 🐾 🐾

Oh, Chappy wanted one of those geese so badly! Who knows what he would have done if he had actually gotten close to one. Or what the goose would have done, for that matter. When we got out of the car, the geese seemed to know of his presence long before he caught a whiff of them. So the flock headed for the little pond, and Chappy, after we took him to the water's edge, simply watched them from the shore, twitching. Otherwise, he was content to sniff around the playground and picnic pavilion, stay on his leash as required, and go home.

Take White's Ferry Road (Route 107) west until it turns into Fisher Avenue in Poolesville. Take a right on Spates Hill Road and go straight through the subdivision to the park. The park is open dawn–dusk daily. 301/495-2525.

Restaurants

Bassett's: There's such a sorrowful-looking basset hound on the big sign out front that you figure that explains the name, but the place is actually named after the owner, whose last name is Bassett. And there's certainly no reason for sadness once you carry out a bucket of eight pieces of juicy fried chicken with biscuits and coleslaw. 19950 Fisher Avenue; 301/972-7443.

POTOMAC

Nightline host Ted Koppel, basketball's Patrick Ewing, actress Lynda Carter, and boxing champ Sugar Ray Leonard are just a few of the famous who own homes in upscale, beautiful Potomac. It's easy to see why. While you can bring your putter but not your pup to some of the internationally famous golf courses in these rolling green hills, this ritzy community affords plenty of grounds for your own canine caddy.

Parks, Beaches, and Recreation Areas

41 Avenel Park 🐾 🐾

Gold lettering graces the stone walls marking the gate to this incredibly pristine park in the middle of the mansion-filled Avenel neighborhood. The Avenel Golf Course, whose long fairways and pristine greens host the Kemper Open each year, is on the other side of the street. The upper-crusty Congressional Country Club, another professional tour stop, is just a few miles away. This is true country -club country. The signs are not for pedestrian or deer crossings, but golf cart and

DIVERSION

Take a Hike: In the fall every year, the Montgomery County SPCA sponsors a **Pet Walk and Pet Fair** to raise money. Founded in 1973, the MCSPCA operates the Washington metropolitan area's only no-kill animal shelter, which means the animals are never euthanized. It is not affiliated with the Montgomery County Animal Shelter or the Humane Society and is funded completely by individual donations.

The Pet Walk is not only a good cause, but it's really fun and makes for prime dog watching, with about 400 dogs participating every year. A group of dalmatians dominated everyone's attention as they pranced around showing their spots. Lots of cute mutts got oohs and ahhs, and there were two mastiffs that everyone steered clear of—although the folks at the SPCA insist only friendly dogs are allowed to participate. Chappy wasn't all that into wearing the spiffy green bandanna all dogs got for entering, but he succumbed.

Chappy was also a little shy during the mix 'n' mingle time before the walk started. He had his tail down and just didn't know what to make of so many fellow canines in one place at one time. A whole lot of sniffing went on. Of course we had to scoop Chappy's poop almost the minute we hopped out of the car. Oh, well. At least we got that out of the way right off.

In addition to checking out the other dogs and owners, the annual 1.5-mile stroll is delightful because it winds around the million-dollar homes in ritzy Potomac. People working in their expansive yards stopped to lean on their rakes and watch the parade of pooches.

The SPCA had buckets of water at the halfway mark—gallon sizes for the big dogs, half-pint sizes for the half-pints. Chappy sniffed them all but would have none of it. He did, however, feel compelled to stop at every tree and post along the way. Needless to say, he wasn't the leader of the pack.

After the walk the contests were held for best bark, owner-dog look alike and other events. We didn't win anything except a fun afternoon. Chappy slept all the way home. For more information about the annual event, call the MCSPCA at 301/948-4266.

---

horse crossings. Two cars were in the park parking lot here, both Mercedes. A nanny was watching a small child play on the playground. Dogs must be on a leash. Leaving a pile of poop on these manicured grasses would be a glaring faux pas. But what a nice place to visit, even if you can't live here.

From the Beltway, take River Road west, turn left onto Bradley Road, and continue as it winds around and becomes Oaklyn Road. The park is on the right and is open daily dawn–dusk. 301/495-2525.

42 McKee-Beshers Wildlife Management Area 🐾 🐾

If that dog don't hunt, think twice about this spot. Once your orange cap is properly in place, then okay, get out of the car—with your hands up. This is a "managed hunting area," and you will find four-wheel-drive vehicles and hunters in camouflage outfits in search of deer (at least during hunting season - which is from September to February for deer and anything else a hunter feels like shooting; turkey season is April through May).

Hunting Ridge Road, the main road through it, is like a Disney World ride through a haunted swamp. The red-clay lane has huge potholes, and water floods so much of the land that at one point we thought it was the road continuing to the right, but it was a stream. Oddly enough, the one animal we saw while driving through here was a tiny black cat in a tree. You would not want to get out here and trek around unless you are into dismal swamp walks with your dog.

Instead, go back out to River Road and take the next left down. The sign is marked pointing to McKee-Beshers, Maddux Island. If you turn in and drive to the end of the road—which is paved, although somewhat rough—you'll find an area where hunting is not allowed and where access to the Chesapeake & Ohio Canal Trail is found. A golden retriever—leashless, although the rule is that dogs must be on a leash—and his family was heading down into the woodsy slope to check out the Potomac River when we visited.

Take water; there are no facilities here. Take towels because you and the dog will probably be real muddy. And take a cellular phone. And take food. And make sure you have plenty of gas. From the Beltway, take River Road west for about four miles, turn left on Sycamore Landing Road, and follow it to the park's parking lot near the Potomac River. The park is open daily dawn–dusk. 301/495-2525.

Restaurants

Chicken Out: If you're in the mood for a chicken and all that goes with it, they've got it here—and they specialize, as the name implies, in packing it up for you to haul off to a nearby tree. 10116-B River Road, in the Potomac Place Shopping Center at the corner of Falls Road and River Road; 301/299-8585.

Old Angler's Inn: People park all around here to access the Chesapeake & Ohio Canal Trail and hike it up to the park and back. This popular and long-time institution has a deck in the sun right out front with an entertaining view of the road and the people carrying kayaks to the river. Tall trees filter the sun and make it a perfect spot for sipping white wine while waiting for one of the restaurant's notable steak or seafood entrees. Dogs are allowed to sit out on the deck with you, but the manager will ask that you take a table on the perimeter, so as not to annoy the other customers. 10801 MacArthur Boulevard; 301/299-9097.

Potomac Pizza: You can also get lots of great salads—chef, Caesar, grilled chicken, turkey—besides the standard pizza disks that Chappy would rather chase than a Frisbee. Everything on the menu is available for carryout. 9812

EARMARK YOUR CALENDAR–APRIL

Doggone MS: This organized group walk that raises funds to fight multiple sclerosis includes Potomac (near Avenel) as one of its starting points. Hikers take four or more hours to trek down the Chesapeake & Ohio Canal Trail to Glen Echo Park, just north of the District line. Friendly, well-behaved leashed dogs are welcome, though the National MS Society that sponsors the walk doesn't advertise it. The event is held on a Saturday in mid-April and usually attracts 3,500 walkers. There is no registration fee. 202/296-5363.

Falls Road; 301/299-7700.

Vie de France Restaurant: Without a doubt, the ham-and-cheese croissants are a family favorite of ours (and that includes Chappy, who probably needs a cholesterol check). But Vie de France is more than a bakery. You can also carry out an appetite-heightening order of delicious sesame noodles, hearty lasagna, and a lovely cold chicken salad, along with lots of other entrées. In the summer, set that pooch down at the outdoor tables in front. In winter, the shopping center benches will have to do. 10146 River Road, in the Potomac Place Shopping Center at the corner of Falls Road and River Road; 301/299-0904.

ROCKVILLE

An incorporated city of its own, with rules and regulations that separate it in letter and spirit from the rest of Montgomery County, Rockville has almost a schizophrenic relationship with canines. On the one hand, it has gone well beyond the call of duty to build a park in every neighborhood, and leashed dogs are allowed, in those parks. On the other hand, it bans dogs from all outdoor special events, such as its Fourth of July celebration and its Hometown Holidays festival in May. Scoop laws are strictly enforced. Yet in a policy that demonstrates genuine care for canines, the city's police department gives demanding off-leash tests that earn dogs and their owners a certificate and tag enabling them to go anywhere within the incorporated Rockville limits without a leash.

Parks, Beaches, and Recreation Areas

43 Cabin John Regional Park 🐾 🐾 🐾 🐕

Cinderella's carriage and her glass slipper are recreated here. One of the most imaginative playgrounds around can be found in this 525-acre park with ropes, ladders, tube slides, and various climbing creations. But that's all kids' stuff.

Chappy was much more interested in the trees that are found throughout the park in the many cool, shady, grassy areas, and in the many other dogs that frequent the paths through the playground and the park. Bird-watchers come to see woodpeckers and other winged creatures. A variety of trees and wild-flowers draw nature lovers.

He was a little worried about the pig machine, a loud motorized trashcan in the shape of a big Porky Pig that gobbles up whatever is thrown its way. He also didn't quite know what to make of the miniature train with its loud bells and whistles. But he was very happy to saunter through the picnic areas and explore the paved paths through the woods.

No one knows who exactly Cabin John is, although some claim it is Captain John Smith, who explored this area in the 1600s. Primitive camping sites not much improved from back then are available by reservation at the Robert C. McDonnell Campground in the park's popular north end, which provide woodsy plots perfect for setting up a tent for $16 a night. In season, these are in demand, however, so don't figure on grabbing one at the last minute. Call 301/495-2525 for reservations.

On the park's quieter south end (which extends into Bethesda) near the Locust Grove Nature Center and tennis courts there are several hiking trails good for dog walks (leashed, please) that loop through the relatively undeveloped woods.

Open daily, dawn–dusk, the park is located about a mile from the Beltway (I-495). Take the Old Georgetown Road exit, go north and turn left on Tuckerman Lane, and continue to the park just past Westlake Drive. 301/299-4555.

44 Calvin Park 🐾

A stray dog sauntered through here when we were visiting, and all he did was lift a leg on a tree and keep on trucking. A small hill with benches, a picnic area, and a grill, the park is clearly used by people in the neighborhood. Otherwise, it's just a pit stop with your leashed dog.

From the Beltway (I-495), take Georgia Avenue north. At Viers Mill Road, turn left, then take a right on Edmondston Drive (about six streets past Aspen Hill Road). Turn right on Baltimore Avenue, right on Gladstone Drive, and look for the park on the left. It's open daily, dawn–dusk. 301/495-2525.

45 East Norbeck Park 🐾

Because this park was overtaken by crows in the fall when we checked it out, it was eerie. The black birds were everywhere, probably because of the remnants of a cornfield right next to the park. The playground area and the walking area for dogs are on the opposite side of the park from the cornfield, so it's not a bad place to stop. Tennis courts, ball fields, picnic tables, and basketball share the grass with the crows.

From the Beltway (I-495), take Georgia Avenue (Route 97) north. Turn left on Norbeck Road (Route 28) and you'll find the park will be on the right. It's open daily, dawn–dusk. 301/495-2525.

46 Maryvale Park 🐾 ½

Look for the little bridge over a small creek leading into the park. You'll have to find a parking space on the street, then walk with your leashed dog into the grassy area, which is long and narrow and stuck in between subdivisions. But it is attractively landscaped.

From Rockville Pike heading north, turn right on Norbeck Road (Route 28) and left on First Street. Follow First Street as it bears to the right, and you'll see the park on the left. The park is open daily, dawn–dusk. 301/495-2525.

47 Rock Creek Regional Park 🐾 🐾 🐾 🐾

Dive right into Lake Needwood. It laps up at the edge of the road and looks inviting. At several spots around this lake, the water is easily accessible. Just shoo those ducks out of the way and have at it.

Needwood is one of two man-made lakes in this 2700-acre park. The other, Lake Frank, is on the other side of Muncaster Mill Road They were both built in the 1960s. Lake Needwood was designed for families, anglers, and boaters. Lake Frank, a little smaller, is more suited to nature study and education. Thirteen nature trails will take you throughout the park.

The Meadowside Nature Center, a favorite with kids for its fun exhibits, is near Lake Frank. There is a collection of log buildings made from local oak and hickory logs that shows the way early Americans farmed. There are also 7.5 miles of trails around the center.

At Needwood, you can get on the hiker-biker trail, which at that point is 13.5 miles from the District line. It's a paved trail that is basically downhill and winds through suburban Maryland following Rock Creek. If a shorter trek is what you had in mind, try the half-mile jaunt along a stream to the Muncaster mill ruins by the nature center. Even the longest trail is only 3.13 miles—around Lake Frank.

There is something for everyone here, especially dogs, who must be on a leash. No boats are permitted on Lake Frank. Stick to grilling burgers over by Lake Needwood. The park is open dawn–dusk daily. From I-270 north, take Exit 9 (Route 370/Shady Grove Road) and head north about two miles; turn right on Muncaster Mill Road, then right again on Needwood Road to Beach Drive and the park. To reserve picnic shelters call 301/495-2525; to reach the park manager call 301/948-5053.

48 Rockville Civic Center Park 🐾 🐾 🐾

The sheer beauty of the perfectly manicured lawns surrounding the Rockville Manor and the Civic Center building, which perch at the top of the hill in the heart of Rockville, makes this worth a visit. Signs warn Sled at your own risk, which gives you an idea of the dramatic hills that spread out from the manor. The gardens are manicured and the sculptures add elegance. There's no shortage of shade trees along the woodland trail nearby. Tennis courts give it a country-club feel and the stone wall surrounding the complex suggests hunt country. Go to the groomer's and put on your Sunday duds before heading here.

From Rockville Pike heading north, turn right on Norbeck Road (Route 28), right on Baltimore Avenue, and left on Edmonston, and make an immediate right up into the grounds. The park is open daily dawn–dusk. 301/309-3001.

49 Silver Rock Park 🐾

This park literally spans several backyards. Still, if your pooch needs to stop long enough to feel the grass in his paws, or lift a leg, this wide gully of land does an adequate job. Otherwise, it's hardly worth snapping the leash on your dog.

From the Beltway (I-495), take Georgia Avenue north. At Viers Mill Road, go left. Turn right on Edmonston where one entrance to the park will be on the right. Or stay on Edmonston until you reach Maple Avenue and turn right. A bigger entrance to the park will be on the right. 301/495-2525.

Restaurants

Ambrosia: No reason to eat on the premises since dogs can't and the decor ranges from minimalist to deconstructionist, but the Greek-Italian-American food is everything the atmosphere isn't. And it's cheap! Carry out a gyro or souvlaki sandwich for lunch or head this way for the full-blown Athenian chicken entrée at dinnertime. 1765 Rockville Pike, in the Congressional South Shopping Center; 301/881-3636.

Bombay Bistro: Carry out Indian food on a picnic in a park with a dog who appreciates the exotic aromas? Why not? And this friendly restaurant excels in the culinary arts of Indian sauce making. The lamb *rogan josh* and the lamb masala are rich and fiery. Take along a tandoori chicken order from the clay ovens for the Mahatma pooch who isn't into spicy food. 98 West Montgomery Avenue at the Bell's Corner Shopping Center; 301/762-8798

Crisp & Juicy: Decisions are very simple at this superb Argentine rotisserie chicken carryout: Pick up a whole or half of the marinated and herb-rubbed chicken to go. Ask for extra hot sauce, an order of the crisp yuca (instead of French fries), and if you're sharing the chicken with your pup, get some rice and beans to fill out the picnic. 1331-G Rockville Pike at the Sunshine Square Shopping Center; 301/251-8833.

Hard Times Cafe: I wouldn't feed this chili to a dog. But humans? Well, that's another matter. Don't mind if I do, 'cause this rowdy little chili parlor serves a hearty bowl that you can carry out to be with your no-hot-stuff-for-me puppy pal, who probably can make do on its unspicy chicken breast sandwich. 1117 Nelson Street, in the Woodley Gardens Shopping Center; 301/294-9720.

House of Gyro: Chappy loves gyros. Chicken, lamb, beef—he isn't picky. So look for the Gyro Man sign out in front of this little restaurant and try the special house gyro, or maybe the shish kebab. Or even try the souvlaki and the spicy, delicious red sauce. Everything can be carried out, or sit at one of

DIVERSIONS

Certified for Off-Leash?: The registration for the City of Rockville's **off-leash testing** of dog and designated dog handler costs $5. Pass it and your pup can go anywhere inside the incorporated city limits without a leash. The tests are given by the police department's Neighborhood Services every fourth Saturday of the month, excluding holidays. Two judges run the both of you through lots of hoops, as it were, from testing whether your dog can ignore a Frisbee zooming past him to another nearby dog to seeing if your dog can handle strangers reaching for him. It tests basic "good citizenship," and those who pass earn a tag and certificate—plus freedom. City of Rockville Police Department, Neighborhood Services, 111 Maryland Avenue; 301/309-3115.

Pass the Pert, Please: The **Montgomery County Humane Society** sponsors several annual dog events. The Dog Wash is one of the most fun to witness. For $5, they'll scrub up your pooch. And for $5 more, they'll do his nails. That happens every summer at the society. In fall they sponsor a doggy Olympics, patterned after the Alexandria Canine Games. Other fund-raisers for the society include an annual golf tournament and a flea market—but no dogs are allowed at those. Of course, if you buy your dog license here, you can get a free rabies shot. Well, your dog can. 14645 Rothgeb Drive; 301/279-1823.

---

the white tables out front if it's sunny. 4007-C Norbeck Road (Route 28); 301/929-9211.

La Madeleine French Bakery: Yet another of these take-your-time fast–French food cafés, it's hard to look past the incredible breads to see the soups—but you won't regret it. The tomato basil is *magnifique!* 11858 Rockville Pike; 301/984-2270.

O'Brien's Pit Barbecue: Call it the pits if you like, and happily so, because this smoky joint has been around since 1972 and offers authentic Texas-style, closed-pit barbecue to go. 387 East Gude Drive; 301/340-8596.

Places to Stay

Cabin John Regional Park Campground: See Cabin John Regional Park, above.

Woodfin Suites: Dogs are accepted, with a reasonable $5 fee per night. A double room includes a two-room suite with two TVs and a VCR (tapes are available at the front desk). There's no room service, but the front desk suggests using the Waiter-on-the-Way service, which will deliver from area restaurants. There is a complimentary breakfast served each day. A double costs $99. 1380 Piccard Drive; 301/590-9880.

SILVER SPRING

Back in the 1800s, Francis Preston Blair discovered a spring in a heavily wooded area north of the city of Washington. He purchased the land around it, built a home, and named it Silver Spring after the sparkling water. By 1899 Blair became the first postmaster of the community. Now Silver Spring means sprawling suburb.

Parks, Beaches, and Recreation Areas

50 Argyle Park 🐾

If your dog could be leashless, the 17 acres of open grass would be great for Frisbee. As it is, it's just a good pit stop.

It's open dawn–dusk daily. From the Beltway (I-495), take Route 29 north (Columbia Pike) and turn left on Lamark Way, followed immediately by a left on Sutherland Road, which winds around to the right and turns into Forest Glen Road. The park will be on your left. 301/495-2525.

51 Glenfield Park 🐾

It's a good thing the park is up on a hill because Layhill Road gets busy. The height makes it less noisy up on the exercise course and ball fields. Leashed dogs will also like the picnic area in the trees.

The park is open dawn–dusk. Take Layhill Road north to the park, which is just past Georgia Avenue (Route 97). 301/495-2525.

52 Indian Spring Terrace Park 🐾

Cars whizzing by on the Beltway don't enhance the park's ambience, but the grass and trees for the dog aren't bad. Check out the neat boulder that sits right in the middle of the park.

The park is open during daylight hours. Take the Beltway (I-495) to Route 29 south. Turn left on Hastings, right on Granville, left on Fairway, and the park is on the left. 301/495-2525.

53 North Four Corners 🐾 ½

Kick up the leaves in this small but tree-filled neighborhood park. The wooden playground and the log cabin community center surrounded by a low stone wall give the park a rustic look. And a large white whippet was taking it all in one day, as he walked over the little bridge from the subdivision and headed around the park on its paved path.

The park is open daily dawn–dusk. From Route 29 south, go left on Southwood, which dead-ends into the park. 301/495-2525.

54 Saddlebrook Park 🐾

The park police headquarters is located here, and there's a teensy park in back with playground and some overgrown grass. Dogs can find a place to raise a leg and that's about it. Only thing is, since this is the headquarters, dogs had darn well better be on their leashes, even if they're only relieving themselves.

The park is open daily dawn–dusk. From the Beltway (I-495), take Georgia Avenue north. Turn right on Randolph Road, then the second left on Glenallan Avenue. Then turn right at the first right, Layhill Road. The park is on the right. 301/495-2525.

55 Sligo Creek Park 🐾 🐾 🐾 🐾

It may seem odd to give this park four paws, because it is a narrow stretch of woodland that winds along Sligo Creek and Sligo Creek Parkway. But it is truly a delight for leashed dogs (as required). Walking the trails and bridges that go back and forth across the creek in several spots is an excursion into the gurgling sights and sounds of nature at its best. Groupings of maples and oaks encircle open grassy fields. Playgrounds and wooded areas become stops for chatting between the longer stretches of communing with nature. And always there's the mesmerizing creek.

Take the Beltway (I-495) to Route 29 south and make a right on Sligo Creek Parkway. That's the start of the park on the left. As you begin to drive up the parkway, you'll be driving right alongside a winding paved trail following the water. One good place to park is the small lot across from Dallas Avenue. If you prefer, go up a little farther to the parking lot opposite Sligo Golf Course, a public course, with a snack bar and outdoor tables. Grab a Bud and have a snack with your leashed bud. And if you want to see a round white sculpture of two little kids whispering, follow up the parkway a little bit more to the Sligo Dennis Avenue Park. Basketball courts, tennis courts, phone, water fountain, benches, picnic tables, and a bridge over to a wide-open area plus the trail continuing in a more woodsy setting can be found there. A final stopping point is just south of University Boulevard, which marks the end of the trail and the creek. The park is open daily dawn–dusk. 301/495-2525.

Restaurants

Crisfield: One of the great plain-old seafood restaurants around allows you to carry out steamed shrimp, grilled fish, or any of the other menu items originating on Maryland's eastern shore. In season, the crabs and crab dishes such as the crab imperial are hard to beat. 8012 Georgia Avenue (Route 97); 301/589-1306.

Crisp & Juicy: If you're heading out to Olney for some antiquing, skip the marvelous marinated rotisserie chicken this smoky Argentine place makes and go for the less messy but no less satisfying chorizo or chicken breast sandwiches. 3800 International Drive at Leisure World Plaza; 301/598-3333.

Manny & Olga's Pizza: Chicken souvlaki and pizza to go can accompany you wherever you go. 12134 Georgia Avenue (Route 97); 301/942-2299.

Negril—The Jamaican Eatery: In the heart of downtown Silver Spring and only a block off the main drag, this funky little counter and restaurant does more take-out business than sit-down, partly because only a few tables line its front window. But don't pass by without taking out some of its modestly priced Caribbean fare. The best carryout item to eat while driving to a nearby park is the Jamaican meat loaf, a sweetened doughy turnover filled with ground beef seasoned mildly enough that Chappy can eat some without neg-ative effects. The jerked chicken sandwich is tasty but way too peppery for pups. So is the Jamaican beef pattie, a flaky turnover filled with hot and spicy ground beef. For more substantial meals, give the curried goat or goat roti at least one try, or stick to the less-demanding dishes such as curried shrimp or steamed red snapper. If you can't tell from the saliva on this page, this is one of our must stops anytime we're in the Silver Spring neighborhood around lunchtime. 965 Thayer Avenue; 301/585-3000.

SPENCERVILLE

Parks, Beaches, and Recreation Areas

56 Spencerville Local Park 🐾

Right off Good Hope Road, the park is deceiving. It seems small, but it has 18 acres tucked in and that's plenty for a hour or so of fun on a sunny afternoon in a neighborhood park. But there's not much to do other than run about—leashed, of course.

The park is open dawn–dusk daily. From New Hampshire Avenue north-bound, turn right on Good Hope Road and look for the park on the right once you've crossed Briggs Chaney Road. 301/495-2525.

TAKOMA PARK

Known as Azalea City, a name you'll agree it deserves if you visit during the height of spring, this unlikely town on the outskirts of the District started in the late 19th century as a neighborhood of cool summer homes for government officials. Among those early pioneers were Department of Agriculture officials who brought their specialty with them, planting not only the flora that today distinguishes this neighborhood from others, but also the seeds of the green soul still present in this town. One of the first towns in the nation to declare itself a nuclear-free zone, Takoma Park has a reputation for liberal politics and diverse population. Its Victorian houses and bungalows create a backdrop from another era for alternative thinking.

Parks, Beaches, and Recreation Areas

57 Jequie Park 🐾 🐾

Chappy met several new furry friends (a couple of them not leashed as required) when we stopped by this lovely landscaped triangle of parkland where neighborhood tykes learn their first slide and swing experiences while their older sibs shoot baskets or play on the ball field. The field between the ball diamond and picnic structure and the boxwoods edging the park make it a popular doggy destination among locals. Chappy was momentarily intrigued by the passing Metroliner train across the street before he dived back into to his incessant turf sniffing.

The park is open dawn–dusk and is located along Eastern Avenue about three blocks west of Piney Branch Road. 301/495-2525.

58 Lee Jordan Athletic Field 🐾

This expansive area encompassing football and baseball fields is a great place to settle into one of the benches that line the playing fields and watch some sports with Spot. Leashed dogs can also hike along the periphery of these neighborhood-use grounds and on the great hill next to the Takoma Park Middle School—a popular sledding spot in winter.

The park is open daily dawn–dusk. To reach the park, take Georgia Avenue (Route 97) to Piney Branch Road and head north. Turn right on Grant Avenue and follow it until you see the park on the left. 301/495-2525.

59 Old Town Park 🐾

In the middle of the town center, this sweet dink of a park is all bricked walkway, benches, and a gazebo at the top of the hill, and farther down a wood-chip playground and more benches under shade trees. This is the park to park at when coming to Takoma for the antique shops, bookstore, or specialty eateries in the town center. The park is open in daylight hours and is located at the corner of Carroll Avenue and Westmoreland Street. 301/495-2525.

60 Opal Daniels Memorial Park 🐾 🐾

It's hard to find, but for a respite from a bright and hot sunny day, this shady hillside of lawns surrounded by thick woods provides a calming effect, like stumbling into a tiny bit of Shangri-la. And, believe us, any suggestion of Shangri-la, even on a leash, perks up our Tibetan pooch's shaggy ears.

This daylight-hours park is located off Carroll Avenue, west on Sherman Avenue and north (right turn) on Sheridan Avenue. 301/495-2525.

61 Takoma Piney Branch Park 🐾 🐾 ½

Well hidden in the depths of residential neighborhood that characterizes Takoma Park, the vast green spaces here are actually about two stories below the parking-lot level at the entrance. Once Chappy tugged us down the series of steps to the bottom where the park begins, we found a roomy runabout with a few folks playing tennis, others dribbling along the basketball court—not what you'd call high use, at least on this particularly cool fall day. A good guess is that come warm weather, the picnic facilities and playground see plenty of people. We walked the long stretch on the park's opposite length that's lined with woods and where Chappy found a rubber ball that he refused to drop.

Open daily dawn–dusk, the park is located at the dead end of Hancock Road just off Grant Avenue, about a half mile behind the Takoma Park Middle School. 301/495-2525.

Restaurants

Everyday Gourmet: With fine coffees and superb croissants, this nookish eatery is part coffeehouse hangout, part grocery, and a must on Sunday mornings, especially when the farmer's market draws the crowd. 6923 Laurel Avenue; 301/270-2270.

Middle Eastern Market: Tabbouleh, *baba ghanouj,* and falafel platters are the right choice at this friendly ethnic grocery where you can carry out authentic delights. The selection of imported fetas alone is worth the visit—and you 'hought feta is feta? 7006 Carroll Avenue; 301/270-5154.

EARMARK YOUR CALENDAR–OCTOBER

Old Town Takoma Park Street Festival: The annual early-October blowout of neighborhoodliness fills the streets of the town center with dozens of kiosks of ethnic foods, arts and crafts stalls, entertainment, and other attractions. Loads of family fun and Chappy adores the attention he and other dogs get. The festival takes place along Cedar and Carroll Avenues. 301/270-4821.

Taliano's Restaurant and Bar: Carry out this best pizza in town to a nearby town-center park bench and give the pooch some pepperoni. Dogs can't come in, but you needn't worry about tying your pup to the nearby parking meter when you go in to pick up the pie, because carryouts are rung up at the front window so you'll never lose sight of your precious. 7001-B Carroll Avenue; 301/270-5515.

VIERS MILL

Parks, Beaches, and Recreation Areas

62 Dewey Park 🐾

A narrow, five-acre park, Dewey is split in half by tennis courts where love matches are a common occurrence. On one side is a wide-open area used for soccer. On the other is a playground and basketball area. Although the rule is that pets must be on a leash, two sheepdogs were walking off-leash around the courts. The Rock Creek hiker-biker trail runs through here.

From Connecticut Avenue heading north out of the District, take a left on Wexford Drive, and then a right on Beach Drive north. Take a right on Garrett and a left on Dewey Road until you see the park on the left. The park is open daily dawn–dusk. 301/495-2525.

63 Parklawn Park 🐾

Popping a tire seems like a real possibility when driving in here. It's not a gravel path; it's a rock path. And going over the narrow one-lane bridge over a stream was like something out of an Indiana Jones movie. But if you want adventure and woods and a much more overgrown place, this is an unusual park. No bright orange playgrounds with wood chips here. And no porta-potties, just trees, grass, water, and bugs, as well as access to the Rock Creek hiker-biker trail.

Take Connecticut Avenue north out of the District and turn left on Aspen Hill Raod. Take a right on Marianna Dr, and a left on Renn St. The park is on the right. It's open daily dawn–dusk. 301/495-2525.

64 Viers Mill Park 🐾 🐾

Fitness walkers hit the paved Rock Creek hiker-biker trail here. Everyone else can just run down the hill to the soccer field, head for the playground right near the parking lot, or sniff the trees on either side of the trail without making it a serious exercise effort. Grills and picnic tables mean hot dogs for dogs—and people, too. Dogs must be on a leash.

From the Beltway (I-495), take Connecticut Avenue north to Viers Mill Road. Turn left. At Edgebrook, again turn left and follow it as it becomes Dewey Road. Stay on Dewey Road until it dead-ends into Garrett. Go right and the park will be on the right. The park is open daily dawn–dusk. 301/495-2525.

WHEATON

Parks, Beaches, and Recreation Areas

65 Layhill Park 🐾

Take a right at the cows and you're at this 32-acre park. There are not a lot of trees, just plenty of grass that's not particularly well kept. At the other end of the park is the Trolley Museum, accessible from Bonifant Road, but no dogs are allowed on the antique trolleys, so we don't really give a toot about them.

The park is on Layhill Road, not far past the intersection of Bel Pre Road, on the right. It is open daily dawn–dusk. 301/495-2525.

66 Layhill Village Park 🐾

If you're in the neighborhood, this is an adequate place for making a pit stop or stretching those furry legs. Play on the bright orange and blue equipment while your pup sniffs out those who preceded you. But there's nothing special beyond that for you and your leashed dog.

The park is open daily dawn–dusk. Head north on Layhill from Randolph Road, take a right on Queensguard Road, and follow it down to the park on the right. 301/495-2525.

67 Wheaton Forest Park 🐾 ½

A drive-through parking lot area off busy University Boulevard makes this feel somewhat like a drive-through park. Zoom in, stop, put on the leash, hit the soccer field, check out the trees by the small playground, and you're off again.

The park is open daily, dawn–dusk. From the Beltway (I-495) take Georgia Avenue (Route 97) north, and turn right on University Boulevard. The park is on the right. 301/495-2525.

68 Wheaton Regional Park 🐾 🐾 🐾 🐾 🐾

Trains, playgrounds, and automobiles could be the name of this massive multi-use, 496-acre park. This is truly one of those "Everybody in the car; we're going to the park" parks.

Dogs on leashes will find tall trees to sniff, shady grassy areas to laze around, while the kids tackle the vast mazelike playground. Drink machines as well as water fountains are plentiful. A minitrain and carousel are open in the summer months. On the athletic side of the field are several baseball fields, enclosed tennis courts, and an ice rink.

Trails meander throughout the park and the Shorefield Trail is one of the best for dogs, as it goes around the lake. Or just head off through the grassy areas.

Take the Beltway (I-495) to Georgia Avenue (Route 97) toward Silver Spring. Take a right on Shorefield Avenue into the park. This is the best entrance for dogs. Don't forget the leash. The park is open daily dawn–dusk. 301/946-7033.

EARMARK YOUR CALENDAR–MAY

Chowin' Down: By the time the daffodils have died out in mid-May, Chappy knows it's time to pin down the date of the annual **Taste of Wheaton Festival.** He likes this one especially because some three dozen restaurants from this locale prop up their tables on the sidewalks of downtown and peddle tempting, bite-sized nuggets of their cuisine for as little as 50 cents or a dollar each. And the culinary artistry represented covers so many nationalities it's hard to keep track. Free music and other entertainment round out what adds up to a belchin' good Sunday afternoon. The feast fest happens along Grandview and Ennalls Avenues, and the admission is free. 301/217-4800.

Restaurants

Anchor Inn: This a seafood and steakhouse, the kind people go to on a Saturday night for a big meal. But the surf and turf, as well as pasta and sandwiches, are all available for carryout if you're in need of something hearty for you and your dog. 2509 University Boulevard West, at the corner of Georgia Avenue (Route 97) and University Boulevard; 301/933-1814.

Chicken Basket: Everything is for carryout, so stop in here for the 21-piece shrimp dinner (a specialty) or a grilled chicken sandwich, fries, and a soda, close to $5. It's a popular carryout, and you and the pup can walk a block or two in either direction to find a comfy spot to sit and dine together. 11435 Georgia Avenue (Route 97); 301/949-8818.

Chicken Place: Cheap, crispy roasted chicken and French fries with a Peruvian slant on that rotisserie is a great take-out lunch or dinner—but make sure your pooch does not get the chicken bones! 11201 Grandview Avenue; 301/946-1212.

Tucson Cantina: Even though this is almost right at the extremely busy intersection of Georgia Avenue (Route 97) and University Boulevard, it's still a good place to have a taco on a summer afternoon. Just make sure it's okay with the manager. He says he plays it by ear. 2418 University Boulevard; 301/946-9798.

WHITE OAK

Parks, Beaches, and Recreation Areas

69 Martin Luther King Jr. Recreational Park 🐾 🐾 ½

Quiet and peaceful, there's a lake right in the middle of the grounds. A paved path invites a great stroll around the lake. The park has bathrooms, a drinking fountain, baseball fields, and picnic benches in the shade. There were no dogs in sight on the sunny afternoon we visited with Chappy on a leash. There was just a little kid riding his tricycle around the path, some people fishing, and a couple walking.

The park is open daily, dawn–dusk. Take the Beltway (I-495) to New Hampshire Avenue and turn right on Jackson Avenue (not far past the intersection of Route 29/Columbia Pike). Go past Jackson Elementary School to the park. At the end of the street, there is a wide paved trail that leads into Upper Branch Park for biking and hiking. 301/622-1193.

70 Meadowood Park 🐾

Tucked back behind houses, this is a park for people who know it's there—so you and the pooch will feel a little bit like interlopers entering its charming and sequestered 16 acres. A dog was leashless and playing when we intruded, although the rules are that dogs need to be leashed. This park feels more like a big backyard than a public park.

It's open daily, dawn–dusk. The park is located off upper New Hampshire Avenue on Eldrid Road at the church. 301/495-2525.

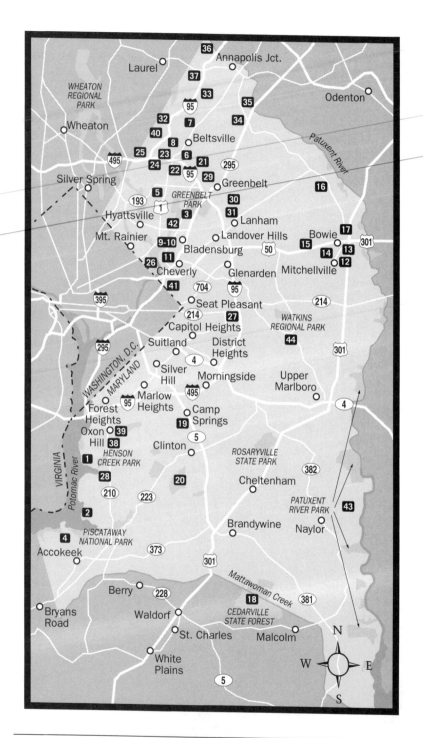

12 PRINCE GEORGE'S COUNTY

To the east and south of the District is Maryland's other bedroom suburb, named in 1696 for Prince George of Denmark. Don't ask why. It's a by-marriage thing, not by royal blood. But those 300-plus years make it one of the nation's oldest counties, and its history remains a clear and present characteristic of these 500 square miles of old land between the Potomac and Patuxent Rivers. Prince George's (PG) County was the path marched by British soldiers on their way to burn the White House in 1814. John Wilkes Booth escaped south into this Confederate-sympathizing territory in 1865 after shooting President Lincoln.

In the past couple of decades, the county has experienced growing pains. Its demographics have shifted it from a once sleepy rural southern county to an urbanite refuge suffering some of the urbanite problems its newer resident bring along as baggage.

NASA's Goddard Space Flight Center and Andrews Air Force Base, where the presidential jet Air Force One parks, have made it their home for decades. In recent years, developers have turned its rolling tobacco fields and riverside wilderness into suburban subdivisions and apartment complexes. When the late Washington Redskins owner Jack Kent Cooke decided to move his foot-

---

ball club to the 'burbs, he chose vacant acreage close to the Beltway in Landover to build the $160-million stadium now called FedEx Field. Meanwhile, traffic jams the county's main highways and roads leading into the District during rush hour—don't even mention the Wilson Bridge to a PG County resident—although underwater ground has been broken on building the second-bridge solution to this frustrating problem.

An exodus of middle-class residents escaping the inner-city crime and poverty that mars neighborhoods in the District has funneled many new residents here into comfortable suburban homes built on land once plowed by slaves. Some of them have brought inner-city inclinations with them. Since the mid-1980s, PG County's violent crime statistics have been second only to the District's in the metropolitan area and outlying counties. While those figures have dropped slightly, there's good reason to watch your step in some neighborhoods when taking your pooch on the road. But many parts of this county remain benign and inviting.

Speaking of dogs, when the county felt the bite instead of the bark of its growing population of aggressive breeds after several brutal attacks on humans, authorities banned residence to any new "pit bulls" born after Feb. 3, 1997 and that restriction continues. Other dog rules are standard: All parks require leashes unless otherwise noted and expect you to keep grounds tidy.

That said, this county is home to some exceptional destinations for dog lovers with a soft spot for history, beauty, and tradition. Both urban and rural, modern and historic (220 historic landmarks), it boasts more than 20,000 acres of parkland and recreation destinations. Some of its acres are home to long-standing southern Maryland traditions such as horse racing, fox hunting, and jousting. This is, after all, a county where George Washington not only slept, he was among the first to wager at its racetracks.

National Parks

1 Fort Foote Park 🐾 🐾

A 50-acre national park that displays partially preserved earthworks of a Civil War fort and several 15-inch cannons that could shoot 400 pound cannonballs four miles, this sweet little park gets overlooked because it exists in the shadow of the much larger Fort Washington nearby. But dog lovers and their pooches will appreciate these mostly wooded and largely unattended acres that nestle directly on the Potomac River—and there have been upgrades recently to clean up the place. It's worth the navigational difficulty you might experience getting there, because strolling on the sandy, rocky beach that bumps out into the river with few folks around is simply a delight.

The park is open dawn–dusk. From the Beltway (I-95), take Exit 3 south on Indian Head Highway (Route 210) and immediately turn right onto Oxon Hill Road heading south; go about two miles and turn right at Fort Foote Road. The park entrance is located about two miles farther on the right opposite Jessica Drive. 301/763-4600.

2 Fort Washington Park 🐾🐾🐾🐾 🐾

Overlooking the juncture where the Potomac River feeds Piscataway Creek, and across the river from Mount Vernon, this stately old fort looks like everything a fort ought to be. Built between 1814 and 1824 to replace the previous Fort Warburton that stood here before British troops destroyed it on their rampage toward Washington, this is a real piece of work and a site worth visiting. Its eight-foot-wide stone walls, ready-for-attack ramparts, earthworks, a drawbridge spanning a protective moat, and cannons are all perfectly in place for the imagination to run wild with history. Just swiping your hand over the massive walls or picking up a scrap of gray slate that more than a century ago roofed its barracks sends chills down the spine. Did we say we love this place? Because we do.

During the Civil War, Union troops occupied the heavily armed battlement here to prevent a Confederate campaign that might target the United States capital just a few miles upriver. Some secondary fortresses built during that time, and since then, remain scattered throughout the national park's 341 acres. Though park authorities have closed some and fenced others for safety reasons, these are great, musty-smelling, crumbling shells of another era that Chappy loved sniffing endlessly. A few dank rooms are still accessible in some—along with creatures that thrive in dankness. The brick-walled tunnel in the main fort that leads down and out into the weed-overgrown front grounds is a cool and amazing little trek.

Standing atop the main fort's cannon turrets, you and the pup (if you can lift him high enough) will take in a dazzling view of the Potomac. Children love to hike down the dozens of steps to investigate the huge dungeon-like rooms directly below the turrets in the fort's bowels—though it's tricky on paws. Some dogs won't be amused. Don't be surprised if you find some odd lizards (as a child here, Don spotted one with a blue sail-like crest on its back) and other unusual life forms. For the seriously curious, park rangers conduct interpretive tours that you can find out about in the visitor center office, underneath the awesome archway leading into the main fort.

DIVERSION

All Together Now: A full schedule of weekly programs and group nature hikes at Greenbelt National Park includes a two-mile **Pet Walk** through the lush wildflower and fern-bottomed forest every two or three weeks in good weather. The rangers don't allow aggressive dogs to participate. The limit is seven people and their seven dogs per hike, so call the visitor center for details. 301/344-3948.

The park has a lot more to offer dog lovers than its remarkably preserved fort and history. This is a recreation mecca. Directly in front of the main fort, you can walk a narrow sandy beachhead and splash your feet in the river (though watch out for the inevitable decaying fish carcass floating by). You'll find anglers trying to hook rockfish, perch, and catfish from the shoreline. Just catching a beautiful sunset across the Potomac works for us.

More than three miles of hiking trails show off the property's extensive and sometimes dense woods, snaking back into wilderness where there's no evidence of a massive masonry fort, or even civilization, for that matter—but where our forefathers walked to protect a upstart nation. Between the park's entrance and the main fort almost a mile of twisting roadway winds through the picnicking area that regularly accommodates large group outings as well as families spending the day in the park. This is where weekend revelers play Whiffle ball and hammer horseshoe spikes into the ground for an afternoon of competition. So bring along a picnic lunch and plan on spending the day, because there's more to see and do here than you could possibly imagine.

Despite the fed's rules requiring dogs to stay leashed, this open space is where you'll find a few pooches racing after Frisbees and playing leash-free fetch. No harm done, generally, but if a park ranger nabs your runaway dog, you could get fined. Also make sure to clean up after your dog.

The park charges an entrance fee of $4 per vehicle and is open 7:30 A.M.–sunset year-round; the main fort is open 9 A.M.–5 P.M.; and the visitor center is open 10 A.M.–4 P.M. (closed Christmas, Thanksgiving, and New Year's Day). From the Capital Beltway (I-95), take Exit 3 south on Indian Head Highway (Route 210) and go four miles; turn right on Fort Washington Road. The park entrance is 3.5 miles at its end. 301/763-4600.

3 Greenbelt National Park 🐾 🐾 🐾 🐾 🐾

What in the world is an honest-to-goodness, beautifully maintained, 1,100-acre national park doing sandwiched among the so-so shopping plazas, gas stations, and fast-food restaurants on Greenbelt Road? Fitting in quite well, thank you. Yosemite it's not, but Greenbelt National Park is a green oasis of the highest degree for any visitor—human or canine—who's weary of suburban sprawl.

Three well-marked nature trails of one or two miles each loop through the park's woodsy interior. On the north side, park in the Sweetgum parking and picnic area and hike with the pup halfway around the Azalea Trail to the Laurel picnic area. There you can peacefully commune with nature and partake of the lunch you packed (tables are first-come, first-served) while listening to singing birds and scrambling wildlife—including herds of deer at times. Continue along the looped trail through the dense pine and hardwood forest and past the North Branch Still Creek to your car.

Chappy liked another easy hiking trail, the centrally located 1.5-mile Dogwood Trail that's dense with ferns and flowering dogwoods in season—but which has no picnic or other facilities. The 1.5-mile Blueberry Trail to the south side cuts through some striking grounds but gets heavy use from the folks staying at the campground near its entrance. During the summer months, the entire park gets crowded by locals who know a good thing when they've got it in their midst. Other visitors drive the 12 miles from downtown Washington (or the 23 miles from Baltimore) to enjoy the natural charms of this land once hunted by Algonquin Indians and farmed by colonists.

Don't bother with the six-mile Perimeter Trail, unless you and the jog-dog go for distance. It is fine for hiking and horseback riding, but traffic-noise pollution from the nearby Baltimore-Washington Parkway along the park's eastern edge disturbs this trail, unlike the others.

Park rules require dogs to be on leashes no longer than six feet (though we've never seen a measuring tape pulled on anything close to that). You must scoop the dog poop, not only for the benefit of those who walk in your footsteps, but also for the upkeep of the natural environment.

The park also provides exceptional camping facilities—probably the closest you'll find to downtown Washington. Camping is restricted to the designated 174-site, year-round campground area near the entrance to the Blueberry Trail, and limits two tents, two vehicles, and six people per site. Dogs must remain leashed in campgrounds, as elsewhere in the park. The sites are a bit cozy on crowded evenings, with campers to the left, campers to the right, and campers behind you. But the environment more than distracts campers from each other. The 10 P.M.–6 A.M. "quiet hours" help to regulate disturbances, along with an obvious presence of rangers in charge at the nearby ranger station. The campsites provide grills for cooking, and clean (heated in winter) bathroom and shower facilities. Sites are available on a first-come, first-served basis. The fee is a great deal for what you get at $14 per night.

The park is open 24 hours a day. To get here from I-95, take Exit 23 onto Kenilworth Avenue (Route 201) and drive south a half mile toward Bladensburg; turn east on Greenbelt Road (Route 193) and look for the sign at the park entrance on the right. A south entrance and parking area for the park is located about a half mile east of Kenilworth Avenue on Good Luck Road. But its distance from the ranger station and proximity to Parkdale High School across the street increases the possibility of vandals messing with your car, so go to the north entrance. For details on camping, call the campground ranger station at 301/344-3948. The park's general number is 301/344-3948.

4 Piscataway National Park 🐾 🐾 🐾 🐾

A favorite of Chappy's for its name alone (though his canine brainine can't quite grasp that Piscataway is Native American in origin and not a fun doggy activity), this rural junction of riverside parkland was created in 1952 as a shoreline park for one reason only: to preserve the undeveloped rural vistas opposite the historic Mount Vernon estate of our first president, located directly across the Potomac River in Virginia. Since then, the park has grown into much more than just a pretty picture to contemplate from a rocker on George Washington's back porch.

The park is divided into three separate and distinct areas. Its southernmost tip extends into Charles County to the south, though the best-laid plans are on the Prince George's side. The most visited of the areas is the National Colonial Farm, a full-scale working farm set in 1775 where there are more than 100 acres of tobacco, corn, wheat, and other crops grown and cultivated using no chemicals. Interpretive staffers dress in period clothing and squire visitors through the fields, living quarters, and buildings. Chappy found the people, antiquated structures, and bucolic scenery by the riverside a lively change of pace from the usual wooded parks with trails. The Woodland Trail through the periphery woods here provides a glimpse of trees and plants, from persimmons to hickory nuts, raspberries to pawpaws that provided food for colonists. History freaks will love the historical placards posted along the trails, where they get a briefing on what happened and can stare into the distant vista and imagine events two and three centuries ago. Full facilities, including restrooms, a visitor center, picnic tables overlooking the river, a fishing pier, and plenty of shade complete a wonderful setting for a day out with the pooch. The entrance fee is $2 per adult, 50 cents per child; interpretive tours of the farm cost extra.

If it's just woods and trails you want, this park has its own unusual brand. As you breeze past the quaint farmhouses and not-so-quaint brick ramblers along Bryan Point Road heading toward the park, pull up a half mile shy of the road's end at the National Colonial Farm where you'll see a brown Piscataway Park sign on the right by a gravel entrance. This is the other side of the park, and it's like day and night. From the unpaved parking area, follow the wood-planked walk through a largely undisturbed riverside marshland near Accokeek Creek, which offers splendid up-close viewing of the odd swamp creatures and water birds that live there. Continue on and you'll discover large expanses of well-hidden parkland farther back where you can hike almost to Mockley Point, which juts out into the fork in the river between the Potomac and Piscataway Creek. During some high tides, the marshlands and boardwalk could be flooded and impassable, but in dry weather it provides sturdy footing for exploring unusual turf.

Never mind the trail leading off from the entrance to the nearby Hard Bargain Farm. Dogs aren't allowed at that environmental study area, nor are most human visitors. It's primarily a school-group destination.

About six miles south of the Accokeek Creek site is the park's third area, the site of what was once Marshall Hall Amusement Park. In the early 1950s the area attracted picnicking families with its huge swimming pool, great wooden roller coaster, carnival games and rides, and slot machines. It now stands barren except for some ruins and the original historic house that pre-dated the screams from the Tilt-A-Whirl. This is a pleasant and uneventful parkland right on the Potomac that lures more anglers to its seawall and boaters to its ramp than it does other visitors.

The park is open year-round dawn–dusk; the National Colonial Farm is open on the weekend from spring through fall, 10 A.M.–4 P.M. From the Beltway (I-95), take Exit 3A onto Indian Head Highway (Route 210) south, and drive about 10 miles to Accokeek. Turn right onto Livingston Road, turn right almost immediately onto Biddle Road, and then left onto Bryan's Point Road. The marshland area is located about 3.5 miles on the right; the National Colonial Farm is about four miles at the end of the road, along the Potomac River. For park information call 301/763-4600 at Fort Washington Park, which administers it. The park ranger office is 301/627-7755, and the National Colonial Farm is 301/283-2115.

ADELPHI

Parks, Beaches, and Recreation Areas

5 Adelphi Manor Park 🐾 🐾 ½

One of the pearls in the string of nature parks strung by the Northwest Branch Stream, one of the two principal branches of the Anacostia River, this stream valley park is mostly undeveloped riparian wilderness. But Chappy likes the trails that run through it. Restoration efforts to stabilize the stream banks and protect the forest are ongoing and have added hundreds of red maple, black gum, sweet bay magnolia, sycamore, and serviceberry trees, plus other trees and shrubs, along both sides of the stream over recent years. Because this park's more natural state offers fewer human attractions than other nearby parks, you can find great solitary hikes with your pup here. The stream isn't bad for a quick doggy dip on hot afternoons.

Open daylight hours, the park is north of University Boulevard (Route 193) at West Park Drive, near Adelphi Plaza. 301/699-2407.

BELTSVILLE

Parks, Beaches, and Recreation Areas

6 Beltsville Neighborhood Park 🐾 🐾

No, wait. You really *are* driving in circles on the great American Capital Beltway. Completed in the early 1960s, the Beltway (I-95/I-495), the Beltway encircles the nation's capital and takes about an hour to drive its entirety.

Motorists and backseat Baskervilles feeling frazzled by that same old chasing-your-tail feeling can pull off this exit and find a lovely respite from all that bumper-to-bumper business. Hidden amid this decent working-class neighborhood overlooking those congested lanes of traffic, this park's only drawback is that it's within earshot of I-95 to the west. A loud white noise shushes nonstop—as if the universe had sprung a big beach ball-like leak (Chappy's theory).

Actually the top of a triangular woodland that to the south is Little Paint Branch Park, this is a shaded stress-free zone that's much larger than first impressions suggest. Next to the parking lot is a playground, including a see-saw so wonderful Chappy marked it as his own. On the ball fields, an off-leash golden retriever and a black Lab raced after a Frisbee the day we visited. Posted rules require dogs to stay on their leashes, as you might expect. But the atmosphere is neighborly, and nearby neighbors bend the leash rules out of familiarity.

The fast-flowing Little Paint Branch Stream borders the western side of the park, and Chappy loved exploring it once he worked up enough courage to navigate past the chicken wire–reinforced bank. With a small beachhead, the stream is actually swimmable for dogs in warm weather. The picnic pavilion near the parking area was clean as a whistle, and so were the clearly marked paths heading into the woods. A major paved trail cuts through the thick woods to the south and leads into Little Paint Branch Park.

The park is open dawn–dusk. From the Beltway (I-95), take Exit 29 east onto Powder Mill Road; turn right on 34th Street and turn right again onto Montgomery Road. The park entrance is on the left. 301/699-2407.

7 Beltsville Park 🔥

A modest park adjacent to the Martin Luther King Middle School, it's a good stop when stopping is a must for the pooch. Otherwise, this is just school-yard grounds better suited for ball playing where a leashed dog doesn't know what to do.

The park is open daylight hours. From the Beltway (I-95), take Exit 29 east onto Powder Mill Road; turn left onto Old Gunpowder Road, then right on Ammendale Road and look for the park and school on the right. 301/699-2407.

8 Little Paint Branch Park 🐾 ½

Much larger than the Beltsville Neighborhood Park that connects to it to the north, this basic stream valley–style woodland's main attraction to dog lovers is the actual stream that runs through it. Your dog can take a dip because this is a mostly natural setting that doesn't draw crowds year-round, despite the community center and play area near Sellman Road. I-95 heading northeast to Baltimore does breeze past its western side, which causes some notice. Follow the stream north through the woods to find the peace and quiet you seek. Dogs are required to stay leashed, as always.

The park is open dawn–dusk. From the Beltway (I-95), take Exit 25 south onto Baltimore Avenue (Route 1); after a quarter mile, turn right on Cherry Hill

Road and go 1.5 miles, where you turn right onto Sellman Road. The park entrance is less than a mile on the left. 301/699-2407.

Restaurants

Gringada Mexican Restaurant: It's the basic south-of-the-border fare of burritos, enchiladas, and tacos fixed in a jiffy and ready to take out to a nearby park. This is a friendly neighborhood Mexican hideaway, though the deck in back doesn't quite accommodate a canine burrito gobbler. 12300 Baltimore Avenue; 301/210-3010.

Sierra's Grill: This Southwestern-style Mexican cantina is happy to make carryout *comida* or *cena* so you and the poochita can dine under a tree at a nearby park. The tacos are plump, and the salsa and tostadas just the right thing on a summer evening. 11619 Beltsville Drive; 301/572-7830.

BLADENSBURG

It's hard to believe, but in colonial times and during the early years of the new republic when large seagoing ships sailed up the Anacostia River from the Potomac, they often docked at the thriving port city of Bladensburg. This was a hub of the county's important tobacco trading commerce. Indeed, Bladensburg was the last line of defense where American militia stood little chance to stop the better-trained and better-equipped British troops marching on the capital city during the War of 1812.

Today, Bladensburg is an old neighborhood minutes outside of Washington that wears its urban decay in plain sight. But the old port town still has a few surprises left.

Parks, Beaches, and Recreation Areas

9 Bladensburg Gardens Balloon Historic Park 🐾

It's cute, it's quaint, and there are benches and nicely shrubbed gardens, but there ain't room for both of us in this minuscule park. Within sight of the Peace Cross Memorial, the park sits adjacent to the George Washington House (circa 1752), often referred to as the Indian Queen Tavern. Built prior to the

Revolution, when Bladensburg was a hot port town, the tavern is where tobacco was traded. Later, when ground travel caught up with the seafarers here, this old stone building served as a stagecoach stop for weary travelers on the Old Post Road.

The park itself is little more than a stop for weary dogs, though it is surprisingly serene considering the three lanes of traffic on each side. What Chappy didn't care much for were the fenced-in yapping guard dogs over at the Spartan Plumbing and Heating building across the street. The only reason this park rates higher than a pee pot is the historical content, so don't go out of the way. If you do, keep the pooch on his leash—for his own safety if nothing else.

The park is open all hours and is located opposite the Peace Cross Memorial at Bladensburg Road and Baltimore Avenue. 301/699-2407.

🔟 Historic Bladensburg Waterfront 🐾 🐾

Because it's on the Anacostia River, the waterfront is a piece of the Anacostia River Park puzzle that provides riverside recreation and wooded acreage through the heart of Prince George's County. Most of the waterfront has at long last been renovated and reopened—along with a nature center and even pontoon rides (though dogs on any given day may not be invited).

For decades, the old waterfront has been the port and launching ramp for small vessels and a lively fishing pier for local fishermen. It has been one of the few places to rent canoes or rowboats to navigate the Anacostia River.

From the District, take New York Avenue east; turn left on Bladensburg Road and drive about two miles to the first right turn after crossing the Anacostia River onto 46th Street, which dead-ends at the waterfront. 301/779-0371.

🔟🔟 Old Port of Bladensburg Community Park 🐾 ½

Across the street from Bladensburg Gardens Balloon Park, this is a popular neighborhood space that extends north of Bladensburg Road from the waterfront. Shade is plentiful and so are picnic tables and a picnic pavilion. Despite leash laws, lots of dogs were running leashless when we visited.

Open dawn–dusk, the park is located north of Bladensburg Road at Baltimore Avenue and Upshur Street. 301/779-0371.

Restaurants

Three Brothers Pizza: This classic, friendly Italian neighborhood eatery-pizzeria has deliciously messy entrees like spaghetti and meatballs, lasagna, and ravioli on its carryout list that's a huge step up from the fast-food drive-in lane. But if your pup is like Chappy, the last thing you want to do when you get home is scrub off tomato sauce from his coat. So go with the good carryout subs and you won't be sorry. 4521 Kenilworth Avenue (Route 201); 301/864-1570.

BOWIE

Some 150 years ago, this was a railroad stop "on the tracks to nowhere" (sorry, but Chappy here invoked his literary license, which hangs alongside his ID and rabies tags). It wasn't even called Bowie then. Now this suburban burg, named after the late 19th-century governor Oden Bowie, is the county's biggest incorporated municipality. But the feel remains decidedly small-town America.

Located along the road to Annapolis to the east and Baltimore to the north, its neat and tidy outdoor recreation areas—some 1,700 square acres of parkland within the city limits—kindly doesn't forget friendly furry four-leggers who stay on leashes and bring a domesticated human along to clean up after them.

Parks, Beaches, and Recreation Areas

12 Allen Pond Park 🐾 🐾 🐾 🐾 🐾

You've heard of planned communities? Well, this is a planned "multi-use" park whose well-configured features just might convince the doggedly skeptical of what good government can do when it puts its heart into it. Pull into the huge parking lot behind the ice rink and just survey the horizon of this park for a moment: 85 acres of graceful beauty include lighted ballparks to the left, an amphitheater to the right, picnic areas at your feet, and playgrounds here and there. The anchor of it all is an idyllic 10-acre stocked pond in the middle, circled by a one-mile paved hiker-biker trail.

On a cold day, Chappy loved the biting breeze coming off this lakelike pond that made the rest of us shiver. So for a few minutes we huddled behind the boathouse that rents paddleboats, rowboats, and canoes in season. Some boathouse attendants will let you and the pooch go out in a rowboat, some won't, we are told. If you get one who won't, just head farther back into the park and explore the sensory and nature trails—with the pooch leashed, as required. And bring along a bag of old bread crusts (not the moldy ones, though), because the pond is home to lots of squawking ducks and honking geese who are willing to entertain you and the bird dog with their quacky antics in exchange for snacks.

Nearby is Opportunity Park, a thoughtful play area with colorful play stations and heavy plastic equipment all designed to accommodate children with disabilities—and loads of fun for any child.

One word of caution: For plenty of good reasons, this park is a popular destination and it can get crowded on perfect sunny days during warm weather. We've seen it busy on sunny winter days when the thermometer didn't reach freezing. So if you figure on a serious picnic that requires a table and space, better call ahead and reserve one.

The park is open daily, 8:30 A.M.–dusk. From the Beltway (I-95), take Route 50 south toward Annapolis, then take Exit 11 south onto Collington Road (Route 197). After 1.3 miles, turn right on Mitchellville Road and look for the park entrance on the right just past Northview Drive. 301/262-6200, ext. 3009.

13 Blacksox Park 🐾 ½

Probably half of these 70-plus acres is dedicated to baseball and softball, and the other half is relatively undeveloped. No problem, since Chappy's a big ball fan and is happy to take a few minutes out from sniffing tree stumps and marking new territory to catch an inning or two. Besides, there's a sniff of history here too: The park was once the home of the Mitchellville Tigers and Washington Blacksox, two teams from the old Negro baseball league.

Besides, during games the concession stands sell inexpensive eats and, we are told, the city is putting in a hiking trail or two for seventh-inning stretchers and their pups who want to roam way back on the property near the stream—on leashes, of course. Meanwhile, keep the pooch off the playing fields for obvious reasons: We don't want some Little Leaguer sliding spikes high into, well, you know . . . .

The park is open dawn–dusk. From the Beltway (I-95), take Route 50 south toward Annapolis. Take Exit 11 south onto Collington Road (Route 197), then turn right on Mitchellville Road. Less than a mile past Allen Pond Park is the entrance on the left. 301/262-6200, ext. 3009.

14 Bowie Dog Park 🐾 🐾

At last, after nearly four years of hard work by the Bowie Dog Park Association, in December 2001, the canines of this planned community finally had dreams come true for them. The fenced one-acre lot—including a fenced area exclusively for smaller and shy dogs and puppies older than four months—is for Bowie residents and their dogs only, just so you know. One word of caution: The town fathers view this as more of an experiment than a done deal, and they intend to review this project every six months to make sure you and your pooches don't cause trouble. So make sure to pipe down on the barking and clean up after you best friend. Generally, stick by the rules and toe the line, or you'll jeopardize this hard-won victory for Bowie's bowsers.

DIVERSIONS

Music to Floppy Ears: Though Chappy is partial to Mozart and the chants of Tibetan monks, he's always eager to take in a free outdoor concert. From Memorial Day to Labor Day, the **Sunday Sunset Concert Series** takes the stage at the Allen Pond Amphitheater, 7–8 P.M. A lot of the music is the military band sound, though local groups play a variety of styles through the summer, from jazz to folk. The series draws big audiences, so show up early with your blanket and snacks. Best spot for dog lovers with a pooch (on a leash, of course), is along either side of the crowd or at the back, where the inevitable sojourn doesn't disrupt other spectators. Allen Pond Park is located at 3330 Northview Drive, just off Mitchellville Road. 301/262-6200, ext. 3009.

The park is located almost directly across from the soccer mania at Enfield Chase Park at Northview Drive and Enfield. 301/249-1347.

15 Foxhill Park 🐾 🐾

Gone fishing? What ranks this park better than the other community tennis-court and ball field parks in town is the seductive lake where you and the leashed pup can lounge and watch the fish jump in the summer sun. A doggy-friendly trail or two lead off from the parking lot, and a picnic area looks clean and inviting. Otherwise, these 45 acres adjacent to the Benjamin Tasker Middle School are consumed with strictly human pursuits.

Open dawn–dusk, the park is located along Collington Road (Route 197) about a half mile north of Exit 11 on Route 50. 301/262-6200 ext. 3009.

16 Town Green Park 🐾

This comely little site is de rigueur for cooling off hot paws after antique hunting with the pooch in Old Bowie's Antique Row area. The little take-a-break park is right on Main Street and features a circular brick walk with park benches and old trees that shade the worn and weary. It's open all hours daily. From Route 50, take Exit 11 north onto Collington Road (Route 197); after 3.5 miles, turn left onto 11th Street and then turn right onto Ninth Street. The park is located along the westbound lane of Ninth Street on the north side of the bridge in Old Bowie. 301/262-6200 ext. 3009.

17 White Marsh Park 🐾 🐾 🐾 🐾

The reality of this big sprawling parkland is hard to comprehend from busy Route 50 as you turn into the modest entrance. But this home of the Bowie Play-house sees plenty of dogs acting as if they were leashless—and some aren't acting, even though it's against the rules. With the Bowie Playhouse (indoors, so no dogs here), four lighted ball fields, rambling picnic areas and pavilions, hiker-biker trails, the White Marsh Stream running through its middle, and a large playground, this 210-acre park on the outskirts of town is a focal point of outdoor activity in Bowie. Park in the lot near the playhouse and follow the trail that loops south and then west across the stream, where on hot days dogs can splash around to cool off—though leash laws govern even the watery parts. Near the stream, that trail connects with Spur Way, which cuts through some thick wooded territory but doesn't loop back to the playhouse. So when you've had half enough, double back. Taking the pooch on a big picnic with lots of friends? Call first about reservations; in warm weather, this park is crawling with people.

From Route 50, take Exit 13 north onto the Robert S. Crain Highway (Route 3); at about 1.5 miles, look for the park sign. Turn left and backtrack on the southbound lane of Route 3 for 0.1 mile and turn right on White Marsh Park Drive into the park. 301/262-6200, ext. 3011.

EARMARK YOUR CALENDAR

Heritage Day: At this family day that occurs simultaneously at the Belair Mansion, the Belair Stable Museum, and the Huntington Railroad Museum, you and the pup (leashed) can browse the colonial craft displays and marvel at the Civil War reenactments to glimpse some of the history that has marched past these venerable Bowie sites. The afternoon event happens the third Sunday in May annually. Built in the 1740s for the governor, the Belair Mansion is located at 12207 Tulip Grove Drive (east of Route 197); the Belair Stable Museum nearby is at 2835 Belair Drive; and the Huntington Railroad Museum is at 8614 Chestnut Avenue; 301/262-6200.

Bowiefest: An annual community celebration not to be missed, it features more than a 100 information booths and food concessions with plenty of freebies, as well as day-long entertainment on the amphitheater stage, carnival and pony rides, endless arts and crafts booths, and contests. Two events draw the canine crowd: Enter your dog in the morning in the SPCA's dog show where pooches will be awarded for various competitions, and in the afternoon, stand on the sideline with your pup and watch a dog-obedience demonstration. The all-day fest occurs the first Saturday in June every year at Allen Pond Park, 3330 Northview Drive; 301/809-3068.

Fourth of July Celebration: A small-town Fourth from simpler times, the day-long celebration of freedom includes pooches (on a leash), though the crowds get thick here by midday and the fireworks get loud after dark. But if your patriotic pupster is into all that, you and she will find lots of eating and entertainment with the amphitheater being the focal point of the day. Allen Pond Park is located at 3330 Northview Drive; 301/809-3068.

Old Bowie Antique and Craft Fall Fling Street Fest: It's Bowser bargains every last Sunday of September when thousands of fest-fanatics head into the historic section of Bowie for this annual street festival. Emphasis is on yesteryear, with more than 100 antique dealers selling from booths, and Antique Row's 20 antique stores getting into the action as well, with markdowns out on sidewalk. Food concessions and crafts vendors fill in the spaces between the dealers. Olde Bowie Antique Row is located at the intersection of Chestnut Avenue (Route 197) and Route 564. 301/464-1122.

Restaurants

Martin's Deli: It's breakfast all day long, which suits Chappy just fine since he's never quite sure what time of day it is when he's waking up again. But once you get beyond the eggs and home fries, stop by this friendly little deli to carry out a tasty batch of barbecue. The shrimp platter with French fries and coleslaw works for our boys, and the crab cake–sandwich deserves consideration. Best yet, you can carry out the beer. No kidding! 8700 Chestnut Avenue; 301/809-9300.

Memphis Bar B Q Company: Pull into this primary pulled-pork BBQ eatery and take out the saucy stuff for you and your pup. Prices are right; the sauces are great! 4449 Mitchellville Road; 301/809-9441.

Rips: This is a veritable institution in this southern Maryland region and "Rips Country" has been making Maryland crab cakes and stuffing flounder fillets and piling on open-faced hot roast beef sandwiches at this crossroads location just about forever. While you can't take the pooch inside to absorb its large wood-paneled interior, these nice folks are more than happy to wrap up your order or have it waiting, if you call ahead of time. We dug into a large order of the spicy buffalo wings, though Chappy wouldn't touch the celery and carrot sticks served with 'em. The left side of the menu is all steaks; the middle, seafood; the right, "home-style favorites" like liver and onions, meatloaf, and grilled pork tenderloin. 3809 North Crain Highway (Route 301) at the intersection of Collington Road (Route 197); 301/805-5901.

Places to Stay

Rips Country Inn: Just behind Rips Restaurant, this old-style motor lodge accepts dogs of any size in its smoking rooms for an additional $3 per night fee. Plenty of wooded acreage surrounds the parking pavement behind, so sleep-in pooches can take a quick hike for relief. And these folks are friendly. Double rooms cost $65. 3809 North Crain Highway (Route 301), Bowie, MD 20718; 301/805-5900.

BRANDYWINE

Parks, Beaches, and Recreation Areas

18 Cedarville State Forest 🐾 🐾 ½

A Maryland state park that allows dogs? You betcha, but there's a technicality: This huge 4,700-acre rough woodland with 19 miles of trails is largely untouched and officially labeled a "state forest." So there's a little more elbow-room for accommodating dogs, though the statewide leash laws still apply. If natural nature is your cup of kibble, this beautiful young woodland setting with freshwater fishing and more than a dozen miles of fairly primitive trails is a worthy drive almost 20 miles into southern Maryland.

Once you turn into the entrance, follow the main paved road 1.5 miles to the proverbial fork in the road—and the end of paving where your bumpy ride begins. Turn right toward the picnic and fishing sites. Try to ignore the sound of gunfire in hunting season; it's allowed in parts of the forest (so wear bright colors). If you keep driving, you'll see several of the trails that intersect the main road. The Blue Trail is about 3.5 miles, and the Orange Trail with its loblolly pines is a good three miles, but they all loop into each other so you've got several options. Watch your step because the trails also are inviting to mountain bikers and horse riders who sometimes help themselves to more than their share of the pathway.

To the east of the main forest, with its own separate entrance, is the Zekiah Swamp where Piscataway Indians once wintered. Pretty cool place to wander. The bog at the headwaters is home to several rare plant species and many unusual swamp creatures, though dogs don't readily take to these soggy grounds and we lost time on our hike waiting for Chappy to shake his paws now and then. Our pooch preferred the grounds surrounding the Cedarville Pond, where several fishermen sat in the tall weeds waiting for a bite while getting bitten themselves by assorted insects, and dragonflies buzzed the scummy waters on one hot afternoon. Bear to the right off the main road and follow rocky Cedarforest Road past the charcoal kiln (where moonshine was once manufactured) all the way to the end where you'll find the pond and several picnic tables nearby.

The state forest allows "family camping" late March–December, with three special holiday weekend campouts scheduled for the summer—during Memorial Day weekend, Fourth of July weekend, and Labor Day weekend. The 130 campsites feature full showers, picnic tables and grills, a playground, water, and a dump station. When you register, make sure to mention you need one of the three sections marked specifically for campers with dogs. Only 10 campsites are held for advance reservations; all others are first-come, first-served. The camping fee is $18 per night.

The state forest is open 6 A.M.–sunset. From the Beltway (I-95), take Exit 3 south onto Branch Avenue (Route 5) for about 17 miles. About two miles past Brandywine, turn left on Cedarville Road. The forest entrance is about 2.3 miles farther on the right at Bee Oak Road. To reserve campsites, call 888/432-2267, or the state forest offices at 301/888-1410.

Places to Stay
Cedarville State Forest Campground: See above.

CAMP SPRINGS

Parks, Beaches, and Recreation Areas
19 Tinker Creek Stream Valley Park 🐾
Largely unattended, this unwieldy natural zone packs plenty of acreage but not much activity, and tends to look like vacant property more than a public park area. The land is undeveloped, but if you're in the neighborhood and the pooch wants to walk the walk, you can walk it here—and some that do disregard leash laws that are in effect even on these wild grounds. Among the inter-

esting things you might find on the property is an old, ramshackle, burned-out frame house that somebody left long ago, plus lots of trail-less woods.

The park is open all hours but try to keep your visits to the daylight. It's located less than a mile south of the intersection of Temple Hills Road and Allentown Road, about 1.5 miles west of Branch Avenue (Route 5). It is accessible near the intersection of Kirby and Temple Hills Roads. 301/699-2407.

Restaurants

GeMelli Deli & Restaurant: You won't find better wood-burning rotisserie chicken this side of the Potomac. While your pup can't come inside, these friendly folks are happy to bag your order for carryout. 6317 Old Branch Avenue; 301/449-1333.

House of Lee Restaurant and Carryout: Says so in its name—this traditional Chinese restaurant will send you packing with little white carryout boxes of your favorite Asian cuisine. Chappy insists on at least one lo mein dish—and they'll mix up the meats and seafood if you like. 6401 Maxwell Drive; 301/899-8252.

Places to Stay

Days Inn–Camp Springs: These friendly folks have no problems putting up you and your dog at this very standard chain hotel, though the pup has to pay an extra $10-per-night charge from his allowance. There's an outdoor pool (dogs aren't allowed to swim, though), laundry facilities, and all the usual amenities, including a complimentary morning newspaper. And, should your pooch look at you with that I-gotta-go look, it's all grass and woods surrounding the hotel, so take a walk. Rates start at $36. The hotel is located along Route 5 (Branch Avenue) at 5001 Mercedes Boulevard; 301/423-2323 or 800/325-2525.

CLINTON

This town is historically noted as the location of the Surratt House, the home of Mary Surratt, who in 1865 was arrested and convicted for conspiring with John Wilkes Booth and others to assassinate Abraham Lincoln. Otherwise, it is a sleepy southern Maryland crossroads that is rapidly growing as this part of the country begins to bulge in population.

Parks, Beaches, and Recreation Areas
20 Louise F. Cosca Regional Park 🐾 🐾 🐾
Wooded terrain meets fields of dreams at this 500-acre park that offers a lot to do for the sporty pup. The tennis courts are usually busy, and the baseball and softball diamonds are a hotbed of hotly contested games that are great for passing time on the sideline. Nearby, the 15-acre lake attracts local anglers hoping to hook a bass or trout instead of the more likely catfish—the thought of which drives

Chappy to squirming. Boat rentals are available during the summer months, but park authorities won't let pooches go out on the lake. Nor are the pups supposed to go swimming (or humans, for that matter), though you will occasionally find a water-happy mutt dog-paddling in the shallows away from the crowds.

The grove of picnic facilities, pavilions, grills, and play areas located about halfway between the athletic fields and the campgrounds is in big demand for group picnics, class reunions, and family get-togethers. So if you're planning something bigger than sitting at a solitary shady table or leaning against a tree while diving into the picnic basket, call ahead and make reservations. Dogs are required to stay leashed and poop must be scooped.

The extensive playgrounds, minitram Cosca train, and Clearwater Nature Center are all attractions for children but offer little for canines. But leashed dogs are welcome at the small campground situated on the park's eastern border, east of the picnic area and just off Thrift Road. The main hiker-biker trail dead-ends near these 23 family campsites (the other camping area is for groups only). There are no reservations, so get there early—though the ranger assured us that, except on big weekends, you can usually nab a site. Campers pay $8–23 per night (a few dollars more if you're not a county resident), depending on accommodations and accessories. Water, bathhouse, and toilets are included.

The park is open year-round, 7:30 A.M.–dusk (later for lighted tennis courts and ball fields). From the Beltway (I-95), take Exit 7 south onto Branch Avenue

(Route 5). Drive four miles and turn right on Woodyard Road (Route 223); at the second light, turn left onto Brandywine Road. After just over a mile, veer right onto Thrift Road, which leads directly into the park. 301/868-1397.

Restaurants

Texas Ribs & Barbecue: Plenty of meaty choices, but if you don't mind getting sauced, go for the ribs. Take your carryout to a nearby park for lunch and dig in up to your elbows—nothing Chappy likes better than messy eating. 7701 Old Branch Avenue; 301/877-0323.

Places to Stay

Louise F. Cosca Regional Park Campground: See Louise F. Cosca Regional Park in this section.

COLLEGE PARK

Call it Terps Territory if you like, but not only is this the town where the University of Maryland's main campus is located, it's also the parklands by the same name. Two hundred years ago, stagecoaches pulled into this rural travel center that's only about three miles northeast of Washington. As the agricultural college grew into the state's largest university, the town developed into a prosperous business district and a dozen surrounding residential neighborhoods.

Today, dog lovers and their pad-footed pals will find a breather from the surrounding academia and in-season basketball frenzy in the natural artery of parklands, streams, lake, and hiker-biker trails that extend for almost two miles through the area. And for the smart pooch, the University of Maryland campus provides vast areas of green space for strolling among the book-toting students.

Parks, Beaches, and Recreation Areas

21 Berwyn Heights Playground and Park 🐾

The ball fields and street hockey area steal the thunder from leashed canines at this playground park located at the north end of the College Park hiker-biker trail near Berwyn Road. But the baseball and softball fields add enough fringe grasslands and entertainment for dog-day-afternoon pups to scratch out a place in the sun. Lake Artemesia also connects here: the 38-acre dog-friendly lake boasts an aquatic garden, fishing, and fishing pier, plus more than two miles of hiker-biker trails which connect it to Calvert Road Community Park and the grounds of the College Park Airport and Aviation Museum. Leash laws are in effect, and you are reminded to clean up after the dog.

Open dawn–dusk. The park and playground are located south of Greenbelt Road (Route 193) at 58th Avenue and Berwyn Road. 301/345-2808.

22 Calvert Road Community Park 🐾 🐾

Chappy likes low-key parks like this one, which is actually the extension of all those laid-back Anacostia River parks that extend nearly five miles from the District line to this comfy recreation site. The still strong Northeast Branch Stream provides the ambience here, where leashed dogs can caddy competition-quality 18-hole disc golf course (about a mile of walking) or just relax with a carryout snack at one of the shady picnic areas. This is a neighbor park to the Berwyn Heights Playground and Park.

The park is open dawn–dusk. From the Beltway (I-95), take Exit 22 south onto Kenilworth Avenue (Route 201); drive almost three miles and look for the park entrance at Old Calvert Road on the right. 301/445-4500.

23 Cherry Hill Road Community Park 🐾

This unmemorable chunk of nature should be considered a drive-by park only, meaning if you and the pooch are driving by and need a stop to stretch, so to speak, this is fine and dandy. It requires a quick eye to make the entrance off busy Cherry Hill Road. The park expands from its entrance into a large area of decent hiking past the rented garden plots on the west side and the tennis courts at the start. Take your leashed dog down the trail on the east side and you'll find benches and picnic tables in shade. Also, if you're camping a half mile north at the Cherry Hill Campground, this is your closest escape.

Open dawn until dark. The park is located about a mile west of Exit 25 south of the Beltway (I-95) on Cherry Hill Road. 301/445-4500.

24 College Park and Trail 🐾 🐾

Engulfed in a sea of greenery, the hiker-biker trail is the lively outdoors connection that strings together the playgrounds, picnic areas, ball fields, a disc golf course, nature zones, and Lake Artemesia. The trail stretches north from Bladensburg through Berwyn and College Park to Paint Branch Golf Course north of the University of Maryland. However, a tornado in September 2001 damaged more than a mile of the trail from the golf course to Cherry Hill Road, which as of press time remains closed indefinitely. In the university area, where there is heavy walking and biking, this trail and accompanying grounds are prime footwork for leashed canine hikers. But watch your step: Some of these two-wheelers are racing to classes, so the grassy sides of the trail are best for four-legged hikers.

The trail is open all hours. From the Beltway (I-95), take Exit 25 south onto Baltimore Avenue (Route 1) and turn left onto Greenbelt Road (Route 193). Just past the train tracks, turn right on 55th Avenue, left on Berwyn Road, and right on Osage Street, which dead-ends near the trail and park. 301/445-4500.

25 Lake Artemesia Natural Area 🐾 🐾 🐾

A walk in Garden of Eden, this park is dominated by the picturesque 38-acre Lake Artemesia and the Indian Creek Stream that sideswipes it. Fishing is good here (largemouth bass and rainbow trout, supposedly), in case you and the pup have spared the rod. Chappy doesn't have the patience to get up early and risk catching nothing more than the sunrise, so we stuck to the hiking trails on the property—more than two miles of them with gorgeous lakeside views and lush flower gardens and landscaping.

One paved trail circles the lake, it's your best choice because there are lakeside spots where the pup can get his feet wet if he's so inclined. Swimming isn't allowed here, human or canine. He is expected to stay leashed and you're expected to clean up after him—an important consideration on these watery grounds, if you catch my drift. A second trail trails off from the grassy zone surrounding the lake and into wooded area, which is a shady relief from a scorching sun, but also a high tick risk.

Keep in mind you can't drive onto this property, so figure on using the pedestrian entrances. And there are no toilet or other facilities here, which is probably why it's called a "natural area" instead of a park.

The area is open daily dawn–dusk. From the Beltway (I-95) take Exit 22 south onto Kenilworth Avenue (Route 201), after three miles turn right on Calvert Road. There's trail access to Lake Artemesia in the 5200 block of Calvert Road. Another entrance on the north side includes a parking lot at Berwyn Road near 55th Street. 301/927-2163.

Restaurants

Alario's: For a quick pickup, this college-town hot spot specializes in subs, pizza, and entrée-size salads. It's located near town hall and across from the formal entrance to the University of Maryland. 8150 Baltimore Avenue; 301/474-3003.

Bagel Place: Don't know about you, but sometimes Chappy just *needs* a bagel. And this great little college drop-in shop makes exceptional bagel sandwiches that you can pick up and eat with your pooch at a nearby bench and recall the old college days. The chicken salad bagels worked for us. 7423 Baltimore Avenue; 301/779-3900.

Cluck-U-Chicken: If the name isn't irreverent enough, try the buffalo wings. Oooh! Carry out the regular fried chicken parts and juicy chicken sandwiches, too, from this great little shop that attracts undergrads and others majoring in the culinary artistry of eating poultry. 7415 Baltimore Avenue; 301/699-0345.

Ledo Restaurant: This place has been serving its saucy pizza here so long it might qualify for a National Historic Pizza Landmark plaque. But the thing Chappy likes most about Ledo is its original square pizzas and the buttery flavor of its crust. They say it's because they don't cut corners, and they don't. If you're going to carry out pizza to a nearby park hereabouts, this is the place. Call ahead and order carryout, because it gets busy. Then go to the carryout counter that's separate from the rest of the restaurant and they'll have it waiting piping hot. 2420 University Boulevard at the Adelphi Plaza; 301/422-8622.

94th Aero Squadron Restaurant: Order the chicken fettuccine Alfredo

DIVERSIONS

The Wright Stuff: Your plans on visiting the **College Park Airport and Museum** still up in the air? Landing at the world's oldest continuously operating airport isn't a hard decision to make when you and the pooch feel like playing Snoopy and the Red Baron. This is no fly-by-night destination, however—the Wright Brothers trained the U.S. military's very first pilots on this airstrip at the turn of the century after they flew their famous Kitty Hawk caper. But you can read all about that in the cozy museum here (the pup may need to stay outside). The landmark airport is now operated by the Maryland–National Capital Park and Planning Commission, the same folks who bring you all the other delightful parklands in the area.

But it's all heads up once here. You and the *Aire*dale (other breeds and mutts, too) are welcome to relax on the lawns near the airstrip and watch the small planes go airborne. "You'd be surprised how much dogs like to watch the planes take off," one regular visitor told us as her schnauzer focused on a single-engine job lifting off. "They can also play in the stream nearby if they get bored."

Also, every second weekend in September is the annual **Open House and Air Fair,** where you and the head-in-the-clouds pooch will witness feats of daring such as wing-walkers and midair aerobatics. There'll be antique planes on display, model rockets (no bottle rockets, however), and other exhibits. Admission is free. If, however, you're inclined to take an airplane ride in one of the antiques, you will have to come up with several ten spots. From the Beltway (I-95), take Exit 25 onto Baltimore Avenue south (Route 1) to Paint Branch Parkway; watch for signs for the airport. It's open 24 hours a day. 6709 Corporal Frank Scott Drive; 301/864-5844.

or any of the easy-to-carry-out pasta dishes. Then walk over to the airport— the longest in-service airport in the nation—and watch the small planes take off and land while you nosedive into this tasty food from the WW I–bunker-decorated restaurant. It's open for lunch and dinner. There's plenty of airplane lore to look at while waiting for the order. It's at Calvert Park, near College Park Airport. 5240 Paint Branch Parkway; 301/699-9400.

Penguin Pizza: This isn't just pizza, folks, nope, this popular restaurant makes everything! Really. Get past the doughy pizza possibilities, and choose from pita sandwiches, gyros, Italian subs, shrimp platters, chicken platters, baked ziti, and an assortment of kabobs. Chappy loves this place, not only for carryout eating, but because it delivers! 7409 Baltimore Avenue; 301/864-7900.

Ratsi's: Couldn't get more college-foodish than this: burgers, calzones, pizza with extra cheese, pizza without cheese, and subs. Chappy recommends "no eggplant" on the 'za. 7400 Baltimore Avenue; 301/864-8220.

Santa Fe Cafe: Too bad the outdoor dining is railed, because that pretty much means the pooch has to stay on the other side while you dine. But these friendly Tex-Mex cooks will wrap up those wonderful steak fajitas for you if you're on your way somewhere else. 4410 Knox Road; 301/ 779-1345.

Places to Stay

Cherry Hill Park Campground: The closest campground to Washington, this huge, 400-site campground is full of amenities and welcomes dogs at no extra fee and even offers a dog-walking service. For humans, the campground offers guided bus tours of nearby attractions, public bus service access, full hookups, a swimming pool, sauna, hot tub, and conference center. For overnight pups, it provides enough grassy knolls to confuse the conspiracy theorists. The tenting area (44 tent-only sites) works best unless you're an RV enthusiast (290 full hookups). There are also a few cabins, as well as conveniences such as the full-service store, laundry, etc. A ringer of a dog, Chappy liked hanging out at the horseshoe competitions until he grasped the concept of how horseshoes are used when not for sport. And we made an escape or two to the Cherry Hill Road Community Park a half mile south of here.

This campground works hard at publicizing itself, and it may be the best known close-in camping area hereabouts, so call ahead for reservations. The cost is $30 per night and up, depending on vehicle and number of people. From the Beltway (I-95), take Exit 25 onto Baltimore Avenue south (Route 1); turn right on Cherry Hill Road. The campground is about a mile on the left. 301/937-7116.

COLMAR MANOR

Parks, Beaches, and Recreation Areas

26 Anacostia River Park 🐾

Extending from the District into Prince George's County, this is the northward continuation of the wide green stretch of parkland bordering the Anacostia River. Its mirror image across the river to the east in a more industrial neighborhood seems nearly deserted. But this side isn't.

When we pulled into the parking lot, we obviously had interrupted what appeared to be the start of a match where English was the second language and soccer was the first. Everybody stopped what they were doing to see what we were going to do. Hey, it's their ball, their rules. The trail heading away from the athletic fields looked far more inviting than the glares we received. Could be this is too much of a neighborhood hangout for outsiders to venture into, so our advice is don't bother—unless you're an incredible multi-lingual soccer player looking for a pickup game.

The park is open dawn–dusk. From the Beltway (I-95), take Exit 25 south on Baltimore Avenue; about six miles south, veer right onto Bladensburg Road.

Immediately past the bridge, turn left into one park entrance; alternately, go five blocks farther and turn left on 38th Avenue and follow Monroe Street and park signs to the second entrance. 301/445-4500.

DISTRICT HEIGHTS

Parks, Beaches, and Recreation Areas

27 Walker Mill Regional Park 🐾

Located in this dusty, industrial, and low-rent retail area, these 226 acres of parkland aren't all that inviting—but the trail system that winds through these wooded grounds is a fine walk in the park for leashed pups. The athletic fields get the most local use, however. Really, this is a local-use park more than any-thing. The pleasant picnic areas and hillside playground are popular summer hangouts for neighbors hereabouts. The acreage and trails alone rate this park a paw, but unless you're already in the neighborhood, there's no compelling reason to go out of your way to get here.

The park is open 7:30 A.M.–dusk year-round. From the Beltway (I-95), take Exit 15 west onto Central Avenue. After a mile, turn left on Ritchie Road, then right on Walker Mill Road, and look for the park entrance. 301/699-2407.

FORT WASHINGTON

Parks, Beaches, and Recreation Areas

28 Harmony Hall Regional Center 🐾 🐾

Only about four miles from Fort Washington Park, this community and arts center is home to the oldest archaeological site ever uncovered in the county. Called Silesia, it is the ruins of a house dating close to the founding of the Maryland colony in 1634. The digs that still continue on this aged property occasionally allow amateurs who sign up for its programs to join in—though no dogs are allowed to dig on the archaeological sites. Nor are canines encour-aged to go inside the community center where a regular schedule of perform-ances, art shows, and classes—including the aikido classes taught by Chappy's Uncle John—make this a happening community resource.

But dogs are welcome to play and explore behind the center, where a huge open field is bordered by the woodlands that extend north into National Park Service grounds along Broad Creek. And don't be surprised if you bump into a dog obedience class that takes place there regularly—because even dogs ben-efit from some schoolin'.

The park is open dawn–dusk. From the Beltway (I-95), take Exit 2A, head south on Indian Head Highway (Route 210) for about three miles, and turn right onto Livingston Road. The entrance to Harmony Hall is almost two miles farther on the right. 301/203-6040.

Restaurants

Antonio's: If you crave real Italian food from a real Italian mama's recipes and cooked by that very same Italian mama, this is the place. Carry out Italian hoagies, calzones, or strombolis, if neatness is a concern. The lasagna and pizza are authentic. Even if you want a bowl of minestrone, these friendly and neighborly folks will package it up for you and send you off to a nearby park. And when you're there, say hello to Sandro, Mariangela, and Mama Joanna. The restaurant is across the street from the Livingston Mall and behind the 7-Eleven store, at 742 Cady Drive; 301/248-9780.

Betty's Place: This is the place where great traditional all-American breakfasts are made daily. So, if you're heading out early for a day at Fort Washington Park, plan on stopping here for the bacon and eggs—though the yawning pooch will have to stay outside. Don't be surprised if people refer to this little restaurant as Steak-in-a-Sack, because it serves that pita-filled pleasure, too. 10745 Indian Head Highway (Route 210), in the Tantallon Center; 301/292-4494.

Charlie's: Carry out made-to-order sandwiches, pizza, and even elaborate meals, though the sandwiches will do fine on the way to one of the riverside parks hereabouts. It's in the Potomac Village Mall where Old Fort Road intersects Indian Head Highway (Route 210); 301/292-0655.

Proud Mary's: Stroll gently into this delectable dockside restaurant and, if there aren't many folks around, the kind folks here might just let your Potomac-particular pooch sit at your feet at one of the many great outdoor tables, or at least nearby opposite the rail. Chappy says the sizzling chicken wings are a great start (though pull those bones out before sharing with your pup). The jumbo crab cake lunch is right for the setting, as you watch the water sparkle. 13600 King Charles Terrace; 301/292-5521.

GREENBELT

With walkways and courtyards lending to a pastoral ambience, Greenbelt is designed after 19th-century English garden cities and named for its surrounding forests (such as Greenbelt National Park to the south) and smaller belts of greenery and nature that run through it. This was the federal government's first experiment in social and community planning some 60 years ago as part of Franklin Roosevelt's New Deal. From the bends in the streets to the location of the shopping malls and baseball fields central to its Art Deco housing, everything was planned that way for a reason.

Parks, Beaches, and Recreation Areas

29 Buddy Attick Lake Park 🐾 🐾 🐾 ½

Greenbelt Lake is the deserving centerpiece of this splendid park. As you stroll from the ample parking lot over the slight ridge and look down the hillside, the beauty of this almost-still body of water stops you in your tracks. Forget the playgrounds and basketball court—the lake is the headliner here. As we circled it on the jogging path, dozens of seagulls that obviously agreed on the lake's merits flew standstill against the wind. Several dogs, all appropriately leashed, as is posted and required, skipped happily along the banks of the lake with jogging humans. A few folks fished the waters; others played with children. The picnic tables were busy with families eating, old-timers reading the paper, and two others playing chess, while soaking up the warmth of a sunny winter day. Undoubtedly designed as a gathering place in nature, that's exactly what it remains today.

The park is open dawn–dusk daily. From the Capital Beltway (I-95), take Exit 23 north onto Kenilworth Avenue; at the first traffic light, turn right on Crescent Road and look for the park entrance on the right. 301/397-2200.

30 Greenwood Park 🐾 🐾

Not an official county or city parkland, this small forest wedged between Greenwood Village and Eleanor Roosevelt High School's grounds is a secret dog park where leashless pooches running free bother no one—because almost no one's ever here. Even on this under-used terrain, taking the leash off your pup is counter to county rules. But our friend Margo Hart's frisky Doberman named Rico gets his exercise playing in the stream that extends north and south through the woods. He zips on and off the rough trail for even more exercise. And few if any folks know the difference. At the northernmost end where Hanover Parkway intersects Mandan Road, there's a small picnic area—but it has been commandeered by the high schoolers, so don't figure it into your plans.

The park is open dawn–dusk. From the Capital Beltway (I-495), take Exit 22 onto Greenbelt Road east; watch for Eleanor Roosevelt High School on the left and soon after turn left on Mandan Road. The park is on the left extending behind the apartments. 301/397-2200.

🔳 Schrom Hills Community Park 🐾 ½

One of those belts of green that's surrounded by neighborhoods with names like English Country Manor, Hunting Ridge, and Windsor Green, this neighborly park reflects the community spirit with something for everyone. The community center and ball field draw the kids, especially in the summer. For doggy visitors, the large open area is great for running off steam, and the trails through wooded glen are good for cooling off from the heat. Despite leash laws, you'll find some folks running their dogs without a leash, but it's not advised if you're from out of the neighborhood.

The park is open dawn–dusk daily. From the Capital Beltway (I-95), take Exit 22 onto the Baltimore Washington Parkway and turn off almost immediately onto Greenbelt Road heading east; turn right at Hanover Parkway, then left on Greenbrook Drive to the park. 301/552-2004.

Restaurants

Chevy's: Those tables you'll see outside of this popular "Fresh Mex" Mexican restaurant are off-limits for dogs unless they're seeing-eye dogs. But you can

---

EARMARK YOUR CALENDAR

Easter Egg Hunt: The annual White House Egg Roll keeps the doggy on the outside, but come the Monday morning after Easter Sunday, you can take your leashed dog to Greenbelt's lovely Buddy Attick Lake Park. The Easter Bunny's helpers hide some 4,000 eggs here, including special golden eggs. Watch the tykes (ages infant through sixth grade invited) scramble for eggs. But the party-poochster shouldn't be encouraged to join the hunt. Nor should he chase the Easter Bunny character who hops around handing out candy to youngsters. Live entertainment usually follows this good excuse to get out to the park in early spring sunshine. Buddy Attick Lake Park is located near the intersection of Crescent Road and Greenhill Road. 301/397-2200.

Greenbelt Labor Day Festival: One of the largest annual Labor Day events in the state, the town of Greenbelt goes all out to celebrate what it considers its blue-collar roots. Bands perform on stage throughout the weekend and late into the night. The carnival atmosphere includes booths, games, bingo, and lots of food. Dogs need to stay leashed and close to their owners because it does get noisy in that carnival way. The festivities break loose in downtown Greenbelt. Call 301/397-2208 for more information.

---

call ahead or swing by, and they'll bag your lunch or dinner for you to carry out. The house specialty is called El Gordo, which loosely translated means "more than enough baby-back barbecued ribs, mesquite grilled chicken, shrimp, and other stuff for you and the pooch, all on one plate." Otherwise, this happy hangout makes the usual south-of-the-border fare of tacos, enchiladas, salads, etc. 7511 Greenbelt Road; 301/220-0078.

Three Brothers Pizza: Quick-'n'-easy pizza to go? Dog lovers who are also pizza lovers can swing by this doughy hangout and carry out a feast with a crust for less than a parking ticket hereabouts. It's located at Beltway Plaza at Cherrywood Lane and Greenbelt Road; 301/474-5330.

Places to Stay

Greenbelt National Park Campground: See Greenbelt National Park in this section.

LAUREL

The beginning of this town was the 10,000-acre land grant by the king of England in 1658 to Richard Snowden, whose entrepreneurial family built the exquisite Montpelier mansion some 100 years later that still stands today. Since then, Laurel's location bordering the Patuxent River on the north side has stood largely on its own as a mining town, a gristmill and cotton mill center, and a racetrack town. Today, it is an independent and incorporated suburban entity that stands apart psychologically and legislatively from the county it's located in.

Within Laurel's borders, dog lovers will find the kind of friendly environment for their dogs that independent-minded locals usually provide. While many of the 17 parks totaling 150 acres are tiny tot parks or small neighborhood green spaces not mentioned here, some of its parkland is prime for pooches—though look for restrictions because some community centers do not allow dogs on the grounds.

Parks, Beaches, and Recreation Areas

32 Fairland Regional Park 😺

Shared with Montgomery County to the northwest, this park's Prince George's County side houses the Fairland Aquatic and Athletic Complex and Gymnastic Center, neither of which will appeal to your pup. But behind all the complexities—the batting cages, tennis courts, and the never-ending parking spaces—are some woods and a long and pleasant hiking trail that wanders through the woods and over the county line.

The park is open daily, 6 A.M.–10 P.M. From the Capital Beltway (I-94/I-495), follow I-95 toward Baltimore. Take Exit 33 west onto Sandy Spring Road and, after about a mile, turn left on Old Gunpowder Road. The park entrance is just over two miles on the right. 301/953-0294.

33 Granville Gude Park 🐾 🐾 🐾

Most of this 29-acre, downtown-Laurel park consists of pretty Laurel Lake, which has a lovely waterside walking path that's a nice hike in good weather. We brought a picnic lunch and hung out at one of the many picnic tables, though for larger events there's a huge picnic pavilion and plenty of grills available as well. Play horseshoes, or let the little ones scamper around the tot lot, but the most fun is renting a pedal boat and heading out on the lake. Only six boats are available, and the kind lake-house manager won't let dogs out in them. He recommends you leash your pup to a tree and take a cruise anyway—depending on whether your pup is a sleeper or barker, of course.

The park is open all hours. From the Capital Beltway (I-95/I-495), follow I-95 toward Baltimore; take Exit 33 east (Sandy Spring Road) and drive about two miles to Baltimore Avenue (Route 1). Turn right and go past the Laurel Shopping Center and Laurel Mall. After the Cherry Lane intersection, you'll see the lake on the right; park in the commercial lots along Baltimore Avenue (the lake itself has no parking) and walk over. 301/490-3530.

34 Montpelier Mansion and Montpelier Park 🐾 🐾

Dog-nitaries are welcome at this 18th-century mansion's surrounding 70 acres of lawns, gardens, and woods where George Washington, Abigail Adams, and Franklin D. Roosevelt, among other historic American dignitaries, once visited. You and the dog can't traipse together into the restored and furnished mansion to take the public tour led by guides in period costumes. But leashed pups can explore this national historic landmark's outdoors of rolling parkland located high upon a knoll overlooking the Patuxent River—maybe the best view of the river you'll find. Across Route 197 is Montpelier Park, separate from the mansion grounds and primarily wooded acreage that goes down to the river's edge.

The mansion is open Sunday, noon–4 P.M., from March–November; the grounds are open dawn–dusk daily. From the Baltimore-Washington Parkway (Route 295), exit at Laurel-Bowie Road (Route 197) north toward Laurel, and go about a quarter mile to Muirkirk Road. Turn left onto Muirkirk Road and make the first right turn into the Montpelier grounds. 301/953-1376.

EARMARK YOUR CALENDAR–MAY

Montpelier Spring Festival: Around the first Saturday in May, hundreds of folks show up on the Montpelier Mansion's grassy grounds to celebrate the coming of spring. Bands and performers play from several stages, people dance, crafters sell their goods, and you and the leashed pup are invited. The Montpelier Mansion, Laurel-Bowie Road (Route 197) and Muirkirk Road; 301/776-2805.

35 Riverfront Park 🐾 🐾 🐾

If you need convincing that a river running through it can transform a few acres of grass and trees into a scenic oasis, walk this way. Chappy couldn't wait to race directly to the edge where the Patuxent laps the good earth. Seems like this narrow and elongated 23-acre park that parallels the river is one of those mind magnets that pulls people into its natural beauty. But there's more here: The 1.5 miles of paved walking paths accommodate lots of joggers and works just fine for hiking dogs on leashes, too. The proximity of eateries in town (Main Street is just two blocks away) makes the picnic tables and grills bordering the open play areas prime luncheon spots. Even the old dam ruins and mill site are worth a look.

The park is open all hours. From the Capital Beltway (I-95/I-495), follow I-95 toward Baltimore. Take Exit 33 east (Sandy Spring Road) and drive about two miles; turn left on Baltimore-Washington Boulevard (Route 1), go less than a mile, and turn left on Main Street. Turn right on Avendale Street and park near the park area. 301/725-5300.

36 T. Howard Duckett Community Park and Supplee Lane Recreation Area 🐾 🐾 ½

With two ball fields, a playground, a small picnic pavilion, and restrooms, suburban Duckett Park is exceptional only because it is a watershed area beside the Rocky Gorge Reservoir. Located at the very peak of Prince George's County where it meets Montgomery County to the west and Howard County to the north and east across the reservoir, this is also the gateway to the Supplee Lane Recreation Area. Geared toward kids and adults with boats to launch, its waterside area is pleasant, and the nearby horseback trails provide a decent wooded walk so long as you keep an eye open for oncoming hoofed creatures. Chappy found some garbage cans more interesting, and he sniffed out the baseball diamond, which has become almost an automatic for him given the number of baseball games he's attended. Dogs must be on a leash here. Unfortunately, swimming in the reservoir is prohibited unless you're a fish.

The park and recreation area are open dawn–dusk, closed December 15–March 1. You might find the gates open on some posted days during the winter, but that's hit and miss. From the Capital Beltway (I-95/I-495), follow I-95 toward Baltimore. Take Exit 35 (Scaggsville Road) toward Laurel, then turn right on Montgomery Street and right again on Supplee Lane. The T. Howard Duckett Community Park actually marks the entrance to the Supplee area. 301/490-3530.

37 West Laurel No. 2 Neighborhood Park 🐾

Honestly, the fact that this park is named "Number Two" has nothing to do with the reason we pulled off I-95 to check it out. Then, again, Chappy's intentions might have been other than ours.

But, like good dog lovers, we picked up after him at this intimate and friendly little park tucked back behind the houses in the subdivision. Yes, it is inherently skippable, but Chappy liked the small circular area carved out behind the houses, and the little play area and a small soccer field. It's surrounded by lots of tall trees as you enter the park. Dogs must be on a leash.

The park is open dawn–dusk. From I-95, take Exit 33 west on Sandy Spring Road (Route 216). Turn right on Bond Mill Road, go about a mile, then turn right on Bradford Road. Look for the park entrance on the right. 301/725-5300.

Restaurants

Bay and Surf: You can't take even the salty dog inside this pricey yet precious little seafood restaurant that has been serving its seafaring fare for three decades now. But you can order ahead and carry out anything from the full and tempting menu and walk it over to a lakeside picnic table at nearby Gude Park. And you can't miss this place: It looks like a lighthouse there on Baltimore Avenue. If you're faring light, take out bowls of the Bay Country crab soup or the New England clam chowder from the long list of seafood soups. There are loads of fish dishes, from orange roughie to salmon cakes Baltimore-style. And, as you would expect of any older seafood restaurant, they serve baked and stuffed jumbo shrimp as their specialty. 14411 Baltimore Avenue; 301/776-7021.

Oriental Express: If Chinese fast food is your cup of tea, this carryout cooks up a great pork lo mein and plenty of other Asian entrées. And it's near the scenic Granville Gude Park. 14713 Baltimore Avenue; 301/604-0000.

Philadelphia Style Restaurant and Carryout: Damn the cholesterol, sometimes you've just got to have a Philadelphia cheese steak, and the version they make at this restaurant that stakes its name on it tastes so good you'll think it came from the City of Brotherly Love. Otherwise, the hoagies, strombolis, pizza rolls, and homemade Italian dinners are all credible and delicious. 42 Washington Boulevard, just north of Main Street; 301/206-2017.

DIVERSION

Sizin' up the Big Trees: Laurel has been designated **Tree City USA,** though we're not sure by whom. Nonetheless, the city's Tree Board has declared dozens of its most spectacular downtown trees as Champion Trees. You and the canine tree connoisseur can stop by City Hall to pick up a walking-tour list of these spectacular examples of arbordom. By the way, every mid-April the city celebrates Arbor Day with downtown festivities. City Hall is located at the intersection of Old Sandy Spring Road and Birch Run. 8103 Sandy Spring Road, 301/725-5300.

Red, Hot and Blue: The benches out front make this a perfect stop for the pulled pork–platter to go, or the hot wings, or any of its barbecued specialties. Besides, if you'd rather lunch over at Riverfront Park, it's just a few blocks away. 677 Main Street; 301/953-1943.

OXON HILL

Parks, Beaches, and Recreation Areas

38 Oxon Hill Manor 🐾 🐾

The stately old Georgian-style brick mansion isn't the doggy attraction. The mansion draws brides and grooms and other such romantics to its resplendent setting. But the wooded property surrounding the mansion built on a hill overlooking the Potomac River is what dogs will love. They're welcome on these pretty grounds, so long as they stay leashed and the poop gets scooped. As soon as you drive through the elaborate brick and wrought-iron gates, you know this place is promising. Immediately off to the left of the huge parking lot is a swath-cut trail leading that way. In front of the manor house is a precious shaded courtyard with sidewalks and benches that alone would constitute a pleasant visit. Some of the art shows and tasteful concerts sometimes spill outdoors, making the exterior all the more a work of art to behold. The riverside of the property is still more inviting, with elegant brick-terraced gardens and formal landscaping leading downhill toward the wooded Betty Blume Neighborhood Park.

Open Tuesday–Friday, 10 A.M.–3 P.M. The manor is located a half mile from Capital Beltway (I-95/I-495) off Exit 3A. Head south on Oxon Hill Road and look for the sign and entrance on the right. 301/839-7782.

39 Tucker Road Sports Complex 🐾 🐾

A multi-recreation complex and parkland, it occupies a hefty portion of the seven-mile-long Henson Creek Park, still mostly undeveloped parkland that borders each side of Henson Creek that branches off Broad Creek. Athletic dogs will focus on the fitness opportunities. The Tucker Road Fitness Trail is a mile-long exercise course that includes 19 workout stations where Chappy loves watching us strain muscles. The Henson Creek Golf Course, which backs up on the complex, is a fun little nine-holer. But leave your pooch with your Big Bertha in the shade of the clubhouse deck because the dog isn't allowed and the driver isn't needed.

Opposite Tucker Road from the golf course are the tennis courts, baseball and football fields, basketball courts, ice rink, playgrounds, and full-facility picnic areas, even a fishing pond or two. Most important to aerobic bowsers is that between all of these high-energy zones is plenty of low-key grassland where a pup and her pal can sit back and watch the games. And, running through these parts is the new Henson Creek Trail—a paved six-mile scenic recreational route for bikers, hikers, joggers, horse riders, in-line skaters, and, of course, doggers.

Except for the lighted courts and fields, the complex is open dawn–dusk. From the Capital Beltway (I-95/I-495), take Exit 3A south. Turn left from the exit ramp onto Oxon Hill Road, cross Indian Head Highway (Route 210), go about a half mile, and turn right on Livingston Road. At Saint Barnabas Road, turn left, then right on Tucker Road; the complex is located about a mile on both sides of the road. 301/248-4404 or 301/292-9006.

POWDER MILL

Parks, Beaches, and Recreation Areas

40 Powder Mill Community Park 🐾 🐾

The woods surrounding the baseball and football fields were more inviting to Chappy than anything else. Nicely kept trails head off to the east and south, though the floor of this forest has been cleaned up enough that going off-trail is no problem at all. From the parking lot, along your left, the forest drops steeply about 50 feet or more to the brisk and burbling Paint Branch. The stream is deep enough in this isolated location for a dog swim on a hot summer day.

The park is open dawn–dusk daily. From the Capital Beltway (I-95/I-495), take Exit 28 north and turn right on Powder Mill Road; the park is located about two miles on the right. 301/445-4500.

RIVERDALE

Parks, Beaches, and Recreation Areas

41 Anacostia River Park 🐾 🐾

Extending northeast from the District line, this elongated riverside parkland balloons in this town to create a natural setting adjacent to the town office. Playground facilities and open fields on the larger north side area make it more people-oriented than dog-perfect, but there's always strolling room. Chappy found some new friends—all of them on leashes that day—and he always likes sniffing out the banks of streams and rivers. Because the parkland extends to the other side of the Anacostia's northeast branch, this site is very pretty.

Open dawn–dusk. The park is located off East-West Highway (Route 410); turn north on Taylor Road and follow Sommerset Road into the park. 301/445-4500.

42 Fletcher's Field Park 🐾 🐾

Turn into this park just off Kenilworth Avenue (Route 201) and you'll see the fenced baseball fields and a playground beyond the parking lot. It's not immediately impressive as a destination for antsy dogs.

But park the car and walk past the playground, and you'll find delightful wooded parkland and soccer fields that borders the eastern side of the northeast branch of the Anacostia River. There are picnicking facilities and a leisurely feel to the park. Walk farther up the Anacostia about a half mile and you'll find the bridge at Riverdale Road, where you can cross into parkland on the other side.

The park is open during daylight hours. It's located off Kenilworth Avenue (Route 201) at Crest Park Drive. 301/445-4500.

UPPER MARLBORO

Parks, Beaches, and Recreation Areas

43 Patuxent River Park—Jug Bay Natural Area 🐾 🐾 🐾 ½

Don't look up the Patuxent River Park on a map. You'll only get confused. More than a half dozen of "them" appear to bulge their natural environments separately all the way up the Patuxent River as it narrows from Chesapeake Bay and connects Prince George's County's southernmost tip at Chalk Point to its northernmost point above Laurel. Right about in the middle of those 70-some miles of river is the one Patuxent River Park area developed enough to accommodate you and the dog for a day in the park. It's called the Jug Bay Natural Area, and accommodate it does.

A wealth of wildlife and plant life overruns this thick-wooded 2,000 acres (of 6,000 total) only an hour south of downtown Washington. Stop by the park office first and pick up the "Bird Checklist" if you want to be wowed by the 250 species of winged creatures that you might cross paths with—from the red-throated loon to the ruddy duck. Let the park rangers know if you intend to explore extensively the eight miles of hiking and horse trails (also a four-mile driving tour of the off-dog-limits Chesapeake Bay Critical Area farther south), so they know you're out there.

From the parking lot, the trail starts next to the Duvall Tool Museum building and soon branches off east and west along the north side of Black Walnut Creek wetlands. About a half mile or so as the right branch begins to loop around, the trail connects to one of the park's two boardwalks that extend into marshy swamplands. Both have observation decks for spotting the ospreys, swans, geese, herons, and other water birds nearby.

The trails are under-used—which is why they can provide up-close observation of nature. Don't be surprised if while trekking through this overgrown outback, you glimpse a red-tailed hawk streaking across the sky and a wild orchid growing at your feet. It's that kind of place.

Chappy took to the wooded trail that snakes and loops through the area all the way south to Mattaponi Creek where there's a 1,000-foot bridge. He wasn't the least bit curious about the swamplands, however, which is for the best, because dogs aren't supposed to go out on the boardwalks anyway. The concern is that they'll disturb the fragile wildlife. A sign at the head of one trail even prohibited pooches from its woodland path. When we asked the park ranger about it, he said if Chappy stayed leashed we could take him along.

Back at the park office, we stepped gingerly down the side of the elevated riverbank, past the Jug Bay observation tower, to get to the river itself. The park rents canoes but prohibits dogs from boating on Jug Bay for their own safety. You can make a day of fishing from its shoreline or boat-ramp area, where largemouth bass and perch number among the catches, but you will need a Maryland fishing license. The primitive camping sites are reserved for organized groups only.

The park is open daily, 8 A.M.–dusk (hours change by season). From the Capital Beltway (I-95/I-495), take Exit 11 south (Pennsylvania Avenue/Route 4) just past Upper Marlboro; follow Crain Highway (Route 301) south about 1.5 miles and turn left on Croom Station Road. Go about 3.5 miles and turn left on Croom Airport Road. The park entrance is about four miles farther. 301/627-6074.

44 Robert M. Watkins Regional Park 🐾 🐾 🐾 ½

This 430-acre park beckons dogs with its array of hiking and biking trails that carve through well-maintained wooded areas; some even lead to rushing streams and a great pond.

From the long entrance road, you can see that the forest bottoms are cleared and maintained so that following a trail isn't even necessary in some parts of the park. Bikers and in-line skaters dominate the paved paths; hikers and dogs stick to the natural paths. The Wetland Trail, for instance, took us about 50 minutes (including Chappy's many stops for sniffing) to walk. It starts from the nature center and is an easy 1.3-mile hike that crosses several marshy areas via boardwalk and past a ridge where you can view 120-year-old tulip poplars and maybe even some deer. About the same length, the Beaver Pond Trail goes by the pond—the habitat of wood ducks, blue herons, and even beavers.

Large and well-marked picnic areas and pavilions are everywhere, including way back in the woods so that you and the pooch, or even a large group of picnickers, can carry on in relative solitude. A modest-sized campground to the left of the main entrance near the park administration offices offers sites to nonresidents for $20 a night, including use of the comfort station, bathhouse, and water spigots (no RV hookups). Your dog must behave herself and stay leashed.

A huge playground area and classic miniature golf course just off the main parking lot lure lots of children. On the opposite side of the lot are a snack shop (in season), an antique Chesapeake carousel and miniature train ride, and the Old Maryland Farm exhibit. For sports-minded visitors, the park provides baseball and soccer fields and tennis both indoor and out—but Chappy had seen enough athletic fields elsewhere. Instead, he yanked us (dogs must remain leashed) to the nature center, built on a scenic hillside overlooking the woods and a lively creek. Behind the nature center was the outside caged section of an exhibit that extended inside (dogs aren't allowed inside). What was in the cage? Amazingly, a red-tailed hawk, a vulture, and an owl, all perched there blinking out at us, unfazed by our curiosity. What a great mix of entertainment and unabashed nature.

The park is open daily, 7:30 A.M.–dusk. From the Capital Beltway (I-95/I-495), take Exit 15 (Central Avenue/Route 214) east toward Upper Marlboro; after 3.1 miles, turn right on Watkins Park Drive (Route 193). About a mile farther, the park entrance is on your right. 301/218-6700.

Restaurants

Cleo's Restaurant: Cleo Curtis started this roadside restaurant just south of Upper Marlboro decades ago, and it still serves Southern open-pit barbecue chicken, ribs, beef, and pork after all these years. Oh, they serve crispy Southern-style fried chicken, too, but gauging how much you can eat is the first decision you have to make at Cleo's. The minced chicken with a hefty side of kale, coleslaw, baked beans, and potato salad makes a highly recommended regional feast. 5909 Crain Highway (Route 301); 301/627-2718.

Grizzly's Restaurant: Make a quick stop here to carry out pizza or sandwiches—a step up from fast food. 9544 Crain Highway (Route 301), maybe six miles beyond Upper Marlboro proper, but close to the Croom Road intersection on the way to the Patuxent River Park; 301/599-0505.

EARMARK YOUR CALENDAR–DECEMBER

Winter Festival of Lights: One of several such holiday light shows in the region, this starts in late November at Watkins Regional Park and is a cheery and beautiful extravaganza for you and the festive Fido. Some 350,000 lights shape holiday themes and decorations. The illumination runs from dark–9:30 P.M. daily and is free, though the park gratefully accepts donations of canned goods that it turns over to charitable organizations.

Places to Stay

Duncan's Family Campground: Location isn't the only plus for this family-oriented campground—it also happily accepts dogs, whether you come in an RV or set up the leaky tent. Of the 317 campsites here, 120 provide full hookups, 117 have water and electricity, and 80 are barebones sites where campers just rough it. But this isn't serious roughing it. Other camping amenities include laundry facilities, a small grocery store, ice, tables, firewood, even a public phone. The grounds also feature a swimming pool, playground, recreation hall, some group activities, horseshoes, and volleyball. Dog lovers will like the modest but pleasant on-site hiking trails and the proximity to the larger wilderness at Patuxent River Park. Prices start at a base rate $19 per family, $23 after Memorial Day; electric costs extra but dogs don't.

The campground is open year-round, though most recreational facilities open Memorial Day through Labor Day. From Upper Marlboro, take Pennsylvania Avenue (Route 4) southeast about two miles beyond the Crain Highway (Route 301) junction; exit onto Route 408 (Mount Zion) and after a half mile turn north on Sands Road. The campground entrance is a quarter mile on the right; 410/741-9558.

Forest Hills Motel: It's small—only 13 rooms. They're clean and tidy and all on one floor, which any dog lover knows is an advantage, since pooches hate walking up steps or taking elevators. This old-style roadside motel doesn't give canine guests a second thought, though it does add on an extra $5 a night. For humans, the cost is reasonable too, just under $50 a night. Wooded areas surround the hotel, so your pup will have plenty of sniffing territory when not watching the tube. It's located about two miles north of the courthouse in downtown, at 2901 Crain Highway (Route 301); 301/627-3969 or 800/793-2828.

Robert M. Watkins Regional Park Campground: See Robert M. Watkins Regional Park, in this section.

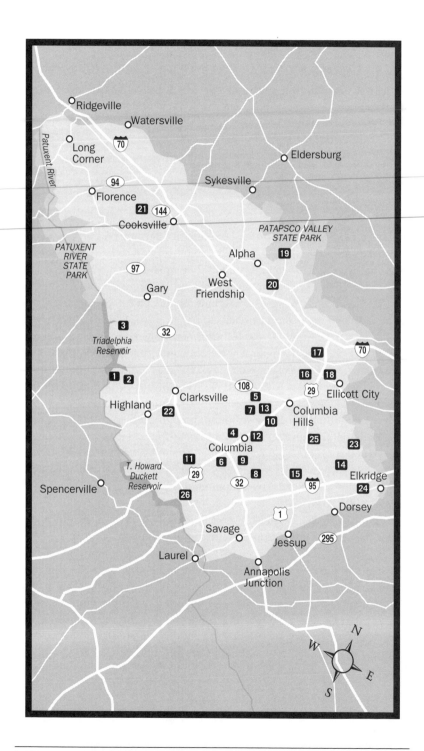

HOWARD COUNTY

Located between Baltimore and Washington, Howard County historically has been a refuge from the city life, an undeveloped countryside. That was before James Rouse designed a planned community in the 1960s to bring people together through its layout, land use, and architecture.

On a tract of land 20 miles north of Washington and 10 miles southwest of Baltimore, Rouse created a suburban community that surrounds a central downtown service area with 10 residential villages. The idea was to create a community offering something for everyone—every race, religion, and economic status.

And dogs, you ask? Today the social experiment of Columbia offers equal recreational opportunity to canines in many thoroughly thought-out green spaces. Even in the terrain beyond Columbia, the Howard County Department of Recreation and Parks is one the most organized of all the park systems in the area. Posted at each of the five county parks and 21 community and neighborhood parks are clear and simple rules: All require dogs be leashed and poop must be scooped. Dogs are not allowed in the picnic and sports areas. Most parks adhere to winter hours (December 1–March 31) of 8 A.M.–

5 P.M., although they gradually extend hours as the days grow longer. Basically, figure they're open dawn–dusk and you'll be close enough.

One group, Howard County Dogs (check out its public bulletin board at http://groups.yahoo.com/group/dogpark), has become very active in opening the county's first off-leash dog park, three fenced-in acres near the Worthington housing development off Newcut Road in Ellicott City. As this edition was going to print, the park was slated to open, but hadn't yet. Neither the park, nor the street it's on, had been named. However, after talking to very devoted president Grant Kalasunas, it promises to be just the beginning for this organization.

BRIGHTON

Parks, Beaches, and Recreation Areas

❶ Brighton Dam 🐾 🐾 🐾 ½

Chappy didn't make it through all of that Neil Simon movie, *Brighton Beach Memoirs,* but it did compel our prolific pup to bark out his own memoir of our visit to Brighton Dam. Loosely translated (and edited for taste), Chap says:

"What's with all the water falling from the wall? Why do we always have to get as close as possible? Oh, no, not bath time in the shower again! Okay, no bath. Hey, I wanna go this way. They must think this is beautiful, I bet. All I want to do is head for that big shady tree over by the creek.

"Wait! What's that I smell? Sniff, sniff, sniff. Cool your rocket, Mom, I wanna sniff here some more. Kinda like the scent of a shih tzu . . . no, wait a second, not shih tzu. I should be so lucky! It was poodle! Hmm. Standard, not miniature, I'd betcha. Sporting clip, not that icky English saddle cut that makes 'em look like topiary. Guess I can top that poodle piddle. Ahhhhhhh! That felt so-o-o good.

"Where next? Hey, I know, let's go to the picnic tables and see if there are any scraps. No, not that plaque. I hate historic plaques. Who cares if this place has been providing water for the area since 1943? Dude! Provide this water!

"Nice walking by the creek here, though. Shady. Cool. Friendly. Maybe I'll pant a while to convince them to get me a drink. Wait? Another dog over there. A golden! No problem, they're nice. Wait! Where're we going? Ain't it hell we canines have to pull our humans around by the leash?

"Oh, well, it's not crowded. They could nix the hunting here, that's for sure. Horseback riders are scary, too. Got no problems with the boaters. Even been out in one myself . . . . "

Enough of Chappy's thoughts. The hunting he refers to is a seasonal issue that might steer you elsewhere, or not. It's mostly separate from the paths of least resistance you're likely to take at this exceptional parkland. Anglers populate this area often. Visitors flock by the thousands around Mother's Day to see the azalea gardens, which were planted in 1949, and the paulownia grove near the picnic area. Said to be an extremely fast-growing tree (up to eight feet in one year) with large heart-shaped leaves two-feet wide, the paulownia tree is a cash crop in the Japanese timber market. This grove boasts beautiful clusters of trumpet-shaped, sweet-smelling lavender flowers in spring.

The area is part of what is called the Triadelphia Watershed. The Washington Suburban Sanitary Commission runs it, which makes it sound like anything but a place where you'd like to go with your dog. But it's one of the best and brightest sojourns in the county. Pets must be on a leash, and the only food available here drops out of vending machines, so bring your picnic basket filled.

Brighton Dam is open from sunrise to sunset. To get there, go north on New Hampshire Avenue (Route 650) nearly three miles past the Capital Beltway (I-495) from the Washington suburbs. About two miles past Brinklow, turn right on Brighton Dam Road. The dam and recreation area are on the right; the azalea gardens are on the left. 301/774-9124.

2 Greenbridge Recreation Area 🐾 🐾

Another boat launching area in the Triadelphia Watershed less than a mile north of Brighton Dam's azalea gardens, this one's smaller than some of the others and offers less to do with the doggy—unless you're boating on the reservoir. It also claims it is *not* a picnic area, and you should take it at its word. But you could easily walk around by the gorgeous water and breathe in some clean air. Dogs must be on a leash, of course, though we've seen some dip on hot days.

The area is open dawn–dusk. Take New Hampshire Avenue (Route 650) north past Brighton Dam Road to Green Bridge Road and turn right. It dead-ends at the water. 410/774-2310.

3 Triadelphia Recreation Area 🐾 🐾 🐾

Two geese honked at Chappy and flapped off onto the water as we got out of the car. The way the parklike area is set up is very appealing to dog lovers: As you pull into the parking lot, you can see a little basin of water and a stone wall around it. Walk around the water to the other side where a hill ascends to overlook the water. Picnic tables dot the grassy slopes under big old trees. There are grills if you're coming to cook out. A swing set and small play area off to the side occupy children. It all provides a pretty view of the water and the craggy water's edge.

Two spots in the area are historic sites. One is where three brothers founded the original water-supply spring for the town of Triadelphia in 1809. The other is a small fenced-in patch of land with two trees, called Ben Franklin trees. They were apparently discovered in 1765 by John Bartram, who named them Franklin trees. They are among the rarest native ornamental trees in the world (it's now extinct in the wild). Come to check these out in spring, however, because in winter they look just like every other tree without leaves or buds.

The park is open from sunrise to sunset. To get to the Triadelphia area, take

Georgia Avenue (Route 97) north to the Montgomery and Howard County border. Turn right on Triadelphia Lake Road. The road dead-ends at the area. 301/774-9124.

CLARKSVILLE

Restaurants

Artie's Ice Cream: Walk up to the window and get a soft-serve cone. You and your dog can share licks, should you desire, while sitting on a bench on the grass in back. 12451 Clarksville Pike (Route 108), across from Saint Louis Church; 410/531-2666.

COLUMBIA

The Columbia Association, which rules the roost in this proud and planned community, created and now oversees 144 toddler's playgrounds, 227 pedestrian bridges, three lakes, 19 ponds, and more than 78 miles of pathways throughout the neighborhoods for biking, jogging, and walking the dog.

Parks, Beaches, and Recreation Areas

4 Atholton Park 🐾 ½

One sunny afternoon we had a good old time at the tot lot, the toddler's playground. We didn't even go on the hiking trails in this 10-acre neighborhood park, where most folks come for the tennis courts and ball field. It was quiet and peaceful just where we were. Dogs must be on a leash.

The park is open from sunrise to sunset. From Columbia Pike (Route 29) north, turn right on Shaker Drive and left on Donleigh Drive. The park is on the left. 410/313-4700.

5 Cedar Lane Park 🐾 🐾 ½

A path through the woods connects two areas where you'll have an enjoyable time at this 100-acre woods. There's no Winnie-the-Pooh and no body of water, which we mention only because so many of Columbia's parks have man-made lakes in the middle of them. This is a park designed for people and what people do—play ball, sit on benches, play tennis, picnic, play.

Still, Chappy liked trotting through the woods. He didn't need anything more than that. Frankly, he says his pads are happy to see a paved trail. He found plenty to sniff along the sides of the concrete path and was glad to have the shade that the woods provided—unlike the wide-open parts of the park where folks play ball.

The concession, restrooms, and drinking fountains are all closed in the winter months. Otherwise, sit back, and have a hot dog with your dog. Just make sure he's on a leash and you clean up after him.

DIVERSIONS

Doggy Day Care: You love your dog, but there are times you might need some help. A little training, a day camp, a special puppy party, The Coventry School offers it all. Billed as a being "for dogs and their people," the folks here offer all sorts of fun events, mostly centered on helping you train your dog. Or is it the other way around? The **Day Camp Just for Dogs** provides an air-conditioned environment in which friendly dogs can play and even get some training, but most of all lots of exercise. The motto here: "A tired dog is a happy dog." Charges per day are $15–25, depending on how many days a week you show up. If you're not a joiner, you can get private classes in your house. Don't forget the **Puppy Parties!** They're a fun way to have the family involved with a new puppy and learn the basics of housebreaking, chewing and destruction control, jumping up and starting on the basic sit, come skills. 7165 Oakland Mills Road; 410/381-1800; website: www.thecoventryschool.com.

Paddle Paws: During the summer months you can rent canoes, rowboats, and paddleboats (flat-bottomed rowboats are best for dogs) from the boathouse located along the west shore of Lake Kittamaqundi in Columbia Town Center—so long as the boathouse manager sizes up your pup as waterworthy. Launch the craft from the wooden pier at the boathouse and row out to Nomanizan Island. Located in the middle of the lake, it can be reached only by boat. Park at Wincopin Circle in the Town Center and walk to the nearby lake and boathouse. 410/381-0194.

The park is open from sunrise to sunset. From Columbia Pike (Route 29), take Clarksville Pike (Route 108) west towards Clarksville, about 2.8 miles. The east area entrance is on your left off Route 108. To enter the west area, turn left off Route 108 onto Cedar Lane; the entrance is three-quarters of a mile on your left. 410/313-4700.

6 Dickinson Neighborhood Park 🔥

Pull over and lift a leg on the side of the soccer field. That's about all that's of interest here. There's no parking lot and not much in the way of facilities. It's just a small park for people who live here.

The park is open dawn–dusk daily. From Columbia Pike (Route 29) north, turn right on Old Columbia Road, and right again on Guilford Road. Then turn right on Eden Brook, and the park will be on the left. 410/313-4700.

7 Hawthorn Park 🐾

People in this community won't want your dog running without a leash on, but the wide-open field that greets you at this park is mighty tempting. Rules are that dogs must be on a leash. So tell the pup she's got to stay tethered; you can still do some running around. Just take it easy; there isn't much shade if the two of you end up huffing and puffing.

The park is open daily, dawn–dusk. From Route 32 west, turn right on Cedar Lane, left on Owen Brown Road, and take the first left, which is Sunny Spring Road. The park will be on the right once you're well into the subdivision. 410/313-4700.

8 Hopewell Park 🐾

This seven-acre park has a little pool and a big open field that sees a lot of local motion and neighborhood activity but not much else. Toward the back of the park, you'll find some trees. Pooch must stay on a leash.

Hopewell Park is open dawn–dusk daily. From I-95 take Exit 41 west onto the Little Patuxent Parkway (Route 175). Turn left on Snowden River Parkway, then right on Rustling Leaf Road, and look for the park on your right. 410/313-4700.

9 Lake Elkhorn 🐾 🐾 🐾

How great would it be to live in the subdivision near here called the Village of Owen Brown and walk the two-mile path around this 37-acre lake every day? The sun sparkles on the water. The lake has a waterfall, a bridge, and docks for launching canoes. The lake (about 15 feet at its deepest) is stocked with trout in the spring, and that attracts schools of folks with fishing gear. On a more practical note, the 23 acres of land surrounding the lake feature water fountains, picnic areas, and a lovely paved path bordered with landscaped flower gardens. On the idyllic breezy day we visited, a small child was flying a kite in one of the open grassy areas and the scene looked almost like an Impressionist painting.

The path sees a lot of action—bikers, joggers, walkers, aerobic fanatics, and fitness freaks. You get the idea: your Arnold Poochenegger would be happy hanging out here. Going down the path from the little parking lot brings out the whippet in all of us. Facilities like restrooms are locked for the winter season. Still, you'll end up having an extremely pleasant outing by the lake. Put the dog on a leash and clean up after him—those are the rules.

The park is open 6 A.M.–10 P.M. To get to Lake Elkhorn, take I-95 to Exit 41 (the Patuxent Parkway/Route 175). Head northwest and turn left (south) on Snowden River Parkway. Take a right when that dead-ends into Broken Land Parkway, and you'll see the lake on the right. 410/715-3161.

10 Lake Kittamaqundi in Columbia Town Center 🐾 🐾 🐾

Another one of Columbia's man-made lakes, this one is 27 acres and named for the first recorded Indian settlement in Howard County. The name actually means "meeting place," according to the Columbia Association.

The lakefront plaza area is well kept. A boardwalk runs around the lake, at times becoming a brick path. Check out those bricks. On them are names of people who live in Columbia, part of a renovation in the early 1990s. The large

Tree of Life sculpture, with 66 abstract human figures, reaches out from a central core in the Lakeside Plaza. Other works of art include a bear and her cub, and one called *The Hug*, which depicts a father and daughter embracing.

A fountain rises up into the air, inspired by Tivoli Gardens in Rome. A sculpture with 12 bells sits closer to the water, and you can hear its chimes every quarter hour. To the right of the carillon is a large abstract steel sculpture known as *Sail*. Once you know its title you'll see the resemblance. Rectangular beds of brilliant red and yellow tulips mark the entrance of the plaza in spring. Other flowers are planted at other times of the year. Ducks waddle around all over the grass and sidewalks, which leads to inevitable chicken matches with Chappy, though the Daffys tend to steer away first. This is one pretty place to walk a dog on a leash, although it tends to be more for people use.

The lake area is open dawn–dusk, though you apparently can walk about there any time. To get to the town center, take Columbia Pike (Route 29) and follow the signs for Merriweather Post Pavilion, Columbia's notable concert hall. If you're coming from the south, you'll turn left into the entrance and right on Little Patuxent Parkway (Route 175). Then make a right into Wincopin Circle. Park there and you can access the walkways and restaurants. 410/381-0194.

11 Martin Road Park 🐾

Pull over when you see the grassy area on the left. This isn't a big park, but a rolling slope on the back side is kind of fun to scramble up. A picnic pavilion with grills means neighborhood picnics with dogs on leashes, and "dogs" on the barbecue grill are the summer staple here.

The park is open dawn–dusk. From Columbia Pike (Route 29) north, turn left on Beechwood Drive and left on Martin Road. The park is on the left. 410/313-4700.

12 Symphony Woods 🐾 🐾

Home of the Merriweather Post Pavilion that is renowned for a jammed and jammin' concert schedule every spring, summer, and fall, this 40-acre park in downtown Columbia is hilly and wooded. In other words, it's a delightful place to roam with the pooch—though it can get crowded and rowdy during shows, so time your visits wisely. Plenty of shade and picnic tables create a lovely casual vista for wasting a few hours bonding with Bowser on a leash.

The park is open just about all hours due to the concert schedule, though you and the pooch will appreciate it most in daylight hours—unless you're there to listen to the music leaking out from inside. It is located off Columbia Pike (Route 29), a half mile north of the Broken Land Parkway intersection. Look for the Merriweather Post Pavilion entrance signs. 410/313-4700.

13 Wilde Lake Park 🐾 🐾 🐾

This park is a polished gem with some fine facets. Originally a low-lying meadow covered with rough grass with a small stream running through it, it's now a 22-acre, man-made lake and dam built by the Columbia Association.

The dam is 200 feet wide and 15 feet high. A path around it is an easy hike of 1.5 miles. The "Wilde" in the name? These grounds are dedicated to Frazar Bullard Wilde, chairman of the board of the Connecticut General Life Insurance Company, and one of Columbia's big supporters.

The park itself isn't huge—only about 16 acres—but the trees and landscaping provide great space and shade. The little lake is picturesque and peaceful. A border collie on a leash—as required—frolicked under a tree the day we visited. Only reason to go here instead of the big parks nearby is that you're more likely to have it all to yourself and the pup—and have just as good a time.

The park is open dawn–dusk daily. From Columbia Pike (Route 29), turn left (west) on Little Patuxent Parkway (Route 175). Turn right on Hyla Brook Road, and the park is just on the left. 410/313-4700.

Restaurants

Akbar Restaurant: Chappy prefers tandoori chicken when he's ordering Indian cuisine because its spices are so subtle and the meat stays moist. He's just not that into curry yet, which is strange considering his breed's origins. Get it to go here and head over to any of the nearby Columbia parks. At the Columbia Marketplace, 9400 Snowden River Parkway; 410/381-3600.

Bertucci's Brick-Oven Pizzeria: It's not just pizza that you can carry out to your favorite park. There are pastas and salads, too. 9081 Snowden River Parkway; 410/312-4800.

Clyde's: Really and truly a Washington institution, the original is located right in the heart of Georgetown—but who's measuring miles and tradition? You hungry? Clyde's in Columbia is just like the Clyde's in Georgetown, with a pub feel and burger atmosphere. We found it was a great place to stop before heading to Baltimore one day for an Orioles game. Get a table by the windows for a view of the lake. With the dog along, however, get it to go and sit on the grass outside, where you'll not only have your pooch begging, you'll attract the ducks as well. On a sunny day, this is a pretty spot for you and Spot. 10221 Wincopin Circle; 410/730-2828.

Famous Dave's: Put a Famous Dave's in every town! That Devil's Spit sauce is the best. Then again, the Rich and Sassy sauce is pretty darn good, too. Whatever your style, this is a great place and they're ready to package it up for you to carry it out. 6201 Columbia Crossing Drive; 410/290-0091.

Friendly's: Who can resist a thick fribble from the carryout window here? If it's super hot, go for one of the refreshing summer coolers that blend sherbet with seltzer water. Need we suggest the original Friendly's menu item, the patty melt? It's better than you remember. 6375 Dobbin Road; 410/997-7219.

Great Wraps: Doesn't the name tell you all you need to know? Give up the Burger King fries (although they drive Chappy nuts because he loves

EARMARK YOUR CALENDAR

Columbia Festival of the Arts: An extravaganza of fine arts and crafts, music, dance, theater, and lakeside entertainment, this big community gathering happens over a week stretch from mid- to late June. Featuring every discipline of the arts (and some undisciplined arts), the evenings include hands-on workshops. The Kittamaqundi lakefront portion is most suitable for four-legged art aficionados who want to stroll among the outdoor exhibits and booths on the weekends. Call the Columbia Association for details at 410/715-3000.

Howard County Fourth of July Celebration: A daytime celebration may be more for a dog's liking than the fireworks at night, but all day long there is stuff to do, including a best-decorated stroller competition. It all happens at Lake Kittamaqundi. Call the Kiwanis Club at 410/740-4545 for more information.

---

them so much) and eat something healthier. 10300 Little Patuxent Parkway; 410/964-1122.

Ledo Pizza: We've always liked the square pizza we get here with the buttery crust, especially when it's topped with extra cheese. Chappy insists on pepperoni, but then he gets thirsty. Hey, it's a dog's life! 6955 Oakland Mills Road; 410/381-5550.

Michael's Pub: Chappy didn't mind staying outside tied to a pillar while we went in, ordered a burger to go, and downed a draft beer at the bar while waiting for the order. It's a neighborhood atmosphere. 8630 Guilford Road; 410/290-7878.

Panera Bread: Fresh sandwiches, soups and salads—get one served in a sourdough bread bowl on a wintry day and there's nothing better—are the order here. In fact, you place your order and then sit down and eat and it's all really easy with the pooch in tow. 10300 Little Patuxent Parkway; 410/730-9666.

Peking Chinese Restaurant: If you want your chicken or shrimp dish spicy, just say so and they'll fix it that way. Call ahead and they'll have it ready for you to carry out. 7060 Oakland Mills Road; 410/381-8580.

Strapazza Italian Restaurant: *Mamma mia!* Go for the chicken cacciatore or the mussels. When they're the special of the night, it's a treat. Nearby benches make it easy to tie up your canine companion, who will be drooling as you dine at the outdoor tables—but at least he'll be nearby. 8775 Center Park Drive; 410/997-6144.

Tomato Palace: You can't sit with your dog at your feet at the outdoor tables, but you can easily station him close by. He'll like the view of the lake

---

and so will you. It's a pretty place to grab a bite on a summer evening. This is right next door to Clyde's and is owned by Clyde's, but it offers more Italian dishes. 10021 Wincopin Circle; 410/715-0211.

Wok 175 Chinese Restaurant: Beef, pork, chicken—name it and they'll wrap it up for you to carry out. Chappy's fond of the sticky rice and gets his own carton but no chopsticks. 6365 Dobbin Road; 410/730-7410.

Places to Stay

Staybridge Suites: Dogs are welcome here and each room has a kitchen, so you'll have some of the comforts of home. There is a large open field in front of the hotel, which makes for a nice little jaunt before you and the dog need to head off to your next destination. A one-bedroom suite with two double beds is only $80. 8844 Columbia 100 Parkway, Columbia, MD 21045; 410/772-9901.

ELKRIDGE

Parks, Beaches, and Recreation Areas

14 Rockburn Branch Park 🐾 🐾 🐾 ½ 🐾

When this park was under construction, the county discovered Native American artifacts, thought to be remnants of encampments from thousands of years ago. Chappy seemed to be imagining himself with war paint and a bow and arrow as he hiked through the 4.25-mile trail that begins right near the front gate off Landing Road. One of three trails in this 387-acre park that nicely mixes athletic areas with wilderness, it meanders through woodlands and by stream valleys. There is no pond or lake. The park is on the flight path of migrating hawks, and bluebirds nest in the area. As you hike, don't just look down for arrowheads, look up for birds. You might also be on the lookout for horses, which use the trails, too.

If you park in the north area off Landing Road, you'll find a concession stand that sells hot dogs, fries, burgers, and drinks at the top of the hill near the parking area. Picnic tables are terraced into the hills by the baseball and softball fields where you and the dog can relax and break bread together.

Off Montgomery Road by Rockburn Elementary School, the south area has more fields, though one trail starts off to the left as you enter the park. It's preferable to go to the north area with a dog. All the trails have signs posting warnings to be careful and walk "with a friend or a dog." Or a dog friend. Dogs must be on a leash and you must scoop the poop, although we saw one dog without a leash near the tennis courts.

The park is open dawn–dusk daily. From Columbia Pike (Route 29) southbound, take Montgomery Road (Route 103) east. From Columbia Pike (Route 29) northbound, you need to take Route 100 to Montgomery Road (Route 103) east. To enter the north area of the park, turn left on Ilchester Road and right on Landing Road; the park entrance will be on your right. To enter the south area, stay on Montgomery Road and turn left into the park. 410/313-4955.

15 Waterloo Park 🐾

Kids were having fun riding their bikes around here, and a team of adults were heavily into a soccer game. So right off it seemed more human-oriented than dog-friendly. Plus, the park is right next to I-95, so the sound of trucks roaring by is constant. Still, a little paved path into these 23 acres of woods earned it a rating that's better than a pit stop. Dogs must be on a leash and the poop must be scooped.

The park is open dawn–dusk. Take I-95 north to Exit 41 (Little Patuxent Parkway/Route 175) west. Turn right on Route 108; then turn right on Lark Brown Road and right again on Old Waterloo Road. The park is at the end of the dead-end road on the left, next to Deep Run Elementary School. 410/313-4620.

Restaurants

Hunan Restaurant: Sick of fast food? Tired of subs? Maybe some Chinese would make for good picnic-and-hike food when you don't want to carry a load later. It's all for carryout anyway, and Waterloo Park is just down the road. 6590 Old Waterloo Road; 410/799-4870.

Pecoraro's: Spaghetti, veal, subs, shrimp, pizza . . . they're more than happy to bag any dish for you to carry out. This is a friendly place. They just say they "don't have dog food." Just as well with Chappy, who'd take veal over his kibble any day. 6270 Washington Boulevard; 410/796-7720.

Waterloo Pizza and Subs: This is just next door to Hunan if you'd rather get a mouth-watering steak-and-cheese sub to take out for a picnic at Waterloo Park. 6590 Old Waterloo Road; 410/799-0067.

Places to Stay

Exec Motel: A $100 deposit is required if you bring a dog to this little 34-room, two-story motel that's only about 12 minutes from Baltimore's Inner Harbor. A double will cost $42. 6265 Washington Boulevard, Elkridge, MD 21227; 410/796-4466.

Hillside Motel: No deposit necessary for your four-legged traveling companion here. And there's a fair amount of grassy area surrounding the place. A double costs $41. 6330 Washington Boulevard, Elkridge, MD 21227; 410/796-1212.

Tip Top Motor Court: Small dogs are allowed here, says management, but expect to pay a $50 deposit. A double room costs $45. 6251 Washington Boulevard, Elkridge, MD 21227; 410/796-0227.

ELLICOTT CITY

In the late 1700s, Joseph, John, and Andrew Ellicott established this town named for them. The historic part of Ellicott City is old, small, and charming. There are steep, narrow streets and some greenery around—like the area near the parking lot at the northernmost point of town, which was good for giving Chappy a break. Many of the original buildings remain, despite a major flood in 1868 and a hurricane in 1972 that almost swept away everything. If your dog likes sniffing out old buildings, he'll be quite happy. Otherwise, the trip is more for the antique lover—although the body-piercing store on Main Street might attract some. In addition to historic Ellicott City, plain old Ellicott City surroundings have some fine parks.

Parks, Beaches, and Recreation Areas

16 Centennial Park 🐾 🐾 🐾 ½ 🐾

The county is extremely proud of this 325-acre park—and well it should be. It has won three awards for its natural design and sensitivity to nature. And it looks like a picture postcard.

The 2.4-mile pathway around the 54-acre lake is the best for hiking with your dog. It's paved and it sees a lot of action—from strollers to pooches. And it's pretty. The sign right at the entrance—the one with a dog on a leash and the reminder to clean up after your pet—was the first place Chappy lifted his leg, obviously following in the footsteps of many a canine park-goer before him.

Though its address reads Ellicott City, this fine park is part of the Columbia planned-community mindset and the county planned for everything—perfect lake, perfect paths, a perfect little bridge, a refreshment area, ducks, geese, seagulls. If you like a rougher, wilder time of it, this isn't the place to go. If you like it nice, tidy, and pretty, this is hard to beat. A dock with refreshment stand is open in summer months—April–October.

The park hours vary by season and scheduled activities. Winter hours are 8 A.M.–5 P.M.; otherwise, figure on dawn–dusk. From Columbia Pike (Route 29), take Route 108 west, towards Clarksville. The main entrance is about one mile on your right. 410/313-4620.

17 Cypressmeade Park 🐾

If there are 20 acres of park here, then Chappy's a monkey's uncle. Then again, we're not betting. But it is hard to find that much property, unless the trails lead much farther into the woods. A small playground, where an overweight black Lab named Bart was cheerfully knocking down small children, is wedged between tennis and basketball courts.

The park is open daily, dusk–dawn. To get to the park, take Route 40 (Baltimore National Pike) east to Greenway Drive. Turn right, then left at the first street, Longview Drive. Turn left again onto Cypressmeade Drive. The park is on the left. 410/313-4620.

18 Dunloggin Park 🐾 ½

A lot of parks are right next to school areas and seem to double as both play fields for the school and for the community. This one is in back of Dunloggin Middle School and Northfield Elementary School, and it didn't seem to be a separate community park at all. Two separate playgrounds and lots of open grassy areas for playing sports suggest phys-ed class rather than pooch property. There are no water fountains, no trees, no picnic tables. Paved trails lead to bridges into the subdivision behind, presumably so school kids can walk there. But the bridges are fun to explore as they go over small streams.

The park is open dawn–dusk daily. From Route 29 (Columbia Pike) north, turn left on Saint John's Lane, until it dead-ends. Then turn left again as Saint John's Lane curves around Saint John's church. Then turn right on Northfield Road, which dead-ends into the school parking lot. 410/313-4700.

19 Patapsco Valley State Park 🐾 🐾 ½

Straddling the county line between Baltimore and Howard Counties, and running through Carroll and Anne Arundel Counties as well, this 15,000-acre state park spans 32 miles along the Patapsco River.

With an intimate, sparkling river snaking that far through the bottom of a canyon of woods, you'd figure this to be a four-paw park, right? Well, not quite. This big and busy park undoubtedly would rate among the best if only the state of Maryland were a tad more generous in its attitude toward canine constituents. As we've pointed out before, Maryland often puts dogs in its doghouse when it comes to its state parks.

The rule for dogs and all other pets at Patapsco: They are allowed only "outside of developed areas." That means dogs get to traipse the trails—on a leash—in areas of the park that avoid picnicking, athletic fields, playgrounds, campground, skiing, disc golf, restrooms, any other facilities or buildings, or anywhere humans are the dominant species. It means you and the hiking hound are relegated to trails used primarily by serious hikers, horseback riders, and mountain bikers. It could be worse. But this also means you and the poor pooch can't go in the main gates of any of the park's main recreation areas, where you'll find signs that just say no to dogs.

How do you get to the undeveloped areas if not through the front door? The trailheads are the trick. Pick up the brochure, *A Guide to Your Pet in Patapsco Valley State Park,* which maps out several undeveloped areas where dogs are welcome. All but two of them are located on the Howard County side of the Patapsco.

So your first stop in tackling this doggy dilemma is to go to the Hollofield Area, located three miles northeast of Ellicott City on Route 40, where the park's headquarters are located. This area is also popular among picnickers, anglers, and campers.

The 76-site campground here actually includes a pet loop of about 12 dog-friendly sites where you and the hike-lovin' hound can set up pup tents and stay a few nights. During holidays, you must stay a minimum of three days, and non-holiday times it's a minimum of two. Make reservations first, because the dog campsites are in demand, depending on when you want to go. Each site features its own picnic table and grill, with full bathhouse and toilets centrally located. Sites with electricity run $20 a day; those without are $15. Make sure when you sign in at the camp ranger's office that you ask for the park's pet brochure, which will direct you to areas near the campground that allow dogs. Alas, that's the only drawback: The hiking trails connecting directly to the campground area are off-limits to dogs. The closest dog-friendly zone, which is an undeveloped half-mile trail that leads down to the river and a small overlook, is two to three miles away. And you've got to drive to it because the area between it and the campground prohibits dogs. It's a classic can't-get-there-from-here quandary that Chappy swears he saw in a Camus novel called *Underdogs,* but don't take his word for it.

Farther north along the river, less than a mile from Marriottsville, is the McKeldin area. Another destination for mountain bikers, hikers, and horse riders, it has plenty for anyone without a dog—picnicking, ball fields, a big pool with rapids, and playgrounds. But if you bring the backdoor pooch to hike its trails, figure on going in on the gravel road called Freezer's Lane, off Marriottsville Road on the north side of the park's main entrance. You'll find a parking area down there and the trailhead where dogs are allowed. Hike that wooded trail north for about 1.5 miles, and you'll arrive at Liberty Dam—the cork at the bottom of the beautiful Liberty Reservoir. You'll find other trails around the reservoir without hiking a whole lot farther.

In central Howard County, the side-by-side Avalon and Orange Grove areas, located two miles northwest of Elkridge on River Road via South Street from Route 1, feature more than 30 continuous miles of fine equestrian, hiking, and mountain-biking trails—but they get crowded, especially on fair-weather weekends. There's a swing bridge that connects the north side of the river in Baltimore County to the Howard County south, plus remnants of the historic viaduct and the Orange Grove mill.

Keep in mind that dogs are something of pariahs on these grounds, so steer the pup clear of the highly peopled points. And if in doubt where to access the undeveloped territories, call the park headquarters.

The park is open daily, 10 A.M.–sunset. To get to the headquarters in the Hollofield Area from I-695, take Exit 15 three miles west towards Ellicott City. Look for signs for Patapsco Valley State Park. 410/461-5005.

DIVERSIONS

Sunset Serenades: From mid-June to mid-August, take your tune-loving animal to **Centennial Park,** spread out a blanket, and listen to live music as part of the park's Sunset Serenade series. Make sure the dog's on a leash, and you certainly must clean up after him, but otherwise have a pleasant musical evening. For more information call the Howard County Department of Recreation and Parks, 410/313-4632.

Puppies, Start Your Engines: You know how happy your dog makes you. So why don't you and your dog companion bring a little cheer to an elderly person by signing up for the **Pets on Wheels** program. The organization is always looking for volunteers who would like to visit nursing homes, assisted living homes, home-bound folks, and senior centers. To volunteer, call the Florence Bain Senior Center and ask to speak to the Pets on Wheels program coordinator. 410/313-7213.

Restaurants

Bippy's: Get a Bippyburger to go and your dog will be one happy camper. But this pub also offers salads (Cobb for $7.95) and even crab cakes to go. Call ahead and then pick up your order. 10194 Baltimore National Pike, in the Bethany 40 Center. 410/465-3633.

Crab Shanty: Too bad Chappy couldn't go inside and see the sled in the Chesapeake Room which Bing Crosby rode in the movie *White Christmas,* or to see the pretty oak beams and large brass-and-copper chandelier. But the good thing is that they'll pack fresh seafood for travelers to make sure it stays okay. And carryout's available. Try the shrimp salad platter with coleslaw and fries for $9.50, or go for one of the bigger meals of sirloin, flounder, crab cakes, or Maryland fried chicken, topped off by a piece of cheesecake. But it's a good idea to call ahead. 3410 Plumtree Drive; 410/465-9663.

Places to Stay

Forest Motel: There is no extra fee for dogs at this small, old-fashioned, and campy 25-room motel. But management has one wish: that you walk the dog in a designated area. There is a soft ice cream stand right next door to the motel and people like to sit at the picnic tables and not be bothered by panting pooches. But get yourself a cone and stroll by the trees and everyone will be happy. There also is the Forest Diner just a few feet away if you want to get a real meal and take it back to your room. A double on a Saturday night is right around $55. 10021 Baltimore National Pike, Ellicott City, MD 21043; 410/465-2090.

Patapsco Valley State Park Campground: See Patapsco Valley State Park, in this section.

FRIENDSHIP

Parks, Beaches, and Recreation Areas

20 Alpha Ridge Community Park 🐾 ½

If that ridge along the hillside at the back of this park wasn't the Howard County Landfill, you'd never know you were anywhere near someone's garbage.

Obviously built for community activities, the park features two beautiful baseball fields, a soccer field, two playgrounds, tennis courts, and picnic pavilions. Porta-potties were very clean and actual restrooms are planned for construction, according to the county. There were no drinking fountains, though, which is tough, considering you're really out in the middle of the country. Still the paved paths lead around the edge of the more wooded areas although it would be easy enough to take a hike into the higher brush if that's really what you want to do.

This isn't a park with character, however. There is no lake. But if you want to have a picnic and play some ball with pals, you can cook up a great afternoon—and never smell a thing, even when the wind shifts. Really.

The park is open dawn–dusk daily. From Route 40 east, turn left on Frederick Road (Route 144). Turn right on Route 32 north and then right on Old Frederick Road (Route 99). The park is on the right. 410/313-4700.

GLENWOOD

Parks, Beaches, and Recreation Areas

21 Glenwood Park 🐾

Truly out in the middle of nowhere, this park sits next to a middle school and a high school and is clearly there for them. Nothing but rolling hills, farmland, and countryside surround this park, making it hard to know where the park begins and ends. There are no trees and no facilities. One set of bleachers marked what must be the sideline of a field used for soccer. But not knowing boundaries seems to be the character of this locale—even from its beginnings. A historical marker said the area was named after Dr. Charles Alexander Warfield, 1751–1813, a Revolutionary War patriot and major of the Elkridge Battalion. The grave, the sign added, "is near here somewhere."

The grass is greener across the street where the county plans to develop what will be called Western Regional Park. But then the grass is always greener.

The park is open dawn–dusk daily. Take Georgia Avenue (Route 97) north until it turns into Roxbury Mills Road, and you'll see the schools on the left. Turn left on Carrs Mill Road, and the park will be on the left. 410/313-4700.

HIGHLAND

Parks, Beaches, and Recreation Areas

22 Schooley Mill Park 🐾 🐾 🐾

Wetlands, woodlands, a sediment pond, and meadows make this a 192-acre park rich in wildlife and a great place for the complacent pupster to get to know his animal kin. Deer, red foxes, opossums, and groundhogs show up here regularly, we're told. But we didn't even see any horses the day we visited, although there is an equestrian ring just as you enter the park.

The 4.5 miles of trails—basically a big loop around the property—provide a vigorous walk, and plenty of wide-open grassy areas surround the tennis courts, the playground, and the ball fields. Even the horse areas provide more than enough room to romp on a leash. But finding the only real shade requires heading down a trail or grabbing a picnic table under the cluster of trees behind the concession area.

The James Marlow House, circa 1840, stands by itself in the middle of the park. The house is significant as a prototype of rural farming architecture, which is why the county restored it to pre-Civil War era configuration.

The park is open from dusk to dawn. From Columbia Pike (Route 29), take Route 32 west to Hall Shop Road and turn left. Look for the park entrance on the left. 410/313-6130.

JESSUP

Places to Stay

Greenway Motel: With only 19 rooms, this is truly the old-fashioned roadside motel, but there is plenty of lawn area, and dogs are welcome. And a double costs $36, tax included. 7731 Washington Boulevard, Jessup, MD 20794; 410/799-2975.

Red Roof Inn–Jessup: Showtime's on cable here and Chappy doesn't get that at home, so he was hoping we'd stay. The three-story motel has no room service, but there's a diner within walking distance and you can get carryout there. Also, free coffee in the lobby, 6–10 A.M., always makes life easier. A double is around $55. 8000 Washington Boulevard, Jessup, MD 20794; 410/796-0380 or 800/843-7663.

Restaurants

Avanti Restaurant: No outdoor tables here, but you can get any of the Italian or American dishes wrapped up to go. 8801 Washington Boulevard; 410/792-0355.

SAVAGE

Parks, Beaches, and Recreation Areas

23 Guilford Park 🐾 🐾 🐾

A little lake, paved paths, and the aesthetically pleasing landscape make this a notch above the usual neighborhood park, even though that's all it really is. Not rough, not rugged, not too athletic, the park offers simple pleasures such as shade, water fountains, and paved walking areas that Chappy really liked.

From I-95, take Exit 38 and watch for the signs for Guilford Road heading back west. Follow the road through the Route 1 intersection. The park, with two separate entrances, is on the left. Either entrance will access the entire park. 410/333-4700.

24 Savage Park 🐾 🐾 🐾

There are seven miles of connecting trails in this 270-acre park, but you wouldn't necessarily know it until you pick one and venture in with the explorer dog.

Paths wind along steep valley walls that are home to white-tailed deer, box turtles, chipmunks, raccoons, and squirrels. Woodpeckers, wrens, and king-fishers are abundant feathered friends. The Middle Patuxent River runs through it and there is great fishing for smallmouth bass, trout, and sunfish. There is a two-trout limit for anglers, though no limit for dogs.

One trail we walked for a bit was the Historic Mill Trail, 1.5 miles long and level. It begins at the Bollman Truss Bridge, built in 1869 and moved to Savage in 1887, the last remaining bridge of its type. The bridge itself is worth the trip. It's red and constructed of wrought iron—railroad tracks go through the middle right next to a little walking path over the rushing river. It's not a big bridge, but it gives you the feeling of another era.

Two other trails, including the wide, wood-chip–covered, steep Wincopin Neck Trail, are accessible from Vollmerhausen Road. The Savage Loop Trail, with some rocky terrain, includes the one-mile River Trail, accessed near the baseball and volleyball courts of the park, which are off Fair Street. This entrance is the main entrance to the park, where the playground, ball fields, restrooms, and concession area are.

The park is open sunrise–sunset. From Route 1, go west on Baltimore Street, which dead-ends at Fair Street. The park entrance is just on the right. Or from Baltimore Street, turn right on Savage-Guilford Road and follow it until you turn left on Vollmerhausen Road and look closely for the right entrance to the trail. 410/333-4700.

Restaurants

Savage Mill Cafe: The chicken salad is gourmet good. The grilled cheese is just right. And you can even just get ice cream, a big soft pretzel, or a bagel, if that's what you're in the mood for. Lots of outdoor tables surround the Savage

Mill, a renovated cotton mill built in the 1800s that now is home to lots of antique shops, artisans' studios, and gift stores. So tie the dog up outside, run in and get some food, and have a pleasant lunch outside. 8600 Founders Street, in Savage Mill; 410/724-0060 or 800/788-6455.

SCAGGSVILLE

Parks, Beaches, and Recreation Areas

25 Hammond Park 🐾 🐾

A Scoop Your Poop sign—the one with the little dog and his pile of poop and a red line through it—was the first thing we saw at this park. Chappy didn't deny us the privilege to do just that. A big field like this one is just a big bull's eye in Chappy's book. The closer to the middle it lands, the more points you score! It gives new meaning to the term "pickup game."

Besides the fields, this park offers tennis courts, basketball courts, and another field used mostly by neighboring Hammond Elementary and Middle

Schools. The stone walls around the playground and picnic area were some of the nicest we've ever seen at a public facility. Chappy, on a leash as required, liked burying his nose in the yellowed, dried-out tall grasses along the edge of the green grassy areas. There were lots of piles left by dogs whose owners weren't concerned about scooping—which is bad form, folks, especially considering kids use the park.

The park is open dawn–dusk daily. Take I-95 north to Scaggsville Road (Route 216) west/north. Then take a right on Leishear Road and left on Glen Hannah. The park will be on the right. 410/313-4700.

26 Scott's Cove 🐾 🐾 🐾 🐾

Who would have thought that an area governed by the Washington Suburban Sanitary Commission (WSSC) would be one of the most rustic and delightful spots in the entire Baltimore-Washington area?

It's absolutely true. What a surprise to emerge from the narrow country road—with no markings pointing the way—to see a gravel parking lot on the side of the road and a few picnic tables. But that's just at the top. From there, you can see the cove area below.

Geese started honking at Chappy as we made our way down the sloped hillside toward the water—the T. Howard Duckett Watershed, a reservoir used as a public water source. It looks more like a lake or river, and visitors are encouraged to come. There are several large brick grills, picnic tables, and a playground right in the middle of the hill. The water's edge is accessible—like a beach. The posted signs say No Wading or Swimming, which is unfortunate because it looks so inviting, especially for a traveling dog. On the other hand, when you figure that someone's going to drink that water . . . . Speaking of which, there are no water fountains and no restrooms—although two portable toilets are tucked into the woods across the street from the parking lot.

There is a lot to explore, whether it's checking out the big boulders by the water's edge off to the left, or walking around the cove to the right where the sun filters through the tall trees a little bit more.

The WSSC says dogs are allowed on a leash. The place closes at sunset. To get to the cove, take I-95 to Exit 35 (Scaggsville Road) heading west. At Leishear Road, turn left until it dead-ends at Scaggsville Road. Turn right onto Scaggsville Road and go only a few feet and turn left onto Harding Lane. Follow Harding as it bears to the right until you see the cove on the left. 301/774-9124.

WOODBINE

Places to Stay

Ramblin' Pines Campground: In a wooded area 25 miles from Baltimore, this family campground rents cabins, RV sites, and tent sites and accepts well-behaved dogs that stay on their leashes. They do ask "What kind of dog is it?"

so if your pal is a breed known for aggressive behavior, don't be surprised if they say, "Sorry." There's a pet walk that follows a trail into the woods about two blocks from the camp office, and there is a stocked fishing pond for those who know a hook and line when they see one. Bathhouse and toilets, game room, and miniature golf are on the grounds. Cabins run about $45 per day and sleep a family of four; tents run $24 for primitive sites and $27 for sites with electricity. 801 Hoods Mill Road, Woodbine, MD 21797; 410/795-5161.

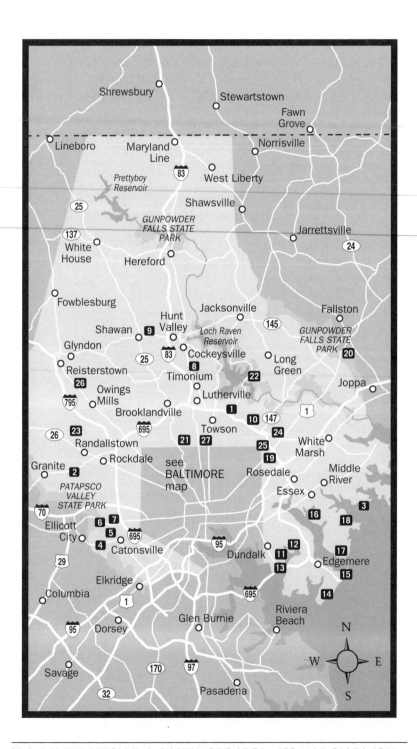

Shrewsbury

Stewartstown

Fawn Grove

Lineboro

Maryland Line ⑧③

Norrisville

Prettyboy Reservoir

West Liberty

㉕

Shawsville

GUNPOWDER FALLS STATE PARK

Jarrettsville

㉔

⑴③⑺

White House

Hereford

Fowblesburg

Jacksonville

Fallston

Shawan ⑨

Hunt Valley

Loch Raven Reservoir

⑴⑷⑸

GUNPOWDER FALLS STATE PARK

㉔

Glyndon

Reisterstown

㉖

⑧③

Cockeysville

Long Green

㉔

⑧

㉒

Owings Mills

Timonium

㉕

Joppa

⑺⑨⑸

Brooklandville

Lutherville

①

⑴

Randallstown

㉖

㉓

⑥⑨⑸

Towson

⑩ ⑴⑷⑺

㉑ ㉗

㉔

White Marsh

Rockdale

see BALTIMORE map

㉕

⑲

Granite

②

Rosedale

Middle River

PATAPSCO VALLEY STATE PARK

Essex

③

⑺⓪

Ellicott City

⑥ ⑺

⑤

⑯

⑱

⑴⑺

Catonsville

④

⑥⑨⑸

Dundalk

⑫

⑴①

⑰

Edgemere

㉙

Elkridge

⑨⑸

⑴③

⑮

Columbia

⑴

⑴④

Dorsey

Glen Burnie

Riviera Beach

⑨⑸

⑴⑺⓪

⑨⑺

N

Savage

W   E

③②

Pasadena

S

BALTIMORE COUNTY

Its 600 square miles surround the city of Baltimore on three sides. The county is smack in the middle of Maryland and in the heart of many canine carousers who like the geographic diversity of close-in suburban neighborhoods, miles of strip malls, beautiful rolling hills and valleys, farmlands, and quaint historic towns.

But the terrain where whiskers really get a-twitching is along the 173 miles of Chesapeake Bay waterfront, where the sun glistening on the bay and the aroma of the renowned blue crabs steamed in beer define the county for many residents and visitors. As they say, "It don't get no better than this." But it does: Most of the county's 10,000 acres of extraordinary parkland, much of it protecting the Patapsco River and the Loch Raven, Liberty, and Pretty Boy Reservoirs, are prime grounds for nature-loving dogs. Off-limits to canines but nationally known are the county's two thoroughbred race tracks at Pimlico and Timonium, which spawn celebrations and events throughout the region that are dog friendly. To get here? Just take any one of the many main arteries out of Baltimore proper and you'll be rollicking and rolling in the countryside of Baltimore County.

The Maryland state parks, you should know, generally aren't very dog friendly. Some don't allow dogs at all, and the ones that do usually restrict them to undeveloped areas and remote trails only.

National Parks

1 Hampton National Historic Site 🐾 🐾 🐾 ◀🐾

Thank goodness they allow dogs here, because this 60-acre park is home to a magnificently furnished 18th-century mansion and elaborately landscaped grounds on what was once an affluent 24,000-acre estate. In other words, these are great digs for dogs, but don't let your pooch actually dig, please.

A fascinating *Gone with the Wind* setting, this place is a feast for the eyes. It's also just a plain-old pleasant afternoon well spent if you're looking for an outdoors excursion that has something way more than trees and trails.

History lesson: In 1745, Colonel Charles Ridgely purchased the original estate. A merchant, he turned the original tract of land into the beginnings of a commercial empire. Fifteen years later the Colonel deeded 2,000 acres to the youngest of his sons, Captain Charles Ridgley, a keen businessman who parlayed the modest inheritance into a huge fortune.

So now we've got the colonel and the captain, right? Not inappropriately titled, as it turns out, because this estate is the story of soldiers of fortune as well as the fortune of soldiers. The colonel got even richer from mining iron ore and selling it to the opposing armies in the Revolutionary War to manufacture camp kettles, round shot, and cannons.

Not enough of a money tree, this place? We kept our eyes down while walking Chappy around, just in case cash started sprouting from the ground. These Ridgelys also raised thoroughbred race horses, livestock, mules, oxen, cattle, swine, goats, and chickens. The Hampton dairy they started continued to milk profits well into the 20th century. At the height of all this venture capitalism, the younger Ridgley built Hampton Hall—the grand-scale Georgian mansion with a main house and two wings surrounded by formal gardens that you and the pooch can wish for on your visit.

Dogs can't go inside for the 30-minute guided tours, because this mansion is all beautiful wood floors and expansive space filled with the original furniture, paintings, and other Ridgely family heirlooms. If you arrive early, it's not usually crowded. You can survey the grounds and decide if you feel comfortable leaving your pup outside. Chappy was happy to relax on the Great Terrace lawn near the marble steps of the mansion's north facade, where we found an old catalpa tree that provided plenty of shade.

Below there are four stately parterres, considered the crowning glory of the Hampton gardens. These geometric, terraced gardens are unique survivors of the 19th-century practice that followed earlier European aristocratic designs rather than the natural designs of American and English gardens after the turn of the century. Check out the roses and peonies of the third and fourth parterres. The roses are an old-fashioned variety called heritage roses, the pioneer of all hybrid roses. Peonies are among the oldest cultivated plants and grew in these gardens 200 years ago. When viewed from the cupola of the mansion, these magnificent parterres create an optical illusion of a gigantic garden all on one level.

Landscaping as artistic expression spreads across the entire estate. Walk your pup around the walkways and notice the Ridgely legacy of unusual trees—from the purple European beech on the mansion's north side to the saucer magnolia and pecan trees to the southwest. Due west is a reconstruction of the original orangerie where the Ridgelys nurtured one of the finest collections of citrus trees in the nation.

By the time we walked the grounds with Chappy on a leash visiting the smokehouse, privies, pump house, herb garden, ice house, stables, and other sites, Chappy was hungry and so were we. Now this is too good to be true, but the lovely tea room inside the mansion serves lunch. Outdoor tables and chairs couldn't have been more accommodating for Chappy to sit with us and share our crab cakes.

The mansion tours begin every hour, 9 A.M.–4 P.M. The grounds are open daily, 9 A.M.–5 P.M., except Thanksgiving, Christmas, and New Year's Day. The tea room is open Tuesday–Saturday 11:30 A.M.–3 P.M. To get to this grand estate, take Exit 27B off I-695. Follow the signs to the right, turn onto Hampton Estate Lane, and look for the grounds on the right. 410/823-1309.

AVALON

Parks, Beaches, and Recreation Areas

2 Patapsco Valley State Park 🐾 ½

Only two of the several recreation areas in this 15,000-acre park are located on the Baltimore County side of the river. The others are in Howard County (see Patapsco Valley State Park under Ellicott City in the Howard County chapter).

The problem with this enormous stretch of woods and wetlands is that the state of Maryland bans dogs from its developed areas—which leaves the backwoods trails and that's about it. Not that we're complaining. There's some good hiking back here. But dog lovers and their pups have to be careful not to cross the wrong path in these woods. And while you might be lured to the Avalon area of the park, where the visitor center houses exhibits panning over 300 years of history, this is actually off-limits to dogs.

The park headquarters near Ellicott City in Howard County provides information and brochures about the dog-friendly areas in the park. In Baltimore County one of them is the Glen Artney Area, located just off Route 1 north of Elkridge via the South Street entrance also used for the Avalon and Orange

Grove Areas across the river in the Howard County. With no formal rec areas like those, however, Glen Artney is mostly rougher trails, creeks, and a pond—the kind of undeveloped turf where dogs can go.

About a mile upriver is the Hilton Area that's located south of Rolling Road in Catonsville. For doggy access to the undeveloped property that goes down to the river, follow Hill Top Road from Frederick Road to the parking lot and pick up either the trailhead used mostly by anglers to go directly to the river, or try the Buzzard's Rock Trail, also near the parking lot, which leads to a scenic overlook of the river.

The park is open daily, 10 A.M.–sunset. To get to the headquarters in the Hollofield Area from I-695, take Exit 15 west (Route 40)towards Ellicott City. Look for signs for Patapsco Valley State Park. 410/461-5005.

BENGIES-CHASE

Parks, Beaches, and Recreation Areas

❸ Miami Beach Park 🐾 🐾 🐾

If you itch for a little sand between your toes, head to Miami Beach. Uh, no, this isn't likely to be mistaken for its Florida namesake—not by a long shot. You won't find many babes in thongs here, no posh high-rise hotels here, nor the fast life of that tropical city here. But this is still a nice park encompassing 59 acres right on the water and walking distance south of Goose Harbor Boatyard. Tucked back in a modest residential neighborhood, the park allows leashed dogs but not in the swimming or picnicking areas when they are open. Sometimes humans aren't around, however, and yours wouldn't be the first dog to take a dip and nobody knew. You do run the risk of a fine, but the fact is that the park is under minimal supervision. The trails that lead into the wooded area are good walks in the shade, which helps on hot days.

The park is open 9 A.M.–7 P.M. and can be reached by taking I-695 to Exit 38 (Route 150/Eastern Boulevard). Head east almost eight miles and turn right on Bowleys Quarters Road; turn left on Good Harbor Road approaching the back side of the park, and then right on Miami Beach Road which dead-ends at the park. 410/887-3873.

DIVERSION

And They Call It Puppy Love: In business for 25 years, Puppy Love—that's the name of the business—has expert groomers whose fingers instinctively reach for the clippers at the sight of a shabby dog. These puppy lovers also sell dog accoutrements, etcetera, that any dog-indulgent dog lover needs. 317 Bowleys Quarters Road; 410/335-3766.

CATONSVILLE

In the early 1800s, this town about eight miles west of the Inner Harbor was a convenient rural rest stop for travelers on the old Frederick turnpike. As the community developed, wealthy Baltimoreans built large summer estates here to escape the summer heat in the city. Today, the town is still a convenient suburban rest stop for travelers—and a peaceful suburb of Baltimore. One off-leash dog park group has been trying to establish a park near the Westowne Elementary School, but has been unsuccessful. There was a one-year trial period during which some fencing went up, but without the backing of the Baltimore County Recreation and Parks Department, it was taken down.

Parks, Beaches, and Recreation Areas

4 Benjamin Banneker Historic Park 🐾 🐾 ½ 🐾

Located midway between Ellicott City and Catonsville, this park is cut from the midsection of the massive Patapsco Valley State Park that extends northward and to the southeast. Here you'll find that the Oella–Benjamin Banneker Site adds a happy *vive la différence* if you're looking for something more from a park—something intellectual, perhaps.

A $2.4 million project, the park pays tribute to Banneker (1731–1806), an African American who lived most of his life in a one-room log cabin here in southern Baltimore County. Unlike many other free African Americans of his time who worked long days in the fields, Banneker worked the fields of advanced science, astronomy, mathematics, and agriculture, and became nationally renowned as a man of knowledge. Among his many accomplishments, he assisted Pierre L'Enfant in designing the District of Columbia.

Check out the visitor center, museum, and the archaeological dig site of the Banneker farmstead for more information and insight into the life of this remarkable pioneer. As the pooch's scholarly interest wanes, head over to the outdoor trails and picnic areas. Trail 9 extends from the north side of the park west for a half mile to the banks of the Patapsco River and east through a thick wooded area that follows the Cooper Branch Creek.

The park is open 9 A.M.–5 P.M. It can be reached by taking I-695 to Exit 13 west (Route 144) and following Frederick Road west about three miles. Make a right turn onto Old Frederick Avenue. Turn left on Oella Avenue, and you'll see the park's brick entrance on the left. 410/887-1081.

5 Catonsville Community Park 🐾

Chappy almost got lonely as we walked around the 40 acres of this tidy community park on a sunny summer weekend afternoon. But we figured a little reflective solitude might be just what the doctor ordered for that annoying habit of his, the one where he . . . ah, never mind.

Keep your furry friend on a leash, even if no one seems to be here, because a senior center rests peacefully right on the property—and that's one apple cart you wouldn't want to upset. Tennis courts, a playground area, a picnic area, ball fields, and some shaded paths give this park more potential than apparent use.

The park is open from dusk to dawn. From I-695, take Exit 15 west, Route 40 (National Pike) into Catonsville; after about a mile, turn left on Rolling Road and look for the park entrance on the left at Old Frederick Road. 410/887-3871.

6 Western Hills Park 🐾

Chappy couldn't wait to jump from the car seat when he saw the grassy fields that let you know you've found this park. But now that you've found it, what do you and the pooch do? It's mostly for ball playing, but it's also great for just running hard and fast and far with your dog on a leash through the grass, which is what we did until we collapsed out of breath to the ground.

The park is open dawn–dusk. To reach the park, take I-695 to Exit 16 (alternately, take I-70, Exit 89) and head west to Rolling Road. The park is on the left at the intersection of Rolling and Crosby Roads. 410/887-3871.

7 Westview Recreation Area 🐾

Rinky-dinky might best describe this park. Its most outstanding characteristic is a large climbing structure for kids that looks like a pirate ship made out of string. Chappy couldn't figure it out either. Dogs will appreciate it for a limited time only.

The park is open dawn–dusk. Take I-695 to Exit 16 (Route 70) and head to Rolling Road. Turn left on Chesworth Avenue and you'll see the park on the left. 410/887-3871.

Restaurants

Dimitri's: In the mood for a little moussaka picnic at the park? This classic Greek restaurant serves the other usuals, too, though Chappy never has gobbled stuffed grape leaves quite the way he inhales other foods. But forget about Chappy a moment. Just don't forget the baklava on your way out. 2205 Frederick Road; 410/747-1927.

Double T Diner: Any time of day or night, return to the culinary glories of a simpler era for this classic American diner food. Sniff out the 400-item menu and order carryout. They will wrap up a big homemade dessert or even a

DIVERSION

Take a Break: If you're out and about Catonsville or even a couple of miles west in the Patapsco Valley State Park's Hollofield Area, and your pup needs a rawhide bone to chew on the ride home, this nearby PetsMart carries just about everything but the kitchen sink. 6501-C Baltimore National Pike (Route 40); 410/747-8570.

breakfast special to go. It's open 24 hours. 6300 Baltimore National Pike at Rolling Road; 410/744-4151.

Indian Delite Restaurant: Kabob masala is always a great dish to try, although it's tough to top a delicious tandoori chicken—probably the least spicy and easiest choice for your pooch. Have a vegetarian or nonvegetarian picnic at the park. 622 Frederick Road; 410/744-4422.

COCKEYSVILLE

Parks, Beaches, and Recreation Areas

⓼ County Home Park 🐾 🐾

If you only went where it says County Home Park in big letters on the concrete side wall near some tennis courts, you would not be thrilled with this county athletic area. But, as we've tried to teach Chappy, things aren't always as they seem. Behind that blah zone is a hidden gem of a park where the Agricultural Building and Historical Society are located.

Park next to the Historical Society, near the brown park sign that says, among other things, that dogs must be on a leash. That's the entrance to a giant segment of the park that backs onto the Longview Golf Course. A little Yorkie was running around without a leash when we visited and was dwarfed by the steep hills. In the valley of the hills is a lovely little pond with a picnic table where Chappy decided to plop down for a spell. Paved paths lead around and into the 220 acres of park area. Blooming trees in spring and summer make it all the more picturesque.

The park is open dawn–dusk. From I-83, take Exit 17 east on Padonia Road; turn left (north) on York Road, turn right on Galloway Avenue, and follow it up and around to the dead end at the parking lot. 410/887-3871.

⓽ Oregon Ridge Park 🐾 🐾 🐾 ½

This place is huge, huge, huge! With at least nine trails winding through 836 acres, the knowledgeable folks at *Baltimore Magazine* once likened it to being in the state of Maine. We didn't find any lobsters, so perhaps they meant it's like a state of mind—which is how Zen trickster Chappy interpreted it.

If so, it's a natural state of mind and not a carefully manicured park. The most you can expect is that the fields will be mowed—at least occasionally—and the trails maintained. This is a beautifully rugged area of trees and mountains that hosts downhill and cross-country skiing in snowy winters—and is an exceptional destination for rugged Rovers any season.

A blast from the past: In the 1800s, Oregon Ridge was the site of iron mines, even of a mining town, if you can imagine that. You don't even have to imagine it, actually. Between the north slope of the ridge and the intersection of Shawn and Beaver Dam Roads, a couple of the old mining town buildings still stand—including the supervisor's house near the park's entrance, whose first floor you can even get into and look around. You can also check out the reproduction of a mining building that has been built as a museum walk-through.

When we visited, we didn't know where to start. Chappy is attention-deficient when it comes to walking through old run-down buildings, and you could spend days exploring this great outdoors. Lucky for us and our couch-potato pooch, none of the hiking trails is very long. Two are more than a mile, the rest under a mile and travel over hills and down along a small stream. At the end of another trail is Ivy Hill Pond, a small drink that will surprise you. One caution: Some of these trails are the abandoned logging roads of yesteryear, and their exposed rock makes poor footing in bad weather.

As you might expect in thickly wooded acres such as these, wildlife is de rigueur. Look for white-tailed deer, red foxes, raccoons, opossums, and bunnies on the trails as you commune with nature. Look skyward and maybe you'll see hawks soaring overhead. You can even glimpse actual bluebirds and Baltimore orioles (the winged ones, not the cleated ones) in these fields. If you hike the Red trail that starts by the lodge and goes past excavation sites, you may see a green heron feeding in the shallow waters. Listen for the chorus of frogs, and you'll know nature's calling.

Chappy pulled us close to the archaeological research site so he could sniff the scents of history, but he had no interest in checking out the outdoor stage or the greenhouse. Dogs must remain on a leash in the park, but that's probably best for your pup 'cause there's so much trouble to get into here. (Consider the launch site for hang gliders.) Dogs are not allowed in the lake area and beach where people frolic.

And, sadly, dogs are not allowed at any of the special events that take place regularly at the park, unless it is specifically billed as a dog event. A couple of years ago, the park hosted a greyhound reunion, and the park hosts special dog walks for charity now and then. Call the nature center to find out about low-key activities such as making real maple syrup and taking moonlight hikes—when dogs might get invites.

The park is open dawn–dusk daily; the nature center is open Tuesday–Sunday, 9 A.M.–5 P.M. To get to the park, take I-83 to Exit 20 (Shawan Road) west; turn left on Beaver Dam Road, and make a right into the park. The nature center phone is 410/887-1815. For more information about the park, call 410/887-1818.

Restaurants

Cafe Isis: This is a sister to the Al Pacino café, which is in Pikesville. And it's a bigger, more grown-up version as well. They'll be happy to wrap up a combination platter to go—with hummus, *baba ghanoush*, grape leaves, falafel, and a chunky Mediterranean salad. It's a perfect summer evening picnic for the park. 12240 Padonia Road; 410/666-4888.

DIVERSIONS

Down on the Farm: No problem with dogs that behave themselves and stay leashed at **Valley View Farm** for its phenomenal lighting and decoration display that goes up every Christmas. Other seasons, the lawn, gardens, and nursery are pleasant strolls for the pup. The farm is open daily, 9 A.M.–7 P.M. 11035 York Road; 410/527-0700.

Imitating Life: While at a festival at Oregon Ridge Park, we couldn't help noticing the eye-catching portraits of pets sketched by artist Diane Bauer. She needs one or more close-up color photographs of your dog to create one of her colored pencil on charcoal paper masterpieces. You can choose the paper color. She sprays the delicate pencil-and-charcoal creation with a protective coating, then mattes it in white. To reach Diane, call 410/569-0221.

San Sushi: While it's not the same as sitting at a sushi bar watching a Japanese chef artistically slice fresh raw yellowtail and tuna, among other delicacies from the sea, you can get sushi and sashimi to go—and be quick about it. Or, if those tasty morsels aren't your catch of the day, this Japanese quick fix serves shrimp tempura, too. 9832 York Road; 410/453-0140.

Places to Stay

Chase Suites by Woodfin: A particularly nice setup for us (Have Kids and Dog, Will Travel), this hotel has nothing but suites with a kitchen and living room in each one. Other amenities include a complimentary continental breakfast (Chappy expects us to steal a sausage for him), an outdoor pool, and cable television. Best of all, Oregon Ridge Park is five minutes away. Expect to pay a $5-per-pet fee, plus a $50 refundable deposit. Rates on weekends are $99 for suites with one double bed. 10710 Beaver Dam Road, Cockeysville, MD 21030; 410/584-7370 or 800/331-3131.

Embassy Suites: Every suite comes with a bedroom and a living room as well as a complimentary cooked-to-order breakfast. But that's not all. Dogs are welcome with a $50 fee. While some grassy fields are outside the hotel, Oregon Ridge Park is only minutes away and enough reason alone to rent a room. Rates are about $150 for a double. 213 International Circle, Hunt Valley, MD 21030; 410/584-1400.

CROMWELL

Parks, Beaches, and Recreation Areas

🔟 Cromwell Valley Park 🐾 🐾 🐾 🐾

This is one of our favorite places in the county. A different kind of park, it's almost like visiting someone's well-tended old farm or estate. History and natural beauty reign on these 367 acres that include a pasture, open fields, woods, a gushing stream, views of rolling hills from higher trail points, an old farm house, plenty of picnic tables, grills, and gorgeous old weeping willows, pines, and oaks.

Used primarily for farming since the early 1700s, the land also attracts a wealth of wildlife. We saw a red-tailed hawk flying overhead—at least, that's what we thought we saw. Great horned owls are said to hunt these woods as well, and as Chappy will attest, the small animals they're hunting for do scurry about the forest bottom. It's not unusual to run across deer moving by, quite uninterested in you and the pup. And if you come out early enough, you might spy a red fox.

At the valley's lowest point, you'll find Minebank Run—so named because of iron ore mining that took place in the stream valley. Your pup can cool his hiked-out pads along its glistening bank and even follow it along one trail for a ways.

Six well-marked trails, none longer than three miles, traverse the property. In fall, when leaves float down and cover the dirt path, it is a beautiful spot. Hold hands. Put the leash on the pooch. Enjoy the sparkling afternoon.

The park is open dawn–dusk daily. From I-695, take Exit 29 (Cromwell Bridge Road) east. Stay on that winding road until you reach the top of a hill; on the left, you can turn in at the Cromwell Valley Park sign. 410/887-2503.

Restaurants

Sanders' Corner: Forgot your picnic? No problem. This is a great place where gruff waitresses make you feel right at home. There's a pretty outdoor deck in back, but it's enclosed so don't expect to sit there with your pup, but you can take advantage of the carryout menu. So get a shrimp salad sandwich and take it to Loch Raven Reservoir right up the street and watch water spill over the dam. (Sanders' likes to call itself "That Dam Place." Get it?! Har har.) Or, take your picnic to Cromwell Valley Park just down the road. Be sure to grab some of the delicious chocolate cookies from the jar at the front (three for $1). You won't regret it. 2260 Cromwell Bridge Road; 410/825-5187.

DUNDALK

Boaters like this modest waterside community because of its many marinas and boat launches—sort of the same reason Captain John Smith liked it when he explored this part of the Chesapeake Bay in 1608. Dogs like its neighborly atmosphere and the many small parks that touch the water and provide scenic relief. We've included only the largest and most inviting of these parks and passed on the others as just more—or less—of the same sweet thang. The town's name, by the way, comes from Henry McShane, who founded the McShane Bell Foundry here in 1895 and named the little railroad depot for his birthplace in Ireland.

Parks, Beaches, and Recreation Areas

🔟 Merritt Point Park 🏃

The park's picnic area juts out into pretty Bullneck Creek and would make a perfect outing for the family. But since your family includes your dog, and he's not allowed beyond the grassy front area where people play Frisbee, let's just say ixnay this arkpay, if you catch our drift. The park seems to be heavily used for picnicking.

The park is open from dusk to dawn daily. Take I-695 west and turn off at Exit 44 onto Broening Highway, turn right onto Mornington Road, then left on Dunmanway Court and into the park. 410/887-3871.

🔟 Stansbury Park 🐾 🐾 ½

At first this looked like nothing much. Or, at best, maybe it was just another little park at the end of the road on the water. But this one actually offers more. Yes, there are big steel structures with power lines overhead that make you feel that you're somewhere in Texas. But there is also Lynch Cove with a path around it leading to the smaller Lynch Cove Park to the north side, and plenty of lawns.

A miniature poodle and a German shepherd both were running without leashes, so leash laws are loosely translated here. Children played in the sand at the playground, big kids played Whiffle ball over in the open area, and people fished by the tall grasses at the water's edge. Chappy was both curious and annoyed at those ducks that waddled around as if they were part of our family. Tucked behind residential streets to the west and Lynch Cove to the east, this park has a nice neighborhood feel to it—both lively and inviting.

From I-95 take Exit 58 and follow Dundalk Avenue south to Holabird Avenue where you must first turn left and then quickly right to get on Merritt Boulevard. About a half mile farther, turn left on Moorgate Road, which will dead-end at the park. 410/887-3871.

🔟 Watersedge Beach Park 🐾 ½

Drive through the working-class neighborhood of small houses all close together and you'll find kids riding bikes and playing games in the teeny yards. During Easter time, decorations were everywhere. The park is indeed located at the water's edge with Bullneck Creek to the north and Peach Orchard Creek to the south—two bodies of water that feed into the Patapsco

River and then into the Chesapeake Bay. This is totally a neighborhood rec park typical of the area. You'll find a ball field, some trees, docks, and boats. That's all, folks. But it's a dandy place to stop and sniff the salt air. Dogs need to stay on a leash, but you can walk right up to the creek and out on the pier that extends off Long Point. Or if you have your own boat, you can take the salty dog out on the water.

The park is open dawn–dusk daily. From I-695, take Exit 44 onto Broening Highway. Turn right on Dundalk Avenue, which will dead-end right at the park. 410/887-3873.

Restaurants

Bill Bateman's Carryout: No pulling up a chair because they don't even want you to sit down. It's all food to go, and it's tasty. Choose from ribs, burgers, cold-cut subs, French fries, onion rings, and lots more. 7620 German Hill Road; 410/282-7980.

Captain Harvey's Submarines: Stop at this neighborhood spot and definitely order one of the captain's famous overstuffed cheese steak subs to carry out to a nearby creek. 3435 Dundalk Avenue; 410/284-7772.

Herman's Bakery: Breads, cookies, and other delectables are baked fresh daily, the old-fashioned way. Pick up a dozen and munch at a nearby cove or park. 7560 Holabird Avenue; 410/284-5590.

Tony's Pizza: Chappy's proclivity for pepperoni and sausage (he doesn't even care about the rest of the saucy pie) kind of makes him an annoyance when ordering a pizza—but he always goes along on the extra cheese. This place makes good and unfancy pizza—no weird toppings or anything like that. 98 Wise Avenue; 410/285-3233.

EDGEMERE–SPARROWS POINT

Parks, Beaches, and Recreation Areas

14 Fort Howard Park 🐾 🐾 🐾

Be sure to veer left when you come to the end of the road at the point (we didn't). Otherwise, you'll wind up in the Veterans' Administration Hospital, and that's not quite the same as strolling through the 92 acres of historic parkland next to it.

The park is named after Colonel John Eager Howard, a heroic soldier in the Maryland Continental Army during the Revolutionary War.

Chappy liked walking the trails, which are mostly paved and run through the wooded grounds. Follow them to the old fortress on a hill. The fort, built around 1900, was the headquarters for the coastal troops who were prepared to defend Baltimore from perilous attacks by sea. It still has two well-preserved World War I cannons overlooking the Chesapeake Bay. Picnic tables grouped under trees near the water look like a great spot to sit a spell and eat lunch. The big jail-like rooms near the fort attracted the boys, who immediately closed the bars on each other. Not Chappy, though. He found the old foot-pedal water fountain more entertaining, and a big dog actually might be able to make it work.

The park is green, it's pretty, and if it were anywhere other than next door to North Point State Park, it would probably get a lot more attention. So if it's fewer people and dogs you're looking for, don't overlook it.

The park is open 8 A.M.–8 P.M. From I-695 take Exit 41 onto Cove Road; turn left on North Point Boulevard and follow it all the way to the end, where you turn left on Blank Avenue and into the park. 410/887-7529.

🐾 North Point State Park 🐾 🐾 🐾 ½

Chappy isn't a beach dog, despite the sunglasses. He's a mountain dog, really. He doesn't appreciate a romp at the water's edge like a water dog or retriever might. But one thing that always fascinates good ol' Chap is any other dog's dried-up poop, no matter where it lies. Because he found what are apparently some choice specimens in this 1,310-acre park, he was mighty happy.

You might want to note that this is one of the few Maryland state parks that offer dogs complete access as opposed to banishing them to a narrow trail or outback wilderness away from the people parts. We found many other things to be happy about here, too.

The Chesapeake Bay lapping up on the rocky shore as the sun glistened on the water is one. But let's go back to the beginning. First off, don't park in the parking lot that is just to the left as you drive in the entrance. You'll have at least a mile hike to the main parking lot, which is much closer to the trails and the long, narrow point that reaches out into the bay. Once in that main parking lot, head for the clearly marked visitor center. Chances are good no one will be there. We knocked, and the door wasn't locked, so we went in and picked up some brochures showing the park's trails.

Anglers had already staked their claim to the little dock near the visitor center, so we hiked along the rocky, granular beach toward the point of it all. The beach turns into a dirt and grass path that leads out on along the precious strip of land surrounded by big rocks, chunks of concrete retaining wall, and choppy water. The farther out you go, the breezier it gets; bring a jacket in cool weather. A half-dozen benches sit at the very end near the water's edge. Waves lap up against the rocks. This is a great view of the Chesapeake Bay and the Chesapeake Bay Bridge in the distance to the south.

Standing at this glorious nexus of sky, water, and earth, you can imagine the little-known history that occurred at this point. As the famous attack on Fort McHenry exploded into the annals of American history, even into our national anthem, a much-lesser-known land battle was taking place east of Baltimore on these grounds. Known as the Battle of North Point, skirmishes occurred here between the British and the American militia over the same two-day period as the attack on Fort McHenry.

Returning from the point (though obviously not the proverbial point of no return), we came across the recently renovated trolley barn. In the early 1900s, trolley cars trundled hundreds of visitors from downtown Baltimore to what was then Bay Shore Park. Fare for the hour round-trip cost 30 cents. Turn-of-the-century families spent weekends walking on Crystal Pier here and around the central fountain that recently was renovated after a 52-year dry spell, and riding a contraption called the sea swing. For most of the first half of this century, these grounds were a popular amusement park and miniresort known for bowling, billiards, and dancing.

Once the carny atmosphere folded, Bethlehem Steel operated the park as a game preserve for its executives. When the state of Maryland purchased the park in 1987, only the trolley barn, the central fountain, and a generator building remained.

Walking its woodsy paths, occasionally you still come across paths that feel and look like old streets where crowds once flocked to this summer fun spot. Markers with pictures and information about the wildlife on the surrounding 600 acres of marshland are reminders that those days are long gone. Instead, blue jays, orioles, great blue herons, horned owls, rabbits, and red foxes are the ones having a heyday here.

Picnic tables and grills near the large parking lot provide shaded partying areas, but there isn't much else in the way of facilities. Porta-potties serve as restrooms. So far, no food or water is available. The park is also a trash-free park, meaning that while there are plastic bags available (we used one to scoop Chappy's poop), you won't find any trash cans. Whatever garbage you generate is supposed to go home with you.

The park is open 6 A.M.–6 P.M., closed Thanksgiving and Christmas Day. From I-695, take Exit 41 south onto North Point Boulevard. Follow it down into the peninsula and turn left on Bay Shore Road into the park; 410/477-0757 or 410/592-2897.

Restaurants

Mariner's Landing: There are tables out front, but even if they're not serving outside, the folks here are friendly and will seat you near the door so you can keep an eye on the pup. That way you can enjoy your shrimp with peace of mind. 601 Wise Avenue; 410/477-1261.

Charcoal Deli East: Tables out front make it easy to have some beef, pork, turkey, ham, chicken wings, ribs, or burgers with the dog alongside. It's a menu made in heaven for Chappy. 7210 Holabird Avenue; 410/285-8326.

Jimmy's Famous Seafood: They don't just have crabs by the dozen. "Oh my God, honey, we've got everything—spaghetti, lasagna, Greek food . . ." said the management. Call to place an order and they'll give you directions on how to get there. 6526 Holabird Avenue; 410/633 4040.

New White Swan Restaurant and Lounge: Hey, you're in the Bible belt of blue crabs! Might as well stop by and have these genuine Bawlmer folks wrap up a few dozen steamed crabs (sold only on the weekends) and other assorted seafood, to carry out to a nearby park. 8821 Miller's Island Road; 410/477-5092.

ESSEX

Parks, Beaches, and Recreation Areas

16 Cox's Point Park 🐾 🐾 ½

Because this park is such a community park and used a lot for picnicking and playground play, we were surprised dogs were allowed. But strap on that leash and go for it. With 25 acres right on the water, there's room for everyone, including the ducks that zoom by like some kind of dive bombers. Most other places, they waddle around the water's edge. Here they fly, and fast. Look out for the squirrels, too.

A man sitting on a picnic bench was feeding three of these bold little creatures from his hand. A young rottweiler on a leash was having a fine time sniffing the grass filled with dandelions. Chappy's all in favor of gazing at the water—which is the view on three sides, along with the housing. So we did a lot of that on a sunny afternoon. No industry here, just fishing. Rocks line the edge, so swimming isn't an option.

The park is open dawn–dusk daily. From I-695, take Exit 38 onto Eastern Boulevard (Route 150), going east. Turn right on Riverside Drive and follow it right into the park. 410/887-0251.

🐾 Rocky Point Park 🐾 🐾

Just another pleasant park on the Chesapeake? Nope. The odd thing about this one is the private home located right at the tip of the parkland, so you feel like you might be intruding on someone's privacy. Oh, what the heck! There are grassy areas, shady areas, restrooms, a boat launch area, a beach, and a little pier.

You can easily find a quiet spot to sit down with the pooch here. For Chappy, who is a low-maintenance date, sniffing the trees along the water was plenty. Dogs aren't allowed on the beach area, where humans can swim from Memorial Day through Labor Day. But that doesn't really matter because there is plenty of other room to roam. This is a popular hangout for anglers, who congregate on the pier; Chappy watched several patiently for about five minutes. Five large picnic areas attract lots of families and corporate outings. And folks also boat from this point, so there's lots to see.

Since 1969, the Baltimore County Department of Recreation and Parks has owned and operated this tranquil, 375-acre waterfront park. Located at the mouth of Back and Middle Rivers, it boasts an inspiring view of the Chesapeake Bay, Harte-Miller Island, and one of the four Craighill lights that mark the channel. Don't be surprised if an osprey or a great blue heron flaps down nearby (but not *too* nearby) and begs for a snack.

Rocky Point Park is open dawn–dusk daily. Daily fees from Memorial Day through Labor Day are $5 for adults, $3 for senior citizens, and $2 for children under 12. From I-695 take Exit 36 onto Route 702 and follow it for about five miles. Route 702 turns into Back River Neck Road. Make the first left on Barrison Point Road and continue less than a mile and turn right on Rocky Point Road. 410/887-0217 or 410/887-3783.

🔥 Turkey Point Park 🔥

This was so confusing. The park is actually part of a person's home. There's the brown park sign marking the entrance, and a big patch of land with trees and grass gives the place a woodsy feel. There's a parking lot. And then there's someone's home—a man watching as his little son rides his tricycle around in the back patio. Beyond the house are picnic tables and a portable toilet. Very strange. With Rocky Point Park not too much farther down the road, maybe it's best to give these folks their privacy.

The park is open dawn–dusk daily. From I-695, take Route 702 south and turn left on Turkey Point Road. Continue on Turkey Point Road, making a sharp left onto Greyhound Road, followed by a sharp right into the park. 410/887-0217.

Restaurants

Island View Inn: It's not a hotel—it's a restaurant, with steaks, seafood, crab cakes, and other goodies you can carry out. During the season, it's open Wednesday–Sunday; out of season, it's only open on weekends. It's located right near Rocky Point Park at the end of Barrison Point Road. 410/687-9799.

River Watch Restaurant and Marina: There's a nice deck here and it's covered in case of rain, but the dog has to stay about two feet down on the ground near your table if you want to sit and eat. It's not too bad a setup, providing the weather's okay and your pooch is into lounging in the deck's shade while you scarf down some crab cakes, hamburgers, or even a lobster tail and take in the simple charm of Hopkins Creek. 207 Nanticoke Road; 410/687-1422.

Runabouts: This place looks so islandy. You feel like you're heading into a Jimmy Buffett song when you pull up into the parking lot. Grab one of the plastic tables out front, have a cold one and a burger with the Margaritaville mutt at your feet, and watch the traffic go by on its way to the end of the road. Then watch it come back because there's no other way out. You could spend a long time wasting away here. 1814 Turkey Point Road; 410/682-5930.

DIVERSIONS

Shave and a Haircut: In need of a bottle of shampoo after a long day at the park? Stop at **Katrina's Doggie Den** and pick up supplies, or make an appointment for grooming. The shop is located at 401 Eastern Boulevard; 410/391-0363.

The Way They Were: The Heritage Society of Essex and Middle River holes up in a charming 1920s fire station and displays more than 1,000 artifacts and replicas of 400 years of local history—including a reproduction of the old general store, a candle shop, a school room, and a jail cell. Pups stay on the front porch, but the visit doesn't take long. 516 Eastern Boulevard; 410/574-6934.

FULLERTON

Parks, Beaches, and Recreation Areas

19 Fullerton Park 🛉

Sitting on the hill above the football and baseball fields on this park is fine, but otherwise this is little more than an area to stretch your legs and relieve your bladder (uh, we mean, the *dog's* bladder).

The park is open dawn–dusk daily. From I-695, take Exit 32 onto Belair Road (Route 1) and go south; turn left onto Fullerton Avenue. The small park is on the left. 410/887-3871.

KINGSVILLE

Parks, Beaches, and Recreation Areas

20 Gunpowder Falls State Park 🐾 🐾 🐾 🐾

More than 100 miles of trails, four trout streams, and 18,000 acres of parkland provide endless scenic vistas and recreational possibilities within Gunpowder Falls in the Gunpowder River Valley. From tidal marshes to steep rugged slopes to heavily wooded forests, there's every which kind of terrain throughout in this long, narrow state park. The property spreads out across the county and even appears in separate chunks—from the Hereford Area about 23 miles directly north of downtown Baltimore City, to the middle Sweet Air Area about 20 miles northeast, down to the Dundee Area about 15 miles due east on the Chesapeake Bay.

Of the several areas in the park, the Hereford Area along York Road between the towns of Hereford and is perhaps the favorite to bring along a park-lovin' pooch. Fly fishers like it, too, and Chappy was intrigued with their casting lines in the big Gunpowder Area downstream from Prettyboy Dam. Probably the dog friendliest of its many trails is the South Gunpowder Falls Trail (blue markers). It travels east along the south bank of the river and eventually turns up into the woods until it meets up with the Panther Branch Trail, which will loop back to the start for about a four-mile hike.

Another favorite is the Northern Central Trail, a 21-mile abandoned railroad bed from the Northern Central Railroad that actually cuts north and east of the Hereford Area and extends to the Maryland-Pennsylvania state line. Horseback riders, hikers, and bikers like its beaten stone-dust surface and it has lots of shade, scenic views, and historic sights along the way, including the restored Monkton Train Station and the Sparks Bank Nature Center. Near White Hall is a small waterfall. This area of the river is perfect for tubing. Though the idea is appealing, Chappy isn't quite ready to float lazily down the river in an inner tube, but he can get his paws wet along the edge and watch the fun. The wildflowers are abundant and breathtaking along this trail in the spring. When you

DIVERSIONS

A Bridge to the Past: Only a mile hike southeast from the Gunpowder Falls State Park headquarters, where Jerusalem Road crosses the river, you'll find the **Jericho Covered Bridge,** a Civil War–era bridge with a Burr arch and cedar roof and walls. Built in 1864 and renovated in 1981, this old beauty is the last of its kind in Baltimore and Harford Counties. It's on the National Register of Historic Places. To see something that is just like those in *The Bridges of Madison County,* take I-95 to Exit 74. Turn left onto Route 152 and cross back over the interstate. Continue to Jerusalem Road and turn left on Jericho Road. Parking is available at the Jerusalem Mill, at the intersection of Jerusalem and Jerico Roads. A nature path leads from the mill along Little Gunpowder Falls to the bridge. An excellent walk into history with your dog. 410/583-7173.

Buy 'em by the Bag: If you've spent the day in the Central Area of the Patapsco Valley State Park, and you remember you're down to the bottom of the kibble bag at home, stop by this **PetsMart** a few miles toward Baltimore City from Kingsville and near White Marsh. And buy the big bag this time! 9921 Pulaski Highway; 410/687-6101.

Ingratiate Yourselves: When **Earth Day** comes around, head over to Gunpowder Falls State Park for its annual "Clean-Up Day." Let the park rangers know you've brought your volunteer puppy along and would like to tackle a clean-up project in an undeveloped area. The activities usually involve trail maintenance, tree planting, easy stuff. Call 410/592-2897.

---

come to the end of the line in Pennsylvania, that state has continued the trail for about another 10 miles.

The Central Area, near Baldwin, about 16 miles from downtown Baltimore and north of Kingsville to White Marsh, is largely undeveloped. But its many hiking trails and the restored structures of the historic village of Jerusalem attract human and canine visitors sightseeing the historic mill where the park headquarters is housed, along with the blacksmith shop and Revolutionary War gun factory. A modest one-mile hike along the Little Gunpowder that branches from the village was just Chappy's speed.

Not so for the Sweet Air Area (via Mountain Road, or Route 152, and Green Road). It is 1,000 acres, but equestrians horse around there too much for Chappy's taste. The Sweathouse Branch Wildlands Area (park at the Route 1 bridge over the Big Gunpowder north of Perry Hall) features several loop trails that meander through hardwood forest and along the banks of the Big Gunpowder. One reader of our first edition says this area, off Route 1 (Bel Air Road), north of Perry Hall, is one of her favorite spots.

Skip the Hammerman Area, near Eastern Avenue, which has a great swimming beach for people, but dogs are prohibited. Instead, for a little Gunpowder fun in the sun, head south to the Dundee Marina Area of the park. Chappy isn't much for sand or water. He's more of a snow-plow pooch and even prefers shag carpeting. But he did love the stiff breeze when we emerged from the marshy trail with 12-foot-tall dry, yellow grasses lining each side. Though we worried about the canoeists fighting the white waters of the bay that day, Chappy worried about the two dead fish that were lying by the lapping waters. He didn't particularly like the mud that was unavoidable on the trail.

Dundee is a great getaway, if that's what you're looking for. It's a place you would go to be alone with your dog, by the water, rough and rustic. This isn't a manicured park with water fountains and picnic tables. This is for walking by the water's edge, or maybe spreading a blanket and having some quiet time. We ran into a few other people and dogs, too, but the feel of the place is remote, because most humans go to the distinctly marked beach and picnic areas or to the marina for boating, instead of the "fishing" area where we hiked. To reach the Dundee Area, which is open dawn–dusk, take I-695 to the Eastern Avenue (Route 150) east exit, and go through Essex. At Grace Quarters Road, turn right and follow it to the end. There are signs marking each entrance.

Dogs are supposed to be on a leash throughout the Gunpowder Falls State Park areas. There usually are trash bags hanging on bulletin boards at the park entrances urging you to take your waste with you. Still we saw big piles of poop and, sad to say, more litter than thoughtful visitors should allow.

Before you set out to any of these areas, it's a good idea to call the park rangers at the Gunpowder Falls headquarters. They can send you trail maps and suggest where would be best to visit. 410/592-2897.

LAKE ROLAND

Parks, Beaches, and Recreation Areas

21 Robert E. Lee Park 🐾 🐾 🐾 🐾

This marvelous expanse of parkland is rather well hidden, so be alert when heading out to it. But dog lovers will find it is well worth the hunt. Those who know it, love it. Some days you'll count three dozen dogs or more running around the spillway and bridge area at the park's entrance—pups lapping water from Lake Roland's stream, some chasing Frisbees on the grassier areas. The only interruption to all this jubilation is when the light-rail train clambers by right next to the park.

This is not an official off-leash park, but it sure is widely known among dog owners in the area as a place for socializing, both for unleashed dogs and humans. The only problems come when nondog owners are intimidated by the bounding dogs or when Animal Control decides to pop in and hand out citations.

Water fountains, picnic tables, paved paths, trees—there is everything here for a happy doggy day out. The entire eastern side of the park borders on Lake Roland, where the sound of water rushing can calm even our attention-deficient Chappy. No swimming or boating is allowed, but fishing is permitted. Large signs remind that dogs must be on a leash and must be cleaned up after.

The park is located less than a mile north of Baltimore City. Take Falls Road (Route 25) north and watch for Hollins Lane and a small sign. You'll make a sharp right and wind around, following the stream to the park at the corner of Hollins Lane and Lakeside Drive. Cars park haphazardly, so make sure you don't block or get blocked in. 410/887-3810.

Restaurants

Glas Z Cafe: Take an outdoor table and have a nice gourmet salad, soup, or sandwich with your dog nearby—but don't show off the pooch because someone might complain. 6080 Falls Road (Route 25); 410/377-9060.

Pepe's: Carry out cheesy pizza till the wee hours anytime, but the salads aren't bad either. The real specialty, however, is a nice, messy steak and cheese sub, preferably with Pepe's home-brewed iced tea. 6081 Falls Road (Route 25); 410/377-3287.

Starbucks: Always a welcome spot for those in need of iced coffee and a cookie, this hangout for anyone with a java jones has outside tables so you and your four-legged friend can rest after a long day at Robert E. Lee Park. It's located right next to the Fresh Fields. 1340 Smith Avenue; 410/435-6530.

LOCH RAVEN

Parks, Beaches, and Recreation Areas

22 Loch Raven Reservoir 🐾 🐾 🐾

The water spilling over the dam is a pretty majestic sight on a sunny spring or summer or fall afternoon. Some people park down at the bottom of the falling water or closer to Cromwell Bridge Road on Loch Raven. But most people with their dogs continue on past the dam on the very windy road and up into the wooded area. After crossing the little bridge over the water, the road widens, and this is a popular spot for parking and picnicking.

You'll often find dogs here, as well as people of all ages, playing, sunning themselves, jogging. The grass is a soft pretty green, there are tons of trees for shade, and the water is right there.

Loch Raven Reservoir, created by damming Gunpowder Falls, has become a fish and waterfowl habitat. You'll see ducks and geese alongside anglers, who even go out in boats that are available for rent. The reservoir is run by the Baltimore City Bureau of Engineering and is the oldest of three city reservoirs still in operation. Of the city-owned 5,600 acres surrounding the reservoir, nearly

DIVERSION

Home is Your Castle: The flat waters of Loch Raven Reservoir don't really cover a sunken castle, as some say around here. **Glen Ellen Castle** and its towers once stood along the shore southeast of the reservoir's Hampton Cove, it is true. More than 150 years ago, Robert Gilmor III, country squire, gentleman farmer, and Harvard classmate of Oliver Wendell Holmes, built his dream castle on 900 acres of land along the shore of Loch Raven Reservoir. He fashioned it after Sir Walter Scott's home in Scotland, Abbotsford. According to historian Charles J. Scheve, Gilmor named the three-story castle after his wife Ellen and the lovely little glen at the nearby hillside. Scheve dismisses what most people think might be the sunken castle as the ruins of possibly the estate's cider mill building that is indeed visible at low tide. The old castle itself? Enlarging the lower Loch Raven dam in 1923 doomed the old stone structure whose foundations are still visible at the site.

If you and the pooch are game for an adventure in history, bring your galoshes along and head east from the Hampton National Historical Site on Hampton Lane, and turn left on Providence Road. After about a mile, turn left on Ellendale Drive. Park near where Ellendale Drive horseshoes to the right and look for the old fire road that heads due west into the reservoir's muddy watershed area. Dirt bikers have cleared some of the way for you. Look for the driveway that slopes sharply downward directly to the water's edge and you will find the castle ruins. If the ruins disappoint you, just take in the view from here of the reservoir itself. The pooch will need a good bath after this trek. If you need to talk to someone about this nonsite, call the kind folks at the Hampton at 410/823-1309.

4,500 are natural woodlands dotted with pine trees. Hikers using the watershed trails throughout the lands should know they're lucky; lots of times hiking's not allowed near municipal water. What's more, dogs are allowed, too.

One of the most popular trails is the Deadman's Cove circuit, which is about two miles long and travels along the shoreline, providing views of the beach and the water with all its wildlife. You have a good chance of seeing kingfishers, turkey vultures, hawks, deer, and ducks. To get to this trail, take Dulaney Valley Road (Route 146) north 3.3 miles from Exit 27 off I-695 to a small parking area on the right, just beyond the Stella Maris private drive. The trail entrance is marked by a bureau sign.

The reservoir is open dawn–dusk. From I-695, take Exit 29 north on Cromwell Bridge Road. Turn left at Sanders' Corner restaurant onto Loch Raven Drive and follow that through the entire reservoir property. 410/887-7692.

OWINGS MILLS

Parks, Beaches, and Recreation Areas

23 Soldier's Delight Natural Environmental Area 🐾 🐾 🐾 🐾

A vast mountain of a park, Soldier's Delight is truly a doggy delight. We met Hunter, a husky–German shepherd mix who's usually at the park three times a week. His dog-lovin' companion likes the clearly marked trails—there are seven miles of them—and the fact that not many people seem to know about the place, even though it covers 1,900 acres.

No one is quite sure why or how the natural environment area got its name. It is said that soldiers in the service of King George III named the place Soldier's Delight because Indians could not surprise them as easily with all the pines giving them camouflage. Either that or they found the cakes and pies baked for them by local householders to be delightful.

The delight part probably had little to do with the fact that the park is actually the site of old chromium mines. Chrome was first discovered in the United States in Baltimore in 1808, and all the world's chromium supply from 1828 to 1850 came from these mines. On the Yellow trail here, which is a three-mile walk, you can see the closed-off Choate Mine.

What's so alluring here are the views of surrounding Baltimore County and the trails, all packed dirt with few rocks and lots of soft pine needles. There are also numerous varieties of rare wildflowers growing all around. Chappy seemed happy to trot along in the bright sunshine, and packs of dogs did the same, except they were leashless. We started on the trail to the right of the visitor center, which led back to an old stone house and some picnic tables. That seemed like a wonderful spot with a view of the valley to take a picnic basket.

Dogs are supposed to be on a leash, but down the hills and into the meadows they run free. Three of them were running wild when we visited. Two black Labs and a mutt bounded up to Chappy and sniffed, but they had little use for him and ran merrily off. The ranger said she doesn't often enforce the leash law. "We really just don't want them running around biting people," she added. Four of the five trails cross streams, so there's really everything here—including lots of poison ivy. So take care.

The park is open weekdays, 8:30 A.M.–4 P.M.; Sunday, noon–5 P.M. From I-795, take Franklin Road west (Exit 7B), turn right on Church Road, left on Berrymans Road, left on Deer Park Road, and right on Ward's Chapel Road. Park in the overlook area or keep going a short way up to the visitor center. 410/922-3044.

Restaurants

China Best: You can find Hunan, Szechwan, and Mandarin cuisine here, and even sushi. Call ahead with your carryout order. 9958 Reisterstown Road, in the Saint Thomas Shopping Center; 410/363-8160.

Dragon House: This place had an appropriate name considering how Chappy was dragging after a long and hot morning at nearby Soldier's Delight. Carry out from its basic Chinese menu before heading to the park. 10349 Reisterstown Road; 410/363-0744.

Due: Moderately priced gourmet dishes of smoked shrimp, mussels, and *osso buco* make this a place you might want to come back to without the dog. That way you could watch what goes on in the open kitchen with the big copper splashboard. Note: Carryout is only available for dinner. 25 Crossroads Drive; 410/356-4147.

Liberatore's Bistro: This Italian food comes by way of California, it seems. Carry out grilled calamari, shrimp, lobster tetrazzini, and other tasty combinations. Even the "wedding soup," a chicken-based broth with tiny meatballs floating in it, gets capped, wrapped, and taken on journeys. 9712 Groffs Mill Drive; 410/356-3100.

Linwood's: How about a little seared foie gras on your onion salad with Asian pear vinaigrette? Then maybe you'd like rack of lamb with vegetable risotto? The menu is deliciously imaginative, to say the least. Call and find out what's available for carryout. 25 Crossroads Drive (right next door to Due, which owns this place, too); 410/356-3030.

PARKVILLE

Parks, Beaches, and Recreation Areas

24 Belmont Park 🐕

If you're a neighbor, here's where dogs on leashes can take a short walk on a paved path, or maybe catch a baseball game on one of the two fields. Dogs are prohibited in the playground area in this 42-acre park, however.

The park is open sunrise to sunset. From I-695, take Exit 31 (Harford Road/Route 147) north. Turn right on Joppa Road and then right again on Walther Boulevard. Turn into the park on the left. 410/887-5300.

25 Double Rock Park 🐾 ½

Two rocks dedicated to the community in 1947 mark the entrance. Obviously they were the inspiration of the name for this deceptively large, woodsy park that's tucked in a very modest suburban neighborhood.

Divided up into several picnic areas, the 102 acres can actually accommodate a lot of people; having the company party here wouldn't be a bad idea. For dogs? It's okay, no great shakes. Make sure they're on a leash. Lots of shade and water make each picnic area its own island in a stream. There are ball fields and playgrounds, but the chopped-up nature of the park makes it more of a people place.

The park is open 8 A.M.–sunset. It's not a good idea to enter from Bel Air Road (Route 1). We tried that, lured in by a sign with an arrow that said The Best pointing into the park. But that was the maintenance entrance. You're better off to take I-695 to Harford Road (Route 147) south; turn left on Texas Avenue, and that will dead-end into the park. 410/887-5300.

REISTERSTOWN

Parks, Beaches, and Recreation Areas

26 Hannah More Park 🐾 ½

Take me out to the ball game, take me out to the. . .park? It only stands to reason that this 63-acre parkland that's practically hidden from the roadside behind a renovated old brick school is in the town where Orioles' "Iron Man" Cal Ripken Jr. is said to live. Besides one of the largest children's playgrounds you'll find

---

DIVERSION

'Til the End of Time: No one likes to think about the passing of a beloved pet. But it happens, and if you need a place of rest for your pet, you can thank Elsie Seeger Barton, founder of the Humane Society of Baltimore County. She started the organization in 1927 and in the 1950s she bought a 365-acre parcel of land in Reisterstown. When she died in 1983, she had already established a trust that allowed the Society to use 22 acres for the good of dogs. Today, the land houses the Spay/Neuter Center, the cemetery that inters about 150 companions every year, and the shelter that houses some 3,000 unwanted animals each year. Think about visiting the site; it's at 1601 Nicodemus Road, Reisterstown, MD 21136; 410/833-8848.

---

anywhere, this park is all about baseball. Follow the road through the parking lots and past the picnic areas toward the wooded backdrop on any warm-weather weekend and, guaranteed, you'll find three or four baseball games happening at once. In between the ball fields are rolling hills of grass where leashed dogs can stroll without getting in the way—other than the occasional home run.

The park is open dawn–dusk, except for the lighted ball fields. From I-695, take Exit 20 north on Reisterstown Road (Route 140). Drive about eight miles, beyond Owings Mills (you can count Dunkin' Donut shops and Taco Bells along the strip malls to pass the time), to the first right past Franklin Avenue and enter the park. 410/887-5300.

TIMONIUM

Places to Stay

Red Roof Inn–Timonium: Dogs are welcome and there's no deposit or fee. There isn't much grass around the hotel, but there is free coffee in the lobby and Cinemax on cable. Rates are about $64 for a double on a weekend. 111 West Timonium Road, Timonium, MD 21093; 410/666-0380 or 800/843-7663.

TOWSON

Two brothers named William and Thomas Towson from Pennsylvania moved into the area in 1750 and started farming the land to the northeast of York and Joppa Roads. Then came a large tavern where the Towson Theater is now. After that was up and running, a small village grew into the original Towsontown. In 1854, Towson officially became the Baltimore county seat, and it hasn't gotten up since. Just joking, folks! The real fun here is Towson University, which draws students—including our nephew Jason—and their parents to events during the school year.

Parks, Beaches, and Recreation Areas

27 Forge Park 🔥

In a pinch you might stop here, but otherwise it's not that easy to find Forge Park behind York Road Plaza. The street leading to it is narrow and a dead end. Once you get there, the seven acres are devoted to ball fields and run-down basketball courts.

The park is open dawn–dusk. To get to the park, take York Road (Route 45) north out of Baltimore, and once you've passed Lake Avenue, look for Schwartz Avenue on the left. Turn left, the park will be behind the shopping center on the left. 410/887-3871.

Restaurants

Bel-Loc Diner: Every college town needs one—an all-night diner with terrific banana cream pie, not to mention great milkshakes and Patsy Cline on the juke box. This casual eatery boxes up carryout orders if the pooch is waiting outside. Loch Raven Boulevard at Joppa Road; 410/668-2525.

Bill Bateman's Bistro: Who knew there were 16 different kinds of chicken wing possibilities? There are also more than a dozen kinds of burgers, pizza, and quesadillas served here. Have one of Bill's microbrews on tap while you wait for your carryout; then make sure you give the pup a big drink of water before heading out. 7800 York Road (Route 45); 410/296-2737.

Cafe Troia: Fans swear by the *osso buco* and risotto. Chappy swears by any food. Stop by this popular Italian restaurant with a neighborhood feel and pick up pasta to go. 28 West Allegheny Avenue; 410/337-0133.

Crackpot Seafood: Steamed crabs and other seafood are available in case you hadn't figured that out from the name of the restaurant. They also offer a full menu of other items like ribs, as well, that you can carry out to a nearby bench. 8102 Loch Raven Boulevard; 410/828-1095.

Frisco Burritos: Using fresh ingredients daily, Frisco's will make any of its burritos to go. Chappy prefers the beans. 3 West Chesapeake Avenue; 410/296-4004.

DIVERSIONS

Downtown Doings: All sorts of thing happen in the Towson Courthouse Plaza. In early May in the courthouse area and surrounding streets, the **Towson Spring Festival** is a street celebration with fun for college students and everyone else. It includes five stages, entertainment, and an antique auto display and is a perfect pooch pastime. Everyone has a blast.

Music to Floppy Ears: Music fills Courthouse Plaza on Sunday evenings from mid-June through mid-September for free concerts in the summer. It's a fun thing to do when out for a balmy summer night's walk with your best friend. Then in winter, caroling, Santa, and refreshments mark the official lighting of the tree in the Towson Courthouse Plaza in early December. Leashed dogs can share in the small-town fun year-round.

Farmer Fidos: Another Towson event is the **farmer's market** with fresh flowers, plants, and produce on Thursday from June to October on Allegheny Avenue. Keep the poochster on a leash and maybe she can test a 'loupe for ripeness right along with you. For information on all the events, call the Towson Business Association at 410/825-1133 or the events hot line at 410/583-7033.

Good Grooming: PetsMart is always a welcome sign if you need stuff from the world of dogs—including some excellent how-to dog books, breed books, and maybe even a regional guidebook for, er, well, let's just say for dog lovers. All the regular well-stocked shelves of food and supplies are here, though it's the tropical fish department where Chappy's fascination never ends. 1238 Putty Hill Avenue; 410/823-4593.

Orchard Market and Cafe: Too bad dogs can't just sit in the restaurant because the running water and elegant tiles give the place great atmosphere. That's okay; the café will make their delicious chicken in pomegranate and walnut sauce to go for you. If it's a nice day and you're lucky, you might be able to snag one of the two tables outside. 8815 Orchard Tree Lane; 410/339-7700.

Strapazza: One in a chain of restaurants in this neck of the woods, Strapazza serves any number of pasta or pizza dishes to go. 10 Allegheny Avenue; 410/296-5577.

Places to Stay

Days Inn–Baltimore East: Dogs are welcome at this five-story hotel, with only a one-time flat fee of $15. There isn't a whole lot of grassy area nearby, but Loch Raven High School is only a five-minute walk away and Loch Raven Reservoir is only a five-minute drive away. The hotel also has a restaurant but no room service. Rates for a double are about $65. 8801 Loch Raven Boulevard, Towson, MD 21204; 410/882-0900.

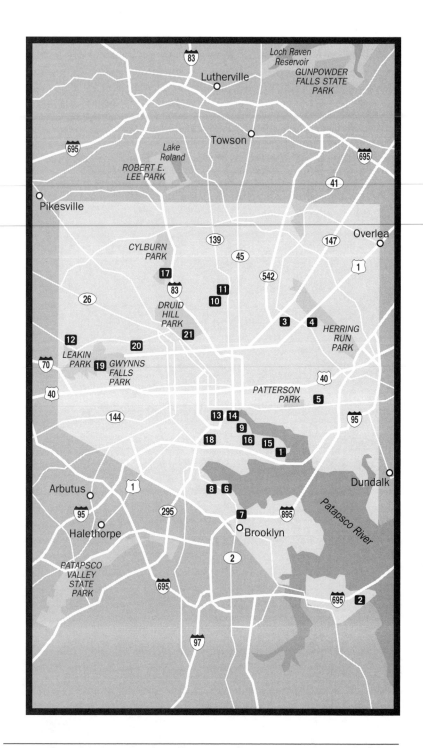

15 CITY OF BALTIMORE

What can we say but, "Hey, hon, welcome to Bawlmer." That's the kind of greeting dog lovers and dogs get in this gritty and beautiful city filled with lots of heart and soul.

Its nickname? "Charm City." And yet, there are those who describe it as "an acquired taste." Baltimore's been called a lot of names and that may be because it's such a mix of identities. A mix of North and South, old-fashioned row houses with sleek modern office buildings, industrial waterfront areas, and busy, revitalized, thriving waterfront areas.

Much of what is Baltimore revolves around the business of the sea. With shipbuilding and manufacturing, it is an important port of call. In 1609, when Captain John Smith explored what's now Inner Harbor and Federal Hill, it was one of the world's largest natural harbors. In the past two decades, the harbor has had a facelift, reinvigorating this city beyond all expectations.

As you walk these city streets with the pooch alongside, you discover that this is a fiercely-loved, old-style city of true neighborhoods, maybe hundreds of them, mostly row houses with hardworking folks who still spend summer evenings on the front porch with radios tuned to the O's game, or grand old historic homes like in Federal Hill and Mount Vernon that exemplify gracious living. Its sprawling ethnic sections still reflect the streets where immigrant groups settled more than a century ago, places of character such as Little Italy. Filmmaker Barry Levinson has called it "colorful"—so colorful he made the movies *Diner, Avalon,* and *Tin Men* on location here. Some would say filmmaker John Waters did it off-color, with cult flicks he filmed here such as *Pink Flamingos* and *Polyester.*

This was the home of Edgar Allan Poe and now the NFL's Baltimore Ravens, of Babe Ruth and the team the Great Bambino played his first season with—the beloved Baltimore Orioles. H. L. Mencken could have found his carping journalistic voice only in this town, which he called a "tottering medieval city"—the same one where Cole Porter found his lyrical key, and Dashiell Hammett his gumshoe imagery. Novelist Anne Tyler, who has lived here for years, uses the city as the setting of her tales as well.

But to more important matters: Did somebody say crabs? This is crab central, hon. It's also the home of the Baltimore Spice Company, maker of Old Bay Spice, which, the uninitiated should learn before venturing further, is the essential condiment when steaming one of the finest dining delicacies you'll ever experience—the Chesapeake Bay blue crab. Just walk up to one of the city's old-time crabhouses and order a dozen No. 1 jimmies for starters. Get yourself a little vinegar, spread some newspapers on a picnic table near a waterfront view, and you'll find out more about Baltimore in the next hour than you could learn any other way.

As for dogs in Baltimore, the city allows pooches to be leashed at all its parks and expects them to be leashed in other public places—walking down the street, sniffing out a market. Laws here also require that you scoop the poop on public property, so don't forget those baggies. As for enclosed dog parks, the Department of Recreation and Parks is considering proposals on the matter.

National Parks

❶ Fort McHenry 🐾 🐾 🐾 🐾 🐾

"Oh, say can you see, by the dog's early light?" After visiting Fort McHenry, the birthplace of "The Star-Spangled Banner," you and your patriotic pooch will be singing it all the way home—even if you don't know all the words.

Jutting out into the waters of the Patapsco River, the fort's grounds are well kept, wide open, and perfectly gorgeous for watching the boat traffic in and out of Baltimore's Northwest Harbor. Along this waterfront, it is nonstop tugboats, sailboats, water taxis, and all manner of vessels. And right across from the fort are parked several large and remarkably gray United States Navy ships. This park is simply great—and the history that unfurled at this spot makes it even better for whiling away most of a day with the dog.

Chappy had to be briefed on the story behind the national anthem, however, and your pup might, too. So here's the nutshell version: Seems just as the

British fleet attacked Baltimore during the War of 1812, Francis Scott Key boarded one of the British ships in Baltimore Harbor to look for a friend being held prisoner. Once the bombardment began, Key hid like a dog. . .uh, no, strike that. . .Key stayed put, stuck on the ship the entire night. By the dawn's early light, so to speak, he was amazed to see "our flag was still there," flying high above the fort. So moved was he that Key wrote the famous poem. At his brother-in-law's suggestion, Key put the words to music. In 1931, our ever-alert and fast-acting United States Congress officially made it our national anthem. Folks have been mumbling through the later verses ever since. Some Baltimoreans who know few other lines in the anthem have shown a true talent for singing out the "Oh" in the lyrics—particularly when the anthem begins an Orioles game.

But back to the fort: This classic stone-walled, five-pointed-star fortress with barracks, guard houses, and other buildings still intact, looks like it could withstand a few more rounds. Certainly being in the presence of so much history moved Chappy. Fortunately, we remembered our scooper baggies so as not to let him desecrate these nationally sacred grounds—and possibly do more damage than the British could muster.

Over the old fort a similar giant American flag (30 by 42 feet) still waves on a massive replica of the original flagpole. Even beyond its inspiring story, this national park is a beaut—and a fabulous destination for a day out with the pooch. Ducks flocked by the pier that extended into the bluish harbor waters; so did people picnicking at the many picnic sites, some of them waiting for the water taxis to the Inner Harbor around the bend at Locust Point. Another popular pastime was walking around the curving, mile-long paved path alongside the water that nearly circles the property.

The fort's interior and its other buildings are off-limits to dogs, but going there didn't interest Chappy anyway. He gets impatient with tour guides who talk too much, though the friendly rangers who talk history here are knowledgeable to the extreme and even have a sense of humor.

No matter: Chappy tugged on his leash (required here) to go examine the big statue of a naked guy (fig leaf positioned) near the park's entrance. No, it's not a tribute to Francis Scott Key. Instead, our federal government, in its inestimable wisdom, commissioned the statue in 1914. The sculptor thought Orpheus, the character from Greek mythology, a poet and musician, would best stand eternally at the fort that inspired the "The Star-Spangled Banner." Huh? Eventually, somebody recognized this makes no sense. The Orpheus Unclothed was moved from the front of the fort back into some very leafy trees. He's still pretty tough to miss. And so is this park, which you should not miss.

The fort and park are open daily, 8 A.M.–7:45 P.M., late June–Labor Day; 8 A.M.–5 P.M. the rest of the year. The entrance fee is $5 per adult, which, as Chappy pointed out, is almost $35 in dog money. Fortunately, dogs and children get in free. From I-95, take Exit 55 onto Key Highway; follow it for a half mile and turn left on Lawrence Street. Go two blocks and turn left on Fort Avenue and continue another mile to the fort entrance. 410/962-4290.

ARMISTEAD

Parks, Beaches, and Recreation Areas

2 Fort Armistead Park 🐾 🐾

The city's southernmost park, this waterside site looks out at the widened Patapsco River as it meets the Chesapeake Bay to the southeast. While it is prime real estate, the park is in the middle of industry, which mars the beauty for walking the nature-loving pooch.

To the left, however, there is a fabulous view of the Key Bridge rising up and off into the horizon. Unfortunately, views don't impress dogs, and that's why this pretty place, with the sun shining on the water all around, didn't rate higher. The park grounds are kind of scruffy and grass is sparse. Piers lead out into the water for fishing. Some wooden benches sit only a few feet back from the water, but a chemical plant right next door can't be ignored when considering the aesthetics. The sound of the water gently lapping against the rocky shore and the cawing of the seagulls gets drowned out by the sound of machinery and trucks beeping in rear gear.

Hike back behind the parking lot and you can go up into a wooded, hilly area. But the grass isn't mowed, and it turns out to be another way to the factory next door. People from the area seem to use the place for a quiet lunchtime break, but sitting and eating in the car doesn't seem like a great endorsement for a park. Some of them do get out, judging from the bits of trash and glass scattered here and there.

The park is open dawn–dusk. From I-695, take Exit 1 (Hawkins Point Road) south. Make a right turn off the ramp and then a left turn on Hawkins Point Road; follow it to Fort Armistead Road. Turn left where the sign directs you back to I-695 and the Key Bridge, and follow Fort Armistead Road until it dead-ends at the park. 410/396-5828.

BELAIR-EDISON

A diverse neighborhood whose main arteries are Belair Road and Erdman Avenue, Belair-Edison is a melting pot of families and singles, blue-collar and white-collar residents, and different ethnicities. Chatting on the stoop of these red-brick row houses seems to be the main pastime, while kids play and do wheelies down its alleys and along its tree-lined streets.

Parks, Beaches, and Recreation Areas

🗒 Clifton Park 🐾

Nearly next door to the larger Herring Run Park and on the south side of Lake Montebello, this site of the former summer home of Johns Hopkins is a grand and rambling parkland that takes golf seriously but not dogs. There is grass along the roadside where your pooch can find immediate relief and maybe bark out "Fore" just for fun. But dogs aren't allowed on the golf course.

The park is open dawn–dusk. From I-95, take Exit 60 (Moravia Road) northwest for three miles; turn left on Harford Road and follow it past Erdman Avenue. The park entrance is on the left at Saint Lo Drive; 410/396-6101.

🗒 Herring Run Park 🐾 🐾 🐾

Stretching nearly four miles, the park is a long green oasis in the northern part of the city not far from Memorial Stadium—once the home of the Orioles and temporarily the home of the Ravens. A paved, tree-lined trail with robust woods on both sides promises pleasant dog walking—and you'll meet many dogs as you stroll along, following the bank of Herring Run.

Occasionally you'll find shady spots where blackberry bushes burst with fruit in season. Daylilies bloom wildly, and poison ivy thrives at every turn. Wide-open and grassy fields line some of the path. On the higher ground of the

EARMARK YOUR CALENDAR

Talking turkey: And if that doesn't float your boat, maybe you prefer something a little later in the season. The Saint Paddy's Day Parade is rivaled only by the Thanksgiving Day Parade, which travels east on Pratt Street and is generally held on a Saturday morning around turkey day. It may not be quite the Rose Bowl Parade or the Macy's Thanksgiving Day Parade that you can watch on television comfortably from the plush cushions of your sofa, but this feels more fun. Call 410/837-4636 or 410/837-0685 to find out details.

Festivals, Races and So Much More: This is a city that prides itself on its ethnic diversity. And what better way to celebrate that than with festivals? There's the Hispanic Festival and Indian Day in August, and that's just to name two. Generally held at Hopkins Plaza, these are day-long events celebrating a culture with music, food, crafts, and plenty of socializing. They're always lively and fun and unusually exotic if you're not of the celebrating nationality. If your dog can handle crowds, take him along. These can be fun.

Chappy's favorite time of year is winter, of course, so that he can stick is nose in it. That's why he prefers the Baltimore on Ice Winterfest, even though the rest of us favor the beachy breezes of Martinique and a glass of nouveau beaujolais from the fridge. This festival is usually held at several downtown locations simultaneously, featuring all sorts of wintry events such as ice carving competitions, a cross-country ski and snowshoe course, and more cold things to do.

In Spring, it's Easter time and that's more reason to celebrate. Head to the Harborplace Pavilion for the annual Inner Harbor Easter Celebration, which features street performers, live music, and costumed characters to celebrate Easter. The kids love it, and Chappy gets way too much attention from them. The fun usually happens the Saturday before Easter.

---

park, you'll find Lake Montebello, fenced in, but still a respite from the concrete surrounding these neighborhoods.

Dog walkers use the trails, as do bikers and lots of hikers. According to *Baltimore Magazine,* the dog community is so into this park that doggy weddings with reverends and matching heart-shaped ID tags are held here. When we visited, no dog was in a tux or bridal gown; no one was dancing to polka music. The only marital bliss there, canine or otherwise, we brought with us.

Take water to this park and be careful. Despite leash laws, lots of big dogs lope around here without a leash, splashing and swimming in the creek. They can be a little daunting—at least for whimper types like Chappy. Even the wimp pooches can cool off their dawgs in the shallow creek, or dive in totally in the deeper spots, if they want.

Another cautionary note: Although poop-scooping is recommended, it's not taken seriously here, judging from the piles we had to sidestep regularly.

The park is open from dusk to dawn. From I-95, take Exit 60 (Moravia Road) northwest for three miles; turn left on Harford Road, cross Argonne and Parkside Drives, and veer immediately right to the small parking area. 410/396-6101.

Restaurants

Cafe Tattoo: Know that kinky tattoo you've been thinking about for a couple of years? The great-lookin' Grateful Dead rose? Those silly biceps barbed wires? Get 'em here and have some barbecued ribs or spicy chili while you're at it, because the café is located below the tattoo parlor. Dogs aren't allowed inside (the café, that is), but you can carry out just about everything except the 200 brands of beer. 4825 Belair Road; 410/325-7427.

Lin's Chinese Carryout: Never mind Sundays and Mondays. They're closed then. Got to rest sometime. But if you're looking for a quick getaway dinner in this neighborhood (no lunch though), you can't do it much quicker than this. Standard Chinese cuisine just as Chappy likes it. 3225 Erdman Avenue; 410/276-5668.

BUTCHERS HILL

Diversity reigns in this residential neighborhood of East Baltimore that's only a few blocks north of Fells Point and about a mile east of the Inner Harbor. The name comes from its once-prosperous population of butchers, merchants, and tradesmen in the mid-1800s—most of them of German and Jewish heritage. Nowadays, heritage and ethnicity are more mixed. Some of its streets look the worse for wear, and the continuing community topic is crime and how to stop it from escalating. But this is also the kind of neighborhood renovators dream of—with a blend of grand residences and row houses, many of them like matted and stray dogs that just need a little loving kindness and attention.

Parks, Beaches, and Recreation Areas
🖪 Patterson Park 🐾 ½

This *sounded* like such a great park. Big. Bold. Beautiful. It promises a funky four-story pagoda that offers a scenic view of the harbor. But, reality bites worse than its bark. Yes, you can quote us on that. While this is indeed the largest of the downtown parks (400 acres right in the city), it is a sadly neglected park. Several of its areas were trashy in that urban-wasteland way. We saw several ne'er-do-well dogs running around without leashes despite signs warning that dogs must be on six-foot leashes. You get the feeling the authorities hereabouts have better things to do than fine the owners of rambunctious Rovers.

One woman we met who said she walked her dogs there every day recommended that visitors stick to the upper side of the park bordering on Patterson Park Avenue. The higher crime zone apparently is the lower side, near the tattered tennis courts, but frankly, night strolling anywhere along these city streets wouldn't seem like a good idea.

The park is open dawn–dusk. From the Inner Harbor, take Eastern Avenue east about 1.3 miles; the park is bordered by Baltimore Street and Patterson Park Avenue. 410/396-3774 or 410/396-5828.

CHERRY HILL

Parks, Beaches, and Recreation Areas

6 Broening Park 😾

This small tract of parkland connects to the larger and more happening Middle Branch Park via a concrete path under the Vietnam Veterans Memorial Bridge. The path is good for a walk or a bike ride. But other than the attractive Vietnam Veterans Memorial with its circular patio, landscaping, and shrubs, Broening Park has only a popular boat launch.

The park is open dawn–dusk. From I-95, take Exit 54 south onto Hanover Street and go across the Vietnam Veterans Memorial Bridge. The road south becomes Potee Street; turn left at Reedbird Avenue, and return north on Hanover until you see the sign for the park on the right, past the Harbor Hospital Center. 410/396-3838.

7 Cherry Hill Park 🐾

Don't go out of your way, really. But if you need to stop desperately, if the dog is in the back seat sitting in a forced lotus position with a crooked smile on his dog lips, plenty of grass awaits here. Tall grass.

The park area is large and unimproved and badly maintained. A small community pool sits in its middle, along with a playground featuring tires to climb on and some tennis courts. This is not a great part of town: Crime statistics mark this area as having some of the highest numbers of murders, rapes, robberies, assaults, and auto thefts.

Run for the Roses: Don't underestimate just how big a deal the **Preakness** is in Baltimore. Nothing makes this city go bonkers quite like Preakness time each May. So get a good spot somewhere along Pratt Street near Charles Street to watch the annual parade with that thoroughbred dog of yours. A busy and crowded street event that you and the leashed dog will find to be lively, it typically features celebrities such as Olympic gold medalists, gigantic helium balloon characters, antique trucks, and horses. Did we say lots of horses?

For kids, the Baltimore Office of Promotion hosts a Preakness all their own at Inner Harbor's Rash Field. They can act like little jockeys (is that redundant?) as they ride hobbyhorses for great prizes and fleeting fame. Dogs can't enter the competition, but they're welcome to watch, even bark on their favorite hobbyhorse to the finish line. No betting please. This is one Preakness week event where the kids are the highlight, and it's free. 410/837-4636 or 800/282-6632.

And not to be left, out there's the **Phillips Preakness Trayfecta,** one more event of Preakness Week. Phillips Harborplace challenges downtown restaurant servers to an obstacle course that rivals a busy Saturday night. In an outdoor caf setting, complete with umbrella tables, potted plants, swinging kitchen doors, and demanding customers, waiters and waitresses have to deliver the goods in the fastest time without spilling. The tables are set at the Harborplace Amphitheater, located by the waterfront at Pratt Street and Light Street. To find out about all Preakness events, try calling 410/837-4636 or 800/282-6632.

When we stopped—in broad daylight on a weekend—nothing seemed terribly threatening. Unless the pup can't hold it, there are finer sights to see just minutes away at Middle Branch Park.

The park is open dawn–dusk daily. From I-95, take Exit 54 south onto Hanover Street and go across the Vietnam Veterans Memorial Bridge. Take Reedbird Avenue south to Seamon Avenue and into the park. 410/396-3838.

8 Middle Branch Park 🐾 🐾

Local folks go crabbing off the docks of this almost undiscovered park just across the Vietnam Veterans Memorial Bridge from Baltimore proper. On the shore of the middle branch of the Patapsco River, it has paved paths, a few benches, a couple of piers, and not many trees. On a breezy afternoon, it is a pleasant spot overlooking the small marina and a different view of the city and the water.

Stroll down the path and you can walk underneath the bridge and over to tiny Broening Park to see the Maryland Vietnam Veterans Memorial statue and watch people launch their boats. The large building by the piers is the Baltimore Rowing and Aquatic Resource Center. But, again, the neighborhood hereabouts struggles with crime, so beware.

The park is open dawn–dusk daily. From I-95, take Exit 54 south onto Hanover Street and go across the Vietnam Veterans Memorial Bridge. Almost immediately turn right onto Waterview Avenue and look for the park entrance on the right. 410/396-3838.

FEDERAL HILL

Overlooking the south side of Baltimore's Inner Harbor, this 19th century neighborhood of large Federal and Victorian period row houses lining its broad main street is National Register territory by any standards. It's also one of the most affluent addresses in the city, attracting dozens of fine restaurants, cafés, bars, and other retailers.

Parks, Beaches, and Recreation Areas

🎯 Federal Hill Park 🐾 🐾 🐾

You want to be part of the Inner Harbor action, but you want to get away from the crowds of tourists? Head up the hill to this classy little park with a picturesque view overlooking the harbor from its south side. Once a military observation point that signaled ships into the harbor, the park is now a charming neighborhood hot spot. It marks the northern boundary of the historic district—roughly 20 blocks of 19th century renovated row houses. Yup, this is high-ticket turf.

There aren't any lakes or long hiking trails here, but it still rates three paws because a happy little dalmatian puppy was having a great time the day we stopped by. He had on a leash but had broken free and was chasing his owner around. There were lots of other dogs, too. You'll see many that go off-leash because at this park, the kids are enclosed and the dogs go free, but watch out for animal control. We talked to one woman who got a $100 ticket a couple of years ago. It prompted an off-leash dog park group to form but nothing was ever designated at this park.

Wrought-iron fences and brickwork give the park a Victorian feel, and appropriately so, since a historic plaque dates this public park to 1880.

The park is open 7 A.M.–midnight. From Inner Harbor, follow Light Street south and around the bend and up to the park at Battery Avenue and Key Highway. 410/396-5828.

Restaurants

Golden City: Whether it's chicken, beef, pork, or shrimp you crave, it's available for carryout at this chopstick eatery. Take lunch or dinner down to the Harborview Marina and Yacht Club where you can sit and watch the boating culture, or go back uphill to Federal Hill Park. 1025 Light Street; 410/685-3511.

DIVERSIONS

Marketing a Piece of History: The historic **Cross Street Market** opened in 1846 and to this day upholds the old-fashioned street market tradition. Chappy likes maneuvering between tables and carts as artisans, farmers, and fishermen sell their wares—from homemade kielbasa and live blue crabs, to fresh vegetables and Atlantic salmon. There are dozens of businesses and eateries at this location—places such as Cross Street Poultry where you can still buy fresh-killed poultry; Nick's Inner Harbor Seafood market which boasts "Baltimore's Best Seafood"; the Cross Street Cheese Company specializing in cheeses and pâtés; and Cornucopia for herbs, mushrooms, gourmet produce, and flowers. Keep your pooch on a short leash, though, and maybe yourself as well, because there are simply way too many temptations at this wonderful other-era marketplace.

Someone Say Treat?: Chappy loves to hear that word. Key Wagner knows lots of dogs love to hear the word—and love to eat 'em. So she invented the **Baltimore Dog Bakery.** It's not a store; it's the actual name of her all-natural dog biscuit. She's a wholesaler who makes the wheat-free goodies and sells them to retailers such as Fresh Fields. After working with the mentally ill for 13 years, she decided she needed a new line of work. Her own golden retriever, Petey, not only was her "best friend in the whole world" but also her inspiration. The biscuits come in four flavors and sell for about $5 a pound. The most popular is the low-fat apple-cinnamon. Key also makes doggy birthday and wedding cakes. "One of the local radio stations last summer had a dog wedding—they had 15 dog couples. Concept is kinda weird, but it was a blast," she says. Her busiest time of the year is Christmas, when she hand cuts all the cookies. Call her at 410/485-2333 and she'll tell you more—unless she's busy pulling a batch out of the oven.

Maria D's Sub Shop: Right by the Harborview Marina, it earns the Chappy Seal of Canine Approval on its turkey, roast beef, and Italian cold-cut subs. You and the pup will have to walk the overstuffs to a bench or seawall site, however. 1022 Light Street; 410/727-5430.

Matsuri: Crowds line up for seats at this popular Japanese restaurant; you'll have to opt for carrying out entrees such as the light and crispy shrimp tempura and colorful fish cake. 1105 South Charles Street 410/752-8561.

Nichiban: One good bow deserves another, so don't overlook the sushi artistry at this Japanese bistro. Tempura is available if you prefer, and you can get any of the menu to go. 1035 South Charles Street; 410/837-0816.

No-Way Jose: Yes, way. Taco? Fajitas? Chimichangas? If you're in the mood for Tex-Mex with some homemade salsa, this is the place to get it and go.

Though it is a little farther out from Harborview, driving the extra few blocks is worth it: *Baltimore Magazine* voted the margaritas Baltimore's best and Baltimore's *City Paper* rates its salsa the best. 1041 Marshall Street; 410/752-2837.

One World Cafe and Art Gallery: Hey, it's Chap-ster and verse at this throwback coffeehouse where our Chappy likes to indulge in a little poetry while he scarfs down a black bean burrito and we sip a dark roasted. Your beatnik Bowser won't get shooed away from the outdoor tables in front where Kerouac might have hung out for hours had the road come this way. 904 South Charles Street; 410/234-0235.

Sisson's Restaurant and South Baltimore Brewing Company: Specializing in Cajun cooking, this brewing company directly across the street from the Cross Street Market whips up its own ales as well. Blackened chicken breasts and gumbos are the choices here. The best beers are the seasonal ales, and you can get a "growler" (Chappy's ears perked up at this historical term for a 64-ounce jug) of brew to go on your way out. Pick up one of Sisson's own root beers if you're driving. 36 East Cross Street; 410/539-2093.

FELLS POINT

Baltimore's most reputed and largely restored waterfront community, this neighborhood dates back to 1726 and is older than Baltimore itself. It is located east of Inner Harbor and Little Italy and is one of the most frequented tourist areas. Broadway, its main street, is lined with understated seafood houses, gentrified specialty shops, and antique stores mixed between rehabilitated old homes—

DIVERSION

Broadway Market: A favorite spot for fresh produce, fresh seafood, and those plump Polish sausages that are culinary legend in these parts, this indoor marketplace is one of several throughout the city. It's a throwback to times when going to market didn't mean a supermarket. Dogs aren't allowed inside. But Chappy knows well that his wait outside along the characteristic Fells Point brick sidewalks will be worthwhile, since many of the counters inside sell mouth-watering odds and ends that any dog will gladly devour. Quibble over the merits of kibble all you want, but Chappy happily scarfs down scraps of those authentic Bawlmer crab cakes anytime. The ice-packed seafood counters inside sell fresh fish and shellfish, but also double as raw bars where you can satisfy that yearning for a quick half-dozen oysters on the half shell. Oh, yeah, did we mention personality? The folks behind these counters are the genuine item. Go and enjoy them. Open Monday–Thursday, 7 A.M.–6 P.M., and Friday and Saturday, 6 A.M.–6 P.M. The market is located on Broadway between Lancaster and Fleet Streets. 410/276-9498.

---

some dating back before the War of 1812. Altogether, the personality-packed neighborhood offers always-interesting dog walks along its red-brick sidewalks.

Thrilled to walk out to the end of Broadway Pier, Chappy stuck his nose in the air and smelled all that he could smell. Two tall, thin Russian wolfhounds came along and intimidated our scruffy little Chap. He still seemed to enjoy the breeze and the wooden slats of the pier under his feet. We did have to watch out for some broken beer bottles; Fells Point is a party place.

Chappy also isn't much into traffic, so he was much happier when we veered off the cobblestone streets and busier sidewalks to walk along the wharf and river. There are benches there and even some patches of grass. He watched curiously as we chatted with a man in a kayak who had just paddled five miles to the harbor and was about to head back home. The four tugboats docked nearby dwarfed the kayaker. The seagulls caught Chappy's attention, but only until he had sniffed out tidbits of leftover crab cake sandwiches and pretzels in a trash can. Right next door, a fake Baltimore police station used to be where the Emmy-winning TV show *Homicide* was filmed.

Restaurants

Bay Cafe: You get a great view of the marina and the water from the outdoor tables, and your pooch can lie low nearby as you dine on sandwiches, burgers, pizza, and salads. "Sure, a lot of people do that," said the management when we asked about Chappy staying tableside. 2809 Boston Street; 410/522-3377.

Bertha's: Famous for its steamed mussels and its bumper stickers that say "Eat Bertha's Mussels," this restaurant is well known and often jam-packed. There's a good beer selection and the menu lists other seafood—but mostly mussels served in a variety of ways. One warning: Bertha's does carryout only when it isn't busy inside, so if the pooch is along and you're heading this way, come extra early. 734 South Broadway; 410/327-5795.

Bohager's: Too bad none of the outdoor decks allows dogs, but it's just impossible when it's an enclosed space. However, this fun-loving spot will fetch you anything from the barlike menu of burgers, grilled pizza, chicken, seafood, and crabs in season—for carrying out and dining with your dog. 515 South Eden Street; 410/563-7220.

BOP: It stands for Brick Oven Pizza, and there are so many varieties of toppings, it'll take awhile to decide what to order. Try one with artichoke hearts and Canadian bacon, and get it to go. 800 South Broadway; 410/563-1600.

Braznell's Caribbean Kitchen: Call ahead to make sure there is still some of its outrageously good jerk chicken left before you come this way for a pick up. That might be a little peppery for the pup, so ask these kind island folks for something less spicy for him. 1623 East Baltimore Street; 410/327-2445.

Daily Grind Coffee House: It's a great name and a great place to hang out. When the cast of *Homicide* used to film across the street at the police station, they would regularly send over granitas on hot summer days. 1726 Thames Street; 410/558-0399.

Ding How: And how! If you're not in the mood for seafood, go Chinese. Carry out a container of chicken lo mein and a pair of chopsticks to eat in marvelous simplicity on the pier watching the water—with the dog at your side. Also, you might expect this in Bawlmer: They serve soft-shell crab dishes in season. 631 South Broadway; 410/327-8888.

Jimmy's Restaurant: A big Jimmy's breakfast or one of his enormous sandwiches has cured many a hangover. Open for breakfast, lunch, and dinner. Carryout is always available. 801 South Broadway; 410/327-3273.

John Steven: This funky little eatery serves up some fine steamed shrimp and some juicy mussels—just the right touch for a waterfront neighborhood. You can get them to go for a waterfront picnic. 1800 Thames Street; 410/327-5561.

Ze Mean Bean Café: It's a tiny coffee shop that serves some delightful Slavic food—*pirozshki* with farmer's cheese or a spicy kielbasa sandwich with onions and sauerkraut. Don't forget the borscht—it is a must. They'll even wrap that up to go, along with one of the many coffee choices. It's perfect for a day by the water—or on the water if you boated this way with the pup. 1739 Fleet Street; 410/675-5999.

Places to Stay

Admiral Fell Inn: For a long time this charming inn did not allow dogs, but it does now, for an additional one-time fee of $35. Note: You will be put on the lobby level, but that's just to make it easier on everyone involved. Chappy feels this is one place where he is treated properly, with custom Federal-style furnishings, cable television, a coffee shop, and valet service. He'd like to book the two-story suite with fireplace and Jacuzzi, but there's that lobby-level rule. Upstairs or down, this is a special place to stay and makes a great weekend hideaway with the pup. And you're right in the thick of things. Rooms run about $215. 888 South Broadway, Baltimore, MD 21231; 410/522-7377 or 800/292-4667.

HAMPDEN

Parks, Beaches, and Recreation Areas

10 Roosevelt Park 🐾

Described by one Baltimorean as "a safe park," this small, neighborhood green has playgrounds for kids and enough leg-stretching room for leashed dogs to get a little exercise.

The park is open dawn–dusk daily. From downtown Baltimore, take Charles Street north, turn left on Falls Road, then turn left on 36th Street. The park is on the left. 410/396-7900.

EARMARK YOUR CALENDAR–OCTOBER

Fells Point Fun Festival: Lots of dogs bring along their humans to this annual outdoor waterfront street festival that quickly gets thick with people, people, and more people. Held the first weekend of October, the fest fills these quaint brick sidewalks with more than 300 arts and crafts booths, music playing from several stages, and food vendors, which is what every one comes for. All proceeds benefit historic preservation. Guys head for the two beer gardens, kids for the children's area. If your dog is a party animal, take him to this street party. Keep him on a leash, though, because it gets packed: Estimated crowds reached 325,000 in recent years.

Howl-A-Ween: People just love to dress up their dogs, we guess, because here's a chance to enter your dog into a contest. Wearing a costume, dogs can compete for scariest, funniest, most Baltimorean, best matching dog and human, and most original at this October event. One year, celebrity judges included people from WHFS radio station and WBAL-TV, a state senator, and a representative of the Maryland SPCA. Proceeds went to benefit the Canton dog park project. For information, call 410/342-0900.

11 Wyman Park 🐾

Walking in Wyman Park is like strolling through the woods next to a college campus, which is exactly what it is. The park extends the entire western length of the John Hopkins University grounds. The first of the urban parklands the city bought to protect its stream valleys just after the turn of the century, this whole stretch is in a gully and dips down to playing fields. Attitudes toward dogs are lax here as they are about many things on college campuses, but it's best to keep the pup leashed when visiting. Also with students lying on the grassy slopes deeply focused on their scholarly endeavors, it is best to clean up after your dog—as it always is.

The park is open all hours—like college students who are up all hours. From downtown Baltimore, take Charles Street north, then turn left on University Parkway, and make a left on the winding San Martin Drive to travel back down through the park. 410/396-7900.

Restaurants

Angelo's: Just Another pizza place? Nope. This neighborhood favorite is known for its gigantic 18-inch slices of pizza. It also offers a variety of other Italian dishes to take home or carry out under a tree. 3600 Keswick Road; 410/235-2595.

Cafe Hon: Known as a true Baltimore experience, this American restaurant serves a creamy dill salad dressing that everyone raves about—and you will,

DIVERSIONS

Brewers' Park: We could have listed this under parks, but it's really more of a museum, or a cluster of museums. Located on the site of an 18th-century brewery, it is the one place on Museum Row where you and your dog can visit for free and soak up some culture.

Dog lovers shouldn't miss the giant RCA dog, Nipper, with his gramophone. Chappy was understandably cautious when approaching the nearly **20-foot-tall Nipper,** who's located in a fenced area by the Nickelodeon Theater across the street from Brewers' Park. Don't miss this photo op!

This area is part of the City Life Museums, six downtown museums probably better tackled without a dog so that you can go inside them. However we had a great time roaming outside with Chappy. He waited patiently while some of us went sightseeing. We never left him alone, though, and we don't think you should, either—because the neighborhood edges on rougher turf. It's also on a very busy street corner; Chappy wasn't comfortable with the traffic whizzing by on President Street. Open daily, 10 A.M.–5 P.M., tickets cost $6, though you can visit the outside areas with the pooch for free. The museums and park are located at 33 South Front Street, between Baltimore and Lombard Streets. 410/396-3156.

Help for the Homeless: Alley Animals is a group of dedicated individuals whose goal is to take homeless animals off the streets of Baltimore. They travel in pairs, picking up animals with the intent of finding good homes for them. The group has periodic food drives, and they regularly place animals for adoption. They could use your tax-deductible contribution. For more information, call 410/823-0899.

Dogged Animal Advocacy: If you're an advocate for your dog, or all animals on God's green earth, you'll want to know that *The Animals' Agenda,* a hard-hitting bimonthly magazine that informs about animal rights and cruelty-free living is published right here in Baltimore. If your love of animals is leading you into animal advocacy, then you might want to contact the dedicated folks at *The Animals' Agenda,* P.O. Box 25881, Baltimore, MD 21224; 410/675-4566.

too. Well, either that or the hot fudge sundaes, which everyone raves about. Leave the dog outside while you pick up the order, then head to the Johns Hopkins campus or Wyman Park. If you're in the mood to pick up some souvenirs, stop by the Hometown Girl gift store right next door, where you can buy a bottle of the salad dressing and trinkets. 1002 West 36th Street; 410/243-1230.

Cafe Pangea: Italian-style sandwiches—like an herb focaccia and panini with smoked Gouda cheese—are much more to Chappy's liking than a big heaping plate of spaghetti with marinara sauce. Add to that a great dessert (for us, not Chappy), and we all leave happy. 4007 Falls Road; 410/662-0500.

Holy Frijoles: They serve only authentic Mexican food here. What does that mean? Famous nachos, mammoth burritos, delectable chile rellenos, and not-to-be-believed chimichangas. It won't matter if this is authentic Mexican or not once you've tasted these dishes. It almost seems as though they're trying to make up for the tiny size of the restaurant with the heaping, fresh plates of food. 908 West 36th Street; 410/235-2326.

HILLSDALE GREENE

Parks, Beaches, and Recreation Areas

12 Hillsdale Park 🐾 ½

Well-manicured lawns made us think "yippee!" Or is it "yuppie?" We soon realized the park is really more of a barely developed backyard to the Forest Park Municipal Golf Course than where you'd find many outdoor amenities that delight dogs.

The park is open dawn–dusk. It's located on the western city line adjacent to the Forest Park Municipal Golf Club, off West Forest Park Avenue. 410/887-3818.

INNER HARBOR/DOWNTOWN

Credit for the rebirth of Baltimore goes to visionary developer James Rouse, who in 1980 designed and built Harborplace—a downtown mall constructed low and made of glass to enhance the vista of the Inner Harbor waterside.

Some Baltimoreans were opposed to the idea of developing the harbor, fearing loss of low real estate taxes and sense of community. Others wanted to retain an open space with empty warehouses and wharfs. Still others didn't want to lose the smell of spices from the McCormick factory, which stood on Light Street and is now demolished.

All the naysayers have been proved wrong by an Inner Harbor that is now alive with sights and smells and activity—one of the great urban renewal success stories. From the old Navy frigate docked there, to its trendy and airy restaurants, to street performers bringing smiles to the many visitors who like walking along the waterfront, Inner Harbor has become the must-see magnet drawing visitors and revenue into the city.

But the biggest attractions at Inner Harbor don't accommodate dogs. Foremost among them is the National Aquarium, located at Pier 3, a few blocks east of Harborplace. This modern building extending into the water has become a model of what an aquarium can be for other cities. Inside, a huge tropical rainforest roofs a coral reef with a 350,000-gallon tank that contains sharks, turtles, and dozens of varieties of other colorful and peculiar fish. The marine mammal exhibit displays amazing beluga whales. No wonder this is one of the most popular attractions in the Inner Harbor area—especially for families with children. Expect to wait an hour or even two after buying your tickets for your precise entrance time; and leave the dog at home. Dogs are prohibited.

Meanwhile, Top of the World on Pratt Street's World Trade Center nearby offers a great panoramic view of the harbor and city, and houses displays describing local history and industry. No dogs allowed in here either.

Never mind the Public Works Museum located in the historic old sewage pumping station on the east side by the big parking lots, because dogs can't go in—even if researching the history of fire hydrants.

Still, the Inner Harbor charm is really the seaside promenade. Even if you can't tour any of the huge seafaring vessels docked there with a dog along, you and the pooch can have a fine time walking along Pier 1 from Pratt Street to look over the amazing U.S.S. *Constellation,* a replica of the Navy's first frigate, *Constellation,* built in 1797 in Baltimore. The Baltimore Maritime Museum is a collection of ships anchored under the sky at Pier 3, where you and the dog can inspect (from the dock) the U.S.S. *Torsk,* a World War II submarine, the last United States vessel to sink a ship in the Big War. The lightship *Chesapeake* and the cutter *Taney* (the *Taney* was at Pearl Harbor when the Japanese attacked) are there, too. When it's in port, definitely check out the *Pride of Baltimore II,* a majestically tall two-masted schooner that is open for tours (not for dogs) on weekends.

Otherwise, Chappy is content to sit back and watch the hustle and bustle of people enjoying themselves in the expansive and tastefully landscaped Inner Harbor, where there always seems to be someone playing music for the passing horde, and where you can grab a sandwich at the many cafés and delis along the promenade and sit in the sun. One thing Chap would really like to try, but he's not allowed to, are the water taxis that zip back and forth from Fells Point to the Light Street Pavilion.

Inner Harbor is mostly a people place where a dog on a leash is no problem. Do make sure to scoop up after your dog if need be. Etiquette and logistics here make it a must.

Parks, Beaches, and Recreation Areas

13 Oriole Park at Camden Yards 🐾 🐕

Okay, okay, it's a ball park, not a dog park. But what a ball park! Camden Yards is well known nationally for being a grand and fairly new stadium, the first of the new ball parks to incorporate modern conveniences with the style and appearance of the great old ball parks of yesteryear. Considered by many baseball fans to be the best stadium built in the past 50 years, it is an outdoor stadium with natural grass and no obstructed views from its 45,000-plus seats. Your pooch's view of this remarkable stadium's interior will be obstructed, however, since you can't take a dog inside the stadium.

But you can walk around the stadium's perimeter and even check out the view from beyond left field behind the wrought-iron gates along Camden Street between Paca and Pratt Streets. On game day, if you and the pooch nudge your way to a strategic spot at those gates (there will be others doing the same), you can catch some of the action on the field. Don't worry when you see the smoke rising from the Eutaw Street corridor behind right field; sniff the air like a hound dog and you'll get a noseful of appetizing aroma from Boog Powell's Barbecue Pit, where the racks of ribs and other good stuff are cooking. More fun are the game-day vendors outside the park hawking their baseball memorabilia, logo caps, and T-shirts. Chappy's fond of those giant, salty, soft pretzels, but there are hot dogs and spicy sausages, ice cream, peanuts in the shell—it's a major league carnival outside.

Check the Orioles' schedule for game times if you want the experience. The stadium is located in between Howard Street and Greene Street, just off Pratt Street, and across from the Convention Center. 410/685-9800.

14 Rash Field 🐾 🐾

Right next to the Maryland Science Center and Davis Planetarium, directly below Federal Hill Park and right on the water is a grassy area with a miniature golf course. It used to be the site of the old wooden shipbuilding yards. Then it was the football field for a nearby high school. Now, it's where the *Pride of Baltimore* memorial stands—a mast and some flowers planted around it. This is in tribute to the clipper ship reproduced in 1976 to sail the globe as a floating advertisement for Baltimore—but it sank in a storm off Bermuda, drowning three of the crew.

The field is named after Joseph Rash, who in the 1950s headed the city's Park Board and was active in the community. Now, Rash Field is a grassy spot that's perfect for taking a break from all the hubbub of the Inner Harbor and still be by the water. You'll often see kids flying kites here, and other dogs (leashed) enjoying this pleasant waterside setting by the Inner Harbor Marina.

The park is open dawn–dusk daily. To get to the park take I-95 into Baltimore; exit onto Russell Street toward the Inner Harbor. Turn right on Pratt Street, and then right again on Light Street, which will veer left and become Key Highway. The field is on the left. 410/396-7900.

Restaurants

Burke's: This is more old-fashioned watering hole dining than trendy new hotel food. You shouldn't leave without an order to go of some of the tastiest onion rings you'll ever crunch on. The crab cake sandwich travels real well to the waterfront. 36 Light Street; 410/752-4189.

Haussner's: Had enough pizza and pasta and seafood? Try this legendary Baltimore restaurant where you'll find an amazing collection of art as well as 90 entrees of German stock—such as traditional schnitzels and sauerbraten (sour beef) with dumplings. There is even a herring cocktail and a fresh pig knuckle you can order. Don't get so full that you can't try a homemade dessert. Even German shepherds are not allowed in the restaurant, however, so plan ahead, and pick it up. 3242 Eastern Avenue; 410/327-8365.

Hollywood Diner: Hollywood filmmaker Barry Levinson filmed much of his movie *Diner* at this location. Note that it's open Monday–Friday, and Sunday for breakfast and lunch only. Chappy's more of a *Seven Years in Tibet* movie location buff (he relates to Brad Pitt, too). But he has yet to object to our running to this old-fashioned diner to pick up a milkshake. 400 East Saratoga Street; 410/962-5379.

Kawasaki: If you get one of the traditional Japanese dishes or fresh sushi to go, you won't get the hot towel for your hands that the sit-down guests get. You won't be able to sip sake. But you still might pass by a Baltimore Oriole or Kathleen Turner, if she's in town. 413 North Charles Street; 410/659-7600.

Louie's Bookstore Cafe: Multimedia, multi-eat-ia, says Chappy. This is one great place that offers a large magazine selection, a book area, an art gallery, and sometimes live music—all in one. On top of that, you can get tasty, be-kind-to-animals vegetarian dishes, or a cup of cappuccino and a piece of homemade pie. There's a new garden area to one side, but dogs aren't allowed, so you'll have to get the reading material and vittles to go. 518 North Charles Street; 410/962-1222.

Paolo's: With a good location, right by the waterside, this place is always busy, but the food is also always good. It specializes in northern Italian dishes made with a little more creativity than usual. Pick up an order of the pastas or a brick-oven pizza wrapped to go. 301 Light Street; 410/539-7060.

Ruth's Chris Steak House: If it's a serious steak you're hankering for, stop here. The bigger the better, Chappy always says. It's no problem to bag one of those babies and take it home or to a park bench for a steakfest with your carnivore canine. 600 Water Street; 410/783-0033.

Tío Pepe: Almost 30 years old now, this extremely popular Spanish restaurant is known for serving a delicious paella, beyond-imagination roast suckling pig, and shrimp entrées for giant appetites. Si, señor, they will wrap it for carryout and have it ready when you and the pup arrive. 10 East Franklin Street; 410/539-4675.

Uncle Lee's: If it's Chinese tonight, walk the block up South Street from the Inner Harbor, just past the Gallery, to this traditional Chinese restaurant that cooks all your favorite Hunan, Mandarin, and Szechwan dishes. Everything's available for carryout. 44 South Street; 410/727-6666.

Wharf Rat: More pub than anything else, it hosts a hopping pre- and post-game crowd at its location directly across from Camden Yards with lots of outdoor tables, perfect for a summer night. Known for its large brew selection, these happy-go-lucky folks will bag a sandwich or fish and chips to go, for you and the sports fan pup. 206 West Pratt; 410/244-8900.

EARMARK YOUR CALENDAR

Don't forget that on July 2, it's Happy Birthday to the harbor as Harborplace celebrates its birthday every year like the rest of us—even if it isn't like the rest of us. Chappy has little patience for the big cake-cutting ceremony, but he always enjoys the street performers—except for the mimes, who make him think he's gone deaf. Two days later is a Fourth of July to-do. Bring your leashed dog if she handles large and loud crowds well. An array of entertainment, including live music and other perform-ances, spreads throughout the promenade area, and soon after sunset the fireworks explode loudly over the water.

And what's the year without celebrating Christmas. Inner Harbor does it up with a Santa's place, Santa's petting zoo, and choirs heralding the sounds of the season.

For the full schedule of all events and to find out which ones are best suited to bringing the dog along, call 410/837-4636 or 800/282-6632.

Bless Me Up, Cap'n: Head to the Harborplace Amphitheater in mid-October on a pretty fall Friday afternoon to witness this quintessential Baltimore event—the **Blessing of Baltimore Work Boats.** Dozens of boats parade along the Inner Harbor shoreline on a late Friday afternoon seeking a benediction and ultimately divine approval. Dogs like Chappy can't expect anything more than an interesting sight. 410/837-4636 or 800/282-6632.

Pickin' and Grinnin': Baltimore loves any excuse for a **crab-picking contest,** and the Preakness works just fine. The best and the brightest of Baltimore's business, media, and sports communities gather to spilt, crack, and pick their way to victory and into the hearts of spectators who flock here not so much for the excitement but for the silly good time. Contes-tants have three minutes to pick the most crab meat at the Harborplace Amphitheater at this free lunchtime event where dogs do nicely on leashes. Afterward, there's something wrong with you if you're not in the mood for a carryout crab sandwich. Just head over to Phillips Restaurant, one of the crabby competition's sponsors. 410/837-4636 or 800/282-6632.

Concerts Your Thing? Finding an outdoor concert is one of summer's great pooch-sharing pleasures. Baltimore makes it convenient and a sim-ple pleasure with its summer series of concerts featuring the region's best modern and alternative music, tropical rhythms, and even patriotic favorites played by military bands They strike up the tunes at the Pier 6 Concert Pavilion, June–September evenings, at Inner Harbor. When you bring the musical mutt, stay at the far back of the crowd where you'll still be able to hear the tunes.

Places to Stay

Baltimore Clarion Hotel: About 12 blocks from the Inner Harbor, this is a neat and tidy hotel that has dropped its $75 deposit if you bring along your dog. Instead, however, it insists that the dog be in a cage. Argh, says Chappy. No thank you. Expect to pay a $10 pet fee per day, too. Rates are about $119 a night. 612 Cathedral Street, Baltimore, MD 21201; 410/727-7101.

LITTLE ITALY

Narrow old streets and generations of neighbors are about all there is in this traditionally Italian section of town—the next neighborhood east of Inner Harbor on Pratt Street. Oh, and one more thing: Some of the best authentic Italian restaurants you'll find this side of the Tiber. We've pointed out only a few representative restaurants. There are many more in this neighborhood—the joy is discovering them.

Restaurants

Amiccis: A little less formal than some, this restaurant serves a mouth-watering chicken cacciatore, tortellini, and other traditional entrées. Everything on the menu is carryout. Inner Harbor's Pier 6 Concert Pavilion is walking distance or pull up a piece of marble at the Columbus statue nearby. 231 South High Street; 410/528-1096.

Antney's Bar and Grill: Goodfellas, godfathers, and compadres gather here for a neighborhood beer. No, no, we mean good fellas, as in good guys. There are two dinner specials nightly that you can get to carry out. 10108 Eastern Avenue; 410/685-8649.

Chiapparelli's: Its many regulars know the place and know Mom Chiapparelli's ravioli. But they also know to get the house salad with Parmesan and peperoncini. Veal comes about a dozen different ways—all of them so good you can't help but say, "Now that'sa Italian!" Chappy can't sit close enough when we carry out these dishes. 237 South High Street; 410/837-0309.

Della Notte: Don't overlook the excellent homemade pastries just because you're full from eating the fresh pastas, pizza, and seafood. Check out the giant artificial tree rising up in the middle of the dining room while you wait to get your sweets wrapped to go. 801 Eastern Avenue; 410/837-5500.

Sabatino's: Friendly hosts and staff are only one reason to stop by this Little Italy institution of higher culinary learning. Another is the delicious food: One of our favorites here is the hearty pasta puttanesca—"whore's pasta"—made with a sauce of tomatoes, black olives, capers, and anchovies (never had it better than this). When you're carrying out your order, keep your eyes open for Orioles players or sportscasters who stop by after a game, because this is a favorite haunt for local luminaries. 901 Fawn Street; 410/727-9414.

Vaccaro's Italian Pastry Shop: You have to stop by and see them to believe them. Confections have names like Lost at Sea. All sorts of taste treats await with your espresso, your gelato, your whipped cream–topped cappuccino. It's coffee and dessert only, and you'll have to take it with you and the pastry-lovin' pup. 222 Albemarle Street; 410/685-4905.

Vellegia's: This favorite is among the oldest in the neighborhood, serving traditional pasta and seafood dishes in true Baltimore fashion—but they'll also serve it to you in containers to carry out. 829 East Pratt Street; 410/685-2620.

LOCUST POINT

Parks, Beaches, and Recreation Areas

15 Latrobe Park 🐾

Long green benches under trees dot this city park, where kids can play on a small playground. One field hosted a pickup football game. A small rec center sits at the corner of the property. If you're looking for a great park, this isn't it. You might as well keep going to Fort McHenry about a half mile farther east on Fort Avenue, which is probably why you're in this neighborhood anyway. But if you can't wait, you could certainly stop here.

The park is open dawn–dusk daily. From I-95, take Exit 55 onto Key Highway; follow it for a half mile and turn left on Lawrence Street. Go two blocks and turn left on Fort Avenue and continue about a half mile until you see the park on the right. 410/396-6694.

16 Leone Riverside Park 🐾

If you don't want to run with the big dogs—big, tough, bully dogs—don't think about stopping at this large and very neighborhoodish old park. A pair of rottweilers set the tone at this park as soon as we got out of the car. Then an Akita, a German shepherd, and several other mixed breeds acted like we'd invaded their territory—which, of course, we had. One gray-and-black big dog was playing football—and, like the other local toughs, ignoring the dogs-must-be-on-a-leash rule that is posted.

Chappy wasn't going to argue the point with any of them. No one was mean or actually picked a fight. But the intimidation factor was high—sort of like walking into a bar and the only empty stool is between Mike Tyson and Evander Holyfield. . .and they're having an argument.

A big swimming pool sits midpoint in the park near where a large, old-fashioned gazebo crowns the top of the grassy hill. Trees and park benches are plentiful, though some of the benches are weathered and worse for the wear. There's a view of the Winans Cove to the south, but it's obstructed by the cars zooming to New York or Washington on I-95.

Hey, what do you expect from an urban park in South Baltimore? Row houses in the neighborhood are small, some of them kept nice and neat, some of them not. Kids using the park weren't a problem. The traditional Baltimore neighborhood bars nearby, with names like the Empty Pocket Saloon and Stumblin' Inn, add to the homey surroundings. You get the feeling this well-used neighborhood park is well used mostly by the neighbors.

The park is open at all hours, though all hours aren't recommended. From I-95, take Exit 55 onto Key Highway; follow it for a half mile and turn left on Lawrence Street. Go two blocks and turn right on Fort Avenue, then go five blocks and turn left on Covington Street. The park is a block farther at Covington Street. 410/396-6694.

MOUNT VERNON

You'll know you're in this neighborhood when you see the 178-foot monument dedicated to George Washington—actually the first such tribute to the first president. It's called the Washington Monument, but this is no obelisk like the tall one in the nation's capital (although the same person, Robert Mills, designed it). Well known to Baltimoreans, this monument is worth seeing because if you climb the 228 steps to the top, you'll find one of the best views of the city. On each of its four sides are small landscaped lawns and gardens—momentary retreats from the concrete hereabouts.

The Mount Vernon area itself displays fine old architecture dating back to 1827; this was once the city's most fashionable residential district and still is an elegant address. It's also home to many of the city's oldest churches, as well as the world-renowned Peabody Conservatory of Music and the Walters Art Gallery. There are monuments to Lafayette and others nearby as well, along a street appropriately named Monument Street.

Restaurants

Akbar: With mirrored walls and those big cold bottles of Kingfisher beer from India, it's always worth stepping into the clove-scented basement of this restaurant to pick up some lamb *vindaloo* to go. 823 North Charles Street; 410/539-0944.

Minato: This mix of Vietnamese and Japanese cuisine cooks a variety of crispy rolls as its specialty. Not only can you carry these out to enjoy with the dog on a nearby bench, but they're also easy to eat without making a mess. 800 North Charles Street; 410/332-0332.

Helmand: Vegetarians and nonvegetarians walk away happy with a plate of Afghan food like *kaddo borawni*—pumpkin with yogurt garlic sauce—from this friendly place. The staff will even brew a special pot of cardamom tea just for your private little picnic with the pup if you bring a thermos for them to pour it into. 806 North Charles Street; 410/752-0311.

Owl Bar: Owls stare at you from everywhere. Chappy isn't thrilled about that, but he's not invited in anyway. You can stop by and get anything from the menu—from pizza to steamed shrimp—for carryout. 1 East Chase Street; 410/347-0888.

Paper Moon: A funky diner that's open 24 hours every day but Sunday, it has outdoor tables where you can sit with your dog, but no waiters serve outside. Get the food to go and then sit outside. 227 West 29th Street; 410/889-4444.

Tony Cheng's Szechwan: No problem carrying out any dish you'd like. Just make sure they're open, because they close down between lunch and dinner for a break. 801 North Charles; 410/539-6666.

Places to Stay

Biltmore Suites: This 18th-century, Victorian-style bed and breakfast has only 16 rooms but goes first class and dogs are allowed. Rooms run about $79. 205 West Madison Street, Baltimore, MD 21202; 410/728-6550 or 800/868-5064.

MOUNT WASHINGTON

Restaurants

Desert Cafe: For inexpensive Middle Eastern fare and great desserts, this restaurant has an outdoor porch for lunch or sultry summer nights, but dogs aren't allowed on it. Still, you can get your pita and hummus to go. 1605 Sulgrave Avenue; 410/367-5808.

Ethel & Ramone's: Sip tea steeped in a china pot and get philosophical. Chappy loves to do that. He looks fairly regal when listening, especially after a bath. The management said it was okay to sit outside at one of the outdoor tables with him while he enters the enlightened state. 1615 Sulgrave Avenue; 410/664-2971.

Hoang's: You can get Thai food, Vietnamese soup, or Chinese dishes here. Or sit at the sushi bar while you wait for your carryout order. This is a place any mixed-breed pooch could relate to. 1619 Sulgrave Avenue; 410/466-1000.

Stone Mill Bakery: Salmon on brioche? Goat cheese and cucumbers on baguettes? This is not your run-of-the-mill bakery. It's the Stone Mill Bakery and it's known for its gourmet baked goods. Just run in and pick up the goodies. There are two stores. 1609 Sulgrave Avenue, 410/452-2233; and 5127 Roland Avenue, 410/532-8669.

PIMLICO

This is the home of the internationally known Pimlico Race Course where every May the horsey world focuses on one of the crown jewels of racing.

Parks, Beaches, and Recreation Areas

🐾 Cylburn Arboretum 🐾 🐾 🐾 ½

About a mile due east from the famous Pimlico Race Course, you'll find this incredibly pretty getaway. The arboretum itself is off-limits to dogs, but that's no big deal, because the 176 acres of gorgeous, tree-filled parkland surrounding it welcomes leashed dogs and is totally loaded with cultivated plantings, wildflowers, and nature trails.

On a spring day when the daffodils are blooming and the tulips are in their glory, you cannot find a more beautiful park setting in Baltimore. It's well worth a visit. Pick one of the nine trails and set out on a nature hike. The wood chips make you feel as if you're walking on sponges—which Chappy's weary pads appreciated. The trails are clearly marked, and robins, squirrels, and other creatures will hop across the path before you. Otherwise, all you hear is the wind in the tall pines.

The lawn surrounding the mansion feels like a grand place for a wedding. You can easily imagine a Victorian-era picnic taking place here. It all looks and feels so civilized. Stone benches are perfectly placed for taking a rest in the sun, but there is also plenty of shade along the paths and near the maple groves. The mansion has restrooms and a museum and gift shop. Take water for your dog, although you could easily fill a bowl in the mansion. Then, after exploring the civility of it all, sit on the porch and marvel at the beauty surrounding you.

The grounds are open daily 6 A.M.–9 P.M. From I-83, take Exit 9 west onto

Cold Spring Lane; go about a half mile and turn right on Greenspring Avenue. The park is located on the right opposite Sinai Hospital grounds. 410/396-0180.

SoWeBo (South West Baltimore) AND HOLLINS MARKET AREA

Though just a couple of blocks from the immaculate Inner Harbor and the excitement of Camden Yards, this urban working-class neighborhood suffers from urban decay and the usual inner-city troubles spurred by poverty. Washington Boulevard is the main drag where a few shops and some crab carryouts conduct business alongside check-cashing and bail bondsmen shops and boarded-up storefronts next to crumbling row houses. In other words, this isn't a tourist 'hood.

Parks, Beaches, and Recreation Areas

18 Carroll Park 🐾 ½

A vast and grassy park of hillsides criss-crossed with paved roadway, the park attracts all types from the neighborhood—kids trying to ride bikes for the first time, mutts without leashes charging around, locals from the 'hood waxing their cars in the shade of its old trees. The big, fenced-off playground at one end gets lots of use, and the six rusty-pole tennis courts in the middle don't. Some guys were playing a pickup game of baseball on the north side near the woods, and in one of its many wide-open spaces, a half-hearted football game was underway.

If you want to get out and let the dog run, it's against ordinances, but no one is around to stop you. This park isn't as kept-up as some of the other city parks to the north and east. This neighborhood, which came to be known unofficially as Pigtown in the days when they herded pigs through the streets to the slaughterhouses, isn't exactly upscale. You'll want to watch your step. Most of

---

EARMARK YOUR CALENDAR–MAY

Cylburn Market Day: Held each year on a Saturday in early May at the Cylburn Arboretum, this annual "yard" sale is timed conveniently for home-landscaping dreamers anxious for springtime planting. The sale includes large variety of plants—vegetables, annuals, perennials, wildflowers, ferns, herbs, even some rare selections. The usual artsy-craftsy suspects show up to vend for themselves to the thousands of green-thumbers who flock here. Keep your dog on a leash—not only is it the rule, but in this crowd you want to know where the pooch is. Admission is free. From I-83, take Exit 9 west onto Cold Spring Lane; go about a half mile and turn right on Greenspring Avenue. The park is located on the right opposite Sinai Hospital grounds. 410/367-2217.

DIVERSIONS

The Sage of Baltimore: H. L. Mencken, one of Baltimore's favorite sons, was an author, journalist, and literary critic who lived for nearly 70 years in a 19th-century row house in the Hollins Market neighborhood. The place is restored and includes many of the writer's original belongings, among them a baby grand piano. There is a small admission fee and, of course, your dog isn't welcome to come in. Sadly, at press time, the house has been closed due to lack of funds. But it's worth a stroll by with your literary-minded pooch in tow. Located at 1524 Hollins Street, the Mencken house is directly across from the grassy lawn of Union Square, but you don't need to hang out around this community. 410/396-3100.

Edgar Allan Poe: Although he lived here for only three years (1832–1835), this famous writer did pen some of his greatest works in this tiny house on the neighborhood border of Hollins Market and Harlem Park. This isn't a great neighborhood for walking the dog, unless she's a rottweiler. The museum has extremely limited afternoon hours, so call before you visit. 203 North Amity Street; 410/396-7932.

the folks at the park seemed to mind their own business and do their own thing. We were told, however, that there are exceptions and that some shady characters do roam onto the park grounds.

Still, Mount Clare Mansion draws its share of curious tourists to the highest point in the park. Its columned portico is impressive. Its history: The only pre-Revolution mansion still standing in the city, it frequently hosted the likes of George Washington and Lafayette.

The park is open dawn–dusk daily. From Inner Harbor, take Lombard Street west; turn left on Monroe Street, go past the railroad tracks and the park entrance is on the left at Washington Boulevard. 410/396-5828.

Places to Stay

Sheraton International Hotel–Baltimore: Dogs may stay here, for a price. A $30 fee, to be exact. One nice feature is 24-hour room service that allows you and the craving canine to stay in for dinner. It's less than a mile from Carroll Park and nearby I-95. Doubles run about $130 a night. 7032 Elm Road, Baltimore, MD 21240; 410/859-3300 or 800/638-5858.

WAVERLY

Restaurants

Alonso's: No problem getting one of this little northside neighborhood's favorite hamburgers to go. They are one-pound large and juicy, but they'll find a way to wrap it for you. Same goes for the crab cakes or the chili. 415 West Cold Spring Lane; 410/235-3433.

Loco Hombre: Families from the neighborhood come for the Tex-Mex tacos with shrimp or salmon with red banana salsa. 413 West Cold Spring Lane; 410/889-2233.

Sam's Bagels: Some folks think Sam makes the best bagels bar none. Breakfast, lunch, or whatever you want to call it, Sam's will serve them plain or with any kind of cream cheese you can think of. 500 West Cold Spring Lane; 410/243-1774.

WEST BALTIMORE

Parks, Beaches, and Recreation Areas

19 Gwynns Falls–Leakin Park 🐾 🐾 ½

The Gwynns family and the Leakin family held adjoining property long ago, and they both donated more than 1,200 acres of tree-filled undeveloped land to the park system to create Gywnns Falls–Leakin Park. While a couple of pretty little rivers run through it (two-miles of Dead Run Stream and six miles of Gwynns Falls Stream), the problem is that this wilderness park really is mostly wilderness.

One of the largest parks of its kind in the nation, it is home to large meadows, fragile wetlands, thickly forested terrain, quarries, springs, and marshes. Plenty of wildlife lurks here, too, including deer, raccoons, beavers, opossums, and red foxes. You find birds ranging from hawks to songbirds as you hike the 15 miles of trails. Some development on the north side includes picnic sites by a historical estate. Work is under way to develop the Gwynns Falls

---

EARMARK YOUR CALENDAR

Wearin' O' the Green: It's not Chappy's heritage (and only a bit o' ours), but he'll eat a green doggy biscuit any time it's thrown his way. Baltimore goes all out (because it's that kind of city) for its **Saint Patrick's Day Parade,** held on or around the day (March 17) depending on how the calendar falls. The Paddy parade rolls past the Washington Monument at Mount Vernon Square (West Pratt and North Charles) in the afternoon, so just pull up a piece of curb.

Gets Your Backfin Up: At the **Old Bay Crab Soup Stakes** in October, Baltimore area residents can present their special recipes and culinary experiments. The smell of these soups will make any dog's nose quiver in delight at this wonderfully provincial competition. It takes place outdoors at Harborplace Amphitheater, so you and the leashed canine soup sniffer can attend—so long as no one ends up shouting, "Waiter! There's a dog in my soup!" 410/837-4636 or 800/282-6632.

Trail, a 14-mile "linear park," as they like to call it, that will one day, when funded to completion, start in Gwynns Falls–Leakin Park and travel through 20 west Baltimore neighborhoods.

Leakin Park actually picks up to the west where Gwynns Falls Park leaves off. Both parks are open dawn–dusk daily. To get to Leakin Park, take I-695 to I-70 east and continue one mile to the Security Boulevard (Route 122) off-ramp. Turn right on Forest Park Avenue; turn right on Windsor Mill Road and turn into the park on the right. Gwynns Falls Park is located at Windsor Mill Road and Forest Park Avenue. 410/396-5828.

20 Hanlon Park 🐾

Next to the cool blue waters of Lake Ashburton, this park offers some open grass areas where pups can frolic a bit (though leashes are required). But the neighborhood isn't that inviting, so it just adds up to a perfect pit stop if that's what your pooch needs.

The park is open dawn–dusk daily and is located off Gwynns Falls Parkway along Longwood Street. 410/887-3818x.

WOODBURY

Parks, Beaches, and Recreation Areas

21 Druid Hill Park 🐾 🐾 🐾

Once a private estate, these 650 acres are now Baltimore city's largest park and one of its most popular. On this land is the Baltimore Zoo. Taking your pooch

---

EARMARK YOUR CALENDAR

A Buncha Hot Air: That's right, and it's all in a dozen magical **hot air balloons** that will lift off from Druid Hill Park each May as part of the fun-filled Preakness week that spreads such crazy joy all over the city. It's a contest of skill and accuracy and great fun to watch.

Picnic in the Park: In August join the giant family reunion when the **Stone Soul Picnic** takes place in the park. It's an annual event. For information on these and other events, call the City of Baltimore Department of Recreation and Parks for more information at 410/396-7900 or the park at 410/396-6106.

Looking for a Good Deal? The idea of a **flea market** isn't appealing to Chappy, who gets that rear paw a-scratchin' just at the thought of it. But this is a fun market to visit every Saturday and Sunday in September—and relatively free of fleas far as we can tell. It's held around the reservoir area, and there's an artist's corner, a marketplace, and, of course, the one-man's-treasure area.

---

there would be a little like taking coals to Newcastle, so save that for a day when the dog's dozin' at home.

Instead, turn right at the beautiful Conservatory building at the entrance off Gwynns Falls Parkway and take the pooch to the vast, hilly, wide-open areas for a walk. Or head around Druid Lake, bordered nicely by a wrought-iron fence. The walk around this reservoir is a favorite of keeping-fit locals who like the 1.75-mile loop it provides.

Avoid the guys sleeping on the picnic tables. The miniature Safety City—a replica of a city block complete with downsized stoplights and crosswalk markings—is not for teaching dogs the rules of the road, but is instead a learning center for school kids and day care groups.

But don't worry, this park is home to the city's police K-9 unit, so you'll be safe and your dog might make some high-powered connections.

The park is open dawn–dusk daily. From I-83, take Exit 7 onto Druid Park Lake Drive and follow the signs into the park. 410/396-6106.

BEYOND
THE BELTWAYS

DAY TRIPS

Unlike some urban centers, one of the great things about Washington and Baltimore is that if you drive an hour or so away from the city lights, you're not just in suburbia, you're in a whole different world of small historic towns, rural countryside, ancient mountain ridges, even sunny ocean beaches.

We've narrowed the overnight possibilities for dog lovers who want to get away from it all—except from their dogs. We've mapped out enough for you and the pup to tackle for a day, maybe two or three, in some of the most inviting day-trip destinations outside of Washington, Baltimore, and the counties we've covered elsewhere in the book.

While we direct you to some parks and recreation areas, to hotels and places to stay that welcome dogs, even some restaurants and things to do where the pup won't feel like an underdog, these day trips aren't as inclusive as the other chapters. They're grounds for a day away or a weekend jaunt. They span from the beaches to the mountains.

The good news: the farther out from the urban blur you take your dog, the friendlier it seems to get. With a few notable exceptions, swank hotels turn away the most pampered of pupsters without even a pat on the noggin. Not that we've got a bone to pick with those snobbish policies, but a surprising number of rustic country inns and rural bed-and-breakfasts go to great lengths to include the pooches in weekend getaway plans. Chappy loves a fluffy comforter (if ours at home is any indication) as much as the next well-bred guy.

We've passed over otherwise wonderful municipal parks and even state parks, for instance, and gone straight for the really nice one or two places you shouldn't miss. We suggest only a few activities, a festival or two that might sway the timing of your trip, a historic site or natural wonder worth detouring to from the beaten path. So think of this chapter as a starter kit for your weekend getaway. And you and the pooch can ad lib from there.

HITTING THE BEACH

The smell of salt air, the feel of the sun's warmth on your skin, the sound of seagulls calling—how can you enjoy a trip to the beach unless your dog's along? No fair working on that tan without Chappy, who is a certified son of a beach. He has been on many a week-long vacation to Bethany Beach, one of the more low-key, family-oriented shoreline locales that he loves.

The Atlantic Coast beaches of nearby Delaware are among the most popular Washington and Baltimore escapes, but taking your dog to the beach can pose some problems. Where to go? Where to stay? These beaches are less than a three-hour drive from either Baltimore or Washington. The young and hardy can easily make it a day trip. But to really enjoy it you probably need to stay a weekend, a week, maybe two.

One problem is finding a place to stay. For several years, we rented a house we found through an ad in the *Washington Post.* The owner had no problem with our bringing a dog. However, if you go through any of the rental agencies that handle most of the beach rental properties, you will find they all have stern no-pet policies. The Internet may help provide you with a dog-loving house owner. Some hotels will allow dogs and we've listed them.

But even after you find a dog-friendly house to rent, you have to be careful. While these beaches can be great trips from the months of wintry solitude through crowded high season, remember that the summertime excursions get hot. Never leave your dog alone in a closed house or hotel room. We heard stories about one dog chewing out part of a door in a rental house in only a few hours of loneliness. We also have a friend whose beautiful golden retriever overheated and died when the room-unit air-conditioner broke down while the owner spent the afternoon at the beach. So if you take your dog with you on your beach vacation, keep him out of the heat. And always make sure there's plenty of water and shade. Dogs can wear themselves out quickly at a sunny summer shoreline, especially if they're swimming in ocean surf.

Another note: Because ownership of eating establishments at the beach turns over faster than in nonresort areas, we didn't attempt to include every restaurant that has outdoor tables (so many of them do), or every pizza and sub carryout shop. In beach communities even the good ones come and go like the tide. As is so often the case when traveling with a dog, you might find a gem of a place with great food and friendly management simply because you happened by at the right time.

Speaking of the right time, dogs are not allowed on any town beaches during the day in season. As a rule of thumb, from Memorial Day to Labor Day— no dogs 9 A.M.–5 P.M.—but check each beach's rules, which are subject to change from one season to the next. Some are stricter than others. On the other hand, it's probably too hot for them at that time, so figure the municipal authorities are doing dog lovers a favor instead of an injustice.

Chappy likes the beach best at twilight anyway, when the toasted crowds have limped off in search of Margaritaville, and the barren beach serves a few kite fliers and surf anglers. Swimming is usually as good as it gets at that hour, too. So plan your dog-along vacation, slather on the SPF, and hit the evening surf with the beach Bowser.

BETHANY BEACH, DE

Parks, Beaches, and Recreation Areas

The Beach 😊 😊 ⬤

No dogs are allowed on this quiet resort town's beach or boardwalk during the season (April through the end of September) and at other times, dogs are allowed all hours if they are on leashes. Okay, mea culpa, we have bent this rule—but only a little bit and never so much that anyone would notice. This is our favorite vacation spot of all the Atlantic Coast beaches because it is such a family-oriented town. Everything is within walking distance and the main street is low key. No wild bars line its main street. Nightlife means buying a glow stick at the kite shop and watching your kid spin it around on a string while the dog goes bonkers. Buying an ice cream cone and watching the players at the pitifully funky, concrete, mini-golf course right in the middle of town is a big night on the town.

The boardwalk is delightful in the early morning hours when you'll find aging joggers and bikers flirting with fitness there—one of the many scheduled activities posted on the town-center calendar board. The boardwalk stretches along the beachfront housing and bandstand area at the heart of town. The beach here is not real wide and almost always takes a beating during bad storms (we had to evacuate one summer when a hurricane came close). Folks on vacation generally love a well-behaved dog like Chappy, and he's never the only one. Lots of dogs accompany their sun-soaking humans to this beach, and you'll see them out walking, on leashes, at all hours.

Although Chappy would take a snowstorm over a tropical island breeze any day—completely unlike the rest of his family—he is usually curious about the sand and the seagulls and sandpipers. But he's timid when it comes to the water—whether it's a bath at home or the ocean on vacation. He's usually happier on our morning walks through town, where he can sniff the sidewalk outside the French fry stand and maybe find a few leftovers. He also likes to leave his mark right in the middle of town on sidewalks that see millions of bare feet as the day gets going. We scoop carefully in this town. It's the law, and it's well posted. Besides, anything less would be awful for everyone—though a few ingrates have yet to learn that lesson.

Dogs on a leash are allowed on the beaches off-season—and October is an optimum month for brisk and breezy solitude here and a little surf fishing. From the Bay Bridge, stay on Route 50 for about 15 miles, then turn left onto Route 404 east. Follow Route 404 to Georgetown; turn right onto Route 113 for about 12 miles, then take Route 26 east 10 miles into Bethany. For more information, contact the Bethany-Fenwick Area Chamber of Commerce, Route 1, Bethany Beach, DE 19930; 302/539-2100 or 800/962-7873.

Restaurants

Di Febo's Cafe and Deli: Carry out subs and even bigger Italian pasta dishes from this sweet little restaurant, which is also a cool refuge on a hot day. 789 Garfield Parkway; 302/539-4550.

Fisher's Popcorn: Yeah, it's not really a restaurant, and popcorn isn't exactly a meal, but for beach eats, this qualifies. This particular brand of caramel popcorn with peanuts is unbeatable. You and the popcorn puppy can stroll right up to the stroll-up window without going inside. 108 Garfield Parkway; 302/537-0155.

Grotto Pizza: Get it to go or have it delivered. Everyone does. Good pizza's one reason. This chain now rules the beaches, though Bethany's Grotto is off the main drag enough that you may have to drive—or let them drive to you. Route 1 in the York Beach Plaza; 302/537-3278.

McCabe's Gourmet Market: Cheese, French bread, pâté, salads, muffins—you can pull together a fancy picnic without going to the grocery store or calling for Grotto's Pizza at this specialty eatery a short jaunt south of downtown Bethany. It's always fun to see what they've got. Route 1 in the York Beach Plaza; 302/539-8550.

Sedona: This southwestern-bent upscale restaurant does things up pretty fancy, but you can convince them to wrap up one of its specialties to take across the street to the Bethany park and dine with your pooch. 26 Pennsylvania Avenue; 302/539-1200.

South Bethany Seafood Market: You can pick it up fresh here to take home and cook yourself, or you can pick up completely made meals—steamed

EARMARK YOUR CALENDAR

Fourth of July Fun: The annual Fourth of July parade is a charming, small-town family affair and everyone's invited. Fire engines turn on the sirens, kids ride their decorated bikes, and families show off homemade floats touting the number of years they've been returning to Bethany Beach. The whole thing lasts about an hour and rolls straight up Atlantic Avenue. For more information call the Bethany-Fenwick Area Chamber of Commerce at 800/962-7873.

Bethany Beach Boardwalk Arts Festival: Stretching from one end of the boardwalk to the other, more than a hundred artists and crafts people set up booths displaying their talents—all of it for sale. And just when you think you can't possibly bear to look at another stained-glass ornament, you come across a watercolorist whose delicate paintings are beyond any expectations you had coming to this fun annual event, generally held the first weekend after Labor Day. 302/539-2100.

Entertainment Extravaganza: Just about every night during the summer, there is some sort of free entertainment on the boardwalk at the central bandstand area. It might be a local dance school or a barbershop quartet or a bungling magician. On good nights we've caught legit bluegrass bands well worth hearing and military bands that were right on key. Stroll up with the dog and check it out around 8 P.M. For more information call the Bethany-Fenwick Area Chamber of Commerce at 800/962-7873.

crabs, fresh-caught tuna, salmon, shrimp, swordfish, and several homemade soups. Call ahead and they'll have it waiting for you. Route 1 in South Bethany; 302/537-1332.

Surf's Up: The best-known and longest-surviving sub and pizza joint in Bethany Beach, this carryout is where you go for foot-long Philly cheese steaks—the best you'll find around here and better than some in the City of Brotherly Love. Other subs are loaded, too. But if the pooch is sharing, tell the lads behind the counter to lighten up on the hot peppers, because they are toasty green ones and too many will definitely hurt. Bethany Town Center at Atlantic Avenue and Garfield Parkway; 302/539-5742.

DEWEY BEACH, DE

Parks, Beaches, and Recreation Areas

The Beach 😺 😺 😺 🐾

Dewey is the beach hangout for young professional singles, where group houses abound and twentysomethings look for summer romance and tanlines.

Capitol Hill workers zoom in every weekend on Thursdays and Fridays during the season, blow off some steam, then zoom out in just enough time to arrive back in D.C. for work Monday morning. People usually spill out the doors of the bars along the Dewey strip on balmy nights. It makes great people-watching and not bad dog watching because this happens to be a most dog friendly beach, too. In tourist season (Memorial Day weekend–Labor Day weekend), dogs are allowed on the beach before 9:30 A.M. and after 5:30 P.M., and out-of-season, they are allowed on the beach all day, every day.

From the Bay Bridge, stay on Route 50 for about 15 miles, and then turn left onto Route 404 east. Follow Route 404 to Georgetown; turn left onto Route 9 and follow it for about 12 miles to Route 1. Turn right and follow Route 1 south about six miles to Dewey Beach. For more information, contact the Rehoboth Beach–Dewey Beach Chamber of Commerce, 5010 Rehoboth Avenue, Rehoboth Beach, DE 19971; 302/227-2233 or 800/441-1329.

Restaurants

Rusty Rudder: Casual tables outside on the dock overlooking the bay, where in the summertime you find bands covering Jimmy Buffett tunes, this long-standing institution just south of Dewey proper will fix up its fried shrimp, crab cakes, cheeseburgers, and just about anything else on its large menu for carryout. And on slow days, you might even get away with the pooch cozying by your feet at one of the dockside tables. Dickinson Street and the Bay; 302/227-3888.

Starboard Restaurant: Open for its all-American breakfast, but Chappy prefers to wait for lunch and the crab cakes, burgers, and wings. Carry it out or on slow days maybe the pooch will catch a break at sitting at one of the rustic deck tables. 2009 Route 1; 302/227-4600.

Sunnyside Up Breakfast Grille & Carryout: In the Ruddertowne complex, this eatery's name pretty much is its menu. Best thing is you can carry out anything they can make—from scrambled eggs in the morning to burgers at night. Dickinson Street and the Bay; 302/227-6644.

Places to Stay

Sea-Esta Motel I and III: Two different hotels with the same name, both accept dogs for a fee of $6 extra per night. Sea-Esta Motel I is closest to the beach and offers 10 ocean-view units in the residential section of Dewey. 2306 Route 1 at Houston Street; 302/227-ROOM (302/227-7666). Sea-Esta Motel III is in downtown Dewey, and its rooms have refrigerators and balconies. 1409 Route 1 at Rodney Street; 302/227-4343.

Rates at the hotels range from about $37–159 per night and go up to $810 weekly during peak season. For more information about any of the Sea-Esta Motels, write P.O. Box 394, Rehoboth Beach, DE 19971 or call 800/436-6591.

FENWICK ISLAND, DE

Parks, Beaches, and Recreation Areas

Fenwick Island State Park 🐾 🐾 🐾 🐾

A concrete submarine observation tower from World War II marks this park with 344 acres of ocean and bay shoreline on either side of Route 1 between Bethany and Ocean City, MD. Dogs are not permitted on the swimming beaches from May 1–September 30, but otherwise they are allowed if on a leash. You'll see signs warning Pets Must Be on a Leash. Generally these are fishing areas but okay for dogs. Walk past the always fragile dunes and you'll find the same pretty beach as elsewhere, just fewer people. The bathhouse has showers. There is a snack food concession and an umbrella and chair rental stand. The day-use fee at the park is around $2.50.

From the Bay Bridge, stay on Route 50 for about 15 miles, then turn left onto Route 404 east. Follow Route 404 to Georgetown, turn right onto Route 113 for about 12 miles, and take Route 26 east 10 miles into Bethany. Turn right on Route 1 and go about five miles south to Fenwick Island. 302/539-1055.

Restaurants

Nick Idoni's: On that night when you're tired of seafood and have a craving for some ribs, go to Nick's and get a rack to go. It comes with all the trimmings, and these ribs will stick to your, ah, hmm. Let's just say they're great barbecued ribs. 145th Street and Coastal Highway; 410/250-1984.

Places to Stay

Sands Motel: Dogs are allowed here in any of the rooms, which range from the deluxe apartment (includes a full-size refrigerator and stove) to an efficiency. This family-owned and cordial motel is on the ocean side of Ocean Highway (Route 1) but is not directly on the oceanfront. Most rooms on the second floor provide a view of the ocean, and it's only a short walk to the beach. Rates in season for a deluxe apartment start at around $135 a night. A standard room starts at around $85. R.D. 3, Box 2093; Fenwick Island, DE 19944; 302/539-7745.

LEWES, DE

Parks, Beaches, and Recreation Areas

The Beach 🐾 🐾 🐾

A small coastal town without the beachy tourist cheesiness and traffic of the sandy locales farther down coast, this seagoing spot has a rustic downtown of shops and wood-paneled restaurants and a small beach past the marina. If peace and quiet are a priority, this might be your destination. Dogs are allowed on the

Fur-Faring Ferry: Of course dogs can ride the **Cape May–Lewes Ferry.** They have to get from here to there, too. Taking the ferry is so much fun that we do it almost every time we vacation in the area. The payoff—a day in Cape May—is a walk back into Victorian times. So if you like boating but couldn't begin to sail or motor your own, try the ferry ride for a day trip. If you happen to get on a refurbished boat (which runs on the weekend), the inside glass-enclosed restaurant offers gourmet meals and hot dogs and hamburgers. But no dogs are allowed inside. The rules ban dogs from where food is being served, but you can take out a quick bite from the food court and sit on deck while the seagulls squawk at you overhead, begging for a bite.

The cruise across Delaware Bay from Lewes to Cape May takes 70 minutes, which is just enough to enjoy it but not enough to get tired of it. The price for a car and driver is $20 in-season. Vehicle passengers 6 and over pay $6.50 each on top of that. Children 5 and under, and dogs, ride free. Call 302/426-1155 or 800/64-FERRY (800/643 3779) for information.

---

beach only before 8 A.M. and after 6:30 P.M. in season (May 1–September 30). From Route 1 follow Savannah Road (which is also Route 1) to the ocean. 302/645-8073.

Cape Henlopen State Park 🐾 🐾 🐾 🐾 👣

This is one of the few places where dogs are allowed year-round, so it's a must-visit spot. It is also Delaware's largest state park with almost 4,000 acres.

Surf fishing is big here, so it's a good idea to abide by the leash law to keep the pooch from getting hooked. No pets are permitted on swimming beaches from May 1 through September 30, but the Point Crossing area is open to them. It tends to be much less crowded but doesn't have the nice bathhouse, snack bar, or other amenities. The dunes rise up majestically, and the views of the ocean are spectacular. No dogs are allowed on the nature trails in the park, which wind through many of the dunes, but dogs are allowed on the roughly paved Salt Marsh Spur.

The park is home to many plants and animals and contains historic and prehistoric features, which is the reason for a lot of the rules. But it's wild looking, and it's a beach that allows dogs. So just stick to the designated areas and have a great time. Fees are collected in the summer and on weekends and holidays. Be sure to call before you come because the beach sometimes closes in June and July to protect endangered shorebird nesting areas. And you'll want to make sure its dog policies haven't changed.

Camping, which is about one mile from the beach, is available for tents, trailers, and RVs. The only rule is that pets must be attended to at all times. Picnic

---

tables, electric and water hookups, and a bathhouse are available. The park does not take reservations, and the fees for non-Delaware residents start at $18 for one of the 159 sites. For more information on camping, call 302/645-2103. The park is located north of Rehoboth Beach. From Route 404, take Route 1 for about five miles, turn right onto Route 9, and follow the signs to the park. 302/645-8983.

Restaurants

Lighthouse Restaurant: That deck overlooking the canal would be *so* nice, but don't expect to be able to sit there, especially at the height of the season. Rules prevail. You can, however, carry out whatever seafood or other menu item tempts you. At the corner of Anglers Road and Savannah Road (Route 1), just over the Lewes-Rehoboth Canal; 302/645-6271.

Places to Stay

Cape Henlopen State Park Campground: See Cape Henlopen State Park, above.

MILLVILLE, DE

Parks, Beaches, and Recreation Areas

Holts Landing State Park 🐾 🐾 ½

You've left the beach and decided to take a different route to avoid the traffic. You're heading out Route 26 from Bethany and you see the brown state park signs pointing to Holts Landing. Go ahead and turn in. You won't find a very crowded place. What you will find is 203 acres right on Indian River Inlet Bay. Picnic tables are plentiful under large shade trees throughout the park. There are also two ball fields and a boat ramp. We almost always see someone fishing or crabbing at low tide here, too. It's a very peaceful spot that offers a grand view of the entire bay. The only drawback is that it can get a little buggy, but the horse flies bothered us more than they did Chappy. Expect to pay a small fee during the summer season, and remember to keep your dog on a leash.

The park is open dawn–dusk. From Route 13, take Route 26 toward Millville and look for the signs on the right. P.O. Box 76, Millville, DE 19970; 302/539-9060.

REHOBOTH, DE

Parks, Beaches, and Recreation Areas

Delaware Seashore State Park 🐾 🐾 🐾 🐾

The park actually straddles both sides of Route 1 two miles south of Rehoboth Beach and covers some 2,500 acres. Dogs are permitted in any nonswimming parts of the beach areas all year around (there are six miles of ocean beaches), but they must be on a leash and attended to at all times.

The campground has 434 sites open to campers with tents, trailers, or RVs. About a quarter of the sites provide water, electric, and sewage hookups from mid-March to mid-November. While it's good camping, there won't be any weenie roasts with the dog there, because fires are prohibited on the beach.

Located right at the Indian River Inlet, this is a great spot because you're about as close to it all as you can get. Watch the boats come and go. Watch anglers try to pull in some blues. But don't expect to take a dip here; it's too rocky. There are 144 sites with water, electric, and sewage, 133 sites with no hookups. Rates start at about $25 a night.

Open 8 A.M.–sunset year-round. From Route 50, take a left on route 404 and then a right on Route 1 to the Indian River Inlet between Dewey and Bethany. Route 1 Inlet 850, Rehoboth Beach, DE 19971; 302/227-2800.

Rehoboth Public Beach 🐾 🐾 🐾

One of the more elegant beach scenes along the mid-Atlantic, Rehoboth is home to gourmet restaurants, wide beaches, more shopping than any of the others, and the reputation as being the favorite gay destination out here. Like most of the Atlantic beaches, dogs are not allowed on the beach or boardwalk from April through October. Rehoboth Beach–Dewey Beach Chamber of Commerce, 501 Rehoboth Avenue, Rehoboth Beach, DE 19971; 302/227-2233 or 800/441-1329.

Restaurants

The Camel's Hump: In the mood for Middle Eastern decor and Mediterranean food? You can get it to go. 21 Baltimore Avenue; 302/227-0947.

Denardo's by the Sea: Seafood and crabs all ready for you to carry out. 330 Rehoboth Avenue; 302/227-0947.

Obie's by the Beach: A Rehoboth institution for two decades, this friendly boardwalk restaurant serves great burgers, Caesar salads, crab-cake sandwiches and ribs, and will package it up for you and the pooch. On Wednesday nights, there's usually a band, so don't go off too far. Olive Avenue and the Boardwalk; 302/227-6261.

Places to Stay

Cape Suites: A two-bedroom unit goes for $115–135 a night, and dogs are fine at this "gay friendly" hotel. No restrictions. No extra fees. 47 Baltimore Avenue, Rehoboth Beach, DE 19971; 302/226-3342.

Corner Cupboard Bed and Breakfast: A few rooms are available for dogs, with a $20-per-day charge. Rates range from $90–230 a night, but that includes breakfast at this friendly inn. However, dogs are not allowed in the dining room. 50 Park Avenue, Rehoboth Beach, DE 19971; 302/227-8553.

EARMARK YOUR CALENDAR

A Whale of a Time: Held annually for about 20 years, the **Whale Sandcastle Contest** is worth seeing on Fisherman's Beach at the north end of Rehoboth in early August. The detailed artistry is phenomenal—and all destined to wash away at high tide. Just don't let your pup wet down one of these amazing sand sculptures ahead of time. For more information, call 302/645-2265.

Out of Season: If you like the beach in the fall when it can still be quite beautiful and warm, plan for an early October visit and hit the annual **Fall Sidewalk Sale.** The Chamber of Commerce can give you more details at 302/227-2233 or 800/441-1329.

Delaware Seashore State Park Campground: See Delaware Seashore State Park, above.

Holly Lake Campsite: About 10 miles from Rehoboth, dogs are welcome if on a leash and under control (well, let's hope so). But it offers a lot, including 1,100 sites, pool, playgrounds, petting zoo, and bathhouses. Rate is $35 per night. It's on Route 24, about six miles west of Route 1, about a 15 minute drive to the beach. (There is no lake, by the way; it's "more like a swamp," says the manager. R.D. 6, Box 141, Millsboro, DE 19966; 302/945-3410.

3-Season Camping Resort: West of Rehoboth by about two miles, this is for trailers and RVs only; prices start at $40 a night. Dogs are allowed, but tents aren't. The resort has a swimming pool, arcade, miniature golf, and beach shuttle. It's located on Route 273 out of town. 727 Country Club Road, Rehoboth, MD 19971; 302/227-2564 or 800/635-4996.

ANNAPOLIS, MD

Annapolis became Maryland's capital in 1695 but has been here since 1649, when it got its start as an early American seaport. In other words, it's older than old by American standards. Many of the quaint houses and public buildings were built more than 200 years ago, but now house stylish boutiques and quaint shops. It's easy to spend a day tracing the abundant history through town, shopping, eating, or just strolling with your dog.

But it's just as easy to connect with the Chesapeake Bay culture that thrives in this port town. The Bay is the heartbeat of Annapolis. About 45 minutes from Washington and from Baltimore, this quaint capital city looks much the same as it did way back when. The State House dominates and is the oldest state capitol in continuous legislative use in the country. At night if you're walking around the waterfront, look up at the lighted dome for a postcard-perfect view.

Don't be surprised if you meet new canine friends walking these historic cobbled sidewalks. You might even meet a gorgeous Chesapeake Bay retriever, the sporting breed named the official dog of Maryland in 1964.

The city is all the more charming for its collection of 17th- and 18th-century houses—the most in a single city in the country. The National Historic District is a tapestry of modest and great buildings, all within walking distance of each other. Archaeologists constantly are roping off areas for historic digs.

The best starting place for a doggy tour is the City Dock. This area along the waterfront lined with fine restaurants, a marketplace, and quaint shops that stretches up Main Street and Maryland Avenue is the center of historic Annapolis. It has been for 300 years, and since the time when warehouses, shipbuilding shops, and taverns circled the dock, its skyline has changed remarkably little. Check out the dockside plaque honoring Kunta Kinte, the ancestor of the late Alex Haley, author of *Roots*, whose research into the 18th-century slave trade and his family's past brought him to this dock.

Pick up the free walking-tour guide from the Maritime Museum, located near the City Dock at 77 Main Street, if you and the dog want to follow the footsteps of history through town. Chappy recommends it because this is a great strolling town. The bottom line in Annapolis really is the simplest of pleasures—sitting by the dock of the bay, wasting time.

Parks, Beaches, and Recreation Areas

Baltimore & Annapolis Trail 🐾 🐾

Stretching 13.3 miles from near Annapolis to Glen Burnie, this trail runs through old forests, working farmlands, and urban and suburban neighborhoods that today line the old rail bed of the old Baltimore & Annapolis Short Line Railroad. Available to walkers, runners, cyclists, equestrians, roller skaters, and skateboard enthusiasts alike, this eight-foot-wide, paved swath through parkland that measures 66 feet across can get crowded. Two drawbacks: The Annapolis Trailhead starts about three miles from downtown across the Severn River, and dog lovers who tire of bicyclists zooming by and not knowing trail-passing etiquette will grow weary. When less crowded, however, this is a relaxed hike with the dog in which you'll spot rabbits and squirrels scampering and lots of birds, including owls. There are remnants of the old railway here and there.

The trail is open from sunrise to sunset. From historic Annapolis, take Roscoe Rowe Boulevard to Route 50; head east across the Severn River Bridge. Immediately exit onto Ritchie Highway (Route 450) toward Severna Park and turn left immediately past the underpass onto Boulters Way and Winchester Road where you see signs for parking. Trail headquarters and the ranger station are located about seven miles up the trail on Earleigh Heights Road, in Severna Park. 410/222-6244.

Quiet Waters Park 🐾 🐾 🐾 🐾 🐕 🦴

This extraordinary park is anything but quiet. The whistling of frogs in the tall grasses near the entrance made Chappy's ears perk up on his first visit. But keep cruising into the park because it only gets better at these 336 acres of woodlands, grassy areas, beaches and hiking and biking trails. It's a beautiful park, an artistic park. And it's got everything.

There are more than six miles of trails, some of them just footpaths. But there's one exceptional paved trail around the park that dogs, in-line skaters, and bicyclists use—not to mention lots of strollers.

DIVERSIONS

Walking State Circle: The cobbled old brickwork underfoot and the historic buildings in every direction make this a quaint environment for strolling with the leashed pup. At the center of it all is the oldest state house in the country in continuous use—since 1772. Chappy's sense of history ends where the previous dog's scent begins, but this historic quadrant in the middle of Annapolis just brims with the past. It's the site of George Washington's resignation as commander-in-chief after the Revolution; it's where the Treaty of Paris was signed; and the State House served as the capitol of the United States from 1783 to 1784. These days, it's also the center for the best shopping. 410/974-3400.

Chaos Theory: Annapolis is home to one of the most laid-back dog-friendly hiking clubs you'll find anywhere. It's called CHAOS partly because that's the acronym for the Chesapeake Hiking and Outdoors Society. The club has no rules, bylaws, or requirements for membership—that's the other reason for the name. These down-to-earth folks go hiking, biking, camping, canoeing—hey, whatever, as long as it's outside and fun. Experienced hikers are welcome on the monthly Sunday trip, and so are beginners—and so are dogs. Usually CHAOS members go for day trips an hour or two outside of Annapolis. Typically they meet at Graul's Market at Taylor Avenue and Rowe Boulevard and carpool to the site. The first Wednesday of each month they potluck at a member's home and decide where the next trip will be. Anyone can join: Just pay $12 a year, which helps pay for the monthly newsletter and trip schedule. Guests can join in on trips, too, for $1. For more information, call 410/867-0183.

Say Plebes: The beautiful grounds of the U.S. Naval Academy are dog friendly so long as you clean up after your leashed pup. Beneath the chapel, which the dog can't visit, is the tomb of John Paul Jones. Out in the "Yard," however, dogs can sniff the many monuments to naval heroes—as well as the statue of Tecumseh, the midshipman's saint of academics. The U.S. Naval Academy is located at King George Street and the Severn River; 410/263-6933.

Take a walk around the park and you'll find it is beautifully landscaped with sculptures tucked into meadows and clearings through the park. The visitor center is air-conditioned and doubles as an art gallery, party place, and cafeteria. In winter, a fire roars in the fireplace. There are indoor tables where the dog can't eat, as well as tables outside where the dog can dine with you on the grand Victorian porch overlooking a pond that becomes a skating rink in winter.

Check out the fancy English gardens next to the visitor center, where you and the proper pupster can walk the brick paths, find more sculpture, and lounge undisturbed on the wooden benches with wrought-iron sides next to the old-fashioned street lamps.

One of the best playgrounds we've seen is a short walk over a slight hill from the pond; adjacent to the playground was a small open field where a couple and their child played with a golden puppy who had leash on. Paths take you through woodsy settings—some down to the river.

Though dogs aren't supposed to go leashless at this lovely waterside parkland, the totally dog-friendly management here opened a 1.3 acre dog park within the park in December 2001. It's a high-quality, fenced-in dog run that dedicates about a third to smaller dogs. But get this—because so many dog owners had previously let their pooches swim down at the river's edge, this park also opened a "dog beach" that is exclusively for dog swimming down on the South River, about a quarter mile from the dog park.

The dog-community response? "We have been swamped with people. We've seen attendance and revenue go up 25 percent and a fair portion of that is attributable to the dog park," says Michael Murdoch, superintendent of the Quiet Waters Park who lobbied for the dog park. He and his wife, Dee Dee Miller, take their own two dogs—Flowerpott Murdoch, a golden-lab-hound mix, and Hazel Teapott Miller, a rat terrier—everywhere they go and fully understand other people who do. But he also thinks it's important that dog lovers keep in mind that everyone who visits a park like Quiet Waters doesn't want someone else's pooch jumping up on them. "We hardly go anywhere without our dogs," he says, "but I do realize people come to parks like this for a lot of different reasons."

The park is open 7 A.M.–dusk, but it is closed on Tuesday. From Route 50, take Route 665 (Aris T. Allen Boulevard, which becomes Forest Drive) and go about 3.5 miles. Turn right on Hillsmere Drive; the park entrance is about 500 feet on the right. Admission is $4. 410/222-1777.

Thomas Point Park 🐾 🐾 🐾

What was making that foghorn-like noise out in the water? Don's 83-year-old mother, Alice, had some interesting theories even the second time around. This park stands the test of time: Walking out to the end of this 44-acre park and sitting on the narrow peninsula stretching out into where South River meets Chesapeake Bay, we again and again are awed by the power and the beauty of the Bay. The noise? Thomas Lighthouse offshore still blasting its sea-sounding warning signal like clockwork.

Benches on the point are the perfect spot to watch the sunset with your dog or any significant other—human or otherwise. The big picnic pavilion and grill would be a perfect place for a large family reunion or picnic. Walking, biking, jogging, bird-watching, and fishing are all allowed—but you've got to stop at the log cabin at the entrance to get a permit for these uses. Expect a $10 fee in the summer months.

Only the narrow main road (the big dinosaur sculpture tucked into the woods by the side of the road is an odd surprise) and one trail lead out into this fragile environment that extends into the bay. It's so fragile, in fact, that you can expect the front gate to be closed when you arrive. That's standard here to discourage tourists from tromping through. This little park, you see, is for the pure-hearted, ecology-lovin' traipsers only. For dog lovers, that means bring the baggies to pick up any poop and make sure Fido doesn't run wild (leashes are required) and give coronaries to the many waterfowl that call this home. This great place doesn't provide all the conveniences of some developed parks, but its location can't be beat.

The park is open daily, 8 A.M.–sunset; the park office is open Wednesday–Sunday, 10 A.M.–noon. From Route 50, take Route 665 (Aris T. Allen Boulevard), which turns into Forest Drive about three miles thereafter (past Carrolton and Edgewood Roads). Take a right on Arundel on the Bay Road and make a sharp left turn on Thomas Point Road. The park is at 3890 Thomas Point Road. 410/222-1969.

Truxtun Park 🐾 🐾

This 70-acre wooded area with 12 tennis courts, four basketball courts, three ball fields, an outdoor swimming pool, and picnic sites is tucked into a housing area, running lengthwise down the side of one street. It's not a big, beautiful park, but it does seem to see a lot of use from neighboring apartment buildings and from anglers and boaters who use the ramp for launching. The quaint waterside scene will impress you. Although the leash law is in effect, if your dog is a swimmer, no doubt a little dunk would be fine with everyone here. This is a water-lovin' locale where folks own boats bigger than their apartments.

Back behind the ball fields, a very bumpy road leads down to a more swampy area and a wooden bridge that cuts through over to another neighborhood. It's a nice enough walk, but watch out for bugs.

The park is open dawn to dusk. From Route 50, take Route 665 (Aris T. Allen Boulevard), which turns into Forest Drive about three miles thereafter (past Carrolton and Edgewood Roads). Turn left on Bay Ridge Avenue and left again on Tyler Avenue, which forks into Hilltop Lane. The park is on the right. 410/263-7958.

Restaurants

Ego Alley: With checkered tablecloths and shrimp by the pound, this is a funky, in-your-face, late-night place that will wrap to go its crab cakes, salads, burgers, whatever's on the menu. Probably wrap it in a menu if you like. It's open until 2 A.M., even on weekdays. 133 Dock Street; 410/263-3353.

Einstein Brothers Bagels: With sidewalk benches along this stretch of shops and eateries across the street from where the leisure boats tie up, this is a great place to grab one of the bagel sandwich concoctions these folks are noted for and have a seat outside with the pooch. Don't forget to buy one of the hard-chew doggy bagels for about a buck to keep the sidekick occupied. 122 Dock Street; 410/280-3500.

Harris Crab House: Okay, technically this longtime institution is indeed located at Kent Narrows, but we love it so much we just needed to add it in the mix. A traditional Maryland crab house that covers its picnic tables inside and out with brown butcher paper, this is a popular destination for the boating set, who tie up at the dock beside the drawbridge and dine. Other choices on the menu are excellent, including the burgers and the Styrofoam cups filled with spiced steamed shrimp, but it's nearly an atrocity to order anything but the crabs here. If you're nice, the bartender who oversees dockside tables outside just might let your well-behaved pup sit by your feet, while you watch the fishing boat crews flip the day's catch of blues or rockfish on the dock. And order one of the large, hard-frozen, homemade Nutty Buddy ice creams for dessert. It's well worth the short drive from Annapolis over the Bay Bridge to the Kent Narrows exit. 425 North Kent Narrows Way, Grasonville; 410/827-9500.

Mangia: You can hardly walk past this enticing pizzeria without getting lured into its downstairs clamor of people jammed at the carryout counter, people eating at the stand-up counter, people shopping from the grocery shelves and drink cooler. Upstairs, there's casual dining with tables, where the menu selections range from bruschetta to spicy shrimp to traditional Maryland-style crab cakes. The upstairs doesn't include dogs, so stick to the disorderly downstairs where you can get pizza and hoagies to go. 81 Main Street; 410/268-1350.

Market House: If you have any doubt where to tell someone to meet you, this is the answer. If you and the wharf rat are strolling dockside and require a little nourishment, tie him outside and step into one of the must-visit eateries in historic downtown. Like an old-fashioned marketplace with stalls and kiosks selling different to-go foods and stand-up eating counters for those who want to eat there, it is located at the head of City Dock. Fresh seafood is the main thing—steamed shrimp, crab cakes, raw bars. There are also pizzas and pastries, deli sandwiches and fried chicken, cheeses and fresh-baked breads. City Dock; 410/269-0941.

Middleton Tavern: Amazing but true—this rustic, wooden-paneled tavern began serving ale in 1750 as the last watering hole before catching Samuel Horatio Middleton's ferry over to Maryland's Eastern Shore across the bay. George Washington stopped here; Thomas Jefferson stopped here; so did Benjamin Franklin; and so can you, though your loyal pup can't enter these hallowed halls of history with you—nor are dogs allowed to sit by the outside tables. But the kitchen will bag your lunch or dinner to go, so order the seafood chowder and the touch-spicy Maryland crab cakes. The burgers are old-fashioned good, and the crab balls are a smart alternative to the cakes if you've got to share with the pup. 2 Market Space; 410/263-3323.

Pony Espresso: If you're in the mood for just a snack and a latte, stop in here across the street from the visitor center. Besides fresh-roasted coffee just about every which way, Annapolis's original espresso bar also carries accompanying baked goods and pastries. 33 1/2 West Street; 410/280-6160.

Starbucks: These friendly java joints will perk up your dog hikes with a tasty morning café au lait or an afternoon Frappuccino, plus the assortment of edible accessories. 124 Dock Street; 410/268-6551.

Storm Brothers Ice Cream Factory: Ice cream coneheads absolutely must stop by this ice cream parlor for a taste of its homemade, creamy blends and shakes. 130 Dock Street; 410/263-3376.

Places to Stay

Capitol KOA Campground: About 15 to 20 minutes from Annapolis, you can camp here with your dog. It's a nice wooded area, including a pool, hiking trails, game room, and more. They ask that you have only one pet per site and that you keep your happy camper pooch on a leash at all times. The fee is $25 a night with no hookup; $30 with a hookup. Shuttles are available to Washington and Baltimore mass transit—but someone will have to stay behind with the pup, who isn't allowed on the bus. The campground is closed during the winter months (November–March). 768 Cecil Avenue, Millersville, MD 21108; 410/923-2771.

Days Inn–Bay Bridge: Located about one mile from the Bay Bridge, this two-story motel welcomes dogs and charges no fee or deposit. There are two stipulations: You must stay in a smoking room (definitely something to keep in mind), and you must not leave your dog unattended in the room—always a good rule. Hotels sometimes relegate doggy guests to smoking rooms because they think other guests who are allergic to pets are also bothered by cigarette smoke and odors. Tibetan terriers like Chappy are danderless and shed-free dogs that rarely trouble people with allergies (other hypo-allergenic breeds include Wheaten terriers and Portuguese water dogs). Because we have very low tolerance of cigarette smoke and odors, this hotel doesn't work for us and Chappy. Rates start at $99 for a weekend night, depending on the season. 1542 Whitehall Road, Annapolis, MD 21401; 410/974-4440.

EARMARK YOUR CALENDAR

No Boat Dogs: The **Spring Boat Show** is one of the biggest festivals in Annapolis, usually held in April. But the problem is: no dogs allowed. But there's no law against walking around with your salty dog, just to check out the scene. Or, leave the pooch at home if you're hot on checking out the boats. Otherwise, flaunt the pooch outside the gate and have fun in town anyway. Yeah! Power to the pooches! The event takes place at the City Dock. 410/268-8828.

Deck the Sailboats with Boughs of Holly: Every year about two Saturdays before Christmas, a procession of yachts and sailing vessels all decorated for the holidays makes its way around the inner harbor of Annapolis. Best spots for viewing are the City Dock and the marinas of Eastport. We're not sure Chappy quite knows what he's seeing, but we like it, and he enjoys sniffing the salt air. Plus it's free. 410/280-0445.

Jonas Green House Bed-and-Breakfast: In 1738 colonial printer and patriot Jonas Green and his new bride moved into this charming house on what is now Charles Street. The house remained in the Green family through the years and is now considered one of the oldest residences in Annapolis. When you stay with your dog and whomever else you bring along, you'll see the original floor, fireplace area, and old cooking fireplace. The antiques add to making it feel like you're taking a step back in time. It's said to be one of Annapolis's two oldest residences, but the amenities are first-rate, with bathrobes and radios in the rooms. In the large Anne Catherine room, with a good view of the State House dome, there is a private bath and the rate is around $160, including tax, breakfast, and parking. That's the most expensive room. The other two are $115 and $140. 124 Charles Street, Annapolis, MD 21401; 410/263-5985.

Radisson Inn–Annapolis: Whether staying in Annapolis or just driving through, this is a convenient dog-friendly hotel. There are walking areas outside this six-story hotel and room service when it's time to chow down. A special one-time dog rate of $25 covers the pooch, though management does ask that before checking out, you have housekeeping come by the room and check for damage (not that it's necessary with our well-behaved Chappy). Other little rules concern dogs as well. Rates start at $99. 210 Holiday Court, Annapolis, MD 21401; 410/224-3150 or 800/465-4329.

Residence Inn–Annapolis: Maybe it was the continental breakfast that lured Chappy in. Most likely it was just that, yes, dogs are welcome here, and out back there's even a pet run, as they call it at the front desk. A nice little path with some grass and woods, this "pet run" is to a big dog what the landing strip in Saint Bart's is to a big plane—but it's the thought that counts. The only real drawback is that you need to drive 10 minutes to get to downtown Annapolis. But finding a nice place like this to stay with the sleepy pooch is probably worth it. You have to ante up a $100 nonrefundable deposit for cleaning. Rates start at $149. 170 Admiral Cochran Drive, Annapolis, MD 21401; 410/573-0300 or 800/331-3131.

ASSATEAGUE, MD

This celebrated beach home of the feral horses is one of the nicest untouristy and natural beach areas along the Atlantic Coast—so natural, in fact, that some stretches of it are known as clothing-optional beaches. Located on a barrier island south of Maryland's beach towns, this idyllic and sometimes buggy destination is also home to some endangered wildlife, so domesticated canines are invited to limited areas only.

Parks, Beaches, and Recreation Areas

Assateague Island National Shoreline 🐾 🐾 🐾

Pets are prohibited in the Chincoteague National Wildlife Refuge, Assateague State Park, and all backcountry camping areas on these two side-by-side islands at the southernmost end of the coastal stretch of where Maryland meets Virginia. That leaves the town of Chincoteague and the Assateague Island National Seashore on the Maryland side of the island for dog lovers and their sun-loving pups to explore. Dogs must stay on six-foot leashes, even when swimming these waters.

In fact, they're so itchy about dogs visiting the largely undisturbed natural beauty of Chincoteague and Assateague that the brochure put out by the National Park Service starts with these ominous words: "Please leave pets at home." The rules are strictly enforced here because dogs and other domestic animals can disturb the famous wild ponies that live on the islands, as well as the shorebirds that nest in the sand and in the marsh grasses. The National Park Service warns that blowing sand and salt spray are hard on the eyes and feet of dogs anyway, and that insects that can get especially nasty here can endanger your pooch's health—or at least drive him to chasing his tail in circles. Poison ivy, mosquitoes, and ticks are abundant on the islands from spring through fall. Yikes!

Make a drive-by visit to Assateague's dog-friendly and beautiful national seashore, but don't set foot in the state park next door, and don't even think about crossing through the chain-link fence into Chincoteague's wildlife refuge. You can decide if those restrictions are inviting enough to stay overnight on either side.

The Assateague shoreline and town of Chincoteague are open all hours. To get to Assateague from the Maryland's other Atlantic beaches, take Route 50 west out of Ocean City; go about 1.5 miles and turn left on Route 611. Drive six miles south past the visitor center to the Island. To reach the town of Chincoteague, take Route 50 west out of Ocean City, drive about six miles, and turn left onto Route 113 south. Drive about 35 miles, turn left onto Route 175, and go another seven miles into the town. For more information, call Assateague Island National Seashore, 7206 National Seashore Lane, Berlin, MD 21811; 410/641-1441. You can also contact the Chincoteague Chamber of Commerce, P.O. Box 258 (Maddox Beach Road), Chincoteague, VA 23336; 804/336-6161.

Places to Stay

Assateague National Park Campground: Despite the fact that dogs cannot go a lot of places on the island, they are allowed here in the 104 oceanside and 49 bayside sites with picnic area, nature trails, fishing, boating, and beach. Just call for a reservation; sites start at $14 a night. 7206 National Seashore Lane, Berlin, MD 21811; 410/641-3030 or 800/365-2267.

Garden and Sea Inn: Pets aren't just allowed; they're welcome at this charming 1802 inn, complete with gingerbread trim. Dogs often come to visit Chincoteague but are not permitted on the south end of Assateague. Here's a place for those visiting to stay. Large rooms with luxurious linens, antiques, fresh flowers, stained-glass windows, and private bath and air-conditioning are among the amenities. Chef/owner Tom Baker is known for his elegant entrees prepared with fresh local seafood. A hearty breakfast is included in the rates, which range from $75–185. P.O. Box 275, New Church, VA 23415; 800/824-0672.

Tom's Cove Campground: Dogs are allowed here, and it's right on Chincoteague. The typical sorts of rules are in effect: walk only in designated dog-walk areas, clean up after your dog, keep your dog on a leash at all times, and do not take her into buildings or swimming areas. Please don't leave the dog unattended. Otherwise, have fun at the 914 sites, some without hookups, many with water, electricity, and cable. Amenities include shower rooms, an Olympic-size pool, saltwater swimming area, live bands on weekends, bingo on some Fridays, church services on Sundays, a playground, fishing piers for crabbing or dropping a line, a marina, and an air-conditioned pavilion. No phone reservations are accepted, and a $20 deposit per campsite is required. Rates start at $27 per day. Mail your request to Tom's Cove Park, P.O. Box 122, Chincoteague, VA 23336; 757/336-6498.

EASTERN SHORE, MD

This picturesque territory where time almost stands still sprawls eastward from the Chesapeake Bay to the Atlantic Coast and is the stuff of novels and water-color landscapes—not to mention dog-friendly inns and bed-and-breakfasts. Home of the blue-crab culture, it boasts charming and historic little Bayside and rural towns, from the seaside Saint Michaels and time-warped Tilghman Island to the urban Easton and breezy Salisbury. Driving through its heartland along Route 50, travelers go through sight-shifts as dramatic as skipjack-sailed Bay inlets and rivers, acres of tobacco and cornfields, even forests and marshes.

Places to Stay

Combsberry: Giant weeping willows stand guard over this 18th-century English country manor on the Eastern Shore. Built in 1730, Combsberry is set among the magnolias on the banks of Island Creek, so walks with your dog are filled with inviting sights, sounds, and smells. Being a half-mile off the road, there's plenty of room to roam. When you come back, you'll probably be staying in the Oxford cottage, which has a view of the water—as do all the rooms. Jacuzzis, fireplaces, and the English garden mix old and new graciously. A full breakfast, as well as afternoon tea or wine and cheese, is included in the rate. Expect to pay about $350 a night, depending on the season. 4837 Evergreen Road, Oxford, MD 21654; 410/226-5353.

Huntingfield Manor: You and your dog are welcome to stay in the guest cottage but not in the actual manor house, which is the centerpiece of a 70-acre working farm that dates back to the middle 1600s on the Eastern Shore. We're talking old. The farmhouse is 136 feet long and only one room wide. The inn has six rooms, each with its own private bath, but if you come with the pooch, you'll be in your own cottage about 50 feet from the main house. Walk through the peacocks wandering the grounds to get there. It's got its own kitchen, air-conditioning, and full bath. 4928 Eastern Neck Road, Rock Hall, MD 21661; 410/639-7779 or 800/720-8788, which is a reservation service.

Kemp House Inn: The little town of Saint Michaels is well known as an Eastern Shore getaway. It's a quaint little place, and dogs are welcome at the Kemp House Inn, which is right in the middle of it all. Expect to stay in the cottage with queen bed and cathedral ceiling; it's reserved for travelers with pets. But do check out the main house, which is filled with period antiques, patchwork quilts, and wing chairs. There is a two-night minimum. Rates for one of the seven rooms in the historic home are $95, but you should expect to pay $140 a night for the cottage. 412 South Talbot Street, Saint Michaels, MD 21663; 410/745-2243.

River House Inn: A dog could have his day here on Maryland's Eastern Shore. Generally dogs are asked to stay in a cottage separate from the main house. Lucky dogs! The cottages have breathtaking views of the Pocomoke

River, not to mention fridges, coffee makers, and whirlpool tubs. Call ahead and discuss it, which is always a good idea anyway. The cottage rates are $225–250 a night and that includes a full breakfast. There is a $10 pet fee per night. In the town of Snow Hill you can canoe, boat, bike, fish, or golf. The old brick sidewalks of the little village, incorporated in 1686, will take you and your four-legged friend past homes that are well over 100 years old. Chincoteague, Assateague, Ocean City, and Crisfield are all only about a half hour away. Canoes and boats can be rented one block from the inn for exploring the Pocomoke River, or use the inn's pontoon boat to cruise around and check out the wildlife. 201 East Market Street, Snow Hill, MD 21863; 410/632-2722.

River Inn at Rolph's Wharf: Dogs are welcome to come visit the River Inn's five acres right on the Chester River. The Victorian farmhouse was built in the 1830s and features six guest rooms, each with a private bath. There is a swimming pool, or you can take a dip in the river. Tennis, antique shops, bike rentals, and hiking trails, as well as shopping, are all within one mile. The inn is only two miles from historic Chestertown, which makes a nice little jog. Rates are $105–125, and a continental breakfast with home-baked breads is included. There is a $10 pet fee. The inn is located at 1008 Rolph's Wharf Road, Chestertown, MD 21620; 410/778-6389.

FREDERICK, MD

Less than an hour's drive from Washington or Baltimore, it seems like a wonderfully small town, yet it's one of the state's biggest cities. The streets in the attractive, 33-block historic section are so quaint that you can spend pleasant hours strolling with the dog (leashed, as required) while window-shopping antique stores and reading menus in restaurant windows. Stately mansions and restored brick town houses built like they don't build them anymore set the tone for downtown. On the outskirts, the roads are like easy rollercoasters passing through open fields and horse farms contained by white fences. As the poet John Greenleaf Whittier put it, "The clustered spires of Frederick stand, green-walled by the hills of Maryland."

It is easy to believe this town dates back to 1745, then called Fredericktown for Frederick Calvert, the sixth Lord of Baltimore. This was a colonial frontier settlement, the gateway for pioneers who ventured into the dangers over the mountains and westward. Patriots in this town claimed the first defiant act of open rebellion against the British Crown: They burned a copy of the Stamp Act at the courthouse steps. Other American heroes called this home, too—Francis Scott Key was born here; John Hanson, technically the nation's first president, lived here. It was also the home of Barbara Fritchie, whose flag-waving defiance of Confederate General Stonewall Jackson and his troops Whittier embellished in his poem about the town.

Today Frederick's history attracts tourists and Civil War buffs, Hood College (ranked one of the nation's best small colleges) attracts scholars and students, and its friendly restaurants, tolerant accommodations, and excursion opportunities make it ideal for dog-day afternoons.

National Parks

Catoctin Mountain Park 🐾 🐾 🐾 🐾

The 18-mile drive from historic Frederick to this 6,000-acre national park is a must for dog lovers in search of the complete forest-hiking side trip. In itself this is reason enough to spend a day or two based in Frederick. The park is located on a spur of the Blue Ridge Mountains just west of tiny Thurmont, Maryland. The sight of the broad white-water streams and rock formations watercolorists paint will make keeping your eyes on the road difficult as you drive into the parklands.

About two miles from Thurmont, you can pull into a small side-of-the-road parking area and tackle the strenuous, uphill trail to Chimney Rock (elevation 1,419 feet). The 2.6-mile round-trip hike will take about 75 minutes. Unless your pooch is a conditioned hiker, however, Rover won't make this steep ascent—and neither will you. So follow lounge-dog Chappy's lead and take one of the longer but less steep paths from inside the park. It will take twice as long, but the footing is better and the flatter path is easier to hike.

Stop by the visitor center about 3.5 miles in, and the rangers will give you a trail map. The rugged grounds and gorgeous eastern-hardwood forest will amaze you. Until the 1930s mountain farmers, lumber companies, and charcoal manufacturers worked these acres. When the Great Depression came, the federal government bought the property and put people to work recreating it into a recreational parkland—that eventually included Camp David, the presidential retreat.

What is open to the public is 25 miles of dog-friendly hiking trails. They range in difficulty from the easy half-mile Blue Blazes Whiskey Trail to the hard-core Wolf Rock Trail that takes two hours to hike to its scenic overlook.

For the less rigorous, the park has well-planned picnic areas, such as the small Hog Rock and huge Chestnut (grills, tables, bathrooms) picnic areas. Dogs on leashes are welcome here. Head all the way back to Owens Creek (about 11 miles from the visitor center), where the pooch can take a dip along Foxville-Deerfield Road near the Owens Creek picnic area.

You and the happy camper can even put up the pup tents at the Owens Creek Campground, open April 15–early November. Each of 51 first-come, first-serve sites in this family-oriented campground provides a picnic table, grill, lamppost, and tent pad. No water or electrical hookups, but there are centrally located bathrooms and hot showers at one station. The park prohibits dogs in the 29 rustic log cabins down the road at Camp Misty Mount.

The park is open daylight hours year-round. The visitor center is open Monday–Thursday, 10 A.M.–4:30 P.M.; Friday, 10 A.M.–5 P.M.; and Saturday and Sunday, 8:30 A.M.–5 P.M. It is closed on winter federal holidays. From Frederick take Route 15 north, turn left on Route 77 (look for the exit sign to Catoctin Mountain Park). Along Route 77, don't venture to the woodlands south of the highway with the pooch because that's Cunningham Falls State Park, and it strictly prohibits dogs. The visitor center will be about 3.5 miles on the right. 301/663-9330 or 301/663-9388.

Monocacy National Battlefield 🐾 🐾 ½

Only a small part of this 11,050-acre battlefield turned parkland is open to the public. The rest of its rolling hills and pretty woods are making swords into plowshares, so to speak. They're federal agricultural leases.

Stop at the visitor center just across the Monocacy River Bridge to orient yourself on the electric orientation map of "The Battle That Saved Washington." It was here in July 1864 that Union General Lew Wallace and his infantry gallantly resisted Confederate General Jubal Early's surprise advance on the nation's capital. A bloody battle ensued. The Confederates overwhelmed the Union forces, but not before their strategic assault was delayed by a day—long enough for General Ulysses S. Grant to reinforce the defenses of Washington.

Today the green valley east of the Monocacy River looks about the way it did during the battle—including several houses and ruins of buildings from back then. There are war monuments to the east side of the park near Araby Church Road and Urbana Pike. You and the pup (leashed) can take in the vista and walk the trails through the battlefield. The park rangers conduct a full schedule of programs, some of which might allow you to bring along your Wishbone history dog.

The battlefield park is open daylight hours daily. The visitor center is open daily, 8 A.M.–4:30 P.M., from Memorial Day to Labor Day and Wednesday–Sunday the rest of the year. From Frederick take Market Street south to Route 355 (Urbana Pike), which goes into the battlefield. From I-270, take Exit 26 (Urbana) and turn left onto Route 80. Turn left onto Route 355 north and go about 3.5 miles to the visitor center. 301/662-3515 or 301/663-8687.

Parks, Beaches, and Recreation Areas

Baker Park 😺 😺 ½

You're not coming to Frederick to visit this or any other of its perfectly lovely city parks because you've got bigger fish to fry. But if the pup's sitting at the hotel begging for some fresh green grass to scruff up or if you're downtown anyway, this is convenient and pretty. Located downtown, these 44 pleasant acres include a large lake, tennis courts, a 49-bell carillon next to a ball field, and a swimming pool. It's the open fields you came for, plus your on-leash companion will go for a refreshing "paws" along Rock Creek. The bonus is the lovely low-lying townscape surrounding the property.

The park is open from sunrise to sunset. From historic Frederick, take Church Street west to Bentz Street, turn left, and then almost immediately turn right on Carroll Parkway to the park. 301/694-1646.

Sugarloaf Mountain 😺 😺 ½

We have been to the mountaintop. That's the primary reason you and the pup might want to drive through these narrow, winding roads to get to this privately owned 3,000-acre mountain.

Like nearly everywhere around here, the place has a history. It got its name from early 18th-century pioneers who reckoned its shape resembled the sugar loaves that were common food then. During the Civil War, Union and Confederate armies both posted lookouts from its peak vantage point—though not at the same time.

Today, this Registered Natural Landmark is most popular for picnics with a view. Picnicking areas near and at the summit provide vistas of the valleys below that are stunningly beautiful—so don't forget to bring lunch. Also, bring water; there's none beyond the entrance below. Trails through the rocky low-bottom woods provide hikers with abundant nature—including two kinds of poisonous snakes, timber rattlers and copperheads, according to park bulletin board notices. There's poison ivy, too, so take care out there.

Dogs must stay on leashes. Admission to the mountain is free. The park is open sunrise–sunset. From Frederick, take I-270 south toward Washington; go west at Exit 22 (Hyattstown) and follow Old Hundred Road (Route 109) to Comus. Turn right on Comus Road and drive about two miles to the Sugarloaf Mountain entrance. 301/869-7846 or 301/874-2024.

Restaurants

Brewers Alley: You can't go inside this classy microbrewery restaurant with a hungry dog alongside. But on the raised patio outside next to the leaded-glass-and-oak front doors, there are tables where the management will let you tie the pup on the other side of the wrought-iron railing if he behaves himself, we were told. So he's kind of sitting with you as you dine on creative sandwiches, antipasto, wood-oven pizza, Louisiana boudin, and freshly brewed beer (the Oatmeal Stout is swamp black and sweet as they come). 124 North Market Street; 301/631-0089.

Crabapples Delicatessen: They do it like New York City at this old-style deli where the cold-cuts are top-notch and the sandwiches stacked. Carry it out to eat with the pup. 101 West Patrick Street; 301/694-0208.

Famous Cozy Restaurant: If you're going or coming back from Catoctin Mountain and just can't wait to eat, take the Thurmont exit off Route 15 onto Route 806, and you can't miss Cozy Village. It's a complex of shops, trinkets and crafts, memorabilia of presidents and the press who stopped on their way to Camp David, dog-friendly cabins you can stay in, and a restaurant. When the weather's good, the kind proprietors might let you leash your pup off the deck and across the railing from one of those outdoor railside tables. Then you can toss that cozy pooch scraps from the mountain of food on your plate that you filled from the 1950s-inspired buffet table inside (meat loaf, fried chicken, ham, turkey, mashed potatoes). 103 Frederick Road; 301/271-4301.

Frederick Coffee Company and Cafe: Just around the corner from the visitor center, this place makes a great cup of coffee and has the food to go with it—croissants, muffins, *et al.* At one of the little tables out front on the sidewalk you can hitch the pup and read the Frederick *Gazette.* 100 East Street; 301/698-0039.

La Paz Mexican Restaurant: Located just behind the Church Street parking deck, stop by this south-of-the-border eatery and carry out the loaded fajitas—Chappy's favorites because there are actual cuts of meat inside. You can get tacos, enchiladas, and other messy stuff, too. 18 Market Space; 301/694-8980.

Province Too: A dog lover's prayer answered, this great little catering restaurant makes all sorts of wonderful yet moderately priced baked goods. It also specializes in deli creations, soups, stews, pies, and cakes. Try the honeyed ham. Call ahead, and they'll put together a tasty picnic lunch for your excursions. 12 East Patrick Street; 301/663-3315.

Places to Stay

Blue Bird on the Mountain: Catoctin Mountain breezes and vistas are what you and your well-trained, well-behaved dog will find at this 1900 elegant bed-and-breakfast and spa retreat, located about eight miles from Thurmont

EARMARK YOUR CALENDAR

Frederick Festival of the Arts: Every spring this is a big deal over in Carroll Creek Linear Park in downtown Frederick. If yours is an art-loving dog, the juried exhibits of art from around the country mix graciously with the scenic promenade downtown. There's food, too. Admission is charged. Call 301/663-8687.

and Catoctin National Park. The inn is a great base for exploring not only the park, but also the Appalachian Trail and the battlefields in Gettysburg and Antietam. Or just go out hunting for morel mushrooms, visit an apple festival, or take a fall foliage tour. Walter Taylor, an aide to Robert E. Lee, formerly owned the 1900 manor house. Sit on the big old-fashioned porch or relax by a fire on a chilly day. There are French doors, antique armoires, and cozy rocking chairs. You can even get a massage for $50, if you reserve it two days in advance. Rooms are in the neighborhood of $125 a night. 14700 Eyler Avenue, Cascade, MD 21719; 301/241-4161.

Catoctin Mountain Park Campground: See Catoctin Mountain Park, above.

Crow's Nest Campground: If there's no room at the Catoctin Mountain Park Campground, and you and the outdoor pup had your hearts set on sleeping under the stars, these folks are just outside Catoctin in Thurmont. They gladly accept pets, and they have sites for RVs and tents and a lake where you can take a hike. 355 West Main Street, Thurmont, MD 21788; 301/271-7632.

Hampton Inn–Historic Frederick: On the edge of Frederick proper, this 160-room, national chain hotel attracts many Civil War buffs who favor its location a mile west of Monocacy Battlefield. Dog lovers will find this hotel outright hospitable toward its four-legged guests who can stroll through the clean and tidy lobby without anyone looking askance. Besides, it gets the Chappy Seal of Canine Approval on the gratis continental breakfast alone. Pooches can't sit in the American-food restaurant downstairs (health-code inspectors develop facial twitches when that happens), but you can take its entrees up to your room and eat alongside his royal caniness. Rooms run $84 per night plus a $10 per night pet charge. The hotel has no restrictions on dogs. There's not a lot of fringe grass around the parking lot but enough for quickie dog relief. Otherwise, drive the three miles into downtown Frederick to Baker Park, where the woods, lawn, and two miles of stream are perfect for a longer stroll for the dog and you. 5311 Buckeystown Pike, Frederick, MD 21701; 301/698-2500.

Holiday Inn–Frederick: Talk about experienced in handling dog guests, this large conference center hotel hosts more than a half dozen dog shows annually, including the ABC Boxer Nationals every year, plus Labrador, dalmatian, and dachshund shows. Another dog in the hotel? No problem. They've had days when *hundreds* of dogs are in the hotel. The digs here are pristine, the pool area cheery, the in-house Harrigan's Restaurant (American cuisine) convenient for room service between 6:30 A.M. and about 9 P.M. There are no extra dog charges, no dog restrictions. The only rule is that if you don't take your dog with you when you leave the room, keep him in a crate or kennel. The grounds outside are adequate for a dozen dogs doing their business. Room rates run $89 per night. 999 West Patrick Street, Frederick, MD 21702; 301/694-7500 or 800/465-4329.

Quality Inn–Frederick: About a mile southwest of the historic downtown area, just down from the Festival at Frederick Shopping Center, this tidy chain hotel doesn't even flinch at dogs staying overnight. There are no restrictions, no extra charges. The relief lawn is sparse hereabouts, but there's enough for an emergency. Chappy gives two thumbs up on the free HBO, CNN, and ESPN cable connection and a coffeemaker in every room. Rooms run about $79. 420 Prospect Boulevard, Frederick, MD 21701; 301/695-6200 or 800/221-2222.

OCEAN CITY, MD

Less refined than the family and professional destinations along the coast to the north, Ocean City has forever been the beach where high schoolers head at prom time, where college hunks and bikini beauties get summer jobs, where bikers swagger along the boardwalk showing off tattoos and big boots in the summer sun. It's where little kids squeal on the roller coaster that dips steeply toward the ocean at the boardwalk amusement park and bars do a booming business every night. You might think this is fun city, depending on your definition of fun. Or you might head down this way for a change of pace from the beaches to the north.

Parks, Beaches, and Recreation Areas
The Beach 🐾 🐾 🐾 ◀●

No matter what you think of the town's honky-tonk atmosphere, this is where the beach is biggest, with a wide expanse of sand between the water and the street or boardwalk. Never mind that someone is likely to have his boom box cranked nearby or that sand flies when you're having fun; this is a beachy beach for sun and play.

As for dogs on the beach, they allowed on the beach and boardwalk October–April, and prohibited May–September. To reach the beach from the Bay Bridge, take Route 50 all the way (there may be faster ways but none more brainless). For more information, contact the Ocean City Convention and Visitors Bureau, 4001 Coastal Highway, Ocean City, MD 21842; 410/289-8181 or 800/626-2326.

Northside Park 🐾 🐾 🐾

You're at the beach, but your dog really needs a park, something with green grass and paved paths. Northside is almost suburban-esque in that it features manicured green areas and paths that wind around a lagoon with a fountain before they go out toward the bay. The ball fields attract kids, and the paths attract in-line skaters, strollers, and walkers. A picturesque pier extends into the bay. Your dog's sand-worn paws will be happy there's no sand in sight. 127th Street on the Bay side; 410/289-8181.

Restaurants

Big Pecker's Bar and Grill: A fairly large number of tables on an outside front deck set back from the main highway and the casual menu of burgers, wings, crab cakes, and tacos make this a fine eatery for you and your dog. Popular with many who stop here is the "Famous Frozen Chicken Plucker." That's a drink. Just don't let your dog drive home after having one—or you, for that matter. Needless to say, the Big Pecker T-shirts are a big seller. At the corner of the Coastal Highway and 73rd Street, Ocean City; 7301 Coastal Highway; 410/723-0690.

Dumser's Dairyland Ice Cream Parlor and Restaurant: Since 1939, the sign says, they've been serving up thick, delicious milkshakes. That's actually what you order, a "thick milkshake," as opposed to an ice cream soda, float, or yogurt treat—just a few of the treats from the menu. Makes your mouth water just to type in the words. They also offer complete breakfast, lunch, and dinner menus. Several outdoor tables allow good viewing of the miniature golf course next door, and they are lenient when it comes to pups sitting alongside. 123rd Street and the Coastal Highway; 12305 Coastal Highway; 410/250-5543.

Galaxy Bar and Grill: Starry, starry night . . . . Take a trip through the galaxy when you step in here to carry out your basic American dinner. 6601 Coastal Highway; 410/723-6762.

Hanna's Marina Deck Restaurant: The grouped couches and chairs make a pleasant place to sip a pi-a colada with your pooch. But they can't allow it. So get a nice, fat lobster to go and make your drinks at home with your faithful companion by your side. 306 Dorchester Street; 410/289-4411.

J.R.'s The Place for Ribs: This place gets so packed you don't even need to think about trying to eat inside here—you *or* your dog. Just get some of the baby back ribs, chicken, and a big loaf of onion rings to go. They'll put it all in a big shopping bag and send you on your way. That ride home drives Chappy nuts. 6104 Coastal Highway, 410/524-7427; or 13101 Coastal Highway, 410/250-3100.

Places to Stay

Barefoot Mailman Motel: Forget about trying here in July or August, because demand is so high that they don't even think about dogs those

St. Patrick's Day Parade and Festival: What else but Irish singing, dancing, and eating? It's at the Coastal Highway and 61st Streets, and is held around March 17. Call 410/289-2800 for more information.

White Marlin Parade and Festival: High school bands, floats, and other festivities take place in mid-May along the boardwalk from 15th Street to the inlet, with an outdoor festival held on North Division Street, Baltimore Avenue to the boardwalk. Call 410/289-1413 to find out more.

Arts Atlantica Festival: This fine arts festival on the boardwalk also features live musical performances for a few days during Memorial Day weekend. For more information, call 410/289-2800.

SunFest: Sponsored by the town of Ocean City, these are four mid-September days of celebration, music, arts, crafts, kids' activities—all under big-top tents except for the kite festival. It's generally held from a Thursday through Sunday on the beach at the Inlet lot, at the south end of the boardwalk. In May, there's the mirror-image SpringFest as well. Tickets required. For more information, call 410/289-8311 or 800/626-2326.

---

months. Otherwise, the motel keeps a limited number of pet rooms available for those who make reservations early. Most of the rooms are efficiencies with kitchenettes or refrigerators, and all have their own balconies. Peak season rates run about $175 per night. Add an extra $10 per night for a pooch. Because the motel is on the ocean side of the Coastal Highway, you and the pup don't have to cross any busy streets to get to the beach. 35th Street and the Coastal Highway, Ocean City, MD 21842; 410/289-5343 or 800/395-3668.

Clarion Resort Fountainebleau Hotel: This fancy luxury hotel happily accepts dogs for an extra $25 a night. This is one of the grander spots on the Ocean City beach, located at the northern end of town where it's much more residential and quiet. A double with an ocean view runs $250–270 a night in season, but you've got to call well in advance. This place books fast soon as spring hits and people start thinking beach time. And the pet rooms go quickly, too. 10100 Coastal Highway, Ocean City, MD 21842; 800/638-2100.

Frontier Town Campground: Situated right along the Sinepuxent Bay, this place offers a lot for you and your leashed dog. There are 225 sites with hookups, a bathhouse, laundry facilities, a restaurant, pool, water slide, dock, and the Western Theme Park, which is a replica of a circa 1860 cowboy town on 38 acres of woodlands. Campers get a discount at the theme park. Primitive sites for tents are $26; with water and electric hookup, they're $37. P.O. Box 691; Ocean City, MD 21842; 410/641-0880 or 800/228-5590.

Ocean City Travel Park Campground: This is the only campground within the city limits, and therefore sites book up fast, so call for reservations. There are 200 sites with hookups, but only 70 are available for short-term stays. There is a bathhouse, laundry facilities, arcade, and boat dock. Rates start at $32 for a tent site and $37 for small RVs. Pets must be on a leash at all times, walked outside the camping area, scooped up after, and never left alone. They are happy to allow pets, but if you and the pooch break any of these rules, the management will ask you to leave. 105 70th Street, Ocean City, MD 21842; 410/524-7601.

Safari Motel: Noisier and closer to where the action is but the management is friendly, and they were ready to take our medium-sized Chappy. You might pay a small fee (around $10 a night), or at the height of the season you can expect a three-night minimum at about $160 a night that will include your dog. At 13th Street and the Boardwalk, Ocean City, MD 21842; 410/289-6411.

FREDERICKSBURG, VA

Virginians like nothing better than to name-drop about the famous political leaders who lived, slept, or even just passed through their town. George Washington spent his youth at Ferry Farm here. Thomas Jefferson penned his Statute for Religious Freedom while staying here. President James Monroe began his promising career as a young lawyer in this town.

If there's something Virginians like to boast about even more than famous residents, it's battlegrounds. During much of the Civil War, over four bloody years, Fredericksburg was an armed encampment and the hub of four major battles in the area.

Yes, the Civil War passed through this town. You and your dog can trace the footsteps of weary soldiers. While you feel the history, your dog will just have a really nice walk. Beyond that, the historic district of Fredericksburg, founded in 1728 on the Rappahannock River, is a charming old town center. Lined with antique shops and cozy restaurants, it's surprisingly dog friendly. But, then, rural towns generally know how to value dogs. The historic downtown visitor center can help you know how to value what this historic excursion has to offer you and the pup.

National Parks

Fredericksburg and Spotsylvania National Military Park 🐾 🐾 ½
If it's battlefields you came for, it's battlefields you get. Lucky for curious dog lovers who lack the historian's fervor to revisit each of them step by step, you and your on-leash dog can stop and smell the cannon smoke without getting battle weary. On the other hand, you can traipse as much as you want and absorb more Civil War history here in a short time than just about anywhere this side of Gettysburg. This National Military Park consists of 8,400 acres and

DIVERSION

Vintage Virginia: When in the neighborhood of beautiful Lake Anna, stop by one of Virginia's growing number of wineries. **Lake Anna Winery,** only about two miles from the lake itself, is in a renovated barn on the Heidig family farm. It's no problem to stop by with your pooch and taste a few of their award-winning reds, whites, and blushes. 5621 Courthouse Road, Spotsylvania. 540/895-5085.

four distinct and partly preserved battlefields: Fredericksburg (in 1862), Chancellorsville (in 1863), Wilderness, and Spotsylvania (both in 1864).

First stop is the visitor center near the famous stone wall at Marye's Heights in the Fredericksburg Battlefield. Some maps will confuse you by not distinguishing the battlefield from the national cemetery where more than 15,000 Union and Confederate soldiers are buried. Fact is, the battlefield is where they built the cemetery. Helpful park rangers will steer you in the right direction and provide brochures with directions and descriptions for self-guided tours, skirmish by skirmish, through the battlefields.

The battle of Fredericksburg was Robert E. Lee's most one-sided victory of the war. While attacking Prospect Hill about three miles south of Fredericksburg, Union troops under the command of Ambrose Burnside also advanced on Marye's Heights. As Lee's artillery shelled the Union army from elevated ridge positions, his infantry fired from behind stone wall. They slaughtered masses of Union soldiers. You and the pooch take a much safer and more leisurely 30-minute stroll up the shaded Sunken Road to the original stone wall. Along the way, you'll find several monuments to the brave and the dead, a panoramic painting that helps you envision what occurred here, and the old Innis House where bullet holes are evidence it got caught in the crossfire.

If that little dab won't do you, there are more embattled acres 12 miles west of Frederick at Chancellorsville Battlefield, another five miles beyond that at Wilderness Battlefield, and 14 miles southwest of Fredericksburg at Spotsylvania Court House Battlefield—all part of this national military park. The park rangers recommend you take two days minimum to cover these historic grounds adequately, more if you sign on to the weekend guided walking tours offered during the summer months—leashed dogs welcome. The park service has thoughtfully provided picnic tables at each battleground, so bring your lunch.

The battlefields are open sunrise–sunset. The visitor center is open daily 9 A.M.–5 P.M., with expanded hours in the summer. From I-95 take the Route 3 exit east into Fredericksburg. When the road divides, veer right onto Hanover

and follow it for a half mile; turn left on Littlepage Street, then right on Lafayette Boulevard. The visitor center will be on the right. 540/373-6122.

Parks, Beaches, and Recreation Areas

Lake Anna State Park 🐾 🐾 🐾 🐾 🐾

Feeling surrounded by too much history on your little jaunt into the old Confederacy? A half-hour drive southwest of downtown Fredericksburg into Spotsylvania County is one of Virginia's most beautiful and popular lakes. About three miles into the neatly kept forest of this off-the-beaten-path state park, you catch your first glimpse of the blue waters of Lake Anna—13,000 picturesque acres of water sports and recreation.

The park itself offers just about everything a hiking dog might hope for—except for off-leash free running. Virginia state parks, remember, require dogs on leashes no longer than six feet. Confidentially, there's plenty of space to race here and many unpopulated areas—especially in the fall when this large lake is framed by red and yellow leaves.

Dogs are welcome everywhere but on the protected beach area. The best treks are the woody trails that are well marked and maintained. Chappy liked the two-mile Railroad Ford Trail that you pick up on the south side of the pond behind the visitor center. It loops alongside the lake's edge most of the way and provides a few spots where a rambunctious dog (not Chappy) might find her way into the lake for a dip. The 1.1-mile Fisherman's Trail beyond the parking area by the boat launch is another waterside hike. But take heed: Shallow water hazards and rough bottoms might be good enough reason to keep your dog dry.

Plenty of picnic tables overlooking the lake are great for lunching and day-dreaming. There's a food concession complex in season if you forget your picnic basket. Ask at the visitor center which direction to go to pan for gold. Lake Anna today is close to the nuclear power plant named for it, but historically this land was known for its gold mines—and folks still occasionally pan precious specks out of its mucky shoreline. If you and your sidekick have come to fish, the lake is home to bass, perch, pickerel, and walleye, among others—but check what fishing licenses you need.

The park is open 8 A.M.–dusk. Getting here is a little tricky, but enough signs are posted along the way. From Fredericksburg, take I-95 south 11.5 miles to Exit 118 at Thornburg. Turn right on Route 606; drive 5.3 miles to the intersection of Route 606 and Route 208. Go straight through the light and stay on Courthouse Road (Route 606) for 11.3 miles (even as it turns left at the Lake Anna sign). Turn right onto Lawyers Road (the sign says only State Park) and look for the park entrance down 3.5 miles on the left. 540/854-5503.

Restaurants

Walking in the footsteps of all those Civil War soldiers made Chappy weary and hungry. We include all of the eateries below because they have outdoor tables where you and your dog can take a break to refuel.

J. Brian's Tap Room: Just around the corner from the main traffic of Caroline Street, this laid-back place offers beefy or vegetarian burgers, lovely salads, the works. You can often find dogs at the wrought-iron tables outside where you get a view of the foot traffic while being out of the way. 202 Hanover Street; 540/373-0738.

Merriman's: "Absolutely!" says the staff. Go ahead and take one of the outdoor tables and enjoy a burger or crab cakes with your dog resting comfortably next to you. 715 Caroline Street; 540/371-7723.

Old Towne Wine and Cheese Deli: Stop in for some yummy deli sandwiches and then sit outside and watch the people go in and out of the visitor center right across the street. 707 Caroline Street; 540/373-7877.

Sammy T's: Vegetarians will go for the salads; others should go for any of the fresh soups, sandwiches, breakfasts, and dinners here. 801 Caroline Street; 540/371-2008.

Spirits, Pasta and More: One of our sons will always eat a sub. Whether it's breakfast, lunch, or dinner, J. B. is ready for a nice turkey sub, and Chappy becomes his most loving best friend when he's eating one. This place makes great subs, and also serves pizza and pasta dishes right in the heart of the historic district. 816 Caroline Street; 540/371-9595.

Places to Stay

Aquia Pines Camp Resort: A few miles north of Fredericksburg on Route 1,

EARMARK YOUR CALENDAR

Pear Blossom Festival: Fairly low-key, with crafts, food, and lively entertainment, this annual springtime fling in the old-town district is a pleasant way to visit Fredericksburg with the leashed pooch. The festival blossoms in mid-April; call 800/678-4748.

Fredericksburg Dog Festival: Every dog has its day in October at one of the town's public parks. Pups parade around, join in the contests and games, and generally bring together dog lovers for a fall day in the sun. Also in October, is the annual parade and show to commemorate the 1600s when Virginia settlers would meet with Indians to trade hunting dogs for gold. Also interesting to see is an auction of nearly every breed of dog imaginable. Representatives of the two local tribes of Native Americans usually come, as is the custom, and often sell their handcrafted goods and jewelry. The location changes from year to year; in 1998, it was at the Isaak Walton League Park off Route 17.

Old Town Season's Greetings: A great time to head into Old Town Fredericksburg is in mid-November when the town kicks off a full schedule of holiday events with this all-town open house. Town folks bring out decorations. Bagpipers, other musicians, entertainers, and peddlers fill the streets. Some merchants provide free refreshments from their seasonally decorated boutiques and restaurants in this 40-block historic area where more than 350 of the buildings date back to the 18th and early 19th centuries. For more information, call the Fredericksburg Visitor Center at 540/373-1776.

---

this all-amenities campground considers itself a resort and not just a place to pitch a tent. Lots of folks make this their hub while exploring the countryside as far north as Washington and south to Richmond—and everything in between. RV and tent sites are available, starting at $21.25 for tent sites with no hookups and another $2 for water and electricity. Dogs are welcome so long as they stay leashed and you clean up after them. At the fenced swimming pool, you can tie the pooch on the outside in the shade while you take a dip. Otherwise, there's a playground, miniature golf course, basketball court, a full-service store, and lots of stars in the sky. 3071 Jefferson Davis Highway, Stafford, VA 22554; 540/659-3347.

Best Western–Central Plaza: If your dog is small and into Civil War battlefields, you might want to stay here. There is a free continental breakfast included, and there's no deposit for dogs if you pay with a credit card. If you're paying cash, you need to have a spare $25 for them to hold. Rooms are about $59 a night plus tax for your smoking room. A bonus: Nearby is a 24-hour Waffle

House Restaurant. 3000 Plank Road, Fredericksburg, VA 22407; 540/786-7404.

Econo Lodge–Fredericksburg South: They allow only one dog per room—and only one night per dog. Kind of odd, and not all that friendly, but those are the rules. There is a $5 pet fee for lodging in this two-story motel, on top of rates that range from $42–49 a night for a double. You and the pup get a smoking room, however (hate it when they do that). The continental breakfast is free. 5321 Jefferson Davis Highway (Route 1), Fredericksburg, VA 22408; 540/898-5440.

Fredericksburg KOA Campground: Located 10 miles south of Fredericksburg in the heart of Civil War country, this family-oriented campground has 115 sites. Rates for tent sites are $27 with no hookup, $29 if you want a hookup. Leashed dogs are welcome everywhere but in the seven cabins. There's even a dog-walk area just for the pooches. There's a pool, a stocked pond for fishing, a game room, and a playground. A free shuttle will take you to the train to Washington. The train won't allow your pup unless he's a guide dog, so someone had better stay home and tend the campfires with Mr. Pooch. 7400 Brookside Lane, Fredericksburg, VA 22408; 540/898-7252.

Ramada Inn–Fredericksburg: Amid all this history, with Washington an hour north, Richmond an hour south, and Williamsburg less than two hours away, this place makes an excellent base camp. They allow dogs with a $25 refundable deposit. Not only that, but there are 130 rooms decorated with a sort of colonial hotel flair, HBO, pool, and Aunt Sarah's Restaurant right next door. 2802 Plank Road (I-95 and Route 3 west), Fredericksburg, VA 22404; 540/786-8361.

Rocky Branch Marina and Campground: Located on Lake Anna, this is a beautiful setting for pitching a tent. The owners ask that you "not let the dogs run wild"; otherwise, they're welcome. There are 38 water- and electric-hookup sites, and those are $18 a night. Without the hookup expect to pay $14 a night at one of the 25 tent sites. No reservations are necessary; it's first-come, first-serve. A bathhouse and store are on the property, too. 5153 Courthouse Road, Spotsylvania, VA 22553; 540/895-5475.

Roxbury Mill Bed-and-Breakfast: From when it was built in the 1720s until 1962, the Roxbury Plantation was a working mill, right on the Po River about 10 miles south of Fredericksburg. Now it's a bed-and-breakfast where pleasant, not-large dogs are pretty much welcome. There is a big suite upstairs and two rooms downstairs available. And the Virginia country ham biscuits are scrumptious. The only thing the innkeepers worry about is fleas. So please, make sure your dog doesn't have any before heading here. (You'd probably want to make sure anyway, but we promised we'd mention it.) 6908 Roxbury Mill Road, Thornburg, VA 22553; 540/582-6611.

SKYLINE DRIVE AND SHENANDOAH NATIONAL PARK, VA

About an hour west of Washington and about two hours from Baltimore, Shenandoah National Park is 300 square miles of hardwood forest where nature rules and Chappy drools. The 105-mile Skyline Drive winds through the middle of the parkland from Afton Mountain near Charlottesville north to Front Royal. One of the most scenic roadways you'll find anywhere in America, it's guaranteed to keep you and your pooch's noses pressed against the windshield.

This remarkable, four-paw-rated forest spans much of Virginia's Appalachian and Blue Ridge Mountains and attracts some two million visitors annually. Many of them don't venture off the paved, two-lane Skyline Drive where spectacular vistas, roadside drop-offs, and fleet-footed deer make the 35-mile-an-hour speed limit a safety necessity. It twists and turns through the heart of the park past more than 50 scenic overlooks with pull-off areas. But this massive and mostly rugged parkland offers much more than a pretty drive in the countryside.

For dog lovers the trails are the way to go. More than 500 miles of maintained paths and hiking trails cut through the thick underbrush and dense forest to sideswipe breathtaking views from ridges overlooking farm valleys eastward and ridge tops opposite the Shenandoah River westward. What you'll see is the landscape that once covered most of the northeastern United States. A ranger told us that 300 years ago a squirrel could have crossed from the Mississippi River to the Atlantic Ocean and never touched the ground due to thick forests such as this. Seems like squirrels could still roam the treetops of the Shenandoah's acres without coming down to earth.

Along the trails visibility can become so limited that it's hard to see the forest for the trees. You can, however, expect to see some of the parkland's zillions of species (or so it seems) of wildlife—often with little or no notice before you cross paths. That poses no problem for you and the pup when you come face to face with one of the 200 or so varieties of birds that have been sighted here. But bears walk these woods, too. The two species of poisonous snakes that live here—the timber rattler and copperhead—aren't often encountered. Watch your step anyway. Best advice is to stick to the marked trails that will steer you clear of the worst rocky and steep locations and will keep you from getting totally lost.

Many dog lovers have a misconception about the Shenandoah National Park's dog policy. Unlike most national parks that prohibit dogs, Shenandoah welcomes dogs—but with a few restrictions. Dogs have to stay on leashes no longer than six feet and always must be attended. They must stay off trails designated as No Pets at the trailhead—happily the exceptions in this glorious nature sanctuary. Most of the off-limit hikes are on nature trails (including Fox Hollow Trail,

Traces Trail, Stony Man Trail except for where it overlaps the Appalachian Trail, Story of the Forest Trail, and Deadening Trail). A few of the most heavily used hiking trails are also no-goes, such as the popular hike up Old Rag Mountain, Dark Hollow Falls Trail, Bearfence Trail, and Limberlost Trail.

General warning: If your dog is noisy or goes on wild rampages frightening visitors or disturbing wildlife, you and the pooch will be shown the door. The Shenandoah's kind and helpful park rangers are dog-friendly folks, but they're sensitive to anything that disrupts nature here—from mid-winter ice storms leveling trees to rambunctious Rovers running like crazy through a quiet meadow. They can and will impound dogs caught running without leashes and fine the owners, so don't push your luck (and everyone else's) by trying to take advantage of this pastoral paradise. Every dang-dog incident adds fuel to the regularly raised argument in favor of closing off more trails and areas to pets.

When to go? Spring is all pastel and an awesome time to hike the pup through all the newly broken-out foliage as leaves still carry those lighter, finer pigments. You also get the flowering trees in spring—the chokecherries, red-buds, mountain laurels, and dogwoods. One springtime drawback is that as the remnants of winter snow melt from the top of the mountains, the trails can get muddy. The trade-off is that the waterfalls get more dramatic—and some of these are accessible to you and your mud-puddle pooch.

In the summer, green takes over and the animals are harder to see. The wild-flowers grow like weeds, however, making summertime visiting easy. We'd recommend autumn for the spectacular beauty of the changing leaves, but the intolerable crowds that jam Skyline Drive during peak weeks are the stuff of evening TV news reports, so don't even go there then. You and the pooch will leave in awe of nature's beauty, but you'll probably wind up a misanthrope.

The only time the park closes, by the way, is when winter storms knock out sections of the roadway or forest and make traveling hereabouts dangerous. Yet the solitude and still beauty of winter can be an inspiring time to visit.

Easiest way to explore the Shenandoah National Park for more than a day is to stay at a hotel in one of the nearby charming and historic towns, or if you and the dog are more adventurous, camp out under the stars in one of the park's campgrounds.

Your choice of towns ranges from the city-ish Winchester on the north end to Mr. Jefferson's charming Charlottesville to the south. We chose the smaller rural town of Staunton west of Skyline Drive as our base of operation. Tucked between the Blue Ridge and the Allegheny Mountains near the junction of I-81 and I-64, Staunton dates back to the 1740s and played a key role in the Civil War. Today, this town of 25,000 is called the "Queen City of the Shenandoah Valley." Pronounced STAN-ton (only Yankee spies pronounce it STAUN-ton), it is a hilly town whose architecture dates back to before the War Between the States. We like it because it has a lot to offer after you've been to the mountaintop: good restaurants, dog-friendly lodging, people-friendly people. It's even hometown to the Statler Brothers, those country-singing siblings who know how to make the big dogs howl.

Parks, Beaches, and Recreation Areas

Appalachian Trail 🐾 🐾 🐾

The 2,160-mile long AT, as it's commonly referred to by hard-core hikers, twists through some 95 miles of the Shenandoah Mountains on its footpath from Maine to Georgia. Inevitably, it crosses several of Shenandoah National Park's hiking trails and at some points is easily accessible from Skyline Drive.

Dogs are allowed on all parts of the AT as it cuts through the Shenandoah—but they must stay leashed. But be forewarned: When hiking with dogs, the AT can stand for "Awfully Treacherous." Unless you and your pooch are experienced hikers and backpackers, other than taking a short hike along the AT, you'd do well to stick to some of the tamer trails of the Shenandoah. Besides, dog hikers aren't very common on this rugged terrain.

That's because the AT requires serious and strenuous hiking that can quickly turn more venturesome than the novice hiker and canine sidekick are up for. The trail often gets so steep many dogs can't continue; its surface can change to loose rocks that make for unforgiving footing. Stories abound of couch-potato pups such as Chappy venturing onto the AT only to struggle home with cut paw pads or dehydration.

Folks who regularly backpack segments of this challenging trail with their dogs know what they're in for and prepare for it. Both they and their dogs are in shape for hiking, and they pack first-aid items, food, and plenty of water.

The Appalachian Trail is open year-round, 24 hours a day. You can enter the AT at several locations off Skyline Drive and from trails in Shenandoah National Park, including at the 21-mile marker near the Hogback Overlook; between the Rattlesnake Point Overlook and the 22-mile marker (and off Piney Branch Trail); just north of the Elkwallow Service Station at the 24-mile marker; behind the lodge and picnic area at Big Meadows; and behind the campgrounds and picnic area at Loft Mountain. White-blazed trees mark the AT. For more information on the Appalachian Trail, contact the Appalachian Trail Conference, P.O. Box 807, Harper's Ferry, WV 25425-0807; or call 304/535-6331.

Big Meadows 🐾 🐾 🐾 🐾 🐾

Cleared into a huge meadow by torch-wielding Indians long before colonial times, this hub of facilities and activities is an excellent place to center your inside-the-park adventures with the pup. Located at about the halfway point at the 51-mile post along Skyline Drive, in Shenandoah National Park, it houses the Byrd Visitor Center (one of the park's two largest), a decent restaurant–coffee shop where you can buy box lunches for hiking, a wayfarer's camp store, a service station, even a gift shop.

These 1,000 acres are also where you'll find pleasant picnicking areas. We saw several dogs properly leashed but playfully prancing about with their humans in the mowed area of nearly 300 acres back toward the campgrounds where folks were picnicking along the edge in the shade. Several trails begin under the abundant hemlocks, gray birches, pines, and oaks at this location. The tricky, 2.5-mile Lewis Run Falls Trail that leads to twin falls and back was just the right distance on one cool spring afternoon, though Chappy got a little weirded out trying to navigate steep embankments.

Dogs are prohibited from the Big Meadows Lodge and Dining Room a mile back from Skyline Drive. But if overnight is in your plans, you and the pooch can share a sleeping bag and pup tent at the Big Meadows Campground. Better make reservations for peak camping seasons (May–October), however, or prepare to be shut out. You can always try at the 32-site Lewis Mountain Campground or the 32-site Loft Mountain Campground—both located south of Big Meadows. Tent and trailer sites cost $14–17 per night, depending on the season, but none provides hookups, so bring your own drinking water. Shower and flush toilet facilities are centrally located. The campgrounds generally close in October for the winter.

All Shenandoah National Park locations are open year-round and all hours except in bad weather. The entry fee is $4 per car. For information and to reserve a campsite, call Biospherics at 800/365-CAMP (800/365-2267), the reservation company for the park. To get to Shenandoah National Park from Baltimore, take I-95 to Washington. Then take I-66 west from the Capital Beltway (I-95) to the Front Royal Entrance Station. To enter the park in the central area near Staunton, take I-66 west from Washington and drive south on I-81; Staunton is about 75 miles south at the intersection of Route 250. The Rockfish Gap Entrance Station to Skyline Drive is off I-64 east 18 miles from Staunton and just south of Waynesboro. 540/999-3500.

Gypsy Hill Park 🐾 🐾

Sure, it pales by comparison. Staunton's sprawling 214-acre in-town park and recreation haven is no Shenandoah National Park. But if you're overnighting in this town and need a less overwhelming park experience, this is the place. The golf course at the far side from the entrance is off-limits to canine caddies; so is the swimming complex. The rest of the hilly park is good for roaming around and following the rippling creek down to the duck pond. Chappy watched the children's train go 'round for a while before we settled in by the right field fence to watch a couple innings of a Babe Ruth League baseball game at the third ball field in this handsome three-field complex. There are plenty of picnic tables and even a couple of picnic shelters near the little kids' playground. (Burgers and country ham sandwiches from the Tastee-Freez two blocks outside the park satisfied Chappy's appetite.) Leashed dogs can even sit in the ball-field bleachers—like Nancy and Doc Bonoccorso's pup Holly, the cutest, most baseball-savvy cocker spaniel we ever saw, patiently watching from the third-base stands.

The park is open 6 A.M.–11 P.M. From I-81, take Exit 222 (Route 250) east into Staunton and stay on Churchville Avenue or Route 250 (the business route, not the 250 Bypass,) as it turns and jockeys through the old town area, and you'll see signs posted to Gypsy Hill Park. Once inside the park entrance, follow the one-way road around the perimeter and park the car near the baseball fields. 540/332-3945.

Skyline Drive 🐾 🐾 🐾 🐾

For strictly a day trip of driving to scenic overlooks, the Front Royal Entrance Station is the closest to Washington—about a 90-minute drive max—and from Baltimore. Stop by the Dickey Ridge Visitor Center about four miles south of the entrance for a map and info from the rangers first. You and the pup can sit at the picnic tables there and carb up on the picnic lunch you wisely brought along. Then drive south on Skyline Drive to experience some breathtaking beauty. After another mile, you will come to Signal Knob Overlook, where the view of Massanutten Mountain and the Shenandoah Valley awed even our Himalayan hound. Go the next mile and take in Gooney Run Overlook and Gooney Manor Overlook, both grand views of Shenandoah territory owned 300 years ago by Lord Fairfax, who named it for his faithful dog, Gooney.

If you're looking for an excuse to stretch your legs, go three more miles and you'll find Lands Run Falls Trail. The trailhead starts just off Skyline Drive. This quick hike down an old fire road takes you and the pup to lovely, cascading falls. But don't get too close because these slopes are slippery. Round-trip is less than 1.5 miles, but this doggy detour will take almost 90 minutes with the hiking pooch.

Back in the car, go another seven miles south to the Range View Overlook and check out the ridge-upon-ridge effect of the Shenandoah's highest peaks—including Stoney Man Mountain, the Blue Ridge Mountains, and Hogback Mountain to the far south. But that's about it for the day, folks. Turn around and go back home now. To drive the entire Skyline Drive, including several Kodak moments at the scenic overlooks, takes about five hours.

Skyline Drive is always open, except when bad weather intervenes. There is a $5-per-car entrance fee, and $3 per pedestrian; yearly passes are also available. To get there via the Front Royal entrance, take Exit 13 off I-66, turn right on South Street (Route 55) into Front Royal, then left onto Royal Avenue (Route 340), and follow the park signs about a mile to the Skyline Drive entrance. 703/999-2266.

Restaurants

The following restaurants are all in Staunton. Endless other eateries serve the hungry and the restless there and in most of the other towns along I-81's long stretch parallel to the Shenandoah Mountains. We recommend you grab a bite

DIVERSIONS

Caving in: None of the Shenandoah's many spectacular caverns that are open for public tours allow dogs inside the cool recesses of Mother Earth. But many of them are located in parks with picnic areas and hiking trails—not to mention the mandatory cheesy souvenir shops. We stopped at **Grand Caverns,** about a half-hour drive north from Staunton near Grottoes, Virginia. Even though Chappy was feeling very subterranean that day, he stayed outside and strolled the hiking trails. But he would have loved the steady 50° F down under (bring a jacket, even in the dog days of summer), where gigantic stalactites reached down from limestone ceilings and massive columns shaped room after room of stunningly beautiful formations created by ancient flowing rivers and millennia of slowly dripping water. Probably the best known and most spectacular are **Luray Caverns,** near the Shenandoah National Park's headquarters at Front Royal. Grand Caverns is open daily, April–October; some caverns are open year-round. All require guided tours; Grand Caverns' took about an hour, with a new one starting every 30 minutes. From I-81, take Exit 235 east to Grottoes, turn right on Route 340 and look for the entrance on the right. The entrance fee is $13.50 for adults and $7 for children. 68 Grand Caverns Drive, Grottoes, VA 24441; 540/249-5705.

Cultural Detour: Right in Staunton and visible from I-81 is the **Museum of American Frontier Culture**—a re-creation of four working farms spanning the 17th to the 19th centuries. A historic interpretation of the farm life that evolved into the pre–Civil War life in this valley, this outdoors display is fascinating. Dogs, however, aren't invited inside this outside museum. The museum provides self-serve kennels for those who would lock up their pooches and leave them there for an hour or so. We wouldn't and didn't. If your pup isn't along for this ride, the museum is a quick trip into the past. Open daily 9 A.M.–5 P.M., with shorter winter hours in effect December–mid-March. Admission is $8 for adults, $4 for kids. The museum is located just off Route 250 west from I-81 (Exit 222). Look for the signs. 540/332-7850.

to eat wherever you may be and take it along to any of the many picnic areas along Skyline Drive, where you and the dog can munch in view of nature at its most awesome.

Beverley Restaurant: Drop by this simple home-style restaurant, and they'll box a lunch or even hot meals for you to take along to the wilderness. Breakfast is always served here; otherwise it's a meat-and-potatoes kind of place. 12 East Beverley Street, in downtown Staunton; 540/886-4317.

Blue Mountain Coffees: Stop here with the pup in the morning for bagels, pastries, and fresh-brewed coffee. 12 Byers Street, in Staunton; 540/886-4506.

Pullman Restaurant: This classy restaurant's menu of steaks and chicken also flirts with Cajun food, and the shrimp étouffée wasn't too spicy for Chappy to nibble. But the white tablecloths and view from inside this restored C & O train station isn't for dogs. Seating outside on the old station concourse seems relaxed enough that on a slow day the waiter just might let your well-behaved pup sit nearby. If you can't stay for a sit-down meal, tie the pup outside long enough to carry out a couple of cones from the antique soda fountain at the front of the restaurant. 36 Middlebrook Avenue, in downtown Staunton; 540/885-6612.

Places to Stay

The places listed below are spread out throughout the area near that would access Skyline Drive and Shenandoah. Check your map before heading out.

Acorn Inn Bed & Breakfast: Snuggle in for a wintry weekend or head here to watch the leaves turn in fall at this inn nestled in the foothills of the Blue Ridge Mountains. The inn, a converted stable, is a beautiful art-filled lodge with 10 cozy bedrooms that used to be horse stalls. Travelers with well-behaved dogs usually stay in Acorn Cottage, which has a full kitchen and costs $95–125 a night, plus a $10 pet fee. There is skiing nearby at Wintergreen Resort. P.O. Box 431, Nellysford, VA 22958; 434/361-9357.

Anderson Cottage Bed & Breakfast: "Hammocks and rocking chairs typify the place," says Jean Randolph Bruns, the lovely innkeeper of this 200-year-old log tavern with 19th century additions. Dogs are allowed, but she urges that you call to talk to her about your visit.

"Golden retrievers are the best guests," says Bruns, speaking from experience. She adds that she does have many border collies visit when they're in town for trials. "They're so well trained; they're better than human guests." She'll steer you toward staying in the kitchen cottage, a separate building with two bedrooms and two bathrooms. She also asks that you crate the dog if you go out, say, to the warm spring pools that are just half a mile away. But when you get back, you'll still feel the warm breeze from the baths, and you and your dog can have a relaxing time in the big back yard area.

A full breakfast is included in the price of the rooms, which ranges from $60–100 in the main house and $125 in the cottage, with a small per-person fee added to that. Old Germantown Road (no street number necessary),Warm Springs, VA 24484; 540/839-2975.

Ashton Country House: Dogs are welcome at this circa 1860 bed-and-breakfast, which is very close to the junction of the Blue Ridge Parkway and Skyline Drive. The 25 acres of land surrounding the inn are great for doing some hiking with the pooch. The home is lovely, with high ceilings and pine and maple floors. There are no extra fees and no problems having the dogs, but you will likely be put in one of the two downstairs rooms to make it easier for you to come and go. Rates are from $70–125 and include a full country breakfast. 1205 Middlebrook Avenue, Staunton, VA 24401; 540/885-7819 or 800/296-7819.

Comfort Inn–Staunton: Sometimes chain hotels surprise you, and this one does. The service and small amenities impressed us—from the roomy rooms to the enclosed pool area. Dogs are welcome for $10 a night extra—expect to be put in a smoker's room. There are lots of local restaurants nearby and the Waffle House on the other side of the hotel parking lot is convenient for breakfast, though the hotel serves a complimentary continental breakfast in its lobby. Chappy gives high marks for the free HBO and newspaper. Rates run about $80 per night. 1302 Richmond Avenue (Route 250 west), Staunton, VA 24401; 540/886-5000 or 800/228-5150.

Days Inn–Staunton: Not really in Staunton, this clean and friendly bare-bones hotel overlooking I-81 is closer to Mint Springs and about equal distance to Stuarts Draft. The drive down I-81 into Staunton takes 10 minutes. Dogs are welcome for a $6 per night charge in its 121 rooms and with no restrictions. We even saw a passive little spaniel sitting quietly to one side of the small dining room just off the lobby where the free continental breakfast is served, though the manager told us that was pushing the welcome because other guests complained. Outside, plenty of grass zones and wooded hillsides surround the hotel. Rates start at about $59 per night. 372 White Hill Road, Staunton VA 24401; 540/337-3031.

Deerlane Cottages: You can get your own cottage here and dogs are welcome for a $10 fee. Two of the 10 cabins are right on the Shenandoah River and feature full-size kitchens, full-size baths, and decks on the backs. The smaller cabins sleep up to six; the three-bedroom cabins sleep up to 12. Nearby you'll find canoe, kayak, and tube rentals, or you can just have some great walks along the river with your dog. Skyline Drive is about 20 minutes away. Chappy has no interest in nearby Luray Caverns, but they're not far from here; nor is he much for horseback riding, which is about 10 minutes away. The inn is less than two hours from Washington, near Warrenton, Virginia. P.O. Box 188, Luray, VA 22835; 540/743-3344 or 800/696-3337.

Econo Lodge–Staunton: Great location is everything, and this clean and comfortable budget-chain hotel is just off the I-81 at Exit 222 heading into Staunton. It's also across the street from the biggest Wal-Mart Chappy's ever laid eyes on. Dogs are welcome at no extra charge and with no size restrictions, "just so long as they don't bark all night long and keep everyone up," the friendly desk clerk said. The continental breakfast is free and served daily, so is the morning newspaper. Rooms run about $62 per night. 1031 Richmond Road, Staunton, VA 24401; 540/885-5158 or 800/55-ECONO (800/553-2666).

Gay Street Inn: This restored 1860 farmhouse, a classic Virginia house, is in the heart of historic Washington, nestled in a valley surrounded by the Blue Ridge Mountains. Because they're from Nantucket, Donna and Robin Kevis have filled the place with New England antiques, along with the wallpaper from the Shelburne Museum in Vermont. Dogs are welcome in what Donna says is a "very dog-friendly town." The big downstairs room has a fireplace if you want to come in winter, but spring and fall are the busiest, and the rooms with a mountain view go quickly. All rooms have queen beds, and there's a peaceful garden conservatory breakfast room. The rooms range from $95–135. Breakfast is included, and picnic lunches are available. 160 Gay Street, Washington, VA 22747; 540/675-3288.

Graves' Mountain Lodge: Rustic. Countrylike. Offering Southern hospitality. A family-run business for five generations, this mountain lodge has 38 motel rooms and 11 cabins. Family-style meals served three times a day are included in the room rate. Dogs are welcome, but innkeepers Jim and Rachel Graves will put you and your dog in specially designated cottages. There are many cottages, ranging from Pete's House, an 1800s four-room cottage with fireplace and bunk beds, to Rose River, a two-story log cabin that is two miles from the lodge along the Rose River. It has central heating and air, a stone fireplace, and large front and back porches. So being in a cabin is hardly a hardship. There is a wide range of rates, depending on which cabin you want and how many people are in your party. There is a $25 pet fee, along with a $50 deposit, which you get back if there's no damage done. Hikers have a wealth of trails to choose from, and golfers have an 18-hole course nearby. Chappy likes to throw a horseshoe or two himself. Route 670, Syria, VA 22743; 540/923-4231.

High Meadows Inn: Take a walk back in time to a full-service country inn, about 18 miles south of Charlottesville on 50 acres of country tranquility surrounded by rolling hills, trees, and trails. Elegance is the trademark here. Dogs are welcome in designated pet rooms. Don't ask what the "rate" is— rather the "tariff." Gourmet breakfasts, candlelight dining, and evening Virginia wine tastings are all part of the experience along with spacious rooms and suites with fireplaces and private baths with whirlpool tubs. The house, part of it built in 1832 and another part built in 1882, then joined by a hallway, is a registered Historic Landmark. The innkeepers will happily provide supper baskets by the pond, in the gazebo, or at the vineyard, and breakfasts by the fire or on the terrace if that's what you and your dog would like. The inn is located at 55 High Meadows Lane, Scottsville, VA 24590; 434/286-2218 or 800/232-1832.

Hummingbird Inn: Located in Goshen, in the southern Shenandoah region, the Hummingbird is a Gothic villa that dates back to 1780, with the main Victorian part built in the 1850s. Diana and Jeremy Robinson, the innkeepers, accept dogs, since collies have been a part of their lives, but please call ahead and chat a little bit about your pet. There are five rooms (rates from $110–155) filled with antiques, and each has a private bath. A full breakfast will satisfy you and your dog's appetite. Candlelight dinners are available by reservation. The inn is near historic Lexington, Goshen Pass, and Warm Springs. P.O. Box 147 (Wood Lane), Goshen, VA 24439; 800/397-3214.

Inn at Meander Plantation: Thomas Jefferson slept here. Yes, really. He was, the innkeepers say, a frequent guest of this historic colonial country estate, dating to 1726. So was George Washington, who camped here with the Virginia militia. Lafayette as well. That's why a re-enactment in June has become a popular draw for the inn. Although there's a gang of cats and dogs living on the property, some 80 acres surround the inn, so there isn't a problem if you want to bring your dog. Expect to pay a $25 pet fee and be put in a designated pet room, and be sure to mention it when you reserve a room so that everyone knows to roll out the red pooch carpet. Rates are about $120–195 and include a full breakfast. HCR 5, Box 460A, Locust Dale, VA 22948; 540/672-4912 or 800/385-4936.

Milton Hall Bed and Breakfast Inn: Nestled in the Allegheny Mountains just 10 miles from the West Virginia border, this English country manor built by Lord and Lady Milton is a wonderful place for dogs. Dating to 1774, it's a Virginia Historic Landmark, listed on the National Register.

The inn sits on 45 acres and adjoins a national forest where you can hike, fish, golf, and ski. Afternoon tea is available. A full breakfast is included in the room rates, $120–150 a night. Dogs are welcome on a "dog-by-dog" basis, so call ahead and brag about yours. 207 Thorny Lane, Covington, VA 24426; 540/965-0196.

Natural Chimneys Regional Park Campground: The 120 camping sites with hiking and biking trails and all the other amenities (swimming pool, hot showers, camp store, playgrounds, and picnic shelters) are all the more special here because of the remarkable natural rock formations that resemble gigantic chimneys or even a grand medieval castle. Dogs are welcome so long as they are leashed and behave themselves.

The visitor center is open daily, 9 A.M.–5 P.M., and weekends during the summer 9 A.M.–8 P.M. From I-81, take Exit 240 west to Bridgewater and follow the signs. 540/350-2510 or 888/430-2267.

Shenandoah National Park Campground: See Shenandoah National Park, above.

Sleepy Hollow Farm Bed and Breakfast: Dogs are no problem here in the heartland of American history, where evidence of Native Americans as well as Revolutionary and Civil War soldiers can be found. Expect to stay in the cottage, not the main farmhouse, and expect the three dogs that live on the property to say hi to your dog. It's not bad, though, because the cottage has a fireplace and whirlpool tub. The property is nestled in its own unique hollow, surrounded by pastures and woods. There's a spring-fed pond that some people and dogs take dips in. Just look out for the bigmouth bass named Bubba, who likes to tease anglers. Nearby are wineries, horseback riding, Skyline Drive, and Monticello. Rates range from $65–150, including a full breakfast. 16280 Blue Ridge Turnpike, Gordonsville, VA 22942; 540/832-5555 or 800/215-4804.

Widow Kips Country Inn: The folks who run this inn couldn't be nicer, providing a friendly, pretty surrounding for a visit with your dog. Betty Luse, the innkeeper here who bought the 1830 inn with her husband, Bob, from the Widow Kip herself in 1986, says dogs are more than welcome in the four cottage suites on the property. Visit their website: www.widowkips.com and you'll see a whole section telling you just how welcome your pet will be. It's a refreshing thing to see. Located in the Shenandoah Valley, Widow Kips even boasts a five-acre fenced-in area for dogs to run around leash-free. Can't beat that! There's a 32-foot in-ground pool, along with five antique-filled bedrooms with private baths and working fireplaces. October, when the leaves turn, is a very busy month on the property, which happens to be the oldest dairy farm in Shenandoah County. The two cottages have fireplaces. One is a two-bedroom with its own kitchen, sitting porch, and cable TV, which runs about $100 a night, including full breakfast. There is a $10 pet fee. Skiing, golf, wineries, and battlefields are all nearby. 355 Orchard Drive, Mount Jackson, VA 22842; 540/477-2400 or 800/478-8714.

HARPER'S FERRY, WV

A quaint town that bleeds history from every nook and cranny, Harper's Ferry is located in the foothills of the Blue Ridge Mountains where the Shenandoah and Potomac Rivers meet at the nexus of West Virginia, Virginia, and Maryland. The town got its start in 1761 when an early entrepreneur named Robert Harper built the first ferry across the Potomac River at this site. Soon the makings of a settlement grew up around the ferry as frontiersmen and settlers passed this way heading into the virgin lands of the Shenandoah Valley and beyond.

When he became the new nation's first president, years after visiting Harper's Ferry in his youth, George Washington assigned the small town to host one of the United States Army's first arsenals, where military rifles and muskets were manufactured. The town grew larger by the 1830s when the Chesapeake & Ohio Canal reached it on the Maryland side of the Potomac, attracting more commercial interests.

Despite its fascinating early history, nothing defines Harper's Ferry more than when John Brown and his makeshift army of abolitionists captured the armory and arsenal in 1859 to steal arms and munitions to free the slaves in the South. Brown's failed raid proved to be a precursor to the outbreak of the Civil War less than two years later.

Parks, Beaches, and Recreation Areas

Harper's Ferry National Historical Park 🐾 🐾 🐾

Located about 65 miles northwest of Washington and about the same west of Baltimore, the historic town of Harper's Ferry today is a restored 19th-century town operated by the National Park Service. Without indulging in a Disney-ization of history, the NPS has restored key elements of the town to their past appearance, such as the engine house of the armory where Brown's violent standoff took place. This faithful restoration lends an interpretive hand in presenting the history of the event. All of that and the shops that line its two main avenues attract a couple of million visitors annually.

While dogs aren't allowed inside the historic buildings where artifacts and facts are on display, they can walk around the streets (leashed) and revisit this blast from the past. But do everyone a favor and bring along a baggie so that nobody steps in your pooch's own history. Also, dogs aren't allowed on the buses that run from the parking area, so someone will have to drop off you and the dog and then go drive to the parking area and take the bus back and meet you, but having the dog there on a leash is just fine, we were told.

Meanwhile, the natural beauty of the river and nearby parkland is an attraction in itself. Thomas Jefferson once described Harper's Ferry as "per-haps one of the most stupendous scenes in nature." The panoramic view he described came from the top of what is now called Jefferson Rock, located just northwest of the old town which it overlooks. You and the pooch can climb the rock and take the same view and judge for yourselves. At the river's edge of Harper's Ferry, you and the explorer pup can follow the foot-path that begins at the end of Hamilton Street and hike the trail on Virginius Island, where you'll find the ruins of the 19th-century industrial town that once prospered there.

Cross over the footbridge from the old town and up to Maryland Heights, a hike that had Chappy panting but proved well worth the aerobics required. Bring along the camera because from these cliffs the views of the old town across the river and the Potomac below are spectacular. This is a prime doggy photo opportunity, though the round-trip is just over four miles and some of it is uphill. You'll also find the ruins of a Civil War stone fort if you make it back that far—in which case you might not make it back to Harper's Ferry; the round-trip there is about six miles. Even beyond that is where the Appalachian Trail converges with the Chesapeake & Ohio Canal—a good access points to serious AT hikers.

The historic park is open daily during the summer, 8 A.M.–6 P.M., and during the winter, 8 A.M.–5 P.M.; it is closed December 25. The entrance fee is $5 per vehicle or $3 per person if you bike or walk in and is good for seven days. From Washington take I-270 north past Frederick and exit onto Route 70; less than a mile later turn left on Route 340 and watch for signs to Harper's Ferry after

Bloodiest Battle: Once in the West Virginia panhandle, it's a short drive to **Antietam National Battlefield,** located in Sharpsburg on the Maryland side of the Potomac and across from Shepherdstown. This was the site of the brutal battle that ended General Robert E. Lee's first invasion into the North in 1862. In one day of fighting, some 23,000 men were killed or wounded. Today, except for the preserved battlefield, the area is mostly farmland, pastures, and forest. A paved road runs through it for driving the nine miles of self-guided tour—or walking part of it with the pooch. Rent the audiotape guide at the visitor center if you want the whole story.

The park is closed at dark (20 minutes after sunset). Summer office hours are 8:30 A.M.–6 P.M. daily; winter hours are 8:30 A.M.–5 P.M. The entrance fee is $3 per person or $5 for a family pass (passes are good for three days). From Washington take Interstate 270 to Interstate 70; take Exit 29 onto Route 65 south and drive 10 miles into Sharpsburg. 301/432-5124.

Small-Town Experience: About a 25-minute drive north of Harper's Ferry is charming and historic **Shepherdstown.** One of the oldest towns in West Virginia, it dates back to 1730, and today its main street (East German Street) still reflects those beginnings with quaint town houses, small inns and restaurants, and antique shops. It's also home to Shepherd College. Browse a while with the pup on a leash, and then sit down at one of the sidewalk tables in front of the Uptown Café for lunch. Or carry out some of the fabulous fresh-baked goodies from the Old Sweet Shoppe to eat down by the riverside where you'll find the James Rumsey Monument at the site where in 1787 Rumsey previewed a steamboat for the public. From Harper's Ferry, take Route 340 west and turn right onto County Road 230 north into Shepherdstown. 304/876-2786.

crossing into West Virginia. From Baltimore take Route 70 west for about 40 miles, turn left onto Route 15 outside of Frederick, and continue on Route 340 for another 14 miles and look for the sign on the right. 304/535-6298.

Places to Stay

Cliffside Inn: About one mile outside of historic Harper's Ferry, this 100-room hotel sits on, well, the side of a cliff. Actually it's more like a wooded hill, but it's a great place to walk around with your dog, who is welcome to stay in the annex buildings, providing he pays his $8 fee. Rates are about $55 for a room on a Saturday night. The racetrack at Charles Town is only a short drive, though even a speedy greyhound won't be allowed inside. P.O. Box 786, Harper's Ferry, WV 25425; 304/535-6302.

Harper's Ferry KOA: If you want to rough it, a tent site at this relaxed campground just outside Harper's Ferry goes for around $30 for two people per night—and the pup stays free. Pupster also stays on a leash. This under-the-stars place to stay features amenities from fishing to line dancing, and free movies to Sunday morning church services.

It's open year-round. Just make the left after driving west over the bridge instead of the right that takes you into Harper's Ferry proper; then make the next right onto Campground Road. Route 5, P.O. Box 1300, Harper's Ferry, WV 25425; 304/535-6895 or 800/KOA-9497 (800/562-9497).

INDEX

ACCOMMODATIONS INDEX

RESTAURANT INDEX

GENERAL INDEX

A

Absolutely Awesome Animal Awareness
    Camp of Alexandria 188
Accokeek Creek 270
Adams Morgan 45–48, restaurants 47
Adams Morgan Community Festival 47
Adelphi Manor Park 271
adoption, canine 22–23
African-American Family Day Summerfest 84
Air Fair 286
Air Force One 265
airplane travel 20–21
Alcova Park 130–131
Alexandria 187–203, accommodations 196,
    restaurants 195
Alexandria Red Cross Waterfront Festival
    200
Algonkian Regional Park 219–221
All-Breed Dog Show and Obedience Trial
    213
Allen Pond Park 275
Alley Animals 370
Alpha Ridge Community Park 318
Alpo Canine Frisbee Championships 42–43
Anacostia 99–101

Anacostia Park 100
Anacostia River Park 287–288, 297–298
Animal Welfare League of Alexandria 188
Annadale 149–151, restaurants 150–151
Annadale Community Park and Hidden
    Oaks Nature Center 149
Annapolis, MD 398–406, accommodations
    404–406, restaurants 403–404
Antietam National Battlefield 436
Appalachian Trail 426
aquatic gardens 87
arboretums 82
Argyle Park 255
Arlington County 121–145
Arlington County Fair 129
Arlington Forest 128–129
Arlington Heights 130
Arlington National Cemetery 122
Armistead 358–359
Arts Atlantica Festival 417
Ashburn 206
Assateague, MD 406–407, accommoda-
    tions 407
Assateague Island National Shoreline
    406–407

The Maryland SPCA

Our Mission

The Maryland SPCA's mission is to prevent cruelty and neglect of animals through fostering the humane relationship between animals and people. It is a private, non-profit organization. It operates primarily in the Greater Baltimore Metropolitan area. The mission is to be accomplished through education, advocacy, active direct care, pet population control, and screen adoptions. It receives no government funding, and it is not under the direction of any national animal welfare group. It also is not affiliated with any other SPCA.

Our History

The Maryland SPCA was founded in 1869 to ensure the proper care of working horses in Baltimore City. As the use of horses in commerce declined, the SPCA began focusing on dogs and cats.

PROGRAMS AND SERVICES

Adoptions. We provide screened adoptions to place animals from our shelter into new, loving homes. In 2001 we placed more than 3,400 animals into new homes. All animals are spayed or neutered prior to adoption, and the adoption fee includes all vaccinations for one year.

Lost and found. We shelter lost animals and maintain a list of lost and found pets. If you have lost or found a pet, call us and we will check our lost animal registry.

Free spay/neuter services (Baltimore City only). Our Neuter Scooter provides free spay/neuter services to pets whose owners live in Baltimore City.

Low-cost vaccinations. Reduced-price vaccinations are offered at The Maryland SPCA in June and October. Call 410/889-9331, ext. 1 for exact dates.

EDUCATION

Pet Basics. This free class covers the essentials of pet ownership, including selecting the proper pet, feeding, grooming, house-training, and interacting with your pet.

Ask the Expert. Held once a month, this class is an opportunity to meet with a trainer to discuss behavior concerns such as barking, scratching, litterbox problems, and more.

Best Friends Dog Obedience. Rated "Baltimore's Best" by Baltimore magazine, this seven-week dog training program is offered on the grounds of The Maryland SPCA. Puppy Preschool is available for dogs up to six months of age. Regular obedience training is offered for dogs over six months.

Behavior Advice. Litterbox problems, excessive barking, house-breaking challenges? Help is just a phone call or e-mail away. This free service helps pet owners through their pet behavior questions.

"Pet Friendly" spay/neuter license plates. Show you care about controlling pet overpopulation with special license plates that support spay/neuter programs.

Pet supplies. Our shelter carries food, grooming supplies, pet toys, and other pet care items.

For more information contact us:
Shelter office: 410/235-8826
Administration: 410/889-9331
website: www.mdspca.org

 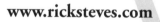

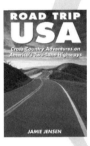

ABOUT THE AUTHORS

If shaggy purebred Tibetan terrier Chappy looks more at home nuzzled into the overstuffed living-room couch than nosing around the newest nature trail at a dog-friendly park, it's because he is. At 11 years old, Chap's not nearly the spry pup he once was, and doesn't move as briskly as he did when researching for the first edition of this book in 1998. His left hind leg gets a little gimpy at times and he needs to catch his breath more often.

But mention the word "park," and Chap still goes directly to the kitchen drawer where his leash is kept. And he still gets excited venturing into the Great Outdoors from Washington to Baltimore and beyond. (Did we mention he's already packed for this summer's trip to Bethany Beach?)

Himalayan legend says Tibetan terriers—traditionally raised by the Dalai Lama—bring good luck to their owners. Perhaps that's how this book came about. But it also made sense. Ann Oldenburg, who grew up with a tough little Maltese named Bo-Bo and a sweet German shepherd named Shelly, is a reporter at *USA Today* and contributes regularly to *Preservation* magazine. Don Oldenburg was born and raised in the Washington metropolitan area with a loyal black cocker spaniel named Inky. He's a feature writer and consumer columnist at *The Washington Post,* and co-edited the book *Dear Mr. President* (Avon, 1993). Both Ann and Don review regularly for the Parents Choice Awards. They live with their three baseball-playing sons, J.B., James, and Cole, in McLean, Virginia.